Communications in Computer and Information Science 510

Commenced Publication in 2007
Founding and Former Series Editors:
Alfredo Cuzzocrea, Dominik Ślęzak, and Xiaokang Yang

More information about this series at http://www.springer.com/series/7899

Susan Zvacek · Maria Teresa Restivo
James Uhomoibhi · Markus Helfert (Eds.)

Computer Supported Education

6th International Conference, CSEDU 2014
Barcelona, Spain, April 1–3, 2014
Revised Selected Papers

Springer

Editors
Susan Zvacek
University of Denver
Denver, CO
USA

Maria Teresa Restivo
Faculdade de Engenharia da Universidade do Porto
Porto
Portugal

James Uhomoibhi
School of Engineering
University of Ulster
Newtownabbey
UK

Markus Helfert
School of Computing
Dublin City University
Dublin
Ireland

ISSN 1865-0929 ISSN 1865-0937 (electronic)
Communications in Computer and Information Science
ISBN 978-3-319-25767-9 ISBN 978-3-319-25768-6 (eBook)
DOI 10.1007/978-3-319-25768-6

Library of Congress Control Number: 2015952065

Springer Cham Heidelberg New York Dordrecht London

Printed on acid-free paper

Springer International Publishing AG Switzerland is part of Springer Science+Business Media (www.springer.com)

Preface

This book includes extended and revised versions of a set of selected papers from CSEDU 2014 (The 6th International Conference on Computer Supported Education), held in Barcelona, Spain, in 2014, which was organized and sponsored by the Institute for Systems and Technologies of Information, Control and Communication (INSTICC). This conference was held in cooperation with the Association for Computing Machinery – Special Interest Group for Information Technology Education, European Council for Business Education (ECBE), and Association des Technologies de l'Information pour l'Education et la Formation (ATIEF). The conference was also technically co-sponsored by the IEEE Education Society – Capitulo Español and SPEE (Sociedade Portuguesa para a Educação em Engenharia).

The purpose of the CSEDU series of conferences is to bring together researchers and practitioners interested in methodologies and applications related to the education field. It had five main topic areas, covering different aspects of computer-supported education, including "Information Technologies Supporting Learning," "Learning/Teaching Methodologies and Assessment," "Social Context and Learning Environments," "Domain Applications and Case Studies," and "Ubiquitous Learning."

CSEDU 2014 received 242 paper submissions from 57 countries in all continents. From these, only 32 papers were selected to be published and presented as full papers and another 69 papers, describing work-in-progress, were selected as short papers for a 20-minute oral presentation. These numbers, leading to a full-paper acceptance ratio of 13 % and an oral paper presentation ratio of 29 %, show the intention of preserving a high-quality forum for the next editions of this conference.

This book contains the revised papers selected among the best contributions, taking also into account the quality of their presentation at the conference, assessed by session chairs. Therefore, we hope that you find these papers interesting and we trust they may represent a helpful reference for all those who need to address any of the aforementioned research areas.

We wish to thank all those who supported and helped to organize the conference. On behalf of the conference Organizing Committee, we would like to thank the authors, whose work mostly contributed to a very successful conference, and the members of the Program Committee, whose expertise and diligence were instrumental in ensuring the quality of final contributions. We also wish to thank all the members of the Organizing Committee, whose work and commitment was invaluable. Last but not least, we would like to thank Springer for their collaboration in getting this book to print.

April 2015

Susan Zvacek
Maria Teresa Restivo
James Uhomoibhi
Markus Helfert

Organization

Conference Chair

Markus Helfert	Dublin City University, Ireland

Program Co-chairs

Susan Zvacek	Fort Hays State University, USA
Maria Teresa Restivo	FEUP, Portugal
James Uhomoibhi	University of Ulster, UK

Organizing Committee

Marina Carvalho	INSTICC, Portugal
Helder Coelhas	INSTICC, Portugal
Ana Guerreiro	INSTICC, Portugal
André Lista	INSTICC, Portugal
Filipe Mariano	INSTICC, Portugal
Andreia Moita	INSTICC, Portugal
Raquel Pedrosa	INSTICC, Portugal
Vitor Pedrosa	INSTICC, Portugal
Andreia Pereira	INSTICC, Portugal
Cláudia Pinto	INSTICC, Portugal
Cátia Pires	INSTICC, Portugal
Ana Ramalho	INSTICC, Portugal
Susana Ribeiro	INSTICC, Portugal
Rui Rodrigues	INSTICC, Portugal
Sara Santiago	INSTICC, Portugal
André Santos	INSTICC, Portugal
Fábio Santos	INSTICC, Portugal
Mara Silva	INSTICC, Portugal
José Varela	INSTICC, Portugal
Pedro Varela	INSTICC, Portugal

Program Committee

Mehdi Adda	Université du Québec à Rimouski, Canada
Shirley Agostinho	University of Wollongong, Australia
Carlos Alario-Hoyos	Universidad Carlos III, Spain
Peter Albion	University of Southern Queensland, Australia
Nelma Albuquerque	People-Inspired Technologies, The Netherlands

Efthimios Alepis	University of Piraeus, Greece
Vassil Alexandrov	Barcelona Supercomputing Center, Spain
Colin Allison	University of St. Andrews, UK
Marilisa Amoia	Saarland University, Germany
George Anastassakis	University of Piraeus, Greece
Terry Anderson	Athabasca University, Canada
Galia Angelova	Institute of Information and Communication Technologies, Bulgarian Academy of Sciences, Bulgaria
Leonard Annetta	George Mason University, USA
Juan Ignacio Asensio	University of Valladolid, Spain
Michael E. Auer	Carinthia Tech Institute, Austria
Anders Avdic	Örebro University, Sweden
Breno Fabrício Terra Azevedo	Instituto Federal de Educação, Ciência e Tecnologia Fluminense, Brazil
Paul M.A. Baker	Georgia Institute of Technology, USA
Adriano Baratè	Università degli Studi di Milano, Italy
Jorge Barbosa	UNISINOS, Brazil
Patrícia Brandalise Scherer Bassani	Universidade Feevale, Brazil
Clemens Bechter	TBS, Thailand
Patricia Alejandra Behar	Universidade Federal do Rio Grande do Sul, Brazil
Kay Berkling	Cooperative State University Baden Württemberg, Karlsruhe, Germany
Marlies Bitter-Rijpkema	Open Universiteit, The Netherlands
Emmanuel G. Blanchard	University of Montreal, France
Lars Bollen	Universiteit Twente, The Netherlands
Andreas Bollin	Alpen-Adria Universität Klagenfurt, Austria
Katrin Borcea-Pfitzmann	Technische Universität Dresden, Germany
Federico Botella	Miguel Hernandez University of Elche, Spain
Jacqueline Bourdeau	Télé-université, UQAM, Canada
Ghizlane El Boussaidi	École de Technologie Supérieure, Canada
Patrice Bouvier	Université de Lyon, France
Claudio da Rocha Brito	COPEC, Brazil
Dumitru Burdescu	University of Craiova, Romania
Santi Caballé	Open University of Catalonia, Spain
Chris Campbell	University of Queensland, Australia
Alberto Cardoso	University of Coimbra, Portugal
Carlos Vaz de Carvalho	ISEP, Portugal
Chia-Hu Chang	National Taiwan University, Taiwan
Amitava Chatterjee	Jadavpur University, India
Weiqin Chen	University of Bergen, Norway
Line Clemmensen	Technical University of Denmark, Denmark
Jo Coldwell-Neilson	Deakin University, Australia
Marc Conrad	University of Bedfordshire, UK
Gennaro Costagliola	Università di Salerno, Italy

Maria Cristina Costa-Lobo	Universidade Portucalense, Portugal
Manuel Perez Cota	Universidade de Vigo, Spain
Caroline M. Crawford	University of Houston-Clear Lake, USA
Beno Csapó	University of Szeged, Hungary
John Philip Cuthell	Virtual Learning, UK
Mats Daniels	Uppsala University, Sweden
Thanasis Daradoumis	University of the Aegean, Greece/Open University of Catalonia, Spain
Sergiu Dascalu	University of Nevada, Reno, USA
Stavros N. Demetriadis	Aristotle University of Thessaloniki, Greece
John Dempsey	University of South Alabama, USA
Giuliana Dettori	Istituto per le Tecnologie Didattiche (ITD-CNR), Italy
Alicia Diaz	La Plata National University, Argentina
Yannis Dimitriadis	University of Valladolid, Spain
Danail Dochev	Institute of Information and Communication Technologies, Bulgarian Academy of Sciences, Bulgaria
Toby Dragon	Ithaca College, USA
Amalia Duch-Brown	UPC – Polytechnical University of Catalonia, Spain
Ishbel Duncan	University of St. Andrews, UK
Erik Duval	Katholieke Universiteit Leuven, Belgium
Olga Dziabenko	Universidad de Deusto, Spain
Martin Ebner	Technische Universität Graz, Austria
Paula Escudeiro	Instituto Superior de Engenharia do Porto, Portugal
Barbara Di Eugenio	University of Illinois at Chicago, USA
Si Fan	University of Tasmania, Australia
Mingyu Feng	SRI International, USA
Richard E. Ferdig	Kent State University, USA
Davide Fossati	Carnegie Mellon University in Qatar (CMU- Qatar), USA
Rita Francese	Università degli Studi di Salerno, Italy
José Ricardo Franco	Universidade Federal de Minas Gerais, Brazil
Jun Fujima	Fraunhofer IDMT, Germany
Serge Garlatti	TELECOM Bretagne, France
Isabela Gasparini	UFRGS and UDESC, Brazil
Xun Ge	University of Oklahoma, USA
Sébastien George	Université du Maine, France
Henrique Gil	Escola Superior de Educação do Instituto Politécnico de Castelo Branco, Portugal
Denis Gillet	École Polytechnique Fédérale de Lausanne (EPFL), Switzerland
Ana González-Marcos	Universidad de la Rioja, Spain
Anandha Gopalan	Imperial College London, UK
Grami Grami	King Abdulaziz University, Saudi Arabia
Angela Guercio	Kent State University, USA
Christian Guetl	Graz University of Technology, Austria

Matej Guid	University of Ljubljana, Slovenia
David Guralnick	Kaleidoscope Learning/Columbia University, USA
Laurence Habib	Oslo and Akerhus University College of Applied Sciences, Norway
Leontios Hadjileontiadis	Aristotle University of Thessaloniki, Greece
Ibrahim A. Hameed	Aalborg University, Denmark
Yasunari Harada	Waseda University, Japan
Andreas Harrer	Technical University Clausthal, Germany
Roger Hartley	University of Leeds, UK
Markus Helfert	Dublin City University, Ireland
Richard Helps	Brigham Young University, USA
George Hloupis	Technological Educational Institute of Athens, Greece
Mark van't Hooft	Kent State University, USA
Janet Hughes	University of Dundee, UK
Kin-chuen Hui	Chinese University of Hong Kong, Hong Kong, SAR China
Nataliya V. Ivankova	University of Alabama at Birmingham, USA
Ivan Ivanov	SUNY Empire State College, USA
Romina Jamieson-Proctor	University of Southern Queensland, Australia
Marc Jansen	University of Applied Sciences Ruhr West, Germany
Stéphanie Jean-Daubias	Université Claude Bernard - Lyon 1/LIRIS, France
Lars Johnsen	University of Southern Denmark, Denmark
Katerina Kabassi	Tei of the Ionian Islands, Greece
Michail Kalogiannakis	University of Crete, Greece
Achilles Kameas	Hellenic Open University, Greece
Charalampos Karagiannidis	University of Thessaly, Greece
Ilias Karasavvidis	University of Thessaly, Greece
Göran Karlsson	KTH Stockholm, Sweden
David Kaufman	Simon Fraser University, Canada
Jalal Kawash	University of Calgary, Canada
ChanMin Kim	The University of Georgia, USA
John Kinnebrew	Vanderbilt University, USA
Dimitris Kiritsis	EPFL, Switzerland
Gwendolyn Kolfschoten	Delft University of Technology, The Netherlands
Rob Koper	Open University of the Netherlands, The Netherlands
Maria Kordaki	University of the Aegean, Greece
Miroslav Kulich	Czech Technical University in Prague, Czech Republic
Chronis Kynigos	University of Athens and CTI, Greece
Jean-Marc Labat	Université Pierre et Marie Curie, France
Timo Lainema	Turku School of Economics, Finland
H. Chad Lane	University of Southern California, USA
Reneta Lansiquot	New York City College of Technology, USA
Rynson Lau	City University of Hong Kong, Hong Kong, SAR China
José Paulo Leal	University of Porto, Portugal
Dominique Leclet	UPJV, France

Newton Lee	Newton Lee Laboratories LLC, USA
Andrew Lian	Suranaree University of Technology, Thailand
Yu-Tzu Lin	National Taiwan Normal University, Taiwan
Andreas Lingnau	Catholic University Eichstaett-Ingolstadt, Germany
Luca Andrea Ludovico	Università degli Studi di Milano, Italy
Heide Lukosch	Delft University of Technology, The Netherlands
Stephan Lukosch	Delft University of Technology, The Netherlands
Philip Machanick	Rhodes University, South Africa
Krystina Madej	Georgia Tech, USA
Massimo Marchiori	University of Padua, Italy
Jacek Marciniak	Adam Mickiewicz University, Poland
Ivana Marenzi	Leibniz University Hannover, Germany
José Couto Marques	FEUP, Portugal
Lindsay Marshall	Newcastle University, UK
Alke Martens	Universität of Rostock, Germany
Manolis Mavrikis	London Knowledge Lab, UK
Bruce Maxim	University of Michigan-Dearborn, USA
Roger McDermott	Robert Gordon University, UK
Rory McGreal	Athabasca University, Canada
Hamid Mcheick	University of Quebec at Chicoutimi, Canada
Bruce McLaren	Carnegie Mellon University, USA, Germany
António José Mendes	Universidade de Coimbra, Portugal
Robert Meolic	University of Maribor, Slovenia
José Carlos Metrôlho	Instituto Politécnico de Castelo Branco, Portugal
Bakhtiar Mikhak	Harvard University, USA
Alexander Mikroyannidis	The Open University, UK
Felix Mödritscher	Vienna University of Economics and Business, Austria
Gyöngyvér Molnár	University of Szeged, Hungary
Roberto Moriyón	Universidad Autonoma de Madrid, Spain
Jack Mostow	Carnegie Mellon University, USA
Antao Moura	Federal University of Campina Grande (UFCG), Brazil
Muhanna Muhanna	Princess Sumaya University for Technology, Jordan
Jogesh K. Muppala	Hong Kong University of Science and Technology, Hong Kong, SAR China
Hiroyuki Nagataki	Okayama University, Japan
Ryohei Nakatsu	National University of Singapore, Singapore
Minoru Nakayama	Tokyo Institute of Technology, Japan
Sotiris Nikolopoulos	Technological Educational Institute of Larissa, Greece
Ebba Ossiannilsson	Lund University, Sweden
José Palma	Escola Superior de Tecnologia de Setúbal, Portugal
Viktoria Pammer	Know-Center, Austria
Pantelis Papadopoulos	Carnegie Mellon University in Qatar, Qatar
Kyparisia A. Papanikolaou	School of Pedagogical and Technological Education, Greece
Iraklis Paraskakis	South East European Research Centre, Greece
Seung Won Park	Texas A&M University – Corpus Christi, USA

Mar Pérez-Sanagustín	Universidad Carlos III de Madrid, Spain
Antonio Ramón Bartolomé Pina	Universitat de Barcelona, Spain
Niels Pinkwart	Humboldt University, Germany
Leonard A. Plugge	Stichting SURF, The Netherlands
Elvira Popescu	University of Craiova, Romania
Philippos Pouyioutas	University of Nicosia, Cyprus
Franz Puehretmair	Competence Network Information Technology to Support the Integration of People with Disabilities (KI-I), Austria
Khalid Rabayah	Arab American University, Occupied Palestinian Territory
Maria da Graça Rasteiro	University of Coimbra, Portugal
Janet C. Read	University of Central Lancashire, UK
Petrea Redmond	University of Southern Queensland, Australia
Manuel José Cabral Dos Santos Reis	University of Trás-os-montes e Alto Douro, Portugal
Manuela Repetto	Consiglio Nazionale delle Ricerche, Italy
Maria Teresa Restivo	FEUP, Portugal
Fernando Reinaldo Ribeiro	Instituto Politécnico de Castelo Branco, Portugal
Martin Rich	Cass Business School, UK
Manuela Raposo Rivas	Universidad de Vigo, Spain
Razvan Rughinis	University Politehnica of Bucharest, Romania
Barbara Sabitzer	Alpen-Adria-Universität Klagenfurt, Austria
Libuse Samkova	University of South Bohemia, Czech Republic
Demetrios Sampson	University of Piraeus and Center for Research and Development - Hellas, Greece
Ian Sanders	University of South Africa, South Africa
Albert Sangra	Open University of Catalonia, Spain
Giuseppe Scanniello	Università Degli Studi della Basilicata, Italy
Sabine Schlag	University of Wuppertal, Germany
Ulrik Schroeder	RWTH Aachen University, Germany
Edgar Seemann	Furtwangen University, Germany
Pei Hwa Siew	Universiti Tunku Abdul Rahman, Malaysia
Martin Sillaots	Tallinn University, Estonia
Juarez Bento da Silva	Universidade Federal de Santa Catarina, Brazil
Peter Sloep	Open University of the Netherlands, The Netherlands
Zacharoula Smyrnaiou	University of Athens, Greece
Filomena Soares	University of Minho, Portugal
Michael Sonntag	Johannes Kepler University, Austria
J. Michael Spector	University of North Texas, USA
Karl Steffens	University of Cologne, Germany
Craig Stewart	Indiana University, USA
Hongyi Sun	City University of Hong Kong, Hong Kong, SAR China
Katsuaki Suzuki	Kumamoto University, Japan

Ekaterina Talalakina	NRU HSE, Russian Federation
Bénédicte Talon	ULCO, Université Lille Nord de France, France
Brendan Tangney	Trinity College Dublin, Ireland
Steven Tanimoto	University of Washington, USA
Pei-Lee Teh	Monash University, Malaysia
Uwe Terton	University of the Sunshine Coast, Australia
Neena Thota	University of Saint Joseph, Macau
Fatt Hee Tie	University of Malaya, Malaysia
Thanassis Tiropanis	University of Southampton, UK
Stefan Trausan-Matu	University Politehnica of Bucharest, Romania
Joseph Trimmer	Ball State University, USA
George Tsihrintzis	University of Piraeus, Greece
James Uhomoibhi	University of Ulster, UK
Carsten Ullrich	Shanghai Jiao Tong University, China
Luis de la Fuente Valentín	Universidad Internacional de la Rioja, Spain
Andreas Veglis	Aristotle University of Thessaloniki, Greece
Ioanna Vekiri	Independent Researcher, Greece
Maria Virvou	University of Piraeus, Greece
Harald Vranken	Open Universiteit, The Netherlands
Pieter de Vries	Delft University of Technology, The Netherlands
Minjuan Wang	San Diego State University, USA
Martin Wessner	Fraunhofer IESE, Germany
Su White	Web and Internet Science, UK
Leandro Krug Wives	Universidade Federal do Rio Grande do Sul, Brazil
Jie Chi Yang	National Central University, Taiwan
Takami Yasuda	Nagoya University, Japan
Katarina Zakova	Slovak University of Technology in Bratislava, Slovak Republic
Diego Zapata-Rivera	Educational Testing Service, USA
Fani Zlatarova	Elizabethtown College, USA
Amal Zouaq	Royal Military College of Canada, Canada
Javier García Zubía	Universidad de Deusto, Spain
Susan Zvacek	Fort Hays State University, USA

Additional Reviewers

Alvine Boaye Belle	Ecole de Technologie Superieure, Canada
José Cordeiro	Polytechnic Institute of Setúbal/INSTICC, Portugal
Nuno Pina Gonçalves	EST-Setúbal/IPS, Portugal
Drew Hicks	NC State University, USA
Timotej Lazar	Univerza v Ljubljani, Slovenia
María del Mar Sánchez-Vera	University of Murcia, Spain
Jian Shi	University of Southampton, UK
Yasuhisa Tamura	Sophia University, Japan
Robert Thompson	University of Washington, USA

Invited Speakers

José Carlos Lourenço Quadrado	ISEL - Lisbon Superior Engineering Institute, Portugal and IFEES - International Federation of Engineering, Education Societies, USA
Steve Wheeler	Plymouth Institute of Education, Plymouth University, UK
Larissa Fradkin	London South Bank University, Brunel University and Sound Mathematics Ltd., UK
Erik de Graaff	Aalborg University, Denmark

Contents

Information Technologies Supporting Learning

Using Wikis to Evaluate Students' Contributions to Collaborative Writing in Teacher Education

Said Hadjerrouit(✉)

Faculty of Technology and Science, University of Agder, Kristiansand, Norway
Said.Hadjerrouit@uia.no

Abstract. Wikis as collaboration tools may serve various purposes in teacher education such as group project, glossary creation, teacher evaluation, and document review. However, despite their potentialities for collaboration, it is still difficult to determine the extent to which students contribute to collaborative writing. Research studies are mostly perception-based and limited to participants' subjective views. Recently, a growing number of research studies have used the data log of the wiki that enables the retrieval of students' contributions to collaborative writing. The data log is inherently more reliable than participants' subjective perceptions to explore collaborative writing activities by means of wiki. This work uses the data log and a taxonomy of category actions to investigate students' contributions to collaborative writing over a period of three years. The work also discusses factors that may influence collaborative writing activities in teacher education, and suggests some recommendations to enhance the level of collaboration.

Keywords: Action category · Collaborative learning · Collaborative writing · Mediawiki · Wiki

1 Introduction

Wikis have been used in teacher education to achieve varied educational goals, such as teacher evaluation, document assessment, or student projects. Wiki-based collaborative writing is a coordinated activity that enables students to edit and revise each other's contribution to the wiki [1–4]. Research studies point out to the potentialities of wikis to support collaborative work [5, 6]. However, in spite of positive experiences that have been reported in the literature [7, 8], a number of researchers are more circumspect about the potentialities of wikis to support collaborative learning and writing. Several hypotheses have been raised to explain the low level of collaboration when using wikis: unfamiliarity with wikis, lack of experience, dominant learning paradigm, limited student contribution, reluctance and resistance to use wiki, lack of motivation and engagement, time management, problem of ownership, and lack of appropriate pedagogy [9–13].

To further explore these hypotheses, this work reports on an empirical study in teacher education that examined the extent to which students collaborated to perform wiki-based tasks associated with collaborative writing over a period of three years. The

S. Zvacek et al. (Eds.): CSEDU 2014, CCIS 510, pp. 3–18, 2015.
DOI: 10.1007/978-3-319-25768-6_1

work uses the data log (or history log) of the wiki, and a taxonomy of action categories to analyse students' contributions to collaborative writing. The main goal is to explore the work distribution among students, the types of actions carried out on the wikis, and the timing of contribution. Influencing factors that may impact collaborative writing with wikis are also discussed, including some recommendations to help students engage in collaboration.

The work is structured as follows. First, the relationship between wiki technology and collaborative writing is clarified. Second, related research work is reported. The next section describes the methodology of the work. Then, the results and discussion are presented. Finally, some remarks conclude the article.

2 Wiki-Based Collaborative Writing

2.1 Wiki Technology

Wikis as a type of Web 2.0 technology is potentially powerful to foster collaborative writing in various education settings. A number of wiki tools are available for use in teacher education. One of the most popular tools is MediaWiki [14]. This tool uses a simplified HTML language and provides an extensive functionality for user authentication, making it appropriate for educational purposes [15]. Another important functionality of MediaWiki is the data or history log that keeps track of students' actions by name, date, and colour coding [16]. In addition, MediaWiki provides a discussion page for written communication, reflections and negotiations.

2.2 Collaborative Learning and Writing

Collaborative learning is an educational approach that requires working together to achieve a common goal. It is grounded in the social-constructivist learning theory [17], and assumes that participants can achieve more in terms of learning benefits than individuals. Collaborative writing describes a learning activity that enables participants to produce a text or a document collectively [4]. Collaborative writing involves the mutual engagement of participants in a coordinated effort to accomplish a writing task collectively [18, p. 160, cited in Judd et al. 2010]. It is opposed to simply splitting up the task, work independently of each other, and then assemble individual contributions to a final product. This activity is called cooperation rather than collaboration [19, cited in Judd et al. 2010].

2.3 Mediawiki and Collaborative Writing

MediaWiki provides a space for collaborative writing by means of a simple interface allowing students to share information, discuss, negotiate, and produce a text by more than one author. MediaWiki provides technical features to support students' collaborative writing activities, such as a simplified user interface to edit the content, track students' actions, and compare differences between two versions of the wiki. It also provides a discussion page for written communication. The content produced by the students and their actions are automatically recorded in the data log of MediaWiki, enabling a statistical analysis of students' contributions to the wiki.

2.4 Taxonomy of Category Actions

A taxonomy developed by Pfeil et al. [20] can be used to analyse students' actions carried on the wiki. The taxonomy included originally 13 actions, of which the following 10 were identified as important for this work [20, p. 101] (Table 1).

Table 1. Taxonomy of category actions.

Name of Category	Explanation
Add Information	Addition of topic-related information (the information must not consist only of links)
Add Link	Addition of links to an existing set of listed links or linking of a word within an existing sentence to a page (links to other Wikipedia pages or to external Internet pages)
Clarify Information	Rewording of existing information without adding new information. Rewording done in order to clarify the content (e.g., substitution of certain words for a better understanding, change of the word order or deletion/addition of words in order to clarify)
Delete Information	Deletion of topic-related information (the information must not consist only of links)
Delete Link	Deletion of links from the set of listed links or removal of the linking function from a word within an existing sentence (links to other Wikipedia pages or to external Internet pages)
Fix Link	Modification of an existing link (can be an alteration of the linked URL or the name of the link)
Format	Contributions that affect the appearance or structure of the whole page (e.g., addition of space lines, sorting/moving of paragraphs or links and addition of subtitles in order to structure the content)
Grammar	Alterations of the grammar (e.g., change of punctuation)
Spelling	Correction of spelling mistakes (e.g., reversed letters or capital letter)
Style/Typography	Contributions that affect the presentation/appearance of the text (e.g., bold/italic/underlined text)

Note that the category "Clarify Information" has been modified to include rewording of existing information with addition of new information. To measure the degree of collaboration, these actions can be classified from the lowest level (that is cooperation as defined above) to the highest level of collaboration. Between these levels, a wide range of actions can be carried out. The lowest level of collaboration is performed when students' actions are limited to add information, add link, delete information, delete link within their own subtask. A high level of collaboration is achieved when students rephrase each other's work, clarify and modify the information of the wiki, correct the grammar and spelling. In addition to rewording and clarifying information as defined in the taxonomy, students can make peers aware of changes and ask them to react to them. These activities can provide a high level of collaborative writing. Between these forms, varied level of collaboration can be achieved, for example when students clarify the meaning of other's work, add information and links, structure some other's work or move sentences. Furthermore, these categories can be divided into four groups of actions (Fig. 1):

1. Actions carried out on entire sentences, which do not change the sentences
2. Actions within sentences, that is actions carried out on specific words within sentences, which in contrast to the first group, alter the meaning of the sentences
3. Actions on navigation and linking
4. Actions on presentation and structure of wiki pages

The two first categories were used by Meishar-Tal and Gorsky [2]. In addition, it is useful to include actions on navigation and structure of wiki pages. Accordingly, actions on sentences are: add and delete information. Actions within sentences are: clarify information, grammar, style/typography, and spelling. Actions on navigation are: add, delete, and fix link. Finally, actions on presentation and structure are those related to format (Fig. 1).

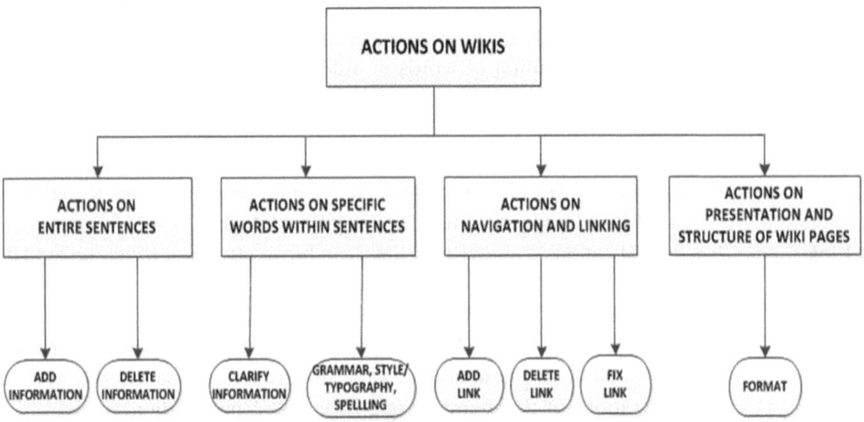

Fig. 1. Types of actions carried out on wikis.

3 Related Work

Wiki-based collaborative writing can be studied from different perspectives and methods. A literature review reveals that most studies use qualitative methods such as interviews and quantitative methods such as survey questionnaires to investigate participants' perceptions of collaborative writing. In recent years, a growing number of studies have drawn on the wiki data log, also called history function, that tracks all students' actions being made on the wiki. The data log is inherently more reliable to analyse students' collaborative writing activities than perception-based studies. This work is a continuation and a synthesis of a research that started in 2010 in the field of wiki-mediated collaborative writing over a period of three years [21–25]. This previous work used both the wiki data log and the taxonomy of category actions. A similar work was done by Judd et al. [12], who analysed data that are automatically recorded in the data log to assess the nature and scope of users' contributions. They found little evidence of collaborative writing among participants, and that many students' contributions were superficial. Likewise, Leung and Chu [26] reported that students worked individually most of the time, and edited each other's contributions if necessary. In some contrast, Meishar-Tal and Gorsky [2] indicated that adding text was carried by a large majority of students, but the percentage of editorial changes was higher than adding sentences, because the students were required to edit each other's work. Nevertheless, most of the work based on the data log pointed out that wikis do not automatically make collaboration happen due to a number of influencing factors in the teaching and learning environment.

4 Methodology

4.1 Research Goal and Questions

This work aims at exploring the extent to which students collaborated to perform wiki-based tasks associated with collaborative writing in teacher education. Relying on the taxonomy of category actions and the data log that tracks all students' contributions to the wikis, this work attempts to address three research questions:

1. What is the level of work contribution of each member of the student groups?
2. What are the types of actions that the groups carried out on the wikis?
3. What is the timing of contributions of each group?

4.2 Participants

The experiments over a three-year period were based on three cohorts of participants. The participative students were enrolled in a Web 2.0 technology course that was offered each year. None of the students experienced wiki-based collaborative writing before taking the course. Some students possessed good technical skills, while other had background in pedagogy and learning paradigms. The first experiment lasted for a whole semester from January to May 2010, while the following experiments in 2011 and 2012 lasted for eight weeks. The number of participants in 2010 was 8 students, divided into 3 groups of 2-4 students (G_1, G_2, and G_3). In 2011, the number of participants was 10, divided into 3 groups of 3–4 students (G_1, G_2, and G_3). The number of participants in 2012 increased in comparison with previous experiments. Sixteen participants were enrolled in 2012, divided into 6 groups of 2–4 students (G_1, G_2, G_3, G_4, G_5, and G_6). Despite these differences, the conditions under which the experiments were carried out were basically similar. Each experiment started with new writing tasks, but the students were encouraged to study previous editions of the course.

4.3 Writing Tasks

The wiki writing tasks were situated within teacher education, including topics related to mathematics, science, geography, history, and other subjects. The specificities and technical features of wikis were introduced to the students during the first week of the course. Lectures on collaborative writing were given in the following two weeks. The students were required to submit their wikis for continuous evaluation on the basis of the following criteria. First, the wikis should follow general usability criteria such as good technical layout, clear linking and navigation. Second, the wikis must contain information of good quality, without linguistic, grammar, and spelling errors. Third, the content of the wikis should draw on recent curricular development in teacher education, and include well-structured study material with images, figures, tables, lists, and references. Fourth, the wikis should be self-explaining, and provide information that is relevant to the target audience. Fifth, the wikis should contain a minimum of 4000 words to ensure that a sufficient quantity of writing is produced. Sixth, the students are required to edit each other's contributions, and take actively part in the discussion of the wiki content and structure. Finally, in line with the wiki philosophy based on collaborations, the students were not assessed individually, but as a group working collaboratively. Nevertheless, the data log can be used to look at the students' individual contributions to the wikis.

4.4 Data Collection and Analysis Methods

In an attempt to provide a consistent evaluation of the experiments, this work used the wiki data log to collect and analyse three types of quantitative data. Firstly, the level of work distribution among members of the student groups to assess the amount of work and frequency produced by each student. Secondly, the total number of actions per group and category, including their frequencies, such as whether an action is an addition, deletion or clarification of information, addition, deletion, or fixation of a link, format, spelling, style, or grammar. Then, data on timing of contribution were recorded to assess the amount of work produced by the students over a period of three years. Finally, observations and informal discussions were used to gain supplementary information on students' collaborative writing activities.

5 Results

The results are described with respect to the experiments that were carried out in 2010, 2011, and 2012. The results are reported in terms of level of distribution, types of actions, and timing of contribution.

5.1 Level of Work Distribution

Table 2 presents the distribution of work made by each member of the student groups over a period of three years (2010–2012).

Table 2. Students' work distribution (2010–2012).

2010			
	G_1	**G_2**	**G_3**
Student 1	634 (39.56%)	292 (87.43%)	152 (70.05%)
Student 2	379 (23.64%)	42 (12.57%)	65 (29.95%)
Student 3	327 (20.40%)	…	…
Student 4	263 (16.40%)	…	…
Total	**1603 (100%)**	**334 (100%)**	**217 (100%)**
2011			
	G_1	**G_2**	**G_3**
Student 1	137 (37.23%)	119 (46.48%)	95 (46.12%)
Student 2	118 (32.07%)	74 (28.91%)	75 (36.41%)
Student 3	113 (30.70%)	63 (24.61%)	27 (13.10%)
Student 4	…	…	9 (4.37%)
Total	**368 (100%)**	**256 (100%)**	**206 (100%)**
2012			
	G_1	**G_2**	**G_3**
Student 1	80 (31.25%)	121 (45.66%)	184 (46.58%)
Student 2	76 (29.69%)	107 (40.38%)	166 (42.03%)
Student 3	64 (25.00%)	37 (13.96%)	45 (11.39%)
Student 4	36 (14.06%)	…	…
Total	**256 (100%)**	**265 (100%)**	**395 (100%)**
	G_4	**G_5**	**G_6**
Student 1	640 (68.38%)	209 (67.64%)	150 (61.48%)
Student 2	296 (31.62%)	100 (32.36%)	94 (38.52%)
Total	**936 (100%)**	**309 (100%)**	**244 (100%)**

In 2010, the percentage of contributions ranged from 39.56 % to 16.40 % of total activities. One student in group 1 (G_1) contributed to almost 40 % of the work, and the rest was distributed among the other students. In group 2 (G_2), one student contributed to 87.43 %. The same situation occurred in group 3 (G_3), where one student contributed to 70.05 %. In 2011, two students in group 3 (G_3) contributed to 82.53 %. In group 2 (G_2), one student made 46.48 % of all contributions. In contrast, the work was more equally distributed in group 1 (G_1) than in the other groups. In 2012, a similar distribution of work can be observed. One student did most of the work in groups 4, 5, and 6 (G_4, G_5, G_6). Two students in group 2 and 3 (G_2, G_3) contributed to more than 80 % of the work. The work contribution of group 1 (G_1) was evenly distributed for three students, with the exception of one student (Student 4). Table 2 shows the level of contribution made by each student in the respective groups. A cross-checking of the results over three years shows that one student did most of the work in groups of 2 students. In groups of 3 students, 2 members did most of the work, with the exception of group 1 (G_1), and in lesser degree group 2 (G_2) in 2011. In groups of 4 students, most of the work was distributed among 2 or 3 students. The table does neither indicate the types of actions or activities performed by the students, nor show the level of collaboration among students. Thus, further analysis is required to gain more insight into the level of collaborative writing and the types of actions carried out on the wikis.

5.2 Type of Actions

The analysis of the results shows that the students carried out all editing actions described in the taxonomy for collaborative writing (add, modify, and delete information; add, fix, and delete link; format; and grammar, style, and spelling) to a certain extent. Table 3 shows all editing actions over a period of three years (2010–2012). Note that grammar, style, and spelling are put together, because these actions are somehow similar. They aim at correcting grammar mistakes and spelling, changing the style, typography, and presentation of the wiki pages. These actions may be considered as collaborative writing activities, though to a lesser degree than clarifying information, especially when students contribute to each other's work.

Table 3. Number and frequency of actions (2010–2012).

	Total 2010	2010 (%)	Total 2011	2011 (%)	Total 2012	2012 (%)	Total 2010–2012	2010–2012 (%)
Clarify information	418	12.89	91	7.49	344	12.04	853	10.81
Delete information	265	8.17	96	8.30	207	7.25	568	7.91
Add information	599	18.47	309	28.27	589	20.62	1497	22.45
Fix link	100	3.09	33	3.81	221	7.73	354	4.87
Delete link	21	0.65	21	1.67	77	2.70	119	1.67
Add link	324	9.99	178	17.72	505	17.68	1007	15.13
Grammar, style/typography, spelling	92	2.84	119	12.08	245	8.59	456	7.84
Format	1424	43.90	228	20.66	668	23.39	2320	29.32
Total actions	3243	100	1075	100	2856	100	7174	100

The most frequent action in 2010 was format (43.90 %), followed by add information (18.47 %), clarify information (12.89 %), add link (9.99 %), delete information (8.17 %), fix link (3.09 %), grammar/style/spelling (2.84 %), and delete link (0.65 %). In 2011, the most frequent action was add information (28.27 %), followed by format (20.66 %), add link (17.72 %), grammar/style/spelling (12.08 %), delete information

(8.30 %), clarify information (7.49 %), fix link (3.81 %), and delete link (1.67 %). In 2012, the most important action was format (23.39 %), followed by add information (20.62 %), add link (17.68 %), clarify information (12.04 %), grammar/style/spelling (8.59 %), fix link (7.73 %), delete information (7.25 %), and delete link (2.70 %).

The average result achieved for the three-year period was a follows. The most frequent action was format (29.32 %), followed by add information (22.45 %), add link (15.13 %), clarify information (10.81 %), delete information (7.91 %), grammar/style/spelling (7.84 %), fix link (4.87 %), and delete link (1.67 %). A total of 7174 actions were performed, but only 853 actions (10.81 %) aimed at genuine collaboration. If grammar/style/spelling (456 actions, 7.84 %) are considered as collaborative writing actions, then the total number of actions that aimed at collaboration is 1309, that is 18.25 % of all actions.

Hence, it appears that cooperation was more evident that collaboration and that no significant progress has been made from 2010 to 2012 regarding the action "modify information" (average score 10.81 %). The action started with 12.89 %, decreased in 2011 (7.49 %), and increased in 2012 (12.04 %). Format (29.32 %) and add information (22.45 %) were the most important actions over three years, in contrast to clarify information and grammar/style/spelling.

Furthermore, the results show that a total of 7174 actions were performed over the period of three years, 2856 actions in 2012, 1075 in 2011, and 3243 in 2010 respectively. Looking at the category of actions over the three-year period, it appears that the following ascending order can be identified (Fig. 2):

- Actions on navigation (add, delete, and fix link) with 1480 actions (20.63 %)
- Actions on presentation and structure (format) with 2320 actions (32.34 %)
- Actions on sentences (add and delete information), with 2065 actions (28.78 %)
- Actions within sentences (clarify information, grammar, style/typography, and spelling) with 1309 actions (18.25 %)

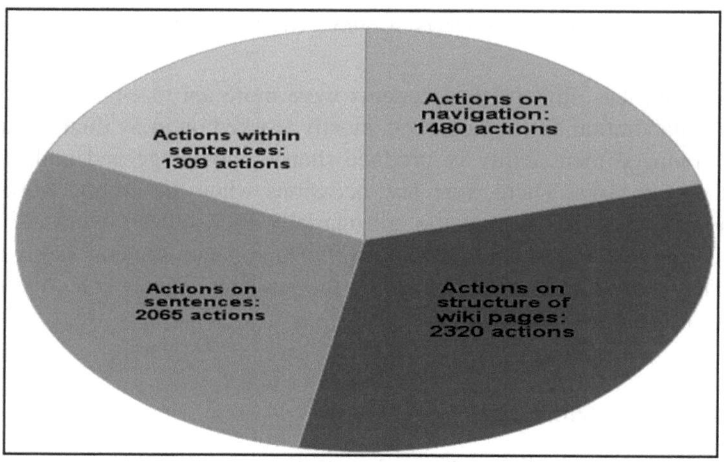

Fig. 2. Types of actions carried out on the wikis.

Looking closely at these categories, it appears that students focused mostly on format, that is actions that affect the presentation and appearance of the wiki pages (addition of space lines, sorting/moving of paragraphs or links and addition of subtitles in order to structure the content). The next common actions were those within entire sentences in terms of addition or deletion of information or content without changing the meaning of the text. This is followed by actions on navigation (addition of links within the wiki and to external Web sites, and deletion or fixing of existing of links). The less common action was clarifying information or content, grammar, and spelling. Figure 2 shows the distribution of actions among these categories. A closer look reveals that addition/deletion of information or content, navigation, and presentation/structure were the most common actions (81.75 % of total actions). The evolution of students' actions over three years confirms the results (Fig. 3).

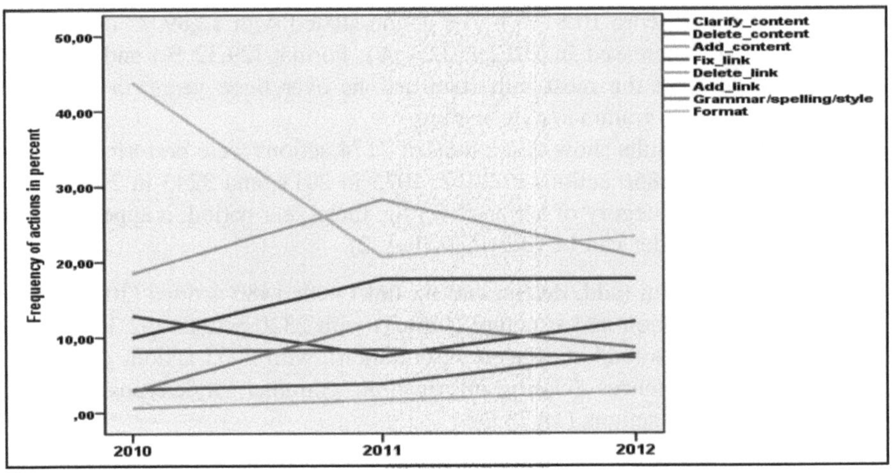

Fig. 3. Evolution of students' actions over three years (2010–2012).

Summarizing, it is obvious that students were more apt to engage in cooperation rather than collaboration. Group members mostly worked on individual sections of the wikis. This reduced their ability to produce shared knowledge and collective documents of the wiki tasks. There were few occasions when the groups worked on the same section of the wiki by revising substantially each other's work. Clearly, this cannot be considered as genuine collaborative writing, since students rarely revised or modified each other's information. Instead, the students were more concerned with format, add information, and add links.

5.3 Timing of Contribution

Table 4 shows the timing of contribution over a period of three years, including the average number of actions per week. Note that in 2011 and 2012, the workload for the month of March was distributed over two weeks, which means that the average number of actions per week must be divided by 2, and not by 4 as it is the case for the month of May in 2010. In 2010, Table 4 shows that all groups worked much as the last deadline approached, and did not follow the schedule assigned throughout the experiment period from January, 19 to May, 14. This was particularly true for group 1 (G_1) and group 3 (G_3). In 2011, a similar tendency was observed, particularly for group 2 (G_2) and group 3 (G_3), in stark contrast to group 1 (G_1). Also here the average number of actions performed in March was much higher than in February and January. This was also the case in 2012, though to a lesser degree.

Table 4. Average number of actions per week (2010–2012).

2010				
	G_1	**G_2**	**G_ 3**	**Average no. of actions per week**
January (2 weeks)	2	1	0	1.5
February (4 weeks)	26	31	19	19
March (4 weeks)	247	43	30	80
April (4 weeks)	323	55	114	123
May (4 weeks)	966	94	172	308
Total	1564	224	335	117.94

2011				
	G_1	**G_2**	**G_3**	**Average no. of actions per week**
January (2 weeks)	91	30	4	62.5
February (4 weeks)	187	97	62	86.5
March (2 weeks)	87	129	140	178
Total	365	256	206	103.37

2012							
	G_1	**G_2**	**G_3**	**G_4**	**G_5**	**G_6**	**Average no. of actions per week**
January (2 weeks)	155	11	0	3	0	1	85
February (4 weeks)	490	207	128	240	148	178	347.75
March (2 weeks)	291	173	116	21	156	79	418
Total	936	391	244	264	304	258	299.62

As a result, it seems that a slight progression has occurred from 2010 to 2012 since the amount of work has not increased drastically the last month in 2012 in comparison to 2011, which achieved a better result than in 2010. This, however, does not automatically mean that students collaborated. It is more likely that they cooperated as a triangulation of the timing of contributions seems to indicate, in accordance with the types of actions carried out on the wikis, and work distribution among students of the respective groups.

6 Discussion

6.1 Summary of Results

A cross-checking of the results shows that the students did not collaborate much in their attempt to perform writing tasks. First, some students did most of the work, while others contributed little to the wikis. Work distribution was not evenly distributed among the students (Research question 1). In terms of actions carried out on the wikis, 81.25 % of all actions were not related to genuine collaboration (Research question 2). Finally, in terms of timing of contributions, the students did most of the work the last weeks before the deadline in 2010 and 2011, and in lesser degree in 2012 (Research question 3).

6.2 Influencing Factors

A number of influencing factors may explain the low level of collaboration. These may be classified in two broad categories: Contextual and personal factors. Contextual factors are those related to the teacher, technology, assessment procedures, and learning paradigm. Personal factors are students' motivation, prior knowledge in collaborative writing, and familiarity with wiki technology. In addition to influencing factors, some recommendations are suggested to improve collaborative writing.

According to Karasavvidis [13], the learning paradigm in higher education is based more on the behaviourist paradigm than collaborative learning. Hence, wiki-mediated collaborative writing may be inhibited when it is introduced into educational settings where traditional views of learning such as behaviouristic practices are actually predominant. As a result, students without sufficient collaborative skills may be disadvantaged even though collaborative writing is potentially possible with wiki technology. Another factor that may have influenced students' collaborative writing activities is the assessment procedure used to evaluate students' contributions to the wikis. Since students were assessed as groups, and not according to their individual contributions, it is not surprising that some students did not fully engage in collaborative writing. As a result, most of the work was done by some students as the distribution of work clearly reveals. It is also possible that some students were more dominant than others [2]. Clearly, collaborative writing requires more group assessment, because it may be necessary to judge individual contributions, which in turn, may influence positively students' contributions to collaborative writing. The third factor is the wiki technology being used, that is MediaWiki. While the tool is based on an interface with a simplified HTML language, it does not offer an advanced WYSIWYG editor, which may facilitate the use of wikis. In addition, the discussion page is not good enough to promote reflections on collaborative writing, influencing thereby students' activities performed on the wikis.

The first category of personal factors comprises perceptions that students hold about wikis, familiarity with the tool being used, its limitations and potentialities for collaborative writing [5, 27]. Informal discussions and observations revealed that some students without technical background were not always comfortable with wikis. On the other hand, students with solid background in information technologies were more confident in using wikis. While students did not feel that they had to know everything about wikis, they did not deny the importance of familiarizing themselves with wikis to the extent of knowing what their functionalities are and how to use them for developing wikis. Some students believed that pre-work and preparation for wiki use before entering collaborative writing would have helped them to tackle some technical problems. The second personal factor is the students' lack of collaborative skills and experience in collaborative learning. Such skills are indeed necessary to foster collaborative learning, which is a prerequisite for collaborative writing. Hence, collaborative learning should not be limited to wikis alone but should be possible using any means found useful, for example let students work together and discuss a topic that can add to each other's knowledge [28]. Another critical factor of success is the students' motivation to effectively engage in meaningful collaborative writing [24]. Motivation is an essential component of wiki-based collaborative writing. Observations and informal discussions revealed that motivated students edited more content and used more wiki features. It seems that motivation is closely related to the wiki task itself, and whether it is relevant and meaningful to the students.

6.3 Recommendations

Based on the results and influencing factors, some recommendations are suggested to help students engage in genuine collaborative writing using wiki technology. Firstly, students need to familiarize themselves with wiki functionality, because not all students possess sufficient pre-requisite knowledge for using wikis [29]. Hence, technical training is still needed to help students acquire the basic knowledge that is necessary to use wikis for collaborative writing. Training includes understanding HTML coding, formatting wiki pages, editing the content, using the discussion page for communicating, and looking at the statistics and information produced by the wiki tool, etc. Students should also be made aware of the shortcomings of existing wiki tools, and their added value as well.

Secondly, wiki technology should be improved to include a WYSIWYG editor and additional features that facilitate collaborative writing. Likewise, the discussion page of existing wiki tools is not good enough to support genuine communication. It should be improved and used in conjunction with other Web 2.0 technologies, such as Google Docs, Twitter, or Facebook, and other information technologies such as mobile phone, Skype, and emails.

Another recommendation that may foster collaborative writing is the students' preparation and prior acquisition of basic collaborative skills [5]. Students should have a sense of how collaboration can be achieved by following a common goal and coordinating their efforts under the guidance of the teacher. Knowing how to collaborative, share information, interact with peers is clearly an advantage in a wiki-based learning environment.

Then, in terms of wiki content, students need to be knowledgeable in the topics being studied in order to create wikis of good quality with relevant references and links to external pages, because those lacking basic knowledge in the wiki topic will not be able to truly contribute to the wiki content. In addition, students should possess some language proficiency to make the writing process easier, especially for those with technical background [30].

Furthermore, collaborative writing needs to benefit from clear assessment procedures and criteria. These may include both peer-assessment and self-assessment, on individual or group basis. To be effective, assessment of students' contributions to the wikis should be mandatory, and based on pre-established quality criteria. Clear assessment procedures may foster both intrinsic and extrinsic motivation to achieve learning goals.

Moreover, the process of creating wikis needs to be carefully planned by teachers to guide and sustain students' collaborative writing activities. The role of the teacher is to create an atmosphere of confidence that helps students take control over their own learning. Teachers in a wiki-based environment should offer students an opportunity to gain practical skills in collaboration.

Finally, in addition to management and planning activities, wiki-based collaborative writing cannot be successful without a sound pedagogy based on collaborative learning or similar learning paradigms such as the sociocultural approach to learning [17]. A pedagogical strategy that supports genuine collaborative writing should engage students in peer editing and meaningful discussions to a greater benefit for the groups.

7 Conclusions and Future Work

Wikis have the potential to foster collaborative writing in teacher education, but wiki-mediated collaborative writing is a demanding task that requires pedagogical changes. These are however difficult to achieve mainly because contextual and personal factors, which can act as barriers to learning, can prevent students from collaborating. Even if it is impossible to draw any general conclusions from the experiments that were performed in 2010, 2011, and 2012, it can be ascertained that students did not make a real progress in their attempt to collaborate. Rather, the experiments show that cooperation was more evident than collaboration. To exploit the full potential of wikis in future experiments, it is important to guide students into all aspects of wiki-based collaborative writing. This entails taking into consideration both contextual and personal factors that affect wiki-based collaborative writing and the suggested recommendations as well. Moreover, progress in wiki-based collaborative writing can be achieved only through the iterative and continuous cycle of experimentations and evaluations in varied teacher education contexts.

References

1. Chao, J.: Student project collaboration using wikis. In: Proceedings of the 20th Conference on Software Engineering Education and Training (CSEE&T 2007), Dublin, Ireland, pp. 255–261. IEEE Press, Washington, DC (2007)
2. Meishar-Tal, H., Gorsky, P.: Wikis: what students do and do not do when writing collaboratively. J. Open Distance Learn. **25**(11), 25–35 (2010)

3. Trentin, G.: Using a wiki to evaluate individual contribution to a collaborative learning project. J. Comput. Assist. Learn. **25**, 43–55 (2008)
4. Witney, D., Smallbone, T.: Wiki work: can using wikis enhance student collaboration for group assignment task? Innovations Educ. Teach. Int. **48**(1), 101–110 (2011)
5. Minocha, S., Thomas, P.G.: Collaborative learning in a wiki environment: experiences from a software engineering course. New Rev. Hypermedia Multimedia **13**(2), 187–209 (2007)
6. Thomas, P., King, D., Minocha, S.: The effective use of a simple wiki to support collaborative learning activities. Comput. Sci. Educ. **19**(4), 293–313 (2009)
7. Kuteeva, M.: Wikis and academic writing: changing the writer-reader relationship. Engl. Specif. Purp. **30**, 44–57 (2011)
8. Naismith, L., Lee, B.H., Pilkington, R.M.: Collaborative learning with a wiki: differences in perceived usefulness in two contexts of use. J. Comput. Assist. Learn. **27**(3), 228–242 (2011)
9. Cole, M.: Using wiki technology to support student engagement: lessons from the trenches. Comput. Educ. **52**, 141–146 (2009)
10. Grant, L.: 'I don't' Care Do Our Own Page!' A case study of using wikis for collaborative work in a UK secondary school. Learn. Media Technol. **34**(2), 105–117 (2009)
11. Elgort, I., Smith, A.G., Toland, J.: Is wiki an effective platform for group course work? Aust. J. Educ. Technol. **24**(2), 195–210 (2008)
12. Judd, T., Kennedy, G., Cropper, S.: Using wikis for collaborative learning: assessing collaboration through contribution. Aust. J. Educ. Technol. **26**(3), 341–354 (2010)
13. Karasavvidis, I.: Wiki uses in higher education: exploring barriers to successful implementation. Interact. Learn. Environ. **18**(3), 219–231 (2010)
14. Kasemvilas, S., Olfman, L.: Design alternatives for a MediaWiki to support collaborative writing. J. Inf. Inf. Technol. Organ. **4**, 87–104 (2009)
15. Su, F., Beaumont, C.: Evaluating the use of a wiki for collaborative learning. Innovations Educ. Teach. Int. **47**, 417–431 (2010)
16. Lund, A., Smørdal, O.: Is there a space for the teacher in a wiki? In: Proceedings of WikiSym 2006, pp. 27–45, Odense, Denmark, 21–23 Aug 2006
17. Vygotsky, L.S.: Mind and Society: the Development of Higher Mental Processes. Harvard University Press, Cambridge (1978)
18. Dillenbourg, P., Baker, M., Blaye, A., O'Malley, C.: The evolution of research on collaborative writing. In: Spada, E., Reiman, P. (eds.) Learning in Humans and Machine: Towards an Interdisciplinary Learning Science, pp. 189–211. Elsevier, Oxford (1996)
19. Scanlon, E.: How gender influences learners working collaboratively with science simulations. Learn. Instr. **10**, 463–481 (2000)
20. Pfeil, U., Zaphiris, P., Ang, C.S.: Cultural differences in collaborative authoring of Wikipedia. J. Comput.-Mediated Commun. **12**(1), 88–113 (2006)
21. Hadjerrouit, S.: Collaborative writing with wikis: evaluating students' contributions. In: Proceedings of the IADIS International Conference on Cognition and Exploratory Learning in the Digital Age (CELDA 2011), pp. 173–180 (2011)
22. Hadjerrouit, S.: Using wikis for collaborative learning: critical evaluation and recommendations. In: Proceedings of the IADIS International Conference e-Society, pp. 91–98 (2012a)
23. Hadjerrouit, S.: Using wikis to foster collaborative writing: exploring influencing factors to successful implementation. In: Proceedings of the IADIS International Conference on Cognition and Exploratory Learning in the Digital Age, pp. 131–138 (2012b)
24. Hadjerrouit, S.: Collaborative writing with wikis: pedagogical and technological implications for successful implementation in teacher education. In: Sampson, D.G., Isaias, P., Ifenthaler, D., Spector, J.M. (eds.) Ubiquitous and Mobile Learning in the Digital Age, pp. 173–189. Springer, Berlin (2013)

25. Hadjerrouit, S.: Wiki as a collaborative writing tool in teacher education: evaluation and suggestions for effective use. Comput. Hum. Behav. **32**, 301–312 (2014)
26. Leung, K., Chu, S.K.W.: Using wikis for collaborative learning: a case study of an undergraduate students' group project in Hong Kong. http://hub.hku.hk/bitstream/10722/127129/1/Content.pdf (2009). Accessed 12 Sept 2013
27. Caple, H., Bogle, M.: Making group assessment transparent: what wikis can contribute to collaborative projects. Assess. Eval. High. Educ. **38**(2), 198–210 (2013)
28. Tetard, F., Patokorpi, E., Packalen, K.: Using wikis to support constructivist learning: a case study in university education settings. In: Proceedings of the 42nd Hawaii International Conference on System Sciences, pp. 1–10 (2009)
29. Harsell, D.M.: Wikis in the classroom: faculty and student perspective. J. Polit. Sci. Educ. **6** (3), 310–314 (2010)
30. Li, M., Whu, W.: Patterns of computer-mediated interaction in small writing groups using wikis. Comput. Assist. Lang. Learn. **26**(1), 61–82 (2013)

Removing the Barriers to Adoption of Social OER Environments

Henri Pirkkalainen[1(✉)], Jussi P.P. Jokinen[1], Jan M. Pawlowski[2], and Thomas Richter[3]

[1] University of Jyväskylä, Mattilanniemi 2, Agora Building, 40014 Jyväskylä, Finland
{henri.j.pirkkalainen, jussi.p.p.jokinen}@jyu.fi
[2] Ruhr West University of Applied Sciences, 45407 Mülheim, Germany
Jan.Pawlowski@hs-ruhrwest.de
[3] University of Duisburg-Essen, Universitätsstrasse 9, 45141 Essen, Germany
Thomas.Richter@icb.uni-due.de

Abstract. Despite the opportunities and benefits of OER, research and practice has shown how the OER repositories have a hard time in reaching an active user-base. The opportunities of experience exchange and simple feedback mechanisms of social software have been realized for improving the situation and many are basing or transforming their OER offerings towards socially powered environments. Research on social software has shown how knowledge-sharing barriers in online environments are highly culture and context-specific and require proper investigation. It is crucial to study what challenges might arise in such environments and how to overcome them, ensuring a successful uptake. A large-scale (N = 855) cross-European investigation was initiated in the school context to determine which barriers teachers and learners perceive as critical. The study highlights barriers on cultural distance, showing how those are predicted by nationality and age of the respondents. The paper concludes with recommendations for overcoming those barriers.

Keywords: OER · Social software · Knowledge sharing · Barriers

1 Introduction

Open educational resources (OERs) and practices to increase the sharing behavior of both educators and learners have been widely discussed in the domain of technology-enhanced learning (TEL) in the recent years. Online OER environments have been receiving attention because they serve as platforms for educators and learners to search and collaborate in. While many initiatives have been rather successful in keeping their OER environments in linear growth with increased amounts of published learning objects [1], maintaining active participation in and use of the OER environments remains the key challenge [2, 3, 4]. Existing research has been discussing various barriers that hinder or negatively affect OER adoption and use in teaching and learning activities. Such barriers relate to lack of awareness of OER and related copyright and intellectual property issues [2, 4, 5], Institutional regulations and restrictions [4, 5], quality of resources [5, 6], and so

S. Zvacek et al. (Eds.): CSEDU 2014, CCIS 510, pp. 19–34, 2015.
DOI: 10.1007/978-3-319-25768-6_2

on. As indicated by Chen [2] and Hatakka [5], not all challenges become significant, and barriers can be highly context-dependent. Therefore, many challenges could occur depending on the types of educational practices in the region or country and depending on the background, experiences, and perceptions of the educators and learners.

The OER movement must consider the implications of knowledge sharing carefully, as many initiatives are basing their OER services and environments on social software-like functionalities that place educators and learners as key users to share, discuss, and collaboratively work on OERs [7, 8]. The established connection between social software and OERs to social OER environments can have multiple potentials. As indicated by research on social software in provision of teaching and in pedagogy, these services can provide positive learning outcomes and intriguing experiences for both educators and learners when applied to teaching practices [9, 10]. However, the connection to OER places educators even more in a key role in OER environments with a strong focus on functionalities for networking and collaboration. As elaborated by Lai and Chen [11] and Zhang [12], adoption of specific social software services can still suffer from many types of organizational and social barriers, and most of all, the adoption might be highly country dependent because of differences in culture and context. As argued by Agarwal et al. [13], there are various challenges to knowledge sharing while so-called cultural distance becomes highly important in a context where people deal within online social environments. However, the current literature has been very limited in studies that could inform the domain regarding how strong those barriers are perceived across nations, within educator and learner communities that adopt these social OER environments. Such information is necessary for any educational institution or educator evaluating the suitability of the OER environments to own purposes.

We address this gap by the means of a large-size exploratory study (N = 855) to investigate how (1) the barriers to adoption of social OER environments are perceived, and (2) how strongly the barrier of cultural distance is perceived by teachers and learners in primary and secondary schools across Europe. Within our study, the aim is not to define culture or different types of influencing factors for it. However, we aim to understand in a cross-national view to what extent teachers and learners perceive cultural distance when dealing with OER online social environments. In addition to observing the barriers, our study strives to understand possibilities to overcome them. These interventions are discussed on a technical and nontechnical level.

The structure of the paper is as follows. The next section describes the theoretical background for barriers to social software focused OER. Then, we will describe the methodology for the study. The results are presented in the fourth section, followed by the discussion of the results. The paper concludes by describing the limitations of this study as well as the key contributions to both research and practice.

2 Theoretical Background

OER has been a widely discussed topic since 2002 when UNESCO coined the term in a global OER forum. OER was described by UNESCO [14] as "technology enabled, open provision of educational resources for consultation, use and adaptation by a community of users for non-commercial purposes." Within this study, the focus is on barriers that prevent educators and learners from adopting OER and in ways to overcome those challenges. These barriers are discussed on various levels, on the missing organizational support mechanisms [2, 4], lack of infrastructure and proper hardware [2, 5], lack of quality of the resources as well as in the provided services [15], and so forth. Existing research is yet to define in which contexts and even in which countries or regions certain barriers are likely to occur. One of the key issues in the literature that could explain contextual differences is culture and specifically, culture of OER sharing [16, 17].

As elaborated by a number of researchers, studying cultural differences can be problematic. Church and Katigbak [18], e.g., argue that while "one needs culture-comparable constructs to make cross-cultural comparisons, their use may distort the meaning of constructs in some cultures or miss their culture-specific aspects." Goldschmidt [19] even goes a step further, claiming that it generally is inappropriate to compare cultures at all, as every "institution" needs to "be seen as a product of the culture within which it developed. It follows from this that a cross-cultural comparison of institutions is essentially a false enterprise, for we are comparing incomparables." As a consequence, most culture comparisons are limited to value systems, as there is a hope that there are general values, which at least play a certain (even if not exactly the same) role across most of the human societies. Within this study, we focus on educational contexts and define culture, according to Oetting [20], as "customs, beliefs, social structure, and activities of any group of people who share a common identification and who would label themselves as members of that group" (herein, perceptions of educators and learners in the educational context).

As cultural issues are constantly raised as critical in OER and knowledge sharing literature [13, 12], our focus will be to understand barriers related to cultural distance. The concept of cultural distance depends on the recipient's perceptions on how strong the difference between the home culture and host culture are; the greater the perceived difference, the more difficult it is to establish a relationship [21]. As an example, such distance can be perceived when educators or learners try to adopt OERs or teaching practices that are exceptional or unfitting to their own context. In the context of OERs, cultural distance becomes a highly relevant issue when educators and learners shall use OERs from different contexts; being constantly exposed to potential learning materials and forms of collaboration that may not fit to their own preferences of working and learning or take place in their own native language.

Recent research in the educational domain shows the increasing interest toward social software. Social software can be described as a set of tools to enable interactive collaboration, managing content, and networking with others [10]. While the application of social environments has been discussed as a support mechanism for pedagogy [9, 11], the connection to OER is rather emerging. The focus of social and collaborative services in OER environments sets educators as key users of the environments. Such "collaborative content federations" [7, 8] often provide materials in various languages, while the environments are not equally translated to support international users. While language skills and preferences vary across educational level and countries, the preferences of educators and learners in terms of language or collaboration are not well known.

OER as well as social software research focuses on understanding particular barriers in order to overcome them. Solutions and interventions have been suggested as possible mechanisms to lower the barriers [2, 4, 5], such as technology and policy-related strategies to be implemented [2] or short- to long-term drivers or enablers from cooperation to OER development [4]. Within this paper, we aim to determine mechanisms for lowering the barriers in social OER environments.

3 Methodology

Our study targeted school education, focusing on teachers and learners in primary and secondary schools across Europe. The aim was to find out (1) what barriers to adoption of social OER environments are perceived as most significant by the teachers and learners, (2) how far cultural distance is perceived as a barrier against the use of social OER environments, and (3) how to overcome the critical barriers.

In our study, we first investigated barriers in general, by asking teachers and learners for their experiences regarding the use of (selected) social OER environments; we wanted to know which aspects in particular were understood as the major barriers against the use of existing OER environments. Second, we asked the participants to determine the improvement potential for the experimentally used social OER environments, in order to identify possible interventions that would be appropriate for overcoming the found barriers.

3.1 Operationalization

There are many types of barriers that might disrupt and stop teachers from adopting and continuing to use social OER environments. A survey needed to be operationalized for this study that would try to capture most essential or likely challenges that teachers might perceive when using social OER environments. The study needed to be extensive to capture essential issues and at the same time, condensed to ensure proper amount of participants. For the study, the key literature presented in the theoretical background on OER and knowledge sharing was used as a basis for the survey. Additionally, a group of experts were addressed to discuss those barriers and to remove the irrelevant for this context. A group of experts was addressed in a focus group session co-located at the Open Discovery Space project meeting in Athens in the spring of 2012. The experts were project partners and coordination team from the Open Discovery Space (ODS)-project. Each participant (26 in total) had large amount of expertise in OER and in development projects around those. During the session, the issues identified in the theoretical background were discussed and additionally, the experts identified other crucial issues or challenges. The discussion was recorded and analyzed for selecting and finding the barriers for the study at hand. Finally, the following barriers were included in the study.

- "Language is the key". I only want to contribute to online communication/collaboration when my own native language is used (newly identified barrier)

- Challenging to apply digital educational resources which are culturally distant (values, symbols, beliefs etc.) from my own (new barrier in relation to adapting and re-using OER)
- Impact of cultural and geographical distance - Lack of trust towards authors of digital educational resources [22], [5]
- Digital educational resources do not give enough information on the context where it is/was created and used [16]
- Do not have enough time to use digital educational resources [23]
- Lack of reward for the efforts made (e.g. not getting paid extra to prepare digital educational resources) [13]
- Lack of common practice - People are not accustomed to use and share digital educational resources within my organization [5]
- Lack of training on how to use digital educational resources for my work [5]
- Lack of support within my own organization on how to use digital educational resources [23]
- Hard to judge the quality of digital educational resources without spending time evaluating them [24]
- Hard to judge the quality of tools and services (around digital educational resources) which I'm unfamiliar with (new barrier for social OER environments)
- Lack of motivation to share own digital educational resources [13]
- Lack of motivation to contribute to discussions around digital educational resources (Adapted to social OER environments based on Noll et al. [25])
- I do not trust digital educational resources that have been produced by others [5]
- Matching digital educational resources to own curriculum is extremely demanding [16]
- Difficult to find relevant digital educational resources for my purpose [5]
- I feel reluctant to use the digital educational resource if there is license or copyright information attached to it [24]

3.2 Operationalization of "Cultural Distance"

To address cultural distance and to observe which aspects can predict its significance, a decision was made to operationalize related barriers into this one latent factor. The focus of the source literature has not fully covered all of the barriers to a culture of sharing and collaborating in OER environments. As discussed, studying cultural influence factors in a holistic setting is impossible because of the wide variety of cultural aspects and the lack of knowledge regarding their distinction (dependencies and interrelations). The approach for the operationalization and selection of related challenges was set based on the previously presented understanding of cultural distance by Ward et al. [21]. For our investigation, we focused on barriers that are related to aspects of sharing and collaboration in social OER environments, the language of collaboration, and the distance of the identified OERs they come across.

As the found literature has not focused on social OER environments, modification of approaches to analyze barriers was necessary. A particular barrier towards cultural distance that was found in the literature was related to knowledge sharing and collaboration [25, 22]. This barrier was related to language component of cultural distance, as well as the perceived difference of the home and host context. As a common language is one of the greatest challenges for organizing distributed work [22, 25], we focused on this in our context. In our setting, teachers and learners are connected within an international community. The first item for our survey was therefore: "Language is the key". I only want to contribute to online communication/collaboration when my own native language is used ([22, 25]).

Richter and Ehlers [6] and Hatakka [5] discussed that teachers might experience an unmanageable distance when adapting resources from other cultural contexts particularly regarding language and culture-specific idioms. The second item chosen for the survey was: Challenging to apply digital educational resources which are culturally distant (values, symbols, beliefs, etc.) from my own (based on Hatakka [5]).

Distance can also result from a lack of trust against the authors of the OERs [5, 22]. While cultural distance can be perceived without geographical or temporal distance [25], the notion of geography was included in the item to highlight the very likely geographic dispersion of users in the social OER environment. Thus, the third item was: Impact of cultural and geographical distance - Lack of trust towards authors of digital educational resources [5, 22].

Another important issue that derived from OER research was that OERs often do not provide enough information on the context where they were created and designed for [16]. This led to our fourth item: Digital educational resources do not give enough information on the context where it is/was created and used [16].

The focus was therefore set to study how the participants perceive OER that is created in a context that is distant from own, whether the distance has impact on the trust for the authors and providers of OER and if language plays a strong role for collaboration. The starting point of our analysis was, that these four culture barrier questionnaire items were indicators of a single latent factor.

3.3 Data Collection

The data collection was conducted within the scope of the Open Discovery Space project (ODS). The ODS [8] is an EU-funded FP7 project that builds a social OER environment for the European school context around a federation of learning content repositories. In the context of the ODS project, workshops for teachers and learners were organized. In the context of these workshops, existing social OER environments were introduced: OERs within their topics of teaching (and interest) exemplarily were used, and the potentials for adopting these environments were discussed. In the end of the workshops, the participants were asked to complete a questionnaire that addressed the particular challenges the participants experienced in this experiment and their expectations toward the upcoming ODS portal. The role of each workshop was to introduce the concepts addressed in the questionnaire. This ensured that the respondents were aware of what was asked from them.

The instrument was operationalized with a total of 23 items and 10 open questions, including the previously presented barriers. The purpose was to see which barriers the respondents perceive as most critical. The second part of the survey included open questions asking for enablers and interventions to overcome such challenges.

Approximately 2300 educators and learners participated in 92 workshops in 19 European countries. While schoolteachers were mainly expected to participate, ODS invited students, educators from higher education as well as policy makers to understand the restrictions and possibilities for influencing the European education system. The selection of schools was based on the longitudinal engagement plan of ODS for the schools of each country. Most of the workshops took place in a face-to-face setting and were organized by the local project partners. Four workshops were conducted online through video conferencing facilities. Each workshop focused on one or more particularly selected OER environment(s). The main criterion for the selection of the OER environments was related to supported social functionalities around the educational resources. The most frequently demonstrated environments within the workshops were:

- OpenScout – OER for business and management (http://learn.openscout.net)
- OSR – Open science resources (http://www.osrportal.eu)
- Discover the Cosmos – Astronomy resources (http://www.cosmosportal.eu)
- Photodentro – A Greek Digital Learning Object Repository (http://photodentro.edu.gr/lor/)

In the study, 1175 individuals from 19 European countries actually completed the questionnaire (nonresponse rate of 49 %). The countries were: Austria, Belgium, Croatia, Cyprus, Estonia, Finland, Germany, Greece, Ireland, Italy, Latvia, Lithuania, the Netherlands, Portugal, Serbia, Spain, and the United Kingdom. The respondents were mainly educators in primary, secondary, and higher education. Additionally, a number of learners and policy makers completed our survey. For the analysis herein, we excluded policy makers and participants representing higher education and only considered the responses of teachers and learners from primary and secondary school education (N = 855). The reason was to avoid mixing differing contexts of higher education and schools together. Additionally, the interventions could also be discussed more accurately when restricting the focus to a certain context. Some questionnaires were only partially completed. Because this was particularly the case in Romania, we finally excluded the country's participants from the evaluation. The mean age of the respondents was 37.4 years (SD = 11.1). Among the respondents, 69 % were female, and 83 % were teachers.

3.4 Data Analysis

The first task within our analysis was to find out how the studied barriers are perceived by teachers. The quantitative data (closed questions) was analysed by applying basic descriptive statistics. As one of the aims of the study was to find out cultural and national differences in the perceptions towards the barriers, variance analysis was applied (Using SPSS software, One way ANOVA) in order to study whether the ranking of the barriers is dependent on the nationality of the respondents.

The second part of the analysis addressed the previously discussed four cultural distance related items that were used in constructing a summated scale to represent the cultural distance barrier for the study at hand. The reliability of the items was confirmed using principal axis factoring. Factor loadings over .50 were expected, as well as loadings relatively comparable in size. The reliability coefficient of the cultural distance scale was calculated using both factor score covariance and Cronbach's alpha. After the reliability inspections, we proceeded to construct a summated scale by calculating the average of the four cultural distance barrier items. The average of all variables was used instead of factor loadings, because the study was exploratory and we wanted to retain the original scale (from one to five). Any missing values for the culture barrier items were imputed to replace missing data. The amount of missing values for the selected four items was between 6.1 % and 7.2 %. Analysis of the missing value patterns revealed no significant differences between the gender and the role of the respondents.

To explore the country differences regarding experienced barriers based on cultural distance, a generalized linear model (GLM) predicting cultural distance barrier was constructed. The fixed factors of the model were, in addition to the country of the respondent, the gender and professional status (teacher or learner). The age of the respondent was used as a covariate. An intercept was included in the model, which was full factorial, e.g., interaction effects between the fixed factors were also tested.

The final part of our study was to look for potential interventions against the critical barriers. This part of the survey applied open questions purposing to understand what could solve or lower the particular barriers reported by the respondents. The following open questions were applied to our survey for this purpose:

- "How could technology solutions around resources solve these problems (e.g., Ones presented to you/which you tried in the workshop)?"
- "How would you improve the current solution?"
- "What kind of help/training/tools would you need?"

Our intention was to find solutions to overcome the barrier of cultural distance and to see which other barriers require special attention. Key interventions against cultural distance barrier were found through clustering of the responses, which was accomplished with a focus on technical and organizational issues. The findings were understood as guiding steps for the ODS implementation.

4 Study Results

The following Fig. 1 highlights the primary and secondary school teachers' perceptions on the barriers selected for the study.

At this point, we wanted to deal with each barrier separately to find out most critical ones. The findings showed how the cultural barriers are not perceived highest when handling each barrier separately. The most critical challenges seem to relate to judging the quality of the resources without spending a lot of time evaluating them and matching OER to own curriculum. Surprisingly, many of the barriers were not generally seen as critical as those fall between somewhat significant (2 on a scale from 1 to 5) and fairly significant (3 on a scale from 1 to 5). The results of the variance analysis showed how the barriers are depending on the nationality of the respondents. The differences in the perceptions vary for each barrier (Fig. 2).

The factor loadings for the four culture barrier questionnaire items are displayed in Table 1. The Kaiser-Meyer-Olkin measure of sampling adequacy was .73, and

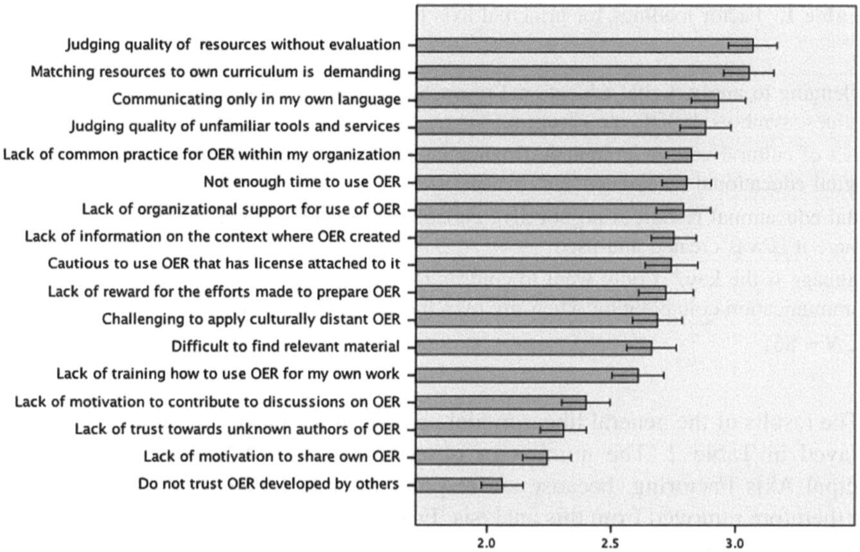

Fig. 1. Means of the barriers in social OER environments.

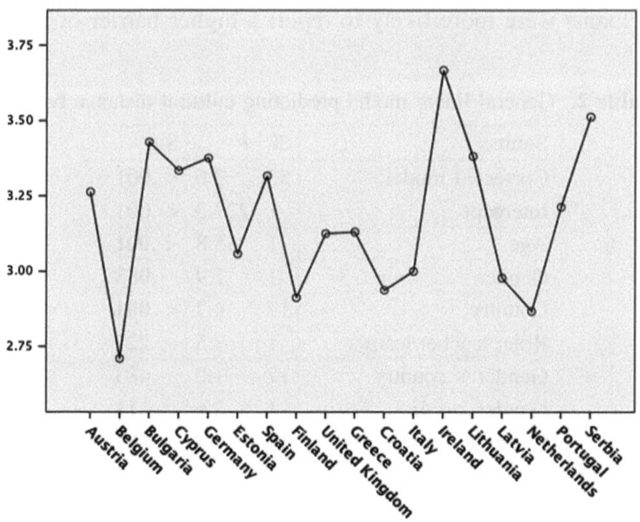

Fig. 2. Judging the quality of the resources without evaluation (country differences).

Bartlett's test of sphericity was statistically significant ($p < .001$). The single factor solution displayed in Table 1 had an eigenvalue of 2.2, and explained 56 % of the variance of the four cultural distance barriers. The reliability of the scale using factor score covariance was .74, and Cronbach's alpha was .72. The mean of the summated scale of culture barrier, calculated as the mean of the four items, was 2.65 (SD = 0.95), and both its theoretical and observed range was 1.00–5.00.

Table 1. Factor loadings for principal axis factoring of cultural distance barrier items.

Item	Loading
Challenging to apply digital educational resources which are culturally distant (values, symbols, beliefs etc.) from my own	.71
Impact of cultural and geographical distance - Lack of trust towards authors of digital educational resources	.69
Digital educational resources do not give enough information on the context where it is/was created and used	.58
"Language is the key." I only want to contribute to online communication/collaboration when my own native language is used	.54

Note. $N = 861$

The results of the general linear model predicting the barrier of cultural distance are displayed in Table 2. The number of observations for GLM was smaller than for Principal Axis Factoring, because six respondents had failed to report their age and were therefore removed from this analysis. From the main effects, age and country were statistically significant. Gender, role (teacher/learner), and the interaction effects between the fixed factors were nonsignificant. The coefficient of the model intercept was 1.88, and the upper and lower bounds of 95 % confidence interval were 1.50 and 2.29, $p < .001$. The coefficient of the age was .01 [.01, .02], $p < .001$. In other words, the older participants were more likely to report a higher barrier of cultural distance.

Table 2. General linear model predicting cultural distance barrier.

Source	df	*F*	Sig.
Corrected model	55	3.6	< .001
Intercept	1	227.3	< .001
Age	1	15.8	**< .001**
Gender	1	2.9	.088
Country	17	4.7	**< .001**
Role: teacher/learner	1	1.5	.227
Gender × country	17	1.0	.483
Gender × role	1	2.6	.111
Country × role	11	0.8	.581
Gender × country × role	6	0.4	.867

Note. $N = 855$. Model R squared = .20, adjusted = .14.

The GLM revealed how the cultural distance barrier depends on the nationality and age of the respondent. Results also indicated how the roles of teacher or learner do not explain the barrier of cultural distance. This implies that teachers are not more likely to perceive cultural distance barrier than learners and vice versa. The mean of the cultural distance barrier variable for learners was 2.52 (SD = 1.03), and for teachers 2.68 (SD = 0.93). For both males and females, the mean was 2.65, and standard deviations, respectively, were 0.93 and 0.96. The findings imply that the perceived cultural distance is not a barrier for majority but is likely to occur depending on the age and nationality of the teacher/learner.

The means of the cultural distance barrier variables between the countries were compared. Based on post-hoc analysis (least significant difference) we identified Croatia, Latvia, and Estonia to be the countries with statistically significantly high means as compared to the countries with relatively low means: Austria, Belgium, Spain, Finland, Ireland, the Netherlands, Portugal, and Serbia. The implications of these results will be discussed in the last section of this paper.

5 Interventions

As previously explained, our research was not limited to investigating the barriers to adoption of social OER environments. In addition, we also studied interventions for the corresponding barriers. The answers we received on the open questions asking for

Table 3. Non-technical interventions.

Key aspect	Explanation
Stimulate teacher and school motivation	OER initiatives to highlight clearly the benefits for different stakeholders, explore ways to offer something the schools wouldn't easily get elsewhere; virtual and physical visits, competitions, awards etc.
Translating/localizing resources to fit the context	Setting a group within small communities and schools to translate the best materials for that purpose into their own language. Setting contests that include translation/localization/adaptation tasks, rewarded by the ODS network in cooperation with the local schools. Rewards could be free access to events such as summer school, training events, or conferences
OER initiative stimulating the creation of knowledge-sharing culture in schools	Teacher's practices still vary, even within their own schools. This process should happen from the bottom-up and then expand to the European level. To create this culture of sharing resources, experiences, and competencies with others, the OER initiatives should reach teachers on local, national, and international levels by showing some good examples of collaboration across countries
	Equality and equity. Offer good, simple and affordable options for schools and teachers with poor access online and low resources
	OER initiatives should aim to be open communities focusing on support and experience exchange. Teachers and learners should feel a sense of belonging and be given something that they feel comfortable using. Otherwise they might feel afraid that they'll be criticized about what they wrote or contributed
	OER initiatives should provide opportunities for teachers to attend international training events, in order to help overcome cultural barriers in trusting resources from different cultures, as well as to feel that they are members of an international community

potential mechanisms to overcome the barriers were related to both technological and organizational/contextual levels: Overcoming the barriers, is not just a technical issue but relates to educators' and learners' own perceptions on the benefits they get from the engagement with OER and the community. The interventions on a non-technical level are in key position towards new sharing practices and change in perceptions towards OER (Table 3).

Also, the usability, the features and the components of social OER environments can help reducing the barriers as expressed by the respondents (Table 4).

Table 4. Technical interventions.

	Key aspect	Explanation
Usability	Speed of the portal, intuitive navigation, secure, stable etc.	Issues that make the user experience free-of-effort
Multilinguality	Resource availability in own native language	Many are unwilling or cannot handle foreign language
	Equal distribution of materials in different languages	Users need to have materials that are easy for them to apply
	Portal translated to own language	Shows that their language is important for the provider/developer
Quality mechanisms	Rich and versatile metadata, Recommendations and other ways to find relevant content, quality material that is pointed out for you	Simple ways to point out quality resources, where the resource comes from, how it can be used.
Curriculum matching	Cherry-picked, pre-selected quality OERs firstly that is linked to different subjects that anyone could enrich and extend	Customized for different countries and regions if necessary
Functionalities	Methods for communication/ collaboration, Sharing and collaborating	Synchronous/asynchronous, Formal/informal With anyone, With selected people/group/community.
Localization, customization	Intuitive and localized for specific user groups	Providing customized views for s/learners from different countries/regions/schools

The results on interventions to potentially overcome or reduce the barriers indicate the key opinions of teachers and learners of our study. As shown in the technical dimension, the provision of functionalities as well as the variety of resources has to match the particular requirements and needs of the individual users. As presented in the previous section, not all users in the different European countries have the experience or are able to collaborate in a foreign language or to adopt OER that might be culturally distant. The key intervention seems still to be stimulating a change in OER knowledge-sharing practices by leading examples through the engagement and training activities of the OER initiatives that also provide the OER environments.

6 Discussion and Conclusions

Within this paper we investigated the barriers against the use of social OER environments and ways to overcome those, focusing especially on the barrier of cultural distance. As the understanding on the barriers was rather limited, the findings of this study can provide a significant contribution to fill this gap. The results indicate how teachers and students in general do not perceive significant barriers to adoption of social OER environments. However, each barrier is strongly depending on nationality of the respondent. Therefore, a barrier for one person is not a critical issue for another. The results also indicated how age and nationality affect the significance of the cultural distance barrier. Younger respondents are more likely to experience a lower level of barrier when dealing with learning resources from and online collaboration with a distant culture. The results also evidence which of the 18 investigated countries' participants perceive cultural distance as a barrier. Interestingly, the professional role of the respondents did not significantly affect the perceptions towards cultural distance barrier.

Our study cannot inform on the reasons for the country differences but some issues could be speculated. The findings indicated that cultural distance is statistically significantly perceived as a barrier, particularly in the Baltic countries of Latvia and Estonia, and in Croatia. However, our study cannot explain why some countries had relatively low means in this context (e.g., Belgium, Spain, Finland, and the Netherlands). More research is needed to indicate the general validity of our results as well as to explain the reasons for the between-country deviations. While one argument could be that language skills and preferences differ between countries, such results might also be explained by awareness on OER in general. If the schools have a strong background in using textbooks, a rapid change to apply and modify OERs provided by an international community might not be realistic or trivial. Such a basic change of thinking and towards practical ways to approach preparation of lectures and teaching can be problematic. However, the findings do indicate how applying OERs that are prepared in/for a specific national/educational context might raise even more significant barrier within another context.

The influence of age regarding the perceived impact of cultural distance barrier is an important finding as it has not yet been reported in the context on OER. However, Onyechi and Abeysinghe [26] reported similar results regarding the use of technology; they found that users under 35 years old are more likely to accept collaborative tools.

Regarding interventions against the barriers in general, we found both technical and nontechnical issues. The respondents elaborated on how social OER environments must fulfill their basic needs in terms of the quality of provided services and resources, and multilinguality. In order to generally reach a higher level of acceptance, OER initiatives should not just provide the technology for the OER usage but additionally foster the change toward openness in education. In this context, intense cooperation with the schools is required, e.g., approaching joint campaigns and collaborative efforts to contextualize/translate OERs for the contexts of the schools.

Our study and the related results have limitations: First of all, our results need to be limited to the context of school education, where the research took place. It is yet unclear to which extent those can be transferred to other educational scenarios. The participating schools were selected from existing networks of the partner organizations in the project. In many cases, only teachers from one specific area of the country participated. Thus, the sample might not be fully representative for all schools in the country. Additionally, we did not investigate the previous experience of the participants with OER. In retrospective, this might have been valuable information for both the analysis as well as the interpretation of the actually received results. We do acknowledge that the actual barriers differ between teachers in different contexts and educational institutions.

As the research was conducted as a part of the requirements analysis for the development of the social OER environment for the ODS project, the practical implications of our study are clear, especially for OER providers and developers: The results are relevant for any engagement activities with teachers and learners in similar OER scenarios. As OER provision through resource-/repository-federations becomes even more frequent, our results support the decisions on how to overcome some typical challenges. The results also give pragmatic suggestions to engage through the younger teachers as early adopters and community builders. Our findings can therefore help to significantly reduce efforts placed for the identification of needs and requirements of teachers and learners during the development of social OER environments.

Our contribution to research lies in the exploration of the barriers to adoption of social OER environments and in the exploratory factor analysis conducted within this study. The identification of the factors representing barriers that are related to cultural distance provides a meaningful construct for future quantitative studies on OERs. Future studies on the topic could apply the proposed construct on variance models to verify and enrich existing theories on, e.g., technology acceptance. It would be important to address further studies to explain which barriers (e.g., lack of support within the organization, lack of awareness on OER) can predict barriers on the level of cultural distance.

Acknowledgements. This Research Has Been Co-Funded by the European Commission through the CIP Programme, Open Discovery Space, CIP-ICT-PSP-2011-5 297229 (Cf. http://www.opendiscoveryspace.eu).

References

1. Ochoa, X., Duval, E.: Quantitative analysis of learning object repositories. IEEE Trans. Learn. Technol. **2**, 226–238 (2009)
2. Chen, Q.: Use of open educational resources: challenges and strategies. In: Tsang, P., Cheung, S.K.S., Lee, V.S.K., Huang, R. (eds.) ICHL 2010. LNCS, vol. 6248, pp. 339–351. Springer, Heidelberg (2010)

3. D'Antoni, S.: Open educational resources: reviewing initiatives and issues. Open Learn. J. Open Distance Learn. **24**, 3–10 (2009)
4. Yuan, L., MacNeill, S., Kraan, W.: Open educational resources – opportunities and challenges for higher education open educational resources. In: CETIS, pp. 1–35 (2008)
5. Hatakka, M.: Build it and they will come? Inhibiting factors for reuse of open content in developing countries. Electron. J. Inf. Syst. Dev. Ctries. **37**, 1–16 (2009)
6. Richter, T., Ehlers, U.-D.: Barriers and motivators for using OER in schools. eLearning Pap. **23**, 1–7 (2011)
7. Ha, K.-H., Niemann, K., Schwertel, U., Holtkamp, P., Pirkkalainen, H., Boerner, D., Kalz, M., Pitsilis, V., Vidalis, A., Pappa, D., Bick, M., Pawlowski, J., Wolpers, M.: A novel approach towards skill-based search and services of open educational resources. In: García-Barriocanal, E., Cebeci, Z., Okur, M.C., Öztürk, A. (eds.) MTSR 2011. CCIS, vol. 240, pp. 312–323. Springer, Heidelberg (2011)
8. Sotiriou, S.A., Agogi, E., Athanasiades, N., Ramfos, A., Stracke, C.M., Richter, T., Pirkkalainen, H., et al.: Open discovery space. http://www.opendiscoveryspace.eu/sites/ods/files/open_discovery_space.pdf (2013)
9. Hall, H., Davison, B.: Social software as support in hybrid learning environments: the value of the blog as a tool for reflective learning and peer support. Libr. Inf. Sci. Res. **29**, 163–187 (2007)
10. De Wever, B., Mechant, P., Veevaete, P., Hauttekeete, L.: E-learning 2.0: social software for educational use. In: Proceedings of Ninth IEEE International Symposium on Multimedia Workshops (ISMW 2007), pp. 511–516 (2007)
11. Lai, H.-M., Chen, C.-P.: Factors influencing secondary school teachers' adoption of teaching blogs. Comput. Educ. **56**, 948–960 (2011)
12. Zhang, L.: Adoption of social software for collaboration. In: Proceedings of International Conference on Management of Emergent Digital Ecosystems, pp. 246–251 (2010)
13. Agarwal, N., Tan, K., Poo, D.: Impediments to sharing knowledge outside the school: lessons learnt from the development of a taxonomic e-learning portal. In: International Conference on Information Systems (2007)
14. UNESCO: UNESCO Promotes New Initiative For Free Educational Resources on the Internet. http://www.unesco.org/education/news_en/080702_free_edu_ress.shtml. Accessed 19 Mar 2014
15. Clements, K.I., Pawlowski, J.M.: User oriented quality for OER: Understanding teachers' views on OER and quality. J. Comput. Assist. Learn. **28**(1), 4–14 (2011)
16. Davis, H.C., Carr, L., Hey, J.M.N., Howard, Y., Millard, D., Morris, D., White, S.: Bootstrapping a culture of sharing to facilitate open educational resources. IEEE Trans. Learn. Technol. **3**, 96–109 (2010)
17. Richter, T.: Adaptability as a special demand on open educational resources: the cultural context of e-learning. Eur. J. Open Distance Learn
18. Church, T.A., Katigbak, M.S.: The Emic strategy in the identification and assessment of personality dimensions in a non-western culture. J. Cross-Cult. Psychol. **19**, 140–163 (1988)
19. Goldschmidt, W.: Comparative Functionalism. University of California Press, Berkeley (1966)
20. Oetting, E.R.: Orthogonal cultural identification: theoretical links between cultural identification and substance use. In: Drug Abuse Among Minority Youth: Methodological Issues and Recent Research Advances, pp. 32–56 (1993)
21. Ward, C.A., Bochner, S., Furnham, A.: The Psychology of Culture Shock. Routledge, Hove (2001)
22. Pallot, M., Martínez-Carreras, M.A., Prinz, W.: Collaborative distance. Int. J. e-Collab. **6**, 1–32 (2010)

23. Humbert, M., Rébillard, C., Rennard, J.P.: Open educational resources for management education: lessons from experience. eLearning Pap. 1 (2008)
24. Hylén, J.: Open educational resources: opportunities and challenges. In: Proceedings of Open Education, Utah State University, Logan, Utah, 27–29 Sept 2006
25. Noll, J., Beecham, S., Richardson, I.: Global software development and collaboration: barriers and solutions. ACM Inroads. **1**, 66–78 (2010)
26. Onyechi, G., Abeysinghe, G.: Adoption of web based collaboration tools in the enterprise: challenges and opportunities. In: Proceedings of International Conference on Current Trends in Information Technology (CTIT 2009), pp. 1–6 (2009)

Vygotsky Based Sequencing Without Domain Information: A Matrix Factorization Approach

Carlotta Schatten(✉), Ruth Janning, and Lars Schmidt-Thieme

Information Systems and Machine Learning Lab,
University of Hildesheim, Hildesheim, Germany
{schatten,janning,schmidt-thieme}@ismll.uni-hildesheim.de
http://www.ismll.uni-hildesheim.de

Abstract. Sequencing contents, like tasks, hints, and feedbacks, is an open issue for Intelligent Tutoring Systems. The common approach is based on domain analysis by experts, who characterize each content with skills involved and a difficulty level. In addition, Machine Learning based sequencers require a specific dataset collection to create users' models and a sequencing policy, which needs to be tested online with strong ethical requirements and a high number of users. In this paper we design a simulated learning environment with customizable scenarios. We also show that a performance prediction method can be used to crate offline fully personalized students' models and sequence contents without domain engineering/authoring effort. The performance prediction method is enhanced by a score-based policy inspired by Vygotsky's concept of Zone of Proximal Development and shows promising results compared to curriculum based policies in the designed simulated environment.

Keywords: Sequencing · Performance prediction · Intelligent Tutoring Systems · Matrix Factorization

1 Introduction

Intelligent Tutoring Systems (ITS) are more and more becoming of crucial importance in education. Apart from the possibility to practice any time, adaptivity and individualization are the main reasons for their widespread availability as app, web service and software. The system generally is composed of an internal user model and a sequencer, that, according to the given information, sequences the contents with a policy. On that side many efforts have been put into Bayesian Knowledge Tracing (BKT), starting with not personalized and single skills user modeling. The limit of this problem formulation became clear soon, also because the contents evolved together with the technology. Multiple skills contents were developed, e.g. multiple step exercises and simulated exploration environment for learning. In order to maintain the single skill formulation systems fell back on scaffolding, i.e. a built in structure was inserted in order to clearly distinguish within the content between the different steps/skills required. As a consequence,

S. Zvacek et al. (Eds.): CSEDU 2014, CCIS 510, pp. 35–51, 2015.
DOI: 10.1007/978-3-319-25768-6_3

the engineering and authoring effort to develop an ITS increased exponentially obliging a meticulous analysis of the contents in order to subdivide and design them in clearly separable skills.

Other efforts have been put into adaptive sequencing. Its main approach, based on Reinforcement Learning, can be reconnected to robotics, which has an availability of accurate simulators and tireless test subjects. The same cannot be said for ITS where, generally, apart from adults, also children of any age are involved.

In this paper we propose a novel method of sequencing based on Matrix Factorization Performance Prediction and Vygotsky's concept of Zone of Proximal Development. The main contributions are:

1. A content sequencer based on a performance prediction systems that (1) can be set up and preliminary evaluated in a laboratory, (2) models multiple skills and individualization without engineering/authoring effort, (3) adapts to each combination of contents, levels and skills available.
2. Simulated environment with multiple skill contents and students' knowledge representation, where knowledge and performance are modeled in a continuous way.
3. Experiments on different scenarios with direct comparison with informed baseline.

The paper is structured as follows: in Sect. 2 one can find a brief state of the art description, in Sect. 3 the explanation of the sequencer problem, in Sect. 4 the simulated learning process, in Sect. 5 the performance based policy and predictor, in Sect. 6 the experimental results and least the conclusions.

2 Related Work

Many Machine Learning techniques have been used to ameliorate ITS, especially in order to extend learning potential for students and reduce engineering efforts for designing the ITS. The most used technology for sequencing is Reinforcement Learning (RL), which computes the best sequence trying to maximize a previously defined reward function. Both model-free and model-based [1,12] RL were tested for content sequencing. Unfortunately, the model-based RL necessitates of a special kind of data sets called exploratory corpus. Available data sets are log files of ITS which have a fixed sequencing policy that teachers designed to grant learning. They explore a small part of the state-action space and yield to biased or limited information. For instance, since a novice student will never see an exercise of expert level, it is impossible to retrieve the probability of a novice student solving some contents. Without these probabilities the RL model cannot be built [2]. Model-free RL, instead, assumes a high availability of students on which one can perform an on-line training. The model does not require an exploratory corpus but needs to be built while the users are playing with the designed system. Given the high cost of an experiment with humans, most authors exploit simulated single skill students based on different technologies like

Artificial Neural Networks or self developed student models [12,16]. Particularly similar to our approach is [12], where contents are sequenced with a particular model-free RL based on the actor critic algorithm [9], which was selected because of its faster convergence in comparison with the classic Q-Learning algorithm [20]. Unfortunately, RL algorithms still need many episodes to converge and will always need preliminary trainings on simulated students.

Our developed content sequencer is based on student performance predictions. An example of state of the art method is Bayesian Knowledge Tracing (BKT) and its extensions. The algorithm is built on a given prior knowledge of the students and a data set of binary student performances. It is assumed that there is a hidden state representing the knowledge of a student and an observed state given by the recorded performances. The model learned is composed by slip, guess, learning and not learning probability, which are then used to compute the predicted performances [4]. In the BKT extensions also difficulty, multiple skill levels and personalization are taken into account separately [5,13,14,24]. BKT researchers have discussed the problem of sequencing both in single and in multiple skill environment in [8]. In a single skill environment the most not mastered skill is selected, whereas in the multiple skill this behavior would present a too difficult content sequence. Consequently, the contents with a small number of not mastered skills are selected. Moreover, [8] points out how in ITS multiple skill exercises are modeled as single skill ones in order to overcome BKT limitations. We would like to stress that the sequencing requires an internal skills representation and consequently, together with the performance prediction algorithm, is domain dependent.

Another domain dependent algorithm used for performance prediction is the Performance Factors Analysis (PFM). In the latter the probability of learning is computed using the previous number of failures and successes, i.e. the representation of score is binary like in BKT [15]. Moreover, similarly to BKT, a table connecting contents and skills is required.

Matrix Factorization (MF) is the algorithm used in this paper for performance prediction. It has many applications like, for instance, dimensionality reduction, clustering and also classification [3]. The most common use is for Recommender Systems [10] and recently this concept was extended to ITS [21]. We selected this algorithm for several reasons:

1. Domain independence: ability to model each skill, i.e. no engineering or authoring effort in individuating the skills involved in the contents.
2. Having comparable results with BKT latest implementations [22].
3. Possibility to build the system with a common data set, i.e. without an exploratory corpus.
4. Small computational time on a 3rd Gen Ci5/4 GB laptop and Java implementation: 0.43 s for building the model with already 122000 lines, negligible time for performance prediction.

3 Content Sequencing in ITS

The designed system consists of two main blocks. The first one is the environment and is represented by the students playing with the ITS. First step toward a working prototype requires testing in a laboratory. Since optimal control problems can only be evaluated online, i.e. the sequence optimality can be measured only after a student worked with it, we designed a simulated learning process that is described in Sect. 4. We excluded the possibility of collecting an exploratory corpus because making practice with very easy and very difficult exercises in random order could be frustrating for the students, who could be children. After a first validation with real students, only a common data set collection will be necessary to set up the system with new contents, giving also the possibility to calibrate the environment and later use it for new sequencing methods. In this paper we use the word content to refer to the activities a student interacts with, although our main focus here is task sequencing. Taking advantage of the simulated learning process characteristics described, we can later interpret contents as different ITS elements. As explained in [17], a content could be a hint, a feedback, a topic or a task, whose sequencing could in each case take advantage of the designed system as we will discuss later.

The second block consists of different modules, i.e. the available contents, the previous interactions of the students with the system (log files), the student Performance Predictor and the Sequencer Policy. We chose a specific Performance Predictor and policy, but nothing is against using other ones in the future. When a student plays with the system the next exercise is proposed to him by the sequencer according to a policy. The Performance Predictor needs the log files of students playing with the contents considered to predict their scores in the next contents. The policy is applied in an adaptive way thanks to the information on

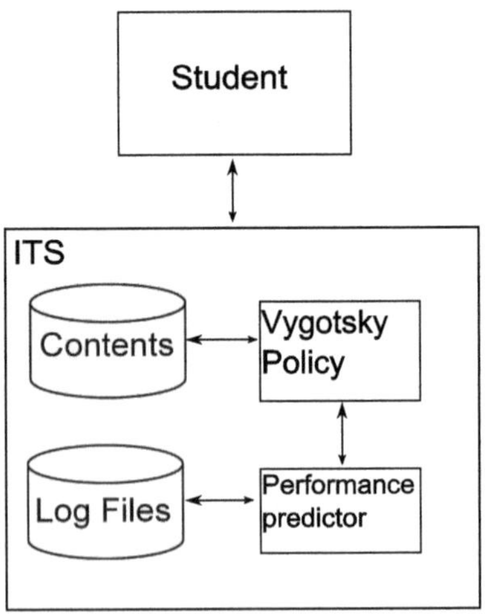

Fig. 1. System structure in a block diagram.

the predicted scores shared between Performance Predictor and Sequencer. In the following Sections we will describe the different blocks represented in Fig. 1.

4 Simulated Learning Process

Given the necessity of preliminary evaluation in a laboratory, it is of crucial importance to have a simulated environment able to model reality with a certain degree of fidelity. For our system we required a score and skill representation between 0 and 1, to be able to test following aspects:

1. Possibility to use score as single success indicator for sequencing.
2. Ability to model a multiple skill domain and students' knowledge by the performance predictor.
3. Possibility to change number of skills involved to test flexibility.
4. Possibility to test also noisy processes.

We designed a simulated student based on the following assumptions. (1) A content is either of the correct difficulty for a student, or too easy, or too difficult. (2) A student cannot learn from too easy contents and learns from difficult ones proportionally to his knowledge level. (3) It is impossible to learn from a content more than the required skills to solve it. (4) The total knowledge at the beginning is different than zero. (5) The general ability on connected skills helps solving and learning from a content. The last assumption is more plausible because we assume to sequence activities of the same domain. For instance, in order to solve a fraction addition, a student needs more related skills: multiplication, fraction expansion etc. It is unlikely for a student to do a fraction expansion without knowing how multiplication works. At the same time the knowledge of multiplication will help him solving the steps on fraction expansion.

A student simulator is a tuple (S, C, y, τ) where, given a set $S \subseteq [0,1]^K$ of students, s_i is a specific student described as a vector $\boldsymbol{\varphi}^t$. The latter is of dimension K, where K is the number of skills involved. $C \subseteq [0,1]^K$ is a set of contents, where c_j is the j-th content, defined with a vector $\boldsymbol{\psi}_j$ of K elements representing the skills required. $\varphi_{i,k} = 0$ means student's i skill level k is zero, whereas $\varphi_{i,k} = 1$ means having full ability. $\tau : \mathbb{S} \times \mathbb{C} \rightarrow \mathbb{S}$ is a function defining the follow-up state $\boldsymbol{\varphi}^{t+1} = \boldsymbol{\varphi}^t + \tau$ of a student $s_i \in \mathbb{S}$ after working on contents c_j^t. In particular $\mathbb{S}$ and $\mathbb{C}$ are the spaces of the students and contents respectively. Finally, a function y defines the performance $y(\varphi_i, \psi_j)$. y and τ can be formalized as follows:

$$\begin{aligned} y(\varphi_i, \psi_j) :=& \max(1 - \frac{||\boldsymbol{\alpha}||}{||\boldsymbol{\varphi_i}||}, 0) \\ \tau(\varphi_i, \psi_j)_k :=& y(\varphi_{ik}, \psi_{jk})\alpha_k \\ \tilde{y} :=& y\epsilon \end{aligned} \tag{1}$$

where

$$\alpha_k^{i,j} = \max(\psi_{jk} - \varphi_{ik}, 0) \tag{2}$$

and ϵ is proportional to the beta distribution $\mathcal{B}(p,q)$. We selected p and q in order to have $\tilde{y} \sim \mathcal{B}(y,\sigma^2)$, where σ^2 is the variance, i.e. the amount of noise. We chose the beta distribution because it is defined between zero and one as the score. Consequently it will not change the codomain of the y function. The characteristic of the formulas are the following. (1) The performance of a student on a content decreases proportionally to his skill deficiencies w.r.t. the required skills. (2) The student will improve all the required skills of a content proportionally to his performance and his skill-specific deficiency up to the skill level a content requires. (3) As a consequence it is not possible to learn from a content more than the difference from the required and possessed skills. (4) A further property of this model is that contents requiring twice the skills level that a student has, i.e. $\|\boldsymbol{\psi_j}\| \geq 2\|\boldsymbol{\varphi}_i\|$, are beyond the reach of a student. For this reason his performance will be zero ($y = 0$). With a simple experiment without noise, we can show the plausibility of the designed simulator. We inserted values in Eq. 1 as follows. Let us consider a system with two skills and represent the student knowledge as $\boldsymbol{\varphi} = \{0.3, 0.5\}$.

Table 1. Simulated learning process with two skills. A simulated student with $\boldsymbol{\varphi} = \{0.3, 0.5\}$ scores y and learning τ after interacting with different contents c_j.

c_j	d_c	y	τ_k
[0.1, 0.1]	0.2	1	[0, 0]
[0.5, 0.6]	1.1	0.617	[0.12, 0.0617]
[0.5, 0.7]	1.2	0.515	[0.1, 0.1]
[0.9, 0.9]	1.8	0	[0, 0]

As it is possible to see in Table 1 with the increase of the content difficulty the learning increases and the score decreases until $\|\boldsymbol{\psi_i}\| \geq 2\left\|\boldsymbol{\varphi}_j\right\|$. The maximal difficulty level is equal to the number of skills since a single skill value cannot be greater than one.

5 Vygotsky Policy and Matrix Factorization

5.1 Sequencer

The designed sequencer is defined as follows. Let $C \subseteq \mathbb{C}$ and $S \subseteq \mathbb{S}$ be respectively a set of contents and students defined in Sect. 4, d_{c_j} be the difficulty of a content defined as $d_{c_j} = \sum_{k=0}^{K} \psi_{j,k}$, $\tilde{y} : \mathbb{S} \times \mathbb{C} \rightarrow [0,1]$ be the performance or the score of a student working on the content, and T be the number of time steps assuming that the student is seeing one content every time step. The content sequencing problem consists in finding a policy:

$$\pi^* : (\mathbb{C} \times [0,1]) \rightarrow \mathbb{C}. \tag{3}$$

that maximize the learning of a student within a given time T without any environment knowledge, i.e. without knowing the difficulties of the contents and the required skills to solve them. A common problem in designing a policy for ITS is retrieving the knowledge of the student from the given information, e.g. score, time needed, previous exercises, etc. The previous mentioned data types are just an indirect representation of the knowledge, which cannot be automatically measured, but needs to be modeled inside the system. Hence, integrating the curriculum and skills structure is the cause of the high costs in designing the sequencer. In this paper we try to keep the contents in the Vygotsky's Zone of Proximal Development (ZPD) [23], i.e. the area where the contents neither bore or overwhelm the learner. We mathematically formalized the concept with the following policy, that we called Vygotsky Policy (VP):

$$c^{t*} = \text{argmin}_c \left| y_{th} - \hat{y}^t\left(c\right) \right| \tag{4}$$

where y_{th} is the threshold score, i.e. the score that keeps the contents in the ZPD. The policy will select at each time step the content with the predicted score $\hat{y}^t$ at time t most similar to y_{th}. We will discuss further in the experiment session how to tune this hyper parameter and its meaning.

The peculiarity of the VP is the absence of the difficulty concept. Defining the difficulty for a content in a simulated environment as ours is easy, because we mathematically define the skills required. In the real case it is not trivial and quite subjective. Also the required skills are considered as given in the other state of the art methods like PFM and BKT, where a table represents the connection between contents and skills required. Without skills information not only BKT and PFM performance prediction cannot be used in our formalization, also sequencing methods [8] have no information to work with.

5.2 Matrix Factorization as Performance Predictor

Matrix Factorization (MF) is a state-of-the-art method for recommender systems. It predicts which is the future user ratings on a specific items based on his previous ratings and the previous ratings of other users. The concept has been extended to student performance prediction, where a student next performance, or score is predicted. The matrix $Y \in \mathbb{R}^{n_s \times n_c}$ can be seen as a table of n_c total contents and n_s students used to train the system, where for some contents and students performance measures are given. MF decomposes the matrix Y in two other ones $\Psi \in \mathbb{R}^{n_c \times P}$ and $\Phi \in \mathbb{R}^{n_s \times P}$, so that $Y \approx \hat{Y} = \Psi\Phi$. Ψ and Φ are matrices of latent features. Their elements are learned with gradient descend from the given performances. This allows computing the missing elements of Y and consequently predicting the student performances (Fig. 2). The optimization function is represented by:

$$\min_{\psi_j, \varphi_i} \sum_{j \in \mathbb{C}} \left(y_{ij} - \hat{y}_{ij}\right)^2 + \lambda(\|\Psi\|^2 + \|\Phi\|^2) \tag{5}$$

where one wants to minimize the regularized squared error on the set of known scores. The prediction function is represented by:

$$\hat{y}_{ij} = \mu + \mu_{cj} + \mu_{si} + \sum_{p=0}^{P} \varphi_{ip}^{T} \psi_{jp} \tag{6}$$

where μ, μ_c and μ_s are respectively the average performance of all contents of all students, the learned average performance of a content, and learned average performance of a student. The two last mentioned parameters are also learned with the gradient descend algorithm.

The MF problem does not deal with time, i.e. all the training performances are considered equally. In order to keep the model up to date, it is necessary to re-train the model at each time step. MF has a personalized prediction, i.e. a small number of exercises needs to be shown to each student in order to avoid the so called cold-start problem. Although some solutions to these problems have been proposed in [11,21], we will show in the experiment session that these aspects do not affect the performance of the system, neither they reduce its applicability. From now on we will call the sequencer utilizing the VP policy and the MF performance predictor VPS, i.e. Vygotsky Policy based Sequencer.

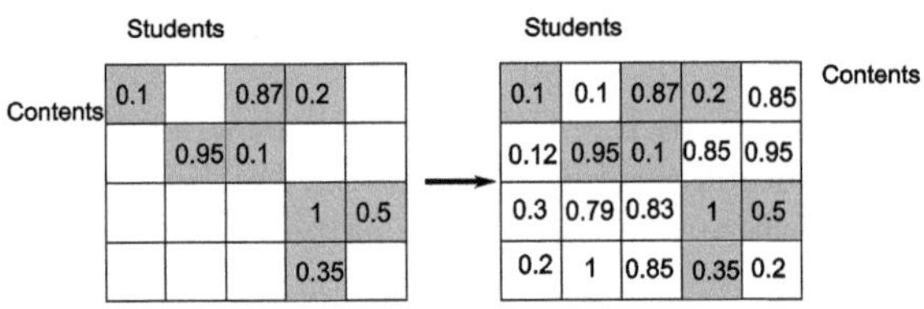

Fig. 2. Table of scores given for each student on contents (left), completed table by the MF algorithm with predicted scores (right).

6 Experiment Session

In this section we show how the single elements work in detail. We start with the student simulator, continue with the VP and end with some experiments with performance prediction in different scenarios and noise. A scenario is represented by a number of contents n_c, a number of difficulty levels n_d, a number of skills n_k, and a number of students for each group n_t[1]. All the first experiments will have no noise, i.e. $\tilde{y} = y$.

[1] The MF was previously trained with n_s students that were used to learn the characteristic of the contents. Consequently, the dimensions of the MF during the simulated learning process are: $\Psi \in \mathbb{R}^{n_c \times P}$ and $\Phi \in \mathbb{R}^{(n_s+n_t) \times P}$, so that $Y \approx \hat{Y} = \Psi\Phi$.

6.1 Experiments on the Simulated Learning Process

To prove the operating principle of the simulator we tested basic sequencing methods in a particular scenario. The one we chose is described in Fig. 3, with $n_d = 7$ and $n_c = 150$. For representation purposes we created the contents with increasing difficulty, so that IDs implicitly indicates the difficulty[2]. The scenario mimics an interesting situation for sequencing, i.e. when more apparently equivalent exercises are available. The two policies we used are (1) Random (RND), where contents are selected randomly, and (2) the in range policy (RANGE), where each second content is selected in difficulty order (see also Table 3). This strategy is informed on the domain because it knows the difficulty of the contents. We initialized the students and contents skills with an uniform random distribution between 0 and 1. Again for representation purposes we show the average total knowledge of the students that is represented by average of the students skills sum at each time step. We chose to perform the tests on 10 skills, i.e. the maximal total knowledge possible is equal to 10. We considered the scenario mastered when the total knowledge of the student group is greater than or equal to the 95% of the maximal total knowledge.

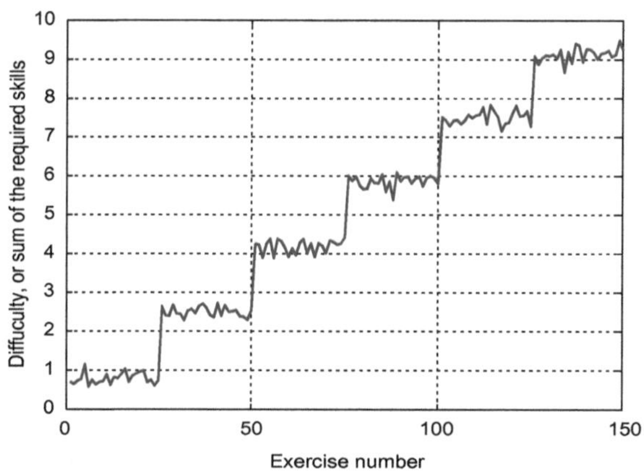

Fig. 3. Scenario: content number and difficulty level.

Figure 4 shows the total knowledge of two groups of $n_t = 200$ students, one group was trained with random policy the other one with the in range policy. RANGE is characterized by a low variance in the learning process. RND, instead, has a high variance because the knowledge level of the students at each time step is given by chance. It is shown that the order in which the student practices on the contents is important for the total final learning. Figure 4 also shows how the practice on too many contents of the same difficulty level, after a while, saturates the knowledge acquisition. All these aspects demonstrate that the learning progress is plausibly simulated.

[2] A content with ID 2 is easier than a content with ID 100, see Fig. 3.

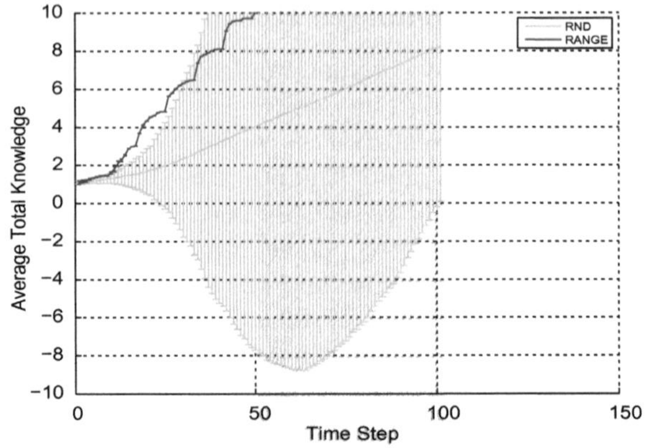

Fig. 4. Comparison between RANGE and RND. Average skills sum, i.e. knowledge, over all the students with variance.

6.2 Sensitivity Analysis on the Vygotsky Policy

In order to evaluate the VP we created two more sequencing methods that exploit information not available in reality. The best sequencing knows exactly which is the content maximizing the learning for a student, for this reason we called it Ground Truth (GT). Vygotsky Policy Sequencer Ground Truth (VPSGT), instead, uses the Vygotsky Policy and the true score y of a student to select the following content. GT and VPSGT can be considered the upper bound of the sequencer potential in a scenario (see also Table 3). In order to select the correct value of y_{th} we plot the average knowledge level at time $t = 11$ for the policy with different y_{th}. From Fig. 5 one can see that the policy is working for $y_{th} \in [0.4, 0.7]$, this because of the relationship between Eq. 1 of the student simulator. In a real environment the interpretation of these results is twofold.

First we assume y_{th} will be approximately the score keeping the students in the ZDP. Second, from a RL perspective, this value would allow finding the trade-off between exploring new concepts and exploiting the already possessed knowledge. Moreover, as one can see in Fig. 6, the policy obtains good results if compared with GT for some y_{th}, but for others the policy is outside the ZPD and the students do not reach the total knowledge of the scenario. In some experiments we noticed that the width of the curve in Fig. 5 decreased so that the outer limits of the y_{th} interval create a sequence outside the ZPD. As consequence we selected the value $y_{th} = 0.5$ that was successful in most of the scenarios.

6.3 Vygotsky Policy Based Sequencer

The scenario we selected for the tests with the VPS has $n_c = 150$, $n_d = 6$, $n_k = 10$ and $n_t = 400$. In order to train the MF-model a training and test data set need to be created. We used $n_s = 300$ students who learned with all the

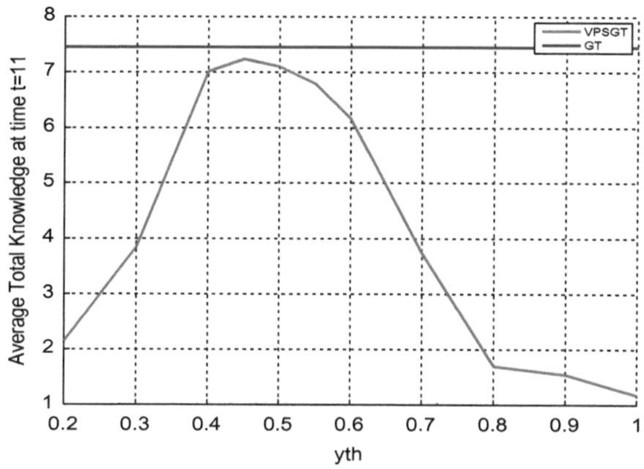

Fig. 5. Policy selection, i.e. the performance of the Vygotsky policy with different y_{th} at the same time step. Different groups of students learned with the Vygotsky policy with y_{th} values going from 0.1 to 0.9. As shown in the figure the knowledge levels change according to the y_{th} selected.

Table 2. Parameters MF.

Parameters	Choice
Learning rate	0.01
Latent features	60
Regularization	0.02
Number of iteration	10

contents in order of difficulty. We used 66% of the data to train the MF-model and the remaining 34% to evaluate the Root Mean Squared Error (RMSE) for selecting the regularization factor λ and the learning rate of the gradient descent algorithm. We performed a full Grid Search and selected the parameters shown in Table 2. The sequencing experiments are done on a separate group of n_t students. In order to avoid the cold start problem 5 contents are shown to them and their scores added to the training set of the MF. For $T = 40$ the best content c_j^{*t} is selected with the policy VP for the n_t students, using the predicted performance $\hat{y}_{ij}^t$. In order to avoid the deterioration of the model, after each time step the model is trained again once all students saw an exercise. A detailed description of the algorithm of the sequencer can be found in Algorithm 1, where Y_0 is the initial data set.

As one can see in Fig. 7 the VPS selects the first content similarly to RANGE. Then the prediction allows to skip unnecessary contents speeding up the learning. Once the total knowledge arrives around 95%, the selection policy cannot find contents that fit to the requirements. Consequently the students learn as slow as the RND group, as one can see from the saturating curve. In Fig. 8 GT selects the contents in difficulty order skipping the unnecessary ones. The average

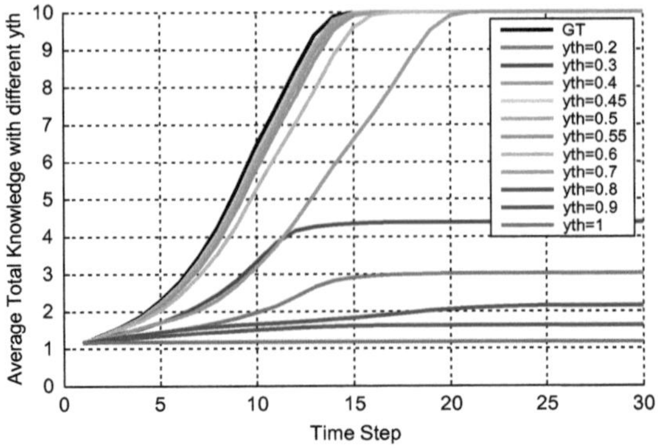

Fig. 6. Effects of the different y_{th} on the final knowledge of the students. The learning curves of the student groups that learned with the different Vygotsky policies.

Algorithm 1. Vygotsky Policy based Sequencer.

Input: $\mathbb{C}$, Y_0 π, s_i, T

Train the MF using Y_0;
for $t = 1$ *to* T **do**
    for *All* $c \in \mathbb{C}$ **do**
        Predict $\hat{y}(c_j, s_i)$ Eq. 6;
    end
    Find c^{t*} according to Eq. 5;
    Show c^{t*} to s_i with Eq. 1;
    Add $y\left(s_i, c^{t*}\right)$ to Y_t;
    Retrain the MF; // Corrects over- or underestimation by the MF
end

---

sequence of the VPS, instead, is also with approximately increasing difficulty but in an irregular way. This is due to the error in the prediction performance. In conclusion the proposed sequencer gains 63% over RANGE and 150% over RND.

The presented experiments show how the MF is able, without domain information, to model the different skills of students and contents and partially mimics the best sequence, which is the one selected by GT in Fig. 8.

6.4 Advanced Experiments

In this section we want to show the correct working of the sequencer changing the parameters of the scenario n_k and n_c and later adding noise. In order to do so we consider the percentage of gain of VPS with respect to RANGE considering a specific time step $t = 30$ with $n_k = 10$ and $n_d = 6$. As one can see in Fig. 10 the gain obtained by the sequencer depends on the available number of contents. Since in RANGE each second content is selected, with $n_c < 60$ there are not enough contents for all time steps. Our sequencer can adapt without problems to the situation. The optimal point for the in range policy is when $n_c = 60$ because

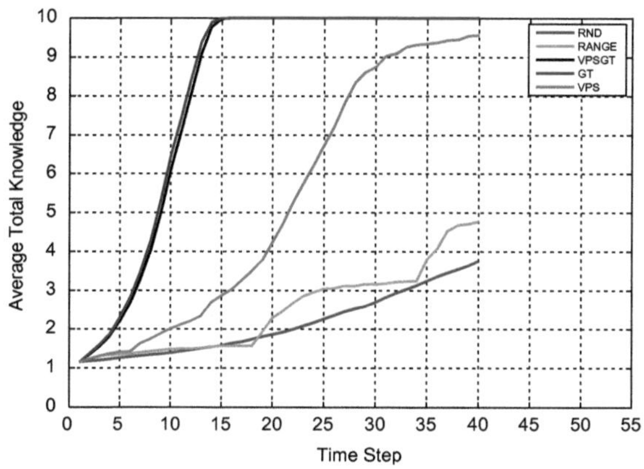

Fig. 7. Average total knowledge. How the average learning curve of the students changes over time.

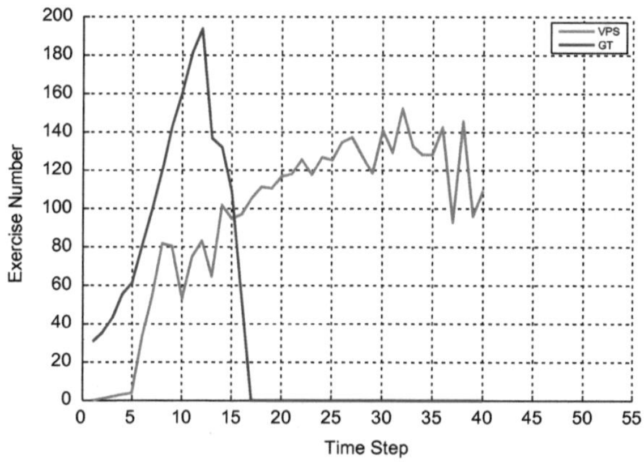

Fig. 8. Average sequence selected by the GT and the VPS. The VPS approximate the optimal sequence that GT computes thanks to the real skills of the students.

Table 3. Sequencers description.

Policy	Description
Random (RND)	Contents are selected randomly
In Range (RANGE)	Each second content is selected in difficulty order
Ground Truth (GT)	Selects the contents according to which is the one maximizing the learning
Vygotsky Policy based Sequencer Ground Truth	Chooses the next content using the policy and the real score of (VPSGT) a student
Vygotski Policy based Sequencer (VPS)	Chooses the next content using the policy and the predicted score of a student

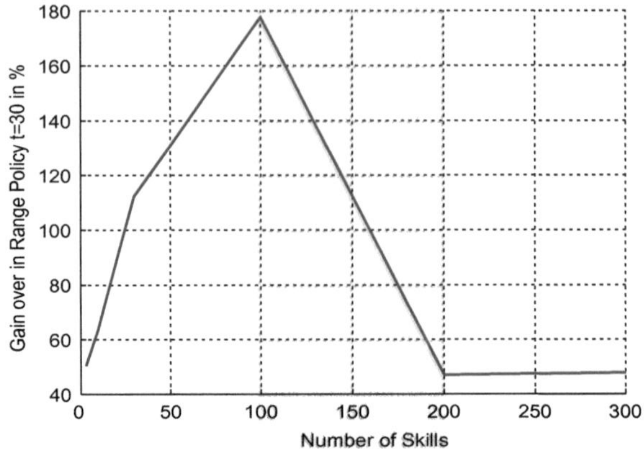

Fig. 9. Gain over RANGE policy varying n_k. The gain is measured at a specific time step in percentage, considering the average knowledge level of the two groups of students, one practicing with the RANGE sequencer and one with the VPS.

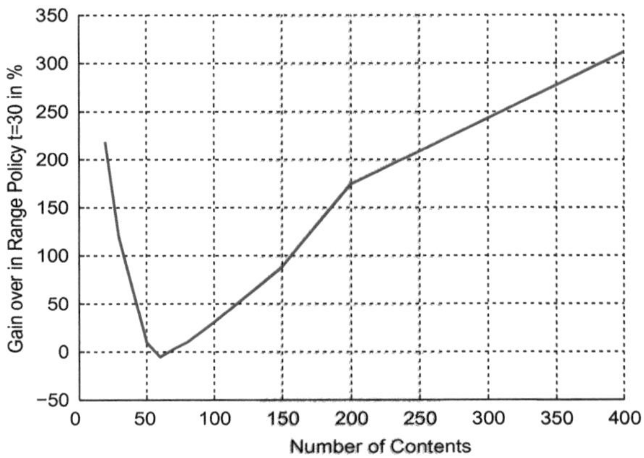

Fig. 10. Gain over RANGE policy varying n_c. The gain is measured at a specific time step in percentage, considering the average knowledge of the two groups of students, one practicing with the RANGE sequencer and one with the VPS.

there is exactly the necessary number of contents for the student to learn. When $n_c > 60$ the students see many unnecessary contents and consequently learn slower. Figure 9 with $n_c = 60$, $t = 30$ and $n_d = 6$ shows the dependencies between skills and gain. The experiments demonstrated a high adaptability of the sequencer to the different scenarios.

Last we experimented the results robustness adding noise, i.e. $\tilde{y} = y\epsilon$. We experimented with $\sigma^2 \in [0, 0.5]$. As one can see in Fig. 11 with $\sigma^2 = 0.1$ the Vygotsky sequencers are still able to produce a correct learning sequence but more time is required. The VPSGT is the one that suffered the most from the introduction of noise, probably related to the selection of y_{th}.

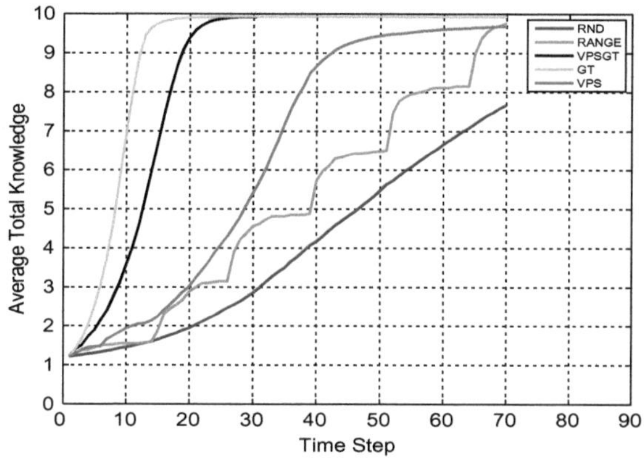

Fig. 11. Effect of noise in the simulated learning process. Beta distribution noise with $\sigma^2 = 0.1$.

6.5 Outlook

VPS has an advantage in comparison to other state of the art methods because it does not require a detailed analysis of the skills involved. Nevertheless, some steps are required for the VPS to be integrated within a learning platform. This aspect has been addressed in [17] for a commercial ITS, where a first offline feasibility discussion was done. Thanks to VPS domain independence, conceptual integration required minor changes. For technical integration we utilized the work in [19] where a novel minimal invasive integration for a Machine Learning-powered sequencer was presented. Another open question is how to select y_{th}. In [17], we explained how this value should be tailored to the available contents exploiting the passing score set by expert. In [6,7] is proposed to personalize the threshold value by means of the output of an affect recognition applied to students speech input. The proposed rule based policy suggests to increase yth if the student felt under-challenged and decrease it if he felt over-challenged. Alternatively a combination of MF and emotion recognition could be designed.

7 Conclusions

In this paper we presented VPS, a sequencer based on performance prediction and Vygotsky's concept of ZPD for multiple skills contents with continuous knowledge and performance representation. We showed that MF is able dealing with the most actual problems of Intelligent Tutoring Systems, like time and personalization, retrieving automatically skills required and difficulty. We proposed VP, a performance based policy that does not require direct input of domain information, and a student simulator that helps in preliminary off-line evaluation. The designed system achieved time gain over random and in range policy in almost each scenario and is robust to noise. This demonstrates how the sequencer could solve many engineering/authoring efforts. Nevertheless, an experiment with real students is required to better confirm the validity of the assumptions of the simulated learning process. A different evaluation is required for the performance prediction based sequencer. Some work was done in this direction and was mentioned in the previous section. In conclusion, to use VPS, no content analysis is required, since the MF will reconstruct the domain information, thanks to continuous score representation. This will allow the integration of the sequencer in ITS whose content analysis is not affordable. With the results obtained in this paper we plan to extend such an approach also to other intervention strategies to further reduce the engineering efforts in ITS after an complete evaluation on real students.

Acknowledgements. This research has been co-funded by the Seventh Framework Programme of the European Commission, through project iTalk2Learn (#318051). www.iTalk2Learn.eu. This paper is an extended version of [18] presented at the 6th International Conference on Computer Supported Education.

References

1. Beck, J., Woolf, B.P., Beal, C.R.: Advisor: a machine learning architecture for intelligent tutor construction. In: AAAI/IAAI 2000, pp. 552–557 (2000)
2. Chi, M., VanLehn, K., Litman, D., Jordan, P.: Empirically evaluating the application of reinforcement learning to the induction of effective and adaptive pedagogical strategies. UMAI **21**(1–2), 137–180 (2011)
3. Cichocki, A., Zdunek, R., Phan, A.H., Amari, S.: Nonnegative Matrix and Tensor Factorizations: Applications to Exploratory Multi-way Data Analysis and Blind Source Separation. Wiley, Chichester (2009). Wiley.com
4. Corbett, A., Anderson, J.: Knowledge tracing: modeling the acquisition of procedural knowledge. UMAI **4**(4), 253–278 (1994)
5. Baker, R.S.J., Corbett, A.T., Aleven, V.: More accurate student modeling through contextual estimation of slip and Guess probabilities in Bayesian knowledge tracing. In: Woolf, B.P., Aïmeur, E., Nkambou, R., Lajoie, S. (eds.) ITS 2008. LNCS, vol. 5091, pp. 406–415. Springer, Heidelberg (2008)
6. Janning, R., Schatten, C., Schmidt-Thieme, L.: Feature analysis for affect recognition supporting task sequencing in adaptive intelligent tutoring systems. In: Rensing, C., de Freitas, S., Ley, T., Muñoz-Merino, P.J. (eds.) EC-TEL 2014. LNCS, vol. 8719, pp. 179–192. Springer, Heidelberg (2014)
7. Janning, R., Schatten, C., Schmidt-Thieme, L.: Multimodal affect recognition for adaptive intelligent tutoring systems. In: FFMI EDM (2014)
8. Koedinger, K., Pavlik, P., Stamper, J., Nixon, T., Ritter, S.: Avoiding problem selection thrashing with conjunctive knowledge tracing. In: EDM (2011)
9. Konda, V.R., Tsitsiklis, J.N.: Actor-critic algorithms. Adv. Neural Inf. Process. Syst. **12**, 1008–1014 (2000)
10. Koren, Y., Bell, R., Volinsky, C.: Matrix factorization techniques for recommender systems. Computer **42**(8), 30–37 (2009)
11. Krohn-Grimberghe, A., Busche, A., Nanopoulos, A., Schmidt-Thieme, L.: Active learning for technology enhanced learning. In: Kloos, C.D., Gillet, D., Crespo García, R.M., Wild, F., Wolpers, M. (eds.) EC-TEL 2011. LNCS, vol. 6964, pp. 512–518. Springer, Heidelberg (2011)

12. Malpani, A., Ravindran, B., Murthy, H.: Personalized intelligent tutoring system using reinforcement learning. In: FLAIRS (2011)
13. Pardos, Z.A., Heffernan, N.T.: Modeling individualization in a bayesian networks implementation of knowledge tracing. In: De Bra, P., Kobsa, A., Chin, D. (eds.) UMAP 2010. LNCS, vol. 6075, pp. 255–266. Springer, Heidelberg (2010)
14. Pardos, Z.A., Heffernan, N.T.: KT-IDEM: introducing item difficulty to the knowledge tracing model. In: Konstan, J.A., Conejo, R., Marzo, J.L., Oliver, N. (eds.) UMAP 2011. LNCS, vol. 6787, pp. 243–254. Springer, Heidelberg (2011)
15. Cen, H., Pavlik, P., Koedinger, K.: Performance factors analysis–a new alternative to knowledge tracing. In: AIED (2009)
16. Sreenivasa, B.H., Ravindran, B.: Intelligent tutoring systems using reinforcement learning to teach autistic students. Home Informatics and Telematics: ICT for The Next Billion. IFIP, vol. 241, pp. 65–78. Springer, New York (2007)
17. Schatten, C., Mavrikis, M., Janning, R., Schmidt-Thieme, L.: Matrix factorization feasibility for sequencing and adaptive support in its. In: EDM (2014)
18. Schatten, C., Schmidt-Thieme, L.: Adaptive content sequencing without domain information. In: CSEDU (2014)
19. Schatten, C., Wistuba, M., Schmidt-Thieme, L., Gutirrez-Santos, S.: Minimal invasive integration of learning analytics services in its. In: ICALT (2014)
20. Sutton, R.S., Barto, A.G.: Reinforcement Learning: An Introduction. Cambridge University Press, New York (1998)
21. Thai-Nghe, N., Drumond, L., Horvath, T., Krohn-Grimberghe, A., Nanopoulos, A., Schmidt-Thieme, L.: Factorization Techniques for Predicting Student Performance. Educational Recommender Systems and Technologies: Practices and Challenges. IGI Global, Hershey (2011)
22. Thai-Nghe, N., Drumond, L., Horvath, T., Schmidt-Thieme, L.: Using factorization machines for student modeling. In: UMAP Workshops (2012)
23. Vygotsky, L.S.: Mind in Society: The Development of Higher Psychological Processes. HUP, Cambridge (1978)
24. Wang, Y., Heffernan, N.T.: The student skill model. In: Cerri, S.A., Clancey, W.J., Papadourakis, G., Panourgia, K. (eds.) ITS 2012. LNCS, vol. 7315, pp. 399–404. Springer, Heidelberg (2012)

The Temporal Change of Attentional Levels Under Different Music Environments

Fumiya Mori[1], Fatemeh Azadi Naghsh[1,2,3], and Taro Tezuka[3](✉)

[1] Department of Children and Families, City of Takasaki, Takasaki 370-8501, Japan
fumiya.mori@gmail.com

[2] Graduate School of Library, Information and Media Studies,
University of Tsukuba, Tsukuba 305-0821, Japan

[3] Faculty of Library, Information and Media Science,
University of Tsukuba, Tsukuba 305-0821, Japan
{atena,tezuka}@slis.tsukuba.ac.jp

Abstract. Keeping attention at a high level is crucial for various tasks that appear in real life. Some existing works pointed out that music helps raise the level of attention. In this work, we conducted experiments to see how music affect the temporal change of attention. To estimate the level of attention, we designed a test based on the conjunction search task, which is commonly used in cognitive science. We monitored the temporal change as the subjects listened to different types of music. We made a comparison among music that they like, that they are uninterested in, and the silence condition. The result indicates that different types of music affect not only on the level of performance but also its temporal change.

Keywords: Attention · Music · Temporal pattern

1 Introduction

The performance of a person is highly dependent on the mental state that she is in. When the person is highly attentive, she can be very efficient, whereas when she is not attentive, she can perform poorly. This is particularly important in education, since the level of attention would affect how much a student can learn within a set amount of time.

Although the change in the level of attention is in part a spontaneous process, it is nevertheless affected by external factors as well. The effect is evident when one considers how productive he can be when the deadline is approaching. Surprisingly, there has not been much work in changing the environmental factors to create higher performance.

Various books describing techniques to enhance attention have been published, but most of them are solely based on personal experiences rather than objective experiments. For example, many students listen to music while they study at home. They seem to have learned from their experience that music

S. Zvacek et al. (Eds.): CSEDU 2014, CCIS 510, pp. 52–67, 2015.
DOI: 10.1007/978-3-319-25768-6_4

increases their level of attention. There has not been, however, much work on evaluating if music could be used to control the level of attention.

In contrast to education, there is an extensive amount of research in the field of sports science, where all efforts are put to win a competition (Katch and Katch 1999). Physical and mental quantities of athletes are measured and analyzed to reach highest performance. The approach here is more objective and quantitative. If such approach was successfully applied to education the effect would be tremendous.

One of the ways to measure the effect of music on performance is to measure how attentive the subject is. In this paper, we describe a system aimed at measuring the level of attention based on the performance of the subject. We compare three conditions, namely playing music that the subject likes, playing music that the subject is not familiar with, and silence. The overall performance of the subject and the temporal change in the performance level will be compared and analyzed, to objectively evaluate if music have positive or negative effect on attention.

The rest of the paper is organized as follows. In Sect. 2 we describe our model of attention, and factors that would affect it. Section 3 is on implementation of our system. It is followed by Sect. 4 where we illustrates the design and the result of the experiment. Section 5 is on related work. Finally, Sect. 6 concludes the paper.

2 Model

In this paper, we employ a task that is assumed to require much attention, in order to measure it. Figure 1 illustrates the overall construction of our model. Arrows indicate causal relationships. Attention is determined by internal parameters, which is affected by external factors. By changing the external factors, we assume it possible to change the level of attention.

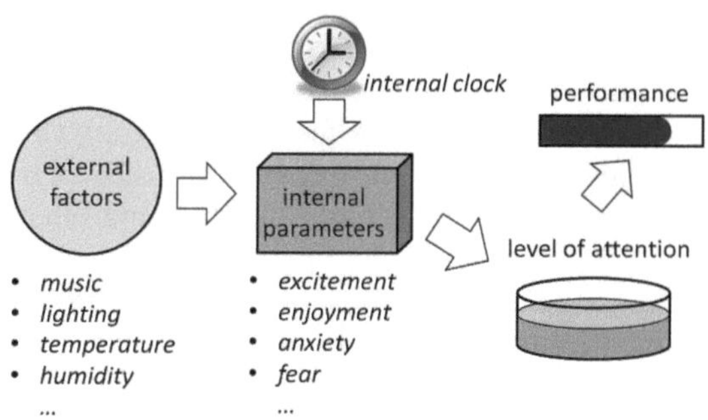

Fig. 1. External factors and internal parameters.

In this paper, we mainly focus on how music and time affect the performance level on a task that requires attention. We discuss the model in more detail in the following subsections.

2.1 Attention in Education

In cognitive science, much work has been done to explain how attention affects different aspects of learning. The main position is even stated that there is no learning without attention (Schmidt 1995). A number of researchers have argued that different types of learning (e.g., explicit and implicit) depend on attention (Tomlin and Villa 1994).

Studies have inferred that attentional mechanisms is essential for all learning even for simple perceptual task (Ahissar and Hochstein 2002) and that more complex learning requires more attention (Schmidt 1995). One established principle of visual attention is that the harder a task is, the more attentional resources are used to perform the task and the smaller amount of attention is allocated to peripheral processing because of limited attention capacity (Huang and Watanabe 2012).

2.2 The Effect of Emotion on Attention

Some researchers have discussed that excitement may enhance attention and facilitate flexibility. On the other hand, it has been pointed out that positive mood may reduce the subject's performance (Schwarz and Clore 1983, 1988; Rank and Frese 2010). When a subject experiences positive affective states, he assumes he is performing sufficiently well thus he withdraws effort. Also, in Cerin et al.'s model predicts that, in general, an affective profile characterized by mild to moderate intensity levels of threat-related affects (e.g. fear and apprehension) and affects conducive to or associated with approach behavior and task-focused attention (e.g. interest, excitement and enjoyment) will be perceived as facilitating performance (Cerin et al. 2000).

We however consider that the balance between excitement and calmness is important. If a person is overexcited, it often happens that he is distracted by any small stimuli and cannot focus on the task. On the other hand, if one's mind is too calm or relaxed, he would not feel like doing anything. The level most appropriate for a task lies somewhere in between excited and relaxed. We assume that listening to music that one likes has a modulating effect, with excitatory and inhibitory factors, helps achieve the best performance. Some music excites and other music calms. We assume that people know from experience which music is best for them to modulate music to sustain her level of attention. We test this hypothesis through experiments described in this paper.

2.3 Temporal Change in the Level of Attention

Time has various effects on cognitive performance (Grondin 2008). For example, it has been pointed out that attention is limited in time (Nobre and Coull 2010).

Humans cannot sustain a high level of attention for a long period of time. Learning is no exception. In practice, it is important to know how the level of attention changes, how it can be recovered, in order to make humans more productive.

Nieuwensetin et al. discussed temporal constraints on conscious vision (Nieuwensetin et al. 2009). If a subject is presented with two visual targets within a short span of time, the second one is often missed, i.e. not recognized by the subject. It is called attentional blink.

It is also known that there are various rhythms in mental processes, from short ones to long ones (Buzsaki 2006). The level of attention does not monotonically decrease either. It may have some rhythm, or it may rise as the end of the task approaches. It may follow different patterns other than rhythms, for example constant decrease in performance. By measuring the temporal change in performance, we try to uncover the temporal change of attention. In this paper, we try to uncover such different patterns through experiments.

3 Implementation

We implemented a system aimed at controlling the level of attention. In this section, we first describe a way to measure it, then describe the actual implementation.

3.1 Measurement of Attention

Our system measures the level of attention using the amount of time required to perform a task that is assumed to require much attention. It is based on a "conjunction search" task, where the subject is presented with signs that have combinations of features, such as shape, color, and orientation (Bergen and Julesz 1983). Figure 2 shows an example of the image presented to the subject when using our system.

The subject is presented with 100 signs, aligned into 10 rows and 10 columns, shown on a computer screen. Signs are in two types, namely T and L, and in two colors, blue and orange. The subject is asked to find a sign that is different from the rest in two aspects. For example, about half of the signs are blue T, and about the half are orange L, but there is one exception, either orange T or blue L. Once the subject finds it, he presses a key, and then the next trial starts. The exceptional sign is presented at different location each trial.

Usually, it is easy for a subject to find an exceptional sign when there is only one feature involved (Duncan and Humphreys 1989). It is an unconscious process, and the exceptional sign "pops out". In other words, the subject notices the exception without paying much mental effort.

On the other hand, one that is exceptional because of a combination of features, it requires much more time to find it. Usually, it requires conscious process for searching it. It means that consciousness is involved in the combinatorial search process. Considering the usual assumption that consciousness is closely related to attention, the task requires much attention. By measuring the time

Fig. 2. Conjunction search task.

required to find the exception, we can quantitatively evaluate the level of attention. This type of test is widely used in psychology to measure the level of attention put by the subject.

In our system, the subject can click a sign by moving a pointer using the mouse. If the clicked sing is not the exceptional one, it is recorded as a mistake. By a preliminary experiment, we checked that time required for moving the pointer to the exceptional sign is negligible compared to time necessary for finding the sign.

3.2 Environmental Factors

As a control factor to affect the internal parameters, we chose to focus on music. Music affects emotion, making a person feel happy or sad. It is natural to think that it may affect internal parameters mentioned above. It has already been pointed out that it improves performance on spatial tasks (Schellenberg et al. 2007). Our experiments are to see if this is also true for tasks that involve attention, and see if it can be quantitatively and systematically measured with an aid of a computer program.

In our experiments, we compared 3 conditions listed below.

1. Silence.
2. Music that the subject likes.
3. Music that the subject is unfamiliar with.

We chose to compare between music that are liked by the subject and that the subject is unfamiliar with. We assume that when the subject is listening to the music that he likes, performing the task becomes more enjoyable.

We asked the subjects to name a song that he/she likes, and used it in the experiment. For unfamiliar music, subjects were provided with music liked by other subjects, after checking that he/she is actually unfamiliar with it.

Using music that the subject likes is to determine the effect of enjoyment on attention. The goal of our experiment is to determine whether the effect comes directly from the music itself, or is strongly influenced by the subject's liking to it.

3.3 Software

For implementing our system, we used PsychToolbox (Brainard 1997; Kleiner et al. 2007), which is a set of functions run on Matlab, aimed at vision research. PsychToolbox contains various functions that could be used for creating psychological tests. For implementation, we used Octave, a Matlab compatible software.

4 Experiments

We performed experiments on 12 subjects. All of them were undergraduate and graduate students, ages around 20, ranging from freshman to 1st year in master's course. Using our system, we measured the number of trials each subject could perform during a set amount of time (15 min), under different conditions. Subjects were asked to perform trials as many times as possible. In other words, they were asked to find exceptional signs as fast as possible.

The types of music that were played were mostly pop music, with lyrics. There were up-tempo ones and slow-tempo ones, depending on the preference of each subject. When we could, we chose unfamiliar music from those that were liked by other subjects. This was to avoid the effect that comes from the types of music, for example the positive effect on attention that may arise from listening to up-tempo music.

4.1 Comparison Among Subjects

The numbers of trials that the subjects could perform under three conditions mentioned in the previous section is indicated in Table 1. The three conditions were silence, playing music that the subject likes, and playing music that the subject is unfamiliar with. Most of the songs used in experiments were with lyrics. This is due to the setup that we let the subjects choose her favorite music. The table shows scores for each condition, which are the numbers of trials that the subject succeeded within the time limit of 15 min. If the subject could complete each trial in a shorter time, he gets a higher score.

To avoid the effect from the subject getting used to the task and performing better in the latter part of the experiment, we arranged the conditions in different orders. The order of conditions the experiment was carried out for each subject is indicated by the second column of Table 1, using order IDs. The order is explained using Table 2.

The result shows that the average score were highest when the subject was listening to the music that he likes. The second highest was when he listened to

Table 1. Scores of subjects under different conditions.

Subject	Order	Silence	Like	Unfam
A	I	98	89	113
B	I	86	84	84
C	II	119	119	96
D	II	54	61	69
E	III	71	72	62
F	III	106	132	109
G	IV	88	96	93
H	IV	109	105	105
I	V	116	131	138
J	V	115	110	112
K	VI	54	51	43
L	VI	40	56	53
Total		1056	1106	1077
Avg		88	92.17	89.75

Table 2. Order of testing.

Order	Silence	Like	Unfam.
I	1st	2nd	3rd
II	3rd	2nd	1st
III	2nd	3rd	1st
IV	2nd	1st	3rd
V	1st	3rd	2nd
IV	3rd	1st	2nd

the music that he is unfamiliar with, and the lowest was for the silence condition. It indicates that performance can be improved using music.

Table 3 shows the number of mistakes made by the subjects when carrying out the test. It shows that the number of mistakes was least when the subject was listening to the music he likes. Figure 3 illustrates the same information as a graph.

4.2 Temporal Change in Performance

In the experiment, each subject was asked to perform the task for 15 min, for each condition. After performing a task under one condition, the subject takes 5 min break.

Since the task is rather simple, so it is assumed that the subjects get tired with the task, or bored, which would lower the performance. Unless a high level

Table 3. The number of mistakes made by subjects.

Subject	Silence	Like	Unfam	Total
A	0	1	1	2
B	1	0	0	1
C	0	0	0	0
D	2	0	2	4
E	0	2	2	4
F	0	0	0	0
G	0	0	0	0
H	1	0	0	1
I	0	0	0	0
J	3	1	1	5
K	0	1	1	2
L	2	0	0	2
Total	9	5	7	21

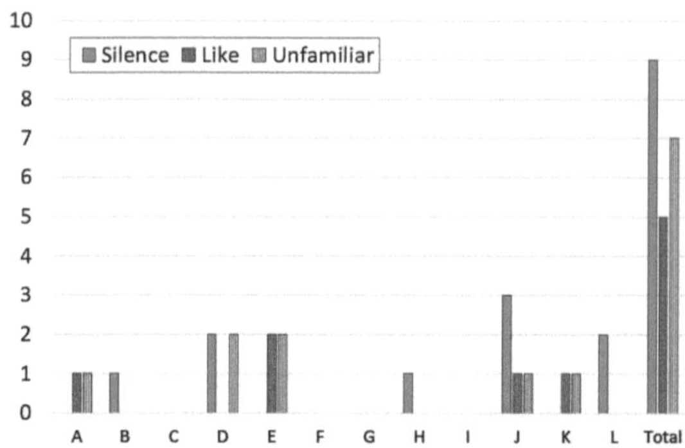

Fig. 3. The number of mistakes made by subjects.

of attention is maintained, the performance level of the subject is unlikely to be constant.

Figures 4, 5, 6, 7, 8 and 9 shows one example of the change in the performance level as a subject did a sequence of trials. The x-axis indicates the trial ID and the y-axis indicates the time it took for the subject to complete that trial, i.e. to find the exceptional sign and click it.

The sequence of the times taken for finishing trials was considered as a function of sample points in time. We applied second order polynomial fitting to this function. The polynomials are also shown in the figures. They show the gradual changes of the performance levels.

Based on an observation, we grouped the result into three types. Type 1 is the case when the performance level does not change much. In this case, the

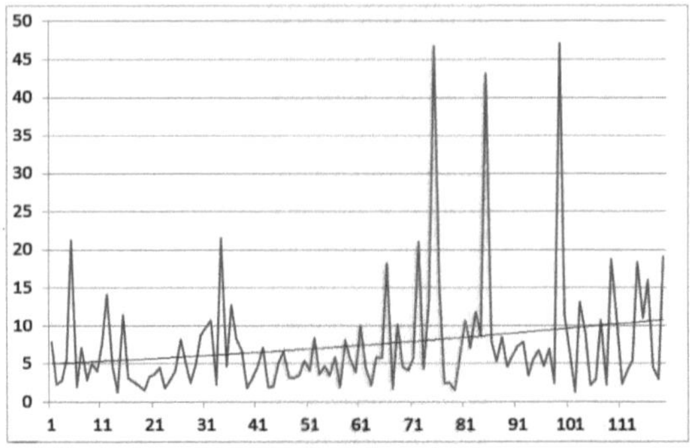

Fig. 4. Temporal change under the silence condition (Subject C, Type 2).

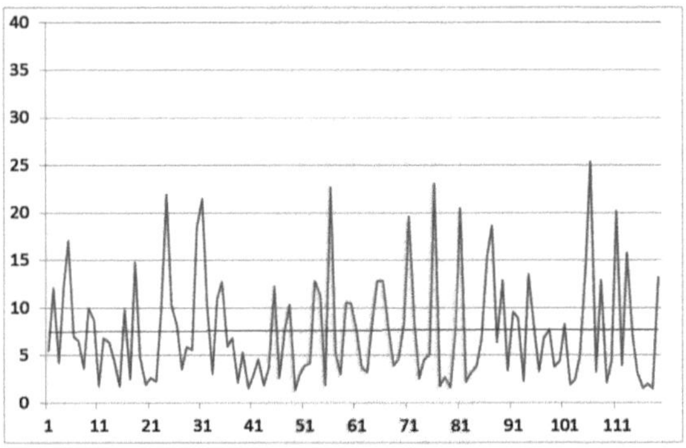

Fig. 5. Temporal change under the liking music condition (Subject C, Type 1).

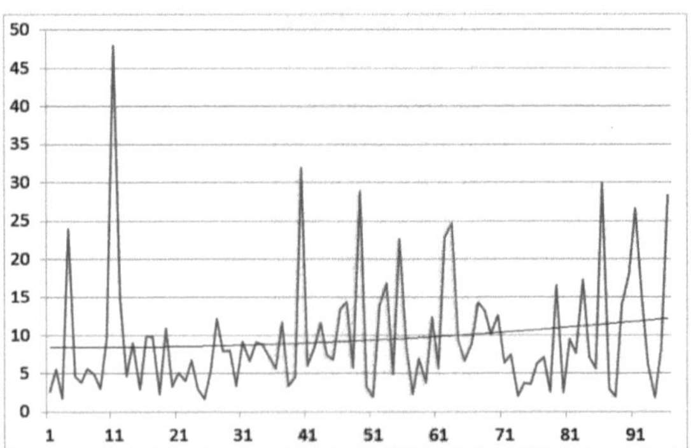

Fig. 6. Temporal change under the unfamiliar music condition (Subject C, Type 2).

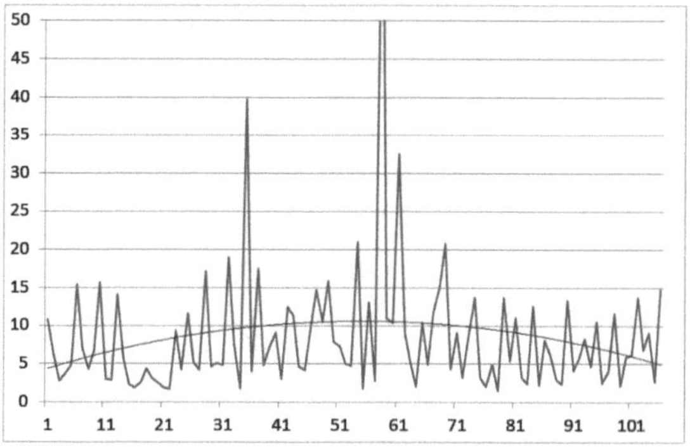

Fig. 7. Temporal change under the silence condition (Subject F, Type 3).

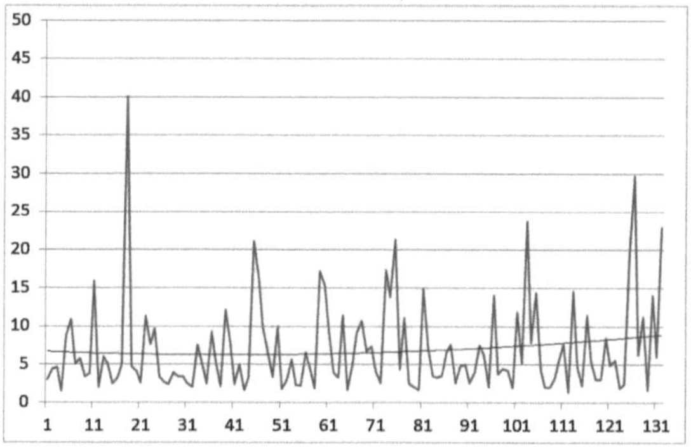

Fig. 8. Temporal change under the liking music condition (Subject F, Type 1).

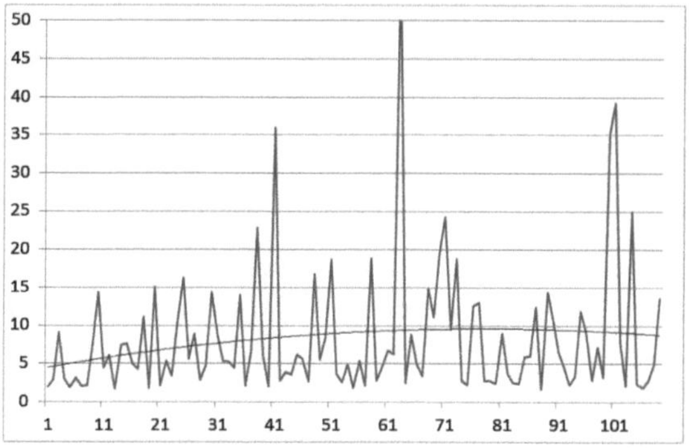

Fig. 9. Temporal change under the unfamiliar music condition (Subject F, Type 3).

polynomial is nearly constant. Type 2 is that the performance worsens as the time passes. In this case, the polynomial is a nearly linear increasing function. Type 3 is when the performance is best near the beginning and near the end, and worse in the middle. In this case, the polynomial is a convex function with its maximum in the middle part of the trial sequence. This is summarized in Table 4. In the table, a_2 is the coefficient of the quadratic term and a_1 is the coefficient for the linear term, for the second order polynomial fitting. Note that the performance is better when the y-value is lower.

The frequent appearance of Type 3 (high in the middle) was interesting, possibly indicating the rise in the performance level when the deadline is approaching.

In general, the overall performance level (the score the subject obtained) was highest for Type 1 and lowest for Type 3. Also, Type 1 was most frequent when the subject was listening to the music that he liked. On the other hand, Type 3 was most frequent when the subject was in the silence condition.

The result indicates that listening to preferred music condition raises the overall performance because it reduces occasions where the subject cannot find the exceptional sign and takes unusually longer time to finish the trial.

Table 4. Types in the temporal change of performance.

Type	Polynomial fitting	a_2	a_1
Type 1	Roughly constant	$a_2 \approx 0$	$a_1 \approx 0$
Type 2	Increasing	$a_2 \approx 0$	$a_1 > 0$
Type 3	High middle, low ends	$a_2 > 0$	

The regression curve may seem to be dependent on large values that intermittently occurs. However, since one of the aims of our experiment was to see the lack of attention, the fact that the subject took a long time to find the exceptional sign does carry information. We did not consider them as outliers.

In some cases, the average performance was better for the without-music condition, if outliers with excess amount of time were ignored. It could be that music distracts on average, but reduces failures that the subject can not find the target.

4.3 Discussion

Our result that music affects the level of attention have various application in real life. When doing self-study, selecting appropriate music would help raise the performance. Even in a classroom, when it is not a lecture-style class but is a practice-style, it might help students by allowing them to listen to music while solving problems.

Teachers may even advice students to try out different types of music while studying, since our result indicates that familiarity to music may affect the temporal change in the level of attention.

Also, the method proposed in this paper to measure the level of attention may be used for other purposes too, for example to know how long a subject can stay attentive.

5 Related Work

In this section, we discuss related work from different aspects.

5.1 Factors that May Affect Mental Attention

Onyper et al. tested a group of subject to solve puzzles or memorize items, while chewing gum (Onyper et al. 2011). They were compared with another group that did not chew gum during the test. The result indicated that chewing gum has positive effect on the subjects' performance. They state that chewing gum may wake you up and increase the level of attention.

Nittono et al. found out that when the subject is presented with a cute ("kawaii", in recent terminology) picture preceding a task, his performance increased (Nittono et al. 2012). Although they hypothesized that a cute picture makes the subject focus on the details of it and increase his performance, it could also be resulting from the increased level of attention due to excitement or enjoyment.

Our work is different from existing work in that it focused on music among many possible factors. It is also different in that it intended to capture the temporal change in the level of attention in a short time span, i.e. in the order of seconds, which is much shorter than usually considered.

5.2 Cognitive Performance While Listening to Music

There has been much work to measure the effect of music on various cognitive activities (Rauscher 1998). As Hill-Clarke et al. (2002) stated, music can help to improve attention span, memory and can enhance learning. Rauscher et al. reported the superior spatial abilities for participants who listened to a recording of music composed by Mozart compared to those who sat in silence or listened to relaxation instructions (Rauscher et al. 1993). Because the performance was better on the spatial tasks after listening to Mozart, this result became known as the Mozart effect (Schellenberg 2005). Reviewing studies that examined effects of listening to music on cognitive performance can be divided to two general group: performance after listening to music and performance while listening to music or background music. Despite the difference, it is pointed out that music influences a wide range of behaviors including cognitive performance (Schellenberg 2012). In these studies, however, it was not checked whether the subjects actually liked Mozart. In comparison, we made a distinction between music liked by the subject and the one that the subject is not familiar with. Our result showed that while music itself raises attention, the one that is liked works even better.

Shih et al. compared how music with, and without, lyrics affects human attention (Shih et al. 2012). Background music with, and without lyrics, was tested for effects on listener in attention testing using a RCT (randomized controlled trial) study. The findings revealed that, if background music is played in the work environment, music without lyrics is preferable because songs with lyrics are likely to have significant negative effects on the attention of worker.

Patston and Tippett examined the overlap between music and language processing in the brain and whether these processes are functionally independent in expert musicians (Patston and Tippett 2011). A language comprehension task and a visuospatial search task were performed under three conditions: music-correct, music-incorrect, and silence for expert musicians and non-musicians. The performance of musicians was negatively affected by the presence of background music compared to silence when performing a language comprehension task. In contrast, the performance of non-musicians was not affected on either the language task by the presence of music played either correctly or incorrectly.

Cassidy and MacDonald studied the effects of HA (music with high arousal potential and negative affect), LA (music with low arousal potential and positive affect), and everyday noise, on the cognitive task performance of introverts and extraverts (Cassidy and MacDonald 2007). Performance was decreased across all cognitive tasks in the presence of background sound compared to silence. HA and LA music produced differential distraction effects, with performance of all tasks being poorer in the presence of HA compared to LA and silence, in the presence of noise than silence across all tasks, and in the presence of noise than LA in three of the four tasks.

Furnham and Strbac examined whether background noise would be as distracting as music (Furnham and Strbac 2002). In the presence of silence, background garage music and office noise, subjects with introvert and extravert personalities carried out a reading comprehension task, a prose recall task and a mental arithmetic task. Results found a significant interaction between personality and background sound on comprehension task only, although a trend for this effect was clearly present on the other two tasks. Participants performed best in silence, background music was second best for performance, and background noise was lowest results.

The existing work mainly focused on making comparison among music, silence and noise, whereas in our work music liked by the subject is compared with unfamiliar one. In this sense, it is more related to the emotion of the subject. Also, the existing work has not discussed much on how listening to music may affect the temporal change in the level of attention. We designed and carried out experiments to check this effect.

5.3 Music for Enhancing Learning

Researchers from psychology as well as sociology have attempted to explain the importance of music for intellectual development by focusing on a variety of cognitive ability. Singer (2008) and Barker (2008) reported that music increased the chance students remembered what they had learned, by assisting the recall of information. Binkiewicz discussed the idea that songs are powerful pedagogical tools that enliven a classroom and enhance student learning in an enjoyable manner (Binkiewicz 2006).

When music is utilized learning, positive results occurred in achievement. Music showed positive impacts on achievement as Southgate and Roscigno assessed three patterns of music participation: in school, outside of school, and parental involvement in the form of concert attendance and possible effects on math and reading performance for both elementary and high school students (Southgate and Roscigno 2009). Their study captured the significant influence of music involvement for both math and reading achievement.

Paquette and Rieg described the benefits of incorporating musical experiences into daily instruction and argued that integrating experiences with music in the childhood classroom supports English language learners' literacy development (Paquette and Rieg 2008). Sims examined the effects of high versus low teacher affect and active versus passive student activities during music listening on preschool children's attention (Sims 1986). Data obtained through observation indicated that children were most attentive during music listening activities when the teacher exhibited high magnitude nonverbal affect, and when they were given a hand-movement activity in which to participate.

Our paper focused on the effect of music on the level of attention, which is related to performance in general, rather than specific tasks in learning. By focusing on a simple task rather than complicated ones, we believe that we could quantify more fundamental parameter that affect the level of performance.

6 Conclusions

In order to increase the attentional level and raise the performance, we implemented a system for measuring it, and examined the effect of an external factor, namely playing music that the subject likes. The result showed that playing music does have positive effects on the level of attention, which would contribute to the performance level.

In future work, we would like to carry out experiments using more subjects, to make our result more statistically reliable. We would also like to look at the temporal patterns of attention in more detail. We would like to see if there is actually rhythms for attention, as mentioned by Buzsaki for different mental processes (Buzsaki 2006). We would like to explore this, for example using frequency analysis. We also plan to carry out more controlled testing, using a larger number of subjects, to validate our hypothesis.

We also plan to explore modulation of the excitement level using music, and see if the attention can be improved. When the subject is too relaxed, we make him listen to excitatory music, and while the subject is overexcited, we make him listen to inhibitory music. We would like to see if the attentional level can effectively controlled that way. We expect the result to provide a fundamental basis for creating the environment that makes people more productive.

Acknowledgements. This work was supported in part by JSPS KAKENHI Grant Numbers 21700121, 25280110, and 25540159.

References

Aheadi, A., Dixon, P., Glover, S.: A limiting feature of the Mozart effect: listening enhances mental rotation abilities in non-musicians but not musicians. Psychol. Music **38**(1), 107–117 (2010)

Ahissar, M., Hochstein, S.: The role of attention in learning simple visual tasks. In: Fahle, M., Poggio, T. (eds.) Perceptual Learning, pp. 253–272. MIT Press, Cambridge (2002)

Barker, C.: Teacher, producer create CD for math success. N.Y. Amsterdam News **99**, 16–32 (2008)

Bergen, J.R., Julesz, B.: Parallel versus serial processing in rapid pattern discrimination. Nature **303**, 696–698 (1983)

Binkiewicz, D.M.: Tunes of the times: historical songs as pedagogy for recent US history. Hist. Teach. **39**(4), 515–520 (2006)

Brainard, D.H.: The psychophysics toolbox. Spat. Vis. **10**, 443–446 (1997)

Buzsaki, G.: Rhythms of the Brain. Oxford University Press, New York (2006)

Cassidy, G., MacDonald, R.A.R.: The effect of background music and background noise on the task performance of introverts and extraverts. Psychol. Music **35**(3), 517–537 (2007)

Cerin, E., Szabo, A., Hunt, N., Williams, C.: Temporal patterning of competitive emotions: a critical review. J. Sports Sci. **18**(8), 605–626 (2000)

Duncan, J., Humphreys, G.W.: Visual search and stimulus similarity. Psychol. Rev. **96**(3), 433–458 (1989)

Furnham, A., Strbac, L.: Music is as distracting as noise: the differential distraction of background music and noise on the cognitive test performance of introverts and extraverts. Ergonomics **45**(3), 203–217 (2002)

Grondin, S. (ed.): Psychology of Time. Elsevier Science, Oxford (2008)

Clarke, K.Y., Robinson, N.R.: Locomotion and Literacy: Effective Strategies to Enhance Literacy Instruction. The University of Memphis, Memphis (2002)

Huang, T.R., Watanabe, T.: Task attention facilitates learning of task-irrelevant stimuli. PLoS ONE **7**(4), e35946 (2012)

McArdle, W.D., Katch, F.I., Katch, V.L.: Essentials of Exercise Physiology, 2nd edn. Lipincott Williams and Wilkins, Baltimore (1999)

Kleiner, M., Brainard, D., Pelli, D.: What's new in Psychtoolbox-3? Perception 36 ECVP Abstract Supplement (2007)

Nieuwenstein, M., der Burg, E.V., Theeuwes, J., Wyble, B., Potter, M.: Paying attention to mindfulness and its effects on task performance in the workplace. J. Vis. **9**(18), 1–14 (2009)

Nittono, H., Fukushima, M., Yano, A., Moriya, H.: The power of Kawaii: viewing cute images promotes a careful behavior and narrows attentional focus. PLoS ONE **7**(9), e46362 (2012)

Nobre, A.C., Coull, J.T. (eds.): Attention and Time. Oxford University Press, NewYork (2010)

Onyper, S.V., Carr, T.L., Farrar, J.S., Floyd, B.R.: Cognitive advantages of chewing gum. Now you see them, now you don't. Appatite **57**, 321–328 (2011)

Paquette, K.R., Rieg, S.A.: Using music to support the literacy development of young English language learners. Early Child. Educ. J. **36**(3), 227–232 (2008)

Patston, L.L.M., Tippett, L.J.: The effect of background music on cognitive performance in musicians and nonmusicians. Music Percept. **29**(2), 173–183 (2011)

Rank, J., Frese, M.: The impact of emotions, moods and other affect related variables on creativity innovation and initiative. In: Ashkanasy, N.M., Cooper, C.L. (eds.) Research Companion to Emotion in Organization, pp. 103–119. Edward Elgar, Cheltenham (2010)

Rauscher, F.H., Shaw, G.L., Ky, K.N.: Music and spatial task performance. Nature **365**(6447), 611 (1993)

Rauscher, F.H., Robinson, K.D., Jens, J.J.: Improved maze learning through early music exposure in rats. Neurol. Res. **20**(5), 427–432 (1998)

Schellenberg, E.G.: Music and cognitive abilities. Curr. Dir. Psychol. Sci. **14**(6), 317–320 (2005)

Schellenberg, E.G., Nakata, T., Hunter, P.G., Tamoto, S.: Exposure to music and cognitive performance: tests of children and adults. Psychol. Music **35**(1), 5–19 (2007)

Schellenberg, E.G.: Cognitive performance after listening to music: a review of the Mozart effect. In: MacDonald, R., Gunter, K., Mitchell, L. (eds.) Music, Health, and Wellbeing, pp. 324–338 (2012)

Schmidt, R.: Consciousness and foreign language learning: a tutorial on the role of attention and awareness in learning. In: Schmidt, R. (ed.) Attention and Awareness in Foreign Language Learning, pp. 1–63. University of Hawai'i Press, Honolul (1995)

Schwarz, N., Clore, G.L.: Mood, misattribution, and judgments of well-being: Informative and directive functions of affective states. J. Pers. Soc. Psychol. **45**(3), 513 (1983)

Schwarz, N., Clore, G.L.: How do I feel about it? Informative function of affective states. In: Fiedler, K., Forgas, J. (eds.) Affect, Cognition, and Social Behavior, pp. 44–62. Hogrefe International, Toronto (1988)

Shih, Y., Huang, R., Chiang, H.: Background music: effects on attention performance. Work J. Prev. Assess. Rehabil. **42**(4), 573–578 (2012)

Sims, W.L.: The effect of high versus low teacher affect and passive versus active student activity during music listening on preschool children's attention, piece preference, time spent listening, and piece recognition. J. Res. Music Educ. **34**(3), 173–191 (1986)

Singer, M.J.: Accessing the musical intelligence in early childhood education. Aust. J. Early Child. **33**(2), 49–56 (2008)

Southgate, D.E., Roscigno, V.J.: The impact of music on childhood and adolescent achievement. Soc. Sci. Q. **90**(1), 4–21 (2009)

Tomlin, R.S., Villa, V.: Attention in cognitive science and second language acquisition. Stud. Second Lang. Acquisition **16**(2), 183–203 (1994)

An Evaluation Methodology for Concept Maps Mined from Lecture Notes: An Educational Perspective

Thushari Atapattu(✉), Katrina Falkner, and Nickolas Falkner

School of Computer Science, University of Adelaide, Adelaide, Australia
{thushari.atapattu, katrina.falkner, nickolas.falkner}@adelaide.edu.au

Abstract. Concept maps are effective tools that assist learners in organising and representing knowledge. Recent efforts in the area of concept mapping work toward semi- or fully automated approaches to extract concept maps from various text sources such as text books. The motivation for this research is twofold: novice learners require substantial assistance from experts in constructing their own maps, introducing additional hurdles, and alternatively, the workload required by academics in manually constructing expert maps is substantial and repetitive. A key limitation of an automated concept map generation is the lack of an evaluation framework to measure the quality of concept maps. The most common evaluation mechanism is measuring the overlap between machine-generated elements (e.g. concepts) with expert maps using *relevancy* measures such as *precision* and *recall*. However, in the educational context, the majority of knowledge presented is relevant to the learner, resulting in a large amount of information being retrieved for knowledge organisation. Therefore, this paper introduces a machine-based approach to evaluate the *relative importance* of knowledge by comparing with human judgment. We introduce three ranking models and conclude that the structural features are positively correlated with human experts ($r_s \sim 1$) for courses with rich content and good structure (*well-fitted*).

Keywords: Concept map mining · Evaluation methodology · Lecture notes

1 Introduction

Concept mapping is recognised as a valuable educational visualisation technique, which assists students in organising, sharing and representing knowledge. Concept maps model knowledge so that it can be expressed externally using set of concepts and propositions (Novak and Gowin 1984). These concepts are organised in a hierarchy with the most general concept at the top and the most specific concepts arranged below (Coffey et al. 2003). The hierarchical nature of concept maps supports Assimilation theory (Ausubel et al. 1978) by identifying general concepts held by learners prior to introduce more specific concepts. Concept maps have been widely used in the educational context, particularly in meaningful learning which integrate relevant prior knowledge to learn new information. Additionally, the adoption of concept mapping

S. Zvacek et al. (Eds.): CSEDU 2014, CCIS 510, pp. 68–83, 2015.
DOI: 10.1007/978-3-319-25768-6_5

into learning, particularly in class room education measured several important aspects such as understanding, misconceptions and knowledge gaps, conceptual changes and problem solving skills (Novak and Gowin 1984; Coffey et al. 2003).

However, '*construct-by-self*', where students are responsible for creating their own concept maps, introduces a substantial difficulty for novice students to correctly identify concepts, relations and hence, requires continuous assistance from academic staff. A common alternative is to provide students with maps constructed by human experts (known as *expert maps*), placing additional load and intellectual commitment on academic staff.

Although constructing a concept map for a lecture is a one-off process, it needs to be updated continuously, to cope with the changing nature of knowledge. However, due to the lack of human awareness of knowledge representations and a general preference for writing informal sentences over creating network models, concept maps are not yet widely used for learning.

Therefore, recent efforts in this area work toward semi- or fully automated approaches to extract concept maps from text (known as *concept map mining*), with the aim of providing useful educational tools with minimal human intervention (Olney et al. 2012; Alves et al. 2002; Chen et al. 2008). However, a significant problem in concept map extraction is the lack of an evaluation framework to measure the quality of machine-extracted concept maps (Villalon and Calvo 2008). At present researchers rely upon human efforts to evaluate machine-extracted concept maps either through manual judgment or comparison with expert maps.

The majority of works in this area focus on the performance of automated tools using the popular Information retrieval metrics - *precision* and *recall*. These forms of measurement evaluate whether the machine extracted elements (e.g. concepts) are *relevant*. However, in the educational context, particularly in course materials, the majority of knowledge presented is relevant to the learner, resulting in large part of lectures or textbooks being retrieved and identified for knowledge organisation (Atapattu et al. 2012). But, according to the definition of concept maps, a concept map should be an overview, which organises most important knowledge according to learning objectives (Novak and Gowin 1984). Hence, the aim of this paper is to discuss a machine-based evaluation technique which studies the *relative importance* of knowledge, focusing beyond the simple measure of *relevancy*.

Current instructional methods widely support verbal learning through linear and sequential learning materials. The literature provides inadequate research to assist transforming linearity of resources into network models such as semantic networks and concept maps. Our approach takes the work that has already been invested in producing legible slides and focus on extracting useful knowledge that are beneficial for both the teacher and the learner. This will be an increasingly important research topic in the decade of Massive Open Online Courses (MOOCs). This paper provides a concise overview of our concept map mining framework using Natural Language Processing (NLP) algorithms.

In this paper, we hypothesize that the natural presentation layout, linguistic or structural features might influence the human expert's judgement of relative concept importance. We developed three ranking models: (1) Baseline methods which use the natural layout of lecture slides (e.g. titles are the most important, sub-points are the least important); (2) Linguistic features such as grammatical structure of English text; and (3) Structural features such as proximity, number of incoming and outgoing connections, and degree of co-occurrence. We compare each of these models with human judgment using Spearman's ranking correlation coefficient (r_s). According to the results in Sect. 5, outcome of the structural feature model positively correlates with human judgment. There is a strong correlation ($r_s > 0.7$) for well summarised courses with rich grammar (i.e. *well-fitted* content). The correlation ranges from *well-fitted* to *ill-fitted* proportionally with respect to the quality and structure of the content. Lecture notes with some potential issues, including excessive information, category headings (e.g. key points, Chap. 1), confusing visual idioms and ambiguous sentences (i.e. *ill-fitted* content) result in poor machine interpretation and hence, poor correlation with human judgment.

The concept map extraction, particularly from course materials, is beneficial for both students and educators. It organises and represents knowledge scattered throughout multiple topics. These maps can be used as an assessment tool (Villalon and Calvo 2008; Gouli et al. 2004) to identify understanding about concepts and relations. Additionally, these concept maps can be used as an "*intelligent suggester*" to recommend concepts, propositions, and existing concept maps from the web (Leake et al. 2004). In the educational context, these maps can provide scaffolding aid for students to construct their own concept maps. Concept mapping has also been utilised widely in question generation (Olney et al. 2012) and question answering (Dali et al. 2009). The preliminary concept maps extracted from this research can also be extended as an ontology for domain modeling in intelligent systems.

This paper includes a background study of various concept map mining evaluation techniques in Sect. 2. In Sects. 3 and 4, we discuss about our core research focus of concept map mining from lecture notes and ranking model respectively. We evaluate our approach with human experts and present results and analysis in Sect. 5 and our study is concluded in Sect. 6.

2 Related Work

The evaluation of the quality of machine-extracted knowledge representations is a challenging and tedious task. This can categorised into three dimensions as structural, semantic and comparative evaluation (Zouaq and Nkabou 2009). In the concept mapping perspective, measuring the effect of structural/graph-based features of concept maps can be classified as structural evaluation. A study of Indiana University and Institute of Human and Machine cognition (IHMC) considered four candidate models to determine which factors have influence for concept importance: baseline model considered map topology and layout as unimportant, Connectivity Root-Distance (CRD) Model (incoming-outgoing links and proximity to the root), Hub-Authority and Root-Distance (HARD) Model (hub has multiple outgoing connections and authority has multiple incoming connections) and Path Counter Model (PC). The results show that layout of the map has no effect, however, CRD outperforms HARD when comparing with human judgment.

In semantic evaluations, human experts are generally involved in judging the validity of machine-extracted maps. In traditional approach, experts are assigning scores to components or structure of the map (e.g. 1 point is assigned for a valid proposition, 5 points for each level of adopted hierarchies, and 10 points for cross-links) (Novak and Gowin 1984). Although, the scoring technique provides information about creator's knowledge structure, this technique is time-consuming when assessing large-scale maps (Coffey et al. 2003). Alternatively, expert generated maps are considered as a gold standard to compare other concept maps either constructed manually or automatically (Villalon and Calvo 2008). This usually compares the overlap between both maps and obtain the relevancy statistics - *precision* and *recall.*

In comparative analysis, the machine-extracted concept maps are compared with other tools, which are built for the same purpose and test using the same corpus. TEXT-TO-ONTO is a popular ontology extraction tool. It is compared with TEX-COMON (Text-Concept map-Ontology) that automatically extracts concept maps from text (Zouaq and Nkabou 2009). In order to use the comparative evaluation, other tools should exist which are built for same purpose. We demonstrate our approach using Microsoft PowerPoint Framework (as a commonly used lecture note format), although our approach is not constrained to PowerPoint but generalises across any common lecture note formats such as OpenOffice, Latex, and Apple Key note with a structured template for headers and text. To the best of our knowledge, there are no existing tools which do this.

However, despite the benefits to the educational context, state of art studies focused on *concept relevancy*, and not their *relative importance*. Our work adapts several structural features (e.g. proximity, incoming and outgoing links) (Leake et al. 2004) and graph-based metrics (e.g. degree) (Zouaq et al. 2012) to rank the concepts according to their importance. However, we also use linguistic features, semantic information and the association between terms to mimic the human judgment using machine algorithms. This resolves syntactically and semantically incomplete information in lecture notes which recognised as a key challenge in applying computer algorithms to semi-structured lecture notes.

3 Concept Map Mining

Our core research focus is on automatically extracting useful knowledge as concept maps from educational materials, particularly from lecture notes to provide variety of learning and assessment/reflective activities for learners. Current concept map mining approaches rely upon statistical methods, linguistic methods or hybrid methods. Statistical methods such as term frequency, C-value/NC-value, co-occurrence of terms (Salton and McGill 1986) suffer from probable semantic loss.

Alternatively, linguistic methods such as syntactic parsing, part-of-speech tagging, named entity tagging and language models (Manning et al. 2008) usually extract nouns or gerund verbs (i.e. some special verbs in its '*-ing*' form which can act as nouns - e.g. *testing*) as concepts. A concept in our context defines an object or an event designated by a label. For an instance, *processor* is unit resides within the computer and *process* is a program that is executing can be identified as an object and an event respectively within the domain of ‘Computing’. Therefore, in general, concept has a ‘meaning’ in a particular context. However, there may be nouns or gerund verbs present that are not concepts in that particular domain. In order to overcome these issues, studies based on linguistic methods utilise external dictionaries and thesaurus.

However, these types of external resources are very limited for specific domains such as Computer Science.

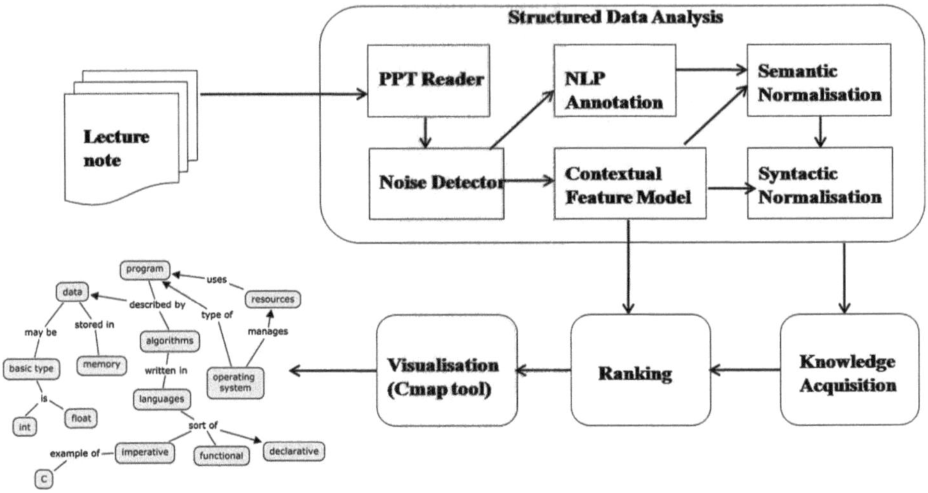

Fig. 1. High-level overview of concept map mining process.

Therefore, our work utilises NLP algorithms to extract concepts and relations using syntactic parsing, part-of-speech tagging (Klein and Manning 2003) and link grammar parsing (Sleator and Temperly 1993). A high-level overview of concept map mining process is shown in Fig. 1. This paper discusses the ranking of concepts included in a triple (concept-relation-concept). We assume that “if the participating concepts in a triple is important, this implies that the relation between these concepts is deemed important”. Therefore, we do not perform a separate relation ranking process.

As shown in Fig. 1, our system relies on the use of the lecture notes presented as set of slides. Therefore, it is capable of extracting rich text features such as underline, font color and highlights and type of text such as a title, bullet point, and sub-point. Lecture notes frequently contain noisy data such as course announcements and assignment details that are irrelevant for a knowledge representation. The system detects and resolves them automatically by utilising co-occurrence between domain-related and unrelated topics. For example, if course title is co-occurred with some terms in body text, that pair of terms has strong relation with the domain, and hence recognised as a domain-specific terms.

Lecture slides occasionally contain incomplete and ambiguous English sentences for machine interpretation. Therefore, it is challenging to apply NLP algorithms to extract knowledge from lecture slides. We implemented a contextual feature model which automatically replaces syntactically and semantically missing entities (e.g. subjects or objects of sentences). Our initial research also focused on resolving pronouns (e.g. *it, their*) and demonstrative determiners (e.g. *these, this*) using a backward search approach (Atapattu et al. 2014).

In contrast to other related works in literature (Chen et al. 2008), which has no relation labels among extracted concepts, our work generates concept-relation-concept triples by analysing subject-verb-object (SVO) in English sentences. We utilise the Stanford parser (Klein and Manning 2003) to extract SVO from simple sentences and link grammar parser to extract triples from complex sentences (Sleator and Temperly 1993) which have more than one nested sentences or dependent clauses. We applied the greedy approach to the remaining text to identify 'key terms' using part-of-speech tagging. The concept and relation extraction along with automated noise detection is broadly discussed in our previous works (Atapattu et al. 2012, 2014).

The extracted concepts and relationships are arranged according to their importance, which is the focus of this paper. Finally, a CXL (**C**oncept map E**x**tensible **L**anguage) file is produced from extracted knowledge, which can be directly exported to IHMC cmap tools[1] for visualisation (Fig. 2).

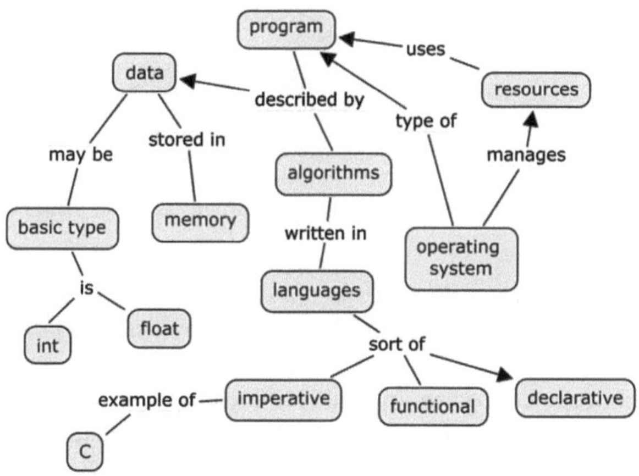

Fig. 2. An example concept map extracted from 'Operating System' topic.

4 Ranking Model

In order to construct a high quality concept map, both domain knowledge and hierarchy are equally significant (Novak and Gowin 1984). This section discusses three candidate models which arrange concepts by their importance.

[1] http://cmap.ihmc.us/.

4.1 Baseline Model

Our knowledge source (i.e. lecture slides) contains a natural layout of presentation title, slide headings, bullet points, and enumerated sub-points. Therefore, one can argue that this layout can directly transfer to a hierarchy. To validate this assumption, we implemented a baseline model by integrating 'text location' in lecture slides (Table 1).

Table 1. Concept importance by location.

Location	Rank
Title	3
Bullet statement	2
Sub-point	1

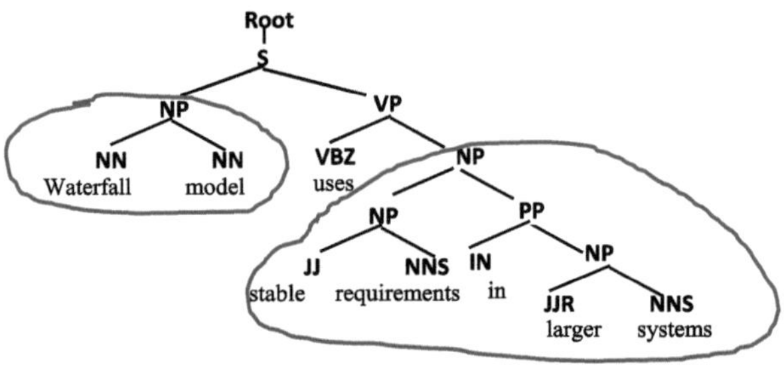

Fig. 3. Syntactic parser tree of an example English sentence.

Hypothesis I: *Text location allocated by the natural layout of presentation slides might influence human judgment of which concepts are most important.*

However, a concept can occur in multiple locations. In order to select the most suitable location for such concepts, we implemented a "link-distance algorithm" which can be found in our previous work (Atapattu et al. 2012).

4.2 Linguistic Feature Model

First, we used the greedy approach to extract nouns and noun phrases using part-of-speech tags (Atapattu et al. 2012). Although, this approach is efficient for extracting isolated nouns or noun phrases, we found it difficult to extract phrases joined by prepositions (e.g. *of, for, in*) and conjunctions (e.g. *and, or*). Therefore, we developed a new approach using the Stanford parser (Klein and Manning 2003), which produces syntactic parse trees (Fig. 3).

It is straightforward to extract nouns (*leaf* nodes) or noun phrases (*pre-terminal* which is one level above *leaf*). This approach outperforms the first method and hence, solves the preposition and conjunction issue.

Table 2. Concept importance by grammatical structure; NP: noun phrase, PP: prepositional phrase, S: sentence, VP: verb phrase (More information can be found in http://bulba.sdsu.edu/jeanette/thesis/PennTags.html).

Feature	Example grammatical structure	Rank
Noun phrase	(NP (NP (NNP **Advantage**)) (PP (IN **of**) (NP (NN **unit**) (NN **testing**))))	3
Simple sentence	(S (NP (NNP **Process**)) (VP (VBZ **is**) (NP (NP (NN **program**)) (PP (IN **in**) (NP (NN **execution**))))))	2
Complex sentence	(S (NP (DT A) (NN **software**) (NN **process**)) (VP (VBZ **is**) (NP (NP (DT **a**) (NN **set**)) (PP (IN **of**) (NP (NP (ADJP (RB **partially**) (VBN **ordered**)) (NNS **activities**)) (CC **and**) (NP (NP (JJ **associated**) (NNS **results**)) (SBAR (WHNP (WDT **that**)) (S (VP (VBP **produce**) (CC **or**) (VBP **maintain**) (NP (DT **a**) (NN **software**) (NN **product**)))))))))))	1

Our hypothesis is based on the recommendation of using the smallest number of words for a concept (Novak and Gowin 1984).

Hypothesis II: *Simple grammatical structures (nouns, noun phrases) of Lecture slides might have higher influence than complex grammatical structures (nested sentences, dependent clauses, indirect objects) for human judgment of which concepts are most important.*

Table 2 shows our rankings based on grammatical structure.

As shown in Table 2, complex sentences contain nested sentences (S), clauses (SBAR) and conjunctions (CC). Therefore, we assume these sentences contain definitions or elaborations rather than the abstract concepts of a knowledge representation. Verb phrase (VP) is the remaining grammatical structure which is usually nested with a verb (or multiple verbs) and a noun phrase. We usually extract NPs from verb phrases.

4.3 Structural Feature Model

In the third candidate model, we integrate some structural features (e.g. incoming, outgoing links and proximity) which have already been proposed in Zouaq et al. (2012), Leake et al. (2004) and new distributional features (e.g. typography and co-occurrence) that are unique to presentation framework.

Hypothesis III: *Structural (Incoming and outgoing links, proximity) and distributional (term frequency, degree of co-occurrence, typography) features might influence the human judgment of which concepts are most important.*

Log Frequency Weight. The system counts the occurrence of *nouns* or *noun phrases* and normalises the term frequency (t_f). This value is significant than typical term frequency measure used in information retrieval applications since our 'terms' are restricted to nouns or noun phrases.

$$W_t = \log(1 + t_f) \tag{1}$$

Incoming and Outgoing Links (I/O Links). We keep track of the number of incoming (n_i) and outgoing (n_o) connections for each node. The 'root' node contains only outgoing links and leaf nodes contain only incoming links. Those that have more outgoing than incoming are identifies as of greater importance.

These metrics are significant to demonstrate disjoint nodes from central concept map. Our system provides this information as a conceptual feedback for teachers. This feedback can be used to reflect on whether their expert structures have been transferred successfully to teaching material. If not, students struggle to organise disjoint information into their knowledge structures since there is no relation between new and existing information.

$$W_o = n_o/\text{total links} \tag{2}$$

$$W_i = n_i/\text{total links} \tag{3}$$

Degree of Co-occurrence. Our hypothesis is '*if two key terms co-occur in many slides (equals to pages in other documents), it is assumed that those two terms have a strong relation*' and hence, can be chosen as domain concepts. To measure the degree of co-occurrence, we use the Jaccard coefficient, a statistical measure which compares the similarity of two sample sets.

In order to measure the degree of co-occurrence between term t_1 and term t_2, first calculate the number of slides, that $t_1$and t_2 co-occurs. This is denoted as $|n_1 \cap n_2|$. Then calculate the number of slides the term t_1 ($|n_1|$), t_2 ($|n_2|$) occurs. The degree of co-occurrence of t_1 and t_2 is denoted by J (t_1, t_2) is,

$$J(t_1, t_2) = |n_1 \cap n_2| / |n_1 U n_2| = |n_1 \cap n_2| / (n_1 + n_2 - |n_1 \cap n_2|) \tag{4}$$

This value is utilised as a key decisive factor for noise detection since key terms such as *announcements, assignments* have low degree of co-occurrence with other domain concepts.

Typography. Lecture slides often contain emphasised texts (e.g. different font color, underline) to illustrate their importance in the given domain. We introduced a probability model to select candidate concepts using their level of emphasis. According to the proposed model, terms which contain infrequent styles are allocated higher weights. More information of this work can be found in our previous work (Atapattu et al. 2012).

Proximity. We consider the 'lecture topic' as the *root* (or central concept) of concept map. Therefore, we hypothesise the concepts that have a higher proximity to the *root* are expected to be more important than those with lower proximity (Leake et al. 2004). We denote the proximity weight (Wp) by calculating the number of nodes (d_n) from root to participating node (inclusive).

$$W_p = 1/d_n \tag{5}$$

Generally, a concept map with 15 to 25 nodes is sufficient to assist learning while not providing an overwhelming amount of information (Novak and Gowin 1984). Thus, the aim of introducing a ranking model is to construct a conceptual overview with the most important domain knowledge from the lecture notes.

5 Evaluation of Concept Importance

We conducted experiments with domain experts (lecturers) to study their judgment of concept importance in their lecture notes. These data are then compared with the machine predictions to assess the accuracy of the auto-generated concept maps.

5.1 Data

Seven computer science courses across different Undergraduate levels (1st year, 2nd year, 3rd year and 4th year) were selected. These courses contain a combination of content types such as text, program codes, mathematical notations, tables and images. The seven courses chosen were *Introductory programming (IP), Algorithm design and data structures (ADDS), Object oriented programming (OOP) (level 1); Software Engineering (SE) (level 2); Distributed systems (DS), Operating systems (OS) (level 3); and Software Architecture (SA) (level 4).* Each participant was provided with approximately 54 slides including one to three topics. Tasks were designed to be completed within 30–45 min, with the variation due to how recently the lecturer had been teaching the course.

Seven lecturers from the Computer Science School volunteered to assist with the experiments. They are the domain experts of selected topics who have extensive experience in teaching the courses.

5.2 Procedure

This study required participants to rate the domain concepts according to their importance. The judgment was expected to reflect personal opinions based on their knowledge and perception. However, we provided a few tips, such as how the importance of a concept can be affected by the learning outcome, course objective, and examination perspective. These instructions did not have any relation with the factors we considered in developing our concept map mining framework.

We provided color pens and printed lecture slides to the participants who preferred working in a paper-based environment. The rest used their computers or tablets to highlight the domain concepts. The three rating scale given to the participants consisted of '*most important*', '*important*', and '*least important*' using three colors '*red*', '*yellow*' *and* '*green*' respectively. Participants tended to rate single concepts as well as noun phrases.

During the experiments, we did not show the machine-extracted concept maps to the participants. They only had access to the course lecture slides. This could prevent any influence arising from structure or layout of concept maps for the human judgment.

5.3 Results

We developed a simple program to extract the annotations of participants. A Java API for Microsoft framework[2] was used to extract highlighted texts. Using this approach, we extracted 678 concepts from 376 lecture slides. The average number of concepts per slide was approximately 2.2 except in IP course. In IP, multiple slides repeated the same content in animations. Therefore, in IP, the average number of concepts per slide is 0.8.

The highlighted texts are categorised and sorted based on their ranks from 3 to 1 (most important to least important). Similarly, our system arranged important concepts according to ranks assigned by each candidate models.

In the baseline model, our ranking algorithm allocated rank 3 for text located in *titles* (see Table 1) and 0 for concepts annotated by human, but not retrieved by machine. The two rankings were compared using ranking correlation coefficient and results are presented in Table 4. The correlation (r_s) is close to 0 for the majority of the courses except for ADDS and SA. This implies there is no linear correlation between human judgment of concept importance and the natural layout of presentation software. This causes us to question and reject the original hypothesis that assumes most important, important and least important concepts are located in titles, bullet points and sub points respectively. Therefore, previous work which performed 'topic extraction' (Kinchin 2006) should focus on fine-grained course contents in addition to lecture headings. The feedback obtained from lecturers regarding concept importance is significant for students. This implies layout of slides is not overlapping with lecturer's judgment of what is more important in the lecture.

However, if we could expand the ranking to a few other levels, we could expect a slightly more positive correlation from the baseline model. This occurs because the ranking model categorises remaining concepts as false positive (rank = 0) that have not been ranked by human and false negative (rank = 0) that have not been retrieved by machine, but annotated by human.

The linguistic feature model assumes the grammatical structure of text (noun/phrases, simple sentences and complex sentences) has an impact for selecting candidate concepts. Similar to the baseline model, this has assigned higher rank (rank = 3) for noun or noun phrases and lower rank (rank = 1) for complex grammatical structures (see Table 2). However, Table 4 shows the correlation is closer to 0 for all the selected courses. This reveals that, in addition to single terms and brief phrases,

[2] http://poi.apache.org/slideshow/index.html.

simple and complex sentences contain candidate domain concepts. Therefore, a deep analysis of all text contents irrespective of their grammatical complexity is significant to extract the useful knowledge from lecture slides.

In the structural candidate model, we normalise weights of each metrics within the range of 0–1. The influence of each metric (discussed in Sect. 4.3) is determined by the parameter values (Table 3). For example, terms with higher outgoing links can be more general, thus more important than terms with higher incoming links. We trained our weighting function using previously annotated data for a previous study (Atapattu et al. 2012). The training data contains slides extracted from recommended text books, University course materials and randomly chosen topics from Web.

Table 3. Best fit parameter values for structural features.

Feature	Best fit parameter values
Outgoing links	0.923
Proximity	0.853
Typography	0.764
Co-occurrence	0.559
Frequency	0.514
Incoming links	0.281

After obtaining best fit parameter values using training set, we calculated the aggregate weight for each concept in the test set and sort them in the descending order of weights. Our system defines *upper*, *medium* and *lower* threshold values in order to rank the *most important* (above upper), *important* (in-between upper and medium) and *least important* (in-between medium and lower) domain concepts. These three threshold values vary depending on the number of concepts retrieved. Finally, similar to other two candidate models, we compare the ranks given by participants with machine prediction. The results can be found in the last column of Table 4.

Table 4. Spearman's ranking correlation (r_s) between candidate models and computer science courses.

Model	**Baseline (r_s)**	**Linguistic (r_s)**	**Structural (r_s)**
Software Engineering	0.193	0.247	0.805
Algorithm design and data structures	0.436	0.252	0.435
Introductory programming	0.113	0.293	0.353
Operating systems	0.325	0.240	0.715
Distributed systems	0.183	0.129	0.455
Object-oriented programming	0.287	0.347	0.521
Software architecture	0.605	0.050	0.806

The results are interpreted as strong positive or strong negative if r_s close to +1 or -1 respectively. There is no linear correlation when r_s is close to 0 and hence, consider as independent variables.

$$r_s = \left(1 - 6\sum d_i^2\right) / \left(n\left(n^2 - 1\right)\right) \tag{6}$$

d = difference between ranks, n = sample size

Since the selected courses contain combinations of content (e.g. text, images, program codes), we claim our data ranges from *well-fitted* (e.g. SE and SA) to *ill-fitted* (e.g. IP and ADDS) contents for 'machine interpretation'.

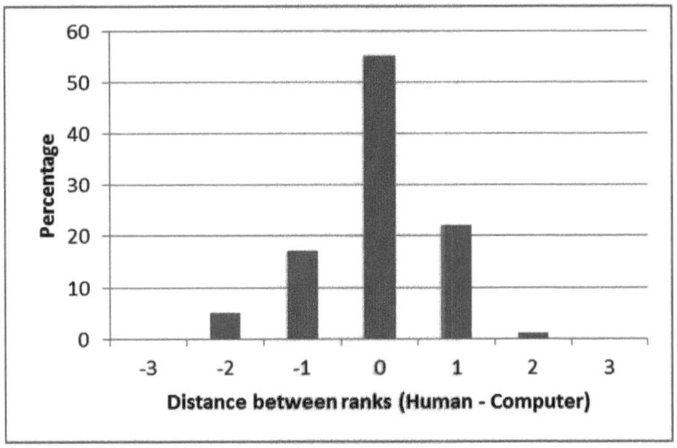

Fig. 4. Distance between human and computer ranking against number of concepts (%) in Software Engineering topic (r_s = 0.813).

In the structural feature model, our results show satisfactory correlation for the majority of the courses and strong positive correlation for SE, SA and OS courses. As an example, in 'Software Testing' topic (Fig. 4), 55 % of concepts (out of 64) overlap between computer and human (distance = 0) and 39 % of concepts indicate one level difference between ranks. This implies 94 % of concepts extracted from machine algorithms are closely aligned with human judgment, resulting in a machine extraction of approximate expert maps. Both OS and SE lecture slides are constructed using popular text books written by Sommerville and Silberschatz respectively and SA lecture slides were well-written and structured. Therefore, those topics contain rich grammar, good summarisation and emphasise domain concepts. These *well-fitted* contents assist relatively straightforward machine interpretation. Thus, our algorithm is more effective for courses categorised as Software Engineering, Computer Architecture, Communications and Security (see the subfields defined by ACM classification[3]).

Other courses which include a combination of good text contents and notations (e.g. DS) with $r_s \sim 0.5$ are categorised as *average-fitted* content.

[3] http://en.wikipedia.org/wiki/Outline_of_computer_science.

Conversely, the remaining course topics include combinations of category headings (e.g. review, summary, welcome), additional text boxes with excessive content, ambiguous texts that are difficult to resolve and repetitive contents in consecutive slides for animations such as programming and mathematical notations are classified as *ill-fitted* content which illustrates $r_s \sim 0$. These types of content reduce the reliability of machine extraction algorithms. Hence, as a general rule, concept map mining from lecture notes provides practical approach for *well-fitted* course contents.

This study highlights the importance of structural features rather than natural layout or grammatical structures. This implies that important information in the lecture should be emphasised, and recapped. Lecturer should also construct probable links with the central idea of the topic. This ensures that approximately reliable machine extraction of concept maps from algorithms developed in this work.

In this study, we only had a single expert participating for the assessment of each course. Therefore, we cannot measure the *inter-rater agreement* (i.e. agreement between human experts) since the author of the material is the only person having an expert knowledge structure of the content.

We received evocative feedback from domain experts during the experiments.

> *"I tend to think that summary generally contains things that have already been discussed. But, I found a new concept in the summary which hasn't seen in the lecture note. I read the lecture from the beginning again to locate that concept, but couldn't find it".*

This comment provides an evident that there can be disjoint concepts included in lecture note which are not fitting with students' knowledge structures.

> *"There are tables which provide comparison between important concepts. How does this handles by the system?"*

This is one of our challenges. The data comes from tabular form include useful domain concepts. However, we have not yet implemented a feature to tackle the comparisons in tabular data.

> *"Examples are very useful to learn concepts, but they are not concepts. Therefore, I am not sure whether they should be included or not. I have included them in cases where I think they are very useful".*
> *"In IP, many domain concepts are introduced via analogy. So, are they also be classified?"*

We do not have an exact answer for this comment. Examples or analogies can be included into the extracted concept map, if they are strongly correlates with domain or emphasised within the context.

In our future work, we plan to extend the evaluation across disciplines to experiment with varied set of data. This allows us to tune our parameter values more accurately. The focus of this study is limited to measure the quality when both concepts of triple or 'start node' of triple is ranked above the threshold value. In our future work, we plan to assess whether the 'end node' of a triple contain important information to the domain in order to reduce information loss. Further, we plan to present the extracted concept maps to lecturers through IHMC Cmap server[1] in order to acquire conceptual feedback regarding deficiencies in knowledge organisation of their courses. This includes disjoint concepts without any relation to the central concept map and relations without proper labeling. This process should improve the legibility of the materials.

6 Conclusions

The primary challenge of concept map mining is the lack of a suitable evaluation framework. The existing approaches utilise the overlap between expert maps (as a whole or as individual elements) and machine extracted maps to determine the *relevancy* using IR metrics - *precision* and *recall*. However, in educational context, the majority of knowledge presented is relevant to the learner. Therefore, *relevancy* is not a good measure to evaluate knowledge acquisition within educational applications. This paper proposes a rank-based evaluation mechanism to measure the rank correlation between human and machine. The results rejects the first two hypothesis developed by us, confirming that concept importance of concept maps extracted from lecture notes determine by the natural layout of presentation framework (baseline) and grammatical structure (linguistic) of text respectively. Thus, we conclude that structural features are positively correlated with experts' judgment ($r_s \sim 1$) for *well-fitted* contents.

This work has potential to be utilised as conceptual feedback for lecturers to have an overview of knowledge organisation of their courses. Machine-extracted concept maps require the assistance of domain experts to validate. However, this effort is substantially smaller than that required to construct a concept map manually. In future work, we plan to provide task-adapted concept maps instead of hints in intelligent tutoring environment. This will help students to identify knowledge gaps and to improve their organisation of knowledge. We believe that this will help to improve the depth of meaning that students can extract from their learning.

References

Atapattu, T., Falkner, K., Falkner, N.: Automated extraction of semantic concepts from semi-structured data: supporting computer-based education through the analysis of lecture notes. In: Liddle, S.W., Schewe, K.-D., Tjoa, A.M., Zhou, X. (eds.) DEXA 2012, Part I. LNCS, vol. 7446, pp. 161–175. Springer, Heidelberg (2012)

Atapattu, T., Falkner, K., Falkner, N.: Acquisition of triples of knowledge from lecture notes: a natural language processing approach. In: Proceedings of the 7th International conference on Educational Data Mining, London, United Kingdom (2014)

Alves, A., Pereira, F., Cardoso, F.: Automatic reading and learning from text. In: International Symposium on Artificial Intelligence (2002)

Ausubel, D., Novak, J., Hanesian, H.: Educational Psychology: A Cognitive View. Holt, Rinehart and Winston, New York (1978)

Chen, N., Kinshuk, Wei, C.: Mining e-learning domain concept map from academic articles. Comput. Educ. **50**, 1009–1021 (2008)

Coffey, J., Carnot, M., Feltovich, P., Feltovich, J., Hoffman, R., Canas, A., Novak, J.: A summary of literature pertaining to the use of concept mapping techniques and technologies for education and performance support. The Chief of Naval Education and Training (2003)

Dali, L., Rusu, D., Fortuna, B., Mladenic, D., Grobelnik, M.: Question answering based on semantic graphs. In: Language and Technology Conference, Poznan, Poland (2009)

Gouli, E., Gogoulou, A., Papanikolaou, K., Grigoriadou, M.: COMPASS: an adaptive web-based concept map assessment tool. In: Proceedings of the First International Conference on Concept Mapping (2004)

Kinchin, I.: Developing PowerPoint handouts to support meaningful learning. Br. J. Educ. Technol. **37**(4), 647–650 (2006)

Klein, D., Manning, C.: Accurate unlexicalized parsing. In: Proceedings of the 41st Meeting of the Association for Computational Linguistics, pp. 423–430 (2003)

Leake, D., Maguitman, A., Reichherzer, T.: Understanding knowledge models: modelling assessment of concept importance in concept maps. In: Proceedings of CogSc (2004)

Manning, C., Raghavan, P., Schutze, H.: Introduction to Information Retrieval. Cambridge University Press, Cambridge (2008)

Novak, J., Gowin, D.: Learning How to Learn. Cambridge University Press, New York/Cambridge (1984)

Olney, A.M., Graesser, A., Person, N.: Question generation from Concept maps. In: Special issue on Question generation, Dialogue and Discourse (2012)

Salton, G., McGill, M.: Introduction to Modern Information Retrieval. McGraw-Hill Inc., New York (1986)

Sleator, D., Temperly, D.: Parsing English with a links grammar. In: Third International Workshop on Parsing Technologies (1993)

Villalon, J., Calvo, R.: Concept map mining: a definition and a framework for its evaluation. In: International Conference on Web Intelligence and Intelligent Agent Technology (2008)

Zouaq, A., Nkabou, R.: Evaluating the generation of domain ontologies in the knowledge puzzle project. IEEE Trans. Knowl. Data Eng. **21**, 1559–1572 (2009)

Zouaq, A., Gasevic, D., Hatala, M.: Voting theory for concept detection. In: Simperl, E., Cimiano, P., Polleres, A., Corcho, O., Presutti, V. (eds.) ESWC 2012. LNCS, vol. 7295, pp. 315–329. Springer, Heidelberg (2012)

An Exercise Assistant for Practical Networking and IT Security Courses in Higher Education

Jens Haag[1,2(✉)], Stefan Karsch[1,2], Harald Vranken[1,2], and Marko Van Eekelen[1,2]

[1] Cologne University of Applied Sciences, Cologne, Germany
[2] Open Universiteit, Heerlen, Netherlands
jens.haag@outlook.de, stefan.karsch@fh-koeln.de, {harald.vranken,marko.vaneekelen}@ou.nl

Abstract. An increasing number of students and the trend to enhance traditional on-campus classes to cover the everytime-everywhere character of modern study programmes require new ideas to support students. Especially when students require support while learning independently from the university, e.g. at home in the evening, this cannot be covered satisfyingly by a human course advisor. As a major step to resolve this, we present our concept of an exercise assistant for practical networking and IT security courses in higher education. This exercise assistant can be preloaded with modelled exercises and is able to provide feedback and guidance, whenever and whereever it is required by a student. We also show, how expert knowledge and description logic can be used by the exercise assistant to verify a students solution.

Keywords: Virtual lab · e-Learning · Exercise assistant · Networking exercises · Description logic

1 Introduction

Computer science curricula for students at universities nowadays include courses on networking and information technology security. Teaching theory on networking and IT security is usually done by means of textbooks and classes (either face-to-face classes or virtual classes, which are popular at universities for distance education). To anchor and deepen the acquired theoretical knowledge, a commonly used teaching method is to hand out practical exercises. The exercises can be worked out in a computer lab, which can be either a traditional on-campus lab or a virtual lab.

Recent evaluation shows that students of a traditional on-campus networking course deem it crucial for their learning success to be able to get support from a course advisor [7]. In the winter semester 2012, a practical networking course

J. Haag—Work has been done as a Ph.D. student of the Open Universiteit.
H. Vranken and M. Van Eekelen are also affiliated with Radboud University Nijmegen.
This paper is an extension of [8].

S. Zvacek et al. (Eds.): CSEDU 2014, CCIS 510, pp. 84–98, 2015.
DOI: 10.1007/978-3-319-25768-6_6

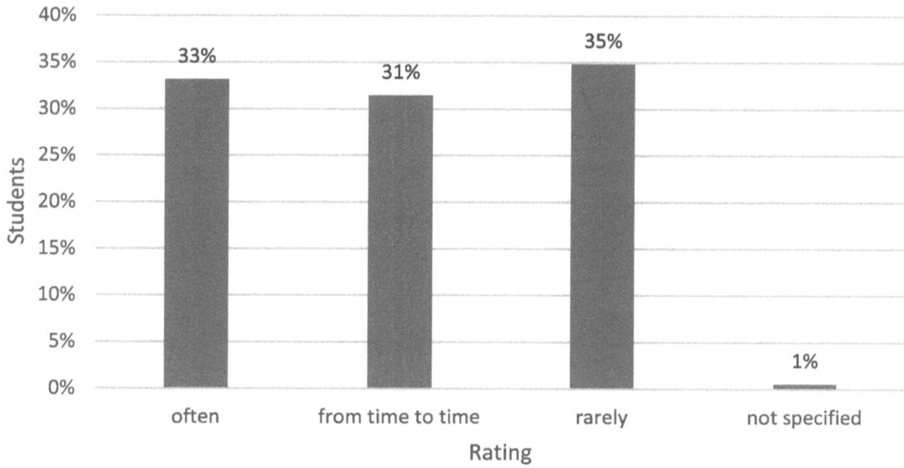

Fig. 1. Utilization of the guided learning hours.

with more than 200 participants was evaluated. While the course was objectively successfull, over 60 % of the students utilized the voluntary so called guided learning hours, at least from time to time (see Fig. 1). While an on-campus university will be able to provide course advisors, which can support a limited amount of students in such guided learning hours, this support is no longer feasible with large groups or if students work e.g. at home in the evening hours, using a virtual lab.

To resolve this issue we introduce an exercise assistant for networking courses which is able to support students while they work on networking exercises. Equipped with a formal model of an exercise, the exercise assistant can be run on a students computer whenever and wherever support is needed. The effort to author such an exercise has to be done once while instances of the exercise assistant equipped with this exercise will then be able to support any number of students.

The remainder is organized as follows: First we introduce our current learning environment in Sect. 2 and an example exercise in Sect. 3. In Sect. 4 we explain our formal model of an exercise. This formal model can be processed by our exercise assistant, whose software architecture we introduce in Sect. 5. After giving a guiding example in Sect. 6 we conclude our work in Sect. 7.

2 Virtual Lab

The virtual computer security lab (VCSL) is a stand-alone environment that each student can install on his or her local computer [13]. It is composed of two virtualization layers, as shown in Fig. 2. The host machine is the students computer, which runs an arbitrary operating system, i.e. the host operating system. The first virtualization layer creates the virtual host machine. It consists of virtualization software such as VMware Player or Oracle VirtualBox, which runs

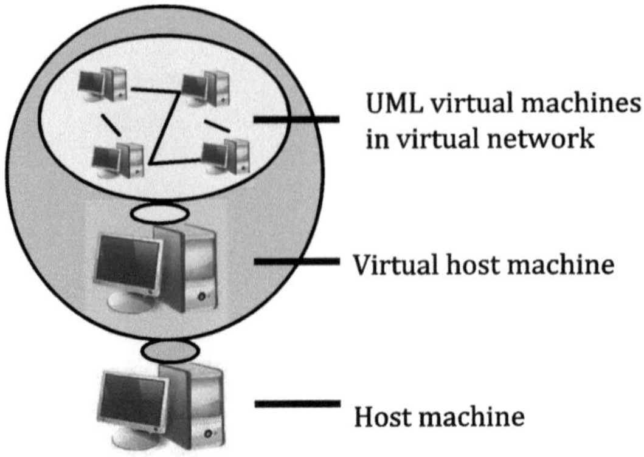

Fig. 2. Architecture of the VCSL.

on the host machine just like an ordinary application. Virtualization software in general introduces an additional software layer with corresponding interface, which creates a logical abstraction from the underlying system software and hardware [10]. Versions of this software are available for free for a large range of platforms and therefore run on nearly all student computers, regardless of the hardware and the host operating system. The virtual host machine runs the guest operating system. For the VCSL, Linux was selected, since it is open source and can also be distributed to students without licensing costs.

The second virtualization layer is a Linux application, called Netkit [9], which runs inside the virtual host machine. This layer allows to instantiate multiple virtual machines that all run Linux. Netkit applies virtualization based upon User Mode Linux (UML). A UML virtual machine is created by running a Linux kernel as a user process in the virtual host machine [4]. Multiple UML virtual machines can easily be run simultaneously, while using minimal resources. The file system is shared by all UML virtual machines using the copy-on-write (COW) mechanism. Hence, the file system is shared read-only by all UML virtual machines. Each UML virtual machine has a second, separate file system in which only the local changes to the shared file system are stored. This saves both disk space and memory, and simplifies management of multiple UML virtual machines. Restoring an initial clean system means to simply remove the second file system.

The VCSL was further developed [5,12] into a distributed VCSL (DVCSL). This DVCSL enables students to work together in a virtual lab by connecting their labs, even if they are physically distant from each other by using an interface to the Netkit environment. This interface consists of a Ghost Host and a Remote Bridge. While the Ghost Host was developed to extract and inject network packets when connected to an existing Netkit virtual network, the Remote Bridge is able to send and receive this packets using an intermediate connection network, e.g. the internet. Using this interface, local Netkit networks can be connected in a transparent and secure manner although they reside on different, distant students computers. This decentralized approach is suited to accommodate any number of students and offers students freedom to run the lab whenever and wherever they want, while preserving the properties of a conventional computer lab (e.g. the isolated network). Therefore, this approach is not limited to distance teaching but could also be useful for universities using a conventional computer lab.

3 Example Exercise

An example assignment of a practical networking course to be solved using the VCSL environment is:

"Setup and configure a scenario with at least three hosts (client, router, server). Client and server should be located within different subnets. The client should be able to intercommunicate with the server by using the intermediate router. The routing should be based on static routing tables."

The minimal requirement for this setup is shown in Fig. 3, consisting of at least three hosts. The client and the server have one network interface card (NIC); the router is equipped with two NICs; one for the client network named n1 and one for the server network n2. Each NIC of each host has to be configured with a valid network configuration.

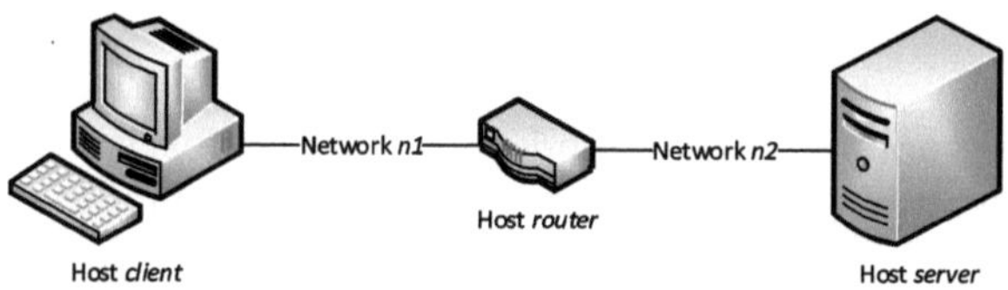

Fig. 3. Valid concept draw for the example assignment.

In this example exercise, students will have to set up hosts and interconnect them accordingly within two different networks. They will then have to assign appropriate IP addresses to these hosts and ultimately configure the routing by altering the routing tables on the hosts. Once the setup is configured properly, students can demonstrate the validity of their solution, e.g. by sending network packets between client and server.

A valid and straightforward solution for this example networking assignment solved in Netkit is stated in Table 1.

4 Exercise Modelling

In the following section we show how the exercises can be transferred into a formal representation, in order to be processed by a computer program. First we will show the partition of our example exercise into activities that will then be organized in a graph structure. This graph will then be extended with conditions

Table 1. Valid solution using Netkit.

 # Create the hosts and networks in Netkit
`vstart client --eth0=n1`
`vstart router --eth0=n1 --eth1=n2`
`vstart server --eth0=n2`
 # Assign IP address on client
`ifconfig eth0 10.0.0.1 up`
 # Assign IP address on the router
`ifconfig eth0 10.0.0.2 up`
`ifconfig eth1 11.0.0.2 up`
 # Assign IP address on the server
`ifconfig eth0 11.0.0.1 up`
 # Set default gateway on the client
`route add default gw 10.0.0.2`
 # Set default gateway on the server
`route add default gw 11.0.0.2`
 # Connection test on client to the server
`ping 11.0.0.1`

that will make the activities verifiable. We also show a way to add feedback attributes to the graph in order to model a certain feedback strategy. Finally we introduce probing, a mechanism to improve the verifiability of activities.

4.1 Activities

Typically, exercises will start with an empty lab. Students have to perform activities that result in a working network environment, configured according to the requirements of the given exercise. While Table 1 shows the commands needed to solve the exercise in Netkit, the minimal conceptual activities needed for solving this exercise are listed in Table 2.

While A10 is the final activity, the order of the activities A1 through A9 shows only one possible sequence. The order can vary because some activities are independent from each other (e.g. A1 and A2), while some other activities have interdependencies (e.g. A1 is a precondition for A3).

These activities and their interdependencies can be modelled as an acyclic, directed graph with exactly one sink (node N with outdegree(N) = 0) and at least one source (node N with indegree(N) = 0). Activities are represented by nodes. A precondition is modelled as a directed edge from the predecessor to the successor, seamlessly indicating the order of the activities. The final activity will be represented by a sink. Activities without a precondition will be represented by sources.

Table 2. Valid solution using Netkit.

Activity	ID
The client network has to be created	A1
The server network has to be created	A2
The client has to be connected to the client network and an appropriate IP address has to be assigned	A3
The server has to be connected to the server network and an appropriate IP address has to be assigned	A4
One NIC of the router has to be connected to the client network and an IP address from the client network has to be assigned	A5
One NIC of the router has to be connected to the server network and an IP address from the server network has to be assigned	A6
The client has to be configured to use the routers NIC in the client network as default gateway	A7
The server has to be configured to use the routers NIC in the server network as default gateway	A8
Routing has to be enabled on the router	A9
Client and server must intercommunicate via the intermediate router using the IP protocol	A10

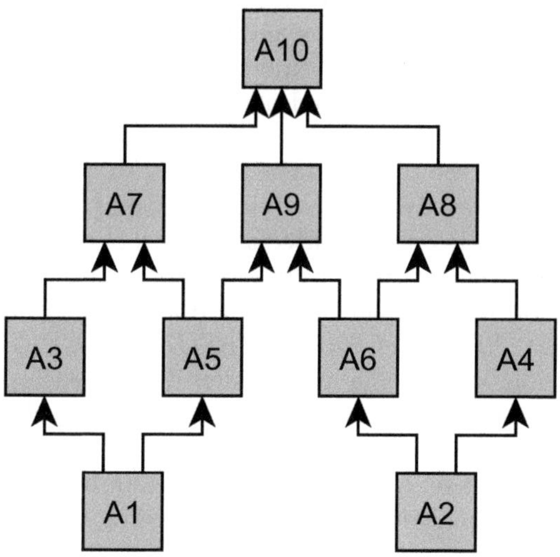

Fig. 4. Example graph.

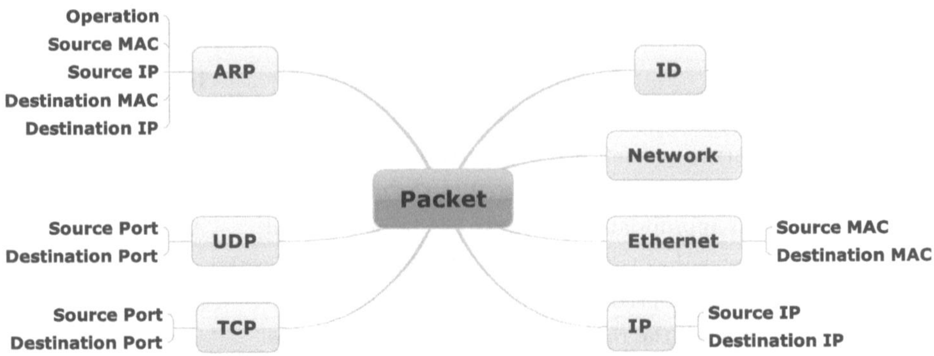

Fig. 5. Ontology excerpt for Ethernet networks.

A valid graph for our example exercise is shown in Fig. 4. This graph is based on the activities stated in Table 2. The interdependencies and thus possible sequences of activities show a valid example. These can of course vary, depending on the exercise and the authors intent, too.

4.2 Conditions

In order to process the graph, the activities have to be verifiable. That means that a condition is needed to detect or to decide, whether an activity is deemed passed, i.e. whether the student has successfully solved a part of the exercise. In [6] we showed, that network packets, obtained from the students Netkit lab, can be used to detect and verify network properties and behaviour of an Ethernet based network. By modelling network specific expert knowledge as predicates and verifying these predicates using the captured network packets, it is possible to detect e.g. the presence of certain hosts and also routing behaviour. While the prototype in [6] demonstrated the technical feasibility of that approach by using SQL queries to model predicates, we improved on it by using description logics [1]. For the terminological box (TBox) we created a network ontology for Ethernet based networks, representing the network layers 2 and above [11], including but not limited to the header and payload fields of the most commonly used protocols, e.g. Ethernet (RFC1042), ARP (RFC826), IP (RFC791), TCP (RFC793) and UDP (RFC768). In addition, we added a unique identifier for each packet and the network origin. An excerpt of our ontology for Ethernet networks is shown in Fig. 5. Using this ontology it is possible to model expert knowledge as predicates using a logic programming language, e.g. Prolog [3]. For example, the expert knowledge to describe the network behaviour "routing" according to [6] is:

"Routing occurs if an OSI layer 3 IP transmission of a network packet between two hosts is based on more than one OSI layer 2 transmissions."

The technical background is shown in Fig. 6. The client wants to communicate with the server using the IP protocol, but the server is located in a different net-

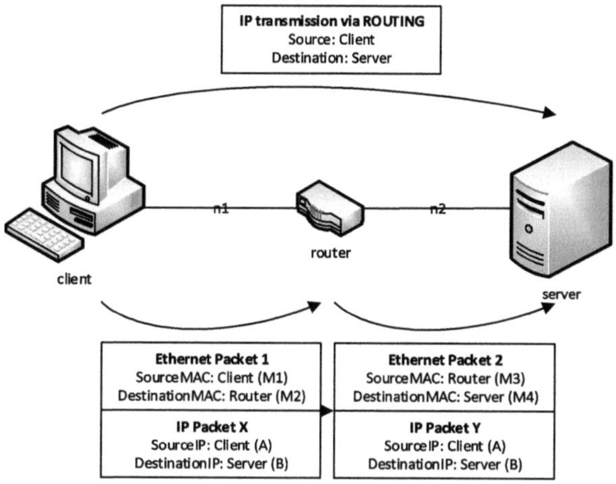

Fig. 6. Routing packet flow example.

work segment. Direct inter-communication between client and server is not possible because the underlying Ethernet protocol does not support communication over network borders. The client has to use a known router located in the same network as itself, and thus reachable by Ethernet. The client now sends an IP packet addressed to the IP address of the server, but the underlying Ethernet packet will be addressed to the router. When the router does receive such a packet, it will forward it to the server. While the two packets that the client and the router send do not differ on the IP layer (both are sent from the client, and addressed to the server), both differ on the Ethernet layer, with different source and destination MAC addresses.

Based on the Ethernet network ontology, this behaviour can be expressed as the following Prolog predicate:

```
routing :-
  ip_packet(X,A,B), ip_packet(Y,A,B),
  ethernet_packet(X,M1,M2), ethernet_packet(Y,M3,M4),
  M1 \= M3, M2 \= M4.
```

This predicate can be read as "routing occurs, when there are two IP layer packets X and Y, both sent from IP address A to IP address B, for which the source and destination addresses differ on the Ethernet layer."

Predicates can be used as conditions to detect activities. E.g. the predicate "routing" can be used to verify the activity A10. We extended the graph, so that every activity can be associated with a condition to verify that activity.

Routing is only one example. We successfully created predicates describing e.g. the presence of hosts and networks, the network behaviour NAT or routing and also higher level usage. E.g. ARP spoofing behaviour can be detected if two hosts within the same subnet having different MAC addresses pretend to own the same IP address using the ARP protocol.

```
arp_spoof :-
   network(P1, AN), network(P2, BN), AN = BN,
   arp_SourceMAC(P1, AM), arp_SourceMAC(P2, BM), AM \= BM,
   arp_SourceIP(P1, AIP), arp_SourceIP(P2, BIP), AIP = BIP.
```

However, this behaviour can also be caused by a misconfiguration of the hosts. For that reason this condition requires preconditions to verify a valid and error-free setup. We also found a trade-off between the shape of an assignment and the capabilities to design predicates. If the assignment is more tightly controlled (e.g. predefined network names and IP addresses), more precise predicates can be designed to detect activities. If the assignment is more generic, the predicates also have to be designed in a more generalized manner.

4.3 Feedback

There are various types of feedback strategies which can be used to support students working on the exercise, e.g. suggestions, complete guiding or an exam mode. The specific shape will be either customized to match the authors aims or customized to the learning style of the learner or a combination. Usually recent progress the student has made in the exercise graph should trigger interaction with the student according to the feedback strategy.

Therefor we extended the graph with feedback attributes. The graph as a whole can be associated with an attribute containing the exercise description; all activities can be associated with different attributes for feedback control, i.e. text messages that give hints about what the next activity might involve (pre messages), or text messages that give feedback about detected activities (post messages). An example for activity A1 from our example exercise look like this:

```
pre_message =
   "You will need at least one host connected to network n1."
post_message = "Network n1 detected."
```

While our message mechanism provides the technical means for the implementation of various feedback strategies, the evaluation and choice of an appropriate strategy resides with the exercise author.

4.4 Probing

While the verification of activities based on passively observed network packets works for many activities, there still are limitations. One such limitation occurs, when an activity needs to be verified that does not have immediate results in the form of network packets.

An example for that would be A9 from our example exercise: the routing functionality has to be activated on the router. Students can do that by setting the appropriate kernel flag on the router if this flag is not enabled by default. This however will not result in the occurrence of observable network packets, until packets are sent to the router for being routed. A possible solution would be to ask the student to send appropriate network packets himself. We followed a different approach. For detecting certain activities we inject special predefined network packets into the Netkit environment to provoke a certain predictable behaviour. This behaviour can also be expressed as a predicate. In the routing example we inject an Ethernet packet addressed to the router into the client network that is addressed to a host in the server network (which does not have to exist) on the IP level. If routing is enabled in the router, the router will try to reach that host in the server network using ARP requests. These packets can be used to verify that routing is indeed enabled on the router.

Such a "probing" packet can be assembled by strictly following the network stack, starting with an Ethernet frame. The destination MAC address must be the routers NIC connected to network n1. In Netkit, the MAC address of a network interface is bound to the name of the client, resulting in a predictable MAC address for the routers first NIC eth0: `0a:ab:64:91:09:80`. The source MAC address can be virtual, e.g. `ee:ba:7b:99:bc:a5`, followed by an IPv4 ethertype identifier (`0x0800`). The encapsulated IP packet starts with the version identifier (`0x4`), followed by mandatory header fields, e.g. length and checksum. The source IP address can be virtual but should be located within the IP range of network n1. The destination IP address can also be virtual but must be part of subnet n2. The IP packet encapsulates an ICMP echo request just to get a complete and valid network packet. This customized packet layout can be represented by a hexadecimal character array, e.g. `0aab6491 0980eeba 7b99bca5 08004500 001c1234 4000ff01 549c0a00 00010b00 00100800 f7fd0001 0001`.

We extended the graph, so that every activity can be associated with a custom network "probing" packet to be sent once before verifying its condition. While that actively alters the environment, it enables the verification of additional activities.

5 Exercise Assistant

In order to support a student while working on an exercise, we developed an exercise assistant, which can be used in the VCSL. As shown in Fig. 7, the exercise assistant is composed of three components: reasoning engine, feedback engine, and an interface to the student's working environment called Netkit interface.

The reasoning engine itself is composed of a reasoner and a knowledge base, which contains a TBox ("terminology box") and an ABox ("assertion box"). The TBox contains knowledge about the domain, i.e. our ontology, in the form of predefined predicates that can be extended by the author with exercise specific extensions, while the ABox contains the concrete instantiations. The data in the ABox is obtained through an interface to the "real world", in our case the Netkit interface. The Netkit interface consists of one or more Ghost Hosts [5] that record network packets from their respective Netkit network, extract the information in them and store that information in the ABox. The Ghost Hosts can also be used to inject special network packets into the environment.

The feedback engine is the part where the activity graph will be processed. Our exercise assistant is able to read an exercise graph stored in the GraphML

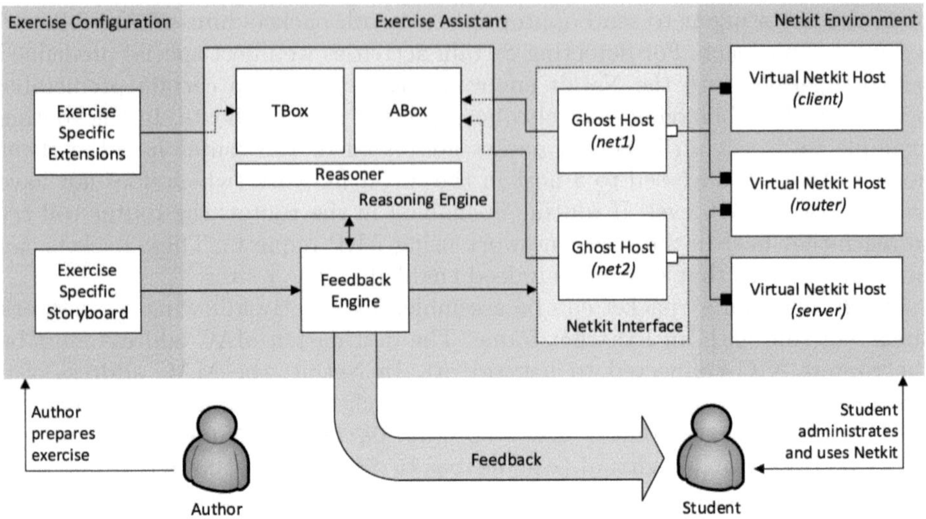

Fig. 7. Architecture of the exercise assistant.

[2] format. Once read, the activities are continuously processed according to their interdependencies, starting at the source nodes which represent activities without preconditions. Processing the activities in this case means verifying their conditions and giving the student feedback according to the feedback attributes of that activity. Once the activity is completed it will be removed from the graph and thus as a precondition for its successors. The feedback engine can also use the Netkit interface, respectively the Ghost Hosts, to insert custom network packets into the environment in order to provoke certain network behaviour to verify an activitys condition using the reasoning engine.

The Exercise Assistant is a software program written in the programming language C using SWI-Prolog [14] as the reasoning engine.

6 Example

Using the VCSL, the window layout of the desktop presented to the students looks like Fig. 8. The exercise assistant shell is a window where the student can keep track of the feedback generated by the feedback engine. The linux shell is a window where the student is able to administrate and use Netkit in order to e.g. create hosts and networks. Once a host is started, it will open a respective shell enabling the student to administrate the host itself. Further hosts, e.g. the router and the server, will open respective shells, too.

The following lines are taken from the exercise assistant shell guiding the example exercise. We authored the activities of Table 2 according to the exercise graph of Fig. 4 and added verbose feedback. The introduced routing predicate is used to verify the final activity (A10). The intermediate activities too have

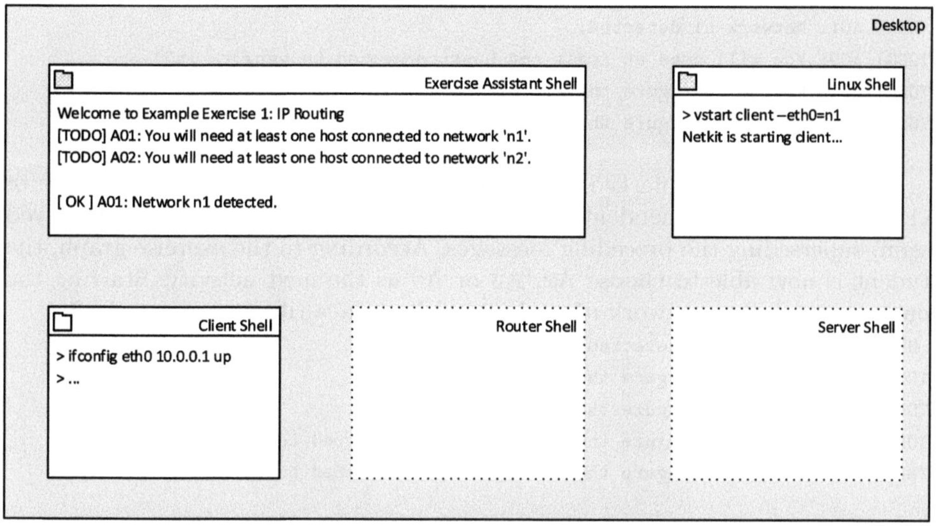

Fig. 8. Desktop draft.

been modelled using our ontology, partially by utilizing probing packets. Once started, the exercise assistant introduces the exercise by displaying the exercise description. Starting with the activities without precondition (A1 and A2), the exercise assistant will prompt the student using the respective pre messages.

```
    Example Exercise 1: IP Routing
Setup and configure at least three hosts (client, router, server).
Client and server should be located in different networks. The client
should be able to intercommunicate with the server by using the
intermediate router. Verify your routing environment by sending routed
network packets between client and server.
Please use the following diagram:
         10.0.0.1                10.0.0.2
         +------+                +------+                +------+
         |client| <-----n1-----> |router| <-----n2-----> |server|
         +------+                +------+                +------+
                                 11.0.0.2                11.0.0.1
Good luck!
[TODO] A01: You will need at least one host connected to network 'n1'.
[TODO] A02: You will need at least one host connected to network 'n2'.
```

The student can start solving the exercise according to Table 1. After the first command `vstart client --eth0=n1` is entered using the linux shell, the exercise assistant is able to confirm this valid activity.

```
[ OK ] A01: Network n1 detected.
[TODO] A02: You will need at least one host connected to network 'n2'.
[TODO] A03: Please configure the NIC of the client.
[TODO] A05: Please configure the router's NIC connected to 'n1'.
```

While A1 is being marked as verified, using the respective post_message of A1, the remaining independent activities without preconditions will be displayed again, superseding the preceding messages. According to the exercise graph, the student is now able to choose A2, A3 or A5 as the next activity. Starting the router connected to network n1 and n2 results in a verified presence of n2.

```
[ OK ] A02: Network n2 detected.
[TODO] A03: Please configure the NIC of the client.
[TODO] A04: Please configure the NIC of the server.
[TODO] A05: Please configure the router's NIC connected to 'n1'.
[TODO] A06: Please configure the router's NIC connected to 'n2'.
```

While the presence of the two networks is verified now, the exercise assistant is not able to detect whether the student has started the server, unless its network interface card gets assigned an IP address. Therefore the pre_messages are authored to prompt the student properly. Choosing to assign the clients IP address as next activity, using the command ifconfig eth0 10.0.0.1 up in the client shell, will result in a verified activity A3.

```
[ OK ] A03: Client host with IP address 10.0.0.1 detected.
[TODO] A04: Please configure the NIC of the server.
[TODO] A05: Please configure the router's NIC connected to 'n1'.
[TODO] A06: Please configure the router's NIC connected to 'n2'.
```

Still missing IP addresses of routers and servers NICs, the student can proceed to configure the routers NICs.

```
[ OK ] A05: Router's NIC with IP 10.0.0.2 detected.
[TODO] A04: Please configure the NIC of the server.
[TODO] A06: Please configure the router's NIC connected to 'n2'.
[TODO] A07: Please adjust client's routing table to use the router.
[ OK ] A06: Router's NIC with IP 11.0.0.2 detected.
[TODO] A04: Please configure the NIC of the server.
[TODO] A07: Please adjust client's routing table to use the router.
[TODO] A09: Ensure, that the router is able to route packets.
[ OK ] A09: Router acts as a router between n1 and n2.
[TODO] A04: Please configure the NIC of the server.
[TODO] A07: Please adjust client's routing table to use the router.
```

Having verified that the two NICs of the router are present, the exercise assistant is able to verify A9 using a probe packet. For the simple reason that routing is enabled per default for hosts in the Netkit environment, the condition of A9 can be verified immediately.

```
[ OK ] A04: Server's NIC with IP 11.0.0.1 detected.
[TODO] A07: Please adjust client's routing table to use the router.
[TODO] A08: Please adjust server's routing table to use the router.
```

After assigning an IP address to the remaining NIC of the server, the student has to alter the routing table on the client and on the server. The exercise assistant is also able to verify these activities by using probing packets.

```
[ OK ] A07: Client uses router as gateway to 'n2'.
[TODO] A08: Please adjust server's routing table to use the router.
[ OK ] A08: Server uses router as gateway to 'n1'.
[TODO] A10: Finally, show me that client and server can intercommunicate.
```

Finally, the student is asked to demonstrate the routing functionality by sending packets between the client and the server using the intermediate router. One valid solution is to use the command ping.

```
[ OK ] A10: Setup verified, exercise completed.
[INFO] Solved in 7 minutes and 42 seconds.
[ OK ] Finished! Well done!
```

Once the final activity is verified, the exercise assistant congratulates the student and then quits.

7 Conclusions

We presented an exercise assistant which improves the learning situation of students solving practical exercises in a networking course. Even when human course advisors are not available, our exercise assistant can recognize learning progress and provide appropriate feedback and support. This significantly improves the learning situation for students working remotely in a virtual environment, which is common at universities for distance education. Besides this automatic support, the exercise assistant can verify intermediate and complete solutions of an exercise. We also presented an approach to formally model exercises in a manner processable by the exercise assistant. For that purpose the exercise author can define possible activities and sequences using a graph structure. Description logic is used to define conditions for the verification of these activities. The exercise author is also able to define a feedback strategy by adding feedback attributes to the graph.

Especially for courses with many participants, our experience shows that teaching staff can benefit from utilizing the exercise assistant. While the teaching method of tutors personally and individually supporting students is certainly one of the most effective for knowledge transfer, it is not feasible for courses of sufficient size.

In such scenarios, the exercise assistant can e.g. be used to offer all students a basic guided tutoring support not only wherever and whenever they want, but also at the speed that best suits their own learning style and their own abilities.

References

1. Baader, F., Calvanese, D., McGuinness, D.L., Nardi, D., Patel-Schneider, P.F.: The Description Logic Handbook: Theory, Implementation, and Applications. Cambridge University Press, New York (2003)
2. Brandes, U., Eiglsperger, M., Herman, I., Himsolt, M., Marshall, M.S.: GraphML progress report. In: Mutzel, P., Jünger, M., Leipert, S. (eds.) GD 2001. LNCS, vol. 2265, pp. 501–512. Springer, Heidelberg (2002)
3. Colmerauer, A., Roussel, P.: The birth of prolog. In: Proceedings of HOPL-II The Second ACM SIGPLAN Conference on History of Programming Languages, pp. 37–52. ACM, New York (1993)
4. Dike, J.: User Mode Linux. Prentice Hall, Upper Saddle River (2006)
5. Haag, J., Horsmann, T., Karsch, S., Vranken, H.: A distributed virtual computer security lab with central authority. In: Proceedings of the CSERC 2011 Computer Science Education Research Conference, Heerlen, The Netherlands, 7–8 April 2011, pp. 89–95. Open Universiteit, Heerlen, The Netherlands (2011)
6. Haag, J., Karsch, S., Vranken, H., Van Eekelen, M.: A virtual computer security lab as learning environment for networking and security courses. In: Proceedings of the 3rd Annual International Conference on Computer Science Education: Innovation and Technology. CSEIT 2012, Singapore, 19–20 November 2012. Global Science and Technology Forum (2012)
7. Haag, J., Witte, C., Karsch, S., Vranken, H., Van Eekelen, M.: Evaluation of students' learning behaviour and success in a practical computer networking course. In: Proceedings of the Second ICEEE 2013 International Conference on E-learning and E-technologies in Education. Lodz, Poland, 23–25 September 2013
8. Haag, J., Witte, C., Karsch, S., Vranken, H., Van Eekelen, M.: An exercise assistant for practical networking courses. In: Proceedings of the 6th International Conference on Computer Supported Education. CSEDU 2014, pp. 97–104. Barcelona, Spain (2014)
9. Pizzonia, M., Rimondini, M.: Netkit: easy emulation of complex networks on inexpensive hardware. In: Proceedings of the ICST International Conference on Testbeds and Research Infrastructures for the Development of Networks and Communities, pp. 1–10 (2008)
10. Smith, J., Nair, R.: Virtual Machines: Versatile Platforms for Systems and Processes. Morgan Kaufmann, Amsterdam (2005)
11. Tanenbaum, A.S.: Computer Networks. Prentice Hall PTR, Upper Saddle River (1985)
12. Vranken, H., Haag, J., Horsmann, T., Karsch, S.: A distributed virtual computer security lab. In: Proceedings of the CSEDU 2011 3rd International Conference on Computer Supported Education, Vol. 1, Noordwijkerhout, 6–8 May 2011, pp. 110–119. SciTePress, The Netherlands (2011)
13. Vranken, H., Koppelman, H.: A virtual computer security lab for distance education. In: Proceedings of the EuroIMSA 2009 5th IASTED European Conference on Internet and Multimedia Systems and Applications, Cambridge, UK, 13–15 July 2009, pp. 21–27. Acta Press, Calgary (2009)
14. Wielemaker, J.: Logic programming for knowledge-intensive interactive applications. Ph.D. Thesis, University of Amsterdam, The Netherlands (2009)

MOOCs: What Motivates the Producers and Participants?

Su White[1(✉)], Hugh Davis[1], Kate Dickens[1], Manuel León[1], and Ma Mar Sánchez-Vera[2]

[1] Centre for Innovation in Technologies and Education, University of Southampton, Highfield, Southampton, UK
{su,hcd,kate.dickens,ml4c08}@soton.ac.uk
[2] Department of Didactics and School Organisation, University of Murcia, Murcia, Spain
mmarsanchez@um.es

Abstract. Within the current educational landscape, Massively Open Online Courses (MOOCs) have stimulated extensive interest and hype in a short time. It has been asserted that these open courses are no more than a prelude to the disruption that traditional Higher Education Institutions will experience from the growth of on-line education. Meanwhile, institutions are making increasingly significant investments to produce MOOCs, and learners are enthusiastically enrolling in large numbers, often in tens of thousands. The analysis presented identifies a spectrum of motivating factors for universities, and suggests likely areas for future attention and developments. It further identifies a range of motivations for learner participation, which may not be identical across cultures and which MOOC providers might wish to take into account.

Keywords: MOOCS · Education disruption · Motivations for learning · Institutional strategy

1 Introduction

In September 2013 the first UK based MOOC platform, FutureLearn, announced twenty new MOOCs. Running in the final quarter of 2013 they included the University of Southampton's first MOOC "Web Science: how the web is changing the world". This paper presents part of our attempt to answer the questions "why are we doing this?" and "why would the learners want to study MOOCs?"

These questions are worthy of discussion at a time when the landscape for higher education is widely predicted to change mainly because of the way the web is changing the world. Some claim that business models for higher education are about to collapse in much the same way that the music industry's business model collapsed in the 2000's; and possibly MOOCs are the Napster in this scenario [1]. One apparent response to these predictions is real financial investment: text book publishers are rapidly re-inventing themselves as purveyors of on-line education, and lobbying government for a level playing field with universities; and venture capitalists are lining up at universities' doors trying to buy into a share of their more popular courses.

S. Zvacek et al. (Eds.): CSEDU 2014, CCIS 510, pp. 99–114, 2015.
DOI: 10.1007/978-3-319-25768-6_7

Venture capitalists expect quick profits, so they are presumably anticipating rapid disruption.

In 2013, universities have invested greater sums of money in developing single MOOCs than they have been accustomed to investing in the development of yearlong courses. If MOOCs are at the frontier of disruption, then what is the motivation for universities to embrace them rather than resist them? Our research on motivations for universities was carried out as a meta-review of the literature. 2012 was the year in which many MOOCs became available, mostly through Coursera, edX and Udacity in the USA. These MOOCs have now been evaluated and we are beginning to see papers published, but at the time we began this research there were few academic articles and to track the emerging phenomena of MOOCs it was necessary to also observe the web-based grey literature of journalistic articles, blogs and social media.

Learners are registering for MOOCs in an enormously wide range of subjects in their tens of thousands. Apparently they are not motivated by grades since in most MOOCs there are no grades. So it is valid to ask why these students are so interested in studying MOOCs.

2 Methodology

Two research perspectives have been adopted.

(1) Investigating the motivations of Higher Education Institutions (HEIs) to engage with MOOCs. A qualitative approach using content-analysis was conducted across a set of around considering whether or not HEIs should foster MOOCs.
(2) Learners' motivations for participation. An online survey was conducted to gather information from MOOC participants. It looked in depth into the reasons why learners decided to register and elicited some reflections on their beliefs, attitudes and behaviours when participating in a MOOC. The questionnaire was analysed primarily by using a quantitative method of frequencies of responses. In carrying out our research on student motivation we wished to get beyond the survey of the set of students that completed a particular MOOC and to investigate some of the cultural differences in motivations, so our results are based on a survey circulated by social media within the UK, Spain and Syria.

2.1 Methodology: HEIs' Motivations

2.1.1 Identification and Selection of Sources

Selected contributions, published in three different domains, were used: namely education technology journals; HE magazines; and blog posts. The sources were identified by using different search strategies depending on the domain where the literature was published. For the peer-reviewed academic literature in journals, the method used was inspired by the identification of sources in the systematic literature review [2] carried out in 2013. The journalistic and blog (grey literature) sources were drawn from the curated collections of four educational technologists via the Scoop.it social media site over the four months prior to August 2013. These MOOC-focused curations drew on a wide range of sources of which a more reduced number were in turn chosen for this project, seeding by provenance and perceived authority and encompassing views which were either for or against the adoption of MOOCs in HEIs. Sources were primarily selected according to their relevance to the topic of MOOCs in HEIs.

(1) Academic literature - to identify the drivers of the emergence of MOOCs.
(2) Grey literature - for identifying current debates.

More rigour was credited to peer-reviewed journal articles, than to journalistic pieces and blog posts. Therefore, the selection of the papers was focused on its content and relevance. The selection of grey literature placed greater emphasis on authorship and provenance because, as noted by Daniel [3], the media contain abundant literature in which the intention of promoting MOOCs as products for profit seeking undermines the objectiveness of the judgements towards their potential to improve the education delivery.

2.1.2 Analysis of Sources

Herring's [4] adaption of Krippendorff's [5] Content Analysis (CA) method for online context was used with the academic and journalistic corpora of MOOC related sources. Apart from identification and selection of sources explained above, CA involves establishing categories into which the arguments in the sources are to be distributed into three contexts. These contexts were (a) open education movements; (b) the evolution of technology in distance education; (c) disruptive innovations in education. Because they were more opinion loaded, non-academic sources were classified into debates of sustainability, quality, and impact of MOOCs from an institutional perspective [6].

2.2 Methodology: Learners' Motivation

Analysing the intrinsic and extrinsic motivation that leads a learner to take the decision to register in a MOOC is not easy because there are many cognitive and affective components involved. A MOOC heavily relies on the autonomy of the student to control their learning process. Termed "Self-regulated learning" (SRL), this concept which emerged in the '80s, addresses the question of how students manage learning process, and includes cognitive strategies, metacognition and motivation [7]. Motivation is an important part of the SRL. Specifically, intrinsic motivation is needed to perform learning tasks as part of the forethought, the strategic process that precedes performance in learning [8]. However, it is more feasible to understand the reasons that may lead a person to consider undertaking a MOOC. The data was gathered through a questionnaire, from an empirical analytical perspective. The questionnaire contains 24 questions, grouped by the following themes:

- About you. This section's goal was to obtain basic information about the participants: residence, age, gender, occupation and kind of learner.
- Education. Focused on level of education and whether parents attended university.

- MOOC providers. To know if people had participated in any MOOC before, when it was, when and where they accessed to materials and what device they used.
- Motivation. Designed to identify which MOOC platform was used, how many MOOCs studied, if they interacted with others, tools used in the MOOC experience, activities developed, and finally, questions relating to reasons for starting a MOOC, and for completion.

The survey was designed and piloted. It was also translated into Arabic and Spanish, to obtain data from those language environments. The questionnaire was published using the University of Southampton web based survey tool iSurvey. The participants were recruited through Facebook, Twitter and email. Once the data was collected, it was analysed through SPSS software. The categorising and coding process of the variables for the questionnaire was related to the type of question (mainly nominal) and a direct reading of the data was made by frequency calculation.

3 Findings: Motivations for Higher Education Institutions

3.1 MOOCs in Context

The analysis of the two sets of sources generated a number of observations on the institutional motivations and reactions to MOOCs. The main observations in terms of the established contexts of the emergence of MOOCs determined by the analysis of academic sources, were as follow:

- Strategic Growth: Marshall [9] argues that developing MOOCs is part of HEI strategic plans to remain competitive in the market for learners seeking an affordable education balancing the 'bargaining power of buyers' and the 'bargaining power of [competitor HEI] suppliers'.
- Marketing: Delarocas and Alstyne [10] observe that MOOCs are often introductory courses that contribute to a marketing recruitment strategy targeting large numbers of potential fee paying students.
- Strategic Collaboration: Universities are gathering in consortia around emerging MOOC platforms, such as Coursera, FutureLearn and EdX. The University of Edinburgh's report [11] identified belonging to peer communities as a way to explore new educational methods, and secure greater reach and more presence for courses.
- Organic Growth/Evolution: Yuan and Powell, [12] argue that MOOCs emerge as a natural evolution of Open Educational Resources (OERs). HEIs, especially those already championing OERs, such as Harvard and MIT are compelled to sustain Open Education within this new format.
- Response to Learners: Castells' influential analyses of contemporary societies [13] emphasises use of available technologies to engage in networked interactions, in the 'networked society'. Williams et al. [14] observe that learners are not only ready to learn collaboratively through social media but also demand it. This trend has permeated the education domain, and leading HEIs must develop pedagogical

approaches that fulfil these demands if they want to maintain their top positions in the rankings.

- Learner Analytics: MOOCs produce large quantities of learner data. This is valuable data that can inform the design of enhanced, customised and effective instructional methods, which may in turn raise the perceived quality of tuition in universities, and hence improve competitiveness. Analysing these datasets can shed light on collective and individual learning processes [15]; learners' engagement levels in different course stages [16]; or their potential for success or failure [17].
- Educational Enhancement: Taken collectively the observations above also suggest that educational enhancement is either a sub-objective or a fortunate consequence of MOOC participation.

3.2 Main Debates on MOOCs

An extensive survey on the contemporary grey literature identified three areas in which the debates were more frequent and intense. Within sustainability two main themes occupied most of the debates, (1) analogies with other business initiatives; (2) learners' sustained participation.

The business analogy of sustainability, championed by Marginson [18], Young [19] and the Economist [20] draws parallels between MOOCs and successful business models of Silicon Valley initiatives such as Google and eBay, who made early investments, provided free services, and now make substantial profit. Weston [21] presents another side of the debate citing the experience of companies who suffered the dotcom bubble; Ptaszynsky [22] suggests that universities will realise that they do not external platforms to run MOOCs, since universities can provide fairly feasible technological solutions without the need for third parties.

The sustainability of learners' participation, debate has optimist commentators such as Lawton and Katsomitros [23] arguing that high numbers of enrolling students provide an opportunity for novel sustainable business models whereby some costs are met by institutions, governments and future employers while students pay for assessment and certification.

However, the interpretation of the high drop-out rates is contentious and relate to the quality of provision as well as sustainability. Sceptics like Tauber [24] see them as a serious issue rooted in poor conceptualisation and design. Kollowitch [25, 26] illustrates the failure of MOOC models with concrete examples, such as the bad experiences with MOOCs of Colorado State University and San Jose State University. However Catropa [27] suggests this sceptical view is mistaken underestimating the high number of students who actually complete a MOOC despite the high drop-out rates while Parr [28] claims it ignores the fact that many learners who do not complete a MOOC still benefit.

There were frequent debates in the media regarding the quality of MOOCs. Sceptics see them as not being able to reproduce the discussions that takes place in small face-to-face group settings, which are deemed as the only way meaningful learning can take place [29]. A frequent counterargument is that seminar discussions can and have been reproduced successfully in web-based environments [30]. Also, many recognise that MOOC tuition quality might be lower due to the ratio of students to teacher, but it is still reasonable for those who will otherwise not access HE [31].

A further motivational factor to HEI involvement in MOOCs is their impact and spread. Lewin [32] compares it with a tsunami; the more universities join the movement, the more universities will be urged to join it. This tsunami will fuel a revolution in HE. However, sceptical views, such as that of Drezner [33], situate the current enthusiasm in the beginning of a hype cycle that will soon deflate.

3.2.1 MOOCs as Distance Education

The literature identifies six distinct generations of distance education associated with the role of technology in each step: [34–38] MOOCs can be considered alongside this timeline.

- First generation: a "correspondence model", studying via mail.
- Second generation: incorporated technologies such as video.
- Third generation: combining tools and telecommunications [34], also referred to as "telelearning", e.g. incorporating the use of videoconferencing. It is also the moment when educational concepts as "open education" and "flexible learning" emerge.
- Fourth generation: "the flexible learning model" Taylor [35] emphasises the use of technology and the Internet in the '90s producing the first eLearning experiences.
- Fifth generation: adds the emergence of Virtual Learning Environments (VLE), the use of Virtual Campus and resources processes characterised by automation systems Taylor [36].
- Sixth generation: based on Web 2.0, like a model of progress of interactive environments technology has changed [38], an increase in social software tools. Blogs, wikis and social networks have changed the way people use the Internet, and represent new opportunities to learn.

Perhaps MOOCs will become the seventh generation in distance education. Clearly they enact a model of distance education. The current "boom" in the university narrative created by MOOCs suggest some turning point in distance education. Although perhaps in terms of a formalized educational understanding of MOOCs it is rather early to make that claim.

3.2.2 MOOCs Structure and Assessment

Two distinct kinds of MOOC are widely recognised: xMOOCs and cMOOCs. The xMOOCs focus on courses content and are typically located on a single web platform. Course development is usually centred on that platform, which provides access to the contents. cMOOCs are related to connectivistm incorporating the design and realisation of networked learning and based on the ideas of Siemens [39, 40] They start from the idea that we learn when we connect with other people, accordingly cMOOCs manifest in a more open format working with social and collaborative tools.

In early MOOCs, the opportunity provided by participating in a MOOC was not to primarily obtain a certificate, but to learn. This aspect of cMOOCs is highlighted because "participation in a MOOC is emergent, fragmented, diffuse, and diverse. There is no credit or certificate offered for completion" [41].

More recently, many MOOCs, particularly, xMOOCs, offer certification (free or charged), providing participants the chance to formally record their learning and thereby to improve their CV. O'Toole [42], in a discussion paper looking at peer assessment, asserts that "whereas in the cMOOC participants are primarily interested in building the collective capabilities of the whole network, and hence are more likely to use feedback and ratings systems honestly, in xMOOCs participants are aiming to get a good personal grade". A demand for validated certification exists and some companies are beginning to sign agreements with institutions to provide MOOC participants with such services e.g. the agreement between Udacity and Pearson to create a network of assessment centres, and a similar agreement between Miriadax, the Spanish MOOC platform and Telefonica.

4 Motivations: Learners

4.1 Findings

A total of 258 questionnaires were completed: 52 English, 193 Arabic, 40 Spanish. The majority of respondents were in the 18–24 age range with variations depending on the language identified in the survey. Majority are male respondents (72.5 %) (Table 1).

Table 1. The majority of respondents were male.

English	67.3 % male
Arabic	77.2 % male
Spanish	48.7 % male

A large volume of interesting data have been obtained from this questionnaire, however, the remainder of this paper will focus on motivation related data, concentrating on reasons that led respondents to participate in a MOOC. In this section, respondents could choose from a number of options and could check more than one. Carefully analysing these data, a number of reasons normally found in the web and scientific discussions, appear to be confirmed. Figure 1 shows all options.

The analysis below explores the findings, indicating whether or not they underpin the widely perceived motivations of learners in MOOCs.

4.1.1 MOOCs are Free and Open

Free availability is the important factor according to the survey selected by 67 % a particularly high number of respondents from the Spanish questionnaire selected this option (72.5 %). Providing educational resources for free is not new and open licensing for software, resources and learning objects is well established. MIT launched the Open Course Ware project (OCW), in 2001 to share web-based teaching materials under Creative Commons licenses. The main difference between MOOCs and OCW is that while initiatives like OCW focus on sharing teaching materials, Universities are using

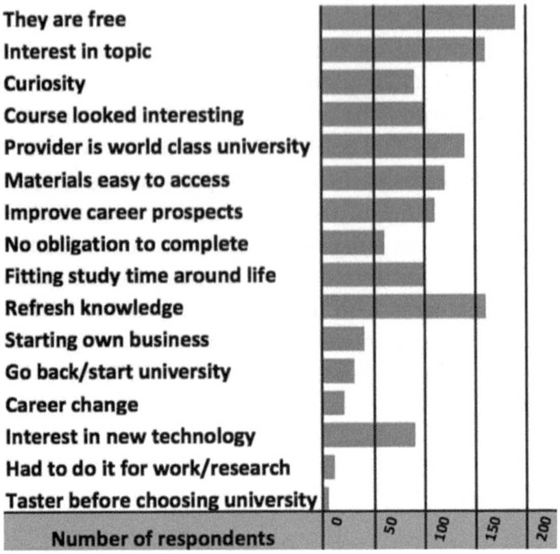

Fig. 1. Distribution of responses identifying motivation.

MOOCs to realise a complete learning process. Learners are not only able to access the material, but they can also follow lessons, develop activities, talk with online-classmates, and even be evaluated. Cost free and usually open.

If free is a fundamental aspect that motivates students to follow a MOOC, and it would be interesting to know which aspect of this liberation is most relevant to them.

4.1.2 MOOCs are Convenient: Fitting Around Life

There are clear differences in motivation related to fitting study time around life, in general, this selection is not chosen by a lot of people (36 %), but it is of interest. The Arabic responses show 27.5 % interested in this aspect, the Spanish represents 65 %. The majority of Spanish participants are in full time employment which may be the reason that they rate this aspect as relevant.

4.1.3 MOOCs for CV and Knowledge Update

There were two possible responses related to professional expertise (1) A MOOC helps to improve my CV (2) A MOOC helps to update knowledge. Both these perspectives may relate to professional expertise.

The question 'A MOOC helps to improve my CV' appears more related to the need for certification to be shown in a CV. In the survey, improving CV is selected by 54.4 % of all participants as one reason to use a MOOC, but the percentage rises to 61.7 % of Arabic participants, probably because the majority are students. This is consistent with other studies, for example findings at Duke University [43] highlights it as the main reason students participated. A MOOC helps to update knowledge. 59.1 % of Arabic and 70 % of Spanish participants said that one main reason to do a MOOC is to refresh knowledge.

4.1.4 The Social Community of MOOCs

MOOCs may have social components that motivate learners to register to participate. Respondents affirm (55.8 %) they were the first among acquaintances, family, colleagues and friends participating in a MOOC. However 124 respondents from 285 found out about MOOCs via social media and then decided to participate. MOOCs can represent an opportunity for socialisation.

4.1.5 MOOCs Satisfying Interest and Usefulness

In a market with a lot of options, MOOCs can represent a new way to learn and access digital content. Interest in the topic is one important reason for participating in a MOOC, specifically 56.8 % overall, 80 % of respondents in the English language selected this aspect. Usefulness also features; 60.6 % of participants overall declare they will use the knowledge gained during the MOOC in a personal project, and 63.2 % in personal development These data follow the same line as other research, such as Duke University, where the topic was identified by 87 % of the students as a motivational aspect [43]. Many students indicated that they thought the course would be fun and enjoyable. This aspect of 'edutainment' where usefulness and fun intersect may be of real importance.

4.1.6 MOOCs Enable Learning with the Best

The origin of MOOCs in prestigious universities, or by the effort of high profile or world leading academics may explain their apparent popularity and rapid growth and their power to attract the attention to many different learners. Although not quite the majority, about half the respondents, 48.1 %, identified 'provider was a word class university' as a reason for participation. There is some difference by origin of respondents. English language respondents show the least interest at 38.5 %; Spanish 43 %; Arabic 51.8 %.

4.1.7 MOOCs Professional Development and Lifelong Learning

The University of Edinburgh report summarising of the experience of their six Coursera MOOCs in May, 2013 [11] observed "In general, we attracted adults with high educational attainments". That is reflected in the survey, 208 of the 282 have a degree (mainly undergraduate 133 of 285. There are more post-doctorate learners in English and Spanish language respondent than in Arabic.

The largest represented age range (50.5 %), is between 18 and 24 but there are a lot of differences depending on the scope: Most Arabic language respondents are in the range of 18–24 years old, this percentage decreases in English and even more so in the Spanish language results, in where the largest represented age range is the 25–34 years old.

Motivations for 18 to 34 years may be closely related to the opportunity to improve their career, moreover, enhance their professional network. Half the respondents indicated that participating in a MOOC enabled them to enhance their professional development and improve their knowledge in the workplace. Among Spanish speaking the percentage identifying this as an important factor rises to 77.5 %.

The survey asked how respondents would use the knowledge gained in the MOOC. The most widely identified factors were personal development and projects. In a world increasingly multidimensional and diverse, MOOCs can work in universities as a piece of the system providing open learning opportunities, forming part of the learners' personal learning network. Professional and personal development needs are increasing alongside rapid business change. Therefore, MOOCs can offer a learning opportunity for people to develop lifelong learning.

5 Issues

5.1 Pedagogic Possibilities or Illusion?

The UK Department for Business, Innovation and Skills extensively reviewed the MOOCs literature in 2013 [44]. They identify two trends in educational press, blogs and general media. One enthusiastically promoting MOOCs, reporting positively on learning experience and innovative forms of pedagogy, focusing on concepts like collaboration and community. But the sceptical view sees two major flaws: the supposed benefits of MOOCs are the victory of content packaging; and the MOOC format itself is exclusive and does not have enough quality to develop skills in learners.

Educational technologists have long argued that learning online is not only about content. Bates [45] suggests that open and flexible education should consist of the provision of flexible learning, built around geographical, social, and time constraints of each student, instead of being built around educational institutions' needs. How can a MOOC, developed for hundreds or thousands of students, meet these aspirations? Educationally, MOOCs are only a small part of the multiplicity of wider international university systems. They cannot be assumed to be the panacea that will solve all educational problems.

Moreover, the very high drop-out rate behind MOOCs is widely recognised. Clow et al. [46] categorise that phenomena as "the funnel of participation". The funnel consists of four stages of participation: awareness; registration; activity and progress. What is not known is the extent of the participants' satisfaction with their (perhaps very limited) participation. However, "bad experiences" with MOOCs have been reported. In July 2013 "Inside Higher Ed" [47] reported that, after six months of high-profile experimentation, San Jose State University plans to "pause" its work with Udacity, because "preliminary findings from the spring semester suggest students [in online joint Udacity/San Jose courses] do not fare as well as students who attended normal classes".

5.2 Assuring Assessment for Learning

The volume of learners in MOOCs perhaps inevitably makes feedback and the assessment two highly debated aspects of MOOCs. MOOCs are demonstrations of assessment online and at scale. Since technologies allow focus upon and tracking of the student learning process, e-assessment need not be an action that occurs only at the end of the course. However, taking into consideration skills and other aspects of the learning process, there is a lack of systems that facilitate a complete assessment, (Strither; Driscoll; Radenkovic et al.) [48–50].

Additionally, the "massive" (independent and remote) nature inherent to MOOCs, makes it more difficult to develop high quality assessment. Although some MOOCs incorporate "peer assessment", O'Toole [42] notes that, rather than peer assessment, it should be called "peer-grading", since it cannot be assumed that an equal or adequate level of understanding about assessment is possessed by all MOOC learners.

Another desirable and thus important aspect of the learning process is feedback, assessment for learning. Feedback on assessment online is not always integrated in the mechanisms that assess students. It is challenging in a MOOC environment to develop effective assessments where, feedback reinforces learning and identifies inconsistencies in the learner process.

5.3 Costs – Benefit or Risk?

MOOCs are in principle free for students, although some platforms now incorporate a fee for a certificate of participation. MOOCs are not free for institutions. Universities have to invest time and money designing and uploading materials, managing the course, providing feedback. It is not clear if this model is sustainable over the time. Luján [51] discusses an interesting perspective that the most important American universities may be using MOOCs to protect themselves against a possible outbreak of "the bubble of Universities". This stresses the hypothesis that a MOOC can work for universities as an initiative to contain costs and enrol more students, thus obtaining more revenue and helping to resolve the crisis in the sector. Yuan and Powell [12] suggest that companies may want to invest in MOOCs in order to enhance the company brand or create a new income stream from Higher Education business. Such motives may lie behind companies signing agreements with institutions to provide services for MOOCs, such as the contract between Pearson and Udacity to create a network of evaluation centres.

5.4 Widening Inequalities

MOOCs can create inequalities at different levels: among students, across educators, between institutions, and even at a global level. Regarding students, Cookson [52] points out that job seekers with MOOC certificates will pose weak competition to those with traditional degrees. Carlson and Blumenstyk [53] note that the skills needed in a tertiary sector driven economy such as talking in public or business etiquette can only be acquired through face-to-face tuition. Those who most need these skills are the most disadvantaged, mainly due to their social backgrounds, and MOOCs may not be able to empower them.

Educators may also face inequalities following a massive adoption of MOOCs. While scalability allows elite 'superstar' professors to reach massive audiences, it may leave the rest of educators in precarious conditions [54]. At institutional level, universities that can afford the costs of engaging in MOOCs may leave competitor institutions with little market share, as massive uptake could lead to centralisation. Although widely contested, Thrun's prediction that only a few universities would be needed in the world [55] may have validity.

Finally, at a global level, Sloep [56] explains that, far from promoting inclusion, MOOCs promote cultural imperialism, because "developing countries lack the financial and human resources to develop an educational system of high quality, so when they are confronted with MOOCs they cannot afford the luxury of refusing them".

5.5 Learners' Digital Competencies

MOOCs require, and develop a range of specific skills. Early reports on MOOCs identify a clear profile of prior-experienced participants who are post-graduates and/or professionals [11, 57]. Brown [58] suggests undergraduate students are less likely to possess the skills needed by an autonomous learner in a MOOC. However, a cross-section of people who are less likely to have these skills can and do enrol. It would be interesting to investigate if the drop-out rates found in MOOCs could be in part explained by the fact that there are people who register who subsequently decide they are not able to complete for lack of skills.

5.6 Certification to Overcome Plagiarism?

Plagiarism is another issue to be borne in mind. If certification and accreditation are to become a significant part of the MOOC business models, the credibility of certificates issued by HEIs might be undermined unless breaches of academic integrity, easily achieved via the anonymity of the web, are prevented. Furthermore it is observed that the concept of plagiarism varies across cultures. Wilkinson notes students in certain Asian countries do not see plagiarism as an academic integrity breach, but as a way to show respect to the authority of the content producer [59]. Therefore, universities not only should incorporate plagiarism detection software in their MOOCs, but also emphasize and clarify the principles of academic integrity expected in their programmes.

6 Conclusions

This paper examines HEIs' motivations of for making MOOCs and the motivations of learners for registering and completing them. It is clear that these are not simple matters so it is not surprising that there are no simple answers. However there are some useful understandings that we gained from our studies, surveys and interactions with other MOOCers that should be borne in mind when considering motivations.

When it comes to considering institutions' motivations to produce MOOCs, we need to understand that institutions are very much aware of predictions for the way the learning landscape will change with the disruption caused by on–line learning; forward thinking institutions understand that they need to respond to these changes.

Creating MOOCs can be seen as a way of enhancing the institution's reputation, not only in the subject area of the MOOC, but also in the area of quality on-line learning. Furthermore, internally, in the university, the enthusiasm and skills that go into producing MOOCs are the same that are needed to grow internal capacity for engaging with and producing high quality on-line learning courses. In the near future we expect to see universities purposefully using of their MOOC material to add value to their accredited courses. Resulting in much softer dividing lines between accredited courses and MOOCs, on-campus education and off-campus education.

From the point of view of learners there would appear to be two important groups – those that see doing MOOCs as a form of Edutainment; providing intellectual stimulation, while another group are those that are seeking educational improvement for the sake of improving their career and life prospects.

MOOCs are much criticised for the high drop-out rates, because small percentages of starters complete their course. But we need to be aware that the motivations of those who register for MOOCS are diverse and may be very different from those who register for university programmes. For a start, many who register have no intention of finishing – they are equivalent to forum 'lurkers', also termed bystanders [60] those who just want to have a look inside the course, and the only way to do this is often to register. Secondly, attitudes to perseverance will vary. Those who find a course less interesting, more time consuming or more challenging than expected may drop-out. Those who signed up at personal cost, believing the study to be critical to their future may persevere.

Finally, we should not assume that all learners intended to complete the whole course. Many learners may only be interested in part of the course, or have time constraints of which they were when they started and thus 'intended' not to complete. Furthermore, MOOCs are free and there is no penalty for failure to complete, many learners are able to drop in (and out) of courses at their own convenience. This should be a cause for educational celebration rather than criticism and represents an opportunity for learner autonomy, choice and independence.

Acknowledgements. The authors would like to acknowledge the work and enthusiasm of Olja Rastic Dulborough and Maraim Masoud two students who worked on internships in the Centre for Innovation in Technologies and Education (CITE) for the summer vacation of 2013, and intern Edmund Baird for subsequent input in 2014. We would also like to acknowledge the respondents who freely gave time to reply to our survey.

References

1. Barber, M., Donnelly, K., Rizvi, S., Summers, L.: An avalanche is coming: higher education and the revolution ahead. Institute of Public Policy Research (2013). http://hdl.voced.edu.au/10707/247391
2. Liyanagunawardena, T.R., Adams, A.A., Williams, S.A.: MOOCs: a systematic study of the published literature 2008-2012. Int. Rev. Res. Open Distance Learn. **14**(3), 202–227 (2013)
3. Daniel, J.: Making sense of MOOCs: musings in a maze of myth, paradox and possibility. J. Interact. Media Educ., 3 (2012). http://jime.open.ac.uk/2012/18
4. Herring, S.C.: Content analysis for new media: rethinking the paradigm. In: New Research for New Media: Innovative Research Methodologies Symposium Working Papers and Readings, pp. 47–66. University of Minnesota School of Journalism and Mass Communication (2004)

5. Krippendorff, K.: Content Analysis: An Introduction to Its Methodology. Sage, Newbury Park (1980)
6. León, M.: Reactions on the emergence of MOOCs in higher education (2013). https://eprints.soton.ac.uk/cgi/users/home?screen=EPrint::View&eprintid=358803
7. Zimmenan, B., Schunk, S.: Self-Regulated Learning and Academic Achievements: Theoretical Perspectives, 2nd edn. Routledge, London (2001)
8. Barnard-Brak, L., Lan, W.Y., Paton, V.O.: Profiles in self-regulated learning in the online learning environments. Int. Rev. Res. Open Distance Learn. **11**(1), 61–80 (2010)
9. Marshall, S.J.: Evaluating the strategic and leadership challenges of MOOCs. MERLOT J. Online Learn. Teach. **9**(2), 216–227 (2013)
10. Dellarocas, C., Van Alstyne, M.: Money models for MOOCs. Commun. ACM **56**(8), 25–28 (2013)
11. MOOCs@Edinburgh Group.2013. MOOCs @ Edinburgh 2013: Report #1 Edinburgh. The University of Edinburgh. http://www.era.lib.ed.ac.uk/handle/1842/6683
12. Yuan, L., Powell, S.: MOOCs and open education: implications for higher education. A white paper. CETIS (2013). www.publications.cetis.ac.uk/2013/667. Accessed 21 March 2013
13. Castells, M.: The Rise of the Network Society: The Information Age: Economy, Society, and Culture, vol. 1. Blackwell, Oxford (1996)
14. Williams, R., Karousou, R., Mackness, J.: Emergent learning and learning ecologies in Web 2.0. Int. Rev. Res. Open Distance Learn. **12**(3), 39–59 (2011)
15. De Liddo, A., Shum, S.B., Quinto, I., Bachler, M., Cannavacciuolo, L.: Discourse-centric learning analytics. In: Proceedings of the 1st International Conference on Learning Analytics and Knowledge, pp. 23–33. ACM (2011)
16. Breslow, L.B., Pritchard, D.E., DeBoer, J., Stump, G.S., Ho, A.D., Seaton, D.T.: Studying learning in the worldwide classroom: research into edX's first MOOC. Res. Pract. Assess. **8**, 13–25 (2013)
17. Barber, R., Sharkey, M.: Course correction: using analytics to predict course success. In: Proceedings of the 2nd International Conference on Learning Analytics and Knowledge, pp. 259–262. ACM (2012)
18. Marginson, S.: Online open education: yes, this is the game changer. The conversation (2012). http://theconversation.com/online-open-education-yes-this-is-the-game-changer-8078
19. Young, J.R.: Inside the coursera contract: how an upstart company might profit from free courses, Chronicle of Higher Education (2012). http://www.chronicle.com/article/ How-an-Upstart-Company-Might/133065/
20. Economist 2013. The attack of the MOOCs. The economist higher education. http://www.economist.com/news/business/21582001-army-new-online-courses-scaring-wits-out-traditional-universities-can-they
21. Weston, C.: MOOCs and other ed-tech bubbles. Ed Tech Now (2012). http://edtechnow.net/2012/12/29/moocs-and-other-ed-tech-bubbles/
22. Ptaszynsky, J.G.: MOOCs: the new internet bubble in education? Microsoft partners in learning (2012). http://pil-tei.com/blog/moocs-the-new-internet-bubble-in-education/
23. Lawton, R., Katsomitros, L.: MOOCs and disruptive innovation: the challenge to HE business models. The Observatory of Borderless Higher Education (2013). http://www.obhe.ac.uk/documents/view_details?id=929
24. Tauber, T.: The dirty little secret of online learning: students are bored and dropping out. Quartz (2013) http://qz.com/65408/the-dirty-little-secret-of-online-learning-students-are-bored-and-dropping-out/

25. Kolowich, S.: How edX plans to earn, and share, revenue from its free online courses. The Chronicle of Higher Education, 21 (2013). http://chronicle.com/article/How-EdX-Plans-to-Earn-and/137433/
26. Kollowitch, S.: The MOOC 'revolution' may not be as disruptive as some had imagined. The Chronicle of Higher Education (2013a). http://chronicle.com/article/MOOCs-May-Not-Be-So-Disruptive/140965/
27. Catropa, D.: Big (MOOC) Data. Inside higher education (2013). http://www.insidehighered.com/blogs/stratedgy/big-mooc-data
28. Parr, C.: MOOC completion rates below 7 %. Times higher education (2013). http://www.timeshighereducation.co.uk/news/mooc-completion-rates-below-7/2003710.article
29. Rheingold, H.: MOOCs, hype, and the precarious state of higher Ed: Futurist Bryan Alexander. DML Central (2013). http://dmlcentral.net/blog/howard-rheingold/moocs-hype-and-precarious-state-higher-ed-futurist-bryan-alexander
30. Davidson, K.: Clearing up some myths about MOOCs. Hastac (2013). http://www.hastac.org/blogs/cathy-davidson/2013/06/11/clearing-some-myths-about-moocs
31. Horn, D.: Failing fast, not spectacularly. Clayton Christiensen Institute for Disruptive Innovations (2013). http://www.forbes.com/sites/michaelhorn/2013/08/15/fail-fast-not-spectacularly/
32. Lewin, T.: Instruction for masses knocks down campus walls. New York Times (2012). http://www.nytimes.com/2012/03/05/education/moocs-large-courses-open-to-all-topple-campus-walls.html?pagewanted=all&_r=0
33. Drezner, J.: Twilight of the MOOCs? Foreign policy (2013). http://dreznerforeignpolicy.com/posts/2013/07/22/twilight_of_the_moocs
34. Nipper, S.: Third generation distance learning and computer conferencing. In: Mason, R., Kaye, A. (eds.) Mindweave: Communication, Computers and Distance Education. Pergamon, Oxford (1989)
35. Taylor, J.: Distance education technologies: the fourth generation. Aust. J. Educ. Technol. **11**(2), 1–7 (1995)
36. Taylor, J.: Fifth generation distance education, in Higher Education Series, report n. 40. Canberra, Australia: Department of Education, Training and Youth Affairs (2001)
37. Fozdar, B.I., Kumar, L.S.: Mobile learning and student retention. Int. Rev. Res. Open Distance Learn. **8**(2), 1–18 (2007)
38. Caladine, R.: Enhancing E-Learning with Media Rich Content and Interactions. Information Science Publishing, Hershey (2008)
39. Siemens, G.: Massive open online courses as new educative practice (2012a). http://es.slideshare.net/gsiemens/open-online-courses-as-new-educative-practice
40. Siemens, G.: What is the theory that underpins our MOOCs? (2012b). http://www.elearnspace.org/blog/2012/06/03/what-is-the-theory-that-underpins-our-moocs/
41. McAuley, A., Stewart, B., Siemens, G.Y, Cormier, D.: The MOOC model for digital practice. University of Prince Edward Island (2010). http://www.elearnspace.org/Articles/MOOC_Final.pdf
42. O'Toole, R.: Pedagogical strategies and technologies for peer assessment in massively open online courses (MOOCs). University of Warwick (2013). http://wrap.warwick.ac.uk/54602/7/WRAP_O%27toole_ROToole
43. Belanger, Y., Thornton, J.: Bioelectricity: a quantitative approach. Duke University´s first MOOC, pp. 1–21 (2013). http://dukespace.lib.duke.edu/dspace/bitstream/handle/10161/6216/Duke_Bioelectricity_MOOC_Fall2012.pdf

44. Department for business, innovation & skills 2013. The maturing of the MOOC: literature review of massive open online courses and other forms of online distance learning. UK. https://www.gov.uk/government/uploads/system/uploads/attachment_data/file/240193/13-1173-maturing-of-the-mooc.pdf
45. Bates, A.W.: Technology, E-Learning and Distance Education. Routledge, Oxon (1995)
46. Clow, D.:. MOOCs and the funnel of participation. In: Proceedings of the Third International Conference on Learning Analytics and Knowledge, pp. 185–189. ACM (April 2013)
47. Inside Higher-ED: Udacity Project on "pause" (2013). http://www.insidehighered.com/news/2013/07/18/citing-disappointing-student-outcomes-san-jose-state-pauses-work-udacity
48. Strither, J.B.: An assessment of the effectiveness of e-learning in corporate training programs. Int. Rev. Res. Open Distance Learn. **3**(1) (2002). http://www.irrodl.org/index.php/irrodl/article/viewArticle/83/160
49. Driscoll, M.: Building better e-assessment, in learning circuits, ASTD (2001). http://www.astd.org/LC/2001/0601_driscoll.htm
50. Radenkovic, S., Krzavac, N., Devedzic, V.: An assessment system on the semantic web. In: Devedzic, V., Gasevic, D. (eds.) Web 2.0 and Semantic Web. Annals of information systems. Springer, USA (2010)
51. Luján, S.: Preguntas y respuestas: ¿Qué son los MOOCS? (2012). http://desarrolloweb.dlsi.ua.es/cursos/2012/que-son-los-moocs/preguntas-respuestas
52. Cookson, P: Are MOOCs the answer? Preserving value of higher education. The quick and the Ed. (2013). http://www.quickanded.com/2013/08/are-moocs-the-answer-preserving-the-value-of-higher-education.html. Accessed 23 August 2013
53. Blumenstyk, G., Carlson, S.: For whom is college being reinvented? The Chronicle of Higher Education, 17 (2012)
54. Engler, C.: MOOCs and megatrends: a prediction comes true. Evolution (2013). http://www.evolllution.com/distance_online_learning/moocs-megatrends-prediction-true/
55. Leckart: The Stanford education experiment could change higher learning forever (2012). www.wired.com/wiredscience/2012/03/ff_aiclass/
56. Sloep, P.: MOOCs, what about them? Some moral considerations. In: Stories to TEL (2013). http://pbsloep.blogspot.nl/2013/01/moocs-what-about-them-continued.html
57. Osvaldo, C.: MOOCs and the AI stanford like courses: two successful and distinct course formats for massive open online courses. Eur. J. Open Distance E-Learn. (2012). http://www.eurodl.org/?article=516
58. Brown, S.: MOOCs, OOCs, flips and hybrids: the new world of higher education. In: ICICTE 2013 Proceedings, pp. 237–247 (2013). http://apps.webofknowledge.com/full_record.do?product=UA&search_mode=GeneralSearch&qid=1&SID=W1xAnAorTZUmTypaXSZ&page=2&doc=14&cacheurlFromRightClick=no
59. Wilkinson, L.R.: ESL academic writing and plagiarism. Internet TESL J. **14**(7) (2008)
60. Anderson, A., Huttenlocher, D., Kleinberg, J., Leskovec, J.: Engaging with massive online courses. In: Proceedings of 23rd International Conference on World Wide Web (WWW 2014), pp. 687–698

Toward an Adaptive Gamification System for Learning Environments

Baptiste Monterrat[1(✉)], Élise Lavoué[2], and Sébastien George[3]

[1] INSA-Lyon, LIRIS, UMR5205, 69621 Lyon, France
baptiste.monterrat@insa-lyon.fr
[2] IAE Lyon, Université Jean Moulin Lyon 3, LIRIS, UMR5205, Lyon, France
elise.lavoue@univ-lyon3.fr
[3] LIUM, LUNAM Université, Université du Maine, EA 4023, 72085 Le Mans, France
sebastien.george@univ-lemans.fr

Abstract. In a learning situation, gamification is a way to motivate learners and enhance their participation to learning activities by adding game elements. But it still pays little attention to the individual differences among learners' preferences as players. This paper presents a generic and adaptive gamification system that can be plugged on various learning environments. The game elements can be automatically adapted, based on an analysis of the interaction traces. The architecture of the proposed system is based on the separation between the control of the pedagogical elements and the control of the game elements. To support the adaptivity of the game elements, we refer to a user model based on a list of player types. The user model is initialized thanks to the traces of interactions, and finally used to predict which game feature will be relevant for the user.

Keywords: Gamification · Adaptation · Learning environment · Motivation · User model

1 Introduction to Gamification in Learning

Many learning environments have been shown to be effective when used, but are quickly deserted by most of the learners because of a lack of motivation. Gamification is becoming a popular way to motivate user participation on web-based activities. "When done well, gamification helps align our interests with the intrinsic motivation of our players" [1]. Although this concept is not new [2], yet little research treats its uses in learning contexts. This paper proposes a generic and personalized gamification system to raise motivation in learning environments that are not intrinsically motivating.

1.1 The Need for Genericity

Turning a learning environment into a game is a complex process. Currently, if the designers of a learning environment are interested in gamifying it, they have to

S. Zvacek et al. (Eds.): CSEDU 2014, CCIS 510, pp. 115–129, 2015.
DOI: 10.1007/978-3-319-25768-6_8

re-design and re-implement the game elements especially for this environment. This could be very complex and require a lot of time, whereas the elements will not be reusable. The existence of generic game elements would address this problem.

Achievements systems like Mozilla OpenBadges [3] address this need for genericity, but using badges only is a poor way to gamify. Maciuszek *et al.* [4] used a component-based framework for implementing educational games. It allows turning a learning software into a learning game by changing only the user interface components. However, the initial software needs to be already compatible with this framework in order to be turned into a game, which is not the case with most existing learning environments. Thus, we aim to develop gamification as an independent layer that could be plugged on learning environments without changing them.

1.2 The Need for Adaptivity

When trying to motivate with games, an important difficulty comes from the fact that people do not have the same expectations, and do not have the same emotional responses to game mechanics [5]. A common approach to fulfill these expectations is to add gamification features for all the player types within the application, but there is a high risk of overloading the user interface. That is why gamification needs to be personalized. Various researches contributed to the field of adaptive games, by adapting the user interface, the level of difficulty [6], the pedagogical scenario [7], or the feedback [8]. We aim at developing an adaptive motivational system addressing the three deficiencies highlighted below.

The first lack identified in existing works is about games genre and dynamics. Game dynamics are defined by Zicherman *et al.* [1] as "the player's interactions with the game mechanics". Related works in adaptive games share the goal of increasing the game acceptance and usability, but the game dynamics remains the same.

The second lack concerns the adaptation of gamification. While many works focus on the adaptation of games, few are interested in the adaptation of gamification. Ferro *et al.* [9] are among the first researchers to conduct works on personalized gamification. They are trying to relate directly game mechanics and game elements to both player types and personality types.

The third lack concerns research on adaptation of multi-player games. It has been shown in the game adaptation techniques review of Hocine *et al.* [10]. As gamification mainly relies on competitive and social features, it is important to consider ways to apply it for groups of users.

1.3 Main Research Questions

Our research works aim at developing a motivating system, adaptive and adaptable to various web-based learning activities. The main research questions related to this goal are:

(1) How to characterize the game elements to make them generic and pluggable to any learning environment?

(2) Which user model can handle the adaptivity of the game elements?
(3) Which architecture can support the tracking, the adaptation, and the integration of the game elements?

Section 2 is dedicated to the state of the art related to gamification and game elements. Then in Sect. 3 we present the overall architecture of the system to make gamification generic. In Sect. 4 we provide details about our user model to make gamification adaptive. We finally conclude about the contribution of the paper and present our future works in Sects. 5 and 6.

2 State of the Art

2.1 Serious Game or Gamification

Games and fun have proven to enhance motivation in learning activities. But various approaches are used to add fun in different cases. The most popular ones are learning games and gamification. Learning games refer to the use of digital games for learning purposes [11]. Gamification has been defined more recently as "the use of game design elements in non-gaming contexts" [2]. These two approaches are often poorly distinguished one from the other. However, they differ by their design process and by the resulting application (see Table 1).

Table 1. Differences between a learning game and a gamified application.

	Learning game	Gamified application
Design process	Designed as a game from the beginning	Adding game mechanics to an existing application
Resulting application	A game with educational elements	A learning application enriched by game mechanics

In this work, we focus on gamification. On the one hand, it can be based on existing learning environments. On the other hand, with gamification the game elements are not central but peripheral, which fosters their adaptivity. Thus gamification can become a "fun layer" that could be plugged on several applications [12].

2.2 Game Adaptation and User Model

2.2.1 Game Adaptation

Research in games adaptation led to a wide range of adaptive features. Togelius *et al.* [13] proposed to make a car racing game funnier by adapting the form of the tracks. Pedersen *et al.* [14] developed a player experience model in order to adapt various parameters in platform games. Marne *et al.* [7] proposed a structure to adapt the scenario of serious games according to the user's profile and learning goals. However, these adaptations do not change the basic game mechanics, i.e. somebody who does not like car racing games in general probably will neither be interested in a car racing game with better tracks.

A review of sixteen game adaptation techniques [10] designed between 2002 and 2009 focused on both entertainment games and serious games. A large majority of them adjusts the difficulty level of the activity under various forms: they adapt the opponent's behavior, the game speed, the scenario or the feedback, but especially to prevent the game from being too difficult or too easy. The rest of the studied works propose a generic adaptation of game parameters values according to player satisfaction, or adapt the learning part of the games rather than the gaming part.

Only one study seems to make a real difference by proposing a scenario adapted to the personality of the players [15]. The personality types are based on the Five-Factor Model (ibid.), and are used to select diverse quests for the players, like defeating other players or solving puzzles. This approach allows the use of various game dynamics for various players. In this paper we aim at transposing it by using a player types model, and proposing gamification features instead of quests.

2.2.2 Distinguishing Learner and Player

In the game-based learning field, user adaptation can focus on the user as a learner, or as a player, because each user is both of them. Research on learner model focus on the relation between the learner and the knowledge. For example, the theory of adaptive hypermedia [16] tends to adapt the content of the user's learning activity.

In our work, the role of user modelling is to adapt the game elements of the gamification layer. Accordingly, we assume that the learner part of the user model is handled by the existing learning application core that manages the learning activity, while the gamification system focuses on the player part. That is why we are particularly interested in player model in next part.

2.2.3 Player Models

Many studies have been conducted about why people play games. For example, Bartle [17] identifies four player types: killer, achiever, socialiser, and explorer. Yee [5] identifies three main motivation components: achievement, social and immersion. Lazzaro (2004) observes four motivational factors for playing games: hard fun, easy fun, altered state and people factor. Moreover, with the growing interest for gamification since a few years, various companies and game designers propose their own types of gamers [18, 19]. In this work, we rely on the classification of Ferro *et al.* [9]: dominant, objectivist, humanist, inquisitive, and creative. Although their proposal is still a work in progress, this classification has the advantage to relate the player types directly to game mechanics and game elements. This link allows us to personalize and adapt our system to the players (see Sect. 4.2).

2.3 Data for Game Adaptation

According to Kobsa [20], we distinguish three forms of adaptation: to user data, to usage data and to environment data. All these parameter are important for the game elements personalization.

2.3.1 User Data

We should pay attention to basic data about users, like their age and gender, as it has an influence on their levels of attention and motivation. Charlier *et al.* [21] focused on the influence of the player's age. They argue that older adults need games without pressing time constraints. There are also gender differences in motivations for playing games. For example, Eglesz *et al.* [22] found that women prefer Role Playing Games (RPG) while men prefer action, adventure simulation and sport games.

2.3.2 Usage Data

Most works presented in the review of Hocine *et al.* [10] base their adaptation mainly on the data from user's interactions with the system. It is not a surprise, as this data is generally available without asking questions to the user. These interactions are the basic information used to fill the user model, which may contain the users' emotional state [23], their way of learning [24], their level of success [6], their level of satisfaction, attention, and engagement. As increasing engagement is our goal in this work, it is also a variable we need to track.

The methods for measuring engagement can be based on humans [25] (observation or self-report), hardware (e.g. eye tracking) or software. The last one is the only one that we can automate in web-based applications. Bouvier *et al.* [26] define a typology of engaged behaviors, to determine if a player is engaged or not, but the interactions tracked are specific to games. Mattheiss *et al.* [27] present a list of specific actions that can predict engagement or disengagement in educational computer games. For example, if the learner asks immediately for help without even reading the question, s/he probably does not want to spend much effort. Cocea [28] also proposed useful examples of behaviors predicting user disengagement, but her approach is qualitative. In this work, we rely particularly on the quantitative and computable method proposed by Beck [29], called engagement tracing.

2.3.3 Environment Data

Kobsa distinguishes the software environment (e.g. the browser), the hardware environment (e.g. the device), and the information about the place (e.g. location and objects in the immediate environment). It is generally harder to get information from the third category, but recent technologies like mobile devices localization can help.

In this work, we are interested in knowing the human context, because people do not play the same way if they are alone, with friends, or colleges. For example, Cheng *et al.* [30] tried to find the good moments to play at work, while some works focus on the uses of games in the classroom [31]. It is also important for us to know the device used and the learning context, as some ways of gamifying can be relevant only in some cases.

3 Architecture for Generic Gamification

In this part, we explain how we design game elements to be generic, adaptable, and pluggable on already existing learning environments.

3.1 Game Elements as Epiphytes

In order to personalize the fun features, the learning application needs to be able to work with or without these features. That is why we propose to use epiphytic functionalities: applications that are plugged in another application without being necessary. Giroux *et al.* [32] define epiphytic systems as follows: (1) the epiphytic system cannot exist without a host, (2) the host can exist without the epiphyte, (3) the host and the epiphyte have independent existences, and (4) the epiphyte does not affect its host.

By implementing the fun functionalities like epiphytes, we can enable or disable them independently for each user, in order to adapt his/her interface without affecting the learning application. This is also a way to foster genericity. We provide below examples of such functionalities that can be activated:

- A leader board of fast learners for competitive users.
- Badges and cups for challenge.
- Ability to leave tips to other users.
- Ability to share scores and success on social networks.
- A chat feature for users interested in socializing.

As shown on Fig. 1, the epiphytes (E1 and E2) are distributed in the user interface, but controlled only by the gamification layer, independently from the control of the pedagogical activity.

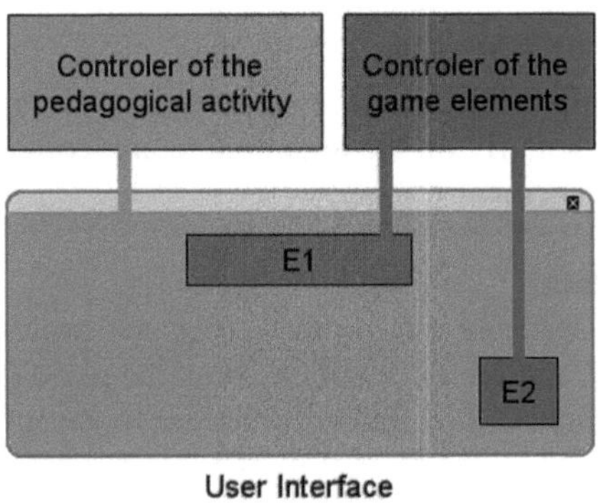

Fig. 1. Independence of pedagogical control and game control.

3.2 Architecture

An overview of the proposed architecture is presented in Fig. 2, which shows the way the gamification system can be plugged in an existing learning environment.

The interactions between the user and the environment are permanently traced (1) and stored in the database. Secondly, the data collected is used by the trace analysis system (2), which calculates frequently the engagement level of the user and stores it in the same base. When the trace analysis system detects user disengagement, it sends an alert to the adaptation engine before the user leaves. When the adaptation engine (3) receives an alert about the low engagement level, it updates the information of the

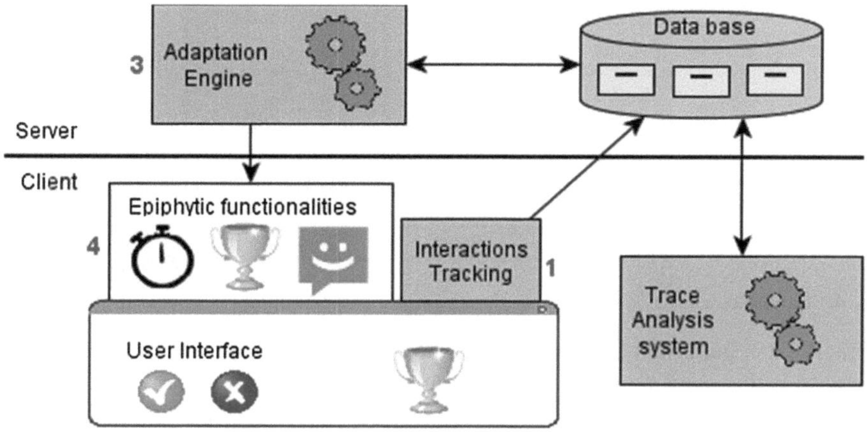

Fig. 2. Architecture of the gamification system.

player model in the same base, according to the history of engagement level and the use of activated epiphytes (see Sect. 4.3.2), and selects the epiphytic functionality which best fits the user's needs. Finally, the selected functionality (4) is introduced in the learning environment (see Sect. 3.3).

3.3 Integration of the Epiphytic Functionalities

There are different possible ways of introducing and integrating the functionalities. On the one hand, the user needs to be aware of the introduction of a new functionality, so we have to inform him/her. On the other hand, the information must not interrupt the learning activity ("the epiphyte does not affect its host"), so a popup window is also not a good solution. As shown on Fig. 3, we propose a small tooltip to inform the user without requiring any interaction.

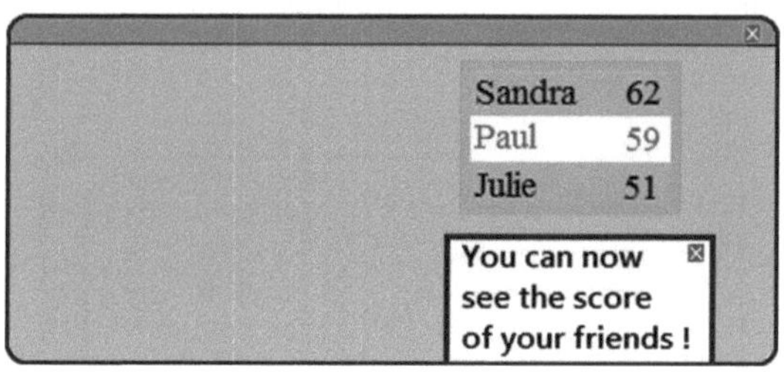

Fig. 3. Tooltip to inform the user of changes.

The web technologies allow us to integrate the epiphytes in various ways on the web pages, like panels for the information displayed permanently, and tooltips for epiphytes based on punctual feedback. Examples are shown on Fig. 4.

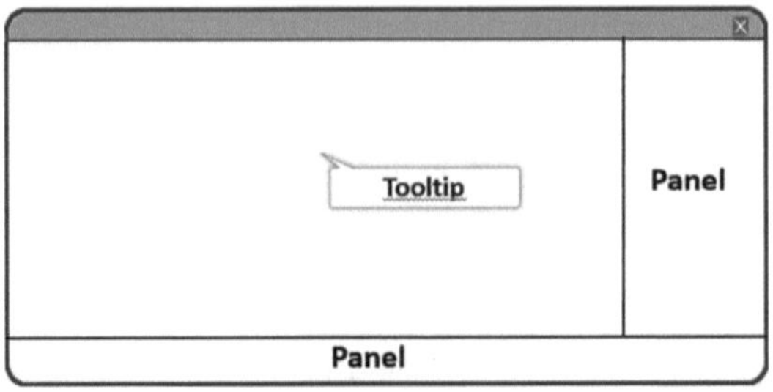

Fig. 4. Examples of ways to integrate the epiphytic functionalities in a web user interface.

Finally, it is important to allow the users to disable the activated functionalities. The first reason is that some people do not want to play, and they should not be forced to, as games are a voluntary activity. The second reason is that the adaptation engine may be wrong during the first uses of the environment, and may propose a functionality that does not feet the player's preferences. Thus, the player can close the functionality. By the way this provides a useful feedback to the system about what the user does not like.

4 Models for Adaptation of Gamification

In Sect. 3.2, we presented the architecture of the system that supports a generic gamification. In this part, we focus on the adaptation process and the player model necessary for this adaptation.

4.1 User Model

An overview of the user model is shown on Fig. 5, and its parts are details in the following subsections.

The data we want to know is registered within the player model (Sect. 4.2), which tells us which game elements the user may like. It is calculated based on the engagement level, and the use of the epiphytes. The collected data is detailed in Sect. 4.3.

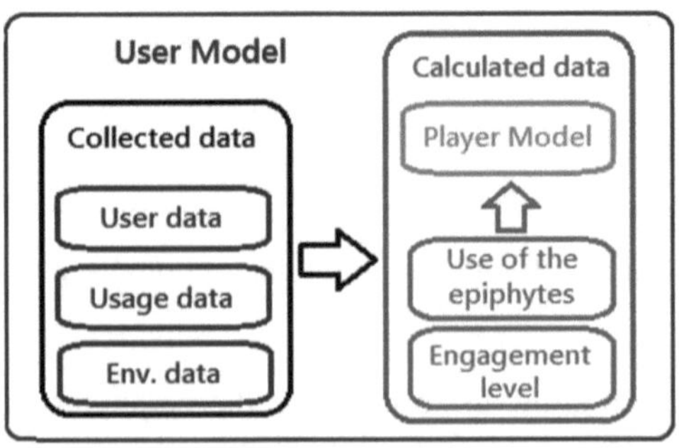

Fig. 5. Overview of the collected and calculated data in the user model.

4.2 Player Model for Adaptive Gamification

In Sect. 2.2 we explained why we chose to base our model on the classification of Ferro *et al.* [9]. The list of its motivational factors is presented in Table 2.

When a new user registers on the learning environment, the values of each motivational factor are initialized for him/her according to user data (see Sect. 4.3.1). During the use of the learning environment, the values will change according to the user's interactions (see Sect. 4.3.2).

In addition, each epiphytic functionality also has a list of values associated with the motivational factors. Table 3 provides an example of such association.

These values are necessary to choose the adequate functionality when we know the user's player profile.

Table 2. Player classification of Ferro.

Classification	Examples of game elements
Dominant	Characters, conflicts
Objectivist	Objectives, challenge
Humanist	Story/Narrative, dramatic art
Inquisitive	Aesthetics, boundaries
Creative	Resources, world building

Table 3. Example of values associating the epiphyte "leader board" to the motivational factors.

Leader board	
Dominant	100 %
Objectivist	40 %
Humanist	20 %
Inquisitive	0 %
Creative	0 %

4.3 Data for Gamification Adaptation

The three types of data we use for adaptation [20] are based on the state of the art presented in part 2.3.

4.3.1 User Data

The user data we use for adaptation are:

- Birth date
- Gender

These data are static, but they have an influence on the initial values of the player model. Adaptation rules can be extracted from our knowledge on the influence of these data, and these adaptation rules can be used to set better values for the player model of new users (see Table 4 for examples).

Table 4. Examples of adaptation to user data.

Tom is a man. When he registers on the learning environment, his value for the motivational factor "competition" is set at 60 %, instead of 40 % for a woman	Nadia is 62 years old. When she registers on the learning environment, we set a limit of 2 epiphytes activated at the same time

4.3.2 Usage Data

We need to track the user's interactions with both the gamification layer and the learning environment, to evaluate the level of engagement.

Concerning the tracking of the epiphytic functionalities, we can assume that the more a functionality is used, the more the player is sensitive to the motivational factor associated with this functionality (Table 5).

As some functionalities do not require direct interactions, the system has to find a correlation between the activation of the functionalities and the engagement of the learner. A functionality is effective if it is correlated with a high engagement (Table 6).

Our way of calculating engagement and disengagement is detailed in Sect. 4.4.

Table 5. Examples of adaptation to the use of epiphytes.

Tom is now able to publish on a social network when he finished a learning session. He uses this functionality many times. Accordingly, his value for the motivational factor "social" increases	The button for sharing activity on social networks has been introduced in Nadia's interface. She turned it off after one minute. Accordingly, her value for the motivational factor "social" decreases

Table 6. Examples of adaptation to the engagement level.

The leader board was added in Tom's environment, but no difference was observed in his behavior. His value for the motivational factor "competition" decreases	Since the leader board was added in Nadia's environment, she is connected more often and makes more exercises to raise her score. Her value for the motivational factor "competition" increases

4.3.3 Environment Data

In addition, some contextual information are crucial for the gamification engine. Firstly, it is useful to know if the learner is at school, at work, or on free time, as this context has an influence about how people learn.

We are also interested in the device used by the player. In the cloud computing domain, various learning environments are available on mobile devices as on computers, but all features are not necessary relevant or available on any device (e.g. because of the screen size) (Table 7).

Finally, the environment data used for adaptation are:

- Device used.
- Learning context (school, work or personal).
- Size of the group (if school or work).

Table 7. Examples of adaptation to environment data.

Tom learns at school in the computer room with his other classmates. Accordingly, a chat feature would be useless because he speaks directly with them	Nadia, whose motivational factor "competition" is high, sometimes learns on her smartphone. Accordingly, we can propose her to compete with players locally near from her

4.4 Engagement Tracking

We have access to one information directly indicating engagement: the session dates. A user who connected very often and for a long time can be considered as more engaged in the activity than others. However, this allows us to know the general engagement but not to compare the engagement level at two distinct times. That is why we need another way to track the real time engagement. We use two metrics:

- Too short time to read texts and to answer questions, based on engagement tracing [29].
- Too long time to read or answer questions.

4.5 Adaptation Process

The role of the adaptation engine is to find the most relevant gaming feature for a user, according to the player model. The gaming features are represented by a vector with values between 0 and 1. For instance, the leaderboard vector could be [dominant 1, objectivist 0.4, humanist 0.2, inquisitive 0, creative 0] (Fig. 3). The users are represented in the same way. Indeed, users are generally interested in more than one game mechanic.

When gaming features have been designed, the values for their player types vector are set according to the game mechanics they implement. When new users register, the values for their vector are set to 0.5 for the five player types. Unlike the game mechanics vector, the player types vector is dynamic: it changes according to the user's interactions with the system. The main adaptation rules for updating the player model are:

- If users disable a feature, their values for the corresponding player types decrease.
- If users interact often with a gaming feature, their values for the corresponding player types increase.

When enabling a gaming feature, the adaptation engine applies this algorithm:

1. Making the list of gaming features that were not enabled yet for this user.
2. Calculating a relevance score for each feature, based on the distance between the player vector and the gaming feature vector.
3. Selecting the feature randomly, by using the relevance scores as odds ratio.

When a user is new, all the relevance scores are closed to 0.5. Thus, the gaming features are selected almost randomly. After some time the player types vector becomes more accurate with high and low values, and some features are more likely to get a high relevance score and to be selected.

Finally, as the epiphytes may induce interactions between users, this engine has to "*take in account the collaborative aspect and heterogeneity between players, while maintaining the overall coherence of the game*" [33]. That is why the adaptation engine checks if several users of the group are interested in competing before activating multi-player functionalities.

5 Conclusions and Discussion

In this paper, we proposed the architecture of a system to motivate learners by integrating game elements in existing web-based learning environments. This system is both generic and adaptive.

The genericity is based on the use of game elements as epiphytic functionalities, which does not affect the host environment when integrated in the user interface.

The adaptivity is based on a player model that defines the player type matching best with the user. The adaptation process has four steps:

1. Tracing data from the learning environment and the game elements.
2. Evaluating the engagement level of the user.
3. Updating the player model, based on adaptation rules, using basic data about the user, data from the use of the environment, and data describing the learning context.
4. Integrating within the user interface the epiphyte matching best with the player model.

This system is not designed with the goal to turn every learning activity into a game, because games need to be played voluntary and people in some contexts are already motivated to learn. Adaptive gamification should be used with non-intrinsically motivating activities, like memorizing vocabulary or mathematical rules.

Despite this system has not been tested yet, it addresses three lacks in the literature and existing software:

- It proposes the adaptation of game dynamics, whereas existing systems (e.g. [34]) adapt the learning path and difficulty level.
- It deals with adaptation of gamification, whereas the literature deals more with adaptation of games.
- It proposes the adaptation of multiplayer features, whereas existing environments propose the same game elements for all the users.

6 Future Works

We plan various evaluations and improvements for the system. Regarding the evaluations, we are currently implementing the system, which will be plugged on "Projet Voltaire", a web-based environment to learn French spelling. For the next step, we will plug the gamification system on other learning environments, in order to evaluate its genericity.

An experiment will allow us to evaluate the system described in this paper. For instance, we plan to compare the automatic adaptation with the "home made" adaptation: what happens if the user can choose the new functionalities by himself? In order to evaluate the gamification adaptation to users' profiles, we plan to compare three cases:

- Case 1: Selecting game elements according to user's profile.
- Case 2: Selecting game elements randomly.
- Case 3: Selecting game elements at the opposite of user's profile.

In this way, we will be able to evaluate the relevance of the proposed adaptation (case 1).

Furthermore, some improvements will concern the flexibility of the player model. Sometimes, the player type is not enough to model the user's needs, as they can change during the day. As an example, two motivational factors of [35] are detailed bellow:

- Hard fun (Players look for challenge, strategy and problem solving).
- Easy fun (Players enjoy intrigue and curiosity).

Whether we expect to relax (easy fun) or to be challenged (hard fun) depends more on our mood than our personality and player type. Some contextual information can help to know about this mood, like the hour and the day. For example, a user may expect a more relaxing activity after lunch. Furthermore, expert systems are limited as they are static. Another improvement we plan to do is the use of machine learning techniques to automatically adapt the adaptation rules themselves, based on the experience with the previous users.

Acknowledgements. The work is supported by a CIFRE fellowship funded in part by ANRT (National Association for Research and Technology) on the behalf of the French Ministry of Higher Education and Research, and in part by Woonoz company.

References

1. Zichermann, G., Cunningham, C.: Gamification by Design: Implementing Game Mechanics in Web and Mobile Apps. O'Reilly Media Inc., Sebastopol (2011)
2. Deterding, S., Dixon, D., Khaled, R., Nacke, L.: From game design elements to gamefulness: defining gamification. In: Proceedings of the 15th International Academic MindTrek Conference: Envisioning Future Media Environments, pp. 9–15 (2011)
3. Mozilla OpenBadges. http://www.openbadges.org/
4. Maciuszek, D., Ruddeck, G., Martens, A.: Component-based development of educational games: the case of the user interface. In: Proceedings of the 4th European Conference on Games-based Learning (ECGBL 2010), Reading, UK, pp. 208–217 (2010)
5. Yee, N.: Motivations for play in online games. Cyberpsychol. Behav. **9**, 772–775 (2006)
6. Andrade, G., Ramalho, G., Gomes, A.S., Corruble, V.: Dynamic game balancing: an evaluation of user satisfaction. In: Artificial Intelligence and Interactive Digital Entertainment (AIIDE), vol. 1, pp. 3–8 (2006)

7. Marne, B., Carron, T., Labat, J.-M., Marfisi-Schottman, I.: MoPPLiq: a model for pedagogical adaptation of serious game scenarios. In: 2013 IEEE 13th International Conference on Advanced Learning Technologies (ICALT), pp. 291–293 (2013)
8. Conati, C., Manske, M.: Evaluating adaptive feedback in an educational computer game. In: Ruttkay, Z., Kipp, M., Nijholt, A., Vilhjálmsson, H.H. (eds.) IVA 2009. LNCS, vol. 5773, pp. 146–158. Springer, Heidelberg (2009)
9. Ferro, L.S., Walz, S.P., Greuter, S.: Towards personalised, gamified systems: an investigation into game design, personality and player typologies. In: Proceedings of the 9th Australasian Conference on Interactive Entertainment: Matters of Life and Death, p. 7 (2013)
10. Hocine, N., Gouaïche, A., Di Loreto, I., Abrouk, L.: Techniques d′adaptation dans les jeux ludiques et sérieux. Rev. Intell. Artif. **25**, 253–280 (2011)
11. Prensky, M.: Digital Game-Based Learning. McGraw-Hill, New York (2001)
12. Monterrat, B., Lavoué, E., George, S., others: Toward personalised gamification for learning environments. In: 4th Workshop on Motivational and Affective Aspects in Technology Enhanced Learning (MATEL 2013) in conjunction with EC-TEL 2013 (2013)
13. Togelius, J., De Nardi, R., Lucas, S.M.: Towards automatic personalised content creation for racing games. In: IEEE Symposium on Computational Intelligence and Games, 2007. CIG 2007, pp. 252–259 (2007)
14. Pedersen, C., Togelius, J., Yannakakis, G.N.: Modeling player experience for content creation. IEEE Trans. Comput. Intell. AI Games **2**, 54–67 (2010)
15. Natkin, S., Yan, C., Jumpertz, S., Market, B.: Creating multiplayer ubiquitous fames using an adaptive narration model based on a user's model. In: Digital Games Research Association International Conference (DiGRA 2007) (2007)
16. Brusilovsky, P.: Adaptive Hypermedia (2001)
17. Bartle: Richard A. Bartle: Players Who Suit MUDs. http://www.mud.co.uk/richard/hcds.htm#1
18. Kotaku: They've narrowed gamers down to eight fundamental types. Which are you?. http://kotaku.com/5938464/theyve-narrowed-gamers-down-to-eight-fundamental-types-which-are-you
19. A new perspective on the Bartle player types for gamification – GCo. http://www.gamification.co/2013/08/12/a-new-perspective-on-the-bartle-player-types-for-gamification/
20. Kobsa, A., Koenemann, J., Pohl, W.: Personalised hypermedia presentation techniques for improving online customer relationships. Knowl. Eng. Rev. **16**, 111 (2001)
21. Charlier, N., Michela, O., Remmele, B., Whitton, N.: Not just for children: game-based learning for older adults. In: 6th European Conference on Games Based Learning, Cork, Ireland, pp. 102–108 (2012)
22. Eglesz*, D., Fekete, I., Kiss, O.E., Izso, L.: Computer games are fun? On professional games and players' motivations. Educ. Media Int. **42**, 117–124 (2005)
23. Poel, M., Heylen, D., Nijholt, A., Trappl, R., others: Emotion based agent architectures for tutoring systems: the INES architecture (2004)
24. Bernardini, A., Conati, C.: Discovering and recognizing student interaction patterns in exploratory learning environments. In: Aleven, V., Kay, J., Mostow, J. (eds.) ITS 2010, Part I. LNCS, vol. 6094, pp. 125–134. Springer, Heidelberg (2010)
25. de Vicente, A., Pain, H.: Informing the detection of the students' motivational state: an empirical study. In: Cerri, S.A., Gouardères, G., Paraguaçu, F. (eds.) ITS 2002. LNCS, vol. 2363, pp. 933–943. Springer, Heidelberg (2002)

26. Bouvier, P., Lavoué, E., Sehaba, K., George, S.: Identifying learner's engagement in learning games: a qualitative approach based on learner's traces of interaction. In: 5th International Conference on Computer Supported Education (CSEDU 2013), Aachen, Germany, pp. 6–8 (2013)
27. Mattheiss, E., Kickmeier-Rust, M.D., Steiner, C.M., Albert, D.: Approaches to detect discouraged learners: assessment of motivation in educational computer games. Proceedings of ELearning Baltimore ELBa 10 (2010)
28. Cocea, M.: Assessment of motivation in online learning environments. In: Wade, V.P., Ashman, H., Smyth, B. (eds.) AH 2006. LNCS, vol. 4018, pp. 414–418. Springer, Heidelberg (2006)
29. Beck, J.: Engagement tracing: using response times to model student disengagement. Artif. Intell. Educ. Support. Learn. Intell. Socially Inf. Technol. **125**, 88 (2005)
30. Cheng, L.-T., Shami, S., Casey, D., Muller, M., DiMicco, J., Patterson, J., others: Finding moments of play at work. In: CHI 2011 Workshop (2–5). Vancouver, Canada (2011)
31. Sanchez, E.: A Game in the Classroom, What did the Students Learn?. ESERA, Lyon (2011)
32. Giroux, S., Pachet, F., Paquette, G., Girard, J.: Des systèmes conseillers épiphytes. Rev. Intell. Artif. **9**, 165–190 (1995)
33. Hocine, N., Gouaïch, A.: Therapeutic games' difficulty adaptation: an approach based on player's ability and motivation. In: 2011 16th International Conference on Computer Games (CGAMES), pp. 257–261. IEEE (2011)
34. Khan Academy. http://www.khanacademy.org
35. Lazzaro, N.: Why we play games: four keys to more emotion without story (2004)

Comparing Multiple-Choice and Constructed Response Questions Applied to Engineering Courses

Dimos Triantis, Errikos Ventouras, Ioanna Leraki, Charalampos Stergiopoulos, Ilias Stavrakas, and George Hloupis(✉)

E-learning Support Team, Technological Educational Institute of Athens, Ag. Spyridonos, Egaleo, Athens, Greece
{triantis,ericvent,leraki,csterg,ilias,hloupis}@teiath.gr

Abstract. A study was performed on the comparison of multiple-choice questions (MCQs) and constructed-response questions (CRQs) in terms of objective grading. A CRQ exam is graded by a tutor though an MCQ is automatically graded. An MCQs drawback is the infiltration of the "guessing" factor during selection thus producing unreliable results that do not reflect students' knowledge. To eliminate this problem MCQs pairs were composed that addressed the same topic. A student who did not possess adequate knowledge could not tell this similarity. A group of undergraduate students enrolled to the "project management" module were examined. A software for electronic examinations was used during the process. A statistical evaluation was performed in order to check whether there was statistically significant difference between the scores provided using CRQs and MCQs. By applying a suitable scoring rule to the MCQs, very similar results are obtained when compared to those of the CRQs examination.

Keywords: Assessment methodologies · Computer-aided examination methods · Evaluation algorithms · Undergraduate engineering modules · Scoring rules · Multiple choice questions · Constructed response questions

1 Introduction

Information Technology can nowadays provide a wide range of tools both software and hardware that enhance the educational process by supporting the production of digital polymorphic content [1–3]. The penetration and incorporation of such tools in the modern academic learning practice has been widely accepted since many years [4] and can essentially contribute to the enrichment of the traditional examination and assessment methods of students by the use of computer aided systems and the introduction of innovative examination techniques [5].

Multiple Choice Question (MCQs) tests belong to the category of objective evaluation methods as the score for each question is predefined and can be rapidly calculated thus relieving the examiner of deciding the grade. Moreover, it does not depend upon the examinee's writing skills (i.e. writing speed etc.) [6–8]. The time efficiency, combined with the objectivity in terms of grading, enables the provision of prompt feedback to the examinee, at the end of the examination. The overall score and other

S. Zvacek et al. (Eds.): CSEDU 2014, CCIS 510, pp. 130–140, 2015.
DOI: 10.1007/978-3-319-25768-6_9

useful information such as correct and incorrect answers are available in a form of a report.

A significant problem of the MCQs is the infiltration of the “guessing” factor whenever the student has to select one of the potential answers. The usual method is to apply a simple grading rule based on adding points to the overall score if a question is correctly answered without losing any for the incorrect ones. This way a part of the points collected, at the end of the examination may be based on guessing or sheer luck and do not objectively reflect the student’s knowledge status. A potential solution to this problem can be the application of special grading rules that may include a penalty (i.e. subtraction of points) in case of wrong answer [8]. Such practices can affect the students’ behavior and mislead them in terms of decision making. Their uncertainty will eventually generate variance regarding the test scores which is related to the expectations of the examinees and not to the knowledge that is tested [9, 10].

One of the widely used examination methods include sets of constructed-response questions (CRQs). The examinee is requested to provide an answer in a form of short text or essay which is evaluated and graded by the examiner. Previous works exhibit that MCQs can be used for validate knowledge if properly constructed and set when compared to the ones that form CRQs while, at the same time, are highly reliable [11–13]. There are two works [14, 15] that compare the results extracted by using both methods (CRQs and MCQs) that are statistically identical when using a special grading rule applied to the MCQs examination. Another work [16] compares oral examination and MCQs examination using the same special grading rule. The modules that the method was applied were core undergraduate engineering courses. The reason was that the students who complete these courses must be objectively evaluated in order to identify any potential gaps in their knowledge that may affect their further studies. A MCQ examination method is based on the formulation of questions in pairs. Every pair that belongs to the set addresses the same topic in a way a student who does not possess adequate knowledge and is not well prepared cannot detect this similarity. A cumulative grade for the pair is calculated by adding bonus points if both questions are correctly answered or by subtracting points as a penalty if only one question of the pair is correctly answered. The aim of that scoring rule is to penalize guessing, in a way that might not positively induce the dissuading effects mentioned above, which are related to the negative marking part of the commonly used mixed-scoring schemes.

The aim of the present work is to further investigate the similarity of results when applying both methods in another engineering course and exploit the possibilities offered by the use of IT in the educational process. An objective of this work is to demonstrate the use MCQs examination methods either in parallel or by substituting CRQ tests that is difficult to be supported by IT.

This study belongs to an ongoing research framework regarding assessment methods and parameters that can be potentially used as indices of reliability and validity markers when performing an examination. Existed studies conclude lead to substantial indications that MCQ provide higher reliability in terms of scoring and their results are as valid as the ones provided by CRQ examinations [11–13]. These indications help promoting the use of MCQ tests in most educational settings where CRQ ones is the preferable examination method. The drawback of the CRQs examination is that the topics examined cannot cover a significant amount of the material taught during the course. Moreover there is an inherent inability of introducing automated grading in essay-like responses to questions. Concerning the interest and motivation of engineering students to use new technological tools as part of their educational process an electronic examination will provide immediate results and could be an essential enhancement in the context of a larger effort already began in the Technological Education Institute of Athens of introducing computer aided and web tools for supporting teaching. This fact requires research and well defined methods for creating objective assessment methods.

2 Examined Course and Sample of Students

During the academic period 2012–2013, a course entitled "Project Management" was selected for applying both examination methods (MCQs and CRQs). The course belongs to the group of supplementary engineering courses taught in the Department of Electronics hosted by the Technological Educational Institute (T.E.I.) of Athens. A group of 37 students were enrolled to this course and participated in both examinations. All students had completed the course and polymorphic material (notes, videos, etc.) in digital format had been provided to them. Moreover, they were familiarized with the electronic examination platform which would be used for both examinations. During the CRQs examination the students had to type their answer into the appropriate text field. For the case of MCQs examination the students had to answer the question by clicking one of the possible answers. The examination took place in a PC laboratory room using an application called "e-examination". This application had been implemented in an effort to introduce at the T.E.I. of Athens proper learning management systems (LMS) and tools to support the educational process [5, 17]. At the end of the MCQs test an electronic report was produced for each student. This report included all questions with the correct answer and the indication of whether it was correctly or wrongly answered, as well as the final score. One copy was given to the student and one to the examiner, for processing the scores.

For the CRQs examination, a set of twenty (20) questions was created. The distribution of CRQs was designed in a way that they covered all topics taught during the course. Their difficulty level varied and a special weight in terms of grading was appointed to each one according to the level of difficulty. The total score that a student could achieve was 100 points.

For constructing the MCQs examination the questions were selected by a database that contained a large number ($N = 300$) of questions which also addressed all the topics taught during the course. By using a special software, a first set of MCQs $\{q_{a1}, q_{a2}, \ldots, q_{ak}\}$ ($k = 20$) was randomly selected from the database. Once again, a weight w_{ai} was assigned to each question $i = 1, \ldots, k$, depending on its level of difficulty. In order to form 20 pairs of questions, another set was selected from the same database $\{q_{b1}, q_{b2}, \ldots, q_{bk}\}$ ($k = 20$). Each pair addressed the same topic and the knowledge of the correct answer for question q_{ai}, from a student who had performed a thorough study implied the knowledge of the correct answer for q_{bi} and vice versa. The total score that a student could achieve was 100 points. The examiners took special care that both examinations were of the same level of difficulty in order that the results could be comparable. During this examination all questions form pairs in order to apply the scoring rules in all the set and trying to eliminate the guessing factor from each and every one of the questions addressed by the students.

3 Scoring Methodology

As mentioned above, the CRQ's examination included twenty questions. Each question corresponded to a certain grade according to its difficulty. The way that the student answered the question was evaluated by the teacher. The overall examination score *m1* was extracted, as the sum of the partial grades, and was by definition normalized to a maximum value of 100. The MCQs final score was calculated as follows:

For each MCQs pair i = 1, …, 20, the "paired" partial score p_i is:

$$p_i = (q_{ai}w_{ai} + q_{bi}w_{bi})(1 + k_{bonus}) \tag{1}$$

if both q_{ai} and q_{bi} were correct ($q_{ai} = q_{bi} = 1$) or

$$p_i = (q_{ai}w_{ai} + q_{bi}w_{bi})(1 - k_{penalty}) \tag{2}$$

if q_{ai} or q_{bi} was correct ($q_{ai} = 1$ and $q_{bi} = 0$, or $q_{ai} = 0$ and $q_{bi} = 1$).

$$p_i = 0 \tag{3}$$

if both q_{ai} and q_{bi} were incorrect, in which case $q_{ai} = q_{bi} = 0$.

The parameters k_{bonus} and $k_{penalty}$ were used for the calibration of the bonus/penalty mechanism applied to the scoring rule. For most pairs, the questions of the pair had the same weight ($w_{ai} = w_{bi}$). In some cases though, the weight of the two paired questions was slightly different (i.e., by 0.5) because it is not always possible to create a pair of questions that referred to the same topic, had the same level of difficulty and the knowledge of the correct answer for question q_{ai}, by a well prepared student implied the knowledge of the correct answer for q_{bi} and vice versa. The total score *m2*, with maximum value equal to 100, was then computed as:

$$m2 = \frac{\sum_{i=1}^{20} p_i}{(1 + k_{bonus}) \cdot \sum_{i=1}^{20} (w_{ai} + w_{bi})} \tag{4}$$

Therefore, for the calculation of score *m2*, a bonus is given to the student that correctly answered both questions of the pair (q_{ai}, q_{bi}) and a penalty if only one question of the pair was correctly answered. In the case that a student left a question intentionally unanswered or the time of examination was expired, a penalty will be applied accordingly. The final score corresponds to the paired MCQs examination method when using the above mentioned algorithm.

A classic scoring rule was also applied to the same group of questions. If a student found the correct answer the points that corresponded to this question were added to the overall score. Otherwise, in case of a wrong answer, no points were added. This method intentionally ignores any relation existed between the questions of a pair. Moreover, no penalty or bonus was considered during the scoring process. The overall score (*m3*) for this method was calculated using the following equation:

$$m3 = \frac{\sum_{i=1}^{20} (q_{ai}w_{ai} + q_{bi}w_{bi})}{\sum_{i=1}^{20} (w_{ai} + w_{bi})} \quad (5)$$

The weights (w) as well as the points assigned to each question in case of a correct answer remained the same. Equation (5) is a special case of Eq. (4) when k is omitted.

4 Validity Threats

Validity is the most important characteristic of assessment data. The most important threats to the validity of the study are discussed below:

The issue of poorly crafted questions is very significant. Constructing effective MCQs and CRQs that properly correspond to certain knowledge is a demanded task. The teacher should be able to create sets of questions comprised of the MCQ type supported by the application. This depends on the structure of the course and the nature of the examination topics. The challenge in our case was to fragmentise big problems and exercises into MCQs covering at the same time a wide range of topics. The questions were categorized into groups of different difficulty levels. The process was based on previous experience in organizing and conducting electronic examinations for the specific course [15]. The teachers of the course had taken special care during the construction of the questions in order to create sets that could not easily answered by guessing. In any case the "paired questions" concept also contributed to the solution of this issue.

Some potential testing irregularities could be that the students had prior knowledge of the questions or the performance of unethical actions (i.e. cheating) during the examination. Such kind of actions if not anticipated could severely affect the score. The students of the specific department were more or less accustomed to new technologies and the use of computers. They were also familiar with the concept of MCQs examined electronically and they had access to sample MCQs tests for self-evaluation purposes. These questions were not part of the current examination. Moreover, the software package used for the electronic examination had the feature to present to each student's monitor the set of the questions along with their corresponding answers in random order. This way any attempt of cheating or communication among the examinees was immediately become apparent to the supervisor.

Test Item Bias refers to the fairness of the test item for different groups of students. In case that the test item is biased different group of students have different probabilities of correctly responding. For the purposes of the current study the same group of students took part in both examinations which were constructed and controlled by experienced teachers.

5 Results and Discussion

In the present study the effects of changing the value of parameter k were investigated. Regarding MCQs examination Eq. (5) was initially used for the calculation of the MCQs examination results. This equation corresponds to the classic scoring rule meaning that no bonus nor penalty points were taken into consideration. This simplified scoring rule produced results that were higher than the ones produced by the CRQs examination. Apart from the top scores that well-prepared students achieved and did not present significant differences, all other scores presented a deviation. A possible explanation could be the absence of a mechanism that fixed the "guessing" factor when answering the questions. In Fig. 1 the regression line of score (*m1*) to score (*m3*) is shown. The fitting is based on a second degree polynomial. It is observed that most students' scores are above the bisector (Fig. 1). A fit for the score can be quantified using parameter R^2 which is related to the regression line of CRQ score of each student (*m1*) to the MCQ score (*m3*) of the same student. Its best possible value is 1. The value of R^2 for this case is equal to 0.9554.

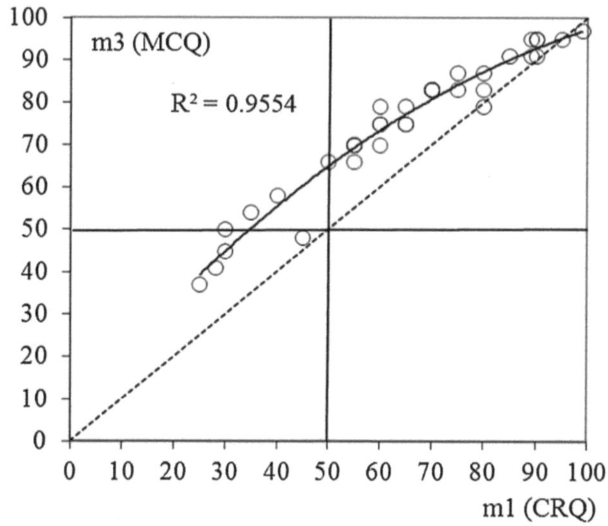

Fig. 1. Regression line of CRQ score of each student (*m1*) to the MCQ score (*m3*).

It must be noted that in order to have comparable results, students had been informed that incorrect answers did not have any additional penalty in terms of negative marking. This way they were encouraged to attempt answering any questions that might have a rough knowledge on the topic. During this examination the students were not aware of the scoring rule based on paired questions as this knowledge might be a factor affecting decision making under uncertainty. In turn, this might produce variance in the test scores that is related to the expectations of the examinees and not to the knowledge that is tested [9, 10]. The final report produced by the system included only the scores calculated based on the classic scoring rule, meaning that no bonus or penalty points were taken into consideration (*m3*).

The bias that is probably caused by the "guessing" factor is clearly corrected when using the scoring rule of paired questions. This is shown in Fig. 2 if the regression line is compared to the one shown in Fig. 1. An attempt to find the optimal values was made in order to have a better fit of the scores achieved by the examinees during both examination methods. For this case the k_{bonus} and $k_{penalty}$ parameters were considered as one (k) and the same value was assigned. This value was added to the score if the student correctly answered both questions of the pair or subtracted if the student failed to answer one question of the pair. The results produced by the system were only available for the examiners in order to perform the research. In Table 1 the results using CRQs and MCQs with paired questions are shown. For the MCQs examination method different values of k parameter were set when calculating the overall score of each student using Eq. (4).

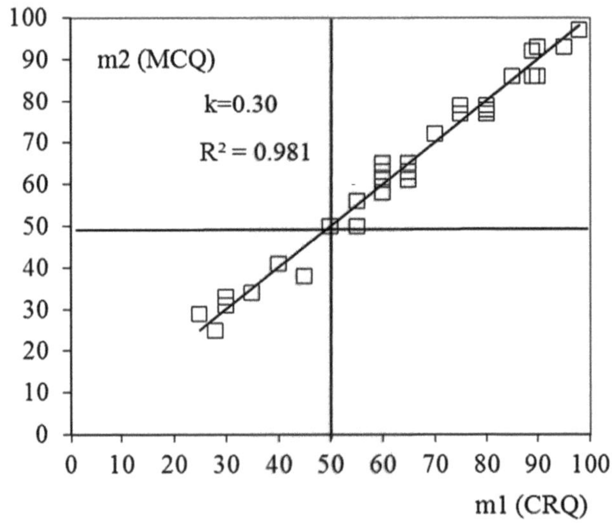

Fig. 2. Regression line of CRQ score of each student (*m1*) to the MCQ score (*m2*).

It is shown that for the parameter $k = k_{bonus} = k_{penalty} = 0.30$ the mean value of the distribution of scores calculated for the MCQ method is very close to the mean value of the distribution of scores of the CRQ method. This is in agreement with the results of previous electronic examinations using the Bonus/penalty scoring methodology [14].

Table 1. Results of the examination methods.

CRQ method	MCQ method (paired questions)				
	k = 0.26	k = 0.28	k = 0.30	k = 0.32	k = 0.34
64.97	65.50	65.14	65.20	64.70	64.41

A statistical evaluation was performed in order to check whether there was statistically significant difference between the scores provided using CRQs *(m1)*, paired MCQs *(m2)*, using the paired MCQ results for k = 0.3, and MCQ without bonus-penalty *(m3)*. The Kolmogorov-Smirnov goodness-of-fit test showed that the distributions of the scores *m1*, *m2* and *m3* were consistent with a normal distribution. Repeated-measures analysis of variance (ANOVA), with one within-subjects factor (method of examination, three levels) indicated that the within-subject effect was significant ($F1.020,36.731 = 6.938$, $p = 0.012$, degrees of freedom were corrected for non-sphericity according to the Greenhouse-Geisser procedure). Therefore, the hypothesis that the overall differences between the means of the scores m1, m2 and m3 are not significant, has to be rejected at $p = 0.012$ level of significance. ANOVA was followed by planned comparisons between each of the examination methods, assessed with post-hoc Bonferroni pair wise comparisons at 0.05 level of significance. Significant differences existed between *m1* and *m3* ($p = 0.031$) and between *m2* and *m3* ($p = 0.042$). Therefore the secondary hypotheses that the difference between the means of the scores *m1* and *m3* is not significant had to be rejected at $p = 0.031$ level of significance and the secondary hypotheses that the difference between the means of the scores m2 and m3 is not significant had to be rejected at $p = 0.042$ level of significance. The same statistical results were obtained when the repeated-measures ANOVA tests were performed using the paired MCQ results for the other values of k that were investigated in the present study. On the other hand, when repeated-measures ANOVA tests were performed for the results obtained using paired MCQ, with one within-subjects factor (k variable, five

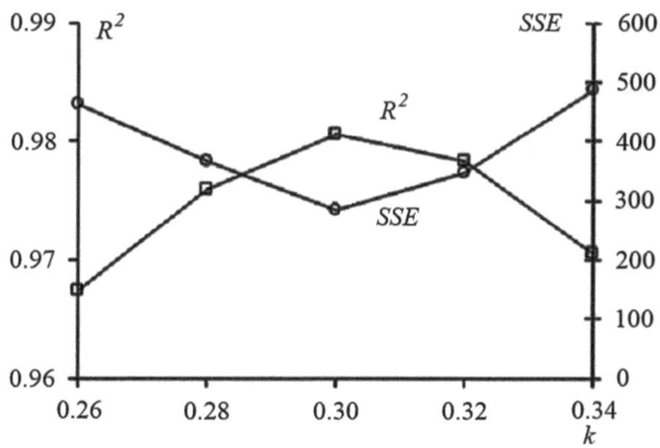

Fig. 3. Sum of squared differences of *m1* and *m2* as related to *k* parameter. R^2 related to *k* parameter.

levels) they indicated that the within-subject effect was not significant ($F2.625,94.492 = 1.360$, $p = 0.261$, degrees of freedom were corrected for non-sphericity according to the Greenhouse-Geisser procedure). These results indicate that the variation of k, to the range and values checked in the present study, does not influence the results of the paired MCQ method in a statistically significant way.

Further research and more examination results of various courses are required in order to evaluate the optimized value parameter k which seems to be approximately equal to 0.3. A fit for the score can be quantified using parameter R^2 which is related to the regression line of CRQ score of each student (*m1*) to the MCQ score (*m2*) of the same student. Its best possible value is 1. In Fig. 2 the regression line of score (*m1*) to score (*m2*) are presented for $k = 0.30$. It is observed that R^2 remained at a high level (>0.98) close to a value equal to 1 for $0.30 \leq k \leq 0.34$. A metric related to the variation of the k parameter value is the sum of the squared differences of the students' scores during MCQs (paired questions) and CRQs examination. The sum of squared error (SSE) is calculated by the following equation:

$$SSE = \sum_{j=1}^{37} (m1_j - m2_j)^2 \tag{6}$$

The optimum value that the sum could have reached was zero. In Fig. 3 it is shown that the function of sum to parameter k is smoothly varying within the space of $k = 0.26$ and $k = 0.34$ having a minimum at $k = 0.30$. This value of k parameter is the optimum one to apply to the scoring rule. In the same figure the relation of R^2 to parameter k is also shown. It is observed that the maximum value of R^2 was also found for $k = 0.3$. This value which seems to be the optimal one and has been also observed during the implementation of this method to other modules already published [14, 15] and optimises the students' overall score in a way that they objectively reflect their level of knowledge.

6 Conclusions

Electronic examinations supported by special software tools are very helpful for the educational process as they provide the means for the automatic production of the results and the ability to easily apply different scoring rules. This way the lecturer can have a clear image of the results which may be used for optimizing the way of teaching and disseminated material.

During the comparison of the CRQs examination method and the MCQs examination method it was observed that the classic scoring rule of positive score for correct answers introduced a bias due to the failure of eliminating the "guessing" factor, a common phenomenon of MCQs examinations. Therefore, such a simple scoring rule cannot advance MCQs examination for potentially substituting a CQRs examination method. Nevertheless, by applying a scoring rule that introduces the use of a special parameter that its value is added or subtracted to the overall score according to the correct or wrong answers along with the concept of pairs of questions addressed the same topic, can give results that are very close to the ones produced by the CQRs method. To the extent of the results of the present study, indication is provided that a value of k parameter approximately equal to 0.3 can optimally give results that clearly and objectively reflect the level of student's knowledge.

The key factor for applying this rule is a thorough preparation of the questions from the examiner in such a way that they cover all topics of interest and can form pairs in a way that their relation to a specific topic will not be evident to a student that is not well prepared.

Part of future work will be the research on results when assigning different values to k_{bonus} and $k_{penalty}$ parameters, respectively. During this research an algorithm might also designed for enhancing the electronic examination application by automatically selecting the optimized value of *k* parameter. The scoring rule has to be tested in other modules as well in order to further verify its usefulness as an objective evaluation tool.

References

1. Reiser, R.A., Dempsey, J.V.: Trends and Issues in Instructional Design and Technology. Pearson, London (2011)
2. Dede, C.: Planning for neomillennial learning styles. Educause Q. **28**(1), 7–12 (2005)
3. Friedl, R., Höppler, H., Ecard, K., Scholz, W., Hannekum, A., Öchsner, W., Stracke, S.: Multimedia driven teaching significantly improves students' performance when compared with a print medium. Ann. Thorac. Surg. **81**(5), 1760–1766 (2006)
4. DeBord, K.A., Aruguete, M.S., Muhlig, J.: Are computer-assisted teaching methods effective? Teach. Psychol. **31**(1), 65–68 (2004)
5. Tsiakas, P., Stergiopoulos, C., Nafpaktitis, D., Triantis, D., Stavrakas, I.: Computer as a tool in teaching, examining and assessing electronic engineering students. In: International Conference on "Computer as a Tool", pp. 2490–2497 (2007)
6. Bush, M.E.: Quality assurance of multiple-choice tests. Qual. Assur. Educ. **14**(4), 398–404 (2006)
7. Freeman, R., Lewis, R.: Planning and Implementing Assessment. Routledge, London (1998)
8. Scharf, E.M., Baldwin, L.P.: Assessing multiple choice question (MCQ) tests-a mathematical perspective. Act. Learn. High Educ. **8**(1), 31–47 (2007)
9. Bereby-Meyer, Y., Meyer, J., Flascher, O.M.: Prospect theory analysis of guessing in multiple choice tests. J. Behav. Decis. Mak. **15**(4), 313–327 (2002)
10. Bereby-Meyer, Y., Meyer, J., Budescu, D.V.: Decision making under internal uncertainty: the case of multiple-choice tests with different scoring rules. Acta Psychol. **11**(2), 207–220 (2003)
11. Lukhele, R., Thissen, D., Wainer, H.: On the relative value of multiple-choice, constructed response, and examinee-selected items on two achievement tests. J. Educ. Measur. **31**(3), 234–250 (1994)
12. Wainer, H., Thissen, D.: Combining multiple choice and constructed-response test scores: toward a Marxist theory of test construction. Appl. Measur. Educ. **6**(2), 103–118 (1993)
13. Wainer, H., Thissen, D.: True score theory: the traditional method. In: Thissen, D., Wainer, H. (eds.) Test Scoring, pp. 23–72. Routledge, London (2001)
14. Triantis, D., Ventouras, E.: Enhancing electronic examinations through advanced multiple-choice questionnaires. In: Babo, R., Azevedo, A. (eds.) Higher Education Institutions and Learning Management Systems: Adoption and Standardization, pp. 178–198. IGI Global, Hershey (2011)

15. Ventouras, E., Triantis, D., Tsiakas, P., Stergiopoulos, C.: Comparison of examination methods based on multiple-choice questions and constructed-response questions using personal computers. J. Comput. Educ. **54**(2), 455–461 (2010)
16. Ventouras, E., Triantis, D., Tsiakas, P., Stergiopoulos, C.: Comparison of oral examination and electronic examination using paired multiple-choice questions. J. Comput. Educ. **56**(3), 616–624 (2011)
17. Stergiopoulos, C., Tsiakas, P., Triantis, D., Kaitsa, M.: Evaluating electronic examination methods applied to students of electronics. Effectiveness and comparison to the paper-and-pencil method. In: IEEE International Conference on Sensor Networks, Ubiquitous, and Trustworthy Computing, pp. 143–151. IEEE press, Taichung, Taiwan (2006)

Design Guidelines for Technology-Enhanced Learning via Mobile Devices in a Tertiary Education Context in South Africa

Patricia Harpur(✉) and M.R. (Ruth) de Villiers

School of Computing, University of South Africa, Pretoria, South Africa
abc@digilearning.co.za, ruth.devilliers1@gmail.com,
dvillmr1@unisa.ac.za

Abstract. Smartphones and tablets are ubiquitous in educational contexts, where students on-the-move access learning material via digital devices, on and off-campus. Successful m-learning experiences can be facilitated by mobile learning environments that are multi-facetted and effective, and that meets students' versatile needs. This study synthesizes a comprehensive set of guidelines for designing and developing mobile-learning environments, with the aim of supporting successful m-learning experiences. The research is a secondary outcome of the development and evaluation of a real-world learning environment for tertiary education, called *Mobile Learning Research* (*m-LR*). An initial set of theoretical guidelines emerged from an extensive literature study and was used in the generation of m-LR. Findings from iterative evaluations of *m-LR*, in turn, contributed to the evolution of a further set of guidelines from real-world practice. These guidelines emerged from positive and negative feedback in the findings of heuristic evaluations by experts and questionnaire surveys among students.

Keywords: Design and development strategy · Design guidelines · Digital devices · Evaluation · Mobile learning environment · Tertiary education

1 Introduction

Smartphones and tablet devices offer ubiquitous mobile-learning (m-learning) opportunities for higher-education students who study while on-the-move [1]. Over and above educational aspects, the perceived usability and user experience (UX) of m-learning platforms depend to a large extent on underlying design and development factors [2]. This study, which extends the work reported in a previous publication [3], proposes a set of guidelines for the design and development of m-learning environments. The research is a secondary outcome of the iterative development and evaluation of a real-world learning environment called *Mobile Learning Research* (*m-LR*) [4, 5]. A *first set* of design guidelines for m-learning was *gleaned from theory in the literature* and used to generate *m-LR*. The purpose of this paper is not primarily to report on the evaluation and redesign of *m-LR* prototypes. However, the findings of the evaluations formed a vital part of the design process and the emergence of *a second set of guidelines*, i.e. *guidelines that emerged from practice*.

S. Zvacek et al. (Eds.): CSEDU 2014, CCIS 510, pp. 141–159, 2015.
DOI: 10.1007/978-3-319-25768-6_10

Ad hoc approaches that ignore design principles in the development of m-learning, may have unfortunate usability and UX implications that designers of the end-product could regret. This study thus contributes to knowledge by synthesising a set of design guidelines that incorporates theoretical guidelines based on acknowledged literature, as well as practical guidelines from the findings of empirical evaluation studies. The composite set of guidelines, emerging from both theory and research, offers a rich broad-based collection of design guidelines that is transferable and adaptable to various mobile- and tablet-based learning situations. Through use and evaluation of *m-LR*, the theoretical guidelines were affirmed by use and new ones emerged.

Section 2 sets the context and outlines the background of this work. The research design is described in Sect. 3. Thereafter we view the guidelines from the lenses of their emergence, application, and evolution. Section 4 lists the initial guidelines that *emerged* from a literature review, while the impact of practically *applying* the guidelines and evaluating the resultant systems, is reported in Sect. 5. Section 6 presents further guidelines that *evolved* from evaluations. Section 7 concludes the study.

2 Background

The primary researcher is a lecturer of undergraduate students taking Software Engineering at a private South African university. She observed that some students were demotivated by traditional face-to-face classroom education. Moreover, the limited access of certain students to the Internet via PCs and laptops hindered effective communication and collaboration on group projects. Yet the majority of students possessed smartphones and/or tablet devices and were proficient in their use. Some depended on these for contributing to group projects when they returned to their distant home territories, thus converting their mode of study to blended learning. This suggested that a mobile technology-enhanced solution might enrich their learning experience. Accordingly, she set out to custom-build an initial mobile-learning (m-learning) prototype on a Moodle platform, producing a distributed digital learning environment, suited to m-learning. Environments such as Blackboard and Moodle provide support for anytime, anywhere learning, but other pertinent issues arose:

- The difficulty of integrating course material from different sources;
- The unwieldy size of digital learning systems;
- Maintenance pressures due to continual addition of learning content;
- A need to accommodate scalability and security requirements;
- Network problems; and
- Limitations posed by the delivery of large multimedia and course content [6].

Guidelines were sought for producing and improving the initial prototype, *m-LR₁*, to optimise the effect of adaptations and to avoid an *ad hoc* design and development strategy. Despite an extensive literature study, no single comprehensive design and development methodology was found. The researchers therefore decided to synthesize a set of design guidelines in parallel with the development of the m-learning environment. Ethical clearance for the research was obtained from the institution where it was conducted and from the university where the primary researcher was enrolled for postgraduate studies.

3 Research Design

The research paradigm used to generate *m-LR*, was design-based research. 'Design science' originated from the Nobel prize winner, Herbert Simon [7]. It led in turn to 'design research', which investigates artificial phenomena and solves complex problems by creating and evaluating man-made products.

Design research is called 'design science research' (DSR) in the Information Systems discipline, [8, 9], and 'design-based research' (DBR) in the educational technology domain [5, 10, 11]. DBR is appropriate for pragmatic contextual research in complex domains, and is implemented by iterative cycles of empirical studies. It has dual outcomes: (i) authentic *practical products* and (ii) *theoretical contributions* that are transferable to other environments. In this research, the practical outcome was *m-LR* and the theoretical outcome was the set of design guidelines presented in this paper.

3.1 Research Question

The research question addressed is:

What are appropriate guidelines to use for the design and development of mobile – learning environments?

The question was answered as follows: First, literature studies provided *secondary theoretical data*, from which the *initial set of guidelines emerged* that were used in generating *m-LR*. Then the empirical evaluation studies of four versions of *m-LR* via heuristic evaluations and questionnaire surveys provided *primary data* that was used to develop a *set of practical guidelines* from evaluation findings. The process of answering the question is shown in Fig. 1, which depicts the iterative development and evaluation processes of *m-LR* versions $m\text{-}LR_1$, $m\text{-}LR_2$, $m\text{-}LR_3$, $m\text{-}LR_4$, and a future final one, $m\text{-}LR_F$. This research reflects on these four versions and four iterative studies: Evaluation Study 1, Evaluation Study 2, Evaluation Study 3 and Evaluation Study 4. A comprehensive set of guidelines was synthesized by combining the two sets.

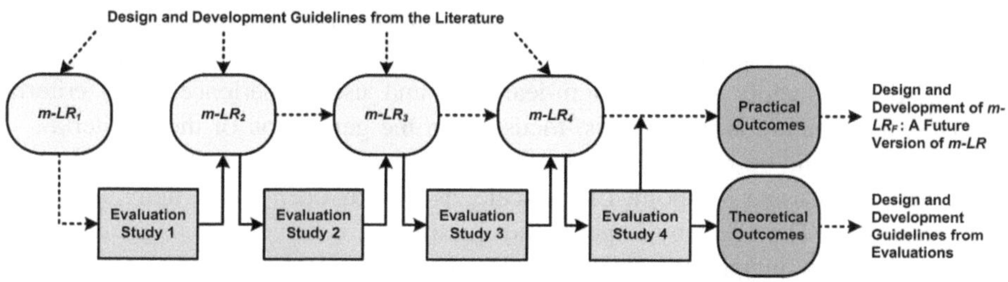

Fig. 1. Development of *m-LR* through four versions and four evaluation studies.

3.2 Research Methods

Evaluations and Participants The research was conducted over two and a half years and entailed four sequential evaluations, each by two different methods, amongst two kinds of participants.

First, heuristic evaluations (HE's) were undertaken, in which between three and five experienced evaluators, so-called 'experts', study a system to identify problems and strengths [12, 13]. Different heuristic evaluators were hand-picked for each of the four studies. All of them were experts in HCI or in digital education or both, so-called 'double experts'. The numbers of heuristic evaluators in the studies were in line with Nielsen's recommendations. Second, questionnaire surveys were conducted amongst end-users, i.e. using students as evaluators. In the first two evaluation studies, samples of experienced software engineering students were purposively selected to participate, while in the third and fourth studies, entire cohorts were used, i.e. the participants were a population, not a sample.

Furthermore, Evaluation Studies 1 to 3 were conducted on a single suburban campus of the university, while Evaluation Study 4 was done on two different campuses of the institution – the suburban one, as well as a campus in a less-affluent area. This enriched the findings, since questionnaires were administered to two varying cohorts.

The use of these research methods aimed to achieve method triangulation (two different methods) and data triangulation (across two different campuses). The evaluations are described in detail in Sects. 5.1 and 5.3.

Evaluation Procedure and Tasks The iterative approach provided sequential evaluations of four different versions of the m-learning environment. Prior to conducting the evaluations, the participants – both expert evaluators and students – completed a defined series of software engineering activities via mobile devices. This familiarised them with the features of *m-LR* and its platform. The activities included: secure login; exploration of specific software engineering course content; a brief review of a lesson, completion of a quiz associated with the lesson; entry of a blog comment; contribution to a forum discussion; a search for particular terms in a glossary; participation in a software engineering chat session; a contribution to a wiki topic; and the viewing of online media. This comprehensive exposure was crucial in helping them contribute meaningfully to the development of new versions and, implicitly, to new guidelines for learning via mobile devices.

Research Instruments The questionnaires were not adaptations of a standard instrument. Instead the evaluation criteria were custom-developed, based on five categories explained in Sect. 5.1, namely: general interface criteria; pedagogical aspects; website specific criteria; factors specific to m-learning; and user experience (UX) criteria. A separate publication is in progress, focusing on the generation of these criteria.

Constructs in the questionnaires were based on these categories. There were evaluation statements using a 5-point Likert scale, as well as open-ended items for qualitative responses. The HE's by experts and questionnaire surveys amongst end-users thus provided both quantitative and qualitative data. The questionnaires and evaluation criteria are not included in an appendix, because of their length.

The quantitative data analysis and the qualitative thematic analysis of free text identified problems in *m-LR*, and highlighted positive factors. This led to a set of practical guidelines, which reflect findings of the evaluations and which are specific to the design of learning environments. The guidelines are presented in Sect. 6.

3.3 Derivation of Design Guidelines

As previously mentioned, the guidelines emerged from two types of sources. Firstly, existing guidelines were garnered from pertinent literature (and synthesized into an initial framework (Sect. 4), presented in Table 1. Secondly, empirical research was undertaken (Sect. 5) by evaluating versions of *m-LR* as described in Sect. 3.2 and illustrated in Fig. 1. The findings of these evaluations (Sect. 6) were used as primary data to generate Table 4, which extends and completes the framework.

4 Initial Guidelines Emerging from the Literature

Literature sources address various challenges within m-learning domains, including the issue of appropriate design guidelines for m-learning applications. A deep and extensive literature review was undertaken for this study, resulting in the structured synthesis of an initial set of design and development guidelines, which are presented in Table 1. The work of many researchers contributed to the formulation of this initial collection of guidelines. Space constraints preclude detailed discussion of the sources consulted, but all of them are acknowledged in Table 1.

The table plays an important role in this paper, in that it is the initial version of the framework of design guidelines, namely the contribution that emerged from theory. It comprises ten categories of guidelines. Within each category, key terms are italicised to emphasise the contributions made by various authors. The contributing authors are cited in alignment in the second column.

5 Empirical Studies: Design, Evaluation and Re-Design

5.1 Evaluation Studies

The guidelines in Table 1 were applied in generating four versions of *m-LR*, namely *m-LR*$_1$, *m-LR*$_2$, *m-LR*$_3$, and *m-LR*$_4$, with a view to a future version, *m-LR*$_F$. Figure 1 in Sect. 3 showed the four sequential evaluation studies, Evaluation Studies 1, 2, 3 and 4, that were respectively implemented on the four successive versions. Participants in these studies were experts who served as heuristic evaluators and end-users, i.e. students, who completed questionnaires.

We present the evaluation framework, followed by brief descriptions of the four evaluations, explaining their context, purpose and impact on the evolution and re-design of *m-LR*. Further findings which are reported in the upcoming Sect. 5.3, focus only on the major studies, Evaluation Study 3 and Evaluation Study 4, which contributed strongly to the evolution of the second set of guidelines.

Table 1. Design guidelines for m-learning environments – emerging from the literature.

Themes	Design and development guidelines
1 Strategy	• Incorporate mobile technologies into *evolutionary planning*, process flows and *road maps* [14, 15]; • Provide *interactivity* via UCD; and improve the environment by implementing *iterative design* [16]; • *Involve experts* in contributing to the design [17]; • Implement ongoing *quality assurance* mechanisms [18]; • Establish an *organisation-wide vision* addressing challenges and economic factors of mobile assimilation [18].
2 Mobile specifications	• Provide *accessible information* to students whilst they are moving to and from locations [2, 19, 20]; • Focus more on *content and m-learning* than on technology [21, 22]; • *Link tasks* to course content [23]; • Include *mobile specifications* with accessibility via all devices [24]; • Aim for compatibility with a *wide range of media* [21, 23]; • Incorporate *security* and *privacy* features [22, 25].
3 User-centricity	• Involve end users in guiding the *design of the interface* [26]; • Consider *users' understanding* of terminology and navigation; incorporate *usefulness* from a user's perspective; and allow *customisation* and *adaptability* for user's preferences and abilities [2]; • Include features that enhance *motivation* [27].
4 Ease of use	• Focus on *simplicity* and *flexibility* [2, 19]; • Aim for easy *assimilation* on the part of the student; and facilitate *availability* of important information [17]; • Present only the *essential* and consistent *information*; make provision for *evaluation* of usability; and implement fluent *navigation* [24].
5 Content	• Include self-contained '*chunks*' of educational material; and provide *accessible* and *compact content*, presented in multiple ways [19, 24]; • Select and structure *categories of information* that are appropriate for mobile delivery [28]; • Facilitate *access, interaction, communication and collaboration* [17, 20, 28]; • *Ground the content* in teaching and learning [17, 27, 29]; • Use mobile technologies to support the achievement of *learning outcomes* [14]; • *Design pedagogical activities* suitable for mobile technologies [30].
6 Context	• Take cognizance of *mobility levels*, usage mode, time and place of learning, budget, and network connectivity factors [2, 27]; • Plan *in-situ social learning* for new, individual and teams with [23]; • Incorporate *a selection of screen and keyboard/touch options*, operating systems, device types, network configurations, and student characteristics [27].

(*Continued*)

Table 1. (*Continued*)

Themes	Design and development guidelines
7 VLEs	• Ensure that the environment reflects academic vision and offers relevant *curriculum content*, providing training and support for staff and students [29]; • Resolve *copyright* and *intellectual property* issues [31]; • Rapidly provide value in a natural way via *mobile services* [2, 17]; • Consider that *digital technology* has changed students' views of writing in the "old-fashioned" way, differing from "pencil and paper" lessons [22, 32]; • Offer *uniform access* to a variety of information sources, e.g. websites, glossaries, reading material, relevant YouTube videos, other student opinions [17, 22].

An evaluation requires both an evaluation method/s and evaluation criteria. As part of this research, a broad generic evaluation framework was synthesized for the purpose of evaluating mobile learning environments [4]. The framework comprises five evaluation categories, each containing criteria that emerged from the literature. They are listed in Table 2, showing the categories and mentioning some of the sources from which the criteria were derived. The issues of contextual factors and user-centricity appear in both Categories 4 and 5. Category 4: *m-Learning* views these aspects from a pragmatic and functional viewpoint, while Category 5: *User Experience* has a hedonic perspective, focusing on the users' emotions, engagement, satisfaction and social experiences. The criteria were then employed in the evaluations of *m-LR*. In Studies 2, 3 and 4, each construct was converted to several evaluation items, which participants rated by Likert scaling. In addition, and importantly, each participant was asked in an open-ended question to list at least five problems they encountered in *m-LR*.

Evaluation Study 1. As the study in 2010 that evaluated the usability of the first version of *m-LR*, a Moodle customised in an ad hoc manner, Study 1 uncovered usability challenges. Its purpose was to evaluate $m\text{-}LR_1$ running on the researcher's own Blackberry 9700 smartphone device, and to produce both quantitative and qualitative findings. Participants were three experts for an HE and ten students in a questionnaire survey, all drawn from a single campus. Subsequent changes to $m\text{-}LR_1$, led to $m\text{-}LR_2$, and included redesign of:

- Course content, providing information in chunks for viewing on mobile devices;
- Log-in features;
- Quantity of information per page;
- Formats of downloadable media and subject matter; and
- Contents of the glossary.

Evaluation Study 2. This small-scale evaluation of $m\text{-}LR_2$ in 2011, was a pilot study for the major Evaluation Study 3. Study 2 was implemented on a single campus with only four students (questionnaires) and one double expert (HE), As in Study 1, each used the same Blackberry 9700 smartphone for their evaluation. Study 2 primarily

Table 2. Design guidelines for m-learning environments – emerging from the literature. (cont.)

Themes	Design and development guidelines
8 Web 2.0 tools and social media	• *Extend* the student's *classroom* experience [33]; • Include *Web 2.0 features* e.g. podcasts, blogs, microblogs, wikis, and social networking sites (SNSs) [33–37]; • Emphasize the *planning* required for implementing social networking applications within an online educational program [35]; • Facilitate *communication* and *collaboration* via synchronous technologies (chat rooms) and asynchronous interactivity (forums and e-mail) [36, 38, 39]; • Investigate and employ blended learning by using accessible *social media*, e.g. Facebook, YouTube, in educational contexts for communication, participation and collaboration [18–21, 23, 40].
9 Integration	• Address *assimilation issues* arising for m-learning implementation [14, 30]; • Ensure *transparent access* to a learning management system; and plan and design *activities for learning* beyond the classroom [41]; • Formulate *common goals* for cross-functional communication [15]; • Plan and provide *anytime wireless connectivity* on campus in and beyond classroom, e.g. libraries, public spaces, residences; incorporate *secure wireless services* supporting all device types [18, 20, 41]; • Incorporate *seamless learning* suited to 21st century skills and seamless technologies [14, 42]; • Orientation programs *to motivate staff and students* for incorporation of mobile devices into teaching and learning [14].
10 Institutional issues	• Incorporate mobile technologies and mobile device skills into *professional development programs* for staff [14, 15, 18]; • Consider *ethical implications* [14]; • Synergise *needs of students* and *expectations of faculty* [28]; • Facilitate *student-staff relationships* [28]; • Facilitate *technology adoption* [14, 30]; • Provide *technological support* for staff and students [30, 41].

served to try out the research procedures, tasks, instruments and evaluation processes, but also led to refinements that resulted in *m-LR*$_3$:

- Privilege levels of the blog;
- Options offered by the glossary;
- Look-and-feel facets such as font styles, size and colour; and
- Open-ended requirements for the quiz.

Evaluation Study 3. This study in 2011, was the largest up to that point. Five HE experts, with their own devices, and seventeen students from one campus, using Blackberry 9700 smartphones, evaluated *m-LR*$_3$ for usability and UX. Adjustments and extensions resulted in the next version of *m-LR*, namely *m-LR*$_4$. Feedback called for new functionalities or changes to:

- The help functionality;
- Built-in documentation;
- Links and navigation mechanisms;
- 'Breadcrumbs', and thus navigability;
- Compatibility of media such as video;
- The range of device types, which needed to be broadened;
- File size, aiming to reduce buffering issues;
- Layout of goals and objectives of learning units;
- Offline reading capability, required by users; and
- Access to social networking applications.

A growing need for storage and collaborative services via cloud technology such as Dropbox and Google Drive became apparent. It was suggested that the addition of these services would increase the appeal of *m-LR* whilst facilitating communication between teams of students doing collaborative projects.

Evaluation Study 4. This final, and largest, study in 2012 used $m\text{-}LR_4$ as input. Its feedback engendered guidelines that, if applied, would produce a future improved version, $m\text{-}LR_F$. Five experts and 32 students from two different campuses completed evaluations, proposing modifications to the:

- Application design;
- Specifications, as participants required compatibility with several device types; and
- The user experience, which could be enhanced by improving ease of use.

The number of problems reported per evaluator was the lowest rate of the four studies, indicating the success of the iterative evaluation and redesign process.

5.2 Features of *m-LR*

Various features were incorporated into the customization of the *m-LR* Moodle, providing collaborative team-based activities; extending the classroom experience; and incorporating Internet links to course-related websites. The features which were largely derived from the themes of guidelines (Table 1), and include:

- *Strategy:* An interactive approach to design, where students contributed to the m-LR content, enabled the assimilation of Software Engineering terminology;
- *Mobile Specifications:* Tasks were linked to course content and comprised weekly lessons supported by a range of compatible media e.g. video - YouTube;
- *User-centricity:* User feedback resulting from evaluation studies was included in the design of the interface, informing adjustments to the m-LR environment;
- *Ease of Use:* A simple and flexible interface supported access to, and navigation through, essential course information via PC, tablet or smartphone;
- *Content:* Hyperlinked chunks, rather than a formal print-style layout of educational material was mapped to Software Engineering modules in the course outline. Forms of content included formative assessment, a glossary, wiki and 'News';

- *Context:* Environment included topic-based forum discussions, where postings gave users the opportunity to contribute, irrespective of the context;
- *VLEs:* The digital platform supported revision exercises with regular click and swipe tests with instant feedback, in preference to handwritten assignments;
- *Web 2.0 Tools, Social Media:* The classroom experience was extended by blogs and links to a Facebook group, customised within *m-LR* for Software Engineering;
- *Integration:* Seamless learning was promoted, coordinating access to 21st century learning resources e.g. lesson summaries, URLs, PowerPoint slides, PDFs; and
- *Institutional Issues:* Secure login screens enabled secure communication between lecturers and learners whilst supporting administrative matters and educational relationships.

5.3 Positive and Negative Feedback

Contrary to expectations, additional themes and guidelines emerged from Evaluation Study 4, despite the maturity that *m-LR* had reached. Twenty five guidelines were elicited from Study 3 on $m\text{-}LR_3$ in 2011 and 27 from Study 4 on $m\text{-}LR_4$ in 2012.

We report first on the *qualitative component* of the studies, combining the expert- and student participants, so that Study 3 had 22 participants and Study 4 had 37. In open-ended responses, considerably more positive comments emerged in Study 4 (132) than in Study 3 (74). Furthermore, in Evaluation Study 4, the number of positives (132) outnumbered the negatives (90), whereas the converse was the case in Evaluation Study 3, with 74 positives and 87 negatives. These aspects are depicted graphically in Fig. 2. Percentage-wise too, the positive comments increased. In Study 3, the positives represented 46 % of total comments, while in Study 4, positives were 60 % of the total. The negative comments decreased from 54 % in Study 3 to 40 % in Study 4. These occurrences imply that the adjustments made after Study 3 were effective.

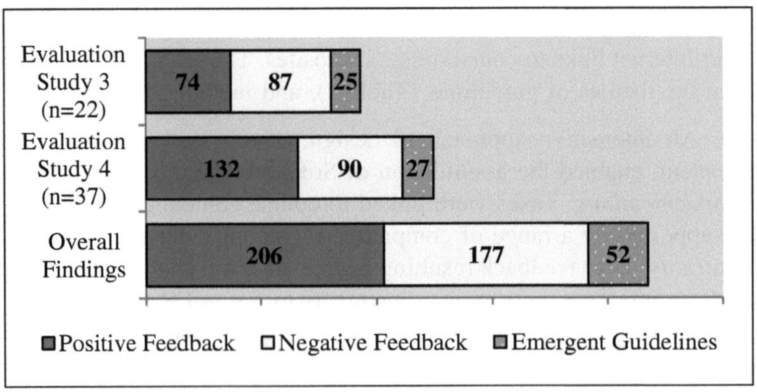

Fig. 2. Relationship between positive and negative feedback and emergent guidelines.

On reflection we established the interesting fact that guidelines emerged from both positive and negative feedback. Many of the guidelines recorded after Study 3 arose from reported negatives, while in Study 4, more of the new guidelines emerged from positive comments made by the participants in their open-ended responses. This shows the value of iterative evaluations, in that evaluations on a mature product can provide positive feedback, as they emphasise and reinforce the strengths.

In qualitative analysis, the problems listed by participants in open responses were structured into themes. There were 87 problems in Evaluation Study 3 and 90 in Evaluation Study 4. The number of problems allocated to the important *Ease of Use* theme, decreased from 29 (33 % of the negative feedback) in Study 3 to 23 (26 % of negative feedback) in Study 4. We single out two other categories for mention, namely *Strategy* and *Mobile Specifications*, where the numbers of problems increased. For Study 3 and Study 4, the *Strategy* category contributed 12 (14 %) and 20 (22 %) respectively of the total problems. Problems in the *Mobile Specifications* theme increased from 6 (7 %) in Study 3) to 20 (22 %) in Study 4 problems).

The increase in reported problems in these two categories can be ascribed to three factors: a dynamically changing digital environment; greater technical acuity of the participants; and a more techno-savvy attitude to mobile technology design concepts.

Table 3 shows *quantitative* findings, indicating the overall mean ratings assigned to each category of criteria for Evaluation Studies 3 and 4 as well as tallies of the problems mentioned in the open-ended responses. The left column lists the five categories given in Sect. 5.1, and the other columns indicate the scores assigned by the expert evaluators in the HE and the students in the questionnaire survey. It is notable that, for the experts, four of the five mean ratings increased from Study 3 to Study 4, with an increase in overall mean from 3.4 to 3.7, where the maximum Likert rating was 5. This demonstrates the impact of the improvements to *m-LR* after Study 3. For the students, four of the five mean ratings decreased marginally from Study 3 to Study 4, with a 0.1 decrease in overall mean from 4.1 to 4.0. The gross problems reported by student participants increased from 46 in Study 3 to 62 in Study 4. But because the number of student participants doubled from 17 to 32, the figures actually represent a decrease per participant from 2.7 in Study 3 to 1.9 in Study 4, this despite the fact that the questionnaire asked participants to report at least 5 problems. Overall, the findings indicate participants' satisfaction with *m-LR*.

6 Evolution of New Guidelines Emerging from Practice

Positive factors from the evaluations shown in Fig. 2 and discussed in Sect. 5, affirm the original guidelines. Other aspects articulated by participants, suggest strengths that should be made explicit by new guidelines, while problems reported in the evaluations, necessitate further guidelines. When the ten new guidelines, particularly those that emerge from qualitative data, are consolidated with the original ten from the literature, the result is a synthesized set of 20 guidelines. The original guidelines are now reviewed, and the evolution of the new set, particularly from Studies 3 and 4, is outlined.

Table 3. A framework for evaluating mobile learning environments.

Category 1: General interface criteria, based on Nielsen's heuristics [43]
1. Visibility of system status;
2. Match between the system and the real world;
3. Learner control and freedom;
4. Consistency and adherence to standards;
5. Error prevention, in particular, prevention of peripheral usability-related errors;
6. Recognition rather than recall;
7. Aesthetics and minimalism in design;
8. Recognition, diagnosis and recovery from errors;
9. Help and documentation.

Category 2: Website-specific criteria [39, 44]
10. Simplicity of site navigation, organisation and structure;
11. Relevance of site content to the learner and the learning process;
12. Information easy-to-access;
13. Content both suitable and of a high quality;
14. System is simple and easy to use (called easiness);
15. Material is of a high quality, i.e. videos and digitisation.

Category 3: Educational criteria [44, 45]
16. Clarity of goals, objectives and outcomes
17. Effectiveness of collaborative learning
18. Cognitive error recognition, diagnosis and recovery
19. Feedback, guidance and assessment

Category 4: m-Learning criteria [46–48]
20. Capabilities of handheld devices and technology;
21. Contextual factors and support of tasks (pragmatic);
22. User-centricity (pragmatic);
23. Flexibility and adaptability of environment;
24. Interactivity, navigational fidelity, means of communication and collaboration.

Category 5: User experience criteria [34, 49–51]
25. Emotional issues: enhancement of engagement and positive attitudes;
26. Contextual factors and individual needs (hedonic);
27. User-centricity: personal approaches and personalised learning (hedonic);
28. Provides social interaction;
29. Meets user expectations and needs;
30. Appealing environment;
31. Induces user satisfaction, pleasure and motivation.

6.1 Emergence of the Original Theoretical Guidelines

Table 1 presented an initial framework of theoretical guidelines for the design and development of m-learning environments, comprising ten themes: 1. *Strategy*; 2. *Mobile Specifications*; 3. *User-centricity*; 4. *Ease of Use*; 5. *Content*; 6. *Context*; 7. *Virtual Learning Environments*; 8. *Web 2.0 Tools and Social Media*; 9. *Integration* and 10. *Institutional Issues*. These themes and guidelines were used in developing *m-LR*$_1$, and also contributed, along with findings of the series of evaluations, to adjustments and improvements of subsequent versions of the m-learning environment – see Fig. 1.

6.2 Guidelines from Evaluation Study 3

The evaluation of in Study 3 by five experts and seventeen students produced positive and negative feedback, resulting in practical principles and guidelines that led to the development of $m\text{-}LR_4$. The positive results firstly affirmed the utility of the initial framework of theoretical guidelines and, secondly, the positive response that emerged for aspects of *m-LR* that had been designed intuitively, showed the need to concretise and formalise certain implicit guidelines. Negative feedback and concerns indicated inadequacies in the design and highlighted the need for further guidelines. Thematic analysis of qualitative data, positive and negative, confirmed existing guidelines, while other evaluation findings were converted to five new categories of guidelines, namely: 11. *Devices*; 12. *Assessment*; 13. *Efficiency*; 14. *Navigability* and 15. *Interactivity*, which are elaborated in Table 4.

Table 4. Quantiative findings of evaluation studies 3 and 4.

Summary of ratings in study 3				
Category of criteria	Expert evaluators (n = 5)		Student evaluators (n = 17)	
	Mean rating	Reported problems	Mean rating	Reported problems
1	3.0	16	4.0	18
2	3.6	9	4.0	7
3	3.5	7	4.1	6
4	3.6	2	4.0	9
5	3.2	7	4.2	6
Overall	**3.4**	**41**	**4.1**	**46**
Summary of ratings in study 4				
Category of criteria	Expert evaluators (n = 5)		Student evaluators (n = 32)	
	Mean rating	Reported problems	Mean rating	Reported problems
1	3.6	14	3.9	27
2	3.5	6	4.0	12
3	3.6	0	4.0	8
4	3.9	4	3.9	8
5	3.7	4	4.0	7
Overall	**3.7**	**28**	**4.0**	**62**

6.3 Guidelines from Evaluation Study 4

The evaluation of $m\text{-}LR_4$ was a major study, with 37 participants, namely five experts and 32 students from cohorts on two campuses. Due to the improvements implemented to $m\text{-}LR_3$ after Study 3, the positive feedback increased, as shown in Fig. 2. Moreover, negativity previously indicated by some initial themes namely: *Mobile Specifications*; *User-centricity*; and *Ease of Use* declined, probably due to the strength of the version $m\text{-}LR_4$, that had resulted from Study 5. Five new categories of guidelines resulted from thematic analysis of the findings of Study 4, namely; 16. *Innovation*; 17. *Visual Factors*; 18. *Satisfaction*; 19. *User Experience* and 20. *Digital Divide*. Finally,

Table 5. Guidelines emerging from findings of evaluation studies 3 and 4.

Theme	Guidelines	Theme	Guidelines
11 Devices	• Ensure *compatibility* with a range of devices; • Support *easy access*; • Consider the limitations of *input mechanisms*; • Consider *screen size* when incorporating features.	16 Innovation	• Offer the user an environment which is perceived as *new and novel*; • Facilitate off-campus *mobile learning*; • Deliver course content in a *creative digital manner*.
12 Assessment	• Design *self-assessment* activities; • Provide *lecturer support* for the correction of errors; • Include multiple choice questions; • Consider short-answer questions • Locate *quiz* options with associated course content; • Incorporate *rapid test feedback* to support users doing revision; • Provide links to online material to facilitate preparation of *coursework* assignments; • Align assessment exercises with *examination preparation*.	17 Visual actors	• Provide a simple and appealing *layout*; • Design a *look and feel* that is user-centric; • Use suitable *colour schemes*; • Make effective use of *white space*; • Where possible and appropriate, enhance the experience with suitable *graphic content*, *headings* and *font choices*; • Strengthen the visual experience, possibly including some *animation* • When constructing a site, design for *logical* page *order*.
13 Efficiency	• Ensure *speedy loading* of site and pages; • Provide *immediate responses* for users accessing features of the application; • Achieve *fast navigation* between links; • Aim for *rapid content delivery*.	18 Satisfaction	• Create a match to user's view of *suitability*; • Provide *consistency* with familiar applications and interfaces to avoid user frustration; • Focus on easy *readability*; • Ensure that *functionalities* operate correctly.
14 Interactivity	• Enable 'on-the-fly' *communication* with classmates; • Support *visibility* of other online users; • Facilitate *collaboration* on group projects; • Allow *sharing* of information;	19 User experience	• Embrace the user's sense of *excitement* and *playfulness*; • Build a learning environment which offers *enjoyable user experiences*; • Create a *rich* and *professional* learning environment; • Use *technology that enhances*, rather than hinders learning;

(*Continued*)

Table 5. (*Continued*)

Theme	Guidelines	Theme	Guidelines
	• Include alternative forms of interactivity, to suit *user preferences*.		• Design lessons that are *fun*.
15 Navigability	• Facilitate *easy and intuitive* navigation; • Ensure visibility of *links*; • Support *browsing* – anytime and anywhere; • Establish an *easy-to-follow flow*, organized logically.	20 Digital divide	• Consider off-campus *Internet access* issues and *data expenses*; • Provide *offline access* to course material; • Ensure equitable availability and affordability of smart devices; • Schedule digital skill workshops.

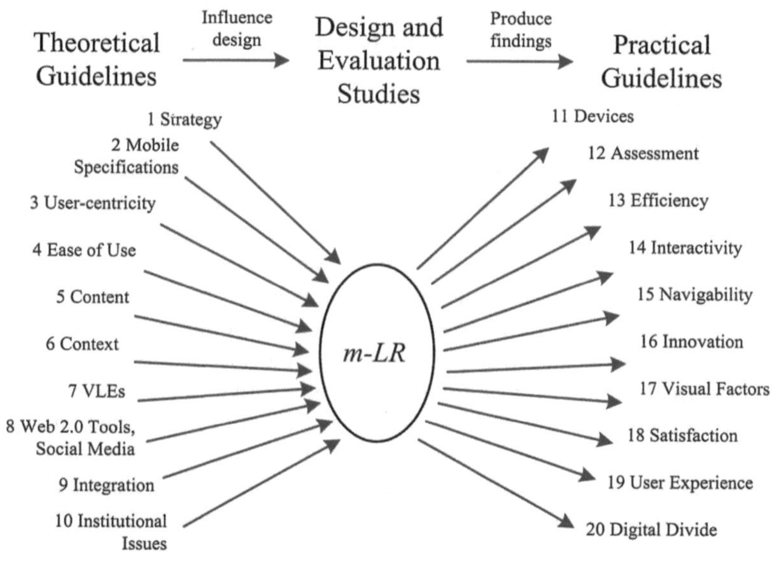

Fig. 3. Theoretical guidelines, design and evaluation of *m-LR* and practical guidelines.

suggestions emerged from Study 4 for improvements to $m\text{-}LR_4$ that would result in a future version $m\text{-}LR_F$.

6.4 Evolution of Guidelines and Extension to the Framework

The new categories of themes and design guidelines, introduced in Sects. 6.2 and 6.3, are listed in Table 4. The original themes that re-emerged, are in Table 1. Table 4, which is the contribution that emerged from practical empirical research, continues the evolution of the framework of design guidelines.

6.5 Final Set of Guidelines

An integration of Tables 1 and 4 would constitute the final and comprehensive set of guidelines in twenty categories for the design and development of mobile learning environments. Such a merged table of final guidelines, though valuable, would be repetitive and is explicitly omitted for the sake of space (Table 5).

7 Conclusions

This study addressed the research question: *What are appropriate guidelines to use for the design and development of mobile-learning environments?*

The primary purpose is thus to produce generic guidelines for the design and development of m-learning environments. Figure 3 shows how the initial theoretical guidelines from the literature, informed the production of *m-LR*. Subsequently, *m-LR* itself, via findings of a series of evaluations, informed the generation of a new set of practical guidelines.

Aggregation of the themes and guidelines in Table 1, based on theoretical sources from the literature, and Table 4, evolving from practical findings from empirical studies, thus contributes to the synthesis of a final set of guidelines and answers the research question.

The research was accompanied by some notable insights. The goalposts moved over the duration of the studies, and target audiences became more 'techno-savvy'. Although students were initially increasingly satisfied with the successive versions, the feedback at later stages began to request sophisticated *refinements and extensions*.

With the acceleration in technology and innovative digital devices, and the increasing capabilities of such devices, further rapid synthesis, evaluation, adaptation and evolution will depend on comprehensive and malleable sets of design and development guidelines. Students who are mobile and on-the-move and accustomed to a plethora of novel apps, expect similar fast, flexible and responsive virtual learning environments. The evolution of these integrated multi-facetted guidelines is in line with these requirements.

Due to the rapidly evolving nature of mobile technology, the task of formulating a set of guidelines is never complete. Hence the guidelines synthesized in Tables 1 and 4, beg augmentation over time and application within other educational contexts.

The guidelines will evolve further as capabilities and affordances of new technologies are accommodated. We acknowledge that the current framework is lengthy due to its comprehensive nature. Synthesis of the categories into a tighter framework could facilitate practical application. Finally in transferring the application of the guidelines to other mobile learning environments, they can be reduced and customized to the context and content.

Whereas literature sources may provide an initial foundational set of guidelines based on theoretical underpinnings, this study demonstrates that empirical findings based on participative user-centric designs can practically extend and enrich a framework of design guidelines.

References

1. Cochrane, T., Bateman, R.: Smartphones give you wings: pedagogical affordances of mobile Web 2.0. Australas. J. Educ. Technol. **26**(1), 1–14 (2010)
2. Oinas-Kukkonen, H., Kurkela, V.: Developing successful mobile applications. In: Proceedings of the IASTED International Conference on Computer Science and Technology, Cancun, Mexico, pp. 50–54. CSA Illumina (2003)
3. Harpur, P.A., De Villiers, M.R.: Synthesis of a framework of design guidelines for m-learning environments. In: Proceedings of the 6th International on Computer Supported Education (CSEDU), Barcelona, Spain (2014)
4. Harpur, P.A.: Evaluation of usability and user experience of an m-learning environment, custom-designed for a tertiary educational context. Unpublished M.Sc. dissertation, University of South Africa, Pretoria, South Africa (2013)
5. De Villiers, M.R., Harpur, P.A.: Design-based research – the educational technology variant of design research: illustrated by the design of an m-learning environment. In: Proceedings of the Annual Research Conference of the South African Institute of Computer Scientists and Information Technologists, East London, South Africa, ACM International Conference Proceedings, pp. 252–261 (2013)
6. Li, Q., Lau, R.W.H., Shih, T.K., Li, F.W.B.: Technology supports for distributed and collaborative learning over the internet. ACM Trans. Internet Technol. **8**, 2, Article 10 (2008)
7. Simon, H.A.: The Sciences of the Artificial. MIT Press, Cambridge (1981)
8. March, S.T., Smith, G.F.: Design and natural science research on information technology. Decis. Support Syst. **15**, 251–266 (1995)
9. Peffers, K., Tuunanen, T., Rothenberger, M.A., Chatterjee, S.: A design science research methodology for information systems research. J. Manage. Inf. Syst. **24**(3), 45–77 (2007)
10. Barab, S., Squire, K.: Design-based research: putting a stake in the ground. J. Learn. Sci. **13**(1), 1–14 (2004)
11. Amiel, T., Reeves, T.C.: Design-based research and educational technology: rethinking technology and the research agenda. Educ. Technol. Soc. **11**(4), 29–40 (2008)
12. Nielsen, J., Molich, R.: Heuristic evaluation of user interfaces. In: Proceedings of the CHI 1990 Proceedings of the SIGCHI Conference on Human Factors in Computing Systems, Seattle, Washington, pp. 249–256. ACM (1990)
13. Nielsen, J.: Finding usability problems through heuristic evaluation. In: Proceedings of the CHI 1992 Proceedings of the SIGCHI Conference on Human Factors in Computing Systems, pp. 373–380. ACM (1992)
14. Pegrum, M., Oakley, G., Faulkner, R.: Schools going mobile: a study of the adoption of mobile handheld technologies in western Australian independent schools. Australas. J. Educ. Technol. **29**, 1 (2013)
15. Campbell, L.: Successfully implementing mobile learning across an entire campus. WCET Frontiers (2014). http://wcetblog.wordpress.com/2013/10/23/mobile-learning/

16. Göker, A., Myrhaug, H.: Evaluation of a mobile information system in context. Inf. Process. Manage. **44**(1), 39–65 (2008)
17. Bri, D., Garcia, M., Coll, H., Lloret, J.: A study of virtual learning environments. WSEAS Trans. Adv. Eng. Educ. **6**(1), 33–43 (2009)
18. Traxler, J.: Mobile learning: shaping the frontiers of learning technologies in global context. In: Huang, R., Spector, J.M. (eds.) Reshaping Learning, pp. 237–251. Springer, Heidelberg (2013)
19. Sharma, S.K., Kitchens, F.L.: Web services architecture for m-learning. Electron. J. e-Learning **2**(1), 203–216 (2004)
20. Mayisela, T.: The potential use of mobile technology: enhancing accessibility and communication in a blended learning course. S. Afr. J. Educ. **33**, 1 (2013)
21. Landers, P.: From e-learning to m-learning. Ericsson (2002). http://learning.ericsson.net/mlearning2/project_one/elearnmlearn.html
22. Pinkwart, N., Hoppe, H.U., Milrad, M., Perez, J.: Educational scenarios for cooperative use of personal digital assistants. J. Comput. Assist. Learn. **19**(3), 383–391 (2003)
23. Parsons, D., Ryu, H., Cranshaw, M.: A study of design requirements for mobile learning environments. In: Proceedings of the Sixth International Conference on Advanced Learning Technologies (ICALT 2006), Kerkrade, The Netherlands. IEEE Computer Society (2006)
24. Low, L., O'Connell, M.: Learner-centric design of digital mobile learning. In: Proceedings of the OLT Conference, Brisbane, Australia, pp. 71–82 (2006)
25. Naismith, L., Lonsdale, P., Vavoula, G., Sharples, M.: Literature review in mobile technologies and learning. Futurelab Series (2004). http://telearn.archives-ouvertes.fr/docs/00/19/01/43/PDF/Naismith_2004.pdf
26. Sharp, H., Rogers, Y., Preece, J.: Interaction Design: Beyond Human-Computer Interaction. Wiley, New York (2007)
27. Botha, A., van Greunen, D., Herselman, M.: A mobile human-computer interaction perspective on mobile learning. In: Proceedings of the 6th Annual International Conference on Computing and ICT Research, Kampala, Uganda, pp. 3–18. Researchspace Software (2010)
28. Chipangura, B., van Biljon, J., Botha, A.: Prioritizing students' mobile centric information access needs: a case of postgraduate students. In: Proceedings of the International Conference on Adaptive Science and Technology (ICAST 2013), Pretoria, South Africa, pp. 1–7. IEEE (2013)
29. Cheung, K.S.: A framework for developing e-learning solutions. In: Proceedings of the Fifth International Conference on Semantics, Knowledge and Grid, pp. 294–297. IEEE Computer Society (2009)
30. Lam, J., Duan, C.G.: A review of mobile learning environment in higher education sector of Hong Kong: technological and social perspectives. In: Cheung, S.K.S., Fong, J., Kwok, L.-F., Li, K., Kwan, R. (eds.) ICHL 2012. LNCS, vol. 7411, pp. 165–173. Springer, Heidelberg (2012)
31. Levy, S.: Six factors to consider when planning online distance learning programs in higher education. Online J. Distance Learn. Adm. **6**, 1 (2003)
32. Lai, C.-H., Yang, J.-C., Ho, C.-W., Chant, T.-W.: Affordances of mobile technologies for experiential learning: the interplay of technology and pedagogical practices. J. Comput. Assist. Learn. **23**, 326–337 (2007)
33. Ebner, M.: Introducing live microblogging: how single presentations can be enhanced by the mass. J. Res. Innov. Teach. **2**(1), 91–100 (2009)
34. Ebner, M., Schiefner, M.: Microblogging - more than fun? In: Proceedings of the International Association for Development of the Information Society (IADIS) Mobile Learning 2008 International Conference, Algarve, Portugal, pp. 155–159. Citeseer (2008)

35. Lockyer, L., Patterson, J.: Integrating social networking technologies in education: a case study of a formal learning environment. In: Proceedings of the Eighth IEEE International Conference on Advanced Learning Technologies, Santander, Spain, pp. 529–533. IEEE Computer Society (2008)
36. Minocha, S., Thomas, P.G.: Collaborative learning in a wiki environment: experiences from a software engineering course. New Rev. Hypermedia Multimedia **13**(2), 187–209 (2007)
37. Safran, C.: Blogging in higher education programming lectures: an empirical study. In: Proceedings of the MindTrek 2008, Tampere, Finland, pp. 131–135. ACM (2008)
38. Jones, P.: Collaboration at a distance: using a wiki to create a collaborative learning environment for distance education and on-campus students in a social work course. J. Teach. Soc. Work **30**(2), 225–236 (2010)
39. MacCallum, K., Kinshuk, K.: Mobile technology in collaboration: evaluation of a web-based discussion board. Int. J. Mob. Learn. Organ. **2**(4), 318–328 (2008)
40. Nykvist, S.S., Lee, K.-T.: Mixing higher education teaching and learning with mobile devices and social media. In: Proceedings of the IAC-ETeL 2013, Prague, Czech Republic (2013)
41. Santos, I.M.: Integrating personal mobile devices in teaching: the impact on student learning and institutional support. Learn. Teach. High. Educ. Gulf Perspect. **10**, 2 (2013)
42. Wong, L.-H.: A learner-centric view of mobile seamless learning. Br. J. Educ. Technol. **43**(1), 19–23 (2012)
43. Nielsen, J.: Heuristic Evaluation. In: Nielsen, J., Mack, R.L. (eds.) Usability Inspection Methods. Wiley, New York (1994)
44. Ssemugabi, S., De Villiers, M.R.: Effectiveness of heuristic evaluation in usability evaluation of e-learning applications in higher education. S. Afr. Comput. J. (SACJ) **45**, 26–39 (2010)
45. De Villiers, M.R.: e-Learning artefacts: are they based on learning theory? Alternation **12**(1b), 345–371 (2005)
46. Sharples, M., Arnedillo-Sanchez, I., Mildrad, M., Vavoula, G.: Mobile learning - small devices, big issues. In: Ludvigsen, S., Balacheff, N., de Jong, T., Lazonder, A., Barnes, S. (eds.) Technology-Enhanced Learning: Principles and Products, pp. 233–249. Springer, Dordrecht (2009)
47. Coursaris, C.K., Kim, D.J.: A meta-analytical review of empirical mobile usability studies. J. Usability Stud. **6**(3), 117–171 (2011)
48. Herrington, A., Herrington, J., Mantei, J.: Design principles for mobile learning. In: Herrington, J., Herrington, A., Olney, I., Ferry, B. (eds.) New Technologies, New Pedagogies: Mobile Learning in Higher Education, pp. 129–138. University of Wollongong, Wollongong (2009)
49. Väänänen-Vainio-Mattila, K., Roto, V., Hassenzahl, M.: Towards practical user experience evaluation methods. ACM (2009). http://research.nokia.com/files/VaananenVainioMattila-VUUM.pdf
50. Hassenzahl, M.:. User experience (UX) towards an experiential perspective on product quality. In: Proceedings of the Proceedings of the 20th International Conference of the Association Francophone d'Interaction Homme-Machine, Metz, France, pp. 11–15. ACM (2008)
51. Botha, A., Herselman, M., van Greunen, D.: Mobile user experience in a mlearning environment. In: Proceedings of the SAICSIT 2010. ACM, New York, USA (2010)

Innovating Academic Knowledge Communication with Social Classroom Response Systems

Bastian Schwennigcke[1], Jonas Vetterick[2](✉), Kristina Marquitz[3], Clemens H. Cap[2], and Wolfgang Sucharowski[1]

[1] Department of Humanities, University of Rostock, Rostock, Germany
{bastian.schwennigcke,wolfgang.sucharowski}@uni-rostock.de
[2] Department of Computer Science, University of Rostock, Rostock, Germany
{jonas.vetterick,clemens.cap}@uni-rostock.de
[3] Department of Mechanical Engineering and Shipbuilding, University of Rostock, Rostock, Germany
kristina.marquitz@uni-rostock.de

Abstract. Classroom Response Systems (CRS) support teachers getting feedback from their students during their lessons, mostly in lessons with large audiences. While this technology is used more and more, it is less known how students really use CRS for feedback. Moreover the aspect of social communication is mostly underestimated. Our research focus on the social communication in modern CRS and provides grounding in the combination of them. We will show how social communication influences learning and feedback. Furthermore we present a classification of CRS learner types based on the results of an evaluation, including the answer which learner type benefits the most of a CRS. In Addition we present a conceptual and technical design of a Social CRS, which is aware of social communication and these learner types.

Keywords: Classroom response systems · CRS · Live feedback · Social learning · Social communication · Class-wide discussion

1 Introduction

Successful learning and therefore successful learners highly depends on social embedding of learning processes. This embedment can be defined in terms of communicative interventions into learning processes. Social embedment of learning allows learners to evaluate their understanding of given contents. Further social embedment allows to compare and conceive the appropriateness of this understanding through communication with other learners as well as with teachers and tutorial attendants in different learning contexts. Additionally academic teaching still often shows a lack of socially embedded learning this way. Even more, academic teaching misses significant strategies to develop this aspect of learning [16,18]. However, the issue of how to overcome this state and enable

S. Zvacek et al. (Eds.): CSEDU 2014, CCIS 510, pp. 160–178, 2015.
DOI: 10.1007/978-3-319-25768-6_11

a significant social involvement of learning is far less trivial and still a serious challenge on quality and success of learning [19].

Classroom Response Systems (CRS) can be regarded as a technological reply to this issue. Whereas the original idea of CRS mainly implements a clicker functionality, where students answer teachers multiple choice questions [11], they now become a wider platform to provide feedback and to elaborate it in direction to a higher social embedment of learning. Although teachers are still able to ask multiple choice questions, modern CRS provide students with the possibility to give more detailed feedback on demand [9,14].

Whilst modern CRS have been extended with many features, we think that CRS currently do not draw on their full potential to support the social embedment of learning. Until know, they are a helpful tool to link more explicitly the presentation and transmission of content on the teachers side with a specific range of receptive reactions on the learners side. In result CRS may support the addressing and solving of understanding problems.

Moreover, experience with CRS with features beyond mere multiple choice tests resulted in participants spontaneously inventing new forms of communication. For example, a public chat-like feedback channel intended originally to pose questions to the teacher was used for tutorial-style communication and for organizing study groups by the students. This demonstrates a demand for increased social interaction in the classroom.

But at this stage of evolution especially social interactions and communication are neither usefully inclosed by CRS learning concepts nor documented for students and teachers further usage on the CRS. In previous work, we recognized a strong need of students to communicate with each other on CRS and to get durable access to the CRS content generated in a lesson [24].

Although the social evolution of CRS seems to be a vital demand as well as an exciting direction of development, the relation between social interaction and learning is widely unexplained, especially in the context of blended and e-learning interventions. This paper shall explore this gap in order to better estimate social phenomena in the evaluation of existing CRS and to provide significant constraints for technological advancements.

This publication describes our position on a current learning model, which covers latest and coming generations of CRS that are aware of social communication and interaction between students and teachers. Based on this discussion we will elaborate which aspects of socially embedded learning CRS currently enable and which aspects are still to be claimed. In Addition we present the results of an evaluation of a common modern CRS, which will cover what types of students really use modern CRS. Furthermore this work outlines how coming CRS should look and act in order to contribute a serious intervention into the social challenge on learning.

2 Modern Classroom Response Systems

As Kay et al. stated in [13] CRS have been voting mechanism in the first place: Teachers ask a multiple choice question and students could answer by clicking the corresponding button on a special voting device. As these voting devices are very expensive and have to be maintained, modern CRS use the mobile devices students already have. Since mobile devices, as smartphones, pads or notebooks, provide a display that can draw more than just buttons for multiple choice questions, CRS evolve to comprehensive feedback systems that are able to implement more complex forms of feedback [8,9,12,14,23] such as:

- Multiple Choice questions asked by the teachers (TQ): Teachers can still use modern CRS as clickers, but without the limitations of a hardware device, so they may label their answers or use a flexible number of answers for example.
- Questions from students (SQ): Students ask specific questions. Other students may vote questions up or down, which can be an indicator for the importance of questions. Based on the number of votes the instructor can address the issues in his lecture. In a variant of this scheme, members of the audience may reply in writing using the system.
- Rating specific presentation parameters (SP): Students mark specific issues, for example when the instructor is moving ahead too fast or the talking volume is inadequate.

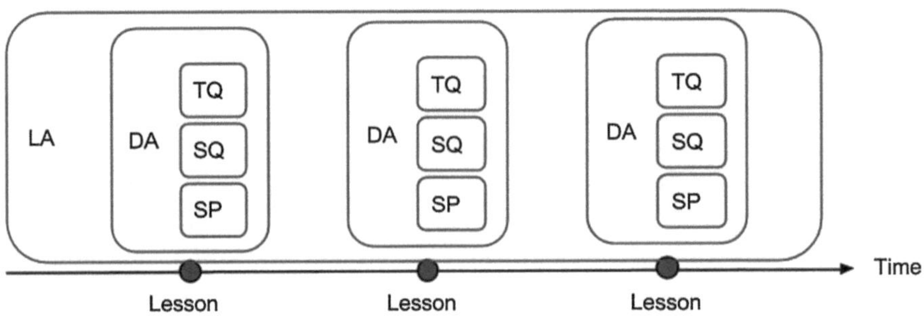

Fig. 1. Demonstrates how the three forms of feedback TQ, SQ and SP are organized by DA and LA.

Moreover modern CRS are able to organize the given feedback to get a deeper understanding. The following methods present current methods for organizing live feedback.

- Durable Access (DA): Students and teachers can later access all the given feedback. Teachers are then able to provide additional material or examples and can improve the presentation. Students can use the feedback to identify important facts, topic or issues for a better preparation for their exams [7,24].
- Identify students learning issues across lessons and terms (LA): By the use of identities (or even pseudonyms) teachers are able to track down how students learn. Interested readers are referred to the field of learning analytics [10].

Figure 1 demonstrates how the three forms of feedback TQ, SQ and SP are organized by DA and LA. Whilst the feedback generated in a lesson can be accessed afterwards (DA), LA allows to identify correlations between the students feedback over lessons or terms.

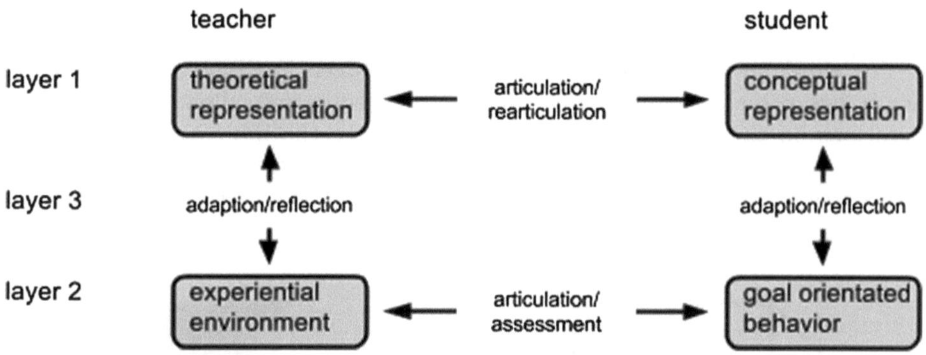

Fig. 2. Conversational framework of learning [15,16,18].

3 Communicative Learning

3.1 Learning

Our main question was if and how modern CRS that operate more socially do affect learning processes in lectures and other forms of university courses. Answering this question requests an exploration of the relation between learning and communication. We grounded our investigation on that relation in a learning model, Diana Laurillard introduced in the late 1990s and has refined up to her present contributions to the debate on academic teaching. It promotes our position in a threefold way [15–18].

- First, it comes from scientifically based efforts for reforms in academic education.
- Second, it uses an educational-driven approach to the use of digital technologies [17].
- And third, it implements important aspects of the social nature of learning.

Her model essentially consists of three layers composed to an conversational framework of learning (Fig. 2). These layers postulate the main functions teachers and learners have in educational settings. The first layer, the layer of conceptual discussion combines the function of content distribution on the basis of theoretical conceptions on the teachers side and the function of content documentation framed by an individual conception on the learners side. Learners even have to reply on distributed content and to control their individual understanding of content in the light of the teachers reactions on their replies.

The second layer, the layer of interaction, is determined by a learning environment constituted by the teacher. Within this environment learners are obligated to solve concrete tasks, such as working out exercises, solving questions or preparing talks or papers. Interaction even includes to observe how learners cope with those tasks on the teachers side. Additionally, learners will admit their processing of tasks while teachers attend to and react on their attempts at a solution.

The third layer establishes a connection between the first and the second one. It has a meta-cognitive function and its realization allows to adopt the operations on the interactive layer with respect to the interchange of content on the conceptual layer. Furthermore it enables to assess the reaches and limits of theoretical concepts in the light of task coping and outcomes as practical experiences on the interactive layer.

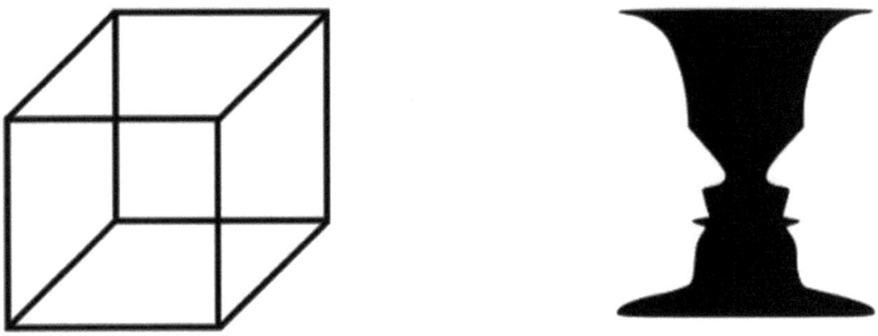

Fig. 3. Picture puzzles convey different information depending on the flexible interplay between fore- and background [22].

Laurillard claims that learning processes based on these three layers go beyond simple instruction. Because any successful understanding of content depends on the ability of teachers and learners to apply a common ontological (object reference) and epistemic (direction of understanding) frame of reference. That means they have to anticipate a common identification of objects and their epistemic treatment in order to use transmitted content the same way. However, a central demand on teaching is not to presume this redundancy of orientation between teachers and learners, but to support its evolution. This evolutionary process has to take into account an iterative progress of adjustment between the differing prerequisites of the participants in an educational process. The core instrument Laurillard suggests to make the outlined adjustment run is giving and handling feedback on each of the frameworks layers.

3.2 Misunderstanding Feedback

First of all, feedback is a way to interrupt the progress of content transmission (layer 1) and task instruction (layer 2) in order to check coherence between transmission and reception of content. Normally, the function of this interruption is seen as an adjustment between intentions behind content transmission on the teachers side and abilities to cope with content on the learners side. Feedback controls the amount of acceptable deviation between intended (teacher) and actually performed (student) understanding of content. This is why feedback is regarded as part of ideal solutions that integrate modern, learner centered teaching into academic education [25].

This perspective on feedback is commonly attended by two major misunderstandings which have to be left behind in order to claim a useful approach to the relation between learning and communication. The first misunderstanding mistakes information for chunked and distinctive unities that can be encoded into and decoded from various types of media data, such as language or pictures. In contrast and accordingly to Gestalt psychology and information theory Gregory Bateson sketches information as a relational term. He says that information always is given as a difference that makes a difference [5]. Firstly, that means any information is an interplay between accentuation (1st difference) and a background that effects its perception (2nd difference). And secondly, different backgrounds can lead to different information. Figure 3 shows an example from perception theory: Switching fore- and background changes the informational structure of the pictures.

Extended research on misconceptions proved that even advanced students have serious difficulties to distinguish e.g. common, everyday from scientific knowledge backgrounds while attending lectures, courses or even texts like scripts or books. In result students regularly fail to derive scientifically appropriate information from what they hear and read in academic education. On the other hand, competences to observe and to reflect those difficulties normally develop slowly. They highly differ on the level of individual availability. In effect content reception and learning is constantly interfered by heterogeneous background knowledge of learners and teachers. Together with organisational as well as epistemic problems to access those differing sources of content reception, handling background knowledge within educational settings is complex and demanding [18].

The second misunderstanding directly follows from not paying attention to the problem of background knowledge. Without this attention feedback could be regarded as the operation of requiring and giving informational repetition and extension. But prior to anything else we have to understand how feedback copes with the problem of complexity and intransparency concerning background knowledge for content reception. That means feedback should be analysed as a way how teachers and learners find scopes within a huge variety of potential repetitions and extensions of content. Therefore feedback should be (re)defined in terms of knowledge strategies which break down the complexity and intransparency of individual background knowledge to socially accountable questions and topics. It also will be necessary to explore if and how feedback processes support reflection of knowledge strategies in academic education. Since feedback is communication we assume that beside formal rules and technical filtering these issues are operated within specific forms of communication. The following section will display these forms from a communication theory point of view.

3.3 Feedback as Communication of Control

If we want to understand how communication operates feedback as a strategy of knowledge organisation we have to understand how communication works. It was Claude E. Shannon who contributed one of the most influencing and yet transdisciplinary discussed model of communication which we choose to provide our basic assumptions on communication. Beyond common reception as a model of message transmission, it allows to access what we said above (Sect. 3.2) about information from a communication theory point of view. The key point is a redefinition of the term message. He say:

The significant aspect is that the actual message is one selected from a set of possible messages. The system must be designed to operate for each possible selection, not just the one which will actually be chosen since this is unknown at the time of design [21].

Shannon added selectivity to be a crucial attribute of messages in a communication system. He modeled a nexus that bounds any single event of communication into a context of other possible and coherent communicative events. Shannon assumed that a single communicative event could be better handled, if it is related to such a context. His concern was technically motivated. He postulated, that the amount of information processing, a communication system has to manage, declines, if it is able to predict or estimate the probability of any other event that could follow to any preceding event. For example, the amount of processed information declines if the probability of b following a is smaller than c following a. In result, the capacity of information transfer and processing could be reduced.

This account on communication is highly interesting for modeling not only technical but human communication. If we apply our previously depicted problem of prior knowledge heterogeneity and intransparency, operation and scope of content reception will always be hardly to predict within educational settings. The main function communication conveys here is not to discover the full potential of an individuals conditions applied to his or her engagement with transmitted content. That would not afford any contribution to better predict content reception. Communication is more than just talking about individual states or sensitivities within learning processes. Communication has used to find a scope of selective topics and issues, which the communicative partners are able to connect with based on their individual state of reception while they are attending to and coping with feedback. To treat feedback by communication implicates a selective way of marking and negotiating feedback. Selective communicative treatment gives feedback a specific meaning and determines its relevance. In result we have to treat feedback not as transmission of messages, but as a way to introduce and to differentiate frames that increase social predictability of content reception. For example it is not important to explore any individuals prior knowledge from everydays life but to introduce the difference of thinking within or without a methodically established paradigm. Understanding feedback as communication means to control the availability of specific frames of content reception and to dispose their perpetuation. We now want to distinguish two major strategies conveying two basic forms of coping with feedback in the outlined way (for general introduction [2,20]).

3.4 Systemic Intervention into Feedback

Lectures normally work on the conceptual layer of learning. Lectures are successful when learners are able to anticipate an intended conceptual order of knowledge out of the way they document presented content (Fig. 4). From a communication theory point of view, this setting could be regarded as systemic setting. Communicative Systems contain an affordance-competence balance [3]. And this is the case, when behavior on the one hand could be regarded as an accomplishment of an affordance setting on the other. The learners activities to document content and to anticipate underlying conceptual orders then are accomplishments to the intentions a teacher has in a specific learning process. Feedback framed by a systemic communication strategy will focus the partners on their knowledge about the structure of demands within that setting. They have to specify and reformulate what they determine to be the right understanding of underlying affordances.

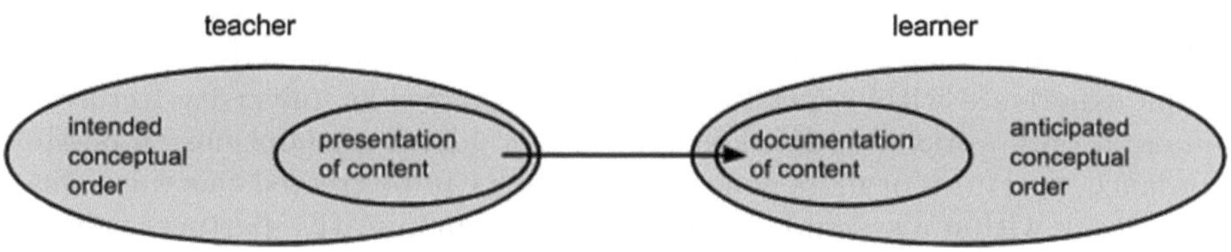

Fig. 4. Conceptual basis of learning based on [16,18].

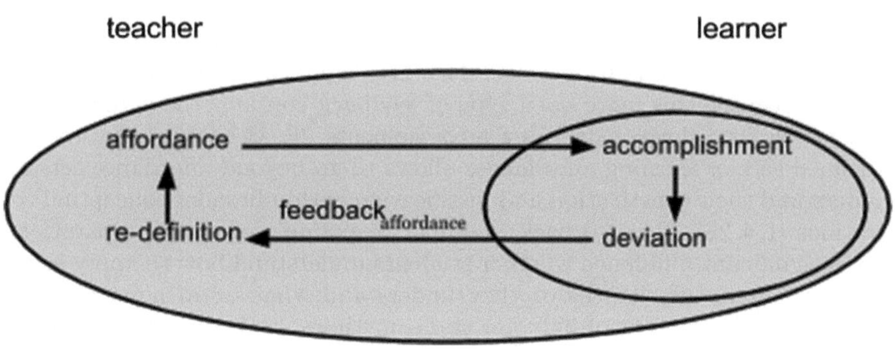

Fig. 5. Systemic feedback process (integrated application of [3,16]).

In result the partners are able to decide whether their behavior is a deviation reclaimable by an accomplishment that fits to their understanding of given demands. Reaction on feedback within this framework will take feedback as a hint on deviation from ideal and it will reclaim this ideal by re-defining the affordance structure behavior should apply to. The problem is, such communicative framework only deals with feedback allowing to connect deviating behavior with redefinitions of given affordances. That means, feedback already has to contain certain links to that affordance structure. In other words, it has to be consciously settled within a given affordance framework, which is shared between the communicative partners in the feedback process.

For example students ask for more explanation within a given topic area because they understand this topic area to be important for their exams and fear to overlook important issues without more explanation. However requesting more explanation could be a deviation from ideal learner performance within a lecture. But it could be handled within the systemic strategy, if the students request already contains knowledge about an intended affordance on the teachers side, e.g. exam preparation, and if this knowledge is shared between teacher and student. Replies to this feedback only have to redefine the affordance structure exam preparation in order to adjust performed and ideal behavior, that means to decide whether requesting more explanation is useful or not within the affordance set exam preparation.

We call feedback annotated in Fig. 5 affordance competent or systemic feedback. We want to suggest that it only can be given by skilled students with enough experience within specific educational settings as university lectures or courses. It only works if feedback is applied to students assumptions on possible affordance structures or more general if feedback can be treated this way. Treating feedback within a systemic strategy needs communicative partners, who are able to find and assume comparable assumptions on a set of affordances in a learning process.

3.5 Concept Critical Interventions into Feedback

Feedback without a strong linkage to socially shared affordances is difficult to handle within a systemic framework. This is a significant problem for learning processes. Because this more open type of feedback contains the highest potential to enable and develop learning advancements [6]. Because deviation from pre-defined sets of learning affordances allows to go beyond affordance sets and to understand their constitution and justification within broader conceptual considerations [1,4,26]. If we go back to our little example of exam preparation it makes a significant difference whether students understand how to apply lecture contents to exam affordances or they understand, that exam affordances are constituted in the context of different and sometimes even competing standards within scientific paradigms or even other perhaps administrative and legal considerations. Feedback that deviates from pre-defined affordance sets contains the opportunity to investigate such contexts and to reclaim a deeper understanding of learning affordances and their range of variation.

The learning theory discussion above suggested to realize such demands by switching between different learning layers and to transfer experiences on one layer to the other. It has been emphasized that such transfer allows to insert experiences on one layer as a hint on the conceptual basis, that constitutes the other layer. For example the quizzes function of CRS can be used to go through a kind of exam like situation in order to help students anticipating the exam affordance set behind lectures. However the main issue here is, that this conclusion has to be worked out in a broader communicative setting. Within this setting communication has to ensure, that deviations are not rejected too soon as interferences into pre-defined systemic frameworks. Instead communication has to be aligned to find contexts which handle systemically deviating feedback as occasion to search for other affordance-accomplishment balances or as occasion to adapt pre-defined affordances.

On a communicative level it also means to find different partners or groups, who are able to pick up and investigate feedback in the outlined way. In effect, this type of communication leads to adaptive processes within given systemic frameworks as well as to distinction and differentiation between varieties of systemic settings. This type of communication additionally unfolds demands on the comparative competences amongst communicative partners. And this demand has to be implemented by parallel investigations into the conceptual basis different systemic settings are based on (Fig. 6).

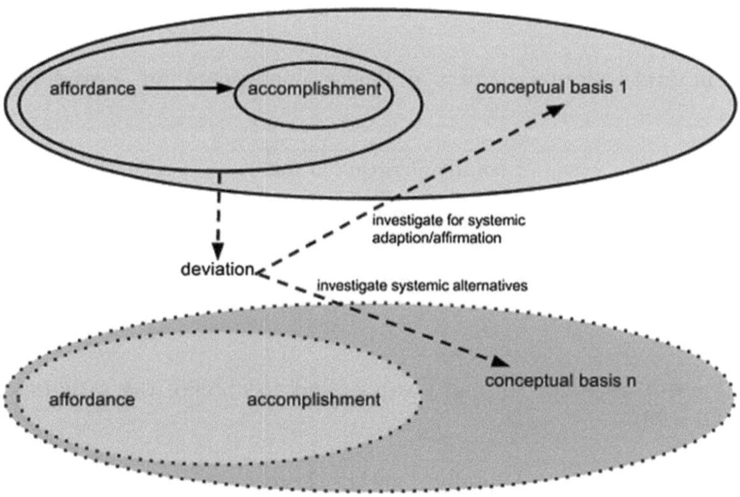

Fig. 6. Concept critical intervention into feedback.

This type of communicative intervention allows to rebind deviations from single affordance settings back into academic lessons and to apply the content and the progress of lessons to different scopes of relevance and function. In effect, the communicative demands on such intervention are more complex. Because given feedback could not only be immediately applied or rejected, but even preserved for later treatment, transferred into other contexts of application and integrated into social discourse about the range of conceptual diversity feedback fits to.

4 Evaluation

Regarding the importance of feedback we evaluated students use of a Modern Classroom Response System called Tweedback. This evaluation has been performed In January 2014 with 76 students. At first we asked the students for their general interest in a Modern CRS, which resulted in a set of 62.1 % motivated students (Table 1). As Table 2 shows, our implication that students use their mobile devices in lectures already has been confirmed (73.3 %). Whereas the students technical equipment and their basic motivation to use a modern CRS are distinctive, these values promote the expectation of a rather extensive usage of Tweedback.

Table 1. I am always interested in new technology like Tweedback (n = 76, valid = 74).

Scale	I totally agree	I rather agree	I am undecided	I rather disagree	I totally disagree
n	26	20	15	8	5
Percentage of valid	35.1	27	20.3	10.8	6.8

Table 2. In every session I carry a device operational for Tweedback (n = 76, valid = 75).

Scale	I totally agree	I rather agree	I am undecided	I rather disagree	I totally disagree
n	48	7	3	7	10
Percentage of valid	64	9.3	4	9.3	13.3

Table 3. I use Tweedback to read postings and to observe the activities of others (n = 76, valid = 73).

Scale	I totally agree	I rather agree	I am undecided	I rather disagree	I totally disagree
n	11	21	12	7	22
Percentage of valid	15.1	28.8	16.4	9.6	30.1

In contrast to these results passive (Table 3) as well as active (Table 4) usage of Tweedback considerably stand back from basic motivation and technological opportunity. What could be reasons for this finding that should be taken seriously. It is obvious that Tweedback is a new technology so that many possible

Table 4. I use Tweedback to post messages, to answer questions or to give feedback (n = 76, valid = 74).

Scale	I totally agree	I rather agree	I am undecided	I rather disagree	I totally disagree
n	8	13	11	14	28
Percentage of valid	10.8	17.6	14.9	18.9	37.8

users may be reserved because of not being used to and trained in its operation and effects. Furthermore the early development stage of Tweedback entails usability issues, which may cause user dissatisfactions. But this is valid for all students in the survey. Only a vanishingly small amount of students already made earlier experiences with Tweedback. Training and adaptation are no sufficient categories for explaining the gap between the motivational and technological potential of Tweedback use on the one side and the actual practice of Tweedback use on the other side. If these categories may be sufficient, we should not have any relevant amount of Tweedback use, which is neither the case.

Accordingly to our learning theory approach, we examined if we had to deal with different types of learners and if different dispositions in organizing learning do affect the motivation and the actual practice of Tweedback usage. As Table 5 shows, we identified clusters of three different learning types based on the specific learning layer they prefer and based on their affinity to Tweedback. We see, that only one group is associated significantly with a high degree of Tweedback affinity (see cluster 2). We call this group progressive learners, because the students in this group are specially characterized by an extended consciousness for combining the content of teaching with concrete scenarios.

Furthermore Table 6 implies a much higher Tweedback use of progressive learners than conservative or double-minded learners. The chi-square-distribution shows a non-significant value of ($X = 2.232$; $p = 0.328$) for passive use, whereas active use has a high-significant value of ($X = 20.529$; $p = 0.000$). Especially the active use is strongly correlated to the progressive learners. This means that Tweedback is interesting for learners, who have great learning skills already. These learning skills mainly bases on the learners ability to put themselves into the situation where the content of teaching is applicable. These learners are able to establish a relation between the contents context and its application. As described in the previous section, the context is defined by the layer a learner is on: On the first layer it covers all the requirements to document and process the content. On the second layer context covers the requirement to formulate the contents aims and issues, so learners can check if their skills are sufficient to apply their knowledge on real problems. Therefore these learners use the relation between the contents context and its application to check their understanding and their need to expand their understanding by learning. In addition they do not primarily depend on the elaboration of the content of teachings application. This type of learners settles for learning knowledge with an existing background

Table 5. Learner types and Tweedback affinity.

	cluster 1 (conservative learners, n = 6)	cluster 2 (progressive learners, n = 31)	cluster 3 (double-minded learners, n = 27)
	Percentage rate of agreement within the cluster	Percentage rate of agreement within the cluster	Percentage rate of agreement within the cluster
Learning layer			
In lectures I attach importance to discussion concerning concepts	16.7	96.8	55.5
In lectures I attach importance to concrete working tasks	50	90.3	81.4
In lectures I attach importance to become aware of different perspectives on one topic	0	87.1	55.5
Tweedback affinity			
I am always interested in new technology like Tweedback	0	100	37
Tweedback should be used in more lectures and courses	0	100	33.3

of application instead of always getting informed about a concrete application. They are able to combine and compact this knowledge. Based on this implication and the results presented in Table 7, we can see that active Tweedback users, who mainly are progressive learners, take advantage of Tweedback because it is supporting them on conceptual discussions (first layer of Laurillards conversational framework of learning).

Table 6. Correlation of learner types with mode of Tweedback usage.

Mode of Tweedback usage	cluster 1 (conservative learners, n = 6)	cluster 2 (progressive learners, n = 31)	cluster 3 (double-minded learners, n = 27)
	Percentage rate of agreement within the cluster	Percentage rate of agreement within the cluster	Percentage rate of agreement within the cluster
I use Tweedback to read posts and to observe the activities of others (passive)	40	67.7	52
I use Tweedback to post messages, to answer questions or to give feedback (active)	0	74.2	23.1

From a communication-oriented view this means, Tweedback is used by learners, who are able to safely combine and compact the content of teaching for extracting concepts. The teaching contents contexts, which are necessary for and leady to reflect and understand the content, are grounded for these learners and are rarely discussed on Tweedback (Concept before Context). Discussing concepts instead of contexts is not uncommon for environments, where Tweedback is used, so we just showed that Tweedback is not strongly changing this type of communication. It seems that a way of communication, which focus on contexts elaboration and additionally supports learners, who have strong deficits in elaborating the content of teachings context (and therefore are not able to extract concepts), needs more than just a Chatwall. The next chapter will cover the didactical and technical implications of this statement.

Table 7. How active users estimate the impact of Tweedback use on learning.

Impact of Tweedback use on learning layer	Percentage rate of agreement
Tweedback helps to promote conceptual discussion (layer 1)	62
Tweedback helps to acquire concrete working tasks (layer 2)	43.3
Tweedback helps to change perspective on topics (layer 3)	37.9

5 Social Classroom Response Systems

Based on the critics and the suggestions for improvement from Sect. 3 and the results we presented in Sect. 4, we will outline a new generation of CRS that is aware of and supports communicative intervention into feedback. The notion of classroom, however, has to be understood in the broader sense of a community of learners; their interaction may occur at the same time and same place (traditional CRS) or at different places (for remote learners) or times (carried over to different cohorts of learners).

This section describes our approach for a social CRS that is aware of social communication. At first we will present the conceptual design for this approach, then we address technical challenges and state feasible implementations for them.

5.1 Conceptual Design

On feedback-events (communicative interventions), when students struggle with an issue, discussions with others can arise. CRS should be aware of these events, because they are a part of students learning process. Similar to bubbles that rise to the surface, discussions can split off the lessons content. Whether or not discussions may not directly related to the lessons content, they are important for their members and can become interesting later on. Moreover, CRS should provide methods to initiate or create such discussion-bubbles. Because students often use their own medium, as social networks or online learning platforms, to discuss an issue, CRS should be able to export discussions. Thereby students are still able to use their known medium for discussion even if they deal with something that has not been created on this medium (enabling concept critical feedback).

In addition to the ability to leave lessons to follow a discussion, CRS have to provide a mechanism to return to a lecture, so students on the one hand can adapt their knowledge generated from the discussion to the current teaching content and teachers on the other hand can react on issues aftereffects. CRS that support to leave to and return from a discussion to a lesson are then able to keep track of learning processes and creation of learners background, respectively. This enables teachers and students to organize and analyze their own and others learning processes and how they built up their context. Furthermore a lecture does now not only consist of teachers knowledge-materials, it also consists of the process how students identify and solve issues. This makes is possible to understand students context.

Whereas traditional technical support in a classroom started with a blackboard and evolved via projector to an electronic presentation of learning material. The next logical step is interactive learning material, where the interaction can take place with a preprogrammed digital tutor (systemic intervention), or with a human docent or co-learner (systemic and concept critical intervention). This communication however must not have the usual digital form of interpersonal exchange (such as email, forum etc.) since in this form it is not centered on the topic to be learned or on the learner but rather on the usual human ritual of communication. Rather, new forms of dynamic lecture materials should be developed, where a Q&A session with a docent of a co-learner is directly connected with that place in the lecture material, where the problem arose.

On this interactive learning material also passive users are able to mark problems. As we presented in the previous sections, active users are able to extract concepts from the content of teaching because they already have a sense of its application. Passive users have strong deficits in extracting these concepts because they lack a sense of application, so they are mostly not able to understand the content of teaching and therefore are mostly not able to formulate this issue. If CRS provide a mechanism to these kind of learners to mark their issues at a place where they lose the plot (marking them directly in the slides), they do not have to struggle with a verbalization of an issue they are not to explain.

Filtering of content, when a participant is able to select the information he will see, and targeting of content, when a participant is able to designate recipients for his questions, remarks and answers, might be necessary to maintain a reasonable signal-to-noise ratio on a social CRS. This is especially important, when the collection and dissemination of contributions is not restricted to real time classroom activities and may span even courses.

5.2 Technical Design

Regarding the concepts previously described there are many technical challenges for implementations of Social CRS. Because modern CRS clients mostly run on mobile devices we assume that every potential user has a web browser and an internet connection, whether mobile or not. Based on this assumption we identify three main technical challenges. First of all there is the teaching content itself, which is the source of most feedback and the main part of interactive learning materials. Second the discussions, including their participants, references and verbalizations have to be implemented. Third the export of discussions is a functionality that highly depends on other technical frameworks, concepts and standards.

The teaching content mainly covers teachers presentation slides, scripts or any other digital documents. Current web technologies are able to present and distribute all of these documents, so the previous assumptions of an existing web browser enables Social CRS to display nearly every digital content teachers are currently using.

Providing a space for discussion or social communication is mainly covered by feedback type SQ (students questions). Even so discussions can arise from issues on other feedback types, so there has to be an implementation to switch to SQ or at least to initiate a discussion on a different medium. Furthermore discussions can include references to the content of teaching, which can be implemented with references to digital objects (pictures, paragraphs, words, videos, etc.) of the digital teaching content. Moreover, social communication needs participants who can be addressable and identifiable. Modern CRS mostly have possibilities for users to use an existing identity, either from their university software system or their social networks. At least all users should be able to address new participants for a discussion and to resign the participation in a discussion. Social CRS can implement this requirement by using the existing identity management.

Exporting discussions or social communication highly depends on targets for an export and needs a specification for addressing. As stated above we recommend a strategy where digital fragments (or digital objects), as paragraphs, slides, pictures, etc., get unique identifiers. Additionally we assign each discussion and each point of discussion an unique id. Over the set of all digital objects and their identifiers Social CRS can span an Application Programming Interface (API), so identifiers are accessible with an unique URL. Thus Social CRS create the ability for a digital ecosystem around the given feedback. Applications of this ecosystem are able to access all the digital objects even if they were not created on them.

6 Conclusions

Our approach claimed that social advancement of CRS is not only a matter of technical development. First of all it is a topic that forces to acknowledge the social character of any feedback process in educational settings and to ask how communication enables and supports feedback as well as how communication effects or maybe interferes learning. We showed that there are two basic types of communication on providing feedback. On the one hand the systemic intervention into feedback, when students need to deviate their accomplishment due to differences between their understanding and teachers knowledge. On the other hand the concept critical intervention onto feedback, which allows to rebind deviations from an affordance settings and to apply the teaching content and the progress of lessons to different scopes of relevance and function.

The evaluation of our system Tweedback indicates a bias for systemic feedback. Active users estimated main effects of Tweedback on the conceptual layer of learning. They used Tweedback to cope with documentation and representation of content while not attending to the application and reflection of content in equal measure. That may surprise because active Tweedback users dominantly were skilled learners with distinctive attention to the other layers of learning. Such findings are critical in a twofold way. On the one hand, skilled learners do not take the opportunity to go beyond established borders of content application and reflection. And less skilled learners on the other will miss the opportunity to explore the interconnection between content representation and application. At least, less skilled learners will fail to join any conversation that implicates such interconnections without accessing them explicitly. They are excluded from such communicative structures of feedback.

The striking conclusion for technical implementation of more socially operating CRS is not how to enable just more interaction. Moreover we presented conceptual and technical designs to create a Social CRS that is aware of these communication challenges on feedback. This includes our approach to handle discussions (communicative interventions), which result from feedback, as important and necessary. CRS should allow to initiate or create discussions as a new part of a lesson that may be progressed in a different medium as well as CRS have to provide a way back to the teaching content. In addition we presented technical solutions for this concept which mainly base on a web application that provides discussion-objects.

In fact of the importance of discussions we are sensible of the distractions Social CRS will create. We see (Social) CRS as a tool for teachers and students that can support the learning process. For this reason one has to be aware that CRS are only able to see a portion of reality. This means that the benefit of feedback and its permanently availability highly depends on students motivation to document their feedback.

Beside this limitation Social CRS and CRS in general are able to become more than just feedback systems. In practice we observed students using CRS to criticize also the system around the lecturer: Some students claimed nuisances on the composition of students with different states of knowledge, which is because the students come from different areas and which is enforced by the university administration. Even if the lecturer recognized this critics as spam at first, he identified it as this critic later on. Keeping this in mind makes it hard to decide if a discussion's level of distraction is worth it or not, even if this discussion might look like spam.

Further research should take up the discussion about social communication with CRS in general. Moreover there are several interesting questions on the discussion export. For example if it is possible to remove an existing export or all related connections. Furthermore it is possible that the ability to document all the social communication can lead to more unrelated information, such as spam, and that such information result in more expense of filtering them. In addition to this question further research can focus on the filtering itself. The filtering itself can be a part of the learning process and may be underestimated.

At least studies on CRS usage remain highly important. On the one hand it has to be evaluated how teachers and students use Social CRS and if they get different benefit from them as we have seen. On the other hand it should be evaluated when students use Social CRS or their documented content respectively. The latter may show that students use their documented social communication mostly for preparation for their exams. Of course this hypothesis is speculative at this point, but such an offline use, however, could require coining a new term, since it no longer is a Classroom Response System.

Acknowledgements. This work was supported in part by the German Federal Ministry of Education and Research (BMBF) and the University of Rostock. We gratefully acknowledge the professional and motivating atmosphere offered by them in supporting our study.

References

1. Baecker, D.: The network synthesis of social action ii: understanding catjects. Cybern. Human Knowing **15**(1), 45–65 (2008)
2. Baecker, D.: Systems, network, and culture. Soziale Systeme **15**, 271–287 (2009)
3. Baecker, D.: A systems primer on universities. Soziale Systeme **16**, 356–367 (2010)
4. Baecker, D.: Observing networks: a note on asymmetrical social forms. Cybern. Human Knowing **19**(4), 9–25 (2012)

5. Bateson, G.: Mind and Nature: A Necessary Unity. Dutton, New York (1979)
6. Bateson, G.: Steps to an Ecology of Mind: Collected Essays in Anthropology, Psychiatry, Evolution and Epistemology, 5th edn. University of Chicago Press, Chicago (2000)
7. Crouch, C.H., Mazur, E.: Peer instruction: ten years of experience and results. Am. J. Phys. **69**, 970 (2001)
8. Draper, S., Cargill, J., Cutts, Q.: Electronically enhanced classroom interaction. Aust. J. Educ. Technol. **18**(1), 13–23 (2002)
9. Feiten, L., Buehrer, M., Sester, S., Becker, B.: Smile-smartphones in lectures-initiating a smartphone-based audience response system as a student project. In: CSEDU, vol. 1, pp. 288–293 (2012)
10. Ferguson, R.: The state of learning analytics in 2012: A review and future challenges. Knowledge Media Institute, Technical Report KMI-2012-01 (2012)
11. Fies, C., Marshall, J.: Classroom response systems: a review of the literature. J. Sci. Educ. Technol. **15**(1), 101–109 (2006)
12. Jenkins, A.: Technique and technology: electronic voting systems in an English literature lecture. Pedagogy **7**(3), 526–533 (2007)
13. Kay, R.H., LeSage, A.: Examining the benefits and challenges of using audience response systems: a review of the literature. Comput. Educ. **53**(3), 819–827 (2009)
14. Kundisch, D., Sievers, M., Zoyke, A., Herrmann, P., Whittaker, M., Beutner, M., Fels, G., Magenheim, J.: Designing a web-based application to support peer instruction for very large groups. In: International Conference on Information Systems (2012)
15. Laurillard, D.: A conversational framework for individual learning applied to the 'learning organisation' and the 'learning society'. Syst. Res. Behav. Sci. **16**(2), 113–122 (1999)
16. Laurillard, D.: Rethinking University Teaching: A Framework for the Effective Use of Learning Technologies, 2nd edn. RoutledgeFalmer, London (2002)
17. Laurillard, D.: Digital Technologies and Their Role in Achieving Our Ambitions for Education. ERIC (2008). ISBN: 978-0-8547-3797-0
18. Laurillard, D.: Teaching as a Design Science: Building Pedagogical Patterns for Learning and Technology. Routledge, New York (2012)
19. Masschelein, J., Simons, M.: The university in the ears of its students: on the power, architecture and technology of university lectures. In: Ricken, N., Koller, H.-C., Keiner, E. (eds.) Die Idee der Universität - revisited, pp. 173–192. Springer Fachmedien, Wiesbaden (2013)
20. Ruesch, J., Bateson, G.: Communication: The Social Matrix of Psychiatry., vol. 114. The Norton Library, Norton, New York (1951)
21. Shannon, C.E.: A mathematical theory of communication. Bell Syst. Tech. J. **27**(3), 379–423 (1948)
22. De Smet, A.: Multistability. Wikipedia, June 2007
23. Vetterick, J., Garbe, M., Cap, C.H.: Tweedback: a live feedback system for large audiences. In: 5th International Conference on Computer Supported Education (CSEDU) (2013)
24. Vetterick, J., Garbe, M., Daehn, A., Cap, C.H.: Classroom response systems in the wild: technical and non-technical observations. Int. J. Interact. Mob. Technol. **8**(1), 21–25 (2014)
25. Weimer, M.: Learner-Centered Teaching: Five Key Changes to Practice, 2nd edn. Jossey-Bass, San Francisco (2013)
26. White, H.C.: Identity and Control: How Social Formations Emerge, 2nd edn. Princeton University Press, Princeton (2012)

Learning/Teaching Methodologies and Assessment

Simultaneously Developing a Serious Game and Its Classroom Use for Fostering Conceptual Understanding of Electrical Circuits: The Effect of the Game 'E&E Electrical Endeavours' on Secondary Students Conceptual Understanding of Electrical Circuits

Ruurd Taconis[1(✉)], Mariette Dubois[2], Lesley de Putter[3,4], and Henry van Bergen[5]

[1] Eindhoven School of Education, Eindhoven University of Technology, Den Dolech 2, Eindhoven, The Netherlands
r.taconis@tue.nl
[2] Sondervick College, Knegselseweg 30, Veldhoven, The Netherlands
[3] Heerbeeck College, Willem de Zwijgerweg 150, Best, The Netherlands
[4] Eindhoven University of Technology, Den Dolech 2, Eindhoven, The Netherlands
[5] Faculty of Electrical Engineering, Eindhoven University of Technology, Den Dolech 2, Eindhoven, The Netherlands

Abstract. Making use of favourable local circumstances an interdisciplinary team of content-experts, educational researchers, game-designers and secondary school teachers was formed. Using a design-research approach, the team simultaneously developed and tested a serious game for the teaching off electrical circuits and effective classroom practice using it.

The project comprised two rounds. In a first round, an open-inquiry teaching strategy was used and the game was observed to have a strong impact on students understanding, though not in the desired way. On the basis of this evaluation and additional expert-review, the game was redesigned. Simultaneously classroom practice was improved accordingly. An extend teacher guide was developed, supporting teachers in switching between 'free' gaming episodes in classroom and episodes of discussion and reflection. In the second round a strong impact on students' conceptual understanding of electrical circuits was observed and the students showed fewer misconceptions. Moreover students spontaneously reported that the game had helped them to understand the subject.

We conclude that multi-disciplinaire collaboration was essential for this result, and that teachers played a critically role in connecting the development of the game and classroom practice. The design research approach taken greatly helped to keep the teams focus on the educational output. Accordingly, the educational expert appeared to be best positioned to play a leading role. It was also concluded that when a suitable mental model is coherently represented in the game's structure and layout (looks included), a serious game may significantly contribute to students' conceptual understanding.

S. Zvacek et al. (Eds.): CSEDU 2014, CCIS 510, pp. 181–195, 2015.
DOI: 10.1007/978-3-319-25768-6_12

Keywords: Design research · Electrical circuits · Conceptual development · Serious games

1 Introduction

Serious games are an inviting new option in education. The game industry is growing spectacularly. However, the characteristics that make games adequate serious games and the pedagogical do's and don'ts of using them in education are still largely uncovered [19]. This paper reports on a design research project conducted using the game 'E&E electrical endeavours'. The project's aim is to help students master the subject of electrical circuits in grade 9 of Dutch secondary education, develop a pedagogical approach to using serious games in secondary education, and to motivate students for science and electrical engineering.

The game was previously developed at the faculty of Electrical Engineering at Eindhoven University of Technology mainly for raising the interest of potential new students. Hence the main focus in the initial version 1.0 of the E&E electrical endeavors game was on student involvement and motivation, excellent graphics and challenging content on electrical circuits. The game can be typified as a simulation based game for individual use. It is not a role-playing game where players are set against each other. In version 1.0 no match with formal science curricula was pursued. A pilot evaluation [4] showed the game was attractive and entertaining for students in secondary school.

Secondary schools were seeking ways to modernize education by implementing ICT, to enrich science education by e.g. serious games, and to bring a lively perspective on scientific practice and careers into the school.

Combining these, the joint conclusion was that both university and secondary school goals could be successfully supported if an attractive serious game could be constructed. The game should fit well into the formal curriculum, clearly contribute to student learning and should be brought into school as a sincere and attractive picture of scientific practice and careers.

To achieve this, a project group was formed comprising secondary school teachers, experts on science education and game-designers. Their task was to: "Construct and evaluate a serious game that is attractive and motivating on one hand and making an adequate contribution to formal learning in secondary education on the other". In line with this, a key research question addressed in this paper is: which characteristics of the game and of the way it is implemented in classroom make it adequate for learning about electrical circuits and dealing with misconceptions in particular? The approach taken to actually develop the game and answer the question was a design research project.

2 Theory

2.1 Building Serious Games and Design Research

Building and implementing serious games successfully requires a broad range of expertise in very different field such as: expertise concerning the content to be learned, expertise on teaching this content and pedagogical issues, practical knowledge of schools and teaching in schools, competence in game design, competence in building/programming the game etc. Moreover these should be brought together synergistically [9].

Design research is well known in both engineering and educational research [12]. In design research on education, education is being (re)designed and evaluated in various rounds. These comprise an alternating sequence of (re)design and evaluation leading to new or refined design criteria. The evaluation adds up to a picture that allows answering previously set research questions, as well as bringing forth new hypothesis and tentative answers. From a methodological point of view, it is a productive experimental design with both explorative and confirmative aspects. From a practitioner's point of view, it has the strong advantage of making a very close connection between research on one hand, and professional practice and professional development on the other.

2.2 Serious Games and Learning

Theory on the design and use of simulation-type serious games in education strongly emphasizes the concepts of flow [2] and experiential learning. A key theory on experiential learning is developed by Kolb [17], and adapted for the case of serious games by various authors [18, 21].

Using insights from general cognitive constructivist learning theories and the five stage model of skill acquisition by Dreyfus and Dreyfus [5], Taconis [24] developed a hypothetical model of experiential learning in serious games. The 'Taconis model' explicitly pictures how the rules underlying and governing the game-engine, through producing the game's 'behavior' and the regularities in the gaming environment, structure the learners experiences while gaming. It also pictures how skilled action by the learner, the acquisition of operational rules and ultimately a coherent reconstruction of the rules underlying the game-engine's may result from the learners 'structured experiences'.

In the model 'skilled actions' (upper box in second column in Fig. 2) are defined as those actions adequate within the gaming environment that do not imply or require conscious declarative knowledge. These actions represent adequate behaviour in standard situations without being underpinned with knowledge. This corresponds to the *advanced beginner* position in the Dreyfus and Dreyfus five-stage-model.

'Operational rules' (middle box in second column in Fig. 2) are – in line with the five-stage-model – considered a next step in development. The operational rules are typified by the involvement of conceptual understanding, though of an operational type, using concepts that are apparent within the experienced game environment. An example would be a learner that acts adequately within the game and is able to explain why and how he performs in terms of the game-world. This could be considered roughly equivalent to the stage of being *competent* within the five-stage-model though this concerns the game-environment only. Reaching this level requires the constructing (learning) of operational rules from experience, and it is presumed to require systematic and reflective thinking. Constructing these rules may be stimulated by asking the students questions, facilitating group discussions and adding tasks that require the construction and verbalization of such rules. Operational rules and skilled actions may transfer from the strict game-environment to other situations/environments, and this is more likely to occur the more akin these situations are [25]. For example, from a serious game that models projectile trajectories, skilled actions and operational rules may relatively easily transfer to projectile shooting experiments in classroom, but less easily to text-book questions on this subject or the context of satellite trajectories (Fig. 1).

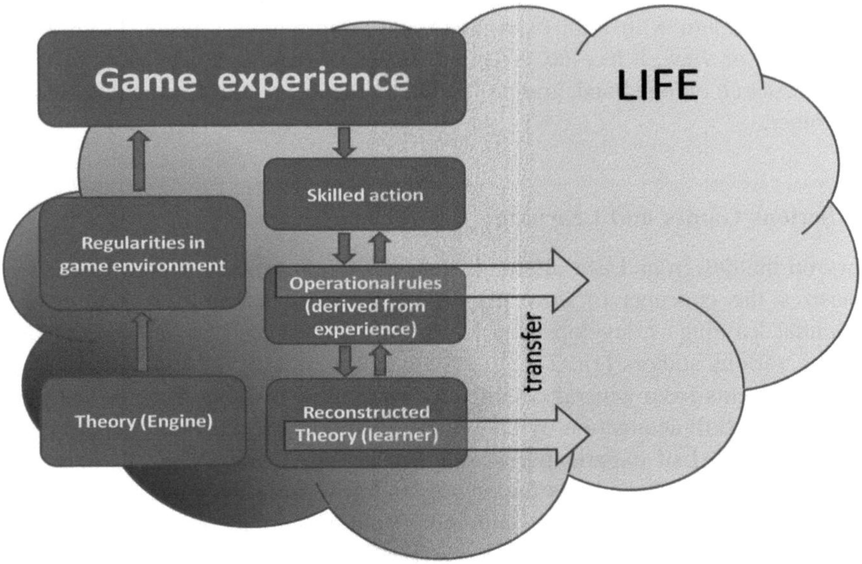

Fig. 1. The hypothetical model of experiential learning in simulation-based serious games by Taconis [24].

The (re)construction of 'theoretical insight' (lower box in second column in Fig. 2), aligns with both *'competent within the game-environment'* towards *'competent in real life'*. This splitting-up of the 'competent stage' in the five-stage-model results from the fact that experiential learning from serious games involves two realities: the real world and the game world that simulates it. By its nature, theoretical insight will formally apply to real-life situations, since the rules a simulation based serious game is built upon apply to real world as well. Even though in many cases the rules underlying the game are in fact simplified versions of real life rules.

But this equivalence will not be automatically clear to the learner. Hence, theoretical insight only principally applies to both the game-world and the real world. In education, the learner should make considerable effort to understand and recognize this difference (transfer) and to achieve a 'competent in real-life' stage.

Constructing or reconstructing theoretical insight definitely requires systematic and reflective thinking as described above, but also making comparisons with contrasting and/or akin situations and theoretical points of view. The confrontation with situations other than the game-environment is needed; both to help constructing the

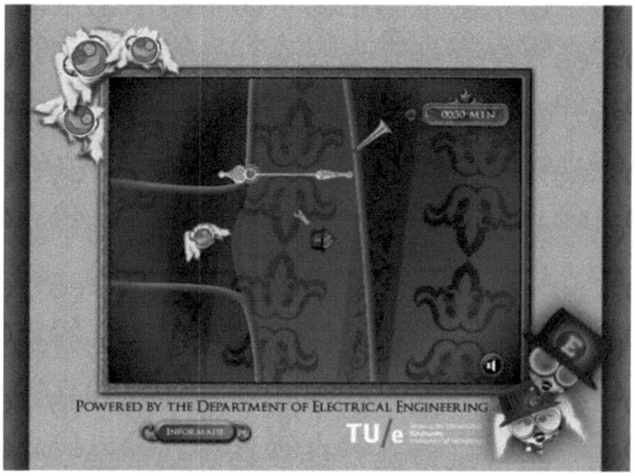

Fig. 2. Characteristic screen shots of E&E electrical endeavors version 1.1.

theoretical ideas independently from the game-world and to facilitate transfer to other situations [25].

The presumed necessity to implement in class these reflective of theoretical components as well as exercises in other learning-environments than the game-environment, conflicts with the fundamental importance of flow for gaming and the use of serious games in education. Put in terms of a concrete design dilemma: how can we have students 'in the flow' while gaming within the game-environment as well as active as critical thinkers on a theoretical level transcending the game-environment. This seems to connect to a fundamental design dilemma in inquiry structured or open education aiming at conceptual development described by various authors [15] and - for the case of education on electrical circuits - Kock et al. [16].

Once attained, theoretical insight opens up an avenue to develop towards proficiency with respect to real-life situations and beyond.

2.3 Learning About Electrical Circuits

Learning problems in electricity have been widely documented: Over the years remedies have been suggested to overcome students' conceptual problems in electricity, but only with limited success [20]. The topic is still receiving attention e.g. [10, 13, 14, 23]. Coming to grips with the scientific concepts in electricity requires an understanding of the physics involved, which is at least partly at odds with the everyday experiences and ways of speaking about electricity [7, 22].

A key problem is the development of inadequate conceptual understanding of various aspects of electrical circuits and particular persistent 'misconceptions' that students tend to develop. In Duit's STCSE bibliography on students' 'misconceptions' and conceptual change [6] several hundreds of publications are listed on learning electricity.

Taconis [24] has described a hierarchical building of concepts concerning electrical circuits based on a review of literature. Each addition to the concepts requires all concepts in the lower floors to be rightly understood.

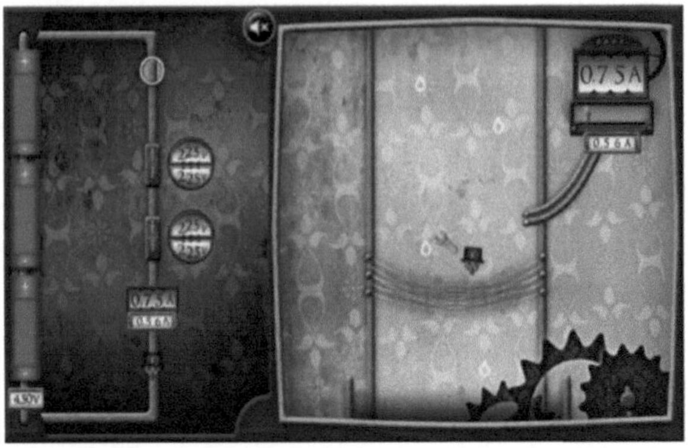

Fig. 3. A characteristic screen shot of E&E electrical endeavours version 3.0.

1. Correct understanding of electrical circuits essentially being closed but not short-circuited, and the electricity circling in the circuit, and the current not being consumed in the circuit,
2. Understanding that two distinct physical quantities are necessary to understand/describe the flow in electrical circuits (and such systems): electrical current and voltage,
3. Understanding of the topological types of electrical circuits; series and parallel and their implications for electrical current and voltage.
4. Understanding of particular electrical components and their properties.

Students may experience problems on either level of this hierarchy and students' alternative ideas often do not correspond to the scientific view and do not easily change through instruction [8, 10, 22, 23]. Kock et al. [16] conclude: when trying to solve problems or explain phenomena in circuits, students frequently (a) confuse important concepts such as current and voltage, (b) use the idea that current is consumed (or use unipolar, clashing or shared current models), (c) view power supplies as a source of constant current instead of constant potential difference, (d) have difficulties building and drawing circuits and (e) do not realize that a change of one element can have an impact on the current in the whole circuit.

A main obstacle here is that students may tend to understand electrical phenomena in terms of the so called 'experiential gestalt of causation' [1]. This basic misinterpretation may underlay many of the observed misconceptions.

In the 'experiential gestalt of causation' there is an *aim*, a *cause* or chain of causes that instigates a process, a *medium/vehicle*, and a *desired effect*. This mental model implies a number of intuitive qualitative rules such as:

- the effect is roughly in the direction of the cause/chain of causes,
- the stronger the initial cause/chain of causes, the stronger the effect – by default proportional,
- the cause/chain of causes costs 'effort', and is weakened in the long run (due to exhaustion) while the effect continues,

- there is a physical connection of the cause to the effect, possibly through the medium (or vehicle), which may damp the effect – by default proportional to its dimensions,
- the better the medium and/or the smaller the distance the stronger the effect,
- as the cause stops, of if the contact is ended or the medium is removed, the effect stops.

A clear source of such ideas is day-to-day life experiences. For example, when a twilight lamp is plugged in (cause) de 'electricity' from the socket is directed to the connected light bulb (aim) via the cord (medium/vehicle) to produce light (the desired effect).

An attempt to counter the misinterpretation of electrical circuits from such a linear causal perspective often made is to explain that the electrical circuit is to be understood in terms of an analogy. Analogies are well known tools for promoting conceptual understanding in science education [11]. Two such analogies are regularly used in science education [13] with their own strengths and weaknesses:

- Fluid current analogies, that of the home heating system in particular,
- Microscopic analogies in which the electrical current is modelled by a stream of electrons depicted as e.g. lorries carrying an electrical load travelling a closed path.

The E&E electrical endeavors game uses the water current analogy.

2.4 Research Questions

The research questions are:

1. Can we built and use for education a serious game that leads to adequate qualitative understanding of electrical circuits without particular misconceptions?
2. What characteristics of the game and the way it is used in classroom facilitate adequate understanding of electrical circuits? In particular:
   (a) in dealing with misconceptions,
   (b) keep a productive the balance between flow-based gaming and reflective and theoretical activities.

3 Methods

In this project we established a close cooperation between various parties within the urban region of Eindhoven in the Netherlands. This region harbors a range of high-tech companies a majority of which work in the fields of electrical engineering, computer hardware, software development or automotive. There also is Eindhoven University of Technology housing both a flourishing faculty of Electrical Engineering and the 'Eindhoven School of Education (ESoE)'. The later institute trains future teachers in cooperation with schools and runs a high standard research program. Hence, the region provides excellent opportunities to establish and maintain the broad interdisciplinary team needed. Moreover the active involvement of schools was supported by SLOA (see acknowledgement), while the city-counsel of Eindhoven supported regional cooperation.

The actual team comprised all partners on an equal basis. It comprised two schools for secondary education providing practical know-how on pedagogical matters, feed-back and testing opportunities. Content was delivered and benchmarked by the faculty of electrical engineering and is a stake holder. ESoE delivers to the team pedagogical know-how and expertise in evaluating learning results and educational processes. Two regional game building companies were involved, one putting its main focus on design issues, the focusing on programming matters.

The set-up of the projects followed the method of design research in which step-by-step improvement and (re)design of the games goes hand-in-hand with research evaluating it. The project was performed in two consecutive rounds each comprising a (re)design and a testing phase. It started with the game version 1.0 as previously build. On advice of the secondary school teachers version 1.0 was upgraded to version 1.1 before starting the project, in order to remove mistakes and smaller difficulties. Version 1.1 was tested by panels of experts in the pedagogy of science, school teachers and students and found adequate for classroom use.

The design research approach taken effectively implied the discussions in the team to focus on the learning impact of the game, a focus guarded by the ESoE participants in particular.

3.1 Description of the Development Rounds

Version 1.1 was taken to the classroom in two Dutch grade 9 classes, one general secondary education and one pre university education. A third one, also pre university education, served as a control group. The lessons were structured to an open inquiry model. The students were allowed to play with version 1.1 during 1½ lesson (approximately 75 min). The lessons for the experimental and control groups were partly the same. They deviated in that the experimental group is playing the game while the control group is following the textbook. This is shown in Table 1. The whole experiment comprised 6 lessons (300 min). Figure 4 a typical screen shot.

In round II, version 3.0 was taken to the classroom in three Dutch grade 9 classes, one general secondary education and two pre university education. Version 3.0 has a renewed level structure that closely follows the regular Dutch grade 9 lesson plan. Also the layout of the game screen is renewed. First, in the left part of the screen the electrical circuit is continuously shown as a closed circuit providing an overview to the students which is much akin to the electrical schemes' usually found in textbooks. Second the working screen on the right is redesigned to more realistically depict voltage and current meters and the way they should be connected. Figure 5 gives an impression.

In round II there was no control group. The lessons were structured according to the teacher guide that was written on the basis of the experiences in the first round and a review of literature. In the first lesson –again- the subject was introduced and the prior knowledge of the students was activated. The students were then allowed to play freely with the game for approximately 40 min, in which they could take op the challenges

Table 1. The quality of the circuits built.

Lesson	Experimental groups	Control group
1	Introduction	
	Activation of basic knowledge from grade 8	
	Inquiry learning playing with version 1.1 *The teacher coaches; no additional teacher explanation of theory*	Individual working from the textbook *The teacher coaches; no additional teacher explanation of theory*
2	Learning task: Build a parallel circuit of two light bulbs	
	Continuation like 1st lesson	Continuation like 1st lesson
3-6	Classical teaching using the textbook	
7	Test	

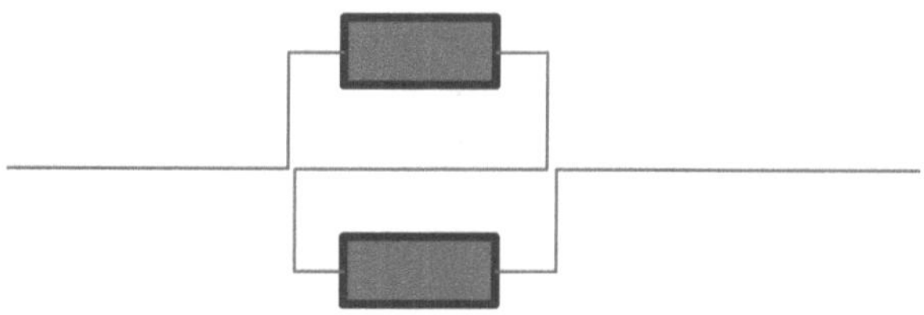

Fig. 4. Optically parallel though not electrically.

built into the games level structure. The next lesson, a classroom discussion was organized evaluating the students various ideas and results, and drawing common conclusions on understanding electrical circuits. In both coaching the students and in the classroom discussions, the teacher could make use of a set of questions in the teacher guide especially designed to stimulate the verbalization/construction of operational rules and theoretical knowledge and to stimulate transfer (see Fig. 2).

A first subset of questions focuses on establishing a comprehensive and correct mapping between the simulation in the game and the electrical system. Examples of such questions are "what is this object in the game?" and "to what element of an electrical circuit does it correspond?". A second subset of questions encourages practical experimentation and fosters conscious observations. Examples are: "what happens if the slider is pushed up?" and "what does not change when the slider is

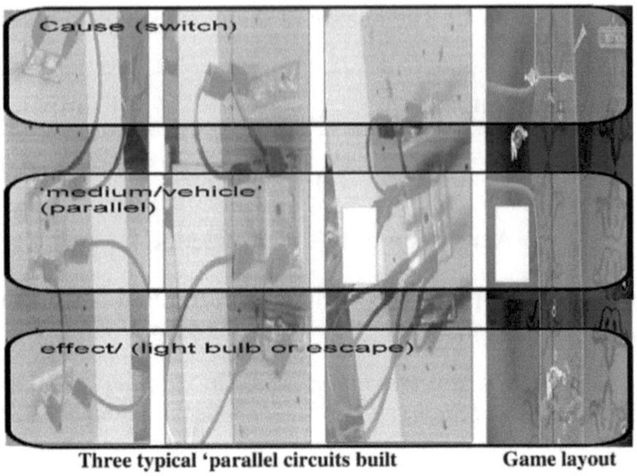

Fig. 5. Students mimicking the games circuit lay-out and linear topology when building a parallel circuit.

moved?". A third group of questions focuses on the active between the 'events' as they occur in the game, and phenomena that may occur in electrical circuits or may focus on 'scientific laws' that emerge from game experience (Fig. 3). For example "what can you conclude on the proportion of the resistors and the proportion of the voltage over the resistors?".

3.2 Analysis of the Circuit Building Test

For both rounds, the learning results were obtained using the standard test results (grades). The same test was completed by all groups in that round. In addition an analysis was made of pictures taken from the circuits built in the learning tasks 'build a parallel circuit of two light bulbs'. The analysis focused on the correctness of the circuits and the presence of misconceptions. Four misconceptions were focused on in particular: circuit not closed/incorrect, short circuit, a circuit lay-out depicting a 'linear causal 'understanding' of electrical circuits, and the type of meaning of 'parallel' the students displayed in the circuit built. Concerning the latter: components may be placed 'visually parallel' though when analyzing the circuit net 'electrically parallel' – see Fig. 6.

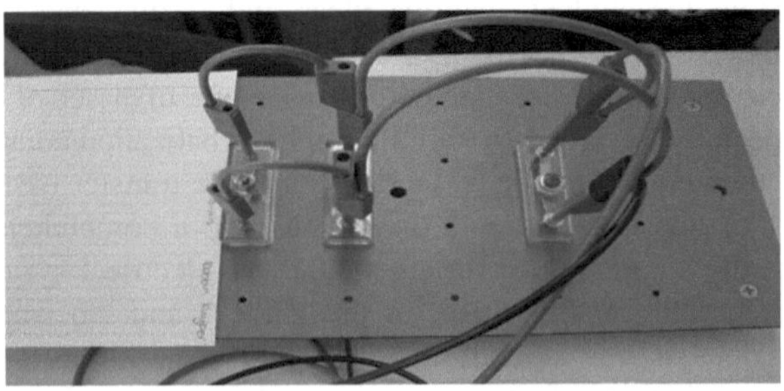

Fig. 6. Typical wrong placement of the switch.

A codebook was used to underpin the various judgements on the circuits and the apparent presence of misconceptions and two researchers cooperated in categorizing the various circuits.

4 Results

In round I, the teacher reported a marked distinction between students that are experienced gamers and other students. The non-gamers experience difficulty in finding their way in the game, while the gamers seemingly effortless solve the problems presented.

The teacher also reported that all students had difficulty recognizing the electrical components in the game. Students in the experimental setting comment: "*it was fun, but I would have preferred an ordinary lesson since then I would have understood it much better*".

The result of the analysis of the 'parallel circuits' built in the second lesson and their quality in general is shown in Table 2.

Table 2. The quality of the circuits built.

	Round I			Round II			t-test
	n*	**M**	**SD**	**n***	**M**	**SD**	
general sec. educ. experimental	13	-0.54	0.75	11	1.68	1.03	5.94***
general sec. educ. control	---	---	---	---	---	---	
pre univ. educ. experimental	11	1.05	1.59	24	1.92	0.70	1.74*
pre univ. educ. control	12	2.75	0.45	---	---	---	
TOTAL	**36**	**1.04**	**1.70**	**35**	**1.84**	**0.81**	**2.54****

* duo's of students; Significance levels: * = 5%, ** = 1%, *** = 0.1%

The control group that worked from the textbook clearly outperformed the two experimental groups. However it was observed that the average grades for the test at the end of the lessons did not significantly differ for the three groups. The teacher commented that she had to make an extra effort in the experimental groups to secure their progress.

An analysis of misconceptions in the circuits built after the second lesson is shown in Table 3, which shows that misconceptions occurred frequently in the experimental groups.

A qualitative analysis of the circuits built revealed a very interesting pattern.

It appeared that a majority of students (54 %) built a circuit in a very particular manner. For general secondary education students this is even 77 %. First they added a switch to the circuit - a component that was not at all mentioned in the assignment. Second they ordered the components in a linear fashion starting with the switch, followed by the 'parallel part' and ending with a light bulb. Figure 7 shows three

Table 3. The occurrence of misconceptions in the first and second round.

		Circuit not closed /incorrect	Short circuit	Causal mental model	Visual view of 'parallel'
Round I	M	0.45	0.39	0.52	1.19
(n*=24)	SD	0.47	0.50	0.45	0.38
Round II	M	0.03	0.14	0.41	0.16
(n*=35)	SD	0.17	0.36	0.35	0.81
t-test		-4.19***	-2.10*	-1.0 (ns)	-6,55***

* duo's of students; Significance levels: * = 5%, ** = 1%, *** = 0.1%

examples (three left columns), as well as the game lay-out (right column). This typical lay-out by the students both resembles the game's screen lay-out and is in accordance with the 'experiential gestalt of causation'.

The disappointing learning result from the game as such, the lack of student and teacher enthusiasm, the frequent occurrence of misconceptions, and the apparent strong but unwanted learning effect arising from the games lay-out that effectively encourages students to understand electrical circuits in terms of 'the experiential gestalt of causation' formed a strong incentive to improve both the game, and the way it is used in classroom. First a panel of teachers was asked to comment on the game and the inquiry based classroom implementation. This resulted in redesigning specifications for the game, and the conclusion that the open-inquiry approach should be replaced by a carefully planned approach combining experiential learning on one hand and reflection, verbalization en additional experience on the other. This criticism was theoretically underpinned by experimental work of Kock et al. [16] and the theoretical insight by Kirschner et al. [15]. A review of literature led to the model by Taconis [24] depicted in Fig. 2, and a extend teacher guide comprising: (a) background information on learning from serious games and understanding electrical circuits, (b) an example time table, (c) concrete questions the teachers could use to stimulate the verbalization/construction of operational rules, theoretical knowledge and their transfer (Fig. 2).

In round II the changes were implemented. The teachers reported the students being enthusiastic about the game, and students reporting that 'it really helped them to understand electrical circuits'. One student for instance stated: 'the game really made me understand what I am doing, and helps me to explain what it is to my friends'. This was supported by a very high mean score on the test concluding the lessons: 7.2 out of 10 (usually 6.3).

The quality of the 'parallel circuits' built is shown in Table 2. It reveals a significant increase with respect to the quality of the circuits built in the first round. Table 3 shows that also the occurrence of misconceptions significantly decreased, except for the occurrence of the 'experiential gestalt of causation'.

A qualitative analysis of the circuits built by the students revealed that in addition many students (54 %) have difficulties with the correct placement of the switch (Fig. 8).

It effectively functions as an optional 'shortcut' directly at the entrance of the powering wires from the power unit. Again, this is in clear accordance with de games lay-out (Fig. 5), were the switch has taken the form of a beam across and blocking the current at the top of the screen.

5 Conclusions and Discussion

We conclude that the close cooperation between school teachers, experts on science education and game-designers was a successful way to a clear improvement in both the game and the way it is adequately used in classroom. Note that enhancing the games contributed to cognitive learning did not imply a decrease in student enthusiasm. The progress made is documented in the projects physical products: the game and guideline for its adequate use in education.

It is concluded that the game when used according to the guideline, probably contributes to improved student understanding. However, misconceptions still occur, those related to 'the experiential gestalt of causation' in particular. In terms of the model by Taconis [24] learning effects seem to concentrate on the level of 'skilled action' (building an electrical circuit) and 'operational rules'. Students do not report on theoretical understanding or models they (re-)constructed.

Concerning the second research question, it is found that the games screen lay-out has a strong though undesired impact on students' mental model of electrical circuits and student learning. The way things are presented apparently strongly influences the students' way of 'looking at things'. This 'topological mimicking' seems to be a very powerful learning mechanism. The games lay-out, and probably its structure as well, sends out a very strong message about 'how things are'. Though not entirely effective in the case of our project, the strength of this mechanism is potentially valuable for designing serious games.

Concerning the use of serious games in classroom, it became clear that 'open inquiry' alone is not the way to go. An approach balancing gaming and deep cognitive processing in alternating phases seems much more fruitful. In this a rule of thumb helping teacher in a practical way could be: "treat serious games as experiments or practical exercises".

Our research has been on a fairly small scale, and as such its outcomes may be easily over generalized. But they point toward two particular issues of importance for larger scale future research:

- developing a pedagogical approaches balancing between play and open inquiry on one hand and stimulating and structuring deep cognitive processing on the other. Put more generally: seeking a productive balance between flow and reflection.
- taking advantage of the strong modelling impact the lay-out and the structure of the game have on student learning.

Acknowledgements. This research was funded by the SLOA fund of the Dutch 'onderwijs cooperation' seeking to promote secondary school teachers doing educational research in cooperation with academic educational researchers.

Appendix: The E&E Game and Its Versions

- 1.0 and 1.1 (http://www.eeee.tue.nl/)
- 2.0 (http://www.eeee.tue.nl/sloa/index.html)
- 3.0 (http://www.eeee.tue.nl/sloa/thebeginning/index.html)

References

1. Anderson, B.: The experiential gestalt of causation: a common core to pupils' preconceptions in science. Eur. J. Sci. Educ. **8**, 155–171 (1986)
2. Csikszentmihaly, M.: Creativity: Flow and the Psychology of Discovery and Invention. HarperCollins, New York (2009)
3. Csikszentmihalyi, M.: Das Flow-Erlebnis. Jenseits von Angst und Langeweile: im Tun aufgehen [Beyond boredom and anxiety], 8th edn. Klett-Cotta, Stuttgart (2000)
4. Dekker, J., Jacobs, A., van Hensberg, V.: Informal user test of E&E electrical endeavours. Internal report (2010)
5. Dreyfus, S.E., Dreyfus, H.L.: A five-stage model of the mental activities involved. In: Directed Skill Acquisition. Storming Media, Washington, DC. http://www.dtic.mil/cgi-bin/GetTRDoc?AD=ADA084551&Location=U2&doc=GetTRDoc.pdf (1980). Accessed 13 June 2010
6. Duit, R.: Bibliography STCSE: students' and teachers' conceptions and science education. http://www.ipn.uni-kiel.de/aktuell/stcse/stcse.html (2009). Accessed 20 April 2009
7. Duit, R., Schecker, H.: Teaching physics. In: Abell, S.K., Lederman, N.G. (eds.) Handbook of Research on Science Education, pp. 599–629. Routledge, New York (2007)
8. Duit, R., Von Rhoeneck, C.: Learning and understanding key concepts of electricity. In: Tiberghien, A., Jossem, E.L., Barojas, J. (eds.) Connecting Research in Physics Education with Teacher Education. International Commission on Physics Education (1998)
9. Duncan, L.R., Hieftje, K.D., Culyba, S., Fiellin, L.E.: Game playbooks: tools to guide multidisciplinary teams in developing videogame-based behavior change interventions. Trans. Behav. Med. **4**(1), 108–116 (2014)
10. Engelhardt, P.V., Beichner, R.J.: Students' understanding of direct current resistive electrical circuits. Am. J. Phys. **72**(1), 98–115 (2004)
11. Emig, B.D., McDonald, S., Zembal-Saul, C., Strauss, S.G.: Inviting argument by analogy: analogical-mapping-based comparison activities as a scaffold for small-group argumentation. Sci. Educ. **98**(2), 243–268 (2014)
12. Gravemeijer, K., Cobb, P.: Design research from a learning design perspective. In: Van den Akker, J., Gravemeijer, K., McKenney, S., Nieveen, N. (eds.) Educational Design Research. Routledge, London (2006)
13. Hart, C.: Models in physics, models for physics learning, and why the distinction may matter in the case of electric circuits. Res. Sci. Educ. **38**, 529–544 (2008)
14. Jaakkola, T., Nurmi, S., Veermans, K.: A comparison of students' conceptual understanding of electric circuits in simulation only and simulation-laboratory contexts. J. Res. Sci. Teach (2010). http://onlinelibrary.wiley.com/doi/10.1002/tea.20386/pdf

15. Kirschner, P.A., Sweller, J., Clark, R.E.: Why minimal guidance during instruction does not work: an analysis of the failure of constructivist, discovery, problem-based, experiential, and inquiry-based teaching. Educ. Psychol. **41**(2), 75–86. http://igitur-archive.library.uu.nl/fss/2006-1214-211848/kirschner_06_minimal_guidance.pdf (2006)
16. Kock, Z.D.Q.P., Taconis, R., Bolhuis, S.M., Gravemeijer, K.P.E.: Some key Issues in creating inquiry-based instructional practices that aim at the understanding of simple electric circuits. Res. Sci. Educ. **43**(2), 579–597 (2013)
17. Kolb, D.: Experiential Learning: Experience as the Source of Learning and Development. Prentice Hall, New Jersey (1984)
18. Koops, M.C., Hoevenaar, M.: Conceptual change during a serious game: using a lemniscate model to compare strategies in a physics game. Simul. Gaming. http://sag.sagepub.com/content/early/2012/09/23/1046878112459261.abstract (2012)
19. Michael, D., Chen, S.: Serious Games: Games that Educate, Train and Inform. Thomson, Boston (2006)
20. Mulhall, P., McKittrick, B., Gunstone, R.: A perspective on the resolution of confusions in the teaching of electricity. Res. Sci. Educ. **31**, 575–587 (2001)
21. Ruben, B.D.: Simulations, games, and experience-based learning: the quest for a new paradigm for teaching and learning. Simul. Gaming **30**(4), 498–505 (1999)
22. Shipstone, D.: Electricity in simple circuits. In: Driver, R., Guesne, E., Tiberghien, A. (eds.) Children's Ideas in Science. Open University Press, Milton Keynes (1985)
23. Taber, K.S., de Trafford, T., Quail, T.: Conceptual resources for constructing the concepts of electricity: the role of models, analogies and imagination. Phys. Educ. **41**(2), 155–160 (2006)
24. Taconis, R.: Using 'E&E electrical endeavors' in teaching on electrical circuits; a guide for teachers (internal communication) (2011)
25. Vockell, E.L.: Educational Psychology: a Practical Approach. Chap. 6. Perdue University. http://education.purduecal.edu/Vockell/EdPsyBook/Edpsy6/edpsy6_transfer.htm. Accessed September 2013

Geometry Question Generator: Question and Solution Generation, Validation and User Evaluation

Rahul Singhal and Martin Henz(✉)

School of Computing, National University of Singapore (NUS), Singapore, Singapore
rahulsinghal@nus.edu.sg, henz@soc.nus.edu.sg

Abstract. Current massively open online courses (MOOCs) are providing several technical challenges for educators. One of these challenges is automated generation of questions, along with the solutions, in order to deal with a large number of students. Geometry is an important part of the high school curriculum. Hence, in this paper, we have focused on the high school geometry domain. We have proposed a framework that combines a combinatorial approach, pattern matching and automated deduction to generate and solve geometry problems for high school mathematics. The system would help teachers to quickly generate large numbers of questions on a geometry topic and may also support the setting of standardized tests such as PSLE, GMAT and SAT.

Our novel methodology uses (i) a combinatorial approach for generating geometric figures from the user input, (ii) a pattern matching approach for generating questions, and (iii) automated deduction to generate new questions and solutions. By combining these methods, we are able to generate questions involving finding or proving relationships between geometric objects based on a specification of the geometry objects, concepts and theorems to be covered by the questions. We propose several algorithms to avoid generation of repeated questions and to avoid questions having redundant information, which increases the effectiveness of our system. We have tested our generated questions on an existing geometry question solving software JGEX, verifying the validity of the generated questions. A survey with the real users such as high school teachers and students on generated questions and solutions shows that our system is effective and useful.

Keywords: Automated deduction · Graph-based knowledge representation · Pattern matching · High school geometry · Axiomatic approach · Constraint handling rules (CHR)

1 Introduction

Geometry, the study of space and spatial relationships, is an important and essential branch of the mathematics curriculum at all grade levels. The study

S. Zvacek et al. (Eds.): CSEDU 2014, CCIS 510, pp. 196–210, 2015.
DOI: 10.1007/978-3-319-25768-6_13

of geometry develops logical reasoning and deductive thinking, which helps us expand both mentally and mathematically. Children who develop a strong sense of spatial relationships and who master the concepts and language of geometry are better prepared to learn number and measurement ideas, as well as other advanced mathematical topics [13].

Euclidean geometry is a branch of mathematics which deals with the study of plane and solid figures on the basis of axioms and theorems employed by the Greek mathematician Euclid. It is important to understand Euclidean geometry when studying a course because geometry does not follow any set pattern. In Euclidean geometry, one can only learn the axioms and results proven from these axioms. The student must apply these axioms with no set pattern or list of steps for solving such questions. Therefore, a question may have (possibly infinitely) many solutions. To practice the required problem solving skills, students require a large number of different types of geometry questions on various concepts. Generally, textbooks and online sites provide a limited predefined number of questions for each topic. Once practiced, these questions lose their purpose of enhancing student thinking. The tedious and error-prone task of generating high-quality questions challenges the resources of teachers. Hence, there is a need for software which assists both teachers and students to generate geometry questions and solutions.

The software can also act as a personalized instructor. It can generate questions that cover the required topic and meet the required level of student proficiency. Apart from helping users, the framework of generating questions has scientific contributions to other research areas, such as Intelligent tutor systems (ITS) and Massive Online Open Courses (MOOCs).

Various research has been performed in automated deduction of theorems at high school level in the geometry domain, although none with the goal of automatic question generation. Instead, they mainly demand users to generate the question with the help of tools. In addition, they mainly focus on solving and assessment of the questions. Our survey shows that the currently available geometry systems, such as JGEX, Geogebra, Cinderella and Sketchpad, are not able to automatically generate questions of user specified geometry topics.

The aim of this paper is to develop a framework that can be used to generate geometry questions based on specific inputs, such as geometry objects and theorems to be involved in their solution. For a given set of geometry objects, the algorithm can generate a large set of questions along with their solutions. The solutions will involve user desired theorems directly or indirectly. Hence the framework can generate questions to test the theorem on various geometry objects and concepts.

The main contributions of this paper are as follows:

1. Our geometry question generator combines the complementary strengths of a combinatorial approach, pattern matching and deductive reasoning. It can generate geometry questions which were not possible previously.

2. A knowledge representation is described for geometry objects and predefined theorems. This representation helps in applying theorem information within the generated questions.
3. The system is made more effective by including algorithms for avoiding repeated questions and handling redundant data.
4. A substantial evaluation is provided that demonstrates the effectiveness of our generator. It can generate various categories of the questions covered in the textbooks and questions asked in SAT and GMAT. A survey is done with the real users (teachers and students) which shows the usefulness of our system.

2 Related Work

In this section, we provide a general review of related works. Computational research in the geometry domain started in the 19th century. However, lack of question generating in geometry in the literature required a principled ab-initio approach in our work. Researchers mainly focused on proving geometry theorems. We are mainly interested in the non-algebraic methods. Non-algebraic methods for automatic discovery and proof of geometry theorems can be further divided into three approaches: coordinate-free methods, formal logic methods and search methods.

2.1 Coordinate-Free Methods

These methods are applicable to constructive geometry statements of equality. Various methods have been proposed under this category, such as the area method [3,12], the full-angle method [2,18], the complex number method, the vector method for Euclid plane geometry [2], the volume method for Euclidean solid geometry [1] and the argument method for non-Euclidean geometry [1]. The area method was further improved and developed into a computerized algorithm [1,2]. These methods can only be applied in constructive geometry, which is outside the scope of this paper.

2.2 Formal Logic Methods

Theorems in Tarski's geometry were proven using Interactive Theorem Prover (ITP) [10], albeit limited to several trivial theorems. ITP is an interactive theorem prover based on the resolution principle, which generates resolution style proofs that resemble traditional proofs. In 1989, Quaife continued the work of McCharen with Otter [14]. Otter is an automated theorem prover based on resolution. A series of tactics such as Hyper-resolution, UR-resolution, paramodulation, support set and clause weight can improve the resolution efficiency. In 2003, Meikle and Fleuriot developed Hilbert's geometry with the theorem prover Isabelle/Isar [11], an interactive and/or semi-automated theorem prover. The greatest disadvantage of formal logic methods is their low reasoning efficiency [9], caused by combinatorial explosion of their search space.

2.3 Search Methods

Fundamentally, the search method is used in a rule-based expert system, which includes a rule database, a fact database and a reasoning engine. The inference rules stored in the rule database include axioms, theorems, lemmas, formula, definitions and algebraic operation rules in geometry. Geometric facts stored in the fact database include geometry predicates such as angle bisector, equidistant points, parallel lines and perpendicular lines. The reasoning engine deduces new geometric facts by applying inference rules to the facts database. There are three ways of performing deduction search, namely forward chaining [18,19], backward chaining [18], and bidirectional chaining [4].

In 1995, Chou, Gao, and Zhang described an integration of a deductive database into the search methods [1,2,6]. The deductive database method can find a fixpoint for a given geometry diagram, containing all properties of the geometry diagrams that can be deduced using a fixed set of geometry rules. They effectively controlled the size of the facts database with structural deductive database techniques.

Each search method has different advantages and disadvantages. Forward chaining is always feasible, but does not have an explicit reasoning goal. Backward chaining has an explicit reasoning goal, but sometimes lacks feasibility. The bidirectional chaining method is feasible and has an explicit reasoning goal, but is hard to implement. We are using forward chaining in our framework as it is most suited for generating previously unknown quantities.

3 Geometry Question Specification

Mathematically, a geometry question Q generated by our system can be represented by a quintuple (Object O, Concept C, Theorem T, Relationship R, Query type qt) where:

- O $\in$ (lines, triangles, square, circle, ...)
- C $\in$ (perpendicular, parallel, midpoint, angle-bisector, circumcircle, ...)
- T $\in$ (Pythagorean theorem, similarity theorem, ...)
- R $\in$ (syntactic, quantitative)
- qt $\in$ (syntactic, quantitative)

In order to generate geometry questions, the user has to provide a set of geometry objects O such as triangles, squares, etc., and a set of concepts C which the user wants the generated question to cover. Optionally the user may select a set of theorems T to be tested by the question. The relationship R can be either syntactic such as perpendicular, parallel, etc., or quantitative such as the length of an object, the ratio of two quantities etc. The query type qt is the type of generated question that can be asked to find the hidden relationship which can be calculated from the given information.

4 Framework

Our framework comprises of three major components along with the knowledge databases used for storing input, geometry figures and a set of predefined theorems. Figure 1 shows the connection of these components. The input consists of geometric objects, concepts and theorems selected by the user. The input is fed into the first component, *Generating Figure (GF)*. This component is used for generation of geometric figures from the input. Each figure constitutes a diagrammatic schema (DS) [8] and a set of unknown variables representing the relationship between geometric objects. The geometric figure is passed to the second component, *Generating Facts and Solutions (GFS)*. This component is used to find values of the unknown variables representing possible relationships to be asked by the generated question. GFS makes use of the predefined knowledge database of axioms. It results in the formation of a *configuration* (Cfg) containing known values for some relationships between its objects.

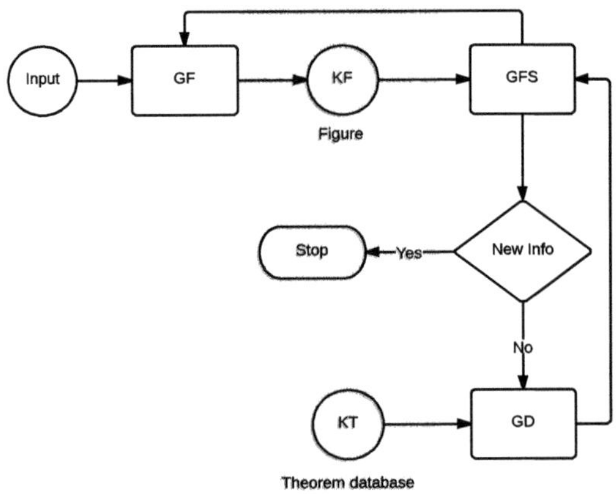

Fig. 1. Connection of the components and knowledge representations.

A question is considered suitable if it covers the essential information such as a new fact and a proper reasoning for the generated fact. Currently, the decision of suitability is taken manually by the user. If the suitability conditions for the generated configuration (Cfg) are not met then configuration is fed into the last component, *Generating data for the figure (GD)*. GD assigns values to unknown variables of relationships. Repeated processing by GD makes the questions generated from Cfg easier and easier, because the values assigned by GD appear as given facts in the generated questions. GD makes use of a predefined set of theorems and makes sure that the assignment results in successful generation of geometry questions. FC generated from this component is again passed to GFS component and this loop continues until a question is found which meets suitability condition.

Along with these components, two knowledge databases are used in the framework, namely the Knowledge database for the generated figures *(KF)* and the knowledge database for predefined theorems *(KT)*.

4.1 Algorithm

Figure 2 shows the step by step execution of the algorithm. We select the following input in our example.

- Object: triangle and line segment
- Concept: perpendicular
- Theorem: Pythagorean Theorem

In the next subsections, we will describe each knowledge database in detail, followed by the three components and their interaction with these databases.

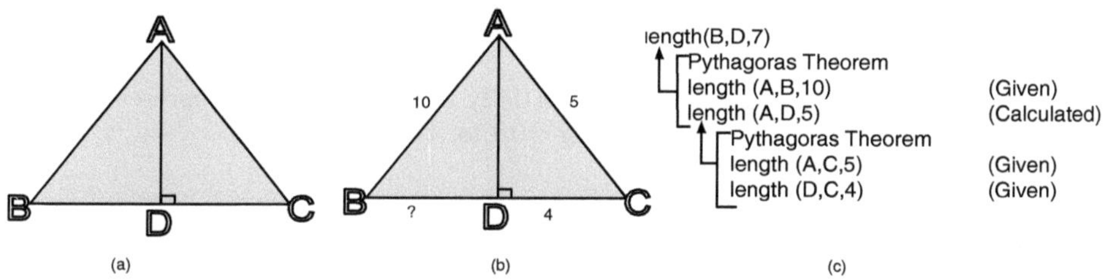

Fig. 2. (a) The figure is generated by using *triangle* and *perpendicular* as the geometry objects using the GF component. (b) The data is generated for (a) using the GD component. (c) The new fact and its derivation using the GFS component is generated from the figure shown in (b).

4.2 Knowledge Database for the Figure/Figure Configuration (KF)

KF contains the question figure and configurations using a graph-based knowledge representation. The nodes of our graph represent the geometric objects. Two nodes can have multiple labeled arcs between them, representing multiple relationships. In addition, an arc can be bidirectional or unidirectional depending on the relationship between the nodes. Following the example of the previous section, Fig. 3(a) shows the geometric figure: a triangle ABC is given and AD is perpendicular to BC. Figure 3b shows its partial representation in a graph format where we focus on the most important relations. Relationships such as "equal angle" and "equal length", which require multiple objects/nodes, are represented by nodes, e.g., the relationship "$\angle ABC$" in Fig. 3(b). In addition, nodes of our graph store the value of quantitative relationships. For example, the node named *"Angle ABC"* stores the value of an angle and is connected to the two nodes representing the sides AB and BC.

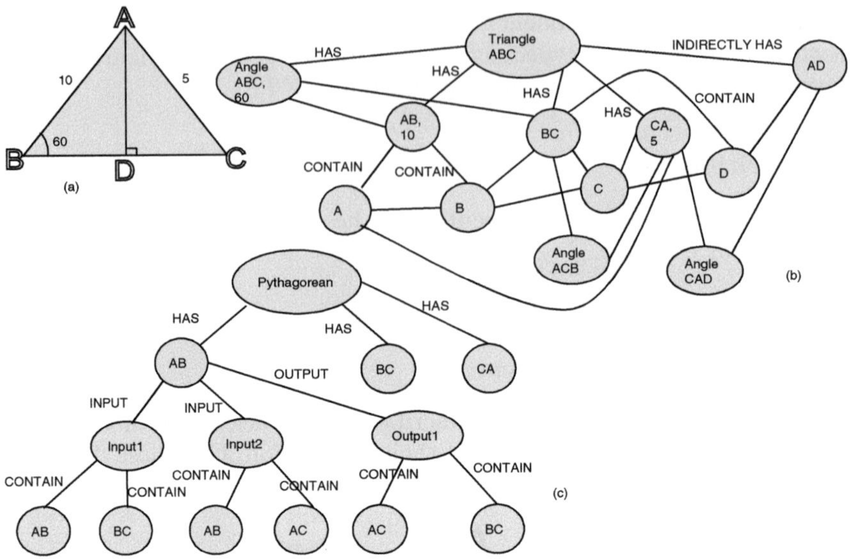

Fig. 3. (a) The geometry figure and (b) Partially drawn knowledge representation of (a). (c) Representation used for generating data for the given figure.

4.3 Knowledge Database for Predefined Theorems (KT)

KT is a knowledge database which contains the predefined database of theorems and is used for assigning values to the unknown variables of configurations generated by the GF component. It uses a graph-based representation similar to KF. However the difference lies in the timing of generation. In order to use KT in the algorithm, some properties of theorems need to be known. Each theorem can be applied to a particular geometry configuration. Each theorem has certain inputs and outputs corresponding to inputs in the geometry configuration. Hence the usage of a theorem requires assigning the variables of input and/or output. In KT, the information of input and output for each theorem is stored along with the geometric configuration in which the theorem can be applied. Nodes represent objects whereas arcs represent the input and output relationships. Input and output are decided offline before the execution of the algorithm and later used for assigning unknown variables to get a useful question. To illustrate the process, the Pythagorean Theorem is taken as an example in Fig. 3c. Given a triangle ABC, where $\angle ABC$ is 90°, Fig. 4 partially shows its usage of KT in generating data. The node representing the side AB has three arcs, two of which represent an input and one of which represents an output relationship. To use the side AB as an input, the length of the sides AB and BC or AC need to be assigned. On the other hand, to use side AB as an output, the length of sides AC and BC needs to be given. By giving this as input or output, we can be sure that the Pythagorean Theorem will give a consistent result.

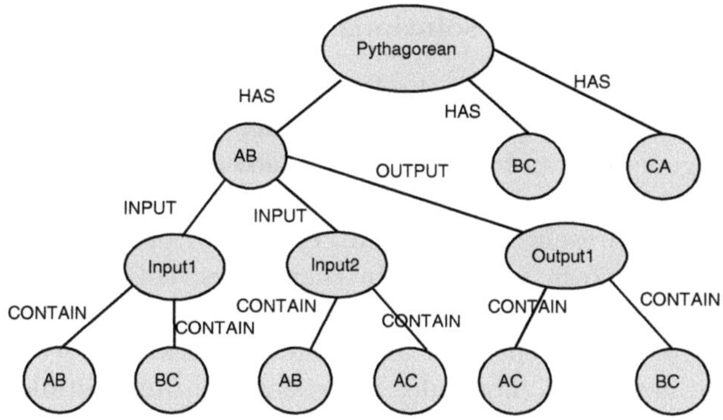

Fig. 4. Representation used for generating data for the given figure.

4.4 Generating Figure Configuration from the User Input (GF)

This is the first step executed by the framework mentioned in the Sect. 4.1. This component generates a figure configuration through the combination of a predefined number of ways to combine geometric objects. Currently, we are focusing on triangles and line segments. Hence our algorithm includes combinations in which various triangles and lines can intersect.

Configuration generation involves the addition of geometry objects, concepts and optionally, user-desired theorems. The detailed algorithm is mentioned here [15].

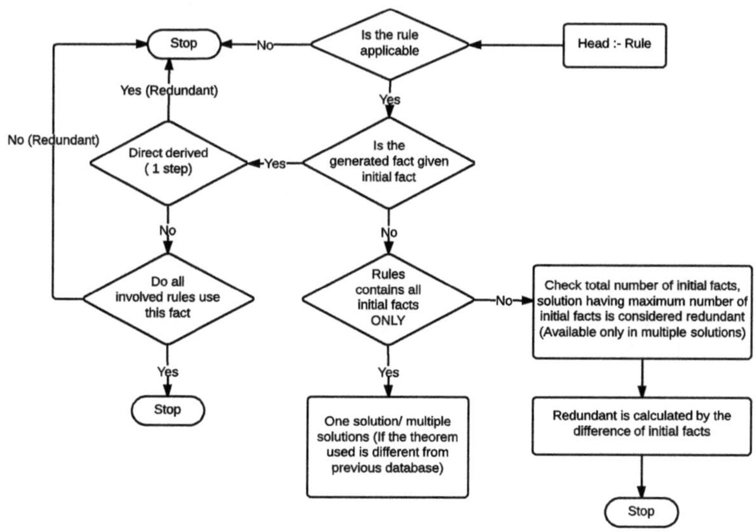

Fig. 5. Figure explaining redundant case

4.5 Generating Facts and Solutions from the Configuration (GFS)

This component is responsible for finding the values of unknown variables of the generated figure/configuration from the other components. This component acts as question generator and solver. The unknown variables whose values have been found represent the generated questions. The steps that leads to finding the unknown variables represent the solution. There can be many ways for finding the values of the unknown variables. In such cases, this component shows all solutions. For generating new facts, it uses a predefined database of theorems.

All theorems are represented in an axiomatic format. Forward chaining is used to generate new facts. The rules representation and detailed algorithm is mentioned here [15].

4.6 Removing the Redundant Data

Redundant data are values assigned to properties of the geometric objects which are not required and can be derived from the previously given data and predefined theorems. It may happen that redundant data is provided in the figure configuration.

Figure 5 shows a flow diagram of an algorithm for detecting and removing redundant data. Figure 6 explains cases with the help of examples. Figure 6a shows an instance of new configuration without redundant data. In Fig. 6b, the length w is redundant, since, by applying the similarity concept, it can be derived from the other two lengths, x and y. In addition, the rules used for generation of w do not previously involve w. However, y is not redundant data, as, the rules used for generating y implicitly requires y. The length AD can be calculated via two ways, Pythagorean Theorem and similarity theorem. Both rules used only initial facts. Hence, both are considered as multiple solutions. Furthermore, the length AB can be derived from two ways. However, in this case, w is consider as a redundant data as w can be generated with other initial facts. Figure 6c shows that w can be obtained from y using the trigonometry rules or vice versa. Hence, one of them can be considered as a redundant data and removed.

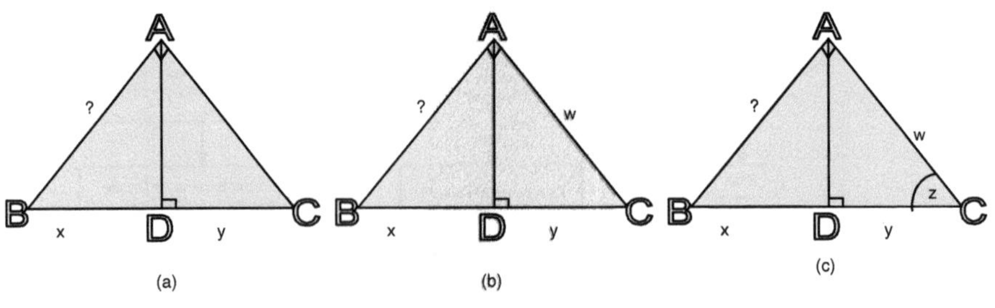

Fig. 6. An example in which redundant data is provided in the given figure.

4.7 Generating New Configurations from an Existing Configuration (GD)

The basic algorithm involves performing pattern-matching of the generated configuration with the predefined set of rules to check which rule can be applied in the given configuration. It makes use of predefined set of rules represented in KR. Each theorem consists of input and output nodes for each variable. Depending on the selected variable and corresponding input and output nodes, the values of unknown relationships are assigned in the configuration. The detailed algorithm is given in [15].

5 Uniqueness

Uniqueness refers to generate non-repeating and non-isomorphic questions. Repetition refers to the same question. Isomorphic refers to the mirror-image of an exiting question (see Fig. 7). Uniqueness plays an important role in terms of the effectiveness of our system. We proposed an algorithm to generate unique question different from all the previously generated questions. The main concept lies in storing all the previously generated configurations and performing efficient configuration matching to maintain uniqueness.

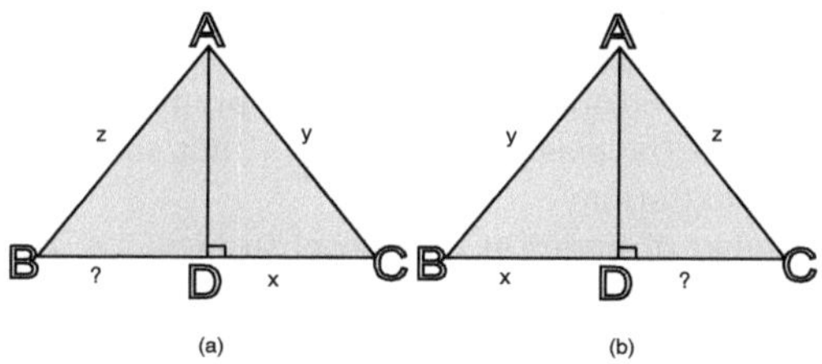

Fig. 7. Figure explaining isomorphic solution.

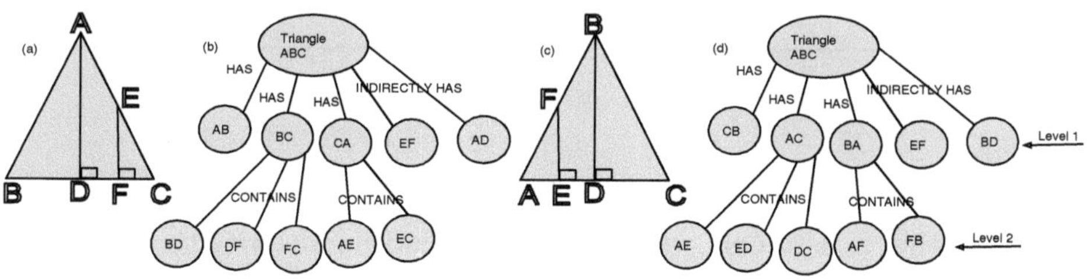

Fig. 8. Figure explaining isomorphic configurations.

Providing Uniqueness in the Question's Figure/Configuration

Uniqueness in the figure configuration involves two cases—the generation of the same figure and the generation of a mirror-image of the previously generated figure. Algorithm 1 describes an algorithm for providing uniqueness in the generated questions. The algorithm is based on checking the equality of configurations at each level. We explain the Algorithm 1 with the help of an example. Figure 8 shows two isomorphic configurations. They have the same number of nodes and relationship links and types at each level. In addition, the number of nodes attached to nodes below and above with equal number of relationship type are the same in both configurations. For example, at level 1, both the figure configuration have three nodes having "HAS" relationships and two nodes having "Indirectly has" relationships. Similarly, at level 2, three nodes are attached to one node at level 1 via the "Contain" relationship. In addition, two other nodes are attached to one node at level 1 via the "Contain" relationship. This equality is same through out each level. Hence, in this case, the algorithm will return true.

Algorithm 1. Algorithm for removing repetition in geometry figure.

Data: A new geometric figure configuration, existing database of previously generated figure configurations
Result: True or false depending on the repetition of new figure configuration with the existing database

1. Check for the number of objects and concepts in the new figure configuration with the existing database. If not same, terminate with false else goto next step.
2. Check the number of nodes at each level to be same. If not same, terminate with false else goto next step.
3. Check the number of relationships at each level to be same. If not same, terminate with false else goto next step.
4. Check the number of nodes and relationships at each level to be same. If not same, terminate with false else goto next step.

Removing Repetition in the Question Data

This algorithm is used only when the above algorithm declares the two figure configurations to be isomorphic. The algorithm is nearly same as Algorithm 1, except, for the additional checking which includes the values of known relationships at each level. Figure 7 shows an example where the two geometric questions would be considered equal. The figure configurations are considered equal following Algorithm 1 and the values of known relationships are equal at each level. For example, AB of (a) with AC of (b) and AC of (a) with AB of (b).

6 Implementation

Each component of our tool is implemented independently, using state-of-the-art languages, libraries and systems. C++ is used for performing calculations and Python is used for implementation of the algorithms used in the GF and GD components. The algorithm in the GFS component is implemented using Constraint Handling Rules (CHR) [5]. CHR are used for generating new facts from the axioms and the given facts. In our implementation, we use the CHR library provided by K.U. Leuven, on top of SWI-Prolog [16]. The theorems used in GFS component are manually converted in the format used by CHR library. For implementing knowledge representation KF and KT, the graph database Neo4j [17] is used. The KF knowledge graph is used and modified by all the components and finally represents the question. Our knowledge databases such KT and predefined ways of intersection of geometric objects are manually generated and stored before the questions generation.

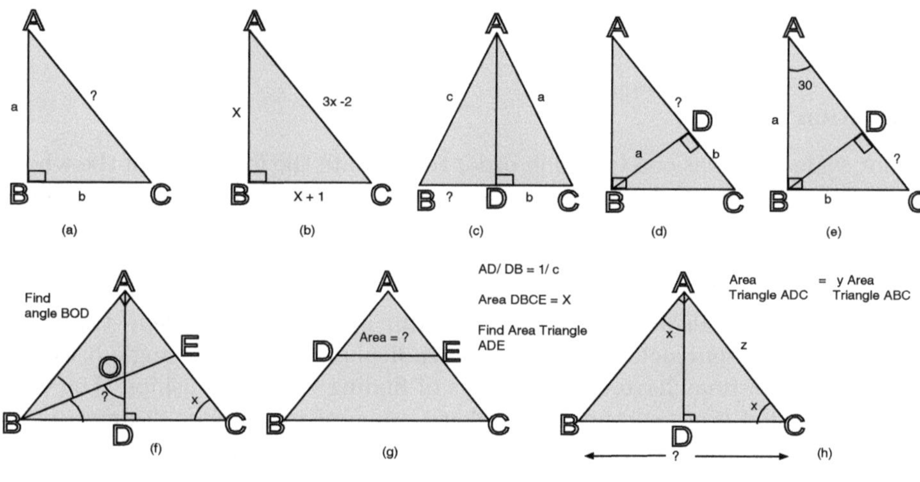

Fig. 9. (a–e) Generated questions based on "triangle", "perpendicular" and "Pythagorean Theorem" as input. Questions in figure (a–c) can be solved using Pythagorean Theorem only. However, questions of figure (d) requires similarity and figure (e) requires trigonometry for finding the unknown value. (f) uses angle-bisector theorem. (g–h) uses similarity theorem. The details can be seen here [15].

Experimental Results

The system can generate geometry questions using the framework described in Sect. 4. Currently, our knowledge database of objects contains line segments and triangles. In addition, we have a predefined set of more than 100 theorems. Figure 9 shows various questions generated by our system on selecting *"triangle"* as object, *"perpendicular"* and *"angle-bisector"* as concepts and *"Pythagorean Theorem"* as a theorem to be covered. The generated questions are tested using the existing geometry solver tool JGEX [7]. For testing in JGEX, the figure configuration is drawn manually by the user and the system is asked to prove/find a certain relationship. The tool is able to prove/solve all the questions generated by our system. Comparing the solutions generated by JGEX with the solutions generated by our system, we found interesting differences that may stem from different representations of geometric knowledge and reasoning techniques and that deserve further investigation.

Table 1. Survey results after real user's testing.

Users	Has seen Online/Textbook (in %)	Appropriateness of solution (in %)	Input used (in %)	Concept used (in %)	Quality (in %)
High school teachers	30	90	99	99	90
College level teachers	80	95	99	99	80
High school students	10	90	99	99	95
College level students	20	85	99	99	90

Evaluation

A pilot evaluation was conducted in order to estimate the feasibility of the whole approach and generated questions. We entered 50 rules in the system, which correspond to specific geometric theorems: Similarity in triangles, Pythagorean Theorem, and Basic Trigonometry formulas.

Different type of inputs are given on order to generate various different problems. Objects include right-angle, equilateral, isosceles and scalene triangles. The covered concepts include triangle perpendicular, median and angle-bisector. Some of the questions have multiple ways of finding the relationships. The prototype generated large number of problems, some of which were "isomorphic", i.e. identical from a pedagogical point of view. All problems were correct, as manually checked by the authors. Ten of the generated questions were selected for evaluation, with the aim of covering a wide range of concepts and objects. The small number of problems was due to evaluator's limited time availability.

The users of the survey were high school teachers, students and professionals involved in standardized exams like GMAT and SAT. The selected problems were given to several experienced High School Mathematics teachers from India, Singapore and US. Hundreds of students, both high school and college level, were involved in the survey.

For each problem, the assumptions, known relationships and unknown relationships to be proved/found as well as generated diagrams were given to the participants. Six survey questions were asked for each generated geometric question, covering aspects such as the quality and the appropriateness of the generated solutions. Table 1 shows the questions asked and the statistics of the user's response. It can be seen that the teachers have different perceptions of the quality and difficulty of the generated questions.

The table shows that half of the users considers these questions as new. However, this depends on the domain knowledge and memory. Several questions were considered new by almost all users. Most of the users consider the generated questions useful and appropriate for high school mathematics. The options for providing objects and concepts of generating these questions matches with those actually provided in the system. Overall, it can be seen that the system is able to fulfill the aim of generating questions quickly from the given input along with the appropriate answer.

Although the number of participants is very limited and the report of the above data is somewhat anecdotal, we see an agreement among teachers regarding both diversity and quality for testing. Although these results should by no means be generalized, they are hopeful initial indicators of the potential validity of the proposed measures for exercise selection, providing a useful basis for further justification and/or adjustment.

7 Conclusions

In this paper, we provide a framework for the automatic generation and solving of questions for high school mathematics, specifically in the geometry domain. Our system is able to quickly generate large numbers of questions on specific topics. Such a system will help teachers reduce the time and effort spent on the tedious and error-prone task of generating questions. Our work aims to develop an automated geometry question generation system that uses a deductive approach for finding the relations between mathematical concepts and for generating and proving these conjectures about concepts.

Future work can be carried in various directions. One of the major work would be generation of relevant questions via user's feedback. Other major work would be generating questions according to the required difficulty level. Another improvement would be the automation of process of knowledge addition in the system. Lastly, solutions readability could be improved.

References

1. Chou, S.C., Gao, X.S.: Handbook of Automated Reasoning. Elsevier and MIT Press, Cambridge (2001)
2. Chou, S.C., Gao, X.S., Zhang, J.Z.: A deductive database approach to automated geometry theorem proving and discovering. J. Autom. Reasoning **25**(3), 219–246 (2000)
3. Chou, S.C., Gao, X.S., Zhang, J.Z.: Area method and automated reasoning in affine geometries (2011)
4. Coelho, H., Pereira, L.: Automated reasoning in geometry theorem proving with prolog. J. Autom. Reasoning **2**(4), 329–390 (1986)
5. Frühwirth, T., Raiser, F. (eds.): Constraint Handling Rules: Compilation, Execution, and Analysis. Books On Demand, March 2011
6. Gao, X.S., Zhu, C.C., Huang, Y.: Building dynamic mathematical models with geometry expert, I. Geometric transformations, functions and plane curves. In: Proceedings of the Third Asian Technology Conference in Mathematics (1998)

7. Gao, X.-S., Lin, Q.: MMP/geometer – a software packagefor automated geometric reasoning. In: Winkler, F. (ed.) ADG 2002. LNCS (LNAI), vol. 2930, pp. 44–66. Springer, Heidelberg (2004)
8. Greeno, J.G., Magone, M.E., Chaiklin, S.: Theory of constructions and set in problem solving. Mem. Cogn. **7**, 445–461 (1979)
9. Jiang, J., Zhang, J.: A review and prospect of readable machine proofs for geometry theorems. J. Syst. Sci. Complex. **25**, 802–820 (2012)
10. McCharen, J.D., Overbeek, R.A., Wos, L.A.: Problems and experiments for and with automated theorem-proving programs. IEEE Trans. Comput. **25**(8), 773–782 (1976)
11. Meikle, L.I., Fleuriot, J.D.: Formalizing Hilbert's Grundlagen in Isabelle/Isar. In: Basin, D., Wolff, B. (eds.) TPHOLs 2003. LNCS, vol. 2758, pp. 319–334. Springer, Heidelberg (2003)
12. Narboux, J.: The area method: a recapitulation. J. Automat. Reasoning **48**, 489–532 (2010)
13. National Council of Teachers of Mathematics: Curriculum and evaluation standards for school mathematics (1989)
14. Quaife, A.: Automated development of Tarski's geometry. J. Automat. Reasoning **5**, 97–118 (1989)
15. Singhal, R., Henz, M., McGee, K.: Automated generation of geometry questions for high school mathematics. In: Sixth International Conference on Computer Supported Education (2013) (Accepted for publication as full paper)
16. Schrijvers, T., Demoen, B.: The K.U. Leuven CHR system: implementation and application. In: First Workshop on Constraint Handling Rules (2004)
17. Vicknair, C., Macias, M.: A Comparison of a Graph Database and a Relational Database (2010)
18. Wilson, S., Fleuriot, J.D.: Combining dynamic geometry, automated geometry theorem proving and diagrammatic proofs. In: ETAPS Satellite Workshop on User Unterfaces for Theorem Provers (UITP) (2005)
19. Zhang, J.Z., Gao, X.S., Chou, S.C.: The geometric information search system by forward reasoning. Chin. J. Comput. **19**(10), 721–727 (1996)

An Analysis of Courses Evaluation Through Clustering

Renza Campagni, Donatella Merlini(✉), and Maria Cecilia Verri

Dipartimento di Statistica, Informatica, Applicazioni, Università degli Studi di Firenze, Viale Morgagni, 65, 50134 Florence, Italy
{renza.campagni,donatella.merlini,mariacecilia.verri}@unifi.it

Abstract. Students of the University of Florence (Italy), before taking an exam, are required to assess different aspects related to the course organization and to the teaching. The data concerning the evaluation of the courses of the Computer Science Program from 2001/2002 to 2007/2008 academic years were collected and linked to the results of students: the grades obtained in the corresponding exams and the delays, with respect to the end of the courses, with which exams were taken. After this preprocessing phase, we used clustering techniques to analyze data and we highlighted a correlation between courses evaluation and the corresponding average student results, as well as regularities among groups of courses over the years. Our analysis can be used to detect possible improvements in the organization and teaching of the degree program and applied to any university context collecting similar data.

Keywords: Educational data mining · K-means clustering · Courses evaluation · Assessment

1 Introduction

The evaluation of university education is an important process whose results can be used in the programming and management of the educational activities by monitoring resources (financial, human, structural and others), services (orientation for students and administrative offices), students careers, courses and occupancy rate. In order to evaluate all these aspects, it is important to analyse the opinion of the *users* of university education, i.e. the students.

The evaluation of the learning process falls in the context of the Educational Data Mining (EDM), an emerging and interesting research area that aims to identify previously unknown regularities in educational databases, to understand and improve student performance and the assessment of their learning process. As described in [11,12], EDM uses statistical, machine learning and data mining algorithms on different types of data related to the field of education. It is concerned with developing methods for exploring these data to better understand the students and the frameworks in which they learn thus possibly enhancing some aspects of the quality of education. Data mining techniques

S. Zvacek et al. (Eds.): CSEDU 2014, CCIS 510, pp. 211–224, 2015.
DOI: 10.1007/978-3-319-25768-6_14

have also been applied in computer-based and web-based educational systems (see, e.g., [10,13]). In this paper, we use a data mining approach based on `K-means` clustering to link the evaluation of courses taken by students with their results, in terms of average grade and delay in the corresponding exams. We also analyse the evaluation of courses over the years in order to identify similar behaviors or particular trends among courses, by using an approach similar to time series clustering (see, e.g., [8]).

This study deepens the analysis presented in [5] and is analogous to that used in [2–4]. The analysis refers to a real case study concerning an Italian University but it could be applied to different scenarios, except for a possible reorganization of the involved data. The data set is not very large but allows us to illustrate a quite general methodology on a real case study. Our approach uses standard data mining techniques, but we think very interesting the concrete possibility of applying these techniques to find and analyse patterns in the context of university courses evaluation, even in large universities.

This paper represents a revised version of [6] which integrates the feedbacks from the presentation at CSEDU 2014.

2 Data for Analysis

In this section, we describe how courses are evaluated by students at the University of Florence, in Italy, with the aim of providing a methodology to search for regularities in data concerning courses evaluation. Therefore, the steps we present can be applied also in other academic contexts. In particular, we refer to a Computer Science degree of the Science School, under the Italian Ministerial Decree n. 509/1999. This academic degree was structured over three years and every academic year was organized in two semesters; there were several courses in each of these six semesters and at the end of a semester students could take their examinations. Exams could be taken in different sessions during the same year, after the end of the corresponding courses, or later.

Table 1 illustrates an example of students data after a preprocessing phase which allow us to integrate original attributes, such as the grade and the date of the exam, with both the semester in which the course was given, **Semester1**, and the semester in which the exam was taken, **Semester2**. Finally, we can

Table 1. A sample of students data: grades in thirtieths.

Student	Exam	Date	Grade	Semester1	Semester2	Delay
100	10	2001-01-14	24	1	1	0
100	20	2002-12-20	27	2	3	1
200	20	2002-06-04	21	2	2	0
300	10	2001-01-29	26	1	3	2
400	10	2002-02-15	26	1	2	1
⋮	⋮	⋮	⋮	⋮	⋮	⋮

compute the value **Delay** as the difference between the semester of the course and the semester in which the student took the exam. We highlight that the values of attributes **Semester1** and **Semester2** are not usually stored in the databases of the universities, therefore this preprocessing phase may be onerous.

At the University of Florence, starting from the academic year 2001/2002, a database stores information about evaluation of the courses quality of various degree programs, among which we find the degree under consideration. The results of this process are available at the address [1], under permission of the involved teacher, and show for each course several pieces of information, such as the name of the teacher who took the course and the average rating given by students on various topics. Before the end of each course (at about 2/3 of the course), students compile, anonymously, a module to express their opinion on the course just taken. This form is divided into the following five paragraphs:

- paragraph 1, concerns the organization of the degree program;
- paragraph 2, concerns the organization of the course;
- paragraph 3, concerns the teacher;
- paragraph 4, concerns classrooms and equipment;
- paragraph 5, concerns the general satisfaction about the course.

Each paragraph is composed by some questions; students can choose among four levels of answers, two negative and two positive levels (disagree, slightly disagree, slightly agree, agree). For details the interested reader can see the sample of the module in [1].

For each course of an academic year and for each paragraph, we can compute the percentage of positive answers, that is, of type *slightly agree* and *agree* by grouping together all questions belonging to the same paragraph and their average percentage value.

To relate data of students careers with courses evaluation, for each course we can compute the average grade and the average delay attained by students who took the exam in the same year. An example of this data organization is illustrated in the first four columns of Table 2. As already observed, the evaluation of courses is anonymous and is done only by students who really take the course, therefore, in this kind of organization, it may happen to consider information

Table 2. Data organization for comparing examination results and courses evaluation.

Exam	Year	AvgGrade	AvgDelay	Par*1*	...	Par*5*
10	2001	25	1	51	...	60
10	2002	26	1	50	...	61
⋮	⋮	⋮	⋮	⋮	⋮	⋮
10	2007	25	1	81	...	67
20	2001	24	0.5	56	...	77
20	2002	26	1	62	...	59
⋮	⋮	⋮	⋮	⋮	⋮	⋮

Table 3. Data organization for analyzing the trend over the years of courses evaluation.

Exam	Par*1*(2001)	...	Par*1*(2007)	...	Par*5*(2001)	...	Par*5*(2007)
10	51	...	81	...	60	...	67
20	56	...	84	...	77	...	84
⋮	⋮	⋮	⋮	⋮	⋮	⋮	⋮

concerning exams of students who may not be the same students who evaluated the courses. As a consequence, we can only compare the results of courses evaluation in a specific year with the aggregate results of students who took the corresponding exams in the same period. However, this data organization does not change a lot if it was possible to identify the students involved in the courses evaluation in order to connect properly the results of the evaluation with those of exams. Obviously, in this case we should ensure the privacy of results, for example by using a differential privacy approach (see, e.g., [7]).

After a preprocessing phase, we can organize students and evaluation data into two different ways by taking into account the following fields:

- **Exam**, the code which identifies an exam;
- **Year**, the year of the evaluation;
- **AvgGrade**, the average grade of the exam;
- **AvgDelay**, the average delay, in semesters, of students exams;
- **Par*k*(t)**, the percentage of positive evaluations of paragraph k at time t.

In particular, Table 2 illustrates a sample of the dataset which can be used to compare examination results and courses evaluation while Table 3 represents a sample of data that can be used to analyze the evolution over the years of courses evaluation. As we will illustrate in Sect. 3, data organized as in Table 2 will be clustered with `K-means` algorithm by using the Euclidean distance to separate the *multidimensional points* representing some characteristic of a course in a specific year; data organized as in Table 3 will be represented in the plane as *trajectories* corresponding to the evaluation of courses over the years and will be clustered with the Manhattan distance. Both these approaches can be used to find regularities in courses evaluations and can highlight criticalities or suggest improvements in the teaching organization.

3 K-means Clustering with Euclidean and Manhattan Distances

Among the different data mining techniques, clustering is one of the most widely used methods. The goal of cluster analysis is to group together objects that are similar or related and, at the same time, are different or unrelated to the objects in other clusters. The greater the similarity (or homogeneity) is within a group and the greater the differences between groups are the more distinct the clusters are.

K-means is a very simple and well-known algorithm based on a partitional approach; it was introduced in [9] and a detailed description can be found in [14]. In this algorithm, each cluster is associated with a centroid and each point is assigned to the cluster with the closest centroid by using a particular distance function. The centroids are iteratively computed until a fixed point is found. The number K of clusters must be specified. In particular, in this paper we use both the *Euclidean* and *Manhattan* distance; in the first case, the centroid of a cluster is computed as the mean of the points in the cluster while in the second case the appropriate centroid is the median of the points (see, e.g., [14]).

The evaluation of the clustering model resulting from the application of a cluster algorithm is not a well developed or commonly used part of cluster analysis; nonetheless, cluster evaluation, or cluster validation, is important to measure the goodness of the resulting clusters, for example to compare clustering algorithms or to compare two sets of clusters. In our analysis we measured cluster validity with correlation, by using the concept of proximity matrix and incidence matrix. Specifically, after obtaining the clusters by applying K-means to a dataset, we computed the proximity matrix $P = (P_{i,j})$ having one row and one column for each element of the dataset. In particular, each element $P_{i,j}$ represents the Euclidean, or Manhattan, distance between elements i and j in the dataset. Then, we computed the incidence matrix $I = (I_{i,j})$, where each element $I_{i,j}$ is 1 or 0 if the elements i and j belong to the same cluster or not. We finally computed the Pearson's correlation, as defined in [14, p. 77], between the linear representation by rows of matrices P and I. Correlation is always in the range -1 to 1, where a correlation of 1 (-1) means a perfect positive (negative) linear relationship.

As a first example, Table 4 illustrates the final grade and the graduation time, expressed in years, of a sample of graduated students. By applying the K-means algorithm to this dataset, with $K = 2$, **FinalGrade** and **Time** as clustering attributes and by using the Euclidean distance, we obtain the following two clusters, in terms of the student identifiers: $C_1 = \{100, 400, 600, 700\}$ and $C_2 = \{200, 300, 500\}$; the centroids of the clusters have coordinates $\mathcal{C}_1 = (107, 3.5)$ and $\mathcal{C}_2 = (96, 5.33)$, respectively. Tables 5 and 6 show the proximity matrix and the incidence matrix corresponding to clusters C_1 and C_2 of the data set illustrated in Table 4. The Pearson's correlation between the linear representation of these two matrices is -0.59, a medium value of correlation.

As another example, Table 7 shows a sample of data concerning courses evaluation: in particular, each row contains the exam identifier and the percentage of positive evaluation of a generic paragraph at time t_i, for $i = 1, \cdots, 4$. We can apply the K-means algorithm to the dataset in Table 7, with $K = 2$, $\mathbf{Par}(t_i)$, for $i = 1, \cdots, 4$, as clustering attributes and by using the Manhattan distance. This means to represent each element of the data set as a broken line connecting the points $(t_i, \mathbf{Par}(t_i))$, for $i = 1, \cdots, 4$, in the cartesian plane. The Manhattan distance between two broken lines thus corresponds to the sum of the vertical distances between the ordinates. By using the K-means algorithm, we obtain the

Table 4. A sample data set about students.

Student	FinalGrade	Time
100	110	3
200	95	5
300	100	5
400	103	4
500	98	6
600	106	4
700	109	3

Table 5. The proximity matrix for data of Table 4.

P	100	200	300	400	500	600	700
100	0						
200	20.12	0					
300	10.25	10	0				
400	7.07	13.08	3.32	0			
500	12.41	8.06	2.24	5.48	0		
600	4.12	16.06	6.16	3	8.31	0	
700	1	19.13	9.27	6.08	11.45	3.16	0

Table 6. The incidence matrix for clustering of data of Table 4.

I	100	200	300	400	500	600	700
100	1						
200	0	1					
300	0	1	1				
400	1	0	0	1			
500	0	1	1	0	1		
600	1	0	0	1	0	1	
700	1	0	0	1	0	1	1

following two clusters in terms of course identifiers: $C_1 = \{200, 500\}$ and $C_2 = \{100, 300, 400\}$; the centroids of the clusters are represented by the sequences $\mathcal{C}_1 = [(1, 72), (2, 68), (3, 67), (4, 73)]$ and $\mathcal{C}_2 = [(1, 82.5), (2, 91), (3, 87.5), (4, 91.5)]$, respectively. Figure 1 illustrates the clustering result by evidencing the centroids $\mathcal{C}_1$ and $\mathcal{C}_2$.

Also in this case we can compute the Pearson's correlation by using the proximity and the incidence matrices computed by using the Manhattan distance.

Table 7. A sample data set about courses evaluation.

Exam	Par(t_1)	Par(t_2)	Par(t_3)	Par(t_4)
100	55	65	67	60
200	85	87	85	92
300	72	68	65	77
400	77	80	70	73
500	80	95	90	91

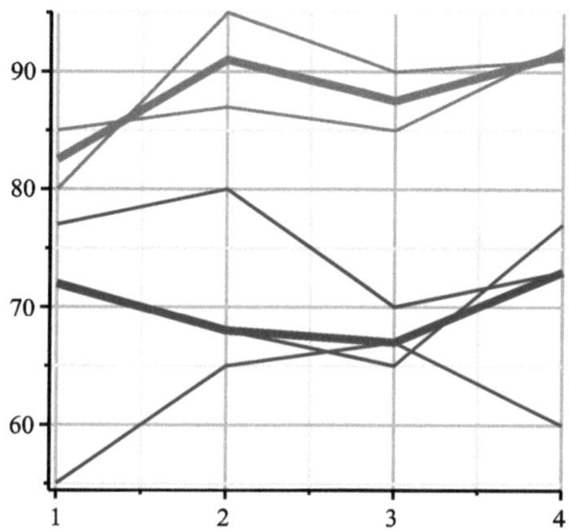

Fig. 1. `K-means` results with data of Table 7 with $K = 2$ and Manhattan distance, centroids in evidence.

3.1 The Case Study

As already observed, the real datasets we analysed concern courses and exams during the academic years from 2001/2002 to 2007/2008 at the Computer Science program of the University of Florence, in Italy. In particular, the first data set is organized as illustrated in Table 2 and refers to the evaluation of 40 courses in seven different years. We explicitly observe that we did not consider in our analysis those courses evaluated by a small number of students. For clustering, we used the `K-means` implementation of `Weka` [15], an open source software for data mining analysis. The aim was to find if there is a relation between the valuation of a course and the results obtained by students in the corresponding exam. We performed several tests with different values of the parameter K and we selected different groups of attributes. We point out that the attributes selection is an important step and should be done according to the preference of an expert of the domain, for example the coordinator of the degree program. For each choice of attributes, we applied the `K-means` algorithm with the Euclidean distance to identify the clusters; then, we computed the Pearson's correlation by using the proximity and incidence matrices. The tests we performed pointed out that the exams having good results, in terms of average grade and delay, correspond to courses having also a good evaluation from students.

In particular, we used **AvgGrade**, **AvgDelay**, **Par*1***, **Par*2***, **Par*3***, **Par*4*** and **Par*5*** as clustering attributes and $K = 2$, obtaining the clusters illustrated in Figs. 2, 3, 4 and 5; each figure represents the projection of the clusters along two dimensions corresponding to the following pairs of attributes **AvgDelay** and **Par3**, **AvgGrade** and **Par3**, **AvgDelay** and **Par4** and, finally, **AvgGrade** and **Par4**. The centroids of the resulting clusters are shown in Table 8, which also contains the average values relative to the full data set.

Table 8. The centroids of clusters in Figs. 2, 3, 4, 5.

Attribute	Full data	Cluster0	Cluster1
AvgGrade	25.31	25.85	24.58
AvgDelay	2.61	1.8	3.68
Par*1*	70.86	77.74	61.67
Par*2*	72.23	82.19	58.94
Par*3*	84.51	90.25	76.86
Par*4*	72.03	74.67	68.5
Par*5*	76.02	80.83	69.61

The cluster number 0, which correspond to 88 blue stars in the figures, contains the courses which students took with *small* delay and that they evaluated positively. On the other hand, cluster number 1, corresponding to 66 red stars, contains those courses which students took with a large delay and that they evaluated less positively. We observe that the centroids of the two clusters are very close relative to the attribute **Par4** which concerns classrooms and equipment. This is also evidenced from Figs. 4 and 5, where the blue and red stars are less separated than those in Figs. 2 and 3. The Pearson's correlation corresponding to these clusters is equal to -0.35. We obtained an improvement by excluding the attribute **Par4** from clustering, in fact in this case we find a correlation equal to -0.51. In general, our tests evidenced that the paragraphs evaluations which are more correlated with students results regard attributes **Par*2*** and **Par*3***, that is, those concerning the course organization and the teacher. We point out that the value $K = 2$ gave the best results in terms of correlation.

Among the courses considered in the previous data set, we selected those evaluated all seven years, for a total of sixteen courses, some in Mathematics and others in Computer Science. This time we are interested in analysing data organized as in Table 3, by considering the evaluation of a particular paragraph over the years. The aim was to find if there are similar behaviors among courses, that is, if we can classify courses according to their evaluations. We performed several tests, by choosing a paragraph at a time. For each choice of attributes, we applied the `K-means` algorithm with the Manhattan distance to identify the

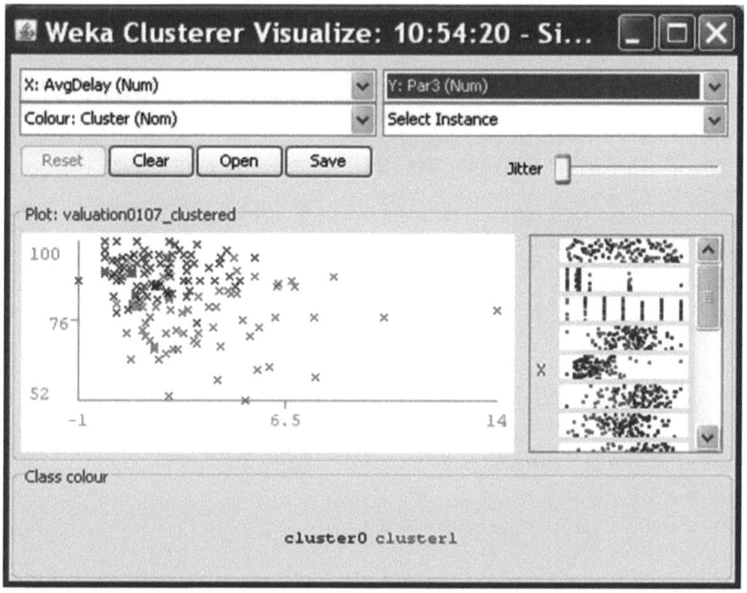

Fig. 2. Clusters of Table 8 with **AvgDelay** and **Par3** in evidence (Color figure online).

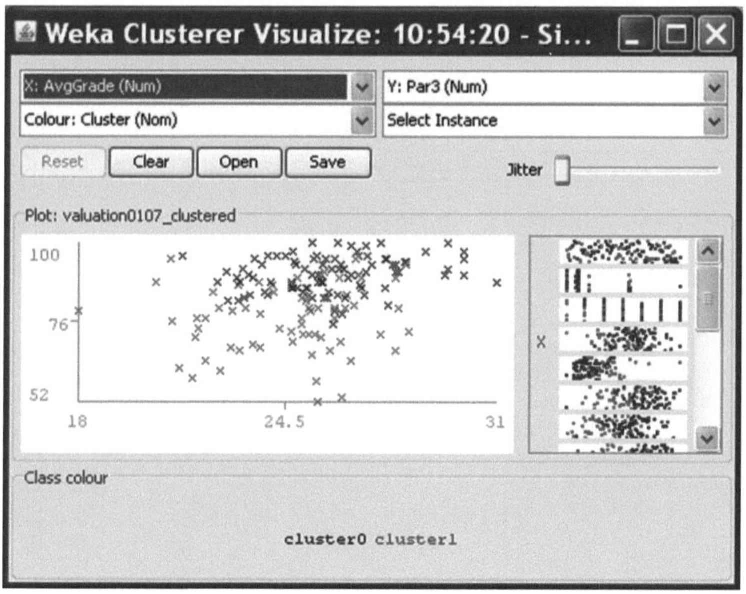

Fig. 3. Clusters of Table 8 with **AvgGrade** and **Par3** in evidence (Color figure online).

clusters; also in this case we computed the Pearson's correlation by using the proximity and incidence matrices.

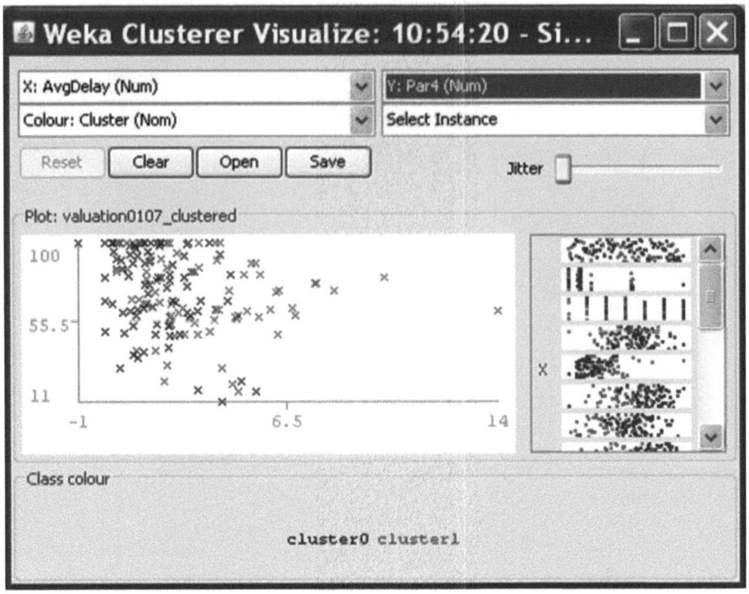

Fig. 4. Clusters of Table 8 with **AvgDelay** and **Par4** in evidence (Color figure online).

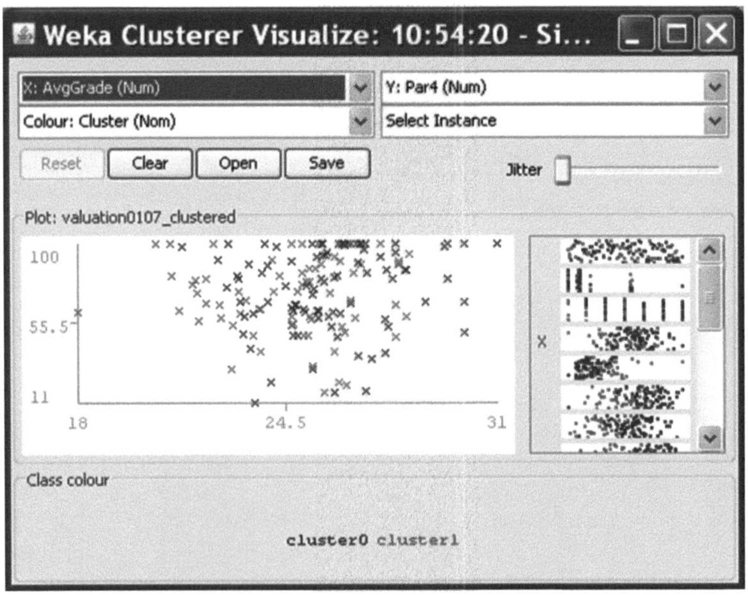

Fig. 5. Clusters of Table 8 with **AvgGrade** and **Par4** in evidence (Color figure online).

Figure 6 illustrates the result of `K-means` with $K = 2$, Manahattan distance and **Par*2*(2001)**, **Par*2*(2002)**, $\cdots$, **Par*2*(2007)** as clustering attributes.

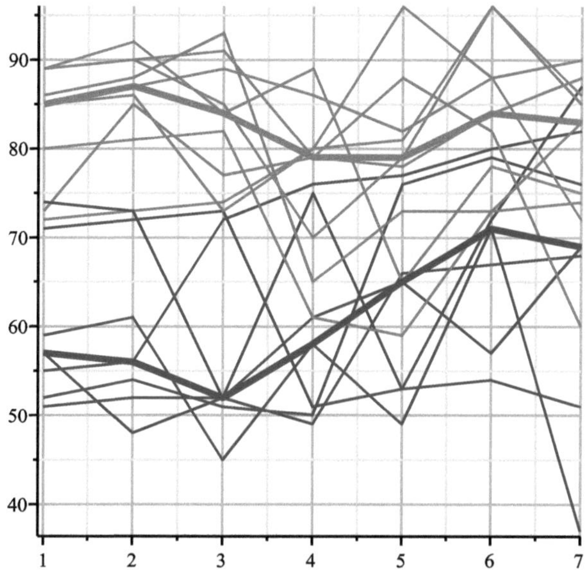

Fig. 6. Clusters of Table 9 with centroids in evidence: each line represents the percentage of positive evaluations about the organization of a course (paragraph 2) over the years 2001–2007 (Color figure online).

The points defining the centroid trajectories of the resulting clusters are shown in Table 9, which also contains the median values relative to the full data set. The Pearson's correlation corresponding to these clusters is equal to −0.64.

The figure puts well in evidence that the courses are divided into two clusters with well distinct centroids. The red cluster contains courses that have been evaluated better over the years while the blue cluster corresponds to courses that students rated worse. What is interesting, though not surprising, is that all courses in the red cluster are Computer Science courses while the blue cluster contains many Mathematics courses. We highlight that the centroids show rather clearly the behavior of the assessment over the years. In particular, the evaluation of the courses in the blue cluster has improved over the years while that of courses in the red cluster has remained more stable.

Also in this case the best results in terms of correlation were found with $K = 2$; however, with $K = 4$ we found the courses rated worse distributed into two clusters, one of which contains only the Mathematics courses. The corresponding centroid illustrates a gradual improvement of the assessment for this type of courses during the years under examination.

Figure 6 illustrates the results of the clustering corresponding to Table 9 with a graphical representation that refers to the natural temporal order, i.e., the values on the horizontal axis ranges from 2001 to 2007. However, since we used the Manhattan distance, the sum of the vertical distances between the ordinates, the trajectories could be represented by taking into account a different time ordering

Table 9. The points defining the centroid trajectories of clusters in Fig. 6.

Attribute	Full Data	Cluster0	Cluster1
Par2(2001)	73.5	85	57
Par2(2002)	77	87	56
Par2(2003)	73.5	84	52
Par2(2004)	72.5	79	58
Par2(2005)	74.5	79	65
Par2(2006)	78.5	84	71
Par2(2007)	75.5	83	69

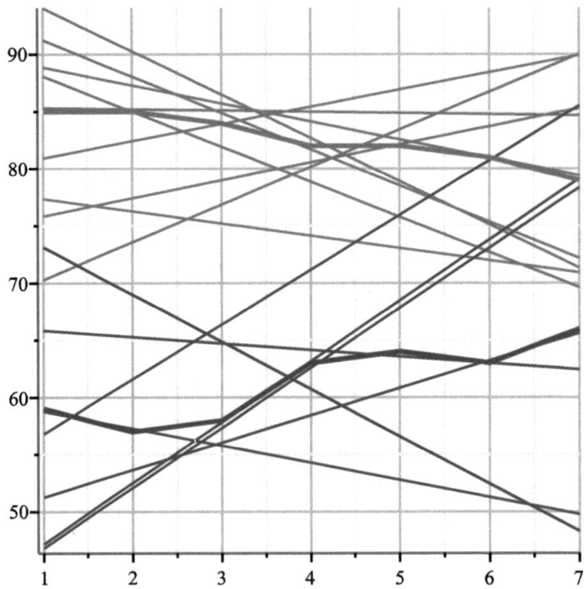

Fig. 7. The regression lines for the trajectories of Fig. 6 with the centroids of the corresponding clustering in evidence.

and the results of clustering would not change. To keep into consideration the temporal values, we can think to compute the regression line corresponding to the points that identify each broken line and then perform clustering with the Manhattan distance. Figure 7 shows the results of clustering with $K = 2$ on the regression lines corresponding to the broken lines of Fig. 6, with the centroids in evidence: the corresponding courses match exactly the same subdivision of the clustering shown in Fig. 6. This new representation provides a better highlight of the courses evaluation over the years and confirms the previous remarks on Fig. 6. Moreover, the analysis could be deepened by clustering courses with respect to the slope values of the regression lines, thus grouping together courses with the same evaluation trend.

4 Conclusions and Future Work

The results of the previous sections show, in a formal way with data mining techniques, that there is a relationship between the evaluation of the courses from students and the results they obtained in the corresponding examinations. In particular, the analysis performed on data related to the Computer Science degree program under examination illustrates that the courses which received a positive evaluation correspond to exams in which students obtained a good average mark and that they took with a small delay. Conversely, the worst evaluations were given to those courses which do not match good achievements by students.

The analysis based on clustering with Manhattan distance allows us to classify courses according to the assessment received by students and can highlight some regularities that emerge over the years or points out some trend reversals due to changes of teachers. In the Computer Science degree program just considered, for example, we observe the trend to give not so good evaluation to Mathematics courses. Results of this type point out a critical issue in the involved courses and can be used to implement improvement strategies.

The correlations highlighted in this paper could be considered predictable, however, we wish to emphasize that our analysis refers to the courses evaluation that students make before taking the exams and before knowing their grades. In fact, as already observed, the evaluation module is given to students before the end of the course. Surely, there is the risk that their judgment is influenced by the inherent difficulty of the course or by the comments made by students of the previous years. To this purpose, it is important that during the module compilation the teacher explains that a serious assessment of the course can increase the quality level of the involved services. Students represent the end-users as well as the principal actors of the formative services offered by the University and the measure of their perceived quality is essential for planning changes. However, the results of courses evaluation should always be considered in a critical way and should not be used for simplifying the contents and to get best ratings. Moreover, we wish to point out again the formal proof of the results with a data mining approach. From this point of view, other cluster algorithms and goodness evaluation measures could be used; for example, an interesting future work could include the use of hierarchical clustering (see, e.g., [14]).

In general, many other factors should be considered for evaluating courses and student success, as addressed in [11]. The approach used in this work could be refined and deepened if it was possible to identify the students involved in the courses evaluation in order to connect properly the results of the evaluation with those of exams. Moreover, it would be interesting to connect the assessment of students with other information such as the gender of students and teachers or the kind of high school attended by students. Starting from the academic year 2011/2012, the University of Florence began to manage on line the evaluation module described in Sect. 2. Therefore, in a next future, it might be possible to proceed in this direction, taking into account appropriate strategies to maintain privacy.

An interesting additional source of information could be given by social media sites, such as *Facebook* or *Twitter*, used by students to post comments about courses and teachers. It would be useful to link this information with the results of students and their official evaluations about teaching, in order to take into account more feedbacks. In such a context, it might be interesting to use text mining techniques to classify the student comments and enrich the database for an analysis similar to that illustrated in this work.

References

1. Progetto SISValDidat. https://valmon.disia.unifi.it/sisvaldidat/unifi/index.php
2. Campagni, R., Merlini, D., Sprugnoli, R.: Analyzing paths in a student database. In: The 5th International Conference on Educational Data Mining, Chania, Greece, pp. 208–209 (2012)
3. Campagni, R., Merlini, D., Sprugnoli, R.: Data mining for a student database. In: 13th Italian Conference on Theoretical Computer Science, ICTCS 2012, Varese, Italy (2012)
4. Campagni, R., Merlini, D., Sprugnoli, R.: Sequential patterns analysis in a student database. In: ECML-PKDD Workshop: Mining and Exploiting Interpretable Local Patterns (I-Pat 2012), Bristol (2012)
5. Campagni, R., Merlini, D., Sprugnoli, R., Verri, M.C.: Comparing examination results and courses evaluation: a data mining approach. In: Didamatica 2013, Pisa, Area della Ricerca CNR, AICA, pp. 893–902 (2013)
6. Campagni, R., Merlini, D., Verri, M.C.: Finding regularities in courses evaluation with k-means clustering. In: CSEDU 2014, Barcelona, Spain, Scitepress, vol. 2, pp. 26–33 (2014)
7. Dwork, C.: Differential privacy: a survey of results. In: Agrawal, M., Du, D.-Z., Duan, Z., Li, A. (eds.) TAMC 2008. LNCS, vol. 4978, pp. 1–19. Springer, Heidelberg (2008)
8. Liao, T.W.: Clustering of time series data: a survey. Pattern Recognit. **38**(11), 1857–1874 (2005)
9. MacQueen, J.: Some methods for classifications and analysis of multivariate observations. In: Proceedings of the 5th Berkeley Symposium on Mathematical Statistics and Probability, pp. 281–297. University of California Press (1967)
10. Romero, C., Romero, J.R., Luna, J.M., Ventura, S.: Mining rare association rules from e-learning data. In: The 3rd International Conference on Educational Data Mining, pp. 171–180 (2010)
11. Romero, C., Ventura, S.: Educational data mining: a review of the state of the art. IEEE Trans. Syst. Man Cybern. **40**(6), 601–618 (2010)
12. Romero, C., Ventura, S.: Data mining in education. WIREs Data Min. Knowl. Disc. **3**, 12–27 (2013)
13. Romero, C., Ventura, S., García, E.: Data mining in course management systems: moodle case study and tutorial. Comput. Educ. **51**(1), 368–384 (2008)
14. Tan, P.N., Steinbach, M., Kumar, V.: Introduction to Data Mining. Addison-Wesley, Boston (2006)
15. Witten, I.H., Frank, E., Hall, M.A.: Data Mining: Practical Machine Learning Tools and Techniques, 3rd edn. Morgan Kaufmann, San Francisco (2011)

Competence Assessment Framework for Project Management Learners and Practitioners

Ana González-Marcos[1](✉), Fernando Alba-Elías[1], Joaquín Ordieres-Meré[2], and Fermín Navaridas-Nalda[3]

[1] Department of Mechanical Engineering, Universidad de La Rioja, C/ Luis de Ulloa 20, 26004 Logroño, La Rioja, Spain
{ana.gonzalez,fernando.alba}@unirioja.es
[2] PMQ Research Group, ETSII, Universidad Politécnica de Madrid, José Gutiérrrez Abascal 2, 28006 Madrid, Spain
j.ordieres@upm.es
[3] Department of Education Sciences, Universidad de La Rioja, C/ Luis de Ulloa 8, 26004 Logroño, La Rioja, Spain
fermin.navaridas@unirioja.es

Abstract. The goal of this paper is to present a competence-based learning and assessment framework that can facilitate the learning of both technical and human project management skills. The proposed competence assessment method is based on the participant's performance and value creation. The information is obtained from assessment forms that relied on at least one piece of evidence and audits conducted automatically. This method can be implemented in an internet-based simulation environment. As the framework that was constructed was tested by students from various universities and locations, this work presents the results obtained, the relationships observed among four transversal competences -teamwork, leadership, motivation and results orientation– and the relationships between those competences and other variables such as the project's final success, the effort ratio and the size of the project team.

Keywords: Project management · Competence assessment · Experiential learning in engineering

1 Introduction

In a constantly changing society, the demands faced by an individual vary from one situation to another and from time to time. Therefore, in addition to possessing the specific basic skills that are necessary to accomplish a certain task, an individual requires more flexible, generic and transferable competences to provide the combination of skills, knowledge and attitudes that are appropriate to a particular situation [11].

In Europe, places of higher learning are immersed in a substantial transformation process of organizational, pedagogical and methodological aspects of

S. Zvacek et al. (Eds.): CSEDU 2014, CCIS 510, pp. 225–241, 2015.
DOI: 10.1007/978-3-319-25768-6_15

knowledge transmission [9]. In this changing context, educational systems are moving from an input- to an output-driven approach, with the quality of education judged on the knowledge and skills that students will require in their professional careers [26]. Thus, competence-based learning and assessment have become one of the main concerns of higher education.

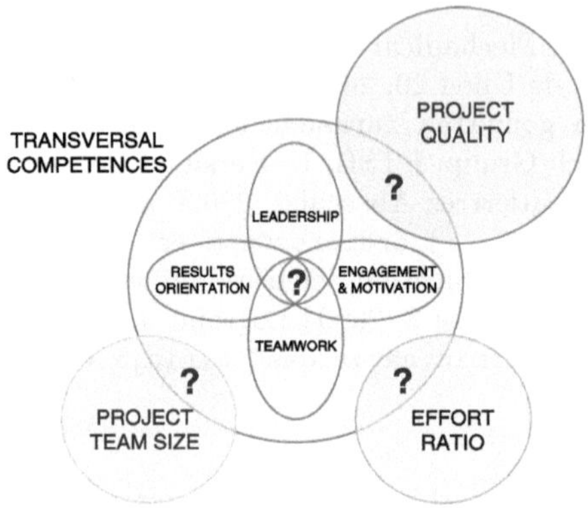

Fig. 1. Relationships investigated in this work.

Competence-based assessment has become the basis for determining instructional effectiveness. However, the availability of valid, reliable and widely accepted indicators and instruments with which to gauge the acquisition of knowledge and skills is proving to be difficult to come by.

In this new concept of higher education, the instructor's role changes from communicating information to students to facilitating and guiding their learning process [5,16]. Thus, the teaching process must be organized in a more learner-centered approach than the classical lecture approach offers.

This work presents a competence-based learning and assessment framework that can facilitate the learning of both technical and human skills for project management. As the framework was tested by students from various university degree programs at various universities and locations, the research questions that were of interest to the authors are as follows (see Fig. 1):

- Are there any relationships among the selected transversal competences: teamwork, leadership, motivation and results orientation?
- Are there any relationships among the selected transversal competences and the projects final success?
- Are there any relationships among the selected transversal competences and the defined effort ratio ratio between claimed and planned effort?
- Are there any relationships among the selected transversal competences and the size of the project team?

The structure of the remaining part of the paper is as follows: Sect. 2 presents a brief review of related works. Section 3 provides an overview of the learning experience. Section 4 is dedicated to present the proposed competence assessment method. Section 5 presents the results and discusses the relationships observed among the four analysed competences, the project's final quality and the other studied variables. Finally, the Sect. 6 presents general conclusions and discusses future work.

2 Background

There are many professional competence frameworks within the project management sector. Some have been published by professional bodies, such as the IPMA [7], and others have been developed within organizations. Most of the frameworks focus on pursuing project success and contributing to organizational success [4]. The project management literature conceptualizes project performance in terms of process performance and product performance. The former refers to development activities that are efficiently and effectively carried out during the course of development. The latter refers to the quality of the project's development work. Thus, project performance is interpreted as staying within the project budget and schedule, achieving operational efficiency, and conducting high quality work [28]. All aspects are important to users because even if the work of the project is of high quality, the project itself may have significantly exceeded the scheduled time and budgeted costs, thereby impacting organizational jobs and resources. On the other hand, well-managed projects that remain within their budgeted costs and schedules can deliver poor systems.

Competences in project management are correlated to performance on the job and can be measured against well-accepted standards and improved by training and other development activities. The underlying assumption is that a competency can be broken down into dimensions of competence, as Project Management Competency Development (PMCD) Framework [22] does. The dimensions considered in this framework are Knowledge, Personal and Performance. Furthermore, the International Project Management Association (IPMA) created the International Competence Baseline (ICB) that consists of 46 elements for knowledge and experience, as well as personal attitudes and abilities for general impression [7]. In addition, the Association for Project Management (APM) developed the APM Competence Framework that provides the technical, behavioral and contextual competence elements required for effective project management [2].

Although human skills -communication, teamwork, organizational effectiveness, leadership, flexibility, creativity, etc.- are acknowledged to be important for project management, the education offered in industrial engineering degree programs concentrates on the control aspects of projects, i.e., the technical skills. It is only recently that authors have begun to discuss how to teach this discipline in institutions of higher learning. Thus, authors in [20] argue for a more balanced approach between technical and human concepts to enhance project management education. The author in [8] discusses the skills that an effective project manager requires, as well as an analysis of four approaches at the M.Sc. level to the development of these skills. The difficulty of learning effective project management skills is discussed in [3]. This author suggests that there is a way to teach project management through properly designed assessment. Similarly, the author in [27] emphasizes that creation of a suitable environment for project learning and the learning of behaviors that will lead to success are most being adequately pursued.

The teaching and learning of project management has grown in interest and popularity [6,18,25]. There are some practical approaches to project management education. For instance, authors in [1] describe a specific experimental approach for information technology students. Authors argue that project activities must mirror the real world for information technology students are to learn what needs to be done in industrial projects. More recently, authors in [10] advocated a combination of theoretical content, individual tasks to provide practical application of the theoretical content, the use of software systems and a strategy of learning by doing in teaching project management. These authors formally introduce negotiating and virtual team management aspects to different teams from different universities in different locations.

3 Methodology and Implementation

The Project and Portfolio Management Learning (P2ML) framework presented in this work is based on the *experiential learning* theory, i.e., learning through action. The following is a list of the main characteristics of the proposed model:

- Students are involved in real-world engineering projects. This provides authenticity and require students to use academic and technical knowledge.
- Students are organized in teams that must develop a solution to satisfy the needs of a client.
- Students are forced to adopt a more active role since they are the ones who must develop a project within specifications and the assigned time.
- The focus is on project management dimension, rather than the problem to solve, which is an instrument.
- The development of an ability to work effectively in a team and the acquisition of human skills, such as leadership, communication or negotiation, are promoted.
- Professional skills that should be developed by a project manager are implemented at scale.

Lectures are focused on providing tools and knowledge to accomplish various activities required by the learner's work in the project. This knowledge may be provided before it is required or only when it is required. On other occasions, it is provided after something happens as a kind of reflective learning approach.

Even when the exam still exists as an individual, self-supported source of information about the quantity and quality of the knowledge that has been acquired, other additional factors are considered when grading students. These may include the quality of work that each student performed on the projects, individual assignments connected to the learning process itself, etc.

Furthermore, as the weight assigned to the reported practical experience is consistent with the effort required, students quickly understand that it is a main part of the learning process

3.1 Simulated Scenario

To reinforce concepts, the simulated scenario involves the student in the development of a real engineering project. Different selected topics are involved in the creation of a product, industry or service, including feasibility analyses and even formal design of the project's products.

Thus, the instructor's team adopts the role of the owner's representatives and deliver the formal documents that make it possible to begin the project.

The final project's expected outcome will be the legal documentation that allows the designed products to be built, but not their physical implementation. Students are involved in the drawing preparation, if required by the project topic, as well as in the formal budget estimation for both the project itself and its implementation.

3.2 Project Management Methodology

For the method to use for project management, PRINCE2^{TM} (Projects IN a Controlled Environment) [17] was selected. It is simple, product-oriented and easy for students, who have no experience in projects or project management, to understand.

As frequently reported [13,30], the use of PRINCE2^{TM} even for academic purposes was not new. Authors preferred it over the most common standard from the Project Management Institute (PMI) -Project Management Body of Knowledge, PMBoK [23]– due to the students' lack of experience. After their initial experience [19], teachers found that concentrating on the products to be developed, instead of a methodology that requires a great deal of effort is of most help to the learning process.

As the students will have an opportunity to test the project managing method, it is expected than they will learn its positive and negative aspects. However, the last lecture of the course deals with different project management methodologies. This will help students to broaden their knowledge of this subject.

The project management method that was adopted addresses a multi-phase life cycle. During the course's first three weeks, students learn the importance of each stage that is established by PRINCE2^{TM}. A general portrayal of the project life-cycle is provided in Fig. 2.

3.3 Competence Framework

The projects provided are basically oriented to learning about project management methodology and developing key competences.

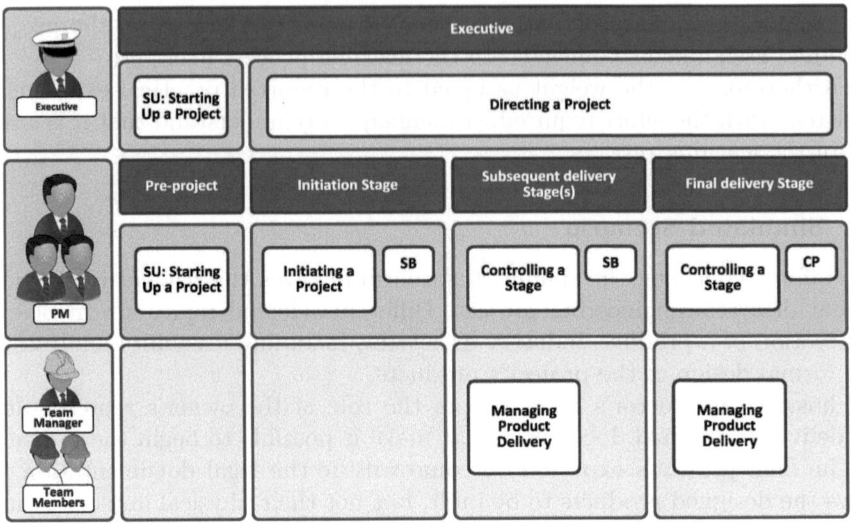

Fig. 2. Project life-cycle: phases and processes.

The authors chosen the IPMA-ICB framework [7] as a reference model for competences in project management because of its flexibility and the taxonomy it provides. IPMA defines the four competences studied in this work as follows [7]:

- *Leadership* includes providing direction and motivating others in their roles or tasks to attain the project's objectives.
- *Engagement & motivation. Engagement* is the project manager's personal commitment to the project and the commitment of other people inside who are associated with the project. *Motivation* of the project team depends on how well the individuals bond together and their ability to deal with both the high and low points experienced during the project.
- *Results orientation* describes the mindset of an individual or group of persons that are concentrating on results that are sought or expected to the exclusion or near exclusion of actions or matters that do assist in their attainment of those results. The PM must ensure that the project's results satisfy the relevant interested parties. To deliver the results required by these parties, the PM must discover what the different participants in the project would like to gain from it for themselves. This aspect of project management behavior is closely linked to project success.
- *Teamwork* covers the management and leadership of team building, operating in teams and group dynamics.

3.4 The Roles of Teachers and Students

Teachers and students are the players in the classical process. However, there are specific functions and roles for them in the proposed framework. The teachers are responsible for defining and establishing the pedagogical project contexts and also for the organization of the group. Teachers are knowledge facilitators as well as academic referees and fill the role of Owner in the PRINCE2^{TM} method, allowing them to 'audit' the work being done. These audits become a major source of applied knowledge as they unveil poorly understood concepts behind the operating procedures as evidence of inconsistencies appear. In summary, teachers must assume the following roles:

- **Owner:** To identify his or her interests and to negotiate various aspects to ensure that his or her interests are carried out.
- **Auditor:** To conduct independent assessments of specific aspects of the evaluation indicators and any corrective action, if necessary.

For the student's learning process, it is necessary to make clear the difference between the various roles of those who work together on the same project, but bear different responsibilities. Because students from different locations – Universidad Politécnica de Madrid (UPM) and Universidad de La Rioja (UR)– and different backgrounds are involved, they are exposed to different participation experiences by assuming four different roles (see Fig. 2, left) –all of which are figures available in PRINCE2^{TM}:

- **EX:** Project Board members -the executive (EX). The Owner (the teacher's role) owns the whole environment, but the EX is charged with effective management of it. Each project is managed by a team of two to four EXs.
- **PM:** Project Manager, with management responsibilities. The PMs have the authority to manage the projects on a day-to-day basis on behalf of the EX. Each project is managed by a team of seven or eight PMs. The number of students playing the role of PM was established according to the need for all students to perform management tasks. It may be noted that the duration of the course is relatively brief. It requires only 120/150 h of work student work (4,8/6 ECTS are assigned to the UPM and UR). This is not very long in view of the students' lack of experience (Warfvinge, 2008).
- **TMg:** Team manager. This is a PM who is temporarily assigned to manage Project Engineers (TM), to produce what was described in the work package document (managing products processes).
- **TM:** Team member, with development responsibilities for engineering tasks. There are ten or twelve TMs in each team.

3.5 Implementation

In order to support learning and monitoring, information and communication technology (ICT) tools were used. The ICT environment provided was constructed by integrating some open source tools as described in [12]. Moreover, specific procedures for operating, doing things, communicating mandatory information, etc., have been developed. Learning these procedures, as well as the use of the ICT system, was the goal of the course's first module, in parallel with learning about PRINCE2^{TM}.

Subsequently, students will develop a direct relationship with PRINCE2^{TM} theory and operational procedures. This module takes three weeks. Its last activity is an individual assessment, which is used as evidence of Project Management Information Systems proficiency and theoretical knowledge of the management of it.

During the period in which the project is being developed, the students continue to learn theoretical concepts for the document structure to be delivered, legal responsibilities and specific techniques that will be useful in their daily work. This procedure also shows how increasing complexity and uncertainty call for a more comprehensive inclusion of managerial and leadership knowledge relative to our teaching of advanced project management [29].

Obviously, most of the work needs to be carried out by groups or teams. However, it is based on individual knowledge. Sometimes this individual knowledge is improved because of the discussions of how to perform the work. Thus, students are responsible for their learning, as well as the learning of others [15].

4 Competence Assessment

Evaluating the learning process is an essential matter not only for students, but also for teachers who are responsible for the learning process. Unfortunately, there is no agreement on the way to integrate different dimensions of learning, knowledge, skills, etc. [14]. Therefore, the authors have incorporated two different assessment methods. The first method is a formal knowledge-based set of tests in different periods of time. The second method is a continuous assessment that is oriented to assessing project management performance and the contribution of each student to it [24]. The project performance is based on the auditing processes carried out by the Project Board and the Owner's representatives (the teachers) and on the competence level gained while the daily work was performed.

The auditing process has two different branches. The first one is automatically performed by a web tool that the authors developed (see Fig. 3). It collects real-time information about the project and students' progress on the Enterprise Program Management Office (ePMO) software that is used during the simulation. It gathers relevant information about each student's performance in their project activities (project planning activities, documents uploaded, effort allocation, use of the communication tools provided blog, discussions, etc.). It also looks for measurable errors, such as the absence of relationships between tasks, the absence of links between documents and deliverables, improper effort allocations, incorrect document codifications, etc. Thus, instructors are able to make periodic reports to better identify mistakes or inappropriate behaviors. In this way, the teachers can more objectively and efficiently monitor and evaluate students throughout the entire course. Furthermore, students were given the right to order an on-line self-audit that is based on the aforementioned automatic checks.

The second branch of the auditing process asks for a more qualitative, but still evidence-based, opinion of the products being produced and how well the

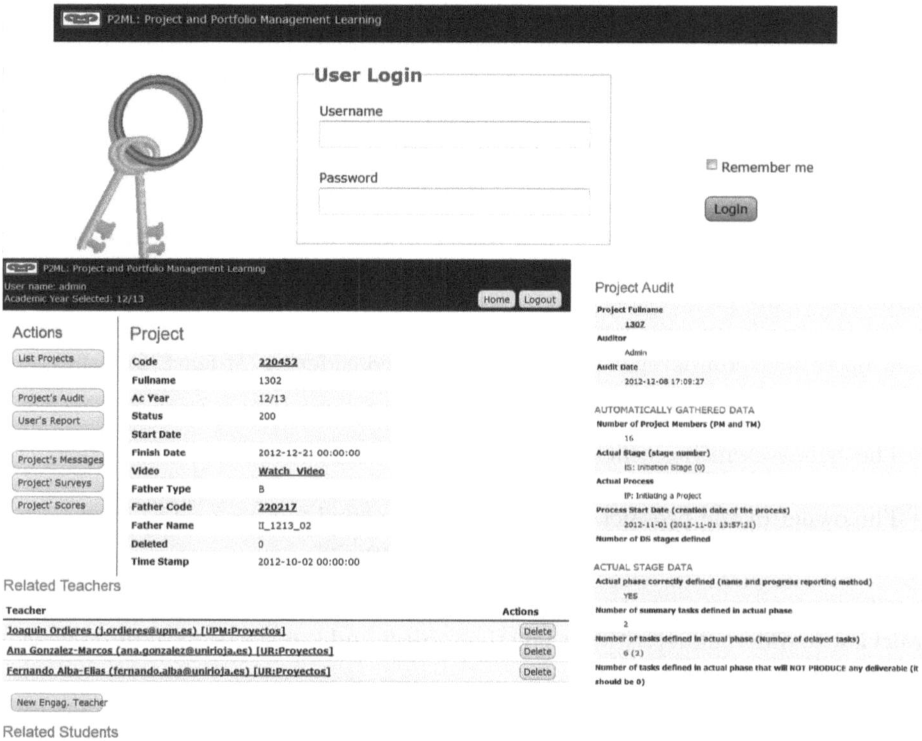

Fig. 3. Screenshots of the auditing tool specifically developed.

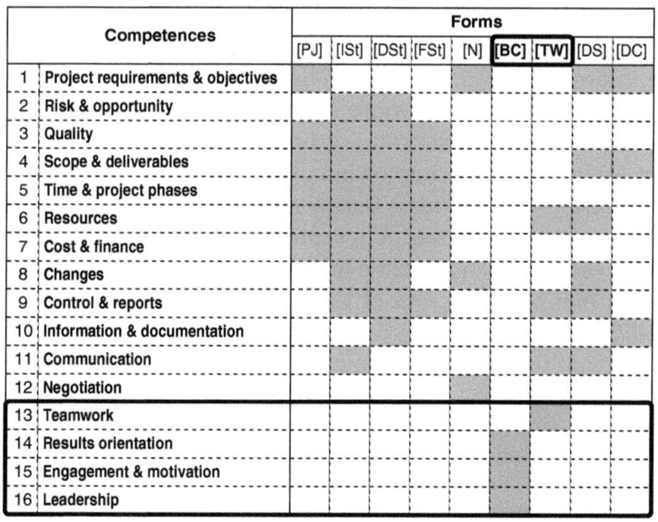

Fig. 4. Competences considered in this framework and forms with which they are assessed (the competences analyzed in this work are in red) (Color figure online).

team is managing the different PRINCE2^{TM} themes -risk, communication, quality and configuration. To determine the competence level, answers to various questions are obtained from different forms that describe products, processes and behaviors (Fig. 4). Most of the responses are Likert-scale-based and opinions come from the producer of the product or those who are responsible for the process implementation, as well as different consumers of those products or participants in the process.

Each competence considered is assessed by several pieces of evidence (at least one) on the previously mentioned forms. The criteria that determine maximum performance are clearly specified.

The numeric assessment of the different pieces of evidence considered as relevant to each competence is conducted after considering, at least, four different roles:

- The self-assessment, which is always a relevant opinion
- The auditor
- The owner of the product that is being developed
- User(s) of this particular configuration or product.

Thus, the competence assessment framework uses some kind of 360-degree overview to different activities inside the project and it collects all these evidences in a weighted integration.

5 Results and Discussion

The project teams consisted of students from two different universities, UPM and UR. They were organized around eight projects (1301 to 1308). Each project team included two EXs, seven or eight PMs and ten to twelve TMs. At the end of the course, more than 450 assessment forms were filled out.

The first step in any multivariate analysis is to graphically represent the individual variables using a histogram or boxplot. These graphic representations are extremely useful for detecting asymmetries, heterogeneity, outliers, etc.

In order to observe differences between perceived PM competences within each project, boxplots were used. They proved a means to summarize a distribution, require less space than other graphical techniques and provide a quick way to examine one or more sets of data graphically (see Fig. 5). The spaces between the different parts of the box help to indicate the degree of dispersion (spread) and skew of the data. A boxplot (also known as a box and whisker plot) is interpreted as follows:

- The box itself contains the middle 50 % of the data. The upper edge (hinge) of the box indicates the 75th percentile of the data set, and the lower hinge shows the 25th percentile. The range of the middle two quartiles is known as the inter-quartile range.
- The line in the box indicates the data's median value

- The ends of the horizontal lines or “whiskers” indicate the minimum and maximum data values, unless outliers are present. In that case, the whiskers extend to a maximum of 1.5 times the inter-quartile range.
- The points that are outside of the ends of the whiskers are outliers or suspected outliers.

In comparing the boxplots across groups, one can summarize by saying that the box area for one group is higher or lower than that for another group. To the extent that the boxes do not overlap, the groups are quite different from one another.

The distributions shown in Fig. 5 illustrate the different opinion that each team project had about the competences exhibited by their PMs. Thus, for instance, the PM team of project 1302 obtained opinions varying from ‘strongly disagree’ (a value of 1 on the Likert scale) to ‘strongly agree’ (a value of 5 on the Likert scale). The other project teams had higher opinions of the competence level of their PMs (from ‘neither agree nor disagree’ (3 on the Likert scale to ‘strongly agree’, with some exceptions).

In general, teamwork (Fig. 5, bottom right) was the competence with the best assessments. In this case, projects 1304 and 1305 exhibited the lowest dispersions with highest assessments (between 3.8 and 5), whereas project 1302 had the highest variability in the assessments (between 1.4 and 5).

It is worth mentioning that the other three competences that were analyzed (leadership, engagement & motivation and results orientation) had very similar distributions per project. Since these three competences were evaluated at the same time by means of the same form, it seems that the evaluation of each person was based on an overall opinion that the assessor had of the assessed person without making any distinction between these competences.

The instructors’ team established the quality of the project (SCORE) according to the content and format of management products (plans, business case, project reports, etc.) and specialist products (feasibility studies, engineering drawings, calculations, etc.). In this case, a 5-point Likert scale (from 1 for “very bad quality” to 5 for “very good quality”) was used.

A visual inspection of all possible pairs of scatterplots in the analyzed variables helps to understand the relationships between variables. If these scatterplots are arranged in matrix format, the type of relationship that there is between the pairs of variables can be understood and the outliers in the bivariate relationship can be identified. Such diagrams are particularly important for identifying non-linear relationships, in which the covariant matrix may not provide a good summary of the dependence among variables [21].

Figure 6 summarizes all of this information and illustrates the relationships between the project quality (SCORE) of each project and the mean value of the assessed PM’s transversal competences. The lower triangle of the matrix contains a scatterplot for each pair of variables with a polynomial approximation according to the nature of their relationship. The histogram of each variable appears on the diagonal. The absolute value of the correlations with size pro-

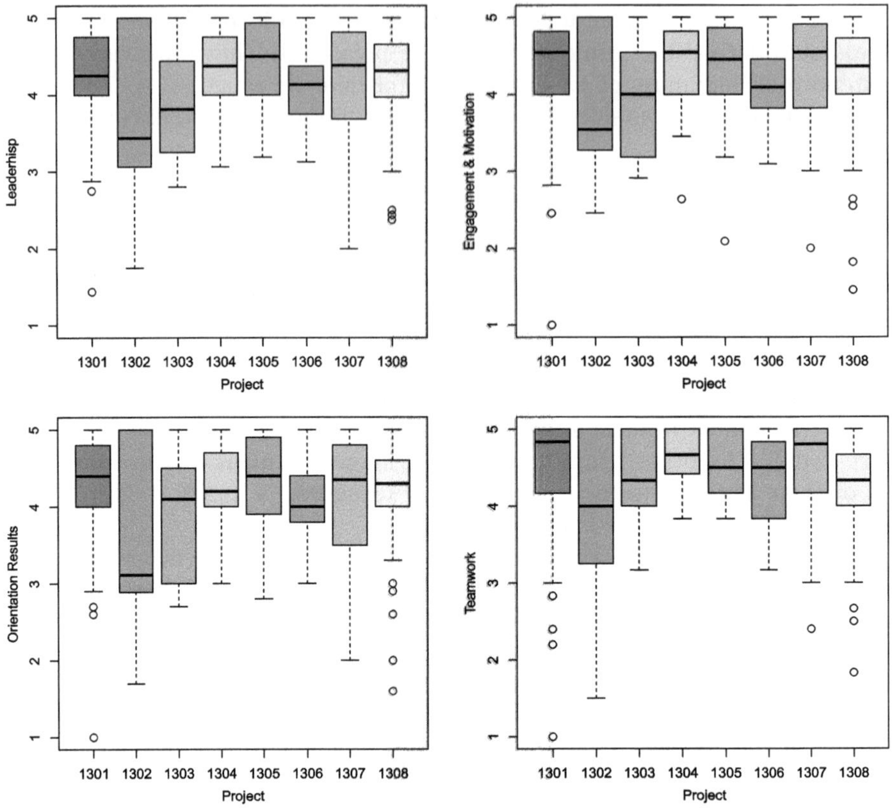

Fig. 5. Competence assessment results per project.

portional to their magnitude is included in the upper triangle. From this figure, the following conclusions can be drawn:

- The project quality (SCORE) is positively correlated with the four transversal competences that were analyzed (Mean_Lider, Mean_CyM, Mean_Ores and Mean_TW). However, as can be seen in the first column of the matrix, these relationships are not perfectly linear (red line). Although projects 1304 and 1305 have the highest means of the four transversal competences (points located at the top of each scatterplot), projects 1307 and 1308 obtained the highest SCORES (points located at the right of each scatterplot). That is, large doses of leadership, engagement & motivation, results orientation and teamwork are important to ensure high quality of the project, but they are not the only relevant variables.
- The highest correlation between the project quality (SCORE) and any of the PM's transversal competences that were analyzed involves the competence named results-orientation (Mean_ORes). This result is consistent with the importance that the IPMA gives to this competence. Results-orientation in

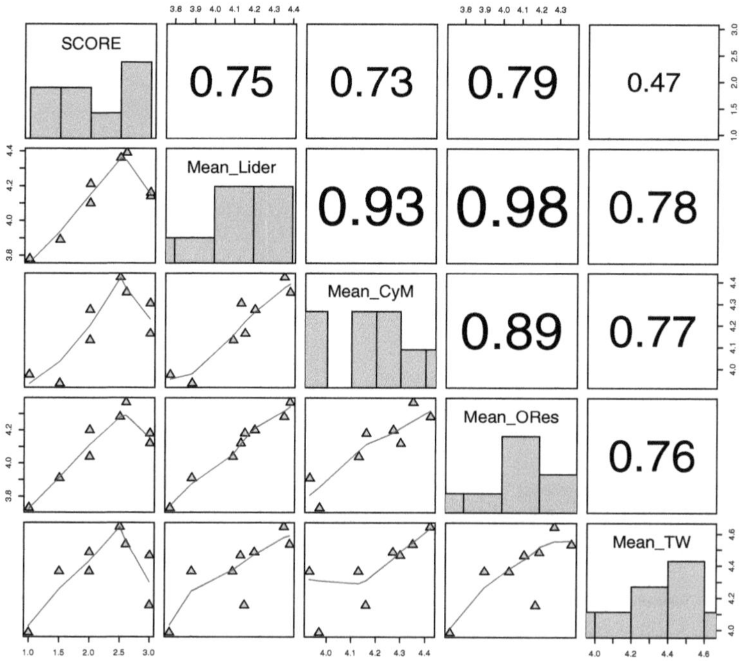

Fig. 6. Relationship between project quality (SCORE) and the transversal competences analyzed (Color figure online).

project management behavior is closely linked to project success [7]. In summary, higher quality projects were attained by PM teams that were able to develop project teams that concentrated on results in the changing environments.

- Project quality (SCORE) and teamwork (Mean_TW) had the lowest correlation (0.47).
- Although there is a high correlation between the four transversal competences that were analyzed, the strongest relationship is that among leadership (Mean_Lider), engagement & motivation (Mean_CyM) and results orientation (Mean_ORes). This is consistent with our previous observation related to the evaluation of these competences through the same form: each assessor evaluated these competences to each person without making any distinction between them.

By defining the effort ratio as the relationship between the total number of hours claimed by the entire project team and the total number of planned hours, a strong correlation (0.83) between this variable and the project quality (see Fig. 7, left) is observed. This result suggests that the lower the deviations between planned and actual activity of the project team are, the higher is the final quality of the project.

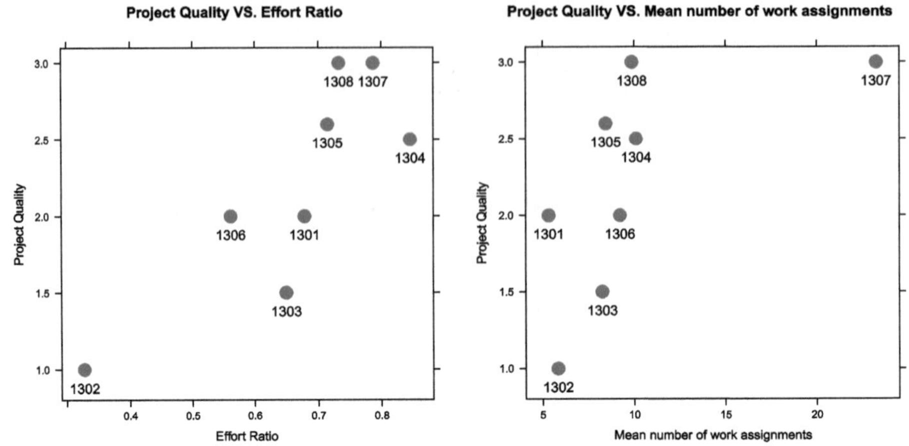

Fig. 7. Relationships between project quality (SCORE) and (left) effort ratio (correlation coefficient = 0.83) and (right) the mean number of work assignments (correlation coefficient = 0.62).

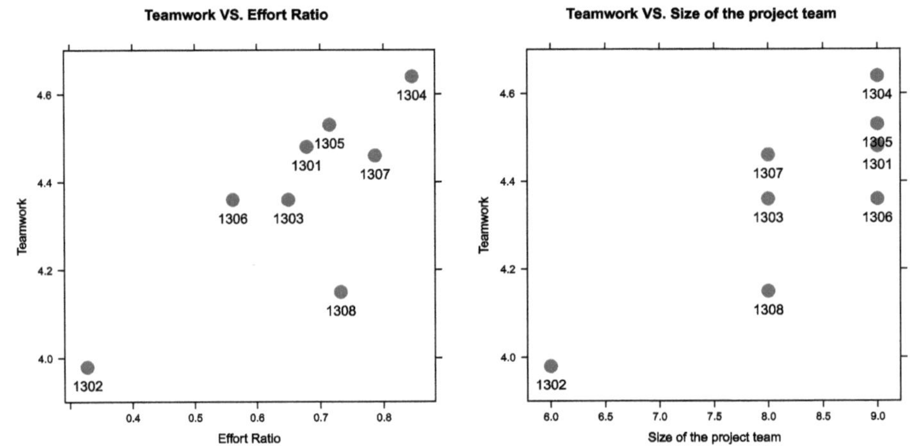

Fig. 8. Relationship between teamwork competence and (left) effort ratio (correlation coefficient = 0.78) and (right) the size of the project team (correlation coefficient = 0.85).

Figure 7 right illustrates the relationship between the mean number of work assignments and the project's final quality. In this case, the correlation between the two variables analyzed is lower. That is, a higher number of work assignments do not necessary mean better project quality. For example, although the number of work assignments defined in the project 1308 was half that of the work assignments defined in project 1307, both projects were of similar quality.

Teamwork competence (Fig. 8) is strongly related to both the effort ratio (correlation equal to 0.78) and the size of the project team (correlation equal to 0.85). These results illustrate how a feeling of teamwork increases as the actual effort approaches the estimated effort (Fig. 8, left). The same feeling was identified taking into account the size of the project team (Fig. 8, right).

6 Conclusions

This paper has introduced an extensible and distributed multi-model-based system for learning and assessing project management competences. The system registers individual activities and promotes reflective learning as participants complete specific forms that are appropriate to activities being performed.

The system is distinguished by the assessment of individual competences by use of a set of performance indicators. The indications of a participant's skills are obtained from analytical evidence and the opinions of other participants in the simulation. The system enables information of the level of demonstrated competences to be obtained not by the measurement of individual knowledge, but by its use in a simulation environment.

An analysis of the PM's exhibited competences have shown a relationship between some transversal ('human') competences and project success. In the academic course analyzed, the strongest relationship was found to be that between results-orientation and project success. Teamwork did not seem to be correlated with project quality. The authors attribute the lowest relationship, namely that between teamwork and project success, to the lower number of pieces of evidence used to assess this competence.

Another interesting result is the strong relationship among leadership, engagement & motivation and results orientation that was found. Considering that these competences were evaluated at the same time by means of the same form, it seems that each assessor relied on an overall opinion of the assessed person in completing the form. No distinction was made between these competences.

In the future, the authors hope to improve the assessment of these competences by using more pieces of evidence. In addition, they will extend the number of competences assessed by the proposed framework and also use the data collected for early detection of problems within the project to improve the learning procedure.

Acknowledgements. The authors wish to recognize the support of the Spanish "Ministerio de Educación" through its research funding program as part of this work was supported by its grant EDU2012-31080. The authors would also like to express their thanks for the financial support of the "Vicerrectorado de Profesorado, Planificación e Innovación Docente" of the University of La Rioja, through the "Dirección Académica de Formación e Innovación Docente" (APIDUR 2013).

References

1. Abernethy, K., Piegari, G., Reichgelt, H.: Teaching project management: an experiential approach. J. Comput. Sci. Coll. **22**, 198–205 (2007)
2. APM: APM Competence Framework. Association for Project Management (2008)

3. Barron, S.: Assessing project management learning -how can it make a difference? In: 2nd Project Management Conference: Excellence in Teaching, Learning and Assessment, Bournemouth (2005)
4. Belout, A., Gauvreau, C.: Factors influencing project success: the impact of human resource management. Int. J. Project Manage. **22**(1), 1–11 (2004)
5. Beltrn, J.: Aprender y ensear en la universidad. Iniciacin a la docencia universitaria. Universidad de Jan (1999)
6. Berggren, C., Sderlund, J.: Rethinking project management education: social twists and knowledge co-production. Int. J. Project Manage. **26**, 286–296 (2008)
7. Caupin, G., Knoepfel, H., Koch, G., Pannenbcker, K., Perez-Polo, F., Seabury, C.: IPMA Competence Baseline, version 3. International Project Management Association (2006)
8. Clark, R.: Project management: the key to engineering employability. In: SEFI - 36th Annual Conference (2008)
9. Council of the European Union: Education and training 2010. the success of the lisbon strategy hinges on urgent reforms. Council document 6905/04, Council of the European Union, 03 March 2004. http://ec.europa.eu/education/policies/2010/doc/jir_council_final.pdf
10. Crespo, E., Alba-Elas, F., Gonzlez-Marcos, A., Ordieres, J., Castejn-Limas, M.: Project management learning in a collaborative distant learning context - an actual on-going experience. In: 3rd International Conference on Computer Supported Education, pp. 105–110 (2011)
11. European Commision: Implementation of "education and training 2010". key competences. Tech. rep., European Commision (2004). http://ec.europa.eu/education/policies/2010/doc/basicframe.pdf
12. Gonzlez-Marcos, A., Alba-Elas, F., Ordieres, J.: A web-based support system for providing effective monitoring, feedback and evaluation in project management education. In: 5th International Conference on Computer Supported Education, pp. 254–257 (2013)
13. Hewagamage, C., Hewagamage, K.: Redesigned framework and approach for it project management. Int. J. Softw. Eng. Appl. **5**(3), 89–106 (2011)
14. Huang, S., Yang, C.: Designing a semantic bliki system to support different types of knowledge and adaptive learning. Comput. Educ. **53**(3), 701–712 (2009)
15. Hughes, J.: The role of teacher knowledge and learning experiences in forming technology-integrated pedagogy. J. Technol. Teacher Educ. **13**(2), 277–302 (2005)
16. Navaridas, F.: Estrategias didcticas en el aula universitaria. Universidad de La Rioja (2004)
17. Office Of Government Commerce: Managing Successful Projects with PRINCE2(^{TM}). Office Of Government Commerce (2009)
18. Ojiako, U., Ashleigh, M., Chipulu, M., Maguire, S.: Learning and teaching challenges in project management. Int. J. Project Manage. **29**, 268–278 (2011)
19. Ordieres-Meré, J., González-Marcos, A., Alba, F.: The use of computers for graduate education in project management. improving the integration to the industry. In: 2011 International Conference on Frontiers in Education: Computer Science & Computer Engineering (FECS11, WORLDCOMP), pp. 233–238 (2011)
20. Pant, I., Baroudi, B.: Project management education: the human skills imperative. Int. J. Project Manage. **26**, 124–128 (2008)
21. Pea, D.: Anlisis de datos multivariantes. McGraw Hill, Madrid (2002)
22. PMI: Project Manager Competency Development (PMCD) Framework. Project Management Institute (2002)

23. PMI: A Guide to the Project Management Body of Knowledge (PMBOK Guide). Project Management Institute, fifth edition edn (2013)
24. Qureshi, T., Warraich, A., Hijazi, S.: Significance of project management performance assessment (pmpa) model. Int. J. Project Manage. **27**(4), 378–388 (2009)
25. Reif, H., Mitri, M.: How university professors teach project management for information systems. Commun. ACM **48**, 134–136 (2005)
26. Seidel, T.: Implementing competence assessment in university education. Empirical Res. Vocat. Educ. Training **25**, 405–412 (2012)
27. Sense, A.: Structuring the project environment for learning. Int. J. Project Manage. **25**, 405–412 (2007)
28. Subramanian, G., Jiang, J., Klein, G.: Software quality and is project performance improvements from software development process maturity and is implementation strategies. J. Syst. Softw. **80**(4), 616–627 (2007)
29. Thomas, J.: Project based learning: a handbook for middle and high school teachers. Buck Institute for Education (1999)
30. Zhang, L., He, J., Zhang, X.: The project management maturity model and application based on PRINCE2. Procedia Eng. **29**, 3691–3697 (2012)

Learning About the Semantic Web in an Information Systems Oriented Curriculum: A Case Study

Daniela Giordano(✉) and Francesco Maiorana

Department of Electrical, Electronics and Computer Engineering, University of Catania, Viale A. Doria, 6, Catania, Italy
{daniela.giordano, francesco.maiorana}@dieei.unict.it

Abstract. Semantic Web technologies are pushing forward the on-going revolution towards Web 3.0 and the semantic Internet of Things. This strong movement must be supported by an adequate educational offer in the IT curriculum of higher education programs, able to fulfill the increasing demand of semantic-oriented job requests expected in the next year. This paper presents a case study about teaching a Master's course entitled "Laboratory in software design and development – Semantic Technologies". A detailed description of the curriculum, which can be easily repurposed, the rationale underlying the choice of content and the software tools used are presented. The main lessons learnt from this experience are also informed by a qualitative analysis of the work that the students were able to produce.

Keywords: Information systems applications · Mash-ups · RDF · RDS · OWL · Linked open data · Knowledge representation and reasoning · Ontology engineering · Triplify · SPARQL · Gruff · Jena · Facebook graph api

1 Introduction

The impact of the World Wide Web (WWW), albeit enormous, is hindered by some problems related to:

- data representation: all the data on the WWW are semantics-free. This gives rise to disaligned, inconsistent and unrelated information.
- entity update: an update on an entity does not affect all the pages that semantically reference it.

The semantic web is able to overcome these difficulties and is gaining momentum day by day. The rise of the semantic web has created a strong demand by industry for people trained in semantic technologies as well as ontologies. This demand is estimated to quickly grow in the following years. Paralleling this strong interest there is a flourishing growth of courses in academia and professional institutions; however, these courses are often single courses within larger programs. [1] identified only one complete academic program completely devoted to education in applied ontology (a Master's program at the University of Buffalo) and 21 programs that offer ontology-centered topics.

S. Zvacek et al. (Eds.): CSEDU 2014, CCIS 510, pp. 242–257, 2015.
DOI: 10.1007/978-3-319-25768-6_16

Applied ontology and the semantic web are relatively young disciplines and therefore there is not yet a general consensus on questions related to several aspects of teaching, ranging from the curriculum to even the terminology.

In the ACM/IEEE computer science curriculum [2], for example, the knowledge required for an ontologist is spread among courses or topics within courses. Examples of such courses are the elective "Advanced Representation and Reasoning" in the field of Intelligent Systems (IS), dealing with ontology engineering and, the elective course entitled "Data, Information and Knowledge", in the field of Computational Science, dealing with "Knowledge: ontologies, triple stores, semantic networks, rules", and so on. First, this paper will briefly review the literature on teaching, curriculum examples and didactic tools in the main areas of the semantic web: ontology design, ontology query languages, ontology programming framework, mash-up and semantic web applications. Then, a case study of the design and the implementation of an introductory lab in semantic web technologies, worth 3 ECTS, will be presented.

Among the several collections of semantic web educational resources to which the reader can refer [3], there exists a repository built by the European Association for Semantic Web Education [4]. In spite of this field being relatively young, there are outstanding experiences in teaching ontology engineering and ontology design. In [5] the authors report the results of a several-years-long experience in teaching the OWL language and ontology design, along with common errors and common design patterns. Several ontologies have been used as didactic examples to teach ontology design and OWL, such as Pizza, Wines and Marsupials.

Recently, a didactic example in the biological domain was proposed by [6], concerning an OWL ontology describing zoo animals. The ontology, with respect to other large biomedical ontologies, has the advantage of reducing significantly the number of classes and the overall complexity, allowing for fast memorization and orientation, yet it uses all the major ontology constructs, with related modelling challenges together with some Ontology Design Pattern (ODP). The proposed ontology uses a light version of Bitop [7] as a top level ontology. Moreover, the ontology covers a domain that involves common knowledge and therefore can be easily understood by the majority of people, especially in the life science domain. The ontology was used in a complete curriculum for ontology design described in [8] where the authors present a teaching experience of a one-week workshop organized around 16 modules, addressing 4 main themes with an increasing level of design complexity: basic principles, practical ontology design, using top-level ontologies and ODP.

Various works address the development of software tools used for training the students in the use of ontology query languages, and examples of clear and didactically sound tutorials are also available. A recent example of a software training tool is described in [9] where the authors propose a web-based SPARQL trainer that allows the tutor to design a course along a set of concepts that are to be tested. The tutor prepares a set of questions and a dataset. Each question is provided with a query solution against which the student's solution is compared. The comparison is based on the result sets: the query solution and the student solution result set must coincide both in the elements and in their order.

For mash-up and semantic web applications, a good tutorial can be found in [10] where the author presents a semantic web application that expects a musical style as input, retrieves data from online music archives and event databases, merges them via a bridge ontology and allows the user to explore events related to artists that practice the required style.

The aim of this paper, which extends the work presented in [11], is to give a detailed overview of the curriculum taught in a Master's-level class in Informatics Engineering in order to "describe in more detail" how some of the knowledge and skills indicated in [1] can be acquired. Our curriculum is "IT-oriented" with a particular emphasis placed on the knowledge and deployment of "IT systems involving many components in addition to the ontology itself" [1]. This type of curriculum fits well with the knowledge and background of Informatics Engineering and Computer Science students and provides a means of broadening both data and knowledge design capabilities, as well as system integration and software development skills.

The paper is organized as follows: Sect. 2 presents the teaching context and the course contents; Sect. 3 analyzes some aspects of the students' submitted assignments to obtain some insights on how they dealt with the wealth of available resources and the freedom they were given to choose the context and scope for demonstrating mastering of the presented techniques; Sect. 4 discusses the lessons learnt, highlighting strengths and weaknesses of the approach used in the course; Sect. 5 offers some concluding remarks.

2 Teaching Context and Contents

The teaching experience pertains to a 30-hour course within the Informatics Engineering Master's degree at the University of Catania. The course was taught in the 2011 Fall term. The course was offered for the first time as a choice to obtain the three ECTS credits that, by curriculum design, are devoted to the acquisition of supplementary ICT skills. It was attended by both first year and second year students. Management of the class was not particularly easy due to the students' varying levels of knowledge and experience. The course schedule was a three hour meeting per week for ten weeks. The course was designed around semantic technologies, with the aim of demonstrating during the classes the main technologies of the semantic web and the main tools used to design and implement semantic applications. As a university rule for this type of credits, the course was graded on a pass/fail basis.

The students attending the course could get acquainted with the following topics and issues:

1. Data transformation from a relational database to RDF. After a review of the main tools, Triplify (http://triplify.org/Overview) was chosen due to its simplicity and its tight relationship with database technologies and the PHP web programming language, tools that are well-known to all the students attending the course.
2. Querying triple stores/RDF files. The main tool used was the SPARQL query language. The Gruff browser was used both in a standalone version and with the AllegroGraph server. Among the different advantages of the Gruff browser, the graph representation capabilities were considered a definitive plus.

3. Relations and ontology design using RDFS and OWL. Protégé was the tool chosen, due to its flexibility, integration with reasoners, rich availability of plugins and its free availability.
4. Linked Open Data: design and implementation of a mash-up from linked data. Jena was the Application Framework selected for this goal.

The course also offered students possibilities to familiarize themselves with the following core skills and knowledge:

- Clarifying the purpose of a given ontology
- Judging what kinds of ontologies are useful for a given problem
- Identifying, evaluating and using software tools that support ontology development
- Using (reading and writing) different representation languages
- Conducting ontological analyses
- Using a modern programming language
- Working in teams

The class activities were supported by an on-line class site developed with the Moodle platform, used for sharing lecture notes, projects and communications and greatly simplified the management of class activities.

The class schedule is reported in Table 1 with an indication of the time devoted to each topic.

The table gives an overview of the curriculum content that was organized into 4 main parts or modules, with an increasing level of difficulty and with a broader view of the covered topics. Each module was further divided into 2 or 3 units. The modularization of the curriculum allows for an easier customization for other courses and classes with different backgrounds.

The first module presents the Semantic Web in comparison to the WWW and its main contributions. The RDF language and RDF graph are presented along with the major serialization languages: N-triples, turtle and XML. Concepts like reification, blank node and list and their impact in designing are presented and applied to examples and exercises. An introduction to the main ontological languages RDFS, RDFS-Plus, OWL and their expressiveness is undertaken.

The second unit deals with data transformation and query techniques. The data transformation technique was appreciated by the students and served as a common thread between their strong background on database and web programming and the course content. After a review of the main tools, such as D2RQ, Triplify was chosen due to its simplicity and its affinity with SQL and the PHP development environment. This allowed students to publish RDF triples from their own databases as well as from data present in Bulletin Board, Content Management systems and so on. The students became acquainted with large RDF files and began to design RDF graphs starting from an E/R schema.

The original work by [12] describing the design of Triplify was used as a main reference. The best works were presented by the students, which benefited the entire class. Figure 1 (a) shows an example of a site created by one team in Wordpress The associated database containing news about course topics and news was used by the team in the conversion process; (b) shows a snippet of the generated RDF triples.

Table 1. Class schedule.

Topic	#H	Tools	Readings	Assignment
Part 1: Basic principles				
The Semantic web	3		[13]: Ch.1	
RDF and RDF graph. Serialization languages.	3		[13]: Ch.2–3	
Reification, blank node, list in RDF. RDFS, RDFS-Plus, OWL	3		[13]: Ch.3–4	
Part 2: Data transformation and querying				
Data transformation tools. Lab session: use of Triplify	3	Triplify Allegro-graph	[12]	Triplify a Database
SPARQL and SPARQL 1.1	4	Allegro-graph/ Gruff	[13]: Ch. 5 [14]: Ch. 6 [15]	Design a set of queries and evaluate their performance
Part 3: Ontology design				
Ontology engineering. Use of Protegè	4	Protegè/OWLViz	[16]: Ch. 4 [13]: Ch. 6 to 12 [14]: Ch. 4, 5, 12	Design an ontology
The Jena framework	4	Eclipse/Jena/MYSQL	[14]: Ch. 12 to 5, [17] [18]	Develop an application integrating data from FOAF and DBpedia
Part 4: Semantic web applications: mash-up, linked data and visualization				
Visualization framework: exhibit	2	Exhibit	[19]	Visualize events data on Google maps
A semantic web application: mash-up and linked data	4	Combination of tools	[20] [21] [10] [16]	Develop a mash-up application (optional)
Total	30			

The subsequent step was the introduction of the SPARQL language to query a RDF triple store. The SPARQL language was selected since it resembles the well-known database query language SQL. The use of triples, graph patterns and other features allowed the students to practice with the underlying RDF graph and with serialization

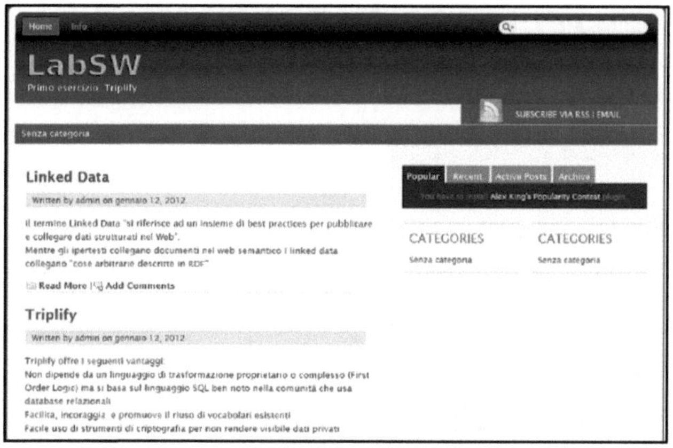

(a)

```
<http://127.0.0.1/wp/triplify/> <http://www.w3.org/2000/01/rdf-schema#comment> "Generated by
Triplify V0.7.1 (http://Triplify.org)" .
<http://127.0.0.1/wp/triplify/><http://creativecommons.org/ns#license>
<http://creativecommons.org/licenses/by/3.0/us/> .
<http://127.0.0.1/wp/triplify/post/3> <http://www.w3.org/1999/02/22-rdf-syntax-ns#type>
<http://rdfs.org/sioc/ns#Post> .
<http://127.0.0.1/wp/triplify/post/3><http://rdfs.org/sioc/ns#has_creator>
<http://127.0.0.1/wp/triplify/user/1> .
<http://127.0.0.1/wp/triplify/post/3> <http://purl.org/dc/terms/created> "2012-01-
12T20:39:04"^^<http://www.w3.org/2001/
XMLSchema#dateTime> .
<http://127.0.0.1/wp/triplify/post/3> <http://purl.org/dc/elements/1.1/title> "Triplify" .
<http://127.0.0.1/wp/triplify/post/3> <http://rdfs.org/sioc/ns#content> "Triplify offre I seguenti
vantaggi:\r\nNon dipende da un linguaggio di trasformazione proprietario o complesso (First Order Logic)
ma si basa sul linguaggio SQL ben noto nella comunit\u00E0 che usa\u00A0
database relazionali\r\nFacilita, incoraggia\u00A0 e promuove il riuso di vocabolari esistenti\r\nFacile
uso di strumenti di criptografia per non endere visibile dati privati" .
<http://127.0.0.1/wp/triplify/post/3> <http://purl.org/dc/terms/modified> "2012-01-
12T20:39:51"^^<http://www.w3.org/2001/
XMLSchema#dateTime> .
```

(b)

Fig. 1. An example of a WordPress site used by one team for the conversion exercise (a) and a snippet of the generated RDF triples (b).

languages. Moreover, the students were free to use OWL and domain ontologies and to practice with large triple stores such as DBpedia. For all these reasons the introduction of SPARQL was considered a beneficial step in this phase of the course. The students were free to choose the RDF store where they published their data, although some suggestions were given, namely, the AllegroGraph RDF store (http://www.franz.com/agraph/allegrograph/) and the Gruff graph based triple store browser (http://www.franz.com/agraph/gruff/) due to the graph representation of the results set. Other common choices were the Sesame (http://www.openrdf.org/) and Joseky (http://joseki.sourceforge.net/) RDF stores. Figure 2 shows the Gruff interface which allows for an easy query experimentation both in SPARQL and Prolog.

Chapter 5 of [13] and chapter 6 of [14] were used as main references. All the types of queries were covered. The unit started with the select query form presenting triple and graph patterns, query modifiers, optional patterns that could be nested, filter conditions on different types and regular expressions, union of graph patterns, background and named graphs to query multiple graphs. The other types of query forms,

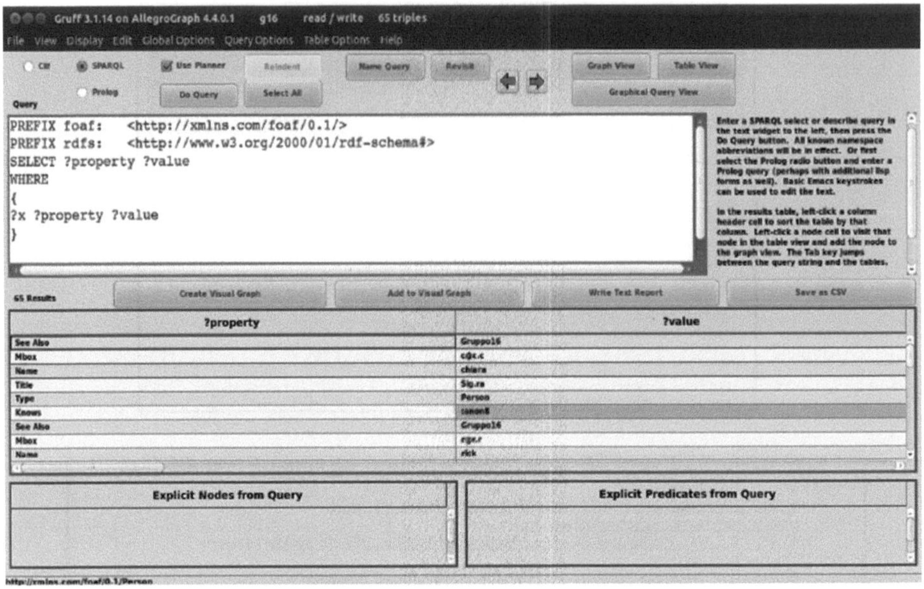

Fig. 2. The Gruff interface.

namely construct and rules, describe and ask, were then covered followed by the new SPARQL 1.1 features: aggregate functions, group by, sample and bound, subqueries, negation, expressions with SELECT, property paths, transitive queries, federated queries and the SPARQL update 1.1 standard.

In order to make the students aware of performance issues in query formulation the problem of benchmarking was presented through studies such as [15, 22]. These works were also used as query examples. Tools such as (http://ftp.heanet.i.e./disk1/download.sourceforge.net/pub/sourceforge/b/project/bs/bsbmtools/bsbmtools/bsbmtools-0.2/) were used by the students to profile queries and experiment with different query formulations. The students experimented with different datasets such as the one suggested in [15], FOAF RDF files, well-known public domain ontologies such as the Wine ontology and so on. Figure 3 shows an example of a graph created with the Gruff browser and Table 2 shows a sample output of the bsbmtools available in the Berlin SPARQL Benchmark.

The third part of the course was divided among two related units. The first dealt with ontology design principles. The main references were Chap. 4 of [16] as well as chapters 6, 7 for RDFS design and Chaps. 8, 9, 11, 12 from [13] for OWL-related design. Finally, Chap. 4 for RDFS design, chapter 5 for OWL design and Chap. 12 for tools and resources from [14] were also suggested to the students for reference. Suggestions on how to present the material are reported in the Lessons Learnt section. Protégé (http://protege.stanford.edu/) was the chosen working tool, with OWLViz (http://www.coode.org/downloads/owlviz/) for class visualization. The approach was to follow the Protegè tutorial [23] as well as sharing suggestions such as those reported in [5, 24], just to cite some examples. An initial methodology and a practical example

```
PREFIX vin: <http://www.w3.org/TR/2003/CR-owl-
guide-20030818/wine#>

SELECT * WHERE {
  ?winery a vin:Chardonnay .
  MINUS{?winery vin:hasBody vin:Medium .}
  ?winery ?property ?value
}
```

(a)

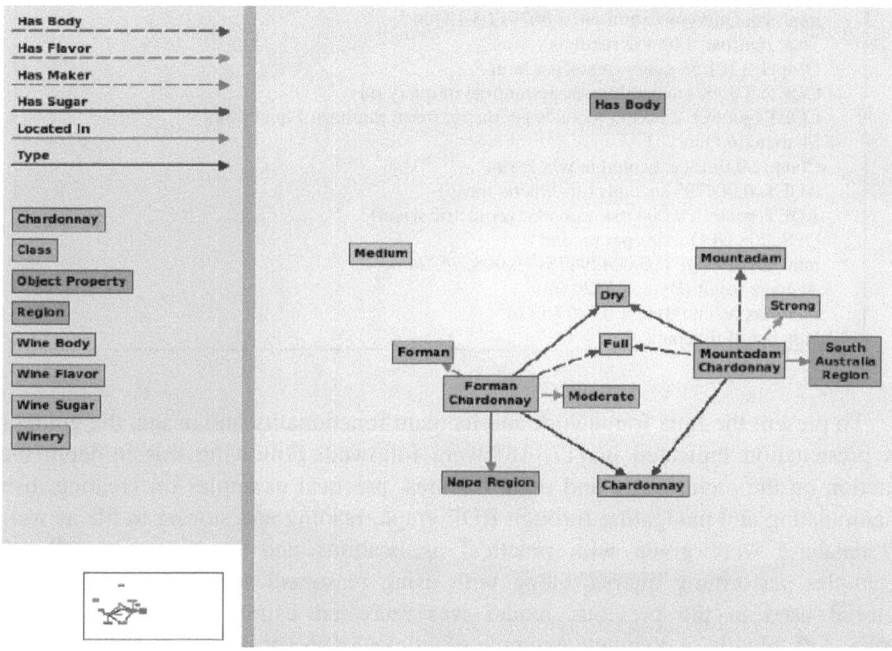

(b)

Fig. 3. An example of a SPARQL 1.1 query (a), with the graph results visualized with the Gruff browser (b).

for converting an E/R model into an OWL model was presented, along with some ODP. Other literature was suggested as further readings, i.e., [25, 26]. Two practical ontology design exercises were also proposed, the first one about the design of an educational portfolio and the second one regarding the sharing of learning objects. As a framework to develop semantic applications and manage ontologies, the Jena framework was chosen due to the large use of Java technologies in both academia and the professional world, as well as its free availability.

The Eclipse IDE and the MYSQL database to store persistent models, were also suggested for data manipulation in a database. As a reference for practical applications, Chaps. 12, 13, 14 and 15 of [14] were suggested.

Table 2. Result of the performance profile of the query on the dataset described in [22] with 1.000 as scale factor. The scale factor used is related to the number of products.

```
Query: Find information of the Person whose label is "reexhibit"
describe ?x
where {
   ?x rdfs:label "reexhibit".
}
```

```
Output of the bsbmtools-0.2
Scale factor: 1000
Number of warmup runs: 20
Seed: 808080
Number of query mix runs (without warmups): 50 times
min/max Querymix runtime: 2.6075s / 3.1330s
Total runtime: 140.452 seconds
QMpH: 1281.58 query mixes per hour
CQET: 2.80904 seconds average runtime of query mix
CQET (geom.): 2.80503 seconds geometric mean runtime of query mix
Metrics for Query: 1
Count: 50 times executed in whole run
AQET: 0.004793 seconds (arithmetic mean)
AQET(geom.): 0.004764 seconds (geometric mean)
QPS: 208.64 Queries per second
minQET/maxQET: 0.00429478s / 0.00822679s
Average result (Bytes): 1320.00
min/max result (Bytes): 1320 / 1320
Number of timeouts: 0
```

To present the Jena framework and its main functionality and usage, the guidelines of presentation indicated in [17, 18] were followed. Following this in-depth introduction on the architecture and main features, practical examples on creating, using, manipulating and navigating through RDF graph, reading and storing to file as well as to database were given with practical applications and working code. Practical examples performing queries along with using reasoners were also presented. The tutorial used in the previous model was recreated using, programmatically, the OWL API. Finally, a complete example of a linked data application in the style of [14] was illustrated. The example was used as a starting point for a linked data application. The practical approach to linked data was followed by a theoretical overview. The books [20, 21] were used as reference material and an overview of the main concepts, design principles, techniques and recipes for publishing and consuming linked data was presented to the students.

Finally, the fourth part completed the picture by presenting visualization tools and strategies to design and implement a mash-up semantic application. Exhibit was selected as the visualization tool due to its simplicity and flexibility in addition to its free availability [19] together with tutorials and other learning material. In particular, Exhibit 3.0 was presented to the students, together with its use in a local environment.

In the original plan, all the technologies tools and techniques had to converge in the presentation of the final project. The aim was to present a mash-up application that integrates different sources of data in different formats, (e.g., relational, XML and RDF) by designing a bridge ontology integrating all these data in a unifying view. The reference material was the tutorial [10] as well as Chap. 9 of [16] where the design principles and main techniques and implementation details are presented. This kind of application should be considered as the concluding and unifying aspect of the course, where all the principles and technologies can be applied to build a working semantic application.

In summary, the guiding factors for choosing the tools were: the efficiency, the ease of use and its connection with the database technologies for Triplify, the visualization aids for Gruff, the free and open source availability together with its large use in ontology development for Jena, and the relative ease of use and rich set of graphical features for Exhibit.

3 Analysis of the Students' Work

Student submissions went far beyond expectations considering the vast amount of lecture notes, readings and mini-projects assigned. In particular this section focuses on considerations regarding the first two assignments: the first one about data transformation techniques using Triplify and the second one about querying techniques using SPARQL.

The students were left free in forming the teams to carry out the assignments and the suggested activities, since they were already experienced in working in groups. The only constraint that was given was about the maximum size of the group, which was set to four. The average group size was 3.16, suggesting that 3 could be a good group size. Overall, the groups worked well together for the whole duration of the course without any change in their composition.

Table 3 reports some key indicators about the first assignment, namely, the distribution of the types of sites and the associated database used in the conversion from a relational to an RDF schema, the average number of queries used in the conversion script and the average number of namespaces used in the conversion process.

Table 4 reports some key indicators for the second assignment, namely: (a) the choice of technology with relative percentages; (b) the repositories, schema and

Table 3. Key indicators for the conversion to RDF assignment, through Triplify.

Test sites	Average number of queries used in the script	Average namespace dimension
– WordPress[a]: 41 % – Drupal[b]: 11 % – Joomla[c]: 11 % – PhpDB[d]: 11 % – Elgg[e]: 7 % – Personal database: 19 %	8.37	11.74

[a]http://wordpress.org/download/
[b]https://www.drupal.org/download
[c]http://www.joomla.org/download.html
[d]https://www.phpbb.com/download
[e]http://elgg.org/download.php

datasets used, with relative percentages; (c) the average number of queries performed; and (d) on average, the maximum number of patterns over all the queries performed by each group of students. According to http://www.w3.org/TR/rdf-sparql-query/ triple patterns are like RDF triples except that each of the subject, predicate and object may be a variable.

Table 4. Key indicators for the SPARQL assignment.

Technologies	Schema and datasets	Average number of queries	Average of max number of patterns
– Allegrograph server and Gruff: 85 % – Joseky: 10 % – Sesame[a]: 5 %	– Foaf[b]: 33 % – Berlin SPARQL Benchmark: 22 % – Wine[c]: 11 % – Personal[d]: 4 % – Deputy Chamber[e]: 4 % – DBPedia[f]: 7 % – Actors[f]: 7 % – Facebook: 4 % – Museum[g]: 4 % – Bible[h]: 4 %	10.41	10.86

[a]http://www.openrdf.org/download.jsp
[b]Different sets of public available personal ontologies
[c]www.w3.org/TR/owl-guide/wine.rdf
[d]Availabe in Allegrograph
[e]http://dati.camera.it/it/progetto.html
[f]http://wiki.dbpedia.org/
[g]http://sparql.linkedopendata.it/musei
[h]http://datahub.io/it/dataset/bible-ontology/resource/a87923c7-1422-46ac-a0d3-fd589f284721

The analysis of the student's work regarding conversion from a relational to an RDF schema revealed a strong interest in the subject and confirmed it as being the right choice for an "ice breaking" activity.

Many groups of students were engaged with different types of datasets, ranging from personal constructed databases to public databases as well as databases in Content Management Systems like Joomla, WordPress, Bulletin Board and so on. Interestingly, the average number of queries submitted by the students was above the reference number queries assigned by the instructors.

Many students experimented with different ontologies and schema both by analyzing them in a separate fashion and in queries with a multi-graph approach. A deeper analysis of the SPARQL queries revealed the covering of all the features of SPARLQ 1.1, ranging from all the types of query forms (ask, describe, construct and select) to federated queries and complex transitive relationships which are augmented by researching the transitivity in SPARQL. Some students experimented with the

Table 5. Snippet of the Python script to retrieve data using the Facebook graph API.

```
def get_friends(uid, token):
    params = "id,name,friends"
    cmd = ["curl",
"https://graph.facebook.com/%s?fields=%s&access_token=%s"
    % uid, params, token)]
    process = subprocess.Popen(cmd,
stdout=subprocess.PIPE,
stderr=subprocess.PIPE)
    result = process.stdout.read()
    try:
        dict_ = eval(result)
    except Exception as ex:
        print "Parsing failed!\n", ex
        return
    print "Looking for %s's" % dict_["name"], "friends"
    my_friends = []
    for new_friend in dict_["friends"]["data"]:
        id_ = new_friend["id"]
        if id_ not in last_friends:
            last_friends.append(id_)
            my_friends.append(id_)
    friends[dict_["id"]] = my_friends
```

Facebook Graph Api (https://developers.facebook.com/docs/graph-api). Table 5 reports a code snippet of the Python script.

The Python script developed by the students automatically retrieves data in Turtle 3 format using a developer Facebook account and different API Key. Other students particularly enjoyed engaging into the query performance evaluation, and took the initiative to extend the assignments by reporting results and considerations from research literature, such as [27].

The observed richness in the scenaria chosen to carry out the assignments and the several initiatives to extend the objectives of the assignments are especially remarkable given the pass or fail grading of the course, i.e., the students pursued these goals not to get top marks but out of genuine interest and will of experimenting with the technologies.

4 Lessons Learnt

The post-hoc analysis of the teaching experience, leads to the following considerations. The initial module on the semantic web, although an interesting and necessary step that gives an overview of the potentiality and breadth of the fields, can be reduced to a minimum and allow the important concepts to emerge from practical case studies such as querying an RDF graph and ontology design.

The use of Triplify was a good ice breaking activity allowing students to start from what they already knew well, namely database design and web programming, bringing them to fast production of their RDF data and hence reading and navigating the data produced. The project assignment can serve as a point of contact between a web-related curriculum such as [28] and an ontology-oriented curriculum.

The use of SPARQL for querying RDF store was a definitive plus, serving as a bridge between different concepts: it allows the student to master serialization languages, ontology representation and navigation, triple and graph pattern, query language, and so on. The use of a benchmarking tool can be of great benefit by allowing the students to place more attention on query design and underlying execution mechanisms. This type of knowledge can help in obtaining a better understanding of both the querying and, more broadly, of the ontology design processes.

The ontology design step is worth further consideration. In the students' submissions we did not observe the same degree of autonomous experimentation and deepening as for the first two assignments. This probably means that more time needs to be allowed for student projects on this aspect and more opportunities to share both their projects and the peer reviews along with the trainer's feedback and comments [29]. At any rate, the use of conversion from E/R to OWL is a good starting point, whereas supplementing ODP by applying it to a real case scenario could be of great benefit. The amount of reference material suggested to the student should be covered through the development of a practical project in order to avoid an overwhelming effect.

Some students reported that they would have preferred to begin with ontology design and then view the querying aspects. The best curriculum may then be designed around a parallel development of query, ontology design and programming framework to converge as soon as possible with the design and implementation of linked data and mash-up in a semantic web application.

The programming side of the linked data and mash-up applications can (and should) be the central aspect of courses for Informatics Engineering and Computer Science students. By leveraging their strong background on software design and programming, by scheduling the necessary time and granting a valid number of credit units, there is the possibility to develop, through group projects, interesting examples of applications.

Due to the breadth and richness of the field along with the cognitive load needed for mastering all the topics and theoretical concepts as well as the set of technical expertise, both as an IS engineer and as designer and programmer, a course with more than 30 h is required. In practice, due to an initial underestimation of the overall workload, the requirement for the final project was turned into an optional one (only 10 % of the students completed it) and the course assessment was performed based on three comprehensive exercises that demonstrated a working knowledge of the techniques and tools showcased during the course.

Less time could be devoted to the first part of the course, and with a course of 40–60 h, more time could be devoted to practical projects with a wider scope, to be developed both in lab sessions, under the guidance of a tutor, and at home, leaving the contents as described.

5 Concluding Remarks

This paper has presented a curriculum, oriented towards Information Technology, suited for a course on semantic web and ontologies. The syllabus is organized around 4 major modules allowing for easy customization. The curriculum, by leveraging on the database, software engineering and web programming backgrounds of the participants, lays the foundation for mastering semantic web theoretical essentials, as well as the tools and techniques necessary to develop applications that exploit the full potential of this emerging field.

The course was designed to engage the students on a fast-pacing approach to master the proposed content, yet leaving a substantial amount of freedom in selecting the technologies and contexts for the assignments. This was done with the intention to foster personal experimentation and critical analysis of the available choices, which is, in itself, an expected learning outcome of the overall curriculum of the MS Program in Computer Engineering. This aspect was taken very seriously by the students, as shown from the quality and variety of the first two assignments; however, it was clearly conflicting with the short time available, resulting in the decision of making the final project an optional one. Overall there was a positive appreciation of the course, particularly from the more motivated students, and several of them expanded upon the course content with a Master's thesis project, often linked to on-going funded research projects in collaboration with the industry, e.g., [30]. Improvements in the course can be certainly obtained either by devoting more time, or by working in synergy with other courses that could take care of the SPARQL and ontology design aspects (typically, an Artificial Intelligence course), at least for the introductory aspects. This would allow to focus efforts on the development of the semantic mash-up application. Yet, as a final note, it is worth reporting some informal feedback collected by students who entered the workforce after graduating and were assigned responsibilities involving semantic web technologies: they consistently commented that although the contents were covered in a very condensed timespan, such contents provided an effective groundwork to join quickly and productively the working teams.

References

1. Neuhaus, F., Florescu, E., Galton, A., Gruninger, M., Guariono, N., Obrst, L., Sanchez, A., Vizedom, A., Yim, P., Smith, B.: Creating the ontologist of the future. Appl. Ontologist **6**, 91–98 (2011)
2. Association for Computing Machinery. IEEE-Computer Society, 2012. Draft Computer Science Curricula (2013)
3. Diederich, J., Dzbor, M., Maynard, D.: REASE—the repository for learning units about the semantic web. New Rev. Hypermedia Multimedia **13**(2), 211–237 (2007)
4. Diederich, J., Nejdl, W., Tolksdorf, R.: EASE: the European association for SemanticWeb education. In: Proceedings of the Semantic Web Education and Training Workshop (SWET 2006), Co-located with the First Asian Semantic Web Conference (ASWC 2006), Beijing, China (2006)
5. Rector, A., Drummond, N., Horridge, M., Rogers, J., Knublauch, H., Stevens, R., Wang, H., Wroe, C.: OWL pizzas: practical experience of teaching OWL-DL: common errors & common patterns. In: Motta, E., Shadbolt, N.R., Stutt, A., Gibbins, N. (eds.) EKAW 2004. LNCS, vol. 3257, pp. 63–81. Springer, Heidelberg (2004)
6. Schober, D., Grewe, N., Rohl, J., Boeker, M.: ZooAnimals.owl: a didactically sound example-ontology for teaching description logics in OWL 2. In: OBML 2012 Workshop Proceedings (2012)

7. Beißwanger, E., et al.: BioTop: an upper domain ontology for the life sciences - a description of its current structure, contents, and interfaces to OBO ontologies. Appl. Ontol. **3**(4), 205–212 (2008)
8. Boeker, M., Schober, D., Raufie, D., Grewe, N., Rohl, J., Jansen, L., Schulz, S.: Teaching good biomedical ontology design. In: Cornet, R., Stevens, R. (eds.), Proceedings of the 3rd International Conference on Biomedical Ontology (ICBO 2012), KR-MED Series, Graz, Austria, 21–25 July 2012. http://ceur-ws.org/Vol-897/sessionJ-paper25.pdf
9. Gerber, D., Frommhold, M., Martin, M., Tramp, S., Auer, S.: Learning semantic web technologies with the web-based SPARQLTrainer. In: Proceedings of the 6th International Conference on Semantic Systems, p. 26. ACM (2010)
10. Della Valle, E.: RSWA realizing a semantic web application. In: Tutorial presented at the 7th International Semantic Web Conference (ISWC 2008), Karlsruhe, Germany (2008)
11. Giordano, D., Maiorana, F.: Getting it fast: an information systems oriented semantic web curriculum. In: Proceedings of the 6th International Conference on Computer Supported Education, Barcellona, Spain, pp. 508–513 (2014)
12. Auer, S., Dietzold, S., Lehmann, J., Hellmann, S., Aumueller, D.: Triplify - light-weight linked data publication from relational databases. In: Proceedings of the World Wide Web Conference (WWW), pp. 621–630 (2009)
13. Allemang, D., Hendler, J.: Semantic Web for the Working Ontologist. Effective Modeling in RDFS and OWL, 2nd edn. Morgan Kaufmann, Burlington (2011)
14. Liyang, Y.: A Developer's Guide to the Semantic Web. Springer, Heidelberg (2011)
15. Bizer, C., Schultz, A.: The Berlin SPARQL benchmark. Int. J. Semant. Web Inf. Syst. **5**(2), 1–24 (2009)
16. Della Valle, E., Celino, I., Cerizza, D.: Semantic Web: dai fondamenti alla realizzazione di un'applicazione. Pearson, New York, Addison Wesley, Boston (2009)
17. McBride, B.: Jena: a semantic web toolkit. IEEE Internet Comput. **6**(6), 55–58 (2002)
18. Carroll, J.J., Dickinson, I., Dollin, C., Reynolds, D., Seaborne, A., Wilkinson, K.: Jena: implementing the semantic web recommendations. In: Proceedings of the 13th International World Wide Web Conference on Alternate Track Papers & Posters, pp. 74–83. ACM (2004)
19. Huynh, D.F., Karger, D.R., Miller, R.C.: Exhibit: Lightweight Structured Data Publishing. In: Proceedings of the 16th International Conference on World Wide Web (WWW 2007) (2007)
20. Bizer, C., Heath, T., Berners-Lee. T.: Linked data-the story so far. Int. J. Semant. Web Inf. Syst. (IJSWIS) **5**(3), 1–22 (2009b)
21. Heath, T., Bizer, C.: Linked Data: Evolving the Web into a Global Data Space. Morgan & Claypool Synthesis Lectures, San Francisco (2011)
22. Schmidt, M., Hornung, T., Lausen, G., Pinkel, C.: SP2Bench: a SPARQL performance benchmark. In: IEEE 25th International Conference on ICDE 2009 (2009)
23. Horridge, M.: A practical guide to building OWL ontologies using Protegé 4 and CO-ODE tools Edition 1.3 (2009). http://owl.cs.manchester.ac.uk/tutorials/protegeowltutorial/. Accessed September 2013
24. Noy, N., Mc Guinness, D.L.: Ontology Development 101: A Guide to Creating Your First Ontology. Stanford University, Stanford (2004)
25. Poveda-Villalón M., Suárez-Figueroa, M.C., Gómez-Pérez, A.: A double classification of common pitfalls in ontologies. In: Workshop on Ontology Quality (OntoQual 2010), Co-located with EKAW 2010, Lisbon, Portugal, 15 October 2010
26. Hammar, K., Sandkuhl, K.: The state of ontology pattern research - a systematic review of ISWC, ESWC and ASWC 2005–2009. In: Blomqvist, E., Chaudhri, V., Corcho, O., Presutti, V., Sandkuhl, K. (eds.) Proceedings of the 2nd International Workshop on Ontology Patterns - WOP2010. CEUR-WS.org, Shanghai, China (2010)

27. Stegmaier, F., Gröbner, U., Döller, M., Kosch, H., Baese, G.: Evaluation of current RDF database solutions. In: Proceedings of the 10th International Workshop on Semantic Multimedia Database Technologies (SeMuDaTe), 4th International Conference on Semantics and Digital Media Technologies (SAMT), pp. 39–55, (2009)
28. Maiorana, F.: Teaching web programming: an approach rooted in database principles. In: Proceeding of the 6th International Conference on Computer Supported Education, Barcellona, Spain, pp. 508–513 (2014)
29. Giordano, D.: Shared values as anchors of a learning community: a case study in information systems design. J. Educ. Media **29**(3), 213–227 (2004)
30. Giordano, D., Torre, A., Alessi, S., Costanzo, A., Faro, A.: Integrating distributed data bases in a semantic framework - the K-Metropolis project. ICEIS **2013**, 322–328 (2013)

Extending the Database Curriculum: From Design Principles to Web and Mobile Programming

Francesco Maiorana(✉)

Department of Electrical, Electronic and Computer Engineering,
University of Catania, Viale A. Doria, 6, Catania, Italy
francesco.maiorana@dieei.unict.it

Abstract. The importance of the World Wide Web is evident from the ubiquitous presence of web-related technologies, from database to programming, from semantic to internet of things, in all aspects of everyday life. For these reasons, providing the new generation of students a strong background is crucial for sustainable development in all countries. This work presents a case study on a teaching experience in a web programming course with an approach suitable for both high school and university students. The first part of the paper describes in detail the curriculum which focuses on small incremental steps built around the management of user login and introduces advanced topics such as transaction, stored procedures and security issues, thus laying the foundation for the application of these concepts in larger projects. Finally, on the basis of this experience, the design and reframing of the curriculum in order to include mobile development is presented.

Keywords: Web programming · Database driven applications · Security · Transaction · Stored procedure · Mobile web programming

1 Introduction

The interest of the younger generation for Science Technology Engineering and Mathematics (STEM), and in science in general, is declining. This waning trend is evident also in Computer Science, as pointed out in many national reports. For example, Fig. 1 shows the trend of search terms on Computer Science performed with the Google Engine from 2004 to nowadays. The decreasing trend is evident and concrete action must be taken to offer high quality education starting from the younger generation. The importance of the education in Science as well as Computer Science education is emphasized by the data on job request forecasting. According to the National Science Foundation [1, 2], the occupational outlook for Information Security Analysts, Web Developers, and Computer Network Architects between 2010–2020 is expected to increase at a rate of 22 %, which is faster than average. The strong interest is confirmed by the increase in web technologies. In [3], for example, during his keynote speech at the Google I/O 2009 conference, the Vice President of Engineering at Google stated that, "The web has won. It has become the dominant programming model of our time".

S. Zvacek et al. (Eds.): CSEDU 2014, CCIS 510, pp. 258–271, 2015.
DOI: 10.1007/978-3-319-25768-6_17

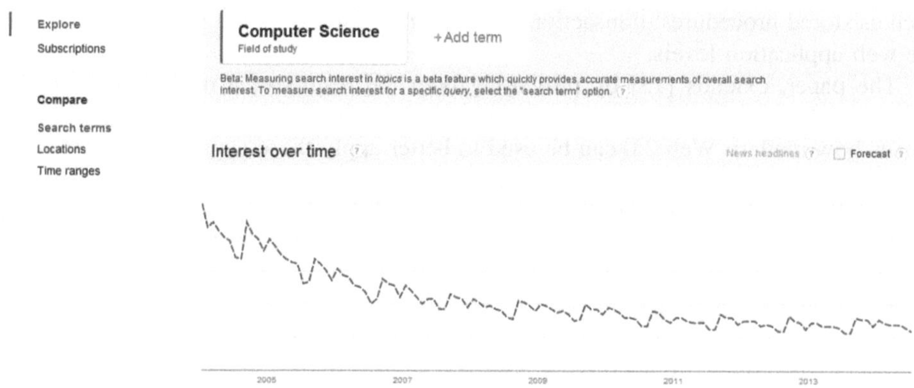

Fig. 1. Trend of Google searches related to Computer Science from 2004.

At the same time, Academia has given web development an increasing level of importance, reflected by the large number of related courses, from entry level to more advanced. Also in research there is a flourishing of conferences and special issue journals such as [4] with "two inter-related aims. The first of these is to communicate current approaches to teaching web development. The second is to reignite the conversation about what role, if any, that web development should have in current computing curricula". The same trend is also evident in K-12 education, where web development is recognized as an important topic in all recently revised curriculum. These include [5–7] as well as new curricula designed at the national level, such as [8] or initiatives developed around innovative ideas on how to teach introductory programming using web technologies such as Code Avengers (http://www.codeavengers.com/) or CodeHS (http://codehs.com/). Web development is also present in undergraduate and graduate curriculum such as [9–11].

From the above cited works, the interest in the subject is evident. However, an analysis of the curricula reveals that it is difficult to cope with all the content and technologies within a single course, especially in high school or in introductory university courses. As proposed by [12, 13], the topics should be covered in three courses: basic markup languages and Cascading Style Sheet in the first course; client side programming in the second course; and server side programming in the third course, with usability and interface design issue spanning all three courses. Other research such as [14] points to the need for subdividing the web programming curriculum into more courses, suggesting a two-course curriculum.

This work presents a curriculum suited for either a university course on web programming or for a third-level high school course, in accordance with the CSTA curriculum. The curriculum was field tested in a high school at the 13th/13th grade with students enrolled in a Computer Science specialization course. The curriculum, by leveraging on prerequisite database knowledge such as Entity Relationship model (E/R) and Data Manipulation language (SQL), focuses on server side web programming and offers the possibility, using simple examples and guided practical lab sessions, to present and practically apply, as well as verify, advanced database concepts such as stored procedures, transactions and security issues, both at the database and at the web application levels.

The paper, extends [15] by presenting both the results of a reflection about the pedagogical approach that leads to the proposal of pedagogical extensions and discusses how modern Web 2.0 can be used to better apply these approaches A proposal for a new curriculum which encompasses modern mobile technologies is also discussed. The work is organized as follows: Sect. 2 briefly reviews the literature on teaching web development; Sect. 3 presents the context of the teaching experience, the pedagogical model, the contents and how the course was taught; Sect. 4 discusses a first course evaluation, highlighting positive and negative aspects; Sect. 5 lays the foundation for designing a database course which includes mobile web development concepts and techniques, by addressing both pedagogical issues and curriculum content; and Sect. 6 presents the conclusions and highlights future work.

2 State of the Art in Teaching Web Programming

In the research carried out by [16], the authors review ten years of research articles on teaching web development in colleges and universities. The authors report that the diversity of protocols and programming languages required for web development presents a problem. Mastering all the knowledge required is deemed "unreasonable" while some practical level of understanding in all the technologies is considered necessary. This conclusion correlates with the necessity to divide, especially in high school, the curriculum into at least three courses. This is reinforced by [17] where a taxonomy of student errors in HTML and CSS is analyzed, reinforcing the pedagogical idea that even entry level languages, not considered as "computationally expensive" as many other languages, require developing computational skills such as checking syntax errors and debugging. The work makes use of an educational tool, openHTML, a web editor developed by the authors. Another e-learning system designed for improving web programming skills, is presented in [18], and offers an integrated environment for web programming.

Among recent case studies and teaching experiences on web programming at the university level, it is possible to recall the following notable research: [19] presenting challenges and tools used; [20] where the authors highlight the challenge of an "efficient delivery of a dynamic web development, database-driven platform"; [21] presenting a course using the PHP language and addressing security issues; [22, 23] and [24] presenting a course focused on server side programming and database interaction; [25] reporting on the positive effect of encouraging students to use code developed by others; [26] where the Google Cloud App was used along with servlets and Java Server Pages (JSP); [27] reporting on an interdisciplinary approach to teaching web programming, graphics and design in a course for non-majors; [28] presenting a CS 1.5 web programming course, and suggesting that educators present form and PHP scripting as early as possible; and [29] presenting a course developed around a Web project. The use of frameworks, recently reviewed in [30], is not recommended in introductory web programming courses.

From this brief literature review it is possible to highlight the following points:

- the difficulty and challenges in selecting the topics and providing sufficient depth [18]
- the rich set of technologies used, the lack of their integration and their development at a fast pace
- the importance of delivering a dynamic, database-driven web development
- the necessity to span the content of the topics among several courses and the interdisciplinary aspect of the topic.

This work reports a detailed practical experience suited for a web programming module and focuses on how these activities offer the possibility to practically explore and experiment with advanced database concepts such as stored procedure, transaction and security in the realm of web programming. The use of these advanced database concepts in web programming represents a unique case compared to other courses described in literature. The application of the blending of the proposed pedagogical approach, although representing a well-established practice, is presented in a particular context and within a particular discipline and will hopefully provide an initial insight in the described setting.

3 Context, Pedagogical Model and Content of the Educational Experience

This work presents a case study dealing with an educational experience in teaching web programming in an Italian high school. The class comprised 14 students, 12 male and 2 female, between the ages of 18 and 20. The students in Italy typically start school at the age of 6, with a few exceptions who start at 5, and after 13 years of school, finish at 19. Among the students, there were two who had to repeat several years of school. The class was the final course of a computer science curriculum lasting five years. In the last three years the students attended two types of courses each year: the first type of course centers on programming and software development and the second type of course centers on hardware and networking. In the third year programming course, the students have to learn basic programming, problem solving and algorithm design in an imperative language such as C, as well as basic web page design using HTML and CSS. In the fourth year the students learn object- oriented programming along with event driven programming. The students extend the web design topic by writing JavaScript code on the client side. In the fifth year the students in the programming course deal with Database design and SQL language in the first term and web programming in the second term. This content is accompanied by the second course where students learn networking architecture, both hardware and software, client server programming and security issues, such as cryptography. The reported teaching experience deals with the second term of the software course focused on web programming technologies, where the students are required to master database design with E/R diagram and SQL languages both for Data Manipulation and for querying. The course in the fifth year was divided into 28 weeks, 12 of which were dedicated to the web programming curriculum. The final two weeks allowed for individual and group project finalization. Each week consisted of a two-hour session for theory, ground discussions and assessment, and three one-hour lab sessions divided into two hours plus a one hour meeting, for a total of three meetings per week.

The course schedule for the first term is reported in Table 1. For a deeper discussion of the database curriculum the reader can refer to [31].

Table 1. Course schedule for the first term.

Unit	Topic	Hours
1	E/R, entity, primary key, attribute	2
	Projection and filtering using one table. Regular expressions	6
	User defined functions	6
	User interface for parametric queries	4
2	Associations 1-N, 1-1; association attribute, multiple associations, association with role	6
	Join and set operations	8
3	Associations N-N	6
	Sub-queries. Nested and correlated sub-queries	6
4	Ternary and n-ary associations	8
	Group by and nested queries	6
5	Associative entity, Normalization	2
	Having clause	4
6	Recursive associations	6
	Total	70

The bibliography for students comprised an Italian book together with selected parts from two leading database books [32, 33], as well as teacher notes. The adopted pedagogical model, in accordance with modern constructivist theory [34], was student-centered, where the students in each lab session are required to design and implement a solution to small problems, presented as specific questions requesting to perform a particular task. The questions guide the students to a final lab session goal of producing an application solving a specific problem or applying a new technology. An example of such questions for the 7th session, as listed in Table 3, is given in Table 2. This approach has the advantage of guiding students in the complex task of mastering different technologies, programming languages, as well as in learning and understanding the deep and fundamental concepts of database and web programming.

According to the revised Bloom taxonomy [35], the questions guide the students in climbing all the levels of the taxonomy: students using self-directed work along with the lab assignment questions are guided in the cognitive process of remembering, understanding and applying. More gifted students are able to analyze and evaluate, while a guided inquiry approach is used during the lab session to allow the other students to analyze and evaluate their solutions. The creative aspect is saved for the end of the lab, in the form of deeper questions, self-directed exploration and experimentation and, most importantly, in the final project, where it is suggested that the students apply all the course knowledge in building a complete, self-chosen web application. The final project can also be done in self-selected groups of students.

Table 2. An example of a lab session assignment.

N	Questions
1	Create, using the SQL language a database called store
2	Create, using the SQL language, the following logical model: Person (id, Lastname, Firstname, age, sex, BornDate, salary, StartTime, CivilStatus) Login (id, idP, username, password) where CivilStatus can only have a value chosen from (single, nubile, conjugated, separated)
3	Insert data in the Person and login table. Verify that the reference integrity constraint works.
4	Create a stored procedure to insert a person. Create a function to insert a person returning the ID of the last inserted person. Verify that the stored procedure and stored function work by calling them
5	Create a stored procedure to insert in the login table and verify it. Verify that the reference integrity constraint works
6	Create an HTML page containing a form to insert the data of a person including username and password
7	Create a PHP page to insert in the database the data relative to the person including the login information. Verify that the transaction mechanism works by forcing the insertion in the login table of a row with a non-existent value for the foreign key
8	Write a stored procedure that, by using the transaction, inserts a row in the person and login table, thus inserting all the information pertinent to the person. Simplify the PHP code in order to perform a single call to this stored procedure. Compare the solutions developed in steps 7 and 8

The lab sessions were designed in an incremental way around the management of the login process and user registration. It was decided, for didactic and security reasons, to divide the user data and the login data (username and password) into two tables allowing the students to present and practically apply important concepts such as stored procedure, transaction, security issues and security advantages in using stored procedure.

A modern object-oriented API such as the Portable Database Object (PDO) was used for database access. The login process allowed students to deal with the main aspects of web programming: HTML, forms, PHP, SQL, session and cookies to keep track of the data across the web pages; data validation took place both on the client side using JavaScript and regular expressions, and on the server side using PHP function and database stored procedures. The choice of the model allowed for the application and verification, with few lines of code, of sophisticated mechanisms such as transactions and stored procedure invoker and creator security models, as well as SQL commands for security management. Possible lab extensions to the basic login page could provide forgotten password functionalities, date and time of last login, count of unsuccessful logins on the basis of the username and a personalized welcome message, just to name a few.

Throughout the entire term an inverted classroom approach [36] was used where the students were asked to pre-read the material, thereby leaving time for practical work during the lab sessions and discussion during the theory sessions. These discussions

Table 3. Course schedule and lab assignments.

N	Topic	Lab assignment	#h
1	Three tier architecture	Install and configure a WAMP framework	3
2	HTML review	Login form creation	3
3	Database connection and data insertion through stored procedure	Stored procedures for insertion in one table and their use with PDO. Parameters. Insert into the person table	6
4	Stored procedure for updating and deleting data	Use of HTML forms and stored procedure to update and delete data. Manage the person and login table. Get and POST method	6
5	Stored procedures for retrieving data with and without parameters	Retrieving data using stored procedures and PDO and presenting them in HTML table. CSS review. List of registered users	6
6	Transaction: begin, commit and rollback	PHP code for managing transaction. SQL code for managing transaction. Insertion in the Person and login table	8
7	Use of transaction to insert, update and modify data across multiple tables	Use of transaction to insert, modify data in multiple tables. Management of the person and login table	4
8	Cookies and sessions	Keep track of username and ID across multiple web pages	6
9	SQL command for security	Granting and revoking privileges to users. Stored procedure for granting and revoking privileges	4
10	Security model of stored procedures: definer and invoker model. Cryptography	Use and comparison of different security models to automatically manage user creation and management. Cryptography functions in PHP	6
11	Client side form validation using JavaScript and regular expressions	Validate the Person and login data at the client side	4
12	Server side data validation	Using PHP and stored procedure to validate the person and login data at the server side	4
		Total	60

included solutions to exercises and case studies with critical comparisons of different approaches to solving the problems. The material was based on the textbook as well as the teacher's notes. Modern web 2.0 technologies (www.blogger.com/) (sites.google.com/) were used to deliver content, encouraging students to use wiki technologies to develop a personal e-portfolio where solutions to case studies and projects were posted to allow peers and instructors to leave formative feedback [37, 38, 39]. The free Easy PHP (http://www.easyphp.org/) Windows Apache MYSQL PHP (WAMP) was used on a Windows platform. Table 3 reports the course schedule with the major lab assignment topics.

The lab sessions were very fruitful and allowed for student self-discovery. For example, during a lab session a student working on a machine with an early version of PHP verified that the foreign key constraint does not work with the MYSQL MyISAM engine. It was suggested that the students use the manual to find a way to change the engine and verify that the foreign key constraint is implemented in other engines such as the InnoDB. The side effect was to push students to improve technical manual reading capabilities, particularly for SQL syntax such as DML instructions [40].

This approach was extended to the PHP manual [41], thus improving a technical skill required in working environments. Overall, the approach was useful in guiding the students in the complex process of designing web applications, allowing for an incremental project that pushed the students to develop limited but working projects in each lab session, refining the solution throughout the semester. This approach avoided teaching each topic individually but rather fostered step-by-step teaching, through incremental integration.

Initially, the students were reluctant to follow the approach due to the added level of abstraction introduced by the stored procedures and hence the higher cognitive effort required to master them. While proceeding with this approach, their opinions changed positively and the students appreciated the benefit of the method in terms of performance and security. Likewise, they appreciated the reduced burden in writing PHP code and the possibility to resolve the basic database management task with the same approach and by using a similar design procedure.

The teachers' evaluation of the experience, by comparison with previous classes with the same coursework and the same teachers, where more emphasis was given to physical database design, indexing and query performance [42] thus leaving less time for more extensive web programming, was positive, mainly due to the possibility of exposing the students to a richer set of technology with a tighter link to database technologies and concepts. Overall, 6 students were able to complete all the guided lab exercises independently, with little guidance in the first lab session, 2 students completed the lab session but required more support from the teachers, 6 students struggled due to the difficulty and deficiency both in concepts such as procedure and functions that were covered in the previous years, and to a deficiency in the mastering of some topics related to the first part of the course and finally 1 student was not able to complete the course and pass the year due to the numerous insufficient results in other disciplines. The final student grades in the discipline were: 4 students received an A, 3 students a B, 5 students a C, 1 student a D and 2 students an F.

4 Course Evaluation and Discussion

The course was evaluated by using student and teacher feedback, obtained by informal discussion and formal colloquia inside the class meetings and by assessing and evaluating student work in each lab session. The feedback from students as well as teachers was positive.

Students were initially overwhelmed by the complication introduced by stored procedure and the necessity to manage and discriminate different working environments such as the MYSQL database, the PHP scripting languages as well as HTML.

When the initial difficulties were overcome, thanks to a series of lab sessions focusing on similar concepts and technologies (e.g., stored procedure for inserting, deleting, updating and retrieving data from a single table), the students particularly appreciated using stored procedure and advanced database concepts which allowed them to use less code, perform canonical tasks such as inserting, updating, deleting and retrieving data in a canonical and recurring way, changing only the SQL command to be used in the stored procedure as well as the number and type of parameters.

From our colleagues' point of view, the approach allowed us to present and master advanced database concepts. The approach allowed for the sharpening and augmentation of database knowledge required by all the students in the final nation-wide state examination. The step-by-step approach avoided students getting lost in the multiple environment scenario typical of Web programming, despite the coverage of advanced topics.

The approach allowed students to experiment and easily verify important topics, such as transactions, by verifying their effects. Examples of this verification approach include: inserting a violating reference key data as the second step in a transaction, thereby allowing students to verify the missing effect in the first step; looking for the data stored on the client side (the cookie) and on the server side (the session file), thus allowing students to distinguish between the two concepts and their effects; verifying the different foreign key mechanisms with different MYSQL engines, and consequently mastering this important topic.

The assessment of the lab sessions revealed, through analysis of the results and of the grades assigned, three levels of achievement: the more gifted students were the first to proceed alone and expand the proposed lab session assignments; a second group of students were able to follow the steps and work through a solution to each step with minimal guidance; finally, a third group of students required particular attention and support to work through the exercises, with some of them falling behind and not meeting the deadlines. This division was reflected in the final grade of the module, as noted before. Despite the increased complexity of the course topic, the results correlate with and are slightly better than past experiences.

Overall, compared to a previous course taught by the same teachers, a deeper mastering of the web programming material was observed. Whereas only two students from the previous course were able to apply and discuss stored procedures and transactions in their final project [42], up to eight were able to do so in this course. This was due to the different teaching approach used, one that did not use the step-by-step assignment method in the lab session and which also dedicated fewer hours to the web programming module in order to explain another important topic, i.e., indexing, which is now an elective course in the new CS curriculum [8].

5 Shifting Towards the Inclusion of Mobile Web Development Concepts

Reflecting on this experience as well as on discussions and brainstorming with professors from a related undergraduate University course in Database Design along with a Masters Course in Human-Computer Interaction, the following considerations have been drawn:

- The curriculum can be improved by integrating the database design principles as well as the querying and the web programming parts as early as possible, in order to get a complete picture. In this way the web programming part can be introduced in the first term.
- Starting with a simple project, the course activity should expand the first solution by adding and applying new concepts.
- Modern mobile technologies such as HTML5 and jQueryMobile should be introduced in the first phase of the course.
- Use of an on-line class site alongside the whole term.

In particular the classroom site can be beneficial in order to:

- Improve communication and collaboration skills
- Encourage students to build a personal portfolio
- Offer a means to extend the class meeting beyond the assigned class schedule and the assigned physical space
- Allows student to ask questions and provide answers, fostering instructor-supervised peer review with a supervision from the instructors. Providing and receiving feedback from peers should improve camaraderie
- Provide the instructors a means to give feedback to the entire class: comments regarding one homework or project must be visible to all members of the class in order to improve and learn from others' experiences. At the same time, students must give feedback and critically revise the work of their peers
- Enhance mutual respect among students and between students and professors. This respect must encompass all aspects, from social interaction to respects of other works in every form, and to avoid any form of plagiarism, for example.

On the pedagogical point of view the classroom site can

- Offer examples of good coding practice and foster student attitude toward critically reading code by using a pedagogical code review approach [43]
- Use it as a medium to achieve a flipped classroom pedagogical approach [44] by publishing resource materials before the lessons.
- Use it as a medium to achieve a collaborative learning pedagogical approach [45]

The pedagogical code review approach is based on small group collaborative activities supervised by an instructor where the students have to read, check and critique the code written by their peers based on a list of best coding practices and discuss related issues. By requesting the students to publish their work on their personal pages on the classroom sites, the instructor has the possibility to ask the students to review the code of a selected group of peers. Likewise, the instructor can lead the discussion in the virtual environment and intervene when necessary.

The flipped classroom approach offers the lecture material via different sensory channels (e.g. text, images, video) before lessons, asking student to pre-read the material, solve homework problems and engage in active group-based class work. The website offers an excellent medium in which to distribute the material before lessons, presents homework problems, collects students' answers to the proposed problems as well as the results of the class activities. The set of on-line tools can take advantage of modern web-based clicker systems [46] that allow to present questions encompassing an extensible number of problem types. The questions can be administered outside the classroom and also during the class activities, thus supporting peer instruction pedagogical practices [47]. The instructor should take care in choosing the questions for the students. Relevant efforts include [48] and recently [49] where the authors present a methodology to find out the set of competencies that every computer scientist should have and how to build a competency model in accordance with these competencies. The competency model is a required step in building quality assessment to measure such competencies and therefore the assessment tool is beneficial in evaluating educational intervention.

The collaborative learning approach [45] can take advantage of cloud-based collaboration tools, as reported in [50].

The content of the curriculum should also be modified in the following ways:

- Modify the schedule of the arguments in such a way as to present concurrently the design of databases with the Entity Relationship (E/R) model, the Structured Query Language (SQL) and the web programming section.
- The web programming section should encompass modern mobile programming techniques favoring applications such as the one proposed in [51]. In line with the conclusion proposed by [52], the introduction of mobile learning and mobile programming both in high school and University courses can be beneficial and reinforce student engagement. For a recent analysis of critical success factors for successful mobile web 2.0 pedagogy the reader can reference [53].

6 Conclusions

A web programming curriculum was proposed, based on the results of a teaching experience in the final year at an Italian high school. The pedagogical approach was based on lab sessions requiring students to design and implement a solution with a small sequence of steps leading to a working artifact. The lab sessions subsequently refined each other by presenting and applying new concepts or techniques and incrementally improving a project spanning all the lab sessions which centered on the management of the login information on a website. In solving the login problem, the students were able to cover all the major topics of web programming, linking them to advanced database concepts such as transaction, stored procedure and security models, topics not usually covered in a high school or undergraduate setting. At the same time the concepts, mastered by the majority of the students, allowed for an easy framing of a solution pattern for the management of data in Web applications. A preliminary course assessment has also been presented.

On the basis of the presented experience, the paper proposes a blending of pedagogical approaches that, by taking advantage of modern Web 2.0 and cloud collaboration technologies, can be used as a guideline for proposing a new web-based curriculum which encompasses modern mobile web programming techniques. The design of the curriculum content is also discussed.

The presented curriculum, according to [13] is suited for a third-level course dealing with server side programming. The course represents the concluding phase, following a tag-based language and Cascading Style Sheet in the first course and client side programming in the second course. The proposed approach presents the advantages of a strong relationship with database concepts, allowing at the same time to present initial issues related to web interfaces and usability.

The proposed curriculum and pedagogical approach can be used in both high school and university courses, allowing the students to present and practically apply all the concepts suited for the third-level curriculum in the proposed three-level course architecture. Regarding further research, the following is planned: a deeper qualitative and quantitative course assessment compared to a previous class with the same coursework.

References

1. National Science Foundation (US) National Science Board: Science and Engineering Indicators (2012)
2. Bureau of labor statistics occupational outlook handbook. http://www.bls.gov/ooh/computer-and-information-technology/information-security-analysts-web-developers-and-computer-network-architects.htm. Accessed September 2013
3. Gundotra, V.: Google I/O 2009 Keynote Day 1 (2009). http://www.youtube.com/watch?v=S5aGZIvk&feature=channel
4. Connolly, R.W., Miller, C.S.: Teaching web development. Spec. Issue ACM J. Trans. Comput. Educ. (2013). http://toce.acm.org/attachments/TOCE-SE-TW.pdf. Accessed August 2013
5. CSTA Standards Task Force: K–12 Computer Science Standards Revised 2011. The College Board, Computer Science: Principles Big Ideas and Key Concepts Learning Objectives and Evidence Statements (2011)
6. The computing at school working group: computer science: a curriculum for schools (2012). http://www.computingatschool.org.uk/data/uploads/ComputingCurric.pdf. Accessed August 2013
7. New Zealand Ministry of Education: Digital technology guideline, dtg.tki.org.nz (2010)
8. Astrachan, O., Briggs, A.: The CS principles project. ACM Inroads **3**(2), 38–42 (2012)
9. Association for Computing Machinery (ACM), IEEE Computer Society: Curriculum Guidelines for Undergraduate Degree Programs in Computer Science (20 December 2013). http://www.acm.org/education/CS2013-final-report.pdf. Accessed July 2013
10. Association for Computing Machinery (ACM), IEEE Computer Society: Information Technology 2008. Curriculum Guidelines for Undergraduate Degree Programs in Information Technology (2008). http://www.acm.org/education/curricula/IT2008%20Curriculum.pdf. Accessed August 2013
11. Association for Computing Machinery (ACM), Association for Information Systems (AIS): IS 2010 Curriculum Guidelines for Undergraduate Degree Programs in Information Systems (2010). http://www.acm.org/education/curricula/IS%202010%20ACM%20final.pdf. Accessed August 2013
12. Connolly, R.: Awakening rip van winkle: modernizing the computer science web curriculum. In: Proceedings of the 16th Annual Joint Conference on Innovation and Technology in Computer Science Education (ITICSE, 2011), pp. 18–22, ACM (2011)
13. Maiorana, F.: Teaching web programming: critical considerations on pedagogical approach and curriculum content. In: Proceedings of International Conference on Sport Science and Computer Science (2013)

14. Wang, Y.D., Zahadat, N.: Teaching web development in the Web 2.0 Era. In: Proceedings of the 10th ACM SIGITE Conference on Information Technology Education, pp. 80–86 (2009)
15. Maiorana, F.: Teaching web programming: an approach rooted in database principles. In: Proceedings of the 6th International Conference on Computer Supported Education CSEDU, pp. 49–56 (2014)
16. Grove, R.F.: Trends in teaching web-based development - a survey of pedagogy in web development courses. In: Proceedings of 3rd International Conference on Web Information Systems and Technologies, Webist, Barcelona, Spain (2007)
17. Park, T.H., Saxena, A., Jagannath, S., Wiedenbeck, S., Forte, A.: Towards a taxonomy of errors in HTML and CSS. In: Proceedings of the Ninth Annual International ACM Conference on International Computing Education Research, pp. 75–82. ACM (2013)
18. Elgamal, A.F., Abas, H.A., Baladoh, E.S.: An interactive e-learning system for improving web programming skills. Educ. Inf. Technol. **18**(1), 29–46 (2013)
19. Liu, Y., Phelps, G.: Challenges and professional tools used when teaching web programming. J. Comput. Sci. Coll. **26**(5), 116–121 (2011)
20. Laverty, J.P.: Implementing a dynamic database-driven course using LAMP. Inf. Syst. Educ. J. (ISEDJ) **9**(7), 33–40 (2011)
21. Baatard, G.: Teaching PHP with security in mind. In: Proceeding of the 5th Australian Information Security Management Conference, pp. 21–27 (2007)
22. Noonan, R.E.: A course in web programming. J. Comput. Sci. Coll. **22**(3), 23–28 (2007)
23. Wang, X.: A practical way to teach web programming in computer science. J. Comput. Sci. Coll. **22**(1), 211–220 (2006)
24. Olan, M.: Web applications: a test bed for advanced topics. J. Comput. Sci. Coll. **24**(3), 72–80 (2009)
25. Tao, Y., Plouff, C.: Work in progress: an opportunistic approach for learning web application development. In: Frontiers in Education Conference (FIE), 2010 IEEE, pp. S2D-1, IEEE (2010)
26. Hollingsworth, J., Powell, D.J.: Teaching web programming using the Google Cloud. In: Proceedings of the 48th Annual Southeast Regional Conference, pp. 76–80, ACM (2010)
27. Gousie, M.B.: A robust web programming and graphics course for non-majors. ACM SIGCSE Bull. **38**(1), 72–76 (2006)
28. Stepp, M., Miller, J., Kirst, V.: A CS 1.5 introduction to web programming. ACM. SIGCSE Bull. **41**(1), 121–125 (2009)
29. Adams, D.R.: Integration early: a new approach to teaching web application development. J. Comput. Sci. Coll. **23**(1), 97–104 (2007)
30. Chao, J., Davey, B.: Navigating the framework jungle for teaching web application development. Issues Inf. Sci. Inf. Technol. **10**, 95–109 (2013)
31. Giordano, D., Maiorana, F.: Teaching database: a pedagogical and curriculum perspective. In: Proceedings of the International Conference on Information and Communication Technology for Education, (ICTE) (2013)
32. Atzeni, P., Ceri, S., Paraboschi, S., Torlone, R.: Database Systems: Concepts, Languages and Architectures. McGraw-Hill, New Delhi (1999)
33. Elmasri, R., Navathe, S.: Fundamentals of Database Systems, 6th edn. Addison Wesley, Reading (2011)
34. Duffy, T.M., Jonassen, D.H. (eds.): Constructivism and the Technology of Instruction: a Conversation. Psychology Press, Hove (1992)
35. Anderson, L.W., Krathwohl, D.R., Bloom, B.S.: A Taxonomy for Learning, Teaching, and Assessing. Longman, London (2005)

36. Gannod, G.C., Burge, J.E., Helmick, M.T: Using the inverted classroom to teach software engineering. In: Proceedings of the 30th International Conference on Software Engineering, pp. 777–786. ACM (May 2008)
37. Giordano, D.: Shared values as anchors of a learning community: a case study in information systems design. J. Educ. Media **29**(3), 213–227 (2004)
38. Giordano, D., Maiorana, F.: An interdisciplinary project in sustainable development based on modern visual programming environments and web 2.0 technologies. In: Proceedings of the 3rd Interdisciplinary Engineering Design Education Conference, IEDEC 2013, pp. 163–167 (2013)
39. Giordano, D., Maiorana, F.: Object oriented design through game development in XNA. In: Proceedings of the 3rd Interdisciplinary Engineering Design Education Conference, IEDEC 2013, pp. 51–55 (2013)
40. MySQL 5.6 Reference Manual. http://downloads.mysql.com/docs/refman-5.6-en.a4.pdf. Accessed August 2013
41. PHP manual. http://us3.php.net/get/php_manual_en.html.gz/from/a/mirror. Accessed August 2013
42. Maiorana, F., Giordano, D.: A constructivist approach to teaching index selection strategies and database design. In: Proceedings of the International Conference on Information and Communication Technology for Education, (ICTE) (2013)
43. Hundhausen, C.D., Agrawal, A., Agarwal, P.: Talking about code: integrating pedagogical code reviews into early computing courses. ACM Trans. Comput. Educ. (TOCE) **13**(3), 14 (2013)
44. Bishop, J.L., Verleger, M.A.: The flipped classroom: a survey of the research. In: ASEE National Conference Proceedings, Atlanta, GA (June 2013)
45. Goodyear, P., Jones, C., Thompson, K.: Computer-supported collaborative learning: instructional approaches, group processes and educational designs. Handbook of Research on Educational Communications and Technology, pp. 439–451. Springer, New York (2014)
46. Hauswirth, M.: Models and clickers for teaching computer science. In: 7th Educators' Symposium@ MODELS 2011—Software Modeling in Education—Pre-Proceedings (2011)
47. Simon, B., Cutts, Q.: Peer instruction: a teaching method to foster deep understanding. Commun. ACM **55**(2), 27–29 (2012)
48. Sanders, K., Ahmadzadeh, M., Clear, T., Edwards, S.H., Goldweber, M., Johnson, C., …, Spacco, J.: The Canterbury QuestionBank: building a repository of multiple-choice CS1 and CS2 questions. In: Proceedings of the ITiCSE Working Group Reports Conference on Innovation and Technology in Computer Science Education-Working Group Reports, pp. 33–52. ACM (2013)
49. Broker, K., Magenheim, J.: Are there competences every computer scientist should have?. In: Global Engineering Education Conference (EDUCON), 2014 IEEE, pp. 999–1002. IEEE (2014)
50. Sun, Y., Lambert, D., Uchida, M., Remy, N.: Collaboration in the cloud at Google. In: Proceedings of the 2014 ACM Conference on Web Science, pp. 239–240. ACM (June 2014)
51. Costanzo, A., Faro, A., Giordano, D.: WI-CITY: living, deciding and planning using mobiles in Intelligent Cities. In: 3rd International Conference on Pervasive and Embedded Computing and Communication Systems, PECCS, Barcelona, INSTICC (2013)
52. Sabitzer, B., Pasterk, S.: Mobile learning for COOL informatics - cooperative open learning in a vocational high school. In: Proceedings of the 6th International Conference on Computer Supported Education CSEDU, Barcellona, Spain, pp. 232–238 (2014)
53. Cochrane, T.D.: Critical success factors for transforming pedagogy with mobile Web 2.0. Br. J. Educ. Technol. **45**(1), 65–82 (2014)

Mathematical Machines and Integrated Stem: An Intersubjective Constructionist Approach

Pratim Sengupta(✉), Gokul Krishnan, Mason Wright, and Cherifa Ghassoul

Mind, Matter and Media Lab, Vanderbilt University – Peabody College, Nashville, TN, USA
{Pratim.Sengupta,Gokul.Krishnan,Mason.Wright, Cherifa.Ghassoul}@vanderbilt.edu

Abstract. In this chapter, we report two studies in which 3rd- and 4th-grade students used a distributed computing infrastructure (ViMAP-Tangible) in order to collaboratively invent "mathematical machines" for generating geometric shapes. ViMAP-Tangible combines the ViMAP visual programming language with a distributed computing infrastructure, in which students collaboratively control the behavior of a virtual agent using both mechanical devices and virtual algorithms. The curricular activities integrate engineering practices such as user-centered design; agent-based computer programming; mathematical reasoning about multiplication, rates, and geometry; and physical science concepts central to learning Newtonian mechanics. In Study 1, we investigate the key affordances of such a distributed computing environment for learning Integrated STEM, and identify the relationships between the various elements of students' physical constructions and computational models, and their STEM learning outcomes. Study 2 is a deeper investigation of the effect of iterative user testing on the refinement of children's designs and their STEM learning.

Keywords: Engineering education · Mathematics education · Agent-based programming · Constructionism · Collaboration · Computational thinking · Integrated STEM

1 Introduction

Integration of the individual domains of science, technology, engineering, and mathematics (STEM) is now recognized as an important goal of engineering and science education reform at the K–12 level [2, 24, 25]. As Nathan et al. [25] pointed out, the emphasis on "integration" implies that diverse fields of knowledge and practice should be merged in a manner that reveals big ideas that transcend specific disciplines [25, 32]. According to this perspective, STEM integration can be viewed as the production and maintenance of *cohesion* of invariant relations across the broad range of cross-domain concepts and representations in the engineering classroom [25]. Berland [2] argued that STEM integration could be brought about by a particular class of activities - *STEM-design challenges* – in

S. Zvacek et al. (Eds.): CSEDU 2014, CCIS 510, pp. 272–288, 2015.
DOI: 10.1007/978-3-319-25768-6_18

which students are posed an engineering design challenge that can only be completed when relevant math and science concepts are applied (e.g., [2, 10]).

This chapter investigates how STEM integration can be fostered using a distributed, agent-based computational programming and modeling platform. In agent-based programming, a user creates a computer program by using simple rules to command the movement and behavior of computational agents, e.g., the Logo Turtle [8, 23, 28, 30, 35, 38]. Consistent with the recent emphasis on computational thinking [41], we have found in previous studies that children can develop deep conceptual understandings in science and math through the construction of domain-specific, agent-based computational models [1, 9, 38]. In this chapter, we extend this argument and demonstrate that a particular form of agent-based programming and modeling, in which control of a single computational agent is socio-technically distributed between two learners in an intersubjective fashion, can be leveraged to integrate diverse STEM domains within a single activity (i.e., a STEM design challenge).

We present a technological innovation in the form of ViMAP-Tangible, and associated curricular activities, in which student dyads design and build mathematical machines for computationally generating geometric shapes using a distributed physical and virtual computing setup. These machines were designed for instructional use – i.e., the intended users of these machines were mathematics teachers (and students) in elementary grades. While tangible and visual programming offer two different interactional modes of programming for the learner, several scholars have argued for introducing a hybrid approach that integrates both modalities [15, 42]. Our pedagogy, grounded in an intersubjective constructionist framework (see Sect. 2), leverages this hybridity. Furthermore, while recent efforts have focused on designing and implementing Integrated STEM curricula at the college level [34], middle school [2] and high schools [25], we demonstrate that younger children (3rd- and 4th-graders) can be brought into the fold of Integrated STEM education that also includes a focus on developing computational thinking.

In this chapter, we report two research studies. Study 1 was an exploratory (pilot) study, in which we investigated the following questions:

RQ 1. How are students' computational and mechanical representations shaped by the following curricular foci:
- 1.1. Collaboration between learners, and
- 1.2. User-Centered Design?

RQ 2. What is the relationship between the structural characteristics of students' physical and computational inventions and their STEM learning?

Study 2 was designed in order to conduct a deeper investigation of several aspects of the user-centered design process, including the involvement of users within the design process. In this chapter, we present an investigation of the following question:

RQ 3. What role does iterative user testing play in the refinement of children's designs, and their STEM learning?

2 Intersubjective Constructionism, ViMAP-Tangible and Integrated STEM

2.1 Theoretical Framework: Intersubjective Constructionism

Our pedagogical framework brings together key ideas from the literature on constructionism, intersubjective and collaborative learning. Intersubjective learning [39] involves collaboration, but goes beyond the conceptualization of collaborative learning as information sharing. Roschelle and Teasley [31] defined collaboration as "a coordinated, synchronous activity that is the result of a continued attempt to construct and maintain a shared conception of a problem" ([31]; p. 70). According to Suthers [39], intersubjective meaning-making takes place when multiple participants contribute to a single composition that is the result of bringing together of interrelated interpretations. Intersubjective meaning-making is different than the notion of "common ground" [4], because it represents a participatory process within which beliefs are enacted (and in this sense are shared from the outset) without necessarily being mutually accepted. There are two key differences between these concepts [39]. First, interpretations can be jointly created through interaction in addition to being formed by individuals before they are offered to the group. Second, in intersubjective learning, cognitive activities underlying learning can be distributed across individuals and information artifacts through and with which they interact [16].

As Berland et al. [3] pointed out, a constructionist approach to learning argues that when learners build creative artifacts that require complex content to function, they develop rich opportunities to learn that complex content in personally meaningful ways [14, 28]. Constructionist learning is typically grounded in generative practices in which learners use generative computational technologies in a deep manner, and further, such forms of learning emphasize the creation of public artifacts, as well as working in social spaces such that learners collaborate to deepen their learning experiences [13, 18]. We explain how our pedagogical approach brings together constructionist, intersubjective and collaborative learning in Sect. 2.3.

There is some evidence that the particular genre of constructionist activity that learners conducted in our studies - designing an artifact for instructional use - can act as an effective pedagogical model for K–12 science education [7, 19]. Some studies have also focused on children designing agent-based instructional software for mathematics (e.g., [13]) and microworld games in science and mathematics (e.g., [19]). In all of these studies, students not only developed a deeper understanding of the target science or math concepts, but also developed substantial expertise in programming. Furthermore, Carver et al. [7] and Kafai et al. [19] also showed that children designers do not regard the involvement of users as a useful component of their design process. These studies therefore suggest that the involvement of users during the design process requires explicit instructional scaffolding.

2.2 ViMAP-Tangible: A Distributed Computational Architecture

ViMAP [36] is a visual programming language with its own integrated development environment (IDE), which allows K–12 students to program agent-based models.

Similar to popular visual programming languages such as Alice [20] and Scratch [23], ViMAP provides a drag-and-drop interface for constructing programs that is easy to use and understand for children. Commands in ViMAP include both domain-general abstractions (e.g., loops, conditionals), as well as domain-specific commands (e.g., for controlling speed, distance and acceleration of the turtles) [9, 36].

ViMAP-Tangible (Fig. 2) enables ViMAP to interact with sensors and actuators, so a user's programs can get data from, and act on, the physical world. ViMAP-tangible uses an Arduino microcontroller to control sensors and actuators. ViMAP employs the popular agent-based modeling program NetLogo [40] as its agent-based simulation engine. ViMAP's embedded NetLogo program runs the NetLogo model and also loads the NetLogo Arduino extension. The NetLogo Arduino extension communicates with an Arduino board through a USB cable. The Arduino board runs an Arduino sketch that interfaces with the NetLogo model. The NetLogo Arduino extension sends integer signals to the Arduino sketch, and it receives strings in reply that encode key–value pairs representing sensor data. The Arduino sketch communicates over wires with sensors such as a distance sensor, and with actuators such as motors or LED's.

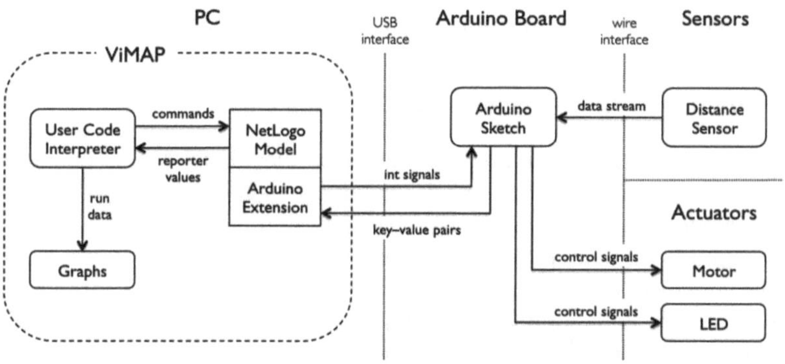

Fig. 1. Architecture of ViMAP-Tangible.

The ViMAP-Tangible environment we used for the studies reported in this chapter consists of the following elements: (a) the ViMAP visual programing language running on a laptop; (b) an Arduino^{TM} microcontroller that is connected to ViMAP using a USB cable; and (c) two Parallax distance sensors, that are both connected to ViMAP via the Arduino^{TM} microcontroller. In addition, learners are also provided with a set of LEGO^{TM} bricks materials for constructing mechanical interfaces (machines) to control sensor readings.

2.3 Building Mathematical Machines with ViMAP-Tangible

During the capstone learning activity in both the studies, learners worked in dyads and constructed a mathematical machine for generating geometric shapes. Each machine consists of two components: virtual and physical. The virtual component is a ViMAP program, that learners construct using visual programming primitives selected from the

ViMAP programming library. The physical component consists of two physical control interfaces, each designed to control the reading on one of the distance sensors. Each sensor controls a distinct Turtle-variable (e.g., color, speed, rotation). Each member of the dyad independently designs one of these physical control structures, using Lego bricks, but the dyad is responsible for jointly designing the ViMAP program.

Intersubjectivity and collaboration are interwoven throughout the learners' design process. Each learner is in charge of designing the physical structure for controlling the readings on one of the sensors, and therefore, keeping in spirit with Suthers' [39] definition of intersubjective learning, is provided with the opportunity to enact their own ideas. However, they have to share resources, such as a set of construction materials (LEGO bricks), and limited physical space (due to the finite length of the USB cables). While these constraints do not require learners to establish common ground, each learner realizes that their actions may impact the scope of work for the other. A clear need for collaboration – i.e., coordinated, non-redundant contributions by each learner towards a shared objective – arises later in the design process, when the dyad has to design the following: (a) a single ViMAP algorithm that links both their machines to the behavior of the virtual agent; and (b) a User Guide, which requires them to understand how to operate each mechanical component in order to generate a particular geometric shape.

2.4 Integration of STEM Practices and Learning Goals

The capstone activity (i.e., designing mathematical machines) can be understood as a *STEM design challenge* [2], because it requires reasoning across different STEM domains, in order to accomplish an engineering design challenge. The learning goals encompass representational and epistemic practices in different domains, as shown in Fig. 1. In the domain of engineering (i.e., "E" in STEM), our goal is to introduce students to two key practices: collaborative (including intersubjective) engineering design, and User-Centered Design. In the domain of technology (T), learners develop computational thinking by developing agent-based programs to control the behavior of the virtual agent (the Turtle), and to link specific agent-variables to sensor readings. The learning goals in science (S) and math (M) are comparatively more *emergent* in nature. We explain these learning goals next, and the interested reader can also find in-depth literature reviews for each of the STEM domains in an earlier paper [37].

Collaboration and teamwork, broadly conceived, hold a significant place in engineering practice [5]. As Johri [43] pointed out, engineers increasingly work collaboratively and in teams around the globe, and technology is a primary driver of such arrangements. Furthermore, in addition to introducing children to a key engineering practice, collaborative design can reflexively support science and math learning through the creation of productive opportunities for shared inquiry and discourse [6, 8, 21, 29].

User-Centered Design [26, 27] emphasizes the importance of understanding the needs of the users in order to design usable systems. This involves (a) providing a good conceptual model to the user, which will allow them to predict the effects of their actions on the designed system; and (b) making controls and hidden rules of the system "visible" to the user. Gulliksen et al. [12] further argued that in addition to involving the user throughout the design process, the following principles are necessary to be enacted in practice in order to support UCD: (1) rapid prototyping during the early phases of the design process; (2) a cyclic iterative process of designing solutions interwoven with evaluation; (3) multi-disciplinary design teams that bring together distributed expertise for the various design components; and (4) an integrated design process, in which the system, the work practices, on-line help, training, and organization should be developed in parallel.

The emergent nature of learning goals in science and math can be understood as follows. In open-ended learning environments, each child's production may employ different structural elements of the technological infrastructure, and this leads to variability among their productions (e.g., [14]). For example, controlling the motion of the Turtle inevitably introduces learners to some reasoning about motion. However, the extent to which operating learners' machines requires an understanding of kinematics, depends in turn on the physical structure of the machines, and on how the agent-variables are linked to sensor readings in the ViMAP algorithm. Similarly, in the domain of math, nearly all learners in our studies were introduced to multiplicative reasoning in their use of programming loops. At the same time, we also noticed that a few children used commands that control the movement of the Turtle by using Cartesian coordinates. This led students to think deeply about Cartesian geometry, in addition to (or in some cases, in lieu of) multiplicative reasoning.

3 Methods

3.1 Study 1

Setting and Data. The study took place in a metropolitan city in the form of an enrichment program for elementary school children, conducted in a classroom on the campus of a large private university in the Mid-Southern USA. Classes met once a week (9:00 a.m. to 11:30 a.m.) on six consecutive Saturday mornings. Students were recruited through an online solicitation sent to the local elementary schools. None of the students in this course had any prior programming experience, and we particularly encouraged female students to apply. Students were admitted on a first-come, first-served basis. There were 16 participants, out of which eight students were in 3rd grade, and eight were in 4th grade. Five of the students were female, and three of them were in 3rd grade. The ethnic composition of the students whose work we analyzed for this paper is as follows: White (7), Asian American (4), and African American (3). Two students were absent for multiple days, and their work has not been analyzed.

The first author acted as the lead instructor. The second author was also present in the classroom. Data was in the form of videotaped in-depth interviews with the participants, the software and hardware artifacts (i.e., ViMAP programs and physical machines) designed by the students, and field notes. The interviews were conducted while the learners were engaged in the modeling and programming activities. In some cases, the interviews ensued when the learner called upon the researcher in order to help him or her with a difficulty. In other cases, researchers conducted interviews in order to ask learners to explain their programs or models.

Curricular Activities. During the first phase of our curriculum, students were introduced to agent-based programming using ViMAP. Students learned to generate "open" and "closed" geometric shapes (e.g. squares, circles, spirals) using ViMAP. In the second phase, students used these shapes to represent models of phenomena involving continuous change over time. This phase was designed to establish shape drawing as a consequential [11] activity that is not only valuable for its visual aesthetics, but that can also be used as a computational model of change over time. In both these phases, each student worked individually. Our previous work has shown that these two phases can effectively introduce students to the basics of agent-based programming, and students also learn to use their programs (i.e., geometric shapes) as models of motion in Phase 2 [35]. The third phase used a STEM design challenge [2], discussed earlier in Sect. 2.3. Emphasis on User-Centered Design was maintained throughout this phase as follows: First, students themselves acted as the users; thereafter, students from other groups acted as users (this is the main user testing phase for the purposes of our analysis); and during the final day of the class, students' parents were invited to visit the class to test their children's designs. Our pedagogical approach emphasized several of Gulliksen et al.'s [12] core principles of UCD: an emphasis on rapid prototyping in the early phases of design; an iterative process of designing solutions interwoven with evaluation; and within-group distributed expertise for different design components.

3.2 Study 2

Setting and Data. The study was conducted in a 4th-grade classroom of a 100 African-American public charter school in the Mid-Southern USA, as part of their regular math curriculum. Fourteen students (8 male and 6 female) participated in the study. Classes met twice a week, for a total of 35 days, for a period of six months (Oct 2013 – May 2014). The class was taught by the homeroom teacher, in collaboration with the first author of the study. In addition, two researchers (the second and fourth author) of the study were present during most of the classes, in order to assist with data collection and to provide logistical support.

Similar to Study 1, data was in the form of videotaped in-depth interviews with the participants, video recordings of user testing, the software and hardware artifacts (i.e., ViMAP programs and physical machines), and the user guides designed by the students. In addition, researchers' field notes were also consulted as necessary.

Curricular Activities. Similar to Study 1, the first phase of the curriculum focused on introducing students to agent-based programming using ViMAP. Students learned to generate "open" and "closed" geometric shapes (e.g. squares, circles, spirals) using ViMAP. This phase lasted for 8 class periods. During this phase, the teacher also emphasized consequentiality of these programming activities by leading regular class discussions on how elements of their programs corresponded to relevant topics in their mathematics curriculum (e.g., multiplicative reasoning and programming loops). For the next 18 class periods, students worked in dyads on the STEM design challenge, i.e., constructing mathematical machines and user guides. We specified that other 4th-grade teachers in Nashville would use these machines, so that students had a specific user in mind. We also invited three graduate students in education with prior math teaching experience in elementary grades, but unaffiliated with our study, to serve as "users". The user testing took place twice: first in mid March (User Testing 1), and in late April (User Testing 2). During both the User Testing events, each user interacted with a dyad's machine for about 20 min, and provided them written and verbal feedback. After User Testing 1, students improved their machines and user guides in order to address the issues highlighted in the feedback. User Testing 2 was also the capstone activity.

It is important to note that, as in Kafai et al. [19] and Carver et al. [7], children were indeed initially unwilling to involve users in their work. For example, in UT1, most groups did not initially let users operate the machines and demonstrated it to the users, and furthermore, did not consider their feedback useful. This is where *teaching* played a significant role. The class teacher designed several instructional strategies in conjunction with the researchers. These included the following: (a) leading class discussions based on design analysis of children's toys, and highlighting the importance of user manuals for making hidden rules explicit to the users; (b) including the development of the user guides as a curricular activity in their literacy (writing) class; and (c) leading class discussions on common suggestions provided by the users to all the groups during UT1 in their written feedback, and relating relevant suggestions to their math curriculum on multiplicative reasoning (e.g., learning and using multiplication tables).

4 Analysis

The first, second and fourth authors analyzed data from each study by identifying themes and sub-themes using the double coding method [22]. Over a period of 6 months, they iteratively developed codes and met several times to discuss their analysis. The analysis presented here represents a consensus among the authors. We answered the research questions (RQs) as follows. In Study 1, in order to investigate the role of UCD and collaboration (RQ1), we compared the intermediate and final products of the students' design activities before and after user testing (during Phase 3) to check for improvements. In order to investigate the affordances of the students' designs in terms of the scientific and mathematical concepts and discourse that the students engaged in their designs (RQ2), we analyze the structure of each group's physical machines, their ViMAP program (i.e., programming commands), and their instructions for users in terms of the type(s) of mathematical measures generated by each group. The children generated these measures in order to provide explicit instructions to users for operating and understanding their machines. These measures in turn were categorized either as (a) mathematical i.e., involving either multiplicative or proportionality-based reasoning, or reasoning involved in understanding geometric coordinate systems; or (b) physics-based, i.e., indicative of reasoning about the measurement of speed and distance.

In Study 2, in order to answer RQ3, we compared the work of each dyad at two stages: User Testing 1 (UT1), and User Testing 2 (UT2). The data included video recordings of both the phases of user testing, and children's designs (mechanical structures, ViMAP programs and written user guides that they developed for each round of user testing). At the broadest level, our iterative coding resulted in identifying a category of improvement in children's work: *communicativity.* In Norman's [26] words, communicativity can be understood as *making hidden rules explicit to the user*. Further analysis revealed that the nature of this improvement was twofold: (a) *mechanistic explanations* evident in their user guides, and their verbal explanations during the user testing process; and (b) *structural improvements* of their mechanical components. A detailed discussion can be found in Sect. 5.3.

5 Findings

5.1 Pedagogical Affordances of UCD and Collaboration (Study 1)

An illustrative case is the work of Chuck and Jerry (Fig. 2A–C). Jerry's machine consisted of a flat LEGO plate that could be lowered or raised above an ultrasonic distance sensor (Fig. 2A), using a pulley, to control the *turn angle* of the computational agent. Chuck's machine comprised a horizontal LEGO surface that could be lowered or raised above a distance sensor (Fig. 2B), using a manually operated crank lift, to control the *step-size* of the Turtle. During Phase 3, students' ViMAP programs became iteratively more refined with fewer bugs and redundancies. For example, in their initial version, Chuck and Jerry had developed each of their mechanical controls independently, and each of them linked multiple Turtle variables to each of the sensors. This resulted in redundancies in their machine, e.g., the Turtle's speed and turn were controlled separately by both their machines during a single iteration of the program. After a few attempts, Chuck and Jerry decided to divide their responsibilities: Chuck's machine would control the turn, while Jerry's machine would control the speed of the Turtle.

We also found that students' ViMAP programs became more generative as a result of user testing, as nearly every user demanded to be able to draw more than one shape. The final designs of six out of seven groups allowed users to draw *multiple* shapes, whereas their initial designs during Phase 3 were more constrained and could only generate a specific shape (typically, a circle). In a few cases, we also noticed that the reliability of the output of a dyad's ViMAP program also improved as a result of improvement of their physical structures. For example, both Chuck and Jerry realized that they had to improve the flatness of the surfaces that were generating the sensor-readings, because their users were unable to generate reliable outputs. This resulted in

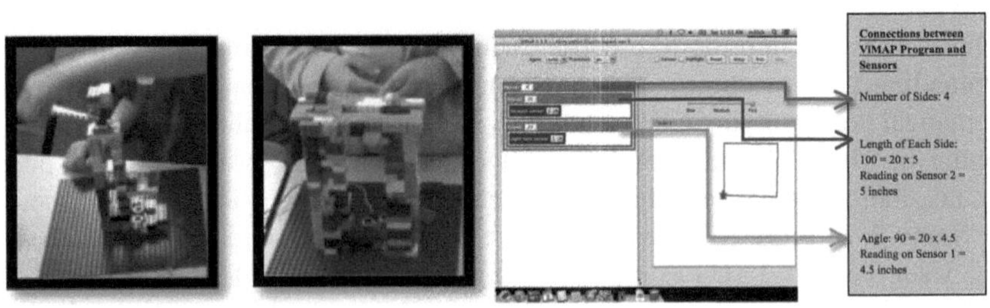

Fig. 2. A (Left). Jerry's pulley mechanism for controlling turn of the Turtle via Sensor 1; **B (Middle).** Chuck's machine for controlling the speed of the Turtle via Sensor 2. **C (Right).** Is a screenshot of their ViMAP program for generating a square, and our annotation makes explicit the multiplicative reasoning involved in generating *angles* and *sides* of the square

Chuck introducing a flat paper strip to cover the bottom of the LEGO plates, while Jerry created a wider plate to control sensor readings more reliably.

5.2 Relationship Between Children's Inventions and STEM Learning (Study 1)

Designs that Primarily Supported Learning Rate and Kinematics. Figure 3A and B show an example of student work in which two students, Seana and Curly, built two separate, manually operated, wheeled cars, with flat surfaces in front (stacked LEGO bricks). The operating mechanism involves pushing the car towards or away from the sensor, where distance of the flat surface (representing the "palm of a hand") from the sensor generates the reading of the ultrasonic sensor. The distance of one of the cars from the sensor controls the speed of the ViMAP Turtle, while distance of the other car from the second sensor controls the rotation of the Turtle. A total of two groups of students developed two cars as their drawing machines.

After user testing, Seana and Curly realized that they had to provide instructions to the user on how fast they would have to move each car in order to generate the desired shape(s). This is because, in their design, moving the two cars at different rates resulted in different shapes. Neither student had any experience in calculating rates or speed prior to this study, nor were they formally instructed during this class to calculate the rates. However, they used the computer clock and cell phones as timers, and figured out by trial and error how fast they had to move each car in terms of the time taken by their cars to travel specific distance(s) in order to generate the desired shape(s). This also resulted in making their designs more communicative by annotating the track at specific positions, along with some written and verbal instructions for users regarding how fast they needed to move the cars between these annotated positions. Although this was a rough measure of rate, we believe that this is a productive entry point into learning kinematics through the development of consequential phys ics talk, as well as mathematical discourse on rates – i.e., through engaging in "conversations for conceptual change" [8].

Designs that Primarily Supported Multiplicative and Proportionality-based Reasoning. An example of this type of design is Chuck and Jerry's work described in Sect. 6.1, and shown in Fig. 2. Jerry's machine controlled the angular turn of the Turtle, and the user could generate readings from 1–10 (inches) by using the pulley mechanism. The user could also alter the numerical parameter of the "Repeat" command in the ViMAP program, which in turn would effectively multiply the sensor reading by that parameter. Chuck used a similar strategy to let users control the step-size of the Turtle; he had created several visible marks on his towers at increments of a third of the maximum height, so that the user can generate shapes of three levels of magnification. Chuck and Jerry, who were both beginning to learn multiplication tables in their regular math class, thus got an opportunity to use and further develop their multiplicative and proportionality-based reasoning in order to make their designs work. We found that three groups of students invented this type of design.

Fig. 3. A (Left) and B (Right). Seana (dressed in black) and Curly (dressed in blue and white) take turns in moving their "cars" towards the ultrasonic sensors.

Designs that Primarily Supported Learning Multiplicative Reasoning and the Cartesian Coordinate System. Two groups of students developed ViMAP programs that employed Cartesian coordinates and programming loops. In each group, one of their Lego plates controlled the translational displacement of the Turtle, while the other controlled the vertical displacement of the Turtle. In each group, one machine used a pulley, and the other a hand crank, as raising and lowering mechanisms (similar to Chuck and Jerry). Each group used ViMAP commands such as "X-Plus-<Sensor-reading>", "X-Minus-<Sensor-reading>", "Y-Plus-<Sensor-reading>", and "Y-Minus-<Sensor-reading>". As they iteratively developed the various combinations of translational and vertical displacements that would generate the different shapes, they became familiarized with the NetLogo XY-coordinate space, and provided users with target coordinates for the vertices of some shapes (e.g., triangle and rectangle). This design also employed algorithmic loops, and therefore multiplicative reasoning. An illustrative case is Barry and Rodney's group, whose written instructions for the users (Fig. 4) explain how to generate a square with sides equal to 180 units. The user has to position both of the mechanical plates 6 inches from the corresponding sensor, and the ViMAP program multiplies each reading by 30 using the "Repeat" command. One of the users con trolled the translational movement (X-Plus-Sensor2 and X-Minus-Sensor2), while the other user controlled the vertical movement (Y-Plus-Sensor1 and Y-Minus-Sensor1).

5.3 Effects of Iterative User Testing (Study 2)

In Study 2, we found that iterative user testing resulted in the improvement in *communicativity* of children's designs. That is, in User Testing 2, the mechanical components and their user guides, as well as their verbal explanations, made explicit to the user the relationships between their actions and the computational output. We found that all the groups accomplished this by making explicit the mathematical explanations corresponding to different sets of actions. As shown in Table 1, this was evident in the following: (a) improvements in the quality of mechanistic explanations, and (b) structural improvements. Mechanistic reasoning involves more than simply mentioning that "X" causes "Y" to happen; it requires that students come to identify how "X" brings about "Y" [33]. Comparison of the UT1 and UT2 user guides revealed a general trend across all groups: the earlier version of the user guides specified user actions, but did not specify *how* the actions were related to the computational desired output. In contrast, the later iteration of the user guides explained relationships between user actions,

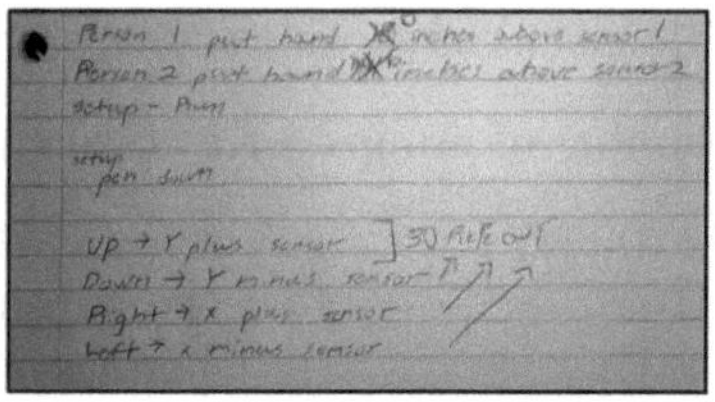

Fig. 4. An excerpt from Barry and Rodney's instructions for the users.

elements of the ViMAP program and the component Turtle behaviors that resulted in the desired shape. This was evident both in their user guides and verbal explanations.

An illustrative example is the case of Jacinda and Tom. Similar to Carly and Seana in Study 1, they also designed a two-car setup. In their user guide for UT1, they wrote down instructions that specified the distance from the sensors at which the user would have to position the two cars in order to generate specific readings (Fig. 5A). In contrast, in UT2, their user guide contained diagrams and written explanations in order to explain the multiplicative reasoning, which in turn explained how actions of the user were related to specific commands and parameters used in their ViMAP program (Fig. 5B). For example, in one of the drawings in their user guide (Fig. 5B), Jacinda and Tom explained that turning 90° involved repeating a turn of 10° (generated by the reading on Sensor 1) nine times. Adjacent to the drawing was a cutout of a color printout of the corresponding ViMAP program, in which the turn-angle was repeated nine times using the "Repeat<number>" command. In their verbal explanations during UT2, both the students were able to point to the relevant parts of their user guide and provide similar mechanistic explanations. That is, we found that their user guide and verbal explanations during UT2 used multiplicative reasoning to explain the following: (a) how user actions generated Turtle behaviors (such as movement and turning), and (b) how the overall shape was generated by repeating these actions computationally using programing loops.

Based on the feedback in UT1, Jacinda and Tom also made structural improvements so that users could operate their machine easily. This included flattening the surface of the track on which users would move the cars, strengthening the base of the cars to prevent it from toppling, and labeling the sensors and different parts of the track. Other changes included adding labels on their machines, which corresponded to, and supported the mathematical explanations in the User Guide. Figure 7 shows the final version of Jacinda and Tom's machine used during UT2, which makes explicit how the labels reflexively supported multiplicative reasoning in their user guides. The labels specified the number of programming loops that the user would need to put in their ViMAP program in order to generate a 90 degree turn, corresponding to three different positions of the car that controlled the turn-angle of the Turtle. Five groups used such labels on their machines in UT2.

Table 1. Improvement in Communicativity of Children's Designs, from UT1 to UT2.

	Number of groups	Key characteristics
Mechanistic explanations	8 (100 %)	User guide (and verbal responses) explains relationships between user actions, ViMAP programs and Turtle behaviors
Structural improvements	5 (63 %)	1. Easier to operate manually
		2. Structural rigidity
		3. Labels

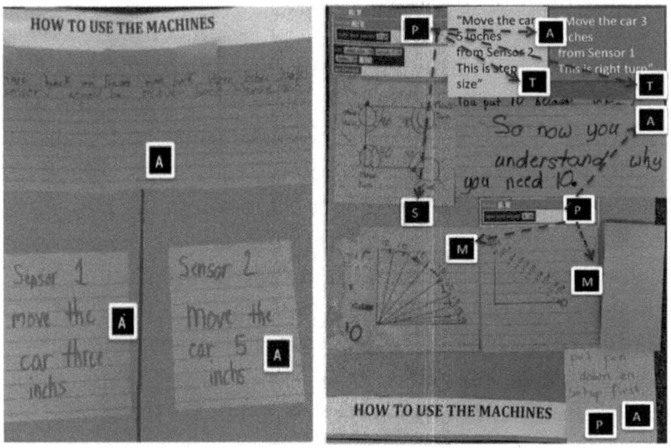

Fig. 5. Jacinda and Tom's user guides in User Testing 1 (Fig. 5A, left) and User Testing 2 (Fig. 5B, right). We annotated their user guides using the schematic shown in Fig. 6.

So, what does this mean for children's STEM learning? To summarize, attending to what the user needs to know resulted in improving greatly the quality of students' mathematical explanations. Their explanations made explicit the mathematical relationships between algorithmic elements (e.g., number of loops in their ViMAP program) and the actions of the Turtle in every step (e.g., right turn), which in turn was directly effected by the users' actions (e.g., sensor reading generated by the user). We consider this as evidence of the reflexivity between user-centered engineering design and mathematical learning.

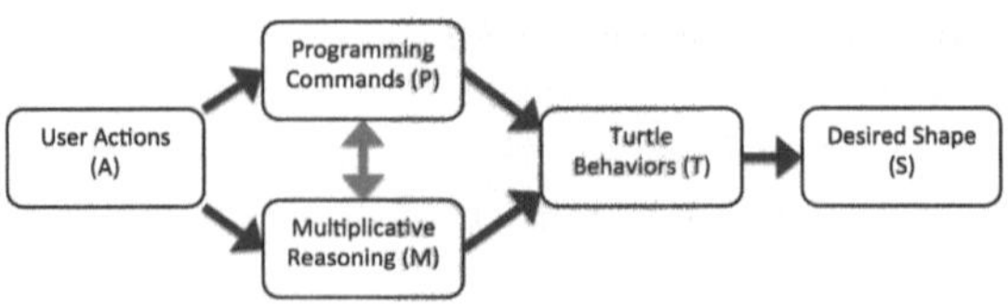

Fig. 6. A schematic for mechanistic explanations used by all groups in User Testing 2.

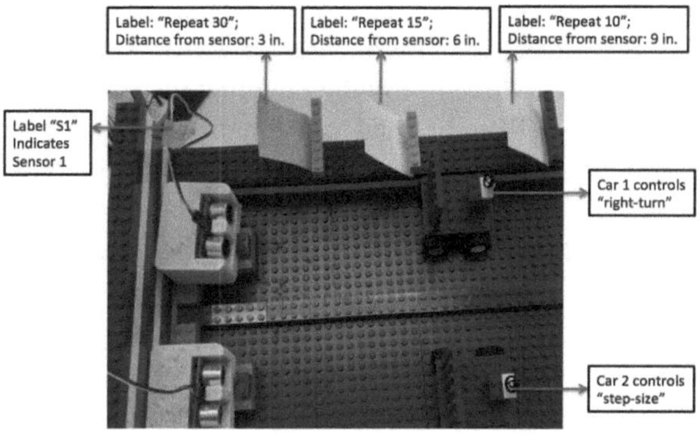

Fig. 7. Final version of Jacinda and Tom's machine used during UT2.

6 Summary and Discussion

In Study 1, we found that the distributed computing infrastructure supported both intersubjective and collaborative learning, where members of each group made coordinated, non-redundant contributions towards a common goal. That is, while thinking about the desired actions of the Turtle provided each dyad with a common objective, the distributed computational infrastructure created opportunities for intersubjective meaning-making, by providing each learner with a certain amount of independence to build their physical control interface. In Study 1, we also found that a focus on User-Centered Design resulted in students refining both their ViMAP programs and mechanical structures by engaging in iterative design cycles. Study 2 was a deeper investigation of what happens when users are involved as part of the design process. We found that iterative user testing helped children attend to making their designs more communicative, which in turn resulted in improving greatly the quality of students' mathematical explanations and computational thinking. As artifacts, the user guides served dual roles: they were key elements of the user-centered design process, by making hidden rules of operation explicit to the user. As Norman [26] pointed out, this is a key characteristic of user-centered design. At the same time, their user guides also served as mathematical inscriptions – e.g., they served as mathematical models of multiplication, as shown in Sect. 5.3.

It was also the process of making hidden rules explicit (to the user) that supported *cohesion* [25] across the different STEM domains: computational thinking, engineering design and physical and mathematical reasoning. Here agent-based thinking and programming acted as the *invariant* [25]: learners designed structures that supported specific user actions to control the movement of an agent; their algorithms repeated results of these actions in order to generate the particular shape; and in reasoning about the behavior of the agent, and its relationship to user's actions, students engaged in domain-specific reasoning in mathematics and science.

Previous studies suggest that the involvement of users during the design process requires explicit instructional scaffolding, especially given children's unwillingness to include users in their design process [7, 19]. Our pedagogy was designed to address this issue by creating opportunities for involving users iteratively during the design process. As we reported earlier, this involved providing explicit instructional scaffolding. Also, none of the previously reported studies had users unaffiliated with the study involved in elementary-grade children's design process. Study 2 therefore breaks new ground by presenting a pedagogical model in which feedback from users from the *"real world"* (to quote a 4th-grade student) can be integrated within an elementary mathematics curriculum.

Acknowledgements. This project was partially supported by NSF CAREER Award #1150230. Contributions of Corey Brady and Leah Embry, and discussions with Rich Lehrer are gratefully acknowledged.

References

1. Basu, S., Dukeman, A., Kinnebrew, J., Biswas, G., Sengupta, P.: Investigating student generated computational models of science. In: Proceedings of the 11th International Conference of the Learning Sciences (ICLS 2014), pp. 1097–1104 (2014)
2. Berland, L.K.: Designing for STEM integration. J. Pre-Coll. Eng. Educ. Res. **3**(1), 3 (2013)
3. Berland, M., Baker, R.S., Blikstein, P.: Educational data mining and learning analytics: applications to constructionist research. Technol. Knowl. Learn. **19**, 205–220 (2014)
4. Clark, H. H., & Brennan, S. E. 1991. Grounding in communication. In: Resnick, L.B., Levine, J.M., Teasley, S.D. (eds.) Perspectives on Socially Shared Cognition, pp. 127–149
5. Bucciarelli, L.L.: Designing Engineers. MIT Press, Cambridge (1994)
6. Carlsen, M.: Appropriating geometric series as a cultural tool: a study of student collaborative learning. Educ. Stud. Math. **74**, 95–116 (2010)
7. Carver, S.M., Lehrer, R., Connell, T., Erickson, J.: Learning by hypermedia design: issues of assessment and implementation. Educ. Psychol. **27**(3), 385–404 (1992)
8. diSessa, A., Hammer, D., Sherin, B., Kolpakowski, T.: Inventing graphing: children's meta-representational expertise. J. Math. Behav. **10**(2), 117–160 (1991)
9. Farris, A.V., Sengupta, P.: Perspectival computational thinking for learning physics: a case study of collaborative agent-based modeling. In: Proceedings of the 11th International Conference of the Learning Sciences (ICLS 2014), pp. 1102–1107 (2014)
10. Fortus, D., Dershimer, R.C., Krajcik, J., Marx, R.W., Mamlok-Naaman, R.: Design-based science and student learning. J. Res. Sci. Teach. **41**(10), 1081–1110 (2004)
11. Gresalfi, M., Ingram-Goble, A.: Designing for dispositions. In: Proceedings of the 8th International Conference for the Learning Sciences, vol. 1, pp. 297–304. ISLS (2008)
12. Gulliksen, J., Göransson, B., Boivie, I., Blomkvist, S., Persson, J., Cajander, Å.: Key principles for user-centred systems design. Behav. Inf. Technol. **22**(6), 397–409 (2003)
13. Harel, I.: Children as software designers: a constructionist approach for learning mathematics. J. Math. Behav. **9**(1), 4 (1990)
14. Harel, I.E., Papert, S.E.: Constructionism. Ablex Publishing, New York (1991)
15. Horn, M.S., Crouser, R.J., Bers, M.U.: Tangible interaction and learning: the case for a hybrid approach. Pers. Ubiquit. Comput. **16**(4), 379–389 (2011)
16. Hollan, J., Hutchins, E., Kirsh, D.: Distributed cognition: toward a new foundation for human-computer interaction research. In: Carroll, J.M. (ed.) Human-Computer Interaction in the New Millennium, pp. 75–94. ACM Press Addison Wesley, New York (2002)

17. Johri, A., Olds, B.M.: Situated engineering learning: bridging engineering education research and the learning sciences. J. Eng. Educ. **100**(1), 151–185 (2011)
18. Kafai, Y.B., Burke, Q.: The social turn in K–12 programming: moving from computational thinking to computational participation. In: Proceeding of the 44th ACM Technical Symposium on Computer Science Education, pp. 603–608. ACM (2013)
19. Kafai, Y.B., Franke, M., Ching, C., Shih, J.: Game design as an interactive learning environment fostering students' and teachers' mathematical inquiry. Int. J. Comput. Math. Learn. **3**(2), 149–184 (1998)
20. Kelleher, C., Pausch, R.: Lowering the barriers to programming: a taxonomy of programming environments and languages for novice programmers. ACM Comput. Surv. **37**, 83–137 (2005)
21. Lai, K., White, T.: Exploring quadrilaterals in a small group computing environment. Comput. Educ. **59**(3), 963–973 (2012)
22. Miles, M.B., Huberman, A.M.: Qualitative Data Analysis: an Expanded Sourcebook (1994)
23. Resnick, M.: Mother's day, warrior cats, and digital fluency: stories from the scratch online community. In: Proceedings of the Constructionism 2012 Conference. Athens, Greece (2012)
24. National Academy of Engineering and National Research Council (NAE & NRC). STEM Integration in K-12 Education: Status, Prospects, and an Agenda for Research. The National Academies Press, Washington, DC (2014)
25. Nathan, M.J., Srisurichan, R., Walkington, C., Wolfgram, M., Williams, C., Alibali, M.W.: Building cohesion across representations: a mechanism for STEM integration. J. Eng. Educ. **102**(1), 77–116 (2013)
26. Norman, D.A.: The Design of Everyday Things. New York (1998)
27. Norman, D.A., Draper, S.W.: User Centered System Design: New Perspectives on Human-Computer Interaction. L. Erlbaum Associates Inc., New Jersey (1986)
28. Papert, S.: Mindstorms: Children, Computers, and Powerful Ideas. Basic Books, New York (1980)
29. Pathak, S.A., Kim, B., Jacobson, M.J., Zhang, B.: Learning the physics of electricity: a qualitative analysis of collaborative processes involved in productive failure. Int. J. Comput.-Support. Collaborative Learn. **6**(1), 57–73 (2011)
30. Repenning, A.: Agentsheets: a tool for building domain-oriented visual programming. In: Conference on Human Factors in Computing Systems, pp. 142–143 (1993)
31. Roschelle, J., Teasley, S.D.: The construction of shared knowledge in collaborative problem solving. In: O'Malley, C. (ed.) Computer Supported Collaborative Learning, pp. 69–97. Springer, Berlin (1995)
32. Roehrig, G.H., Moore, T.J., Wang, H.H., Park, M.S.: Is adding the E enough? Investigating the impact of K-12 engineering standards on the implementation of STEM integration. Sch. Sci. Math. **112**(1), 31–44 (2012)
33. Russ, R., Scherr, R., Hammer, D., Mikeska, J.: Recognizing mechanistic reasoning in student scientific inquiry: a framework for discourse analysis developed from philosophy of science. Sci. Educ. **93**, 875–891 (2008)
34. Sanders, M.: Integrative STEM education: primer. Technol. Teach. **68**(4), 20–27 (2009)
35. Sengupta, P., Farris, A.V.: Learning kinematics in elementary grades using agent-based computational modeling: a visual programming-based approach. In: Proceedings of 11th International Conference of Interaction Design and Children, pp. 78–87. ACM (2012)
36. Sengupta, P., Farris, A.V., Wright, M.: From agents to aggregation via aesthetics: learning mechanics with visual agent-based computational modelling. Technol. Knowl. Learn. **17**(1–2), 23–42 (2012)

37. Sengupta, P., Krishnan, G., Wright, M.: Integrated STEM in elementary grades using distributed agent-based computation. In: Proceedings of the Sixth International Conference on Computer Supported Education, pp. 67–78 (2014)
38. Sengupta, P., Kinnebrew, J.S., Basu, S., Biswas, G., Clark, D.: Integrating computational thinking with K–12 science education using agent-based computation: a theoretical framework. Educ. Inf. Technol. **18**(2), 351–380 (2013)
39. Suthers, D.D.: Technology affordances for intersubjective meaning making: a research agenda for CSCL. Int. J. Comput.-Suppor. Collaborative Learn. **1**(3), 315–337 (2006)
40. Wilensky, U.: NetLogo [Computer Software]. Northwestern University, Evanston, IL (1999)
41. Wing, J.M.: Computational thinking. Commun. ACM **49**(3), 33–35 (2006)
42. Blikstein, P.: Bifocal modeling: promoting authentic scientific inquiry through exploring and comparing real and ideal systems linked in real-time. In: Nijholt, A. (ed.) Playful User Interfaces, pp. 317–352. Springer, Singapore (2014)
43. Johri, A.: Sociomaterial bricolage: the creation of location-spanning work practices by global software developers. Inf. Softw. Technol. **53**(9), 955–968 (2011)

Social Context and Learning Environments

Structuring Collaboration Scripts: Optimizing Online Group Work on Classroom Dilemmas in Teacher Education

Hans Hummel[1,2(✉)], Walter Geerts[2], Aad Slootmaker[1], Derek Kuipers[2], and Wim Westera[1]

[1] Open University of the Netherlands, Valkenburgerweg 177, 6419 AT Heerlen, The Netherlands
{hans.hummel, aad.slootmaker, wim.westera}@ou.nl
[2] NHL University of Applied Science, Rengerslaan 10, 8917 DD Leeuwarden, The Netherlands
{h.hummel, w.m.geerts, d.a.kuipers}@nhl.nl

Abstract. Serious games can facilitate workplace learning, for instance when collaboration on solving professional problems is involved. The optimal structure in collaboration scripts for such games has appeared to be a key success factor. Free collaboration does not systematically produce effective learning, but imposing too much structure by design might easily disturb the genuine notion of spontaneous collaborative learning. In this study we compare a 'high-structured' and 'low-structured' version of a mastership game where teachers-in-training discuss solutions on classroom dilemmas. Adequate solutions are discussed and elaborated during small group play, reported in individual advisory reports, and independently assessed by both two teachers and the group peers. We collected data on the differences in learning effects and student appreciation. The most interesting result shows that reports delivered by students that played the low-structured version received significantly higher teacher grades when compared to the high-structured version. Clear differences in peer-assessments were not found. Practical implications of these findings for future research into collaborative scripting will be discussed.

Keywords: Serious games · Scripted collaboration · Structure · Classroom dilemmas · Teacher education

1 Introduction

Serious games not only support individual learning but also foster the acquisition of soft skills like collaboration and reflection about wicked problems, that are usually not addressed by other learning platforms [8]. Educators call these games 'serious' to denote that they are *not just* fun to play, but *also* hold potential as cognitive tools for learning and professional development (e.g., [17]).

This introduction will describe (1) how serious games may facilitate professional workplace learning when collaboration on practical problems is involved, (2) what is

S. Zvacek et al. (Eds.): CSEDU 2014, CCIS 510, pp. 291–304, 2015.
DOI: 10.1007/978-3-319-25768-6_19

the role of collaboration scripts in such social games, (3) what are ways to define and optimize the structure of such collaboration scripts, and (4) introduce the collaboration game under study (i.e., teachers learning to deal with classroom dilemmas). We will hypothesize that providing structure is a key success factor for effective collaborative learning, and that imposing too much structure by design might have disruptive effects.

1.1 Serious Games for Collaboration in Workplace Learning

Workplace learning is shifting focus from individuals acquiring and updating domain knowledge towards selecting and using this knowledge for certain problem situations in daily practice. Such learning deals with competences like information skills and media literacy, problem-solving, communication and collaboration, and above all critical reflection (e.g., [7]). Today's professionals are becoming lifelong learners that continuously face problem situations that often change dynamically and rapidly. Furthermore, organisations' tacit knowledge plays a crucial role in solving their problems but such knowledge can only be expressed and accessed in direct collaboration on professional tasks (e.g., [18]). Professional tasks that include collaboration, argumentation and negotiation are crucial for vocational education, especially when they aim to connect school knowledge to practical work.

Games are heavily inspired by experiential learning principles which hold potential for contextualised workplace learning. Serious games appear suitable as flexible learning environments where professional tasks can be carried out with little or none direct intervention of experts or teachers (e.g., [1]). We are interested to find out to which extent this holds true in practice and what kind of learner support these learning environments should contain. Such games will take a workplace context (practical problem or authentic case lead) as starting point to stimulate learners acquire new knowledge by sharing and co-creating [1]. How much erroneous or meaningful learning takes place will depend on the learner support that is provided, shared and distributed in the gaming environment. Learner support helps students select most useful information, compare and reflect on multiple perspectives of others, and monitor task progress and quality of learning output. Collaboration support *within* a game has to be enabled by a didactic 'script' which we will name 'scripted collaboration'.

1.2 Collaboration Scripts

Collaboration scripts [16] are an instructional method that structures the collaboration by guiding the interacting partners online through a sequence of interaction phases with designated activities and roles. Scripting collaboration has been examined in CSCL, where it positively influenced learning (e.g., [11]). The group interaction in Computer-Supported Collaborative Learning between learners lead to further elaboration and refinement of individually constructed schemata, since it (a) incites learners to make explicit the actual level of schema development and (b) demands them to explicitly compare their own schemata with schemata of others as to defend or criticize [15].

However, such collaboration scripts have hardly ever been implemented and tested in more open learning environments like serious games [6]. No research has focused on defining or optimizing the essential elements (e.g., of structure) or has measured the learning effects of including such scripting in serious game play. Collaboration scripts in serious games may provide adequate learner support by cueing social processes (elaboration, explanation, argumentation, and question asking) that might otherwise not occur. Dillenbourg [4] mentions that the technological specification of how students should collaborate and solve the problem in an online environment requires five attributes: definition of the task, composition of the group, distribution of the task, the mode of interaction, and the timing of the phases. Regarding the distribution of the task, for instance when a player has to read and understand while another player has to ask questions and give feedback.

1.3 Optimizing the Structure of Collaboration Scripts

The distribution of the task, the mode of interaction and the timing of phases all deal with structure, which we define here as the amount of restriction imposed on the freedom that is allowed in the group collaboration process. An optimal level of structure appears to be a key success factor for effective learner support. A low degree of 'coercion' in 'induced scripts' is elegant but often not sufficient to influence the collaborative process. On one hand, free collaboration does not systematically produce learning (e.g., [4]). But too much educational engineering on the other hand might kill the spontaneity and motivation of genuine collaboration, an effect that Rothkopf [19] denoted as 'mathematanic' (as opposed to 'mathemagenic'). 'Prompted' or 'follow me' scripts have higher levels of 'coercion' and will steer the collaborative process, at the risk of being perceived as too complex or rigid. In a previous study we found that students complained about the complexity and task instruction within for the mastership game [14]. Dillenbourg [4] earlier reported on other scripts (e.g., UniverSanté) that were perceived as too complex. His advice is to keep scripts as simple as possible so that all actors are able to appropriate them. He mentions following risks of over-scripting: disturbing 'natural' interactions by adding too many interaction breakdowns; disturbing 'natural' problem solving processes by segmenting the task; increased cognitive load by the necessity to understand, memorize and execute the script itself as well; 'didactising' collaborative interactions when interactions are played like in the teacher-learner context; and 'goalless' interactions when the script prevents the group to establish a shared goal.

In order to optimize structure, we first have to further define what is structure and what are its elements. Although this might appear evident, a clear definition of structure is not well documented in CSCL literature. Building on Dillenbourg's risks of over-scripting we argue that *segmentation* and *inter-dependency* within the task constitute the main structure elements. Clearly, a holistic task is less structured than a task that has been segmented in various consecutive subtasks. Clearly, a task that can be carried out independently is less structured than a task that depends on synchronisation or approval of peers and/or teachers. We will operationalize these structure elements for this study.

Collaborative learning by some researchers (e.g., [10]) is considered to be overly optimistic or naive. Can we assume that two learners with little knowledge in a domain of study would naturally gain knowledge in miraculous interaction? The recent evolution of CSCL in the direction of using scripting to make collaboration more effective might drift away from this 'natural' process and get us closer to more directive teaching methods. We may question if it is at all possible to combine two pedagogical traditions (collaborative learning and traditional instruction) without losing what makes 'natural' collaborative learning different. In the world of semi-structured communication, optimizing structure plays a key role in this design dilemma. On the positive side, the notion of script might bridge collaborative learning and traditional instructional design.

1.4 Mastership Game: Working Together to Solve Classroom Dilemmas

What should a teacher do, for instance, when a pupil continues to disturb the lesson by insulting his peers. Should the problem be resolved during the lesson, even at the risk of losing valuable time to the expense of the majority of students that is not involved in the conflict? Or should the problem be resolved after the class has been dismissed, even at the risk that disturbances will continue during the lesson? Teaching can be considered to be an exciting game. Teachers without doubt will have to face unexpected situations that demand them to find solutions on the fly. Not all classroom problems present themselves as dilemmas, however as practical contexts dilemmas offer best opportunity for seeing various perspectives, solutions and discussion. Some experienced didactics teachers developed the Mastership game which helps students to find solutions to the most prevailing practical classroom management dilemmas in a playful and collaborative way, a way that will help them become better teachers. The game was originally developed as a card game to be played face-to-face in small groups [9], and was later transformed into on online game to be played synchronously with freedom of place [14].

The Mastership game can be played in small groups of two till six students and does not require any intervention by teachers. After selecting their avatars, students start group play both in the role of player (or problem owner) and of co-player (judging the way that players solve their problems). The game has a structure that consists of five consecutive phases, during which players discuss, elaborate and negotiate solutions to solve each other's problems. Communication is structured by various assignments and rules during these phases, but is possible by unstructured group chat as well. During the *first phase* players select practical classroom dilemmas, either out of a pile of twenty-four, most prevailing practical classroom dilemmas (i.e., "How to maintain control in a good way", "How to deal with negative colleagues", or "How to deal with a pupil that does not want to get coached"). Then each player selects the problem that is considered most important. During the *second phase* players draw an exploratory assignment (e.g., "Provide an exemplary experience that shows why this problem is important for you"). The elaboration is judged by the co-players until the group is satisfied. During the *third phase* players take turns in drawing theme cards (e.g., "professional development", "dealing with losses", or "lesson preparation") that are placed at their co-players while motivating why this theme should be further explored in combination with the chosen dilemma, until every player has received three theme cards. In the *fourth phase* players will negotiate and discuss which theme cards may be declined. Co-players may use jury cards and ask further questions to challenge players to further motivate their declined cards before the group agrees on the final selection. During the *fifth phase* players select a practical assignment and use their co-players' input to further elaborate their solution in a short advisory report (Fig. 1).

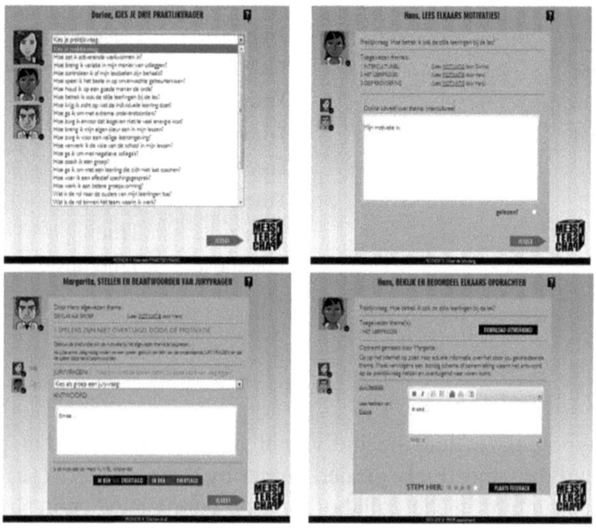

Fig. 1. Screens of the online version of the Mastership game: selecting three practical dilemmas in phase 1 (upper left hand), assigning and motivating themes in phase 3 (upper right hand), motivating and discussing declined themes in phase 4 (lower left hand), and peer assessment of elaborated assignments in phase 6 (lower right hand).

This previous subsection mentioned (a) segmentation and (b) inter-dependency as constituting elements of structure. Following structure elements were identified within the mastership game: (a1) the scenes within a phase (two or three) are consecutive (true) or might be carried out in parallel (false); (a2) the obligatory number of cards to draw (possible values 1–3); (b1) players have to take turns (true) or may work in parallel (false) within the various scenes and phases; (b2) players are being assessed by group members before they may proceed (true), or may decide themselves (false); and (b3) at moments players are dependent on which cards others draw for them (true), or at any time may draw their own cards (false). Most elements only pertain to some of the scenes and phases, with the exception of (b1) which occurs in most phases (see Table 1).

Based on this operationalization of structure we define high-structure as all elements having the value 'true' (and the value of a2 being 3), and low-structure as all elements having the value 'false' (and the value of a2 being 1). We also defined and developed a medium-structured version with a1 being false, a2 being 1, b1 being false, b2 being true, and b3 being true.

The main hypotheses (research questions) to be answered in the next sections are twofold: (1) Will less structure lead to more 'natural' and effective collaborative

Table 1. Possible values of structure elements for each scene/phase.

Scene	a1 (has to finish scene)	a2 (number of cards to draw)	b1 (wait for others)	b2 (feedback required)	b3 (others draw cards)
1_1	True	3/2/1	True/false	False	False
1_2	True	1	True/false	False	False
2_1	False	–	True/false	False	False
2_2	True/false	–	True/false	False	False
2_3	True/false	–	True/false	True/false	False
3_1	True	3/2/1	True/false	False	True/false
3_2	True/false	–	True/false	False	False
4_1	True/false	–	True/false	False	False
4_2	True	–	True	True	False
4_3	True	–	True	True	False
5_1	True	–	True/false	True/false	False
5_2	–	–	–	–	–
6_1	–	–	–	–	–
6_2	–	–	–	–	–

learning? (We hypothesize that the individual reports of those that played the low-structured game will be objectively graded higher by their teachers (1a) and peers (1b)); and (2) Will less structure in the collaboration be appreciated more by students? (We hypothesize that students will subjectively appreciate the low-structured game higher on a number of aspects.)

2 Method

After describing the participants and the learning materials we used, we explain the procedure and assessment instruments we used to measure the effectiveness of learning and the satisfaction with the scripted collaboration in both conditions.

2.1 Participants

Twenty-nine teachers-in-training, third year students of the NHL University of Applied Science in the Netherlands, participated in this case study as part of their regular curriculum. This case study was awarded a study load of about 10 h (half an EC point) as part of workplace learning. Participants are qualifying for a broad variety of first degree teaching positions, ranging from modern languages teaching, teaching didactics to science teaching. All had comparable prior knowledge since all were in the third year of their curriculum. Most students follow education in combination with work (as a dual or flexible learning trajectory) which explains the relatively high average age ($M = 39.5$, $SD = 8.10$), ranging between 26 and 54 years. Twenty-two were female and seven were male students, equally divided over the conditions. Gender and age showed neither to differ over conditions nor to be related to learning outcomes. The effects of gender and age on learning found were $F\ (2,27) = 0.755$, $p = 0.704$ and $F\ (2,27) = 1.286$, $p = 0.267$ respectively.

2.2 Learning Materials

The 'Mastership' game contains a total of 66 'cards' or instructions: 24 practical dilemmas; 13 exploratory assignments; 10 themes, with 10 jury cards containing questions per theme; and 8 final assignments. Instructions and rules for playing the game are provided at the start of each phase. The game will be played by a small group of two till six players, and will take about two hours to play. The five phases with various types of cards involved were explained in the previous section.

We developed the online version of the 'Mastership' game using the ZK toolkit (http://www.zkoss.org). The EMERGO toolkit for serious game development (http://www.emergo.cc) was used for game run management and for storing and analysing data. The toolkit is built in Java and the collaboration script described above was implemented as a separate Java component within the toolkit. The component is designed and built in such a way that it can later be reused and extended for other scripts and cases applying a similar collaboration pattern in their design. Game logic is neatly separated from the rest of the code in so-called GameScene classes. The game can easily be configured by a game author on several aspects like structure.

2.3 Procedure

All students were approached by their teacher (being one of the authors of this article) and invited to be present at a certain place and time at the university for a two-hour meeting. Participants were notified in advance that this meeting would also be used for study purposes, and were randomly allocated to one of three conditions (high-structured, low-structured, control). Participants in the control group had to solve the practical classroom dilemma individually without playing the collaboration game. Each gaming condition contained two groups (of four or five students each). The players received an e-mail before the meeting, containing the URL and their personal account. All playing participants received a questionnaire about their appreciation of the game by e-mail a day after playing the game. At the time of the meeting, playing participants went to a computer room to work together online. A teacher was present in this computer room to control for direct (non)verbal communication beyond the program. During the time of the meeting, students in the control group individually worked on their practical task, without playing the game.

During regular education the fifth phase would be the final phase and outcome of the small group play. Students then elaborate and deliver their reports individually, and get graded by their teacher. For the purpose of this study we included a *sixth* and final *phase* in which students had to grade the reports of their peers, in order to enable a comparison of the assessments by peers (co-players) and teachers. It was estimated that the elaboration of the reports would take about half a day. Students were allowed two weeks to deliver their report and questionnaire, and to grade the reports of the peers in their group (by awarding one to five stars). Playing students were allowed to deliver and grade reports either online or by mail. Students were able to pass through phases without technical problems, with the exception of a group playing the medium-structured version of the game (for this reason the medium-structured condition had to be left out of the research design and primary analyses, although we will mention what was found for this version of the game). All data could be collected two weeks after the meeting took place.

2.4 Learning Effect Correction Model

To measure individual learning output, the quality of the solutions provided for the classroom dilemmas was assessed by using a learning effect correction model, that was developed by the teacher/topic expert (being one of the authors of this article). The elaborated reports can be assessed on 'growth in professional productivity', and the five criteria to establish this growth were inspired by the development of 'design practice' (or practical theory) [3]: A. Ownership (to what extent does student commit to solve this problem); B. Reflection (to what extent does student reflect on his own actions); C. Focus (to what extent does student attach the right amount of context to the problem); D. Nuance/Complexity (to what extent is applying the solution feasible); and E. Richness/Correctness (of the elaborated solution). Table 2 contains indications for the possible scores on these criteria, with total scores ranging from 0 to 10. Sufficient inter-rater reliability of the instrument was determined in a previous study [14].

Table 2. Sub-scales and scoring categories of the learning effect correction model.

Subscales	Insufficient (0 points)	Sufficient (1 point)	Good (2 points)	Score
A. Ownership	Refers to others: "They will solve the problem"	"I will take action"	The answer shows real commitment	0–2
B. Reflection	No reflection	Some reflection, partly rich	Rich reflection	0–2
C. Focus	The problem has not been framed/focused	The problem has partly been focused	The problem is rich and has been correctly focused	0–2
D. Nuance/complexity	The answer does not contain nuance	The answer is correctly linked to one design pattern	The answer is correctly linked to (a network of) more design patterns	0–2
E. Richness/correctness	The elaboration is not correct	The elaboration is partly rich and correct	The elaboration is rich and correct	0–2
Total score				0–10

2.5 Student Satisfaction Questionnaire

The student satisfaction questionnaire was developed for this study by a learning technology expert (being one of the authors of this article). It contains 19 items to establish the students' appreciation of various game aspects, pertaining to the structure (S, 5 questions), user-friendliness and clarity (U, 5 questions), the timing of the phases (T, 2 questions), the quality of the dilemmas and assignments (Q, 5 questions), and the interaction during collaboration (I, 2 questions). The focus on structure and clarity of instruction was inspired by previous studies (e.g., [6]) showing this often to be problematic. Even when structure and clarity of the script (the logistics) are perfect, game play will lead to nowhere when the quality of assignments, players, information exchanged (the content) is of poor quality; this is why we added some items to check for this. (Clearly, the letters referring to these five aspects and +/− signs referring to the positive/negative formulation in Table 3 were not listed in the original questionnaire.) All these items used a Likert-scale with five values, ranging from (1) fully do not agree to (5) fully do agree. The median value (neutral) therefore is 3.0. Depending on the positive (+)/negative (−) formulation of the items, values below can be interpreted as (slightly) negative/positive and all values above as (slightly) positive/negative appreciations. Item 20 was an open question, allowing room for comments and suggestions. Table 3 contains the list of items.

3 Results

This results section provides answers to the twofold research question we posed at the end of the introduction: (1) Will less structure lead to more 'natural' and effective collaborative learning? We hypothesized that the individual reports of those that played the low-structured game will be objectively graded higher by their teachers (1a) and peers (1b); and (2) Will less structure in the collaboration be appreciated more by students? We hypothesized that students will subjectively appreciate the low-structured game higher on a number of aspects. We present the objective learning effect measures (answering the first question) and the subjective questionnaire measures (answering the last question).

3.1 Learning Effect Measures

We found that most individual reports (76 %) could be graded as sufficient. Grades below 6.0 were considered not sufficient, and only seven students received either an 4.5, 5.0 or 5.5 (three times in the high-structured and control conditions, and one time in the low-structured condition). The average grade for all participants was $M = 6.62$, $SD = 1.29$. We added a control group to establish if playing the game does contribute *at all* to learning. As you see in Table 4 the average teacher grades for the control group were indeed lowest, so there appears to be an effect of playing the game. This effect appears significant when we compare the non-playing group to the low-structured ($t\ (18) = 2.97$, $p < 0.01$) and the medium-structured condition (which we left out of the analyses). However, we could not observe a significant difference between non-players and those playing the high-structured version ($t\ (17) = 0.67$, $p = 0.51$).

Table 3. Items of the satisfaction questionnaire.

Item	Aspect	+/−	Statement
1	U	+	The way to play the game is clear, playing rules are clear
2	Q	+	The elaborations (of practical assignments) by co-players were of sufficient quality
3	Q	+	The composition of the group was good (regarding interest and level of expertise)
4	U		The user-interface of the game is clear and user-friendly
5	S	+	Group play was possible without teacher intervention, the collaboration process has been determined well in advance
6	T	−	The time allowed to play was too low
7	S	−	The amount of game structure is too low
8	U	+	The time allowed for each phase was too low
9	S	−	The amount of structure in each phase is too high
10	T	−	The time allowed for each phase was too high
11	U	−	The way to collaborate during each phase was too complex
12	I	+	Mutual interaction and collaboration proceeded well and were useful
13	Q	+	Feedback (assigning cards, peer assessment, etc.) from co-players was useful (in further elaborating my assignment)
14	Q	+	The elaborations of the exploratory assignments by co-players were of sufficient quality
15	S	+	Using jury cards was useful and proceeded well
16	U	+	Collaboration rules (for peer assessment, taking turns, when to proceed to next phase, etc.) were clear
17	S	−	Mutual dependency during collaboration (awaiting feedback, taking turns, etc.) was too high
18	Q	+	The elaborations of the final assignments by co-players were of sufficient quality
19	I	+	It was a fun and effective way to play the mastership game

When looking for an overall effect of condition ($N = 29$) on learning effect we see a clear trend: low-structure scores best, than high-structure, and finally the control group. This effect is 'marginally' significant (F (2, 26) = 3.072, MSE = 4.428, $p = 0.063$, $\eta_p^2 = 0.18$), with values of the partial-eta-squared above .13 showing large effect size according to Cohen [2]. On top of this and even more importantly for the central research question, a significant difference (t (17) = 4,86, $p = 0.042$) is found in favour of low-structure when comparing with high-structure ($N = 19$). When looking at the peer ratings, we do not find any significant differences between conditions. We therefore *accept our first hypothesis* with a positive answer to the first sub question (yes, playing the low-structured game leads to higher teacher grades). We could not find evidence to accept the second sub question (no, peer grading does not seem to differentiate that well between conditions). The average and normalized ratings awarded by peers (co-players) do appear to be correlated to the grades awarded by teachers ($r_S = 0.36$, $p = 0.052$, two-tailed), although this relation is only 'marginally'

Table 4. Average report grades for all conditions, both from teachers and peers.

	High structure (n = 9)		Low structure (n = 10)		Control (n = 10)		All (N = 29)	
Assessment	*M*	*SD*	*M*	*SD*	*M*	*SD*	*M*	*SD*
Teacher grade	6.44	1.59	7.35	1.03	6.05	0.93	6.62	1.29
Peer rating	7.93	.66	7.52	1.04	7.68	0.89	7.70	0.87

significant. Ratings by peers (M = 7.70, SD = 0.87) overall are higher than teacher grades (M = 6.62, SD = 1.29).

The reliability of the learning effect correction model was determined by applying Cohen's Kappa for inter-rater reliability (with k = 2). For the total instrument the standard (and rather strict) Kappa measure appeared poor (K = .16, δ = .09). On the level of the sub-scales of the instrument inter-rater reliability was fair to moderate for four out of five scales. Only on sub-scale B (Reflection) there was poor agreement (K = .19). Excluding this sub-scale would immediately increase the overall Kappa to moderate (K = .48) and acceptable. Closer inspection of the differences in scores between both raters revealed that rater one consistently awarded slightly lower grades (M = 6.48, p = 1.38) in comparison with rater two (M = 6.76, p = 1.41). Since the standard Kappa does not take into account degrees of disagreement between observers (all disagreement is considered as total disagreement) when having ordered categories, we decided it would be preferable to calculate Weighted Kappa's. Since the difference between the first and second category had the same importance as the difference between the second and third category (0, 1, and 2 were the scoring categories in each sub-scale), we used linear weighting. The Weighted Kappa for the total instrument appeared moderate and acceptable (K_w = .47, δ = .08), and when excluding sub-scale B appeared even good (K_w = .68, δ = .09). On a more minute level of interpretation we would like to mention that, when using linear weighting, a good interpretation of the observed Kappa's depends on the maximal Kappa's, which on its turn depend on the marginal distribution of cells for each sub-scale. A smaller observed Kappa (e.g. K_w = .36) then might still be acceptable if the maximal Kappa is just a bit higher (e.g., K_w = .45), yielding a ratio of 0.80. On the other hand a higher observed Kappa (e.g. K_w = .43) might not be that acceptable if the maximal Kappa is much higher (e.g., K_w = .95), yielding a ratio of 0.45. We found ratios of observed and maximal Kappa's for all subscales to range between .51 and .89. We decided it was very acceptable to use the original instrument, even without correction for less agreement on sub-scale B. Kappa's between 0-20 are considered 'poor' or 'light', between 20-40 as 'fair', between 40-60 as 'moderate', between 60-80 as 'substantial' or 'good', and between 80-100 as 'almost perfect' or 'very good' ([12], p. 450).

3.2 Satisfaction Measures

Table 5 presents the average scores on all items of the questionnaire for both conditions. The last colon presents the significances of the difference ($p\Delta$) between both group means on each item after running an ANOVA.

Table 5. Average score on the satisfaction questionnaire items, and significance of difference between versions.

	High structure (*n* = 9)		Low structure (*n* = 10)		All (*N* = 19)		
Item	*M*	*SD*	*M*	*SD*	*M*	*SD*	*pΔ*
1	3.00	1.41	2.70	1.25	2.85	1.30	.64
2	4.00	0.76	4.00	0.82	4.00	0.76	1.00
3	3.50	1.31	4.20	0.92	3.89	1.13	.20
4	2.88	1.25	3.50	1.08	3.22	1.17	.27
5	2.38	1.40	2.67	1.50	2.53	1.42	.67
6	2.25	0.89	1.40	0.52	1.78	0.81	.02
7	3.13	1.25	3.40	1.07	3.28	1.13	.62
8	3.25	1.49	4.20	1.03	3.78	1.31	.13
9	2.75	0.87	2.30	0.95	2.50	0.92	.32
10	2.13	0.83	2.20	1.40	2.17	1.15	.89
11	4.00	0.53	2.90	1.37	3.39	1.19	.04
12	3.38	1.51	2.80	1.23	3.06	1.35	.38
13	2.88	1.36	3.00	0.90	2.91	1.14	.88
14	3.13	0.99	3.33	0.82	3.21	0.89	.68
15	2.88	0.99	2.33	1.16	2.73	1.01	.46
16	2.50	1.31	2.56	1.24	2.53	1.23	.93
17	4.25	1.04	3.56	1.24	3.88	1.16	.23
18	3.00	1.07	3.67	1.55	3.18	1.08	.39
19	3.00	1.19	3.22	1.56	3.12	1.36	.75

Considering the formulation of items (listed in Table 3), we can observe that for both conditions aspects have been valued as slightly positive (above neutral), like items 2, 3, 6, 9, and 10, while others have been valued as slightly negative (below neutral), like items 5, 8, 11, 16 and 17. Although students do not clearly criticize the structure for each phase, they do indicate that collaboration rules were not always clear (item 16) and that mutual dependency was too high (item 17), with the last items clearly being more negative for the high-structured group. For most items we did not find significant differences between both versions of the game, with just two exceptions. The low-structured group showed to be more satisfied with the amount of time to play (item 16). The high-structured group indicated that the overall structure was too high (item 11), a finding in line with what was reported on learning effects. Based on these findings we cannot accept our *second hypothesis*. It did not become clear that low-structure was appreciated more by students on various aspects.

4 Conclusions

Collaboration can be successfully facilitated by scripting serious games when we take into account the importance of good instruction and optimal structure. Also in this study players reported problems with clear task instruction and collaboration rules without teacher intervention. This study found that over-scripting may indeed have disruptive learning effects. Players of the low-structured version of the mastership game produced reports that were graded significantly higher than the ones of those playing the high-structured version (and of those not playing the game). The average grade of a small group playing the medium-structured version (which for methodological reasons we had to leave out of our design) was close to the low-structure group (M = 7.25, SD = 0.61, n = 5). The structure elements that we left out when going from 'high' to 'medium', having to work in a strict order (a1) and having to take turns (b1), appear to have potential disruptive (or mathematanic) effects on the emergence of rich interactions. This result has practical implications for 'designing for conversation' which according to Dillenbourg and Fischer [5] is the holy grail of CSCL.

For the generalizability of these findings it will be useful to carry out studies that research the effectiveness of other types of collaboration scripts and implementations in other domains. For this end we need a dedicated authoring environment that enables us to manipulate elements of scripts. Dillenbourg and Hong [6] proposed 'script families' at a macro level of abstraction. They differentiate three classes of scripts that more or less use the same collaboration patterns: JigSaw (distributing knowledge amongst group members, e.g. by allocating various perspectives or roles), Reciprocal Teaching (using mutual regulation, e.g. by taking turns in contributing to tasks of each other), and Conflict Raising (competing or taking opposing stands, e.g. by negotiation or argumentation). In our research we are currently constructing a dedicated authoring environment to instantiate collaboration scripts for various situations, which is built on the EMERGO platform. Studies into case instances of the JigSaw scripting class [13] and Reciprocal Teaching class [14] have already been realised and reported. For the third family (Conflict Raising) we are currently preparing a study instantiating an argumentation game in EMERGO, based on an existing wiki where players take and defend opposing stands [20]. When user-friendly authoring environments and reusable design patterns become available, the complexity and effectiveness of collaborative learning through serious game play can be further improved.

Acknowledgements. This study was carried out as research activity within the 'Learning Media' program of CELSTEC (Open University of the Netherlands), and within the Lectorate 'Workplace Learning and ICT' (NHL University of Applied Science, The Netherlands). Authors and developers from both institutes worked closely together during development of the game and this study. We express our thanks to both institutes for their funding, and to NHL students for participating.

References

1. Bell, B.S., Kanar, A.M., Kozlowski, S.W.J.: Current issues and future directions in simulation-based training in North America. Int. J. Hum. Resour. Manage. **19**(8), 1416–1434 (2008)
2. Cohen, J.: Statistical Power Analysis for the Behavioral Sciences. Lawrence Erlbaum, Hillsdale, NJ (1988)

3. Copeland, W.D., D'Emidio-Caston, M.: Indicators of development of practical theory in pre-service teacher education students. Teach. Teach. Educ. **14**(5), 513–534 (1998)
4. Dillenbourg, P.: Over-scripting CSCL: the risks of blending collaborative learning with instructional design. Three worlds of CSCL (2002)
5. Dillenbourg, P., Fischer, F.: Basics of computer-supported collaborative learning. Zeitschrift für Berufs- und Wirtschaftspaedagogik **21**, 111–130 (2007)
6. Dillenbourg, P., Hong, F.: The mechanics of CSCL macro scripts. Int. J. Comput.-Support. Collaborative Learn. **3**(1), 5–23 (2008). Springer
7. Garrick, J.: Informal Learning in the Workplace: Unmasking Human Resource Development. Routledge, London (2007)
8. Gee, J.P.: What Video Games Have to Teach Us About Learning and Literacy?. Palgrave MacMillan, New York (2003)
9. Geerts, W., Mitzsche, M., Van Laeken, M. (Red.). Wat zou je doen? Dilemma's in de onderwijspraktijk. Coutinho, Bussum (2009)
10. Glachan, M.D., Light, P.H.: Peer interaction and teaching: can two wrongs make one right? In: Butterworth, G., Light, P.H. (eds.) Social Cognition: Studies of the Development of Understanding. Harvester Press, Brighton (1981)
11. Gunawardena, C.N., Carabajal, K., Lowe, C.A.: Critical Analysis of Models and Methods Used to Evaluate Online Learning Networks. AERA, Seattle (2001)
12. Heuvelmans, A.P.J.M., Sanders, P.F.: Inter-rater reliability. In: Eggen, T., Sanders, P. (eds.) Psychonometry in Practice, pp. 443–471. CITO Institute for Test Development, Arnhem (1993)
13. Hummel, H.G.K., Van Houcke, J., Nadolski, R.J., Van der Hiele, T., Kurvers, H., Löhr, A.: Scripted collaboration in serious gaming for complex learning: effects of multiple perspectives when acquiring water management skills. Br. J. Educ. Technol. **42**(6), 1029–1041 (2011)
14. Hummel, H.G.K., Geerts, W.M., Slootmaker, A., Kuipers, D., Westera, W.: Collaboration scripts for mastership skills: online game about classroom dilemmas in teacher education. Interactive Learning Environments (2013, Online)
15. Jeong, H., Chi, M.T.H.: Does Collaborative Learning Lead to the Construction of Common Knowledge? http://www.ircs.upenn.edu.edu/cogsci2000/PRCDNGS/SPRCDNGS/posters/jeo_chi.pdf (2000). Accessed 9 July 2004
16. Kobbe, L., Weinberger, A., Dillenbourg, P., Harrer, A., Hämäläinen, R., Häkkinen, P., Fisher, F.: Specifying computer-supported collaboration scripts. Comput. Support. Collaborative Learn. **2**, 211–224 (2007)
17. Michael, D., Chen, S.: Serious Games: Games that Educate, Train and Inform. Thomson Course Technology, Boston (2006)
18. Nonaka, I., Takeuchi, H.: The Knowledge-Creating Company: How Japanese Companies Create the Dynamics of Innovation. Oxford University Press, New York (1995)
19. Rothkopf, E.Z.: Control of mathemagenic activities. In: Jonassen, D.H. (ed.) Handbook of Research for Educational Communications and Technology, pp. 879–896. MacMillan Library Reference, New York (1996)
20. Van Rosmalen, P., Westera, W.: Introducing serious games with Wikis: empowering the teacher with simple technologies. Interact. Learn. Environ. **22**(5), 564–577 (2014)

The State of MOOCs from 2008 to 2014: A Critical Analysis and Future Visions

Ahmed Mohamed Fahmy Yousef[1(✉)], Mohamed Amine Chatti[1], Ulrik Schroeder[1], Marold Wosnitza[2], and Harald Jakobs[3]

[1] Learning Technologies Group (Informatik 9), RWTH-Aachen University, Ahornstrasse 55, Aachen, Germany
{Ahmed.fahmy,Chatti,Schroeder}@cil.rwth-aachen.de
[2] School Pedagogy and Educational Research, RWTH-Aachen University, Eilfschornsteinstraße 7, Aachen, Germany
marold.wosnitza@rwth-aachen.de
[3] Center for Innovative Learning Technologies (CIL), RWTH-Aachen University, Ahornstrasse 55, Aachen, Germany
Jakobs@cil.rwth-aachen.de

Abstract. Massive Open Online Courses (MOOCs) are providing limitless opportunities for thousands of learners to participate in free higher education courses online. Indeed, MOOCs have drastically changed the way we learn as well as how we teach. MOOCs have unique features that make it an effective Technology-Enhanced Learning (TEL) approach in higher education and beyond. The number of academic research around MOOCs has grown rapidly in the last few years. The purpose of this paper is to compile and analyze the state of MOOC research that has been conducted from 2008–2014. A template analysis was used to map the conducted studies on MOOCs into seven dimensions, namely concept, design, learning theories, case studies, business model, targets groups, and assessment. This classification schema aims at providing a comprehensive overview for readers who are interested in MOOCs to foster a common understanding of key concepts in this emerging field. The paper further identifies critical challenges that have yet to be addressed and suggests opportunities for future work in the area of MOOCs that will support communication between researchers as they seek to address these challenges.

Keywords: Massive open online courses · MOOCs · OER · Learning theories · Blended learning · Challenges

1 Introduction

Massive open online courses (MOOCs) are an innovative form of video-based learning (VBL) in the sense that they provide opportunities to a massive number of participation to attend free online courses from anywhere all over the world [63, 112]. Over the last few years, the MOOCs phenomenon has become widely acknowledged as crucial for

S. Zvacek et al. (Eds.): CSEDU 2014, CCIS 510, pp. 305–327, 2015.
DOI: 10.1007/978-3-319-25768-6_20

freely accessible high quality courses provided by international institutes for informal as well as formal education [5, 11]. The current published literature around MOOCs discusses different theoretical and practical perspectives on the use of MOOCs, including numerous design and implementation details. These publications are however still in an infancy stage and a systematic classification of the MOOC literature is still missing. This paper is one of the efforts to:

1. Compile and analyze the accumulated literature that has been conducted on MOOCs between 2008 and 2014 to build a deep and better understanding of key concepts in this emerging field.
2. Summarize the main challenges facing MOOC development from pedagogical and technological perspectives.
3. Identify some future research opportunities in the area of MOOCs that should be considered in the development of MOOCs environments.

In the light of these goals, this paper will discuss different angles of MOOCs and is structured as follows: Sect. 2 is a review of the related work. Section 3 describes the research methodology and how we collected the research data. In Sect. 4, we review and discuss the state of MOOCs based on several dimensions. Section 5, summarizes the main challenges facing MOOCs development and highlights possible future directions in MOOC research. Finally, Sect. 6 gives a summary of the main findings of this paper.

2 Related Work

Since research in MOOCs is still an emerging field, we found only two studies analyzing the accumulated academic literature of MOOCs. Liyanagunawardena et al. [62] provides a quantitative analysis of 45 peer reviewed studies that have been conducted from 2008–2012 and provides a general discussion based on a categorization into eight dimensions, namely introductory, concept, case studies, educational theory, technology, participant focused, provider focused, and other.

In addition, the motivations and challenges are the main focus of a study conducted by Hew and Cheung [44]. The authors reviewed the current published literature focusing on the use of MOOCs by instructors as well as students in order to summarize the state of MOOCs concerning the motivations and challenges of using these new learning environments. The main findings of this study were that, the quality of MOOC education and the assessment of student work are the major challenges in MOOCs.

As compared to Liyanagunawardena et al.'s and Hew and Cheung's studies, in this paper, we add a wide range of peer-reviewed publications that have been conducted between 2008 and 2014 and provide a quantitative as well as qualitative analysis of the MOOC literature. Moreover, we apply a template analysis to categorize the state of MOOCs into several dimensions. The paper further identifies critical challenges that have yet to be addressed and suggests new research opportunities for future work in the area of MOOCs. To note, that the paper at hand is an extended version of [114].

3 Research Methodology

The research was carried out in two main phases including data collection followed by template analysis of the literature review.

3.1 Data Collection

We collected data by applying the scientific research method of identifying papers from internet resources [31]. This method includes three rounds. Firstly, we searched 7 major refereed academic databases[1] and secondly 18 academic journals[2] in the field of learning technologies and e-learning indexed by Journal Citation Reports (JCR), using the search terms (and their plurals) "MOOC", "Massive Open Online Course" and "Massively Open Online Course". These two rounds resulted in 148 peer reviewed papers to be included in our study. Thirdly, we applied a set of selection criteria as follows:

1. Research must focus on MOOCs in pedagogical, social, economic, and technical settings. Studies with political and policymakers views were excluded.
2. Experimental or empirical case studies with scientific data on how learners learn with and from MOOCs were included. Studies without analyzed data were excluded.
3. Papers presenting a new design of MOOCs were included. Studies with personal opinions or learner's anecdotal impression were excluded.

This resulted in a final set of 93 peer-reviewed publications which fit the criteria above (88 academic papers, 4 international reports, and 1 dissertation). Table 1 illustrated the number of MOOCs publications between 2008 and 2014 which were found to be relevant for this study.

Table 1. MOOCs papers by publication year.

Year	2008	2009	2010	2011	2012	2013	2014	Sum
Number of publication	1	1	3	8	11	61	8	93

[1] Education Resources Information Center (ERIC), JSTOR, ALT Open Access Repository, Google Scholar, PsychInfo, ACM publication, IEEEXplorer, and Wiley Online Library.

[2] American Journal of Distance Education, Australian Journal of Educational Technology, British Journal of Educational Technology, Canadian Journal of Learning and Technology, Communications of the ACM, Continuing Higher Education Review Journal, Educational Technology Research and Development, Educational Theory, eLearning Papers Journal, Frontiers of Language and Teaching, International Journal of Innovation in Education, International Journal of Technology in Teaching and Learning, International Review of Research in Open and Distance Learning, Journal of Asynchronous Learning Networks, Journal of Computer Assisted Learning, Journal of Interactive Media in Education (JIME), Open Praxis Journal, The European Journal of Open, and Distance and E-Learning (EURODL).

3.2 Template Analysis

The second phase was using Template Analysis as classification technique for mapping MOOCs literature in several dimensions [52]. Template analysis is an iterative process. In the first step of template analysis, we carefully read the MOOCs literature to be familiar with the domain context. Then, in the second level we formulated concrete codes (themes), based on the understanding of the studies domain and using the existing classifications by Liyanagunawardena et al.'s [62] as well as Pardos and Schneider [77] as a reference to test reliability and credibility of the code template. Then, we identified seven codes as follows:

1. **Concept** included aspects in the literature which referred to the concept e.g. definition, history, and MOOCs types.
2. **Design** included design principals e.g. pedagogical and technological features.
3. **Learning theories** that have built the theoretical background of the conducted MOOC studies.
4. **Case studies** e.g. experimental and empirical studies.
5. **Business models** that have been followed in the different MOOC implementations.
6. **Target groups** included aspects which referred to learner characteristics.
7. **Assessment** included different types in MOOCs e.g. e-assessment, self-assessments, and peer-assessment.

After having a stable code template, we had several internal meetings to discuss each code and create a mapping of the 93 publications that were selected in this review into the seven identified codes as depicted in Fig. 1. This template analysis has been done manually using printout tables.

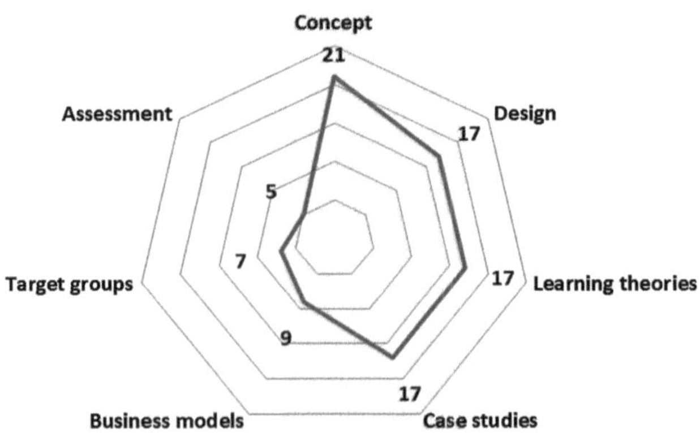

Fig. 1. Classification Map of MOOCs.

4 The State of MOOCs

In this section, we analyze and discuss in detail the state of MOOCs based on the template analysis dimensions (codes) that have been identified in Sect. 3. For the critical discussion part, we apply the meta-analysis method which aims to contrast and combine results from several studies into a single scientific work [31].

4.1 Concept

The first dimension in our analysis is "concept". Nearly 25 % of the literature reviewed in this paper focus on the MOOC concept. To clarify the MOOC concept three aspects have been considered in the reviewed literature, namely definition, history, and types.

4.1.1 MOOC Definition

Dave Cormier and Bryan Alexander coined the acronym MOOC to describe the "Connectivism and Connective Knowledge" (CCK08) course launched by Stephen Downes and George Siemens at the University of Manitoba in 2008 [11, 23]. Various definitions have been provided for the term MOOC by describing the four words in the MOOC acronym. The key elements of MOOCs are depicted in Fig. 2.

- **Massive(ly):** In MOOCs, massiveness reflects the number of course participants. While most of the MOOCs had few hundred participants some courses reached over 150,000 registrations [1, 87]. Massive refers to the capacity of the course to expand to large numbers of learners [3]. The challenge is to find the right balance between large number of participants, content quality, and individual needs of learners [11, 29, 60].
- **Open:** Openness includes four dimensions (4Rs) Reuse, Revise, Remix, and Redistribute [78]. In the context of MOOCs, it refers to providing a learning experience to a vast number of participants around the globe regardless of their location, age, income, ideology, and level of education, without any entry requirements, or course fees to access high quality education. Openness can also refer to providing open educational resources (OER) e.g. course notes, PowerPoint presentations, video lectures, and assessment [3, 94].
- **Online:** the term online refers to the accessibility of these courses form each spot of the world via internet connection to provide synchronous as well as asynchronous interaction between the course participants, [11, 94]. In some variations of MOOCs (e.g. blended MOOCs), learners can learn at least in part face-to-face beside the online interaction possibilities [98].
- **Courses:** The term course is defined in higher education as a unit of teaching. In MOOCs it refers to the academic curriculum to be delivered to the learners, including OER, learning objectives, networking tools, assessments, and learning analytics tools [1, 107].

Fig. 2. Key elements of MOOCs.

The original concept of MOOCs is to offer free and open access courses for massive number of learners. However, scalability issues and low completion rates (less than 10 % in most of the offered MOOCs) constantly concern the MOOC providers [11, 103]. Moreover, several MOOC providers either charge fees for their courses or offer courses for free but learners have to pay for exams, certificates, or teaching assistance from third party partners [11]. Thus, we believe that the original definition of MOOCs will change as a result of the various challenges and rapid developments in this field.

4.1.2 MOOC History

The early MOOC has been driven by Stephen Downes and George Siemens in the CCK08 course [10]. This new form of learning and teaching has led Stanford University to offer three online courses in 2011 [82, 115]. These courses significantly succeeded in attracting a big number of participants, thus turning a qualitative leap in the field of MOOCs. Driven by the success of the Stanford MOOCs Sebastian Thrun and Peter Norvig started to think about MOOC business models and launched Udacity as a profit MOOC model in 2012 [78]. Two other Stanford professors Daphne Koller and Andrew Ng have also started their own company Coursera which partnered with dozens of renowned universities to provide a platform for online courses aiming at offering high quality education to interested learners all over the world [27, 93]. Additionally, Massachusetts Institute of Technology (MIT) and Harvard University launched edX as a non-profit MOOC platform. Figure 3 shows the MOOC and open education timeline [115]. Although these MOOCs platforms have different objectives, they share the focus on building large learning networks beyond the traditional teaching environments.

4.1.3 MOOC Types

The current MOOC literature categorized MOOCs into two main types “cMOOCs” and “xMOOCs” [96]. Moreover, new forms have emerged from xMOOCs. These include “smOOCs” and “bMOOCs” [32, 46]. Figure 4 shows the different types of MOOCs and their underlying learning theories.

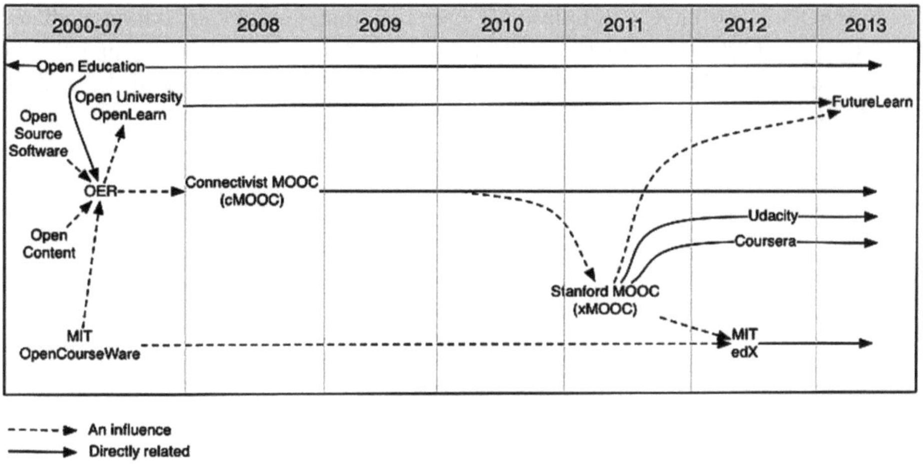

Fig. 3. MOOCs and open education timeline [115].

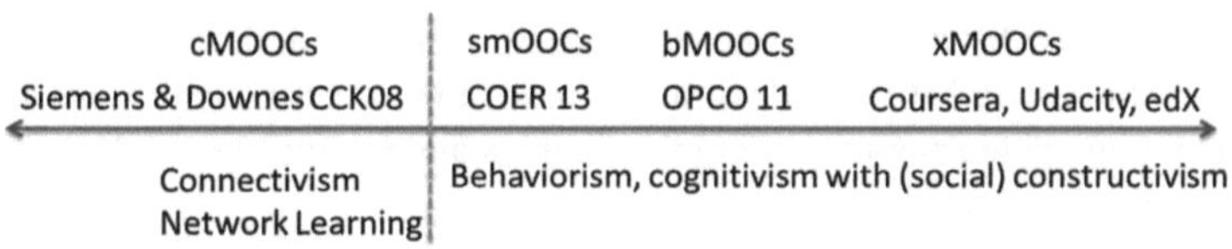

Fig. 4. MOOC types.

The early MOOCs launched by Downes and Siemens (CCK08) were driven by the connectivism theory and were thus referred to as connectivist MOOCs (cMOOCs). cMOOCs provide space for self-organized learning where learners can define their own objectives, present their own view, and collaboratively create and share knowledge. cMOOCs enable learners to build their own networks via blogs, wikis, Google groups, Twitter, Facebook, and other social networking tools outside the learning platform without any restrictions from the teacher [46, 57]. Moreover, peer-assessment was used to grade assignments or tests based on pre-defined rubrics that improve students' understanding of the content. Thus, cMOOCs are distributed and networked learning environments where learners are at the center of the learning process. On the other hand, extension MOOCs (xMOOCs) e.g. Coursera, edX, and Udacity follow the behaviorism, cognitivist, and (social) constructivism learning theories. In fact, in xMOOCs, learning objectives are pre-defined by teachers who impart their knowledge through short video lectures, often followed by simple e-assessment tasks (e.g. quiz, eTest) [23, 47, 57, 98]. Only few xMOOCs have used peer-assessment. Moreover, xMOOCs provide limited communication space between the course participants [38]. Unlike cMOOCs, the communication in xMOOCs happens within the platform itself. Figure 5 depicts the key characteristics of cMOOC vs. xMOOC.

Recently, new forms of MOOCs have emerged. These include smOOCs as small open online courses with a relatively small number of participants (e.g. COER13) and blended MOOCs (bMOOCs) as hybrid MOOCs including in-class and online mediated instruction (e.g. OPCO11) with flexibility ways that learners can interacting in real-time that fit into around their motivation and to build learner commitment to the courses [18, 23, 32, 37].

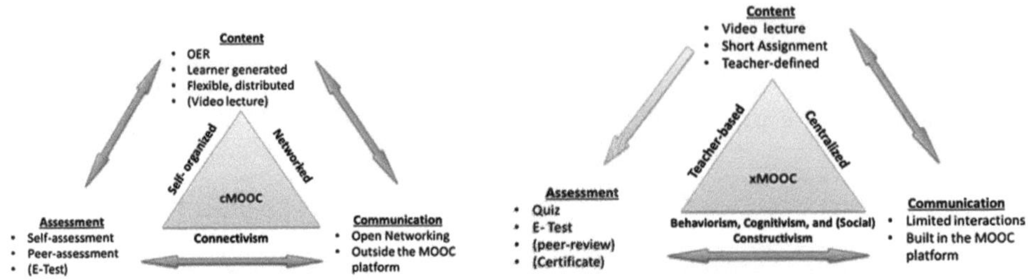

Fig. 5. The key characteristics of cMOOC vs. xMOOC.

4.2 Design

The design aspects of MOOCs are one of the main factors that determine their success. The reviewed studies on MOOCs design distinguish between pedagogical design principles that can engage learners to attend the courses and technological design principles that can make the MOOCs more dynamic.

4.2.1 Pedagogical Design Principles

Most of the teachers and researchers believe that MOOCs cannot completely replace traditional learning [76]. As a consequence, there is an increasing focus on hybrid MOOCs [101]. In order to encourage learners to complete the course, Vihavainen et al. [105] offered bMOOCs with support of scaffolding of learner's tasks using a purpose-built assessment solution and continuous reflection between the learner and the advisor. In other studies, the integration of social networks in bMOOCs added new value in learner's interactions and activities [14, 74].

McCallum et al. [72] designed alphaMOOCs (aMOOCs) as a mix of cMOOCs and xMOOCs by building collaboration teams. Following this design approach, teams were able to receive psychological and emotional support from each other. McAndrew [71] designed a project-based MOOC (pMOOC) by structuring the offered MOOC around a course-related project. Guàrdia et al. [42] analyzed the learners needs in a MOOC and presented a set of pedagogical design principles that focus on improving the interactions among learners. Bruff et al. [12] discussed some pedagogical design ideas that provide guidance on how to design bMOOCs. The authors focused on competency-based design, self-paced learning, pre-definition of learning plans (objectives, schedules, and assignments), as well as open network interaction and collaboration tools that rise motivation and avoid losing interest and drop out from the course. And, Grünewald et al. [41] suggested peer-assistance through the course to solve learning difficulties. Furthermore, Lim et al. [61] stressed that peer discussion groups and scaffolding can support online collaborative learning in MOOCs.

4.2.2 Technological Design Principles

MOOCs are not only providing the opportunity to easily access learning resources but also include several technology features that support different important activities in the learning experience such as interaction, collaboration, self-reflection and evaluation system [25, 35]. The tools used in the reviewed literature can be classified into three main categories, namely collaboration, assessment, and analytics tools.

Most of the MOOCs provide collaboration work spaces that include several tools to support learners in communicating with each other such as forums, blogs, video podcasts, social networks, and dashboards [24, 67, 71]. Different e-assessment methods are applied in MOOCs. While most of xMOOCs use traditional forms of e-assessment like eTests and Quizzes, cMOOCs rather focus on self-assessment and peer-assessment [51, 97]. In MOOCs it is difficult to provide personal feedback to a massive number of learners. Thus, several MOOC studies tried to apply learning analytics tools to monitor the learning process, identify difficulties, discover learning patterns, provide feedback, and support learners in reflecting on their own learning experience [34, 39].

4.3 Learning Theories

How learners learn through MOOCs? In other words, how they absorb, process, build, and construct knowledge? This is a simple question, but the answer is quite complicated. Behaviorists and cognitivists believe that learning experience is a result of the human action with the learning environment [53]. Constructivists, by contrast, believe that learning is an active process of creating meaning from different experiences and that, learners learn better by doing [2]. In the last years, technology has changed the way we learn as well as we teach [28, 106]. And, the social Web has provided new ways how we network and learn outside the classroom. These opportunities are reflected in recent learning theories and models. These include connectivism which views learning as a network-forming process [55, 70, 95, 104] and the Learning as a Network (LaaN) theory which starts from the learner and views learning as a continuous creation of a personal knowledge network (PKN) [16].

Back to the main question how learners learn through MOOCs? As discussed in Sect. 4.1.3, MOOCs are running in two major categories: cMOOCs and xMOOCs. CCK08 was the first MOOC designed based on the principals of connectivism [55]. The aim of CCK08 – and other cMOOCs – is to build and construct knowledge through the interaction in learner networks [6, 54]. This course was unique for several reasons, it was open for everyone, learning happens within large network of 170 blogs, content was created by learners themselves, and different tools including Facebook groups, Wiki pages, and discussion forums were used to motivate learners to be active in the course [13, 15]. Rodriguez [84] pointed out that some cMOOCs indeed succeeded to improve the learner's motivation. On the other hand, xMOOCs were based on the behaviorism and cognitivism theories with some (social) constructivism components that focus on learning by doing (i.e. experimental, project-based, or task-based) activities. This wave of MOOCs is similar to the traditional instructor-led courses offered at universities that are organized around video lectures, and e-assessment. Most of the researchers in the reviewed literature put a heavier focus on xMOOCs as a new model of learning and teaching in higher education [73, 83]. Few researchers stressed the importance of social components in xMOOCs. Blom et al. [9] reported that xMOOCs become more social using collaboration tools e.g. forums and wikis. Purser et al. [81] suggested that the idea of peer-to-peer in collaborative learning helps learners to improve their learning outcome in xMOOCs.

In general, cMOOCs reflect the new learning environments characterized by flexibility and openness. On the other hand, xMOOCs offer high quality content as compared to cMOOCs. To fill this gap, bMOOCs as hybrid MOOCs environment that aims at bringing in-class (i.e. face-to-face) interactions and online learning components (i.e. cMOOCs and xMOOCs) together as a blended environment may resolve some of the hurdles facing stand-alone MOOCs.

The MOOC providers have already piloted the bMOOCs concept within a higher education context. In particular, San José State University (SJSU) has partnered with edX in fall 2012 to provide a "Circuits and Electronics" course as a part of the bMOOC pilot experiment. The 87 SJSU's on-campus students watched the MOOC video lectures on their own. Then they practiced problems as homework. Afterwards, the students met the faculty professor during the class time to discuss the emerged issues. Meanwhile, they took part in small group activities, worked in team projects and did quizzes to monitor their progress. This bMOOC achieved promising results, with 90 % of students who passed the final exam, as compared to 55 % in the traditional class. Even though the overall feedback showed positive results, there were some open issues, such as the lack of interaction between students and the video content [46].

4.4 Case Studies

Several case studies of MOOCs have been discussed in the reviewed literature. In Table 2, we compare different case studies in terms of learning theories, design elements, structure, tools, and assessment [68]. We selected six case studies that are representatives for different MOOC types. To represent cMOOCs we selected CCK08 [7, 30, 66, 84]. From xMOOCs we selected edX as non-profit platform and Coursera as profit platform [21, 48, 65, 80, 84, 100]. In addition, we selected OPCO11 as an example of bMOOCs and COER13 and MobiMOOC as examples of smOOCs [4, 26, 56, 85].

These different MOOCs share some common features. These include the focus on video-based lectures, the support of open registration and informal learning, and the use of social tools (e.g. blogs, forums, social networks). Most of the MOOCs apply traditional e-assessment tools (e.g. E-Tests, Quizzes, MCQ). Peer-assessment is mainly used in cMOOCs and bMOOCs and self-assessment rather in smOOCs. The majority of the reviewed case studies implement the behaviorism, cognitivism, and constructivism learning theories. Only few case studies (e.g. CCK08 and MobiMOOC) include elements that are borrowed from connectivism, such as personal learning environments and open networking.

4.5 Business Models

The initial vision of MOOCs was to provide open online courses that could reduce the cost of university-level education and reach thousands of low-income learners

[22, 102]. Nevertheless, new business models have been launched e.g. in Coursera, Udacity, and Udemy. These business models are heralding a change in the education landscape that poses a threat to the quality of learning outcome and future educational pathways [8, 93, 116]. While a wide range of studies in our review discuss the MOOC concept and design issues, only few studies have considered the role of business models in higher education [36, 43]. Due to the huge budget that has been spent to develop MOOC platforms, MOOC providers are fighting to come up with new business models to satisfy their investors. Most of the MOOCs suffer from low completion rates. This is mainly due to the fact that course participants in general do not get credits for the courses they have attended [33].

Ruth [88] reported his overview of potential business models such as offering courses for free and learners pay for certification, examination, and teaching assistance. Coursera, for instance, offers additional examinations for certificates. The question here is whether these certificates will be accepted. Green [40] believes that if the universities provide MOOC credits, this will be a potential route to accept these certificates in the real market. To achieve this, MOOCs should meet the market needs by providing high quality content as well as high quality outcome [38, 58].

Table 2. Comparison of MOOCs case studies.

Compare Item		CCK08	edX	Coursera	OPCO11	COER13	MobiMOOC
Learning theory	Connectivism	√	-	-	-	-	(√)
	Behaviorism	-	√	√	-	-	-
	Cognitivist	-	√	√	-	-	(√)
	Social constructivism	-	-	-	√	√	-
Assessment	E-Assessment	(√)	√	√	√	√	√
	Peer-Assessment	√	-	(√)	(√)	-	-
	Self-Assessment	-	-	-	-	(√)	(√)
Openness	Profit	-	-	√	-	-	-
	Open registration	√	√	√	√	√	√
	Download Material	-	√	(√)	(√)	(√)	√
Form	Formal Learning	(√)	-	(√)	(√)	-	-
	Informal Learning	√	√	√	√	√	√
Learning Tools	Video Lecture	√	√	√	√	√	√
	Face-to-Face	-	-	-	√	-	-
	Blogs, forums, social network	√	√	√	√	√	√
	Lecture Note, PPT and PDF	√	√	√	√	√	√

√ Completely (√) Partly - Not supported

4.6 Target Groups

Some demographics studies have been conducted to analyze target groups in MOOCs by determining their locations, age group, and learner patterns. One major goal of MOOCs was to reach low-income learners particularly in developing countries. Studies, however, have shown that the vast majority of MOOC participants were from North America and Europe. Only few participate from South East Asia and fewer from Asia and Africa [17, 19, 63, 99]. This is consistent with the analysis of 2.9 million participants registered in Coursera from 220 countries around the globe [109]. Possible obstacles that could prevent learners from Africa and Asia to take part in MOOCs include the poor technology infrastructure. Only 25 % of Africa has electricity access [110]. And Africa has the lowest internet access all over the world with only 7 % [91]. Asia is a continent with many different cultures and languages. Thus, linguistic issues could be a barrier to participate in MOOCs.

Stine [99] and de Waard et al. [25] noted that around 50 % of the participants from 31–50 age groups, which indicates that informal learners have more interest in MOOCs. Several studies have reported a high drop-out rate that reflects the learner patterns in MOOCs [92, 108]. Hill [45] identified five patterns of participants in Coursera, as shown in Fig. 6.

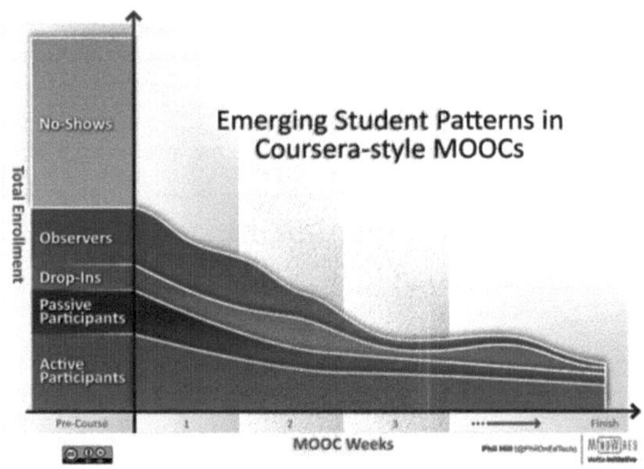

Fig. 6. Pattern of participants in Coursera [45].

The vast majority were No-Shows participants who register but never log into the course. Secondly, observers who read content or discussions without submitting any assignments. Thirdly, Drop-ins participants who are doing some activities but do not complete the course. Fourthly, Passive participants who take the course and do tests but do not participate in the discussion. Fifthly, Active participants who regularly do all assignments and actively take part in the discussions. Some studies explored pedagogical approaches to engage Observers, Drop-ins, and Passive participants to be active learners through e.g. game-based learning [85], social networking that help learners to create their own personal learning environments [42], and project-based learning [49, 71]. Moreover, Rosé et al. [86] explored student dropout behavior in MOOCs and suggested the integration of social tools into MOOCs to engage students in an interactive learning environment.

4.7 Assessment

The ability to evaluate vast number of learners in MOOCs is really a big challenge [111]. Thus, assessment is an important factor for the future success of MOOC-based online education. Currently, MOOCs are only providing a non-credit certificate e.g. completion, attendance, or participation certificate. In the reviewed literature, three main types of assessment were conducted in MOOCs, namely e-assessment, peer-assessment, and self-assessment.

4.7.1 E-Assessment

E-assessment is often used in xMOOCs to gauge student performance. E-assessment in xMOOCs is restricted to closed question formats. These include exams with multiple choice questions and electronic essay assessment based on machine grading [20]. This implementation of assessment is applicable in Science courses. It is, however difficult to apply e-assessment in Humanities courses due the nature of these courses which are based on the creativity and imagination of the learners [90].

4.7.2 Peer-assessment

Peer-assessment was used in cMOOCs and xMOOCs to review essays, projects, and team assignments. These assignments are not graded automatically, but learners themselves can evaluate and provide feedback on each other's work. This method of assessment is suitable in Humanities, Social Sciences and Business studies, which do not have clear right or wrong answers [75]. Cooper and Sahami [21] point out that, some learners in peer-assessment grade without reading the work to be reviewed or do not follow a clear grading scheme, which negatively impacts the quality of the given feedback. Therefore, more criteria and indicators are needed to ensure that peer-assessment is effective.

4.7.3 Self-assessment

Self-assessment is still not widely used in MOOCs. Sandeen [90] and Piech et al. [79] identified some self-assessment techniques. These include model answer as tool to students to cross check if the marks they scored are in tune with the model answers set by the educators, and learning analytics where the learners can self-reflect on their achievements.

5 Challenges and Future Visions

Regardless of the several debates, both for and against MOOC, the fact is that MOOCs have succeeded in attracting thousands of participants worldwide per course. Despite their increasing popularity, MOOCs further require key stakeholders to address a number of challenges. In the following sections, we address critical challenges and outline possible future visions in MOOC research.

5.1 Challenges

In this section, we concentrate on the major challenges from pedagogical and technological perspectives that should be considered in the development of MOOC environments.

5.1.1 Lack of Human Interaction

The first challenge is lack of human interaction. That means participants are effectively cut off from face-to-face interaction during the learning process in MOOCs. Thus, there is a need for solutions to foster interaction and communication between MOOC participants. Social networks and other communication tools should be an integral part of MOOC environments to increase the interaction among learners and keep in contact with their course mates and the teaching staff [33, 46, 59].

5.1.2 Identity Verification and Authentication

Identity verification of MOOCs participants is a crucial challenge in order to authenticate the learners' certificates. Moreover, many learners enrolling in MOOCs are looking for certification to promote their career or complete post graduate studies [44]. Most MOOC providers issue certificates of completion to the course participants. These certificates, however, are not recognized by educational institutions and companies.

Coursera addresses this challenge by providing an identity verification method called "Signature Track" that uses two biometric identity techniques, namely face photos and typing patterns. In this method, the enrollment process requires participants to submit a web cam photo to be checked with the photo from the participant's official ID such as a passport or a driving license. Additionally, the method requires that the participant establish a typing pattern profile by typing a short paragraph that can be used throughout the course to verify that the person submitting the assignment is indeed the participant who enrolled in Signature Track [64].

5.1.3 Plagiarism and Copyright Concerns

Copyright is an important factor for the future success of online education, especially MOOCs [46, 69]. The main challenge is how to validate original work and how to prevent plagiarism? Coursera reported dozens of incidents of plagiarism especially in humanities courses. The technical solution can be a plagiarism-detection software, which is however expensive and time-consuming [46]. Peer reviews can also be an option to solve this problem. In this case, clear criteria and rubrics are needed to ensure that peer review is effective.

5.1.4 Personalized and Adaptive Learning

Due to the massive number of MOOC participants and their diverse learning styles, the possibility of creating adaptive and personalize learning experiences is required [46]. The challenge is how to support self-organized leaning in networked learning environments? How to provide a wide range of educational material to meet the different needs of the MOOC participants?

5.1.5 Completion Rate

MOOCs are facing high drop-out rates in average of 95 % of course participants [28, 45]. One of the potential reasons for that is the complexity and diversity of MOOC participants' perspectives. This requires an understanding of the different patterns of MOOCs participants and their perspectives when participating in MOOCs. Hew and Cheung [44], for instance, reported four reasons why learners sign up for MOOCs: (a) interest in new technology, (b) extend current knowledge, (c) collect completion certificates as many as possible, and (d) learning as a personal challenge. The high drop-out rate can also be explained by the lack of motivation and the failure to follow the course activities. The issue of high drop-out rates could be addressed by targeting specific audiences that are fully interested in the course. This may reduce the number of participants, but can ensure that they are active in the course [28, 92].

5.1.6 Hybrid Education

So far MOOC providers didn't offer official academic accreditation from their home institutions, which might indicate that the quality of learning outcome in MOOCs is different from university courses [38, 90]. On the way to address this gap, the new design paradigm of bMOOCs that aims at bringing in-class (i.e. face-to-face) interactions and online learning components together as a hybrid environment may resolve some of the hurdles facing stand-alone MOOCs [46]. There are currently only few implementations of bMOOCs. Thus, there is a need to conduct more studies around bMOOCs to investigate the impact of blended instruction on learners' performance.

5.1.7 Language Proficiency and Cultural Background

The participants in MOOCs come from all over the world. They speak English in different levels and have different cultural believes. Thus, the examples used in MOOCs should be given in such a way that they can be understood by everyone regardless of the cultural background. Moreover, MOOC providers should consider the diversity in cultural values such as symbols food, animals, and everyday objects [50, 113]. In addition, the level of language proficiency can be a source of misunderstanding the video lectures. MOOC providers, thus, need to have knowledge on how to teach non-native speakers [46, 113].

5.1.8 Learning Analytics

In MOOCs it is difficult to provide personal feedback to a massive number of learners. Several MOOC studies recommended to apply learning analytics tools to provide feedback, monitor the learning process, identify difficulties, discover learning patterns, and support learners in reflecting on their own learning experience [113]. Thereby, issues related data privacy, ownership, sharing, and access need to be resolved [34].

5.1.9 Quality

Quality assurance is a core issue in TEL for providers' as well as participants' communities. Different literature reviews provide a wide range of standards addressing the design of effective TEL environments. These standards include methods for content design, page layout, visual arrangements, use of illustrations, and colors. Nevertheless, not all of them can be used to design a successful MOOC. Hence, the quality of a MOOC design needs to be explicitly and clearly defined. This is the case because MOOC environments have specific requirements which include scalability, openness, and one needs to take into account their processes, products, and services [113].

5.1.10 Libraries Issues

There is a mutual relationship between educational institutions and university libraries. Learning without library resources and services is difficult, if not impossible, and on the other hand, libraries are meaningless if they cannot provide services for the learners. Where and how do these library services fit into the context of MOOCs is a challenge at hand. Higher education institutions are providing MOOCs to thousands of potential learners at a time all over the globe. Does it mean that the libraries should provide these students with their services as well? Moreover, MOOCs raise significant question about legal and policy issues in terms of licensing resources. One can argue that MOOC participants are not officially enrolled in the university, and by this they do not have the rights to access these licensed resources. At the moment, there is no clear answer, or consensus about the position and role of licensed libraries in MOOCs [47].

5.1.11 Costs of MOOCs

If educational institutions and universities decide to use MOOCs for teaching, they will incur additional costs to their budgets. The major cost in MOOC production is not just the nature of the delivery platform. One has to consider about the number of participants in MOOCs, the university administrators, and the teaching assistance offered for supporting the learning activities. Furthermore, the quality of the video lecture is very important for learners' satisfaction and the participants should receive good technical support from the institution. Last but not least, one has to take into account the necessity for implementing special features such as learning analytics, recommendation systems, social tools, virtual labs, and gamification [36, 46].

5.2 Future Visions

Our future vision on MOOCs will have resolute impact on improving teaching with MOOCs and encourage institutions to strive in developing learners' skills for self-organized and network learning. In this section, we convey research opportunities in relation to the dimensions discussed in Sect. 4:

- **Concept:** More theoretical work is needed to achieve a common understanding of the MOOC concept as well as a systematic mapping between the course goals and the MOOC type to be implemented.
- **Design:** it is necessary to conduct research on how to improve the MOOC environments by investigating new learning models (e.g. personalized learning, project-based learning, game-based learning, inquiry-based learning) and tools (e.g. learning analytics).

- **Learning Theories:** It is crucial that future MOOC implementations are backed by a solid theoretical background. A heavier focus should be put on cMOOCs as well as bMOOCs which have the potential to support different learning models beyond formal institutional learning. These include informal learning, personalized learning, professional learning, and lifelong learning.
- **Case Studies:** The field of MOOCs is emerging and it is needed to conduct and share more experimental studies with different MOOC formats and variations.
- **Business Models:** We need to identify new ways to think about business models that preserve the quality of the learning experience supported by MOOCs.
- **Target Groups:** We need to investigate new methods to increase the motivation of observers, drop-ins and passive learners in MOOCs through e.g. learning analytics.
- **Assessment:** it is necessary to go beyond traditional e-assessment methods and apply open assessment methods that fit better to the MOOC environments characterized by openness, networking, and self-organization.

6 Conclusions

The changes in pedagogy in combination with new technologies can be a powerful environment for learning and contribute to change society. MOOCs present an emerging branch of online learning that is gaining interest in the Technology-Enhanced Learning (TEL) community. In the last few years after the launch of the first MOOC in 2008, a considerable number of academic researchers have been conducted to explore the potential of MOOCs to improve the effectiveness of the learning experience. The main aim of this paper was to compile and analyze the state of MOOC research that has been conducted from 2008–2014 to build a deep understanding on what are the educational benefits and effectiveness that MOOCs have on teaching and learning. 93 peer reviewed papers were selected in this study. A template analysis was applied to analyze and categorize the MOOCs literature into 7 dimensions, namely concept, design, learning theories, case studies, business models, target groups, and assessment.

The main findings of our study is that the initial vision of MOOCs as a new learning environment that aims at breaking down obstacles to learning for anyone, anywhere and at any time around the globe is far away from the reality. In fact, most MOOC implementations so far still follow a top-down, controlled, teacher-centered, and centralized learning model. Attempts to implement bottom-up, student-centered, really open, and distributed forms of MOOCs are rather the exception rather than the rule. In general, MOOCs further require key stakeholders to address a number of challenges, including questions about hybrid education, role of the learning analytics, plagiarism, certification, completion rates, and innovation beyond traditional learning models. These challenges will need to be addressed as the understanding of the technical and pedagogical issues surrounding MOOCs evolves. Furthermore, we proposed future visions in relation to the seven analysis dimensions.

This paper is original because firstly it provides a comprehensive review of the development of MOOCs which have been lacking until now and secondly it examines the context within which further work can take place by compiling key challenges and opportunities that lie ahead in this emerging research area.

References

1. Allen, I.E., Seaman, J.: Changing course: ten years of tracking online education in the United States. Babson Survey Research Group and Quahog Research Group, LLC, annual report (2013)
2. Anderson, T., Dron, J.: Three generations of distance education pedagogy. Int. Rev. Res. Open Distance Learn. **12**(3), 80–97 (2011)
3. Anderson, T., McGreal, R.: Disruptive pedagogies and technologies in universities. Educ. Technol. Soc. **15**(4), 380–389 (2012)
4. Arnold, P.: Open educational resources: The way to go, or "Mission Impossible" in (German) higher education? In: Stillman, L., Denision, T., Sabiescu, A., Memarovic, N., (eds.) CIRN 2012 Community Informatics Conference (2012)
5. Beaven, T., Hauck, M., Comas-Quinn, A., Lewis, T., de los Arcos, B.: MOOCs: striking the right balance between facilitation and self-determination. MERLOT J. Online Learn. Teach. **10**(1), 31–43 (2014)
6. Bell, F.: Connectivism: its place in theory informed research and innovation in technology enabled learning. Int. Rev. Res. Open Distance Learn. **12**(3), 98–118 (2011)
7. Bell, F.: Network theories for technology-enabled learning and social change: connectivism and actor network theory. In: Proceedings of the Seventh International Conference on Networked Learning, pp. 526–533 (2010)
8. Bernhard, W., Bittel, N., Van Der Vlies, S., Bettoni, M., Roth, N.: The MOOCs business model. Procedia-Soc. Behav. Sci. **106**, 2931–2937 (2013)
9. Blom, J., Verma, H., Li, N., Skevi, A., Dillenbourg, P.: MOOCs are more social than you believe. eLearning Papers, issue 33 (2013). ISSN 1887-1542
10. Boven, D.T.: The next game changer: the historical antecedents of the MOOC movement in education. eLearning Papers, issue 33 (2013). ISSN 1887-1542
11. Brown, S.: Back to the future with MOOCs? In: ICICTE 2013 Proceedings, pp. 237–246 (2013)
12. Bruff, D.O., Fisher, D.H., McEwen, K.E., Smith, B.E.: Wrapping a MOOC: student perceptions of an experiment in blended learning. J. Online Learn. Teach. **9**(2), 187–199 (2013)
13. Cabiria, J.: Connectivist learning environments: massive open online courses. In: The 2012 World Congress in Computer Science Computer Engineering and Applied Computing, Las Vagas (2012)
14. Calter, M.: MOOCs and the library: engaging with evolving pedagogy. In: IFLA World Library and Information Congress (IFLA WLIC 2013), Singapore (2013)
15. Chamberlin, L., Parish, T.: MOOCs: Massive Open Online Courses or Massive and Often Obtuse Courses? eLearn **2011**(8), 1 (2011)
16. Chatti, M.A.: Personalization in technology enhanced learning: a social software perspective. PhD dissertation, Shaker Verlag, RWTH Aachen University (2010)
17. Clow, D.: MOOCs and the funnel of participation. In: LAK 2013, pp. 185–189, Leuven, Belgium (2013)
18. Coates, K.: The re-invention of the academy: how technologically mediated learning will – and will not – transform advanced education. In: Cheung, S.K.S., Fong, J., Fong, W., Wang, F.L., Kwok, L.F. (eds.) ICHL 2013. LNCS, vol. 8038, pp. 1–9. Springer, Heidelberg (2013)
19. Coffrin, C., Corrin, L., de Barba, P., Kennedy, G.: Visualizing patterns of student engagement and performance in MOOCs. In: Proceedings of the Fourth International Conference on Learning Analytics and Knowledge, pp. 83–92. ACM (2014)

20. Conrad, D.: Assessment challenges in open learning: way-finding, fork in the road, or end of the line? Open Prax. **5**(1), 41–47 (2013)
21. Cooper, S., Sahami, M.: Reflections on stanford's MOOCs: new possibilities in online education create new challenges. Comm. ACM **56**(2), 28–30 (2013)
22. Cusumano, M.A.: Technology strategy and management: Are the costs of 'free' too high in online education? Comm. ACM **56**(4), 26–29 (2013)
23. Daniel, J.: Making sense of MOOCs: musings in a maze of myth, paradox and possibility. J. Interact. Med. Educ. (2012)
24. Dasarathy, B., Sullivan, K., Schmidt, D.C., Fisher, D.H., Porter, A.: The past, present, and future of MOOCs and their relevance to software engineering. In: Proceedings of the on Future of Software Engineering, pp. 212–224. ACM (2014)
25. de Waard, I., Abajian, S., Gallagher, M.S., Hogue, R., Keskin, N., Koutropoulos, A., Rodriguez, O.C.: Using mLearning and MOOCs to understand chaos, emergence, and complexity in education. Int. Rev. Res. Open Distance Learn. **12**(7), 94–115 (2011)
26. de Waard, I., Koutropoulos, A., Keskin, N.Ö., Abajian, S.C., Hogue, R., Rodriguez, C.O., Gallagher, M.S.: Exploring the MOOC format as a pedagogical approach for mLearning. In: 10th World Conference on Mobile and Contextual Learning (mLearn2011), Beijing, China (2011a)
27. Dikeogu, G.C., Clark, C.: Are you MOOC-ing yet? A review for academic libraries. Coll. Univ. Libr. Sect. Proc. (CULS) **3**, 9–13 (2013)
28. El-Hmoudova, D.: MOOCs motivation and communication in the cyber learning environment. Procedia-Soc. Behav. Sci. **131**, 29–34 (2014)
29. Esposito, A.: Research ethics in emerging forms of online learning: issues arising from a hypothetical study on a MOOC. Electron. J. e-Learn. **10**(3), 315–325 (2012)
30. Fini, A.: The technological dimension of a massive open online course: the case of the CCK08 course tools. Int. Rev. Res. Open Distance Learn. **10**(5) (2009)
31. Fink, A.: Conducting research literature reviews: from the internet to paper, 2nd edn. Sage Publications, Thousand Oaks (2005)
32. Firmin, R., Schiorring, E., Whitmer, J., Willett, T., Collins, E.D., Sujitparapitaya, S.: Case study: using MOOCs for conventional college coursework. Distance Education, (ahead-of-print), pp. 1-24 (2014)
33. Fischer, G.: Beyond hype and underestimation: identifying research challenges for the future of MOOCs. Distance Educ. **35**(2), 149–158 (2014)
34. Fournier, H., Kop, R., Durand, G.: Challenges to research in MOOCs. J. Online Learn. Teach. **10**(1) (2014)
35. Fournier, H., Kop, R., Sitlia, H.: The value of learning analytics to networked learning on a personal learning environment. In: LAK 2011 Proceedings of the 1st International Conference on Learning Analytics and Knowledge, pp. 104–109 (2011)
36. Freeman, M., Hancock, P.: Milking MOOCs: towards the right blend in accounting education. In: The Virtual University: Impact on Australian Accounting and Business Education, part B, pp. 86–100 (2013)
37. Gaebel, M.: MOOCs Massive Open Online Courses. EUA Occasional papers (2013). http://www.eua.be/Home.aspx
38. Gallagher, S., LaBrie, J.: Online learning 2.0: strategies for a mature market. Continuing High. Educ. Rev. **76**, 65–73 (2012)
39. Giannakos, M.N., Chorianopoulos, K., Ronchetti, M., Szegedi, P., Teasley, S.D.: Analytics on video-based learning. In: LAK 2013, pp. 283–284, Leuven, Belgium (2013)
40. Green, K.: Mission, MOOCs and money. AGB Trusteeship Mag. **21**(1), 9–15 (2013)

41. Grünewald, F., Meinel, C., Totschnig, M., Willems, C.: Designing MOOCs for the support of multiple learning styles. In: Hernández-Leo, D., Ley, T., Klamma, R., Harrer, A. (eds.) EC-TEL 2013. LNCS, vol. 8095, pp. 371–382. Springer, Heidelberg (2013)
42. Guàrdia, L., Maina, M., Sangrà, A.: MOOC design principles. A pedagogical approach from the learner's perspective. eLearning Papers, issue 33 (2013). ISSN 1887-1542
43. Guthrie, J., Burritt, R., Evans, E.: Challenges for accounting and business education: blending online and traditional universities in a MOOC environment. In: The Virtual University: Impact on Australian Accounting and Business Education, Part One, pp. 9–22 (2013)
44. Hew, K.F., Cheung, W.S.: Students' and instructors' use of massive open online courses (MOOCs): motivations and challenges. Educ. Res. Rev. (2014)
45. Hill, P.: Some validation of MOOC student patterns graphic (2013). http://mfeldstein.com/validation-mooc-studentpatterns-graphic/
46. Hollands, F.M. Tirthali, D.: MOOCs: expectations and reality. Center for Benefit-Cost Studies of Education Teachers College, Columbia University (2014)
47. Hoy, M.B.: MOOCs 101: an introduction to massive open online courses. Med. Ref. Serv. Q. **33**(1), 85–91 (2014)
48. Alario-Hoyos, C., Pérez-Sanagustín, M., Delgado-Kloos, C., Parada G., H.A., Muñoz-Organero, M., Rodríguez-de-las-Heras, A.: Analysing the impact of built-in and external social tools in a MOOC on educational technologies. In: Hernández-Leo, D., Ley, T., Klamma, R., Harrer, A. (eds.) EC-TEL 2013. LNCS, vol. 8095, pp. 5–18. Springer, Heidelberg (2013)
49. Irvine, V., Code, J., Richards, L.: Realigning higher education for the 21st-century learner through multi-access learning. J. Online Learn. Teach. **9**(2), 172–186 (2013)
50. Jona, K., Naidu, S.: MOOCs: emerging research. Distance Educ. **35**(2), 141–144 (2014)
51. Kellogg, S.: How to make a MOOC. Nature (Int. Wkly J. Sci.) **499**, 369–371 (2013)
52. King, N.: Using templates in the thematic analysis of text. In: Cassell, C., Symon, G. (eds.) Essential Guide to Qualitative Methods in Organizational Research, pp. 256–270. Sage Publications, London (2004)
53. Kop, R., Hill, A.: Connectivism: learning theory of the future or vestige of the past? Int. Rev. Res. Open Distance Learn. **9**(3) (2008)
54. Kop, R., Fournier, H., Mak, J.S.F.: A pedagogy of abundance or a pedagogy to support human beings? Participant support on massive open online courses. Int. Rev. Res. Open Distance Learn. Spec. Issue Emergent Learn. Connections Des. Learn. **12**(7), 74–93 (2011)
55. Kop, R.: The challenges to connectivist learning on open online networks: Learning experiences during a massive open online course. Int. Rev. Res. Open Distance Learn. Spec. Issue-Connectivism. Des. Deliv. Soc. Networked Learn. **12**(3), 19–38 (2011)
56. Koutropoulos, A., Gallagher, M.S., Abajian, S.C., de Waard, I., Hogue, R.J., Keskin, N.Ö., Rodriguez, C.O.: Emotive vocabulary in MOOCs: context and participant retention. Eur. J. Open Distance E-Learn. (2012)
57. Kruiderink, N.: Open buffet of higher education. In: Trend Report: Open Educational Resources 2013, pp. 54–58 (2013)
58. Lambert, S., Carter, A.: Business models for the virtual University. In: The Virtual University: Impact on Australian Accounting and Business Education, Part B, pp. 77–85 (2013)
59. Lane, A., Caird, S., Weller, M.: The potential social, economic and environmental benefits of MOOCs: operational and historical comparisons with a massive 'closed online' course. Open Prax. **6**(2), 115–123 (2014)

60. Laws, R.D., Howell, S.L., Lindsay, N.K.: Scalability in distance education: can we have our cake and eat it too? Online J. Distance Learn. Adm. **6**(4) (2003)
61. Lim, S., Coetzee, D., Hartmann, B., Fox, A., Hearst, M.A.: Initial experiences with small group discussions in MOOCs. In: Proceedings of the first ACM Conference on Learning@ Scale Conference, pp. 151–152. ACM (2014)
62. Liyanagunawardena, T.R., Adams, A.A., Williams, S.A.: MOOCs: a systematic study of the published literature 2008–2012. Int. Rev. Res. Open Distance Learn. **14**(3), 202–227 (2013)
63. Liyanagunawardena, T.R., Williams, S., Adams, A.: The impact and reach of MOOCs: a developing countries' perspective. eLearning Papers, issue 33 (2013a). ISSN 1887-1542
64. Maas, A., Heather, C., Do, C.T., Brandman, R., Koller, D., Ng, A.: Offering verified credentials in massive open online courses: MOOCs and technology to advance learning and learning research (Ubiquity symposium). Ubiquity (2014)
65. Machun, P.A., Trau, C., Zaid, N., Wang, M., Ng, J.W.: MOOCs: is there an app for that?: expanding Mobilegogy through an analysis of MOOCs and iTunes University. In: International Conferences on Web Intelligence and Intelligent Agent Technology, IEEE/WIC/ACM, pp. 321–325 (2012)
66. Mackness, J., Mak, S.F.J., Roy Williams, R.: The ideals and reality of participating in a MOOC. In: 7th International Conference on Networked Learning 2010 Proceedings, pp. 266–274 (2010)
67. Mak, S.F.J., Williams, R., Mackness, J.: Blogs and forums as communication and learning tools in a MOOC. In: Dirckinck–Holmfeld, L., Hodgson, V., Jones, C., de Laat, M., McConnell, D., Ryberg, T. (eds.) Proceedings of the Seventh International Conference on Networked Learning 2010, pp. 275–284 (2010)
68. Malan, D.J.: Implementing a massive open online course (MOOC). J. Comput. Sci. Coll. **28**(6), 136–137 (2013)
69. Marshall, S.: Exploring the ethical implications of MOOCs. Distance Education (ahead-of-print), pp. 1–13 (2014)
70. Martin, F.: Will massive open online courses change how we teach?: sharing recent experiences with an online course. Comm. ACM **55**(8), 26–28 (2013)
71. McAndrew, P.: Learning from open design: running a learning design MOOC. eLearning Papers, issue 33 (2013). ISSN 1887-1542
72. McCallum, C.M., Thomas, S., Libarkin, J.: The AlphaMOOC: building a massive open online course one graduate student at a time. eLearning Papers, issue 33 (2013). ISSN 1887-1542
73. Milligan, C., Littlejohn, A., Margaryan, A.: Patterns of engagement in connectivist MOOCs. J. Online Learn. Teach. **9**(2), 149–159 (2013)
74. Morris, L.V.: MOOCs, emerging technologies, and quality. Innovative High. Educ. **38**, 251–252 (2013)
75. O'Toole, R.: Pedagogical strategies and technologies for peer assessment in massively open online courses (MOOCs). Discussion Paper. University of Warwick, Coventry, UK: University of Warwick, (2013). http://wrap.warwick.ac.uk/54602/
76. Ovaska, S.: User experience and learning experience in online HCI courses. In: Kotzé, P., Marsden, G., Lindgaard, G., Wesson, J., Winckler, M. (eds.) INTERACT 2013, Part IV. LNCS, vol. 8120, pp. 447–454. Springer, Heidelberg (2013)
77. Pardos, Z.A., Schneider, E.: First annual workshop on massive open online courses. In: Lane, H.C., Yacef, K., Mostow, J., Pavlik, P. (eds.) AIED 2013. LNCS, vol. 7926, p. 950. Springer, Heidelberg (2013)

78. Peter, S., Deimann, M.: On the role of openness in education: a historical reconstruction. Open Prax. **5**(1), 7–14 (2013)
79. Piech, C., Huang, J., Chen, Z., Do, C., Ng, A., Koller, D.: Stanford University (2013). http://www.stanford.edu/~cpiech/bio/papers/tuningPeerGrading.pdf
80. Portmess, L.: Mobile knowledge, karma points and digital Peers: the tacit epistemology and linguistic representation of MOOCs. Canadian J. Learn. Technol. **39**(2) (2013)
81. Purser, E., Towndrow, A., Aranguiz, A.: Realising the potential of peer-to-peer learning: taming a MOOC with social media. eLearning Papers, issue 33 (2013). ISSN 1887-1542
82. Rhoads, R.A., Berdan, J., Lindsey, B.T.: The open courseware movement in higher education: unmasking power and raising questions about the movement's democratic potential. Educ. Theory **63**(1), 87–110 (2013)
83. Rodriguez, C.O.: MOOCs and the AI-Stanford like courses: two successful and distinct course formats for massive open online courses. Eur. J. Open Distance E-Learn. (2012)
84. Rodriguez, O.: The concept of openness behind c and x-MOOCs (Massive Open Online Courses). Open Prax. Spec. Theme Openness High. Educ. **5**(1), 67–73 (2013)
85. Romero, M.: Game based learning MOOC. Promoting entrepreneurship education. eLearning Papers, issue 33 (2013). ISSN 1887-1542
86. Rosé, C.P., Carlson, R., Yang, D., Wen, M., Resnick, L., Goldman, P., Sherer, J.: Social factors that contribute to attrition in moocs. In: Proceedings of the First ACM Conference on Learning@ Scale Conference, pp. 197–198. ACM (2014)
87. Russell, D.M., Klemmer, S., Fox, A., Latulipe, C., Duneier, M., Losh, E.: Will massive online open courses (moocs) change education? In: CHI 2013 Extended Abstracts on Human Factors in Computing Systems, pp. 2395–2398. ACM (2013)
88. Ruth, S.: Can MOOC's and existing e-learning paradigms help reduce college costs? Int. J. Technol. Teach. Learn. **8**(1), 21–32 (2012)
89. Saadatmand, M., Kumpulainen, K.: Participants' perceptions of learning and networking in connectivist MOOCs. MERLOT J. Online Learn. Teach. **10**(1), 16–30 (2014)
90. Sandeen, C.: Assessment's place in the new MOOC world. Res. Pract. Assess. J. **8**, 5–13 (2013). (summer 2013)
91. Sanou, B.: The World in 2013: ICT Facts and Figures. International Telecommunications Union (2013)
92. Santos, J.L., Klerkx, J., Duval, E., Gago, D., Rodríguez, L.: Success, activity and drop-outs in MOOCs an exploratory study on the UNED COMA courses. In: Proceedings of the Fourth International Conference on Learning Analytics and Knowledge, pp. 98–102. ACM (2014)
93. Schuwer, R. Janssen, B.: Trends in business models for open educational resources and open education. In: Trend Report: Open Educational Resources 2013, pp. 60–66 (2013)
94. Schuwer, R., Janssen, B., Valkenburg, W.V.: MOOCs: trends and opportunities for higher education. In: Trend Report: Open Educational Resources 2013, pp. 22–27 (2013)
95. Siemens, G.: Connectivism: a learning theory for the digital age. Int. J. Instr. Technol. Distance Learn. **2**(1) (2005)
96. Smith, B., Eng, M.: MOOCs: a learning journey. In: Cheung, S.K.S., Fong, J., Fong, W., Wang, F.L., Kwok, L.F. (eds.) ICHL 2013. LNCS, vol. 8038, pp. 244–255. Springer, Heidelberg (2013)
97. Spector, J.M.: Trends and research issues in educational technology. Malays. Online J. Educ. Technol. **1**(3), 1–9 (2013)
98. Stewart, B.: Massiveness + Openness = new literacies of participation? J. Online Learn. Teach. **9**(2), 228–238 (2013)
99. Stine, J.K.: MOOCs and executive education. UNICON, research report (2013). http://uniconexed.org/2013/research/UNICON-Stine-Research-06-2013-final.pdf

100. Subbian, V.: Role of MOOCs in integrated STEM education: a Learning perspective. In: 3rd IEEE Integrated STEM Education Conference (2013)
101. Szafir, D., Mutlu, B.: ARTFuL: adaptive review technology for flipped learning. In: CHI 2013 Conference: Changing Perspectives, pp. 1001–1010, Paris, France (2013)
102. Teplechuk, E.: Emergent models of massive open online courses: an exploration of sustainable practices for MOOC institutions in the context of the launch of MOOCs at the University of Edinburgh. MBA dissertation, University of Edinburgh (2013)
103. Uvalić-Trumbić, S., Daniel, S.J.: Making sense of MOOCs: the evolution of online learning in higher education. In: Hernández-Leo, D., Ley, T., Klamma, R., Harrer, A. (eds.) EC-TEL 2013. LNCS, vol. 8095, pp. 1–4. Springer, Heidelberg (2013)
104. Tschofen, C., Mackness, J.: Connectivism and dimensions of individual experience. Int. Rev. Res. Open Distance Learn. **13**(1), 124–143 (2012)
105. Vihavainen, A., Luukkainen, M., Kurhila, J.: Multi-faceted support for MOOC in programming. In: SIGITE 2012, Proceedings of the ACM Special Interest Group for Information Technology Education Conference, Calgary, Alberta, Canada, pp. 171–176 (2012)
106. Viswanathan, R.: Teaching and learning through MOOC. Front. Lang. Teach. **3**, 32–40 (2013)
107. Voss, B.D.: Massive Open Online Courses (MOOCs): a primer for university and College Board members. AGB Association of Governing Boards of Universities and Colleges (2013)
108. Waite, M., Mackness, J., Roberts, G., Lovegrove, E.: Liminal participants and skilled orienteers: Learner participation in a MOOC for new lecturers. J. Online Learn. Teach. **9**(2), 200–215 (2013)
109. Waldrop, M.M.: Online learning: campus 2.0. Nature (Int. Wkly. J. Sci.) **495**, 160–163 (2013)
110. WEO: International Energy Agency (2012). http://www.worldenergyoutlook.org/
111. Yin, S., Kawachi, P.: Improving open access through prior learning assessment. Open Prax. **5**(1), 59–65 (2013)
112. Yousef, A.M.F., Chatti, M.A., Schroeder, U.: Video-based learning: a critical analysis of the research published in 2003–2013 and future visions. In: eLmL 2014, The Sixth International Conference on Mobile, Hybrid, and Online Learning, pp. 112–119 (2014)
113. Yousef, A.M.F., Chatti, M.A., Schroeder, U., Wosnitza, M.: What Drives a successful MOOC? an empirical examination of criteria to assure design quality of MOOCs. In: Proceedings of the 14th IEEE International Conference on Advanced Learning Technologies, ICALT 2014, pp. 44–48 (2014)
114. Yousef, A.M.F., Chatti, M.A., Schroeder, U., Wosnitza, M., Jakobs, H.: MOOCs - a review of the state-of-the-art. In: Proceedings of the CSEDU 2014 Conference, vol. 3, pp. 9–20, INSTICC (2014)
115. Yuan, L., Powell, S.: MOOCs and open education: Implications for higher education. JISC CETIS (2013a). http://jisc.cetis.ac.uk/
116. Yuan, L., Powell, S.: MOOCs and disruptive innovation: Implications for higher education, eLearning Papers, issue 33 (2013b). ISSN 1887-1542

Technological Imagination for Accessible Design: Invoking Blind Users for Sighted Computer Science Students

Răzvan Rughiniş[1(✉)] and Cosima Rughiniş[2]

[1] Department of Computer Science,
University POLITEHNICA of Bucharest, Bucharest, Romania
razvan.rughinis@cs.pub.ro
[2] Department of Sociology, University of Bucharest, Bucharest, Romania
cosima.rughinis@sas.unibuc.ro

Abstract. We propose a framework for designing computer science courses on accessible design, focusing on blind users. The dominant approach in the literature pursues student motivation for accessible design through three main springs: a 'web of arguments', highlighting utility and morality as key considerations, empathy, and mainstreaming. We introduce aesthetics as a compelling motivational resort, and we appeal to technological imagination to frame sighted students' work in a personal project of weaving a Web of Voices. We present arguments, practices, and online resources to support teachers that introduce accessibility for blind users to sighted students.

Keywords: Technological imagination · Accessibility · Design · Blind users · Aesthetics · Web of voices

1 Introduction

This work represents an updated and extended version of the paper "Introducing accessibility for blind users to sighted computer science students. The aesthetics of tools, pursuits, and characters", presented at the CSEDU 2014 conference in Barcelona, 1–3 April 2014. We are grateful for the rich feedback that enabled us to review our text in the present form.

There is a significant thread of research dedicated to teaching accessibility for computer science and engineering students. We are interested in examining how authors (who, in these cases, are also teachers) justify the importance of teaching accessibility, and how they address students' interests and concerns. We argue that the dominant approach can be enriched in order to support persistent motivation for accessible design – that is, outside of the University campus, after graduation, when IT professionals have to confront competing demands and conflicting priorities. We propose that aesthetic experiences – as regards technological tools, one's own engineering work, and blind user characters – can consolidate the current modus operandi for motivating students, which is mostly focused on considerations of legality, altruism, and profit. Technological imagination can bring further impetus by framing accessibility work into a meaningful personal project.

S. Zvacek et al. (Eds.): CSEDU 2014, CCIS 510, pp. 328–340, 2015.
DOI: 10.1007/978-3-319-25768-6_21

The paper is structured as follows: we first analyze the literature concerning accessibility in the computer science curriculum, and we highlight the dominant motivational approach, identifying three resorts: the 'web of arguments', mainstreaming, and empathy. We then go on to propose aesthetic considerations as an additional resource, in relation to three issues: the aesthetics of the technologies designed by computer specialists, of their work, and of the blind characters with which they establish a relationship through their performance. Students' construction of blind personas can be a useful and flexible learning tool with an aesthetic edge. We then discuss the role of technological imagination in framing accessibility work as weaving a Web of Voices. The final section concludes the paper.

2 Inducing Accessible Design: Three Pillars

Teachers of accessible design appeal to three ways of engaging their students with this perspective: *argumentation*, persuasion through *empathy*, and routinization through *mainstreaming*.

2.1 The Web of Arguments

In articles that discuss various approaches to teaching accessibility, the value of introducing it to students is not treated as a self-evident matter: most authors offer a justification, relying on several arguments [3, 9, 12, 21].

The "social responsibility argument" [21], or ethical reasoning [30], appeals to the goal of universal access for the World Wide Web, as stated by the World Wide Web Consortium (W3C). The "Web for All" design principle stipulates: "The social value of the Web is that it enables human communication, commerce, and opportunities to share knowledge. One of W3C's primary goals is to make these benefits available to all people, whatever their hardware, software, network infrastructure, native language, culture, geographical location, or physical or mental ability" [27]. W3C pursues this goal via the Web Accessibility Initiative (WAI), that develops the Web Content Accessibility Guidelines (WCAG) [28].

The "legal argument" [21, 30] invokes legal requirements for Internet accessibility; for example, in the United States these derive from the Section 508 of the Rehabilitation Act. Rising numbers of impaired students bring to the forefront the issue of legally mandated equal access in education [3]. In countries where such legal requirements exist, skills for accessibility design contribute to employability and can thus be shown to be useful for students' future careers [3, 12].

The market argument stresses the fact that impaired users represent a significant proportion of citizens and customers, which are lost through inaccessible design [12]; this argument also capitalizes on utility, this time from a business perspective, complementing the increased employability.

The "march of technology" argument [21] points to the fact that accessibility does not refer to impaired users only, but also to all users in restricted contexts that become increasingly common as technology permeates more areas of life: "Automobile drivers—who otherwise have normal vision—are blind with respect to the web while they are driving. Likewise, a person surfing the web on a small mobile handheld device is, for all intents and purposes, a low-vision person accessing the web" (ibid., p. 271).

The argument of direct benefits for all users adds that we-as-able-users are likely to become closely involved with impaired users, as we, our parents, and significant others age [12]: "Visually impaired computer users are a minority, but it's a growing minority, and it is growing faster as baby boomers near retirement age. Further, it's a minority that will eventually include us all" ([21], p. 274). This argument lends further support to the market-related considerations.

The "technical reason" [30] indicates that designing for accessibility increases interoperability and standard compliance (also pointed out by [21], thus serving the general public and increasing designers' skills and employability [29]).

Overall, these arguments capitalize on accessibility as a matter of (a) morality – addressing disabled people's needs and rights, (b) abiding the law – and (c) a matter of interest – for developer employees, for businesses, and for the government. In a nutshell, "the audience is growing, the law requires it, and the industry trend is toward it" ([9], p. 23).

Authors also address potential counter-arguments. The issue of cost appears as the most prominent expected hurdle: "I think that all would agree that when faced with an inaccessible website and an accessible website with the same functionality, the accessible website is better. The debate is really over who pays to implement accessibility, and why they should have to bear that cost" ([21], p. 274). How do authors address the issue of cost? There are two main answers. On the one hand, accessibility is deemed "lightweight to introduce" [3] – that is, costs are not high, when introduced skillfully and early. On the other hand, retrofitting accessibility is significantly more costly, therefore it is better to design directly for accessibility [3, 21].

Another expected counter-argument, introduced by Waller et al. [29], is that designing for accessibility might "stifle" creativity (rather than "spark" it), and it might lead into tradeoffs with other important considerations such as "design goals, technological limitations, customer objectives and software objectives" (p. 157). There are no explicit answers advanced for this concern.

Both types of counter-arguments raise the following question: how can students approach accessibility so that they would continue to engage it outside of the classroom, when facing such counter-arguments from team members or leaders (or even from within themselves)? Each project has to navigate a plethora of competing requirements and considerations: how can accessibility stand a chance against issues of beautiful design, or the use of innovative-but-inaccessible technologies to entice large numbers of mostly-able users? Since, for any argument, there is a counter-argument, providing students a set of good justifications for accessible design seems to be necessary, but not sufficient for successful confrontations 'in the field'.

2.2 Empathy

A second resource for strengthening motivation for accessibility consists in cultivating sighted students' empathy with blind people, through a closer experience of their living situations and perspectives. There are several means through which teachers of accessibility cultivate empathy, as discussed in the reviewed publications.

The first such means is *literature*: Rosmaita [21] requires students to read Rod Michalko's memoir *The Two-in-One* [15]; Michalko is a sociology professor who has written compelling accounts of blindness and analyses of the "sighted world" [17], including the University classroom [16], by examining interactions between blind and sighted people.

The second avenue for introducing students to the experiences of blind people consists in face-to-face communication – that is, *actually meeting blind people*. Such encounters can be organized as lectures from blind academics, discussions with blind users of technology [9], possibly also blind students [21], or, at a higher level of complexity, collaboration with blind people in design projects [29].

The third way of cultivating empathy is to ask able students to *simulate blindness* while using computers, for example, by turning off the monitor and navigating with a screen reader [5, 9, 21].

2.3 Mainstreaming

A third resource deemed useful for long term motivation refers to how accessibility is framed through curriculum design. The aim is to cultivate an appreciation of accessibility as a default option, a norm rather than an exception or an add-on feature. A resource for framing accessibility as normality, rather than a feature marked as controversial and optional, consists in mainstreaming it throughout the curriculum [29], by including it in multiple areas and types of learning activities, or throughout a given course [9, 12, 30], by including it in multiple lectures and assignments rather than as a specific, isolated discussion.

Mainstreaming accessibility has two advantages: at a symbolic level, it un-marks it as a special topic, rendering it a normal and strongly normative requirement. As regards skills, students face challenges of accessible design continuously, in multiple tasks and projects. If it becomes routine, accessible design escapes the need for justification: it is just how it's done. Mainstreaming accessibility throughout a course or program curriculum is expected to achieve a routinization of concern, thus going 'under the radar' of competing arguments.

3 Aesthetics: A Fourth Pillar

We propose that there is a fourth pillar for sustaining long-term student motivation, besides the web of arguments, empathy, and mainstreaming. This resource is largely missing from the examined literature: aesthetics.

Taking into consideration the aesthetics of accessibility does not refer strictly to the display of a technology, although this is as stake as well; an essential focus is on the process of technological design itself, and the people with which we are connected through work. We discuss these dimensions in the following sections.

3.1 Aesthetics and Accessibility of Tools: A Trade-off?

When aesthetics of technological tools are invoked in the reviewed articles about teaching accessibility, they are often presented in a trade-off with accessibility. For example, Wang presents designers' perspective as follows: "Without appreciating the social importance of accessibility, Web designers and developers can hardly be motivated to "burden" their design with accessibility limitations" [30].

Along a similar line, Waller et al. report that "[s]tudents are also asked to examine and discuss the trade-offs between good aesthetic design, sound software engineering and the need for accessibility, for example through mock debates on whether accessibility considerations stifle or spark creativity" [29].

These quotes illustrate that the perceived trade-off between accessibility and aesthetic design [13] is often not challenged by teachers; professors accept the assumption that accessibility is a potential hurdle for a beautiful (or otherwise aesthetically interesting) design.

From a statistical perspective on the current state of technology, this trade-off may well exist – although there is research that indicates otherwise. For example, Mbipom [13] analyzed 30 web pages and concluded that those that are perceived as "clean", "clear" and "organized" comply better, on average, with WCAG 1.0, while being seen as "beautiful" or "interesting" does not make a difference. In a similar study [14], the authors analyzed 50 web pages and found that those evaluated as "clean" had fewer accessibility barriers, while the attributes of "pleasing", "fascinating", "creative" and "aesthetic" did not correlate significantly with accessibility.

These correlations are interesting descriptions of the status-quo. Still, they may derive from a general low level of accessibility, rather than from a real independence of accessibility and design. While there are good reasons while cleanliness and clearness associate with higher accessibility, it is possible that the missing correlation between aesthetic sophistication ("interesting", "fascinating", "creative") and access hurdles actually derives from the overall low level of accessibility of all pages under study. That is, if designers do not bother to develop accessible pages and there is a uniform low performance in this respect, accessibility would not correlate with design features because it would not be variable. Low variation can lead to low correlation with any attribute. The challenge remains to cultivate an appreciation for high accessibility that accompanies an interest in cutting-edge aesthetic design. Cultivating performance simultaneously on these two dimensions raises specific challenges.

Regan [20] discusses aesthetics and accessibility, diagnosing a "failure of the imagination". He observes that many accessible sites are indeed aesthetically uninspiring and designers ignore access requirements because they orient their work towards inspiring models. There is a need for aesthetically provocative accessible sites, to infuse professional enthusiasm for accessibility in design work. Such enthusiasm is possible, as he found out by observing a team of designers who set out to create an innovative and accessible site: they saw it as a challenge, and engaged it with full energy. Still, initial frenzy led to confusion and deep concern in the following days, as designers began to struggle with the un-visual world of the screen reader. As Regan insightfully notices, designers are visual professionals: they have fine-tuned their visual sensitivity and orientation skills for years.

Asking them to work in a non-visual environment can easily switch from a challenge to an aggravation. In addition, screen readers are complex applications, which require some familiarity for proper operation, and thus add to the initial vexation. Therefore, engaging designers in accessibility work is not trivial, and not "lightweight": "Designers often spend years honing their instincts for the visual UI. A comparable and parallel effort should be made for alternative environments" ([20], p. 37).

Therefore, while respecting the most important accessibility guidelines (such as adding ALT descriptions to visual content, using headings, avoiding unnecessary tables, and allowing for resizable fonts, among others) is not particularly complicated (although adding captions may come across as tedious and thus 'postponable'), a creative take on accessibility requires a high level of determination to engage with a non-visual environment. Such a creative approach is required in order to transform accessibility from a professional burden to a challenge, and to inspire technology designers rather than to vex them.

Two possible ways to encourage students to think about high accessibility and innovative aesthetics in convergence, rather than in trade-off, are:

- Encouraging a minimalist design aesthetic, based on the "less is more" maxim, and privileging information *structure* and richness of *content* over decoration;
- Emphasizing *flexibility* itself as an aesthetic criterion. Students can learn to understand aesthetics not only through the eyes of sighted persons, but also through the perspectives of screen reader and screen magnifier users, or of color-blind or dyslexic users. Flexibility endows aesthetic value from the possibility of *meaningful use*; there is also an element of *surprise*, as flexibility is not always manifest at a glance.

It is in this spirit that Slatin proposes a warehouse-inspired aesthetics for accessibility design: "My models here are the Centre Pompidou (Beaubourg Museum) in Paris and, more generally, "warehouse style" architecture and design, whereby infrastructural elements-conduits, wiring, ductwork, stairways, elevators, etc., are translated into "exostructure", made visible for all, painted, polished, burnished, or left to weather. We might consider making analogous uses of features in HTML - such as the ALT and LONGDESC attributes for images; the SUMMARY attribute for tables; the LABEL element for forms; captions and audio descriptions for video and animation; and of course headers (H1, H2, etc.) to mark off the formal structural components of our Web-texts. And just as the Beaubourg's pipes are painted in bright primary colors, we can use Cascading Style Sheets to "paint" the accessibility exoskeleton and make it something fun to look at, even while it's being invisibly useful" [23].

3.2 The Aesthetics of a 'Job Well Done': Pursuing Technical Mastery

The aesthetic imagination of computer science students can be energized not only in relation to the tools they create, but also in relation to their own work. The aesthetic value of accessible design as technical wizardry is, we argue, an important motivational resource.

The idea that accessible design is a proof of smart engineering is not uncommon, as we have seen above in the "march of technology" [21] and "technical reasons" [30] arguments. The question is, how to better translate accessibility requirements into a professional challenge for proving technical mastery? This is more a matter of framing and illustrating, than of explicit arguing. For example, the story of dramatically improved accessibility of touchscreen phones brought forward by the iPhone [25] displays accessibility-work as inspirational, from a design perspective.

The "march of technology" argument is particularly valuable to frame accessible design as savvy design, because it transforms the limitations of disability into opportunities of technological reach in ever more diverse situations. This can be a starting point for exercises of UX imagination: in which walks of life can we imagine accessible technologies to be attractive to various types of users? How can accessibility turn into expanded usability? If blind users and 'power users' are alike in their strong preference for using key shortcuts [26], and driving users are for all practical purposes blind to visual information [21], what other similarities can one find across unlike life and work situations?

More concretely, teachers can frame the accessibility designer as a whiz by cultivating a professional appreciation for structure. Structured design is a strong requirement for accessibility, which is enhanced through clear specification of types of entities (for example, through headings) and by a clear prioritization of content according to its importance. The weakest motivational force derives from framing structure as a requirement of WCAG, a requirement of the law, or a need of a group of users – that is, extrinsically mandated. For a more forceful motivation, the requirement of structure can be framed as an aesthetic criterion of design wizardry, along the following lines:

(a) Clear, organized interfaces are highly usable: clarity is a dimension of beauty;
(b) Structure relates to depth rather than surface; understanding how a blind person reads Web pages through assistive technologies that linearize and verbalize content can amount to understanding an alternative, underlying structure of our shared and yet diverging world; the informational structure of visible realities holds a certain aesthetic appeal for computer science students and professionals – as it was maybe best illustrated by the Matrix digital rain (which could be used as a teaching metaphor);
(c) Last but not least, an explicit promotion of minimalism as aesthetic current would support an appreciation of structured, no-frills design that favors accessibility [14]; minimalism has had its ups and downs in web design, for example, but, as Thorlacius argues in his discussion, we can probably agree on a matter of possibility: "A minimalist Web site with no extraneous aesthetics, and visual effects only in the form of typeface and text layout, can be just as aesthetically pleasing as a Web site with lots of pretty pictures and fancy Flash installations" ([24], pp. 71–72).

An important resource for cultivating aesthetic appreciation for structure in design consists in the experience of ridiculousness for poorly designed technologies that mime structure through visual effects (for example, in web design, highlighting headings through font formatting, assembling lists through paragraph formatting, or using tables unnecessarily). As an example of a learning situation in this such humor becomes possible, Benavídez et al. [2] ask students to examine two apparently identical sites, one which is accessible and one which is not. Teachers can create humorous situations that downgrade appreciation for design that is structure-less, tagging it as 'amateurish' or 'lazy', for example. This symbolic fight can then happen again and again when graduates, future professionals, decide consciously or infra-consciously to what extent to structure their technologies, rather than accept older, unstructured versions – which may be already available for revamping, may be easier to delegate to a team member, or may be otherwise more convenient. An aesthetic disregard for 'sloppy, witless work' may counterbalance 'convenience' better than alternative arguments of cost and benefit.

The experiential absurdity of structure-less or otherwise low accessibility design can be brought to life by navigating it through the assistive technologies that blind or low vision people would use. Screen readers' 'non-human voice' [25] is often a topic of amusement among those who experience it, as it is its mechanical 'parroting' of everything written [4]; at the same time, unnecessary repetition of content verbalized by the mechanical voice of the reader can be not only unhumorous, but downright aggravating [7].

3.3 Aesthetics of Blind Characters

A third source of aesthetic appreciation of one's work in accessible design could derive from a feeling of working in connection with blind people, end users and most direct beneficiaries. The question rises, how can empathy and a feeling of sharing experiences across different life worlds be better produced, and turned into an aesthetically valuable experience?

Representing Blind Users. The issue of representation of blind people for sighted students is concomitantly challenging and relatively under-discussed in the literature. As we have seen, teachers of accessible design do stress the importance of meeting blind people and witnessing their experiences of technology, either through lectures or through collaboration. Such encounters generate many insights into the specific worldviews and experiences of blind persons – bringing forward both their problems and their skills and achievements, often unimagined by able students who are not familiar with disabilities.

We propose that such encounters can be consolidated, as an experience, by adding opportunities for explicit reflection on the diversity of blindness, the shared-and-disparate worlds in which sighted people coexist with blind people, and the almost unimaginable skills that blind people develop to master the world.

Sighted students and sighted persons in general are often deeply impressed when meeting blind people, and when their preconceptions are confronted with real lives and actions. At the same time, experiences of direct interaction can be enhanced by mediated interplay.

Firstly, if direct interactions are not reflected upon and if they are not elaborated into narratives, their memories may fade, and their value for out-of-classroom work, which is our focus, declines as the years go by.

Secondly, there is often a limited number of blind people that a sighted student will be acquainted with personally, through her or his University experience or otherwise; while knowledge can be deep, there will remain a certain limitation in breadth, concerning the variety of life situations encountered.

Last but not least, given the extraordinariness of some of these experiences, sighted students may be at some loss of how to make sense of what they have observed, in an existential, rather than a behavioral way. What do the actions and interactions they have been part of tell about human nature – about the diversity or similarity of life situations, the capabilities and limitations of people, the power of individual and the power of relationships or of technologies? There is an important work of sense-making and conceptualization, which is the topic matter of disability studies, which should be at least touched upon in order to reach the full knowledge and motivational potential of such encounters. While there may not be time enough for a familiarization of students with theories of disability, one could probably find some intervals for a more informal exploration. In the following section we aim to indicate some online resources for this work of sense-making, through which blind users become strong characters, sharing the world and the work with skilled technology designers.

Online Encounters. Based on the reviewed literature, it seems that introducing online blind characters to visually able students is a rarely used resource for teaching accessibility. Still, there is a rich blind presence on the Web; as it is to be expected, there is no shortage of narratives, shared experiences, and opportunities for digital interaction.

Online characters can complement meeting blind people face-to-face in at least two respects. On the one hand, there is the narrative richness: there are many deep, insightful, detailed online written accounts of living with blindness, ranging from several paragraphs to book length; they offer students vocabularies for making sense of this condition of being in the world. On the contrary, University-mediated encounters with blind people are often limited in the amount of interaction they can afford for individual students, and in the diversity of topics touched in conversation and narration. On the second hand, there is the diversity of life situations: we can digitally reach people who are blind students, parents, IT professionals, teachers, unemployed, artists and so on; these identities are, of course, overlapping, but usually some of them will be more prominent in a given account.

Online encounters with blind characters are an apt method, for teachers, to reverse the dominant framing of blind persons as needy, vulnerable, and incomplete. Students can experience in so many instances the frustration of blind people when being treated as partially human - illustrated, for example, by Atkinson [1]: "Misconceptions start to spout from even your oldest friends' mouths because negative attitudes about blindness permeate us all. You are about to cross over into the dark side and see what wriggles and writhes on the underbelly of society. Folk will see you as the sufferer, the pitiful, the afflicted, the subhuman – that's you, yes, you. If you use a cane or a dog, people will stare as you walk down the street. People will assume you are more lacking in intelligence than your sighted counterpart. People you have never met before will ask if you want children, and if you do, they will ask if the kids will have the same condition that you have, and whether that is right or wrong. Welcome. Your reproductive autonomy is in the docks of the moral courts of the nation's minds. (…) Going blind (…) is a grand experiment that most don't get to try: to observe as your brain rewires and watch as the human body adapts in infinite ways" [1]. Online encounters facilitate a gradual re-definition of blindness from 'lack' and biological 'disease' to a condition in life that is strongly shaped by how it is defined and acted upon.

The tropes of extra-ordinariness and heroism are very important for making sense, as a sighted person, of blindness; the online environment offers access to many blind characters with extra-ordinary achievements that impress others through their strength, unimaginable skills, and wisdom. It also introduces characters that are ordinary in every respect lest of being blind, and it also introduces characters that are confused, overwhelmed, or otherwise vulnerable; therefore, there is a wider range of emotional responses that the sighted observer or interlocutor could experience.

The online environment also offers a different kind of facility of interaction. Blindness is often experienced, by sighted users, as a stigma – as an embodied feeling that the interaction flow is collapsing, awkward or otherwise difficult. The following account of a blind person renders this obstacle intelligible: "There is an invisible wall between the sighted and the visually impaired", Ms. Squarci said. "One of the women I interviewed, she has been blind since she was 4 years old, she told me sighted people are almost scared to deal with the blind. Being blind is like speaking a language. If sighted people don't find eye contact – which is the first hint of communication – they feel lost and they don't engage" [8]. The online environment allows sighted users the comfort of timing interaction as they see fit, also unidirectionally or asynchronously; of taking time to get acquainted to visually disabled portraits without the anxiety that one might reveal discomfort and therefore appear as prejudiced and socially unskilled. That is, the online medium can be used as a training ground, a sandbox for interaction between sighted students and blind people. This could also provide students the opportunity on reflecting on their emotions when encountering blind people online, helping with the emotional work required for successful interaction in all social situations.

A very specific resource facilitated by the online environment refers to the aesthetics of blind faces. The discomfort of sighted people when looking at a blind person can be confronted and strongly challenged by visiting online exhibitions of visual portraits of the blind, such as, among others Gaia Squarci exhibition [8]; Sam Ivin Photography [10]; Julia Fullerton-Batten, Blind [6]; Charlie Simokaitis, Fade to white [22].

Through online exploration and ventures, various dimensions of interaction between sighted and blind people could be touched: the humor of blindness, through its many mishaps, including the ill-suited reactions of sighted people; its absurdity and, conversely, its capacity to highlight meaning in life; its malleability in being experienced as a disability, as a repertoire of skills, or as utter normality, depending, among others, on the tools and relations that constitute the capability of any human being from the perspective of distributed, 'person-plus' [18] competence.

Blind Personas in Learning Practice. Teachers may dispose of anything from several hours to semesters of study for introducing accessibility, depending on the learning context. Blind personas [11, 19] are a flexible tool to acquaint students with the aesthetics of accessible design and to evaluate their learning and motivation. Students can participate in individual or team projects to construct and present blind personas as users of specific technologies, highlighting relevant background aspects of their lives and concrete details of their experiences with technology. Personas can be sketched in a couple of hours or portrayed through in-depth research, depending on available time. A persona offers a rich ground for expressing the aesthetics of blind characters, accessible tools, and accessible design. Personas are also useful tools for design in general, beyond accessibility concerns. Such learning projects take advantage of the variety of students' aesthetic preferences and professional interests as a resource for collaborative learning about the diversity of blind people's life experiences and technology use.

4 Technological Imagination: Weaving a Web of Voices

If we take forward the metaphor of pillars that we have used by now, we can further complete a motivational architecture for sighted students to engage in accessible design by engaging their *technological imagination* as an overarching structure.

Authors have appealed to imagination in two main guises, while advocating for accessible design: an aesthetic imagination [20], required to overcome the visual bias, and imagining users with various (dis)abilities [23], required to effectively shape accessible technology. We add to the list 'technological imagination', which invites teachers and students to engage with the philosophical and ideological commitments of their projects: how do we hope to change – or at least *nudge* – the world?

One way to formulate accessibility as a dimension of a meaningful project for shaping the world is by using 'voice' as a tool for thought. Students can take part in weaving a 'Web of Voices' – thinking of ways to continually transform the potential Babel-ness of the Internet into meaningful expression, reading, and dialogue.

Web content that is not accessible is thus seen as a site of confusion and loss of meaning. Blind people face the challenge of navigating the Internet and reading, or hearing, *fragmented voices* – losing elements of context, fragments of discourse, and meta information that are present for sighted users. Accessible design aims to present and to afford fuller voices to visually impaired internauts – to let them read and engage with utterances in full awareness of their authors' self-presentations, of others' comments and replies, of illustrations, of message placement in a wider discourse structure.

Time is also an important consideration: blind people navigate the web slower, taking more time to make sense of messages and to find their way in the obscured landscapes of visually designed sites. Un-accessible sites bleed time: exploration, sense-making, overviews are cumbersome as users get lost. Improving speed and efficacy of navigation brings sighted and blind people in a digital universe in which they can share the same temporal flow.

Accessibility is not only a principle of design that clarifies voices to blind readers and listeners – it also enables them to fully participate as conversationalists in web fora. The Web of Voices is thus doubly enriched through accessible design: enhancing *clarity for* – and also inviting *engagement from* visually impaired people.

5 Conclusions

We analyze the literature concerning accessibility in the computer science and engineering curriculum, focusing on the repertories of arguments and practices that authors put forward to support students' motivation. We find a persistent concern for arguing with students and readers that accessibility is a reasonable, efficient, moral and ultimately legally required pursuit. We also identify empathy and mainstreaming as two motivational drives distinct from the logical 'web of arguments', instilling the interest for accessibility in emotions and routines.

We propose two additional resources to consolidate students' persistent motivation. Firstly, we discuss the *aesthetic appreciation* of accessible tools, of working with accessibility in mind, and of characters of blind people – the direct beneficiaries of these pursuits. We advance a first version of an aesthetic motivational repertoire, including arguments, practices, and online resources. Students' construction and presentation of blind personas is a flexible and useful learning tool to this purpose. Secondly, *technological imagination* is a way of invoking blind people in meaningful personal projects of sighted students – for example, the pursuit of a Web of Voices valuing clarity and dialogue.

Harrison [9] writes, reflecting on her teaching: "If students are given the challenge of designing an accessible site, they will rise to meet that challenge" (p. 26). An aesthetic and technological imagination could make this venture even more engaging.

Acknowledgements. This article has been supported by the research project "Sociological imagination and disciplinary orientation in applied social research", with financial support of ANCS/UEFISCDI with grant no. PN-II-RU-TE-2011-3-0143, contract no. 14/28.10.2011.

References

1. Atkinson, R.: Reflections on becoming blind. Braille Monitor (2007). https://nfb.org/images/nfb/publications/bm/bm07/bm0710/bm071004.htm
2. Benavídez, C., Fuertes, J.L., Gutiérrez, E., Martínez, L.: Teaching web accessibility with "contramano" and hera. In: Miesenberger, K., Klaus, J., Zagler, W.L., Karshmer, A.I. (eds.) ICCHP 2006. LNCS, vol. 4061, pp. 341–348. Springer, Heidelberg (2006)
3. Cohen, R.F., Fairley, A.V., Gerry, D., Lima, G.R.: Accessibility in introductory computer science. In: Proceedings of the 36th SIGCSE Technical Symposium on Computer Science Education – SIGCSE 2005, vol. 37, pp. 17–21. ACM Press, New York (2005)
4. Finke, B.: Fade to white. Safe & Sound Blog (2011). http://bethfinke.wordpress.com/2011/07/14/fade-to-white
5. Freire, A.P., de Mattos Fortes, R.P., Barroso Paiva, D.M., Santos Turine, M.A.: Using screen readers to reinforce web accessibility education. ACM SIGCSE Bull. **39**(3), 82–86 (2007)
6. Fullerton-Batten, J.: Blind. Julia Fullerton-Batten Web Site (n.d.). http://www.juliafullerton-batten.com/small.html
7. Gerber, E.: Conducting usability research with computer users who are blind or visually impaired. In: 17th Annual International Conference of CSUN "Technology and Persons with Disabilities" (2002). http://www.afb.org/section.aspx?FolderID=2&SectionID=4&TopicID=167&DocumentID=1718
8. Gonzalez, D.: Guided by blindness. New York Times Blogs (2013). http://lens.blogs.nytimes.com/2013/03/22/guided-by-blindness/
9. Harrison, S.M.: Opening the eyes of those who can see to the world of those who can't. ACM SIGCSE Bull. **37**(1), 22–26 (2005)
10. Ivin, S.: Blind portraits. Sam Ivin Photography (n.d.). http://www.samivin.co.uk/gallery_476907.html
11. Johansson, M., Messeter, J.: Present-ing the user: constructing the persona. Digit. Creativity **16**(4), 231–243 (2005)

12. Ludi, S.: Access for everyone: introducing accessibility issues to students in Internet programming courses. In: Frontiers in Education FIE 2002, vol. 3, pp. S1C–7–S1C–9. IEEE (2002)
13. Mbipom, G.: Good visual aesthetics equals good web accessibility. ACM SIGACCESS Accessibility Comput. **93**, 75–83 (2009)
14. Mbipom, G., Harper, S.: The interplay between web aesthetics and accessibility. In: The 13th International ACM SIGACCESS Conference on Computers and Accessibility - ASSETS 2011, pp. 147–154. ACM Press, New York (2011)
15. Michalko, R.: The Two-in-One. Walking with Smokie, Walking with Blindness. Temple University Press, Philadelphia (1998)
16. Michalko, R.: Blindness enters the classroom. Disability Soc. **16**(3), 349–359 (2001)
17. Michalko, R.L.: Accomplishing the sighted world. The University of British Columbia (1977). https://circle.ubc.ca/bitstream/handle/2429/20966/UBC_1977_A8M52.pdf
18. Perkins, D.N.: Person-plus: a distributed view of thinking and learning. In: Salomon, G. (ed.) Distributed Cognitions: Psychological and Educational Considerations, pp. 88–110. Cambridge University Press, Cambridge (1993)
19. Pilgrim, M.: Dive into accessibility (2002). http://diveintoaccessibility.info/
20. Regan, B.: Accessibility and design: a failure of the imagination. In: Proceedings of the International Cross-Disciplinary Workshop on Web Accessibility - W4A, pp. 29–37. ACM Press, New York (2004)
21. Rosmaita, B.J.: Accessibility first! A new approach to web design. In: The 37th SIGCSE Technical Symposium on Computer Science Education, vol. 38, pp. 270–274. ACM Press, New York (2006)
22. Simokaitis, C.: Fade to White (n.d.). http://www.charliesimokaitisphotography.com/#mi=2&pt=1&pi=10000&s=19&p=1&a=0&at=0
23. Slatin, J.: The imagination gap: making web-based instructional resources accessible to students and colleagues with disabilities. Currents in Electronic Literacy (2002). http://currents.cwrl.utexas.edu/spring02/slatin.html
24. Thorlacius, L.: The role of aesthetics in web design. Nordicom Rev. **28**(1), 63–76 (2007)
25. Tsaran, V.: Victor Tsaran at TEDxSilicon Valley (2009). http://www.youtube.com/watch?v=BsJB73c38yw
26. Vuppala, V., Krishna, A.M.: An aesthetic approach to accessibility testing in enterprise applications (2012). http://www.stepinforum.org/stepin-summit-2012/plenaries/venkata_alluri_track.html
27. W3C: W3C Mission. W3C Site (2012). http://www.w3.org/Consortium/mission.html
28. W3C: Web Content Accessibility Guidelines (WCAG) Overview. Web Accessibility Initiative (2012). http://www.w3.org/WAI/intro/wcag.php
29. Waller, A., Hanson, V.L., Sloan, D.: Including accessibility within and beyond undergraduate computing courses. In: Proceeding of the 11th International ACM SIGACCESS Conference on Computers and Accessibility – ASSETS 2009, pp. 155–162. ACM Press, New York (2009)
30. Wang, Y.D.: A holistic and pragmatic approach to teaching web accessibility in an undergraduate web design course. In: The 13th Annual Conference on Information Technology Education - SIGITE 2012, pp. 55–60. ACM Press, New York (2012)

Designing, Implementing and Sustaining a Technology-Rich STEM Classroom Using Participatory Design Practices

Mary L. Stephen(✉), Sharon M. Locke, and Georgia L. Bracey

Center for Science, Technology, Engineering and Mathematics Research, Education, and Outreach, Southern Illinois University, Edwardsville, IL, USA
{mstepaa,slocke,gbracey}@siue.edu

Abstract. This paper describes a participatory design approach used to create, implement and sustain a technology-rich STEM classroom in a secondary school associated with a U.S. university. Students, teachers, and administrators from the secondary school worked in collaboration with university faculty and staff and with Herman Miller®, an international design company that conducts learning-space research. The goal in utilizing participatory design practices was to maximize the use and sustainability of the classroom. In addition to discussion of the design process and constructed space, a research study conducted in conjunction with this project is described. Implementation challenges and sustainability strategies uncovered through the research and as part of the development of a broader case study focusing on teachers' experiences during this process are outlined along with users' responses to the classroom.

Keywords: Participatory design · Innovative educational space · Technology-rich STEM classroom · Stakeholders

1 Introduction

In February 2012, McCoy High School (pseudonym), a public high school in the U.S. Midwest, opened a high-technology classroom designed to be an innovative environment for teaching and learning in science, technology, engineering, and mathematics (STEM). This STEM classroom was created in response to a call for an increasing focus on STEM education in U.S. schools, as articulated in several high-profile national reports [1–3]. These reports emphasize that STEM education is the foundation for many of the high-growth sectors of the economy. The need for more highly skilled professionals is not limited to the United States [4–6]. Based on 2012 data, European models predict greatly increased demand for such professionals, particularly among the younger generation, in order to meet the challenge of Europe's aging population [7]. At the same time, despite students' personal engagement with technologies, their interest in STEM subjects begins to decline in late primary and early secondary education resulting in fewer than 30 % of males and 15 % of females planning to study STEM subjects in post-secondary education [4]. In response to these reports and to a growing number of national

S. Zvacek et al. (Eds.): CSEDU 2014, CCIS 510, pp. 341–355, 2015.
DOI: 10.1007/978-3-319-25768-6_22

and regional initiatives, local school administrators and teachers are looking for practical solutions to enhance the quality of STEM instruction.

Many schools are turning to computing technologies as a means to improve STEM education because there is a growing consensus that students should be exposed to the advanced technologies and tools used by practicing scientists and engineers [8]. McCoy's STEM classroom provides students who are living in an urban, high-poverty community with access to some of the latest technologies and tools of STEM as part of their learning experience, with the long-term goal of raising student achievement and inspiring students to pursue STEM university degrees and careers. The classroom incorporates design elements that reflect recent understandings of effective ways to promote and support STEM learning and includes features that the STEM teachers and students feel are important for facilitating learning.

In this paper, we describe the design, development, and implementation of McCoy High School's STEM classroom. We discuss some of the challenges encountered during the process, including approaches taken to meet these challenges, and report on student and teacher responses to the completed classroom. Finally, we highlight some additional factors contributing to the sustainability of the project.

2 Background and Vision

The newly constructed STEM classroom is a part of McCoy High School, a public high school located within the local city public school district and sponsored by a nearby public university. The school is located in an economically depressed, post-industrial, Midwestern city which is part of a large urban metropolitan area. All of the school's 120 students are African-American, and over 90 % of students are eligible for free or reduced-price lunches. The school has limited resources and, prior to construction of the STEM classroom, had access to only two outdated computer labs that often were not fully operational. The school is currently on academic watch. In the United States, a school is placed on academic watch if it does not meet proficiency performance standards in academic, attendance, and graduation rate targets defined by the state for four consecutive years.

Students in districts with a high poverty level are especially at risk of being unprepared for university science and mathematics courses [9]. As students advance in grade level, mathematics and science test scores markedly decline. In the McCoy High School district, only 47 % of 7th graders and just 9 % of 11th graders meet performance standards for science on state examinations. Furthermore, schools in low-income communities often do not have the materials, laboratories, and equipment to teach mathematics and science effectively, and many teachers lack the necessary training in their subject areas [10, 11].

In early 2011, the university received a large donation to design and construct a high-technology STEM classroom at the high school, with some of the funds designated for teacher professional development and onsite technology support personnel. The university's STEM Center was charged with overseeing the classroom's design and construction, and it played a key role in gathering together the design team and establishing the project's vision.

The overall vision for the new classroom was developed by experts in STEM education at the university. The stated purpose of the new learning space was to provide students with access to state-of-the-art technology, equipment, and curricula and to support teachers in providing students with hands-on, minds-on science learning. Then, taking a wider view, the team envisioned the classroom as a resource for the entire school district and as a model for excellence in STEM education far beyond the local setting.

The largest portion of the classroom was viewed as a "learning studio," in which movable, flexible seating would enable group work and student-centered discussion. Integrated into the physical space would be state-of-the-art computing and communications technologies and scientific equipment, providing opportunities for authentic learning rarely afforded in low-income communities.

The team also proposed a separate, smaller facility adjoining the main classroom, modeled after the fabrication laboratory, or "FabLab," concept. Originating at the Massachusetts Institute of Technology, educational FabLabs allow students to design objects on a computer using CAD software and then see their creations printed in three-dimensions. FabLabs enhance the learning of a variety of subjects ranging from geometry to engineering to art and design, and help students see the connections between STEM and the creative process [12]. Another goal for the space was to enable teachers to move easily between the main classroom and fabrication area as needed to ensure student engagement and achievement of learning goals.

A final, yet essential, component of the project was the provision of teacher training and support to ensure that the STEM teachers would be fully empowered to integrate the new resources into their teaching. It was intended that university faculty, master educators, and an on-site educational technology specialist would work in partnership with the high school teachers over an extended period of time to ensure that the technology and equipment would be used effectively and with the greatest benefit for student learning.

3 Design Process

The design process for the STEM classroom was participatory, using input from multiple units within a university, business representatives, and the ultimate users of the space, the school's teachers and students. The participatory design process was initially introduced in the 1970s in Scandinavia to empower workers by allowing them to work collaboratively with software designers in shaping the design of the computer systems and technologies used in their workplace. The participatory design process is an iterative process that employs a variety of techniques, ranging from observations, interviews and focus groups to the creation of mock-ups or prototypes. Many of these techniques were used in the design and implementation of the STEM classroom and are discussed later in this section.

A participatory design process relies on stakeholders to generate or create ideas collectively [13]. The major goal in participatory design is to "give a voice" to users in the design process by allowing them to play a meaningful role as informants or co-designers so that the end result will better meet their needs and uses [14–16]. Such a process takes advantage of the users' knowledge and experience, and contributes to a sense of ownership of the end result. This process continues to be used heavily in the design of information systems and technologies. However, participatory design values and practices are also currently embraced in other fields, such as healthcare, communications, business, architecture and curriculum design [17–20].

The physical setting in which teaching and learning take place contributes in practical ways to teacher and student behavior and has been shown to be a mediating factor in student achievement. For this reason, diverse perspectives, especially those of teachers and students, are important when designing educational environments. Using participatory design approaches to involve the users not only in the design phase but also in the evolution of the space has the potential to increase the teaching and learning benefits and sustainability of the space [21–23].

The STEM classroom design and construction involved a large team of individuals representing several units of the university and three businesses. The university's STEM Center director articulated the vision for the space through team meetings, and each unit took responsibility for different aspects of the design. The university's Instructional Technology Services (ITS) assigned two representatives to develop plans for configuring the room to maximize the use of computing technology. Installation of computer projection and videoconferencing systems and networking capabilities was completed by an outside contractor. The university's Facilities Management assigned an architect to design the physical space and to manage the construction schedule and work of carpenters, painters, and electricians.

At an early stage, the university contacted Herman Miller®, known for their innovative furniture designs and interest in research on learning spaces, to request that the project become part of Herman Miller's Learning Studio Research Program. Consequently, McCoy High School became the first secondary school accepted into this program. This formal partnership brought additional resources to the project including interior design expertise. Herman Miller® and an interior design company worked with the project team to turn the vision into reality, providing possible room plans, furniture options, and color schemes.

A critical aspect of the process of designing the STEM classroom involved participation by its end users. The school's three STEM teachers and six student representatives provided feedback on their needs and their vision for an effective learning space. Meetings of the STEM director and the high school team explored teachers' and students' opinions on everything from the educational activities that would take place in the space to possible designs to the aesthetics and feel of the learning environment. The teachers and students participated in exercises to sketch ideas for what the space might look like. Feedback was summarized and conveyed to the larger group and incorporated into the design whenever feasible. The STEM teachers reviewed architectural renderings of the space prior to the beginning of construction. They helped determine technologies, color palettes and furniture fabrics for the classroom. Now that the classroom is in use, the STEM teachers continue to play a role in identifying additional instructional needs and changes in existing technologies and furniture. Through focus groups, students have discussed features and possible changes in the classroom based on their experiences in the space. A summary of key comments from initial meetings with the teachers and students is shown in Fig. 1.

Space and Furnishings

- Colorful
- Bright lighting
- Movable furniture for flexible seating arrangements
- Café-height chairs

Technology

- Work spaces for robotics and other design tasks
- High-speed wireless
- Many electrical outlets
- Separate printer room to reduce noise levels
- Experimental technologies
- Durable equipment

Teaching Environment

- Communication is facilitated by multiple writing surfaces
- Open spaces to move in and form student groups
- Option of two instructors/classes in the room simultaneously
- Respectful attitude towards the room and equipment

Fig. 1. Teacher and student comments.

Four overarching principles guided the design team and are reflected in the final product:

- Fosters creativity and innovation
- Meets the needs of the school
- Appeals to students and teachers
- Integrates innovative technologies

Creativity is increasingly being recognized as a critical skill necessary for success in the 21st Century workplace [24, 25]. The STEM classroom was envisioned as a space that would nurture students' ability to express their creativity, whether through visual representations on white boards, design software, or tinkering with manipulatives such as robotics kits. A goal was to avoid straight lines of desks and the traditional format of a teacher desk at the front of the room, so as to encourage new modes of communication and collaboration during class.

Addressing the needs of the school was deemed critical to the success of the project. Because the school did not initiate the new classroom, it was crucial that administrators, teachers, and students be included as soon as possible to assist with design. Based on the informal needs assessment during focus groups, the design team was able to plan for a functional space that would not be underutilized or generate frustration among the teachers. Similarly, the appeal and comfort of the space was carefully considered so as to encourage the transition into the new space. An inviting environment that reflects the preferences of teachers and students could serve to reduce anxiety associated with the novelty of teaching and learning in a technology-intensive space. The design team reasoned that colors, fabrics, furniture, and layouts that appeal to teachers and students would help motivate use of the space.

The generous gift from an outside donor created a unique opportunity to equip a high-poverty school with innovative and advanced technologies not typically found in similar communities. The design team included technology designers who debated the possible configurations of hardware and software that would allow for an immersive student experience of technology. The goal was to provide access to technologies that would enable students to do background research, collect and analyze data, and collaborate with their peers and outside experts—skills that align with 21st Century learning outcomes for information and media literacy [25, 26].

The next section focuses on how these principles are reflected in the final design of the classroom.

4 Classroom Features

The overall design of the classroom encourages student-centered instruction and group work. The room contains a variety of tables and chairs that are easy to reconfigure for large and small group activities. Movable whiteboards and writable walls provide a large amount of writing and design space.

Computer and information technologies are central to this learning environment (Fig. 2) and can be easily configured for independent and group projects. Laptop computers and tablets can be plugged into the network via floor ports in multiple locations throughout the room, and in turn can be projected onto one of several screens. Additional technology features of the room include a four-screen video wall, an LCD SMART Board, 52-in TV monitor, HD document camera, and ceiling-mounted video cameras to record classroom activities. Sets of iPads, laptops, Botball robotics kits, a programmable humanoid robot, TI-Nspire calculators, and student response systems are available for individual and collaborative work. Additionally, the FabLab contains a 3-D printer and computers with design software to enable students to work with engineering design projects.

The first meeting to begin the design process was in April 2011, and the ribbon-cutting and official opening of the STEM classroom took place in February 2012. In late 2012, The Educational Interiors Showcase awarded the STEM classroom one of its top awards for classroom design, noting the space's "good use of technology" and its "variety of collaboration/presentation spaces and seating options within the classroom."

- Laptop computers
- iPads
- Graphing calculators
- Robotics kits
- Humanoid robots
- Digital cameras
- Document camera
- Multiple flat panel displays
- Video wall
- Classroom recording system
- High definition video conferencing
- 3D printer
- Large format printer
- Desktop computers with 3D design software

Fig. 2. STEM classroom technologies.

5 Implementation

Teaching practice is a product of both the teacher and the teaching environment [27]. Once the room design was completed and construction started, teachers began to consider the question of what they needed to learn in order to make effective use of the new technologies for teaching and learning. They realized that using the technologies within the new space could not only impact current practices, but would require teachers to be open to changing the way they currently teach.

5.1 Researching the Implementation

In conjunction with the design and implementation of McCoy's STEM classroom, researchers from the university's STEM Center designed a research study to understand and document how the STEM teachers capitalized on the potential of the space and available technologies to adopt new or modify existing pedagogical strategies. The research explored factors and challenges that influenced when and how teachers use the room and its technologies. This included examining teachers' concerns and attitudes about using the space over the course of its implementation. It was hoped that findings from this research could be used to optimize the usability of the learning space.

Because of the uniqueness of this complex and dynamic setting, the researchers chose a single case-study design with mixed methods of data collection and analysis. The intention in using this design is that the story developed may provide unusual insights that challenge or reinforce a reader's existing beliefs and promote broader understanding of the issues involved [28–30]. Initially researchers explored the possibility of also studying what, if any, impact the classroom had on students' achievement in STEM subjects and interest in STEM careers. However, the presence of several confounding factors, including initiatives to improve standardized test performance and changes in curriculum introduced at the school at the same time the room was completed, made it impossible to isolate the influence of the classroom from these other factors [21]. These factors did not interfere with the research focusing on understanding the STEM teachers' adoption of the room.

McCoy High School has three full-time STEM teachers. Two of these teachers agreed to participate in the research study. Initially, the study followed all three teachers; however, one of the teachers left McCoy High School shortly after the research study began. While the teacher's replacement agreed to participate in the study, the researchers decided to focus on the two teachers who had been involved from the initial design phase and beginning of the research study. Demographically, the two teachers who are the focus of the study are very different. Teacher A, an African American female in her 60s with extensive experience as an IT professional, participated in the design meetings. She had taught for five years at McCoy High School at the time the room was designed. Teacher B, a Caucasian male in his 20s, also participated in the design meetings. He recently had been hired and began his first year of teaching during the year the room was constructed. In addition, two key administrators at the school agreed to participate through interviews, and 30 % of the students in the school agreed to participate through focus groups and by completing surveys about the features of the room, the technologies, and their teachers' teaching styles.

Data sources include guided and open-ended interviews with teachers and administrators, student focus groups, and observation of sessions in both the STEM classroom and in regular classrooms. Additional data that inform the study were gathered from survey instruments including pre and post student and teacher questionnaires designed as part of the Herman Miller® Learning Spaces Research Program and periodic administration of the Stages of Concern Questionnaire (SoCQ) [31] to STEM teachers. SoCQ is used to create profiles of individuals' evolving levels of concern throughout the process of adopting an innovation.

The data enabled the researchers to identify challenges encountered by the teachers when using this new space and when incorporating new technologies and pedagogical strategies into their teaching. The following section identifies these challenges along with ways these challenges were approached.

6 Challenges to Implementation

1. Lack of Familiarity with Many of the Technologies Available and Ways they Might Effectively Be Integrated into Teaching

Approach: Numerous researchers have identified teachers' confidence and skill in using technologies combined with ability to see value in using technologies as major factors influencing teacher adoption of available technologies [32–35]. One way to build teacher confidence and skill is through professional development. Effective professional development is ongoing, uses peer coaching, and includes teachers in planning activities [36, 37].

At McCoy High School, professional development began during the construction phase and continues today, with the STEM teachers playing a leading role in identifying the type and pace of the activities. Because of other demands on their time, the teachers asked that training focus on one new technology at a time. This would enable them to become familiar with the technology and consider how best to use it with students.

The teachers visited other schools' high-tech classrooms and participated in national conferences, such as the National Science Teachers Association (NSTA) and International Society for Technology in Education (ISTE), as they sought ideas for using the new technologies in their own teaching. Vendor demonstrations occurred, and teachers were given iPads to familiarize themselves with the technology and begin to plan how they might use them in teaching. Teachers from other schools who were experienced with particular technologies led hands-on sessions to introduce teachers to new technologies, such as TI-Nspire graphing calculators and 3-D printers, and shared information on ways they use the technologies with students. An education faculty member from the university worked with the teachers to develop and test lessons incorporating the new technologies and features of the space. Teachers observed and critiqued the lessons for each other. These master technology teachers along with university personnel are an ongoing resource for the teachers. In addition, the teachers continue to identify and participate in conferences, workshops and other related professional development activities.

2. Need for Regular Communication among a Diverse Group of Stakeholders. Stakeholders Included the School Director, STEM Teachers, University Personnel and Researchers

Approach: According to Rogers [38], effective communication channels play a central role in the diffusion of innovations. Communication and sharing of information among the stakeholders involved in the implementation phase proved at times to be problematic as other responsibilities and duties took precedence and delayed email or phone responses. To ensure that all stakeholders are informed on issues related to use of the STEM classroom, periodic meetings occur with key school administrators, STEM teachers, STEM Center director and researchers, and a representative from the university's education department. Albronda et al. [39] found that group meetings are an "effective means of informing and interaction" among stakeholders during adoption of an innovation. The meetings, which are ongoing, provide an opportunity for sharing information, celebrating successes, discussing issues specific to the STEM classroom, planning ways to address STEM teachers' professional development needs, identifying teachers' needs with respect to the STEM classroom and the technologies, scheduling research observations and interviews, sharing of school initiatives by school administrators, and discussing how teachers are using the space and technologies.

3. Limited Technical Support

Approach: Because of technical problems teachers frequently encounter when using technology in teaching and their inability to troubleshoot such problems, they often avoid using technology unless there is a reason for using it or they have technical assistance available [40]. Although teachers and school administrators had input regarding the choice of technologies for the space, the university completed the purchasing and installation. As the teachers began to use the technologies during their first year in the new space,

Teacher B, who had a reputation for being able to fix technology problems, assumed the role of technology support person in addition to his teaching responsibilities. He described this additional role as a "burden." However, during the second year, the university hired a part-time technical support specialist–again with teacher input–to install software and updates, keep the equipment running and provide just-in-time assistance when the classroom is in use. The teachers report that as a result of having the educational technology specialist, they have more preparation and instructional time. Teachers no longer need to interrupt teaching activities to troubleshoot individual students' problems with the technology. Students and teachers have come to rely on his expertise and assistance. According to Teacher A, "the fact that he is here makes everything better."

4. Classroom Management Issues

Approach: A major concern of the teachers was how to handle behavior problems and prevent damage to the technologies in the new space. This is not surprising. Results from a national Teacher Needs Survey conducted by the American Psychological Society show that classroom management and instructional skills rank highest among teachers' self-identified professional development needs [41]. One of the teachers addressed the management concern by only bringing upper division students into the space during the first year and limiting the features and equipment that could be used. This same teacher discovered that the students could be a valuable resource in learning to use particular technologies, and described how "someone would learn something [about the piece of equipment] and everybody else would share it." The teachers developed some general rules that all users agreed to abide by with respect to putting technologies properly away at the end of sessions and keeping the space clean. As the teachers began to make greater use of the room and the technologies, they discovered that management issues were not as major a problem as they had anticipated. They attributed this in part to the students' pride and sense of ownership of the room. Participants in student focus groups described how they felt responsible for keeping the room and the equipment in good condition. One student responded to the question, "Who takes care of this room?" by saying, "I feel like we all do. I feel like it's a community effort… everybody kind of contributes to cleaning up the room."

5. Equitable Use of the Space

Approach: As STEM teachers began to bring their classes into the new space, concerns developed around the fair and practical use of the room. Even though a listing of time slots was made available as a sign-up sheet on Google Docs, one teacher tended to monopolize the schedule so other classes were rarely able to use the room. If a time slot was empty, other STEM teachers would often move their classes in without signing up, resulting in two classes arriving at the room at the same time. Together, the teachers developed a protocol to ensure that each student in the school uses the space and its technologies at least once a week, and that every STEM class has a lesson taught in the classroom every week. They devised a better way of scheduling their time in the classroom, and even found ways for two classes to occasionally use the space simultaneously. Most importantly, they learned to be flexible if a scheduling conflict unexpected occurred. Also, technologies such as iPads, laptops, and calculators can be used in a teacher's regular classroom when not needed in the STEM classroom.

6. Professional and Personal Concerns

Approach: The time required to keep up with rapid changes in technology is an important factor in whether teachers choose to use technology [40], and teachers often worry about how to keep up with such changes in addition to their other teaching duties. For example, Teacher A identified "other responsibilities/priorities and time to learn" as major obstacles to implementing new technologies. There also appeared to be a question of what personal value the new technologies would have. Doubt about whether one can be successful with an innovation such as technology, and whether the administrators will support and recognize effort put into learning to use new technologies are common concerns of teachers faced with adopting these kinds of innovations [42]. Teacher B found balancing responsibilities of being a first-year teacher, assuming the role of the school's IT specialist, and exploring what teaching with new technologies would require from him to be challenging. Teacher A mentioned having to get up at 2 a.m. on occasion to prepare for the day's lessons and grade papers, and questioned where time to learn how to use the technologies would come from.

The teachers completed the Stages of Concern Questionnaire [31] multiple times at different stages of construction and implementation. The profiles created from this data enabled the researchers to note changes over time in teachers' level of concern with professional and personal issues. Initially, the teachers rated these concerns very high. Several aspects of the implementation process addressed these concerns. First, the school provided time and substitute teachers, giving the STEM teachers opportunities to visit other high-tech schools and to attend conferences. Other events such as an open house and various newspaper articles celebrated the STEM classroom and its success, giving the teachers and students a sense of pride. Teacher A commented, "There's a lot of visibility… I think kids were proud to see us in the paper. I think it's always good to highlight the good, and so I think that overall it's been a really positive thing. I get more positive all the time." Awareness of the importance the school's director placed on use of the STEM classroom and preparing the teachers to integrate the technologies into their teaching also contributed to a decrease over time in the teachers' professional concerns.

7 Discussion

One benefit of using a participatory design approach is that it increases the stakeholders' sense of ownership and responsibility as well as motivation to use that which they helped design [18]. This is true in this setting. Teachers regularly comment on students' pride in the room and how being in the room seems to positively affect students' willingness to stay on task and learn. Both teachers and students depict traditional classrooms as 'teacher space' while they view the STEM classroom as 'community space' with teachers and students equally responsible for maintaining the room. In focus groups, students enthusiastically discussed how pleased they were to see their suggestions integrated into the actual classroom along with ideas they had not even considered, such as the video wall. On their own initiative, they have created projects relating to the use of the room and its technologies as a "legacy" for future students. They described the room as "colorful and interactive," and that they "can take charge and teach classes" in the STEM classroom.

One major aspect of the room that both teachers and students praise is the room's flexibility. The furniture can easily be rearranged to accommodate different teaching styles and activities. Students appreciate being able to display their work in different ways using a variety of devices.

The room appears to be having an impact on teachers' teaching style as well. Teachers describe their teaching approach in the STEM classroom as being 'less dictatorial' and more relaxed than when they are in a traditional classroom. Observation sessions in both traditional classrooms and the STEM classroom support this claim. Students mentioned that they "work together much more in the STEM classroom" compared to in a traditional classroom. According to one student, "this room allows one-to-one teacher-student interactions with solving problems and also peer-to-peer."

One STEM teacher who had been somewhat reluctant to use the technologies in the room observed that anticipated classroom management problems did not materialize to the extent expected. Consequently the teacher became more open to identifying technologies in the room that might be used next in teaching. In the STEM classroom, this same teacher encouraged students to learn new features of technologies and share their expertise. The other STEM teacher described how having so many different technologies available made it easier to accommodate students' different learning styles. This teacher noted "I use the STEM classroom typically as a classroom in which I am not the center of focus." The teacher contrasted this with being in a traditional classroom where "my role changes into the more traditional teacher sometimes. I'm not helping them learn as much as teaching them, which is good sometimes, bad other times. I think that the biggest difference is I feel like my role almost changes."

While the researchers noted an impact on the teachers' teaching style as mentioned previously, they also observed that the teachers did not change their underlying teaching philosophy or basic teaching strategies, but found ways to use the technologies and space in the classroom to support those strategies. According to one of the teachers, "The actual actions have not, probably have not changed as much as they will, but the vision has changed. You know, where we are headed has changed for sure." The teacher added "I can't say that I have changed much yet, but the vision has changed… it's just the space and the availability of lots of writing space that I can see what students are doing at the time they are doing it …. I can envision that the multimedia in terms of the screens and the individual computers because some of the work that I have for them can be done on the individual basis and that's where I'm headed."

The design and implementation process for the STEM classroom is ongoing. Often stakeholders' involvement ends once construction has been completed. However, an important aspect of the process described in this paper is that university and STEM Center personnel continue to be actively involved during the implementation phase in a variety of ways, including participation in the periodic meetings, facilitation of professional development requests, and continuation of the research study. The presence of a technology specialist has alleviated technological problems and allowed the teachers to focus on ways to integrate the technologies into teaching and learning. Administrators and STEM teachers continue to identify additional resources needed in the room and in their professional development. The room itself was not designed to be static, but rather to continue to evolve as users experiment with different ways to teach and learn in the space. The presence- of mobile technologies in particular will enable upgrading the technologies as newer devices become available.

One final consideration is the importance of leadership. Byrom and Bingham [43] identified strong, supportive leadership as one of the most important factors in teachers' willingness to adopt innovations. The leadership role played by stakeholders from the university–especially the Director of the university's STEM Center–was crucial during design and construction of the classroom and continues during implementation.

The leadership of McCoy High School also played an important role. The construction and implementation coincided with the appointment of a new director for the school. In discussing the room, the director stated that continued student input would be very important to the success of the room. She stressed to the teaching staff that because the room contains the best and the latest of technologies, activities within the STEM classroom should be "project-based, utilizing the technologies and features of the room to the fullest". She emphasized the importance of seeking out appropriate professional development to achieve this goal. Throughout the implementation process she has encouraged the teachers to decide how best to use the space and technologies and to play a major role in designing the content and pace of their professional development. She has arranged substitute teachers when these activities conflicted with their teaching schedules.

The director takes great pride in the room and has made it integral to setting future priorities for the school. The availability of the STEM classroom made it possible for the school to introduce the pre-engineering program, Project Lead the Way, into the curriculum. She has been instrumental in publicizing to parents, community members, media and university personnel what teachers and students are accomplishing in the room. In describing the impact on the students, the director said of the STEM classroom it will "… change lives. We have an advantage of educating minority and underprivileged students with this advanced technology. They are going to have more options because of the STEM experience at the high school level."

The successful implementation of a technology-rich educational environment requires a participatory process that doesn't end when construction is complete and the technologies are in place. Continuing to engage in participatory design practices beyond initial implementation ensures maximum usability and sustainability of this type of project. Regular meetings and communications keep stakeholders actively involved. Focus groups, observations, and discussions as part of ongoing collaborative research elicit, monitor, and attend to the concerns of the teachers and students. Most importantly, the participatory design techniques still in use with this STEM classroom allow the users voices to continue to be heard and their learning environment to continue to evolve to meet their needs, giving teachers and students the resources to meet the challenges of STEM education together, both now and in the future.

References

1. National Research Council: Successful K-12 STEM Education. National Academy Press, Washington, D.C. (2011)
2. National Science Board: Preparing the Next Generation of STEM Innovators: Identifying and Developing Our Nation's Human Capital. National Science Board, Washington, D.C. (2010)

3. President's Council of Advisors on Science and Technology: Prepare and Inspire: K-12 Education in Science, Technology, Engineering and Mathematics (STEM) for America's Future (2010)
4. Bergaud, C., Kurop, N., Joyce, A., Wood, C. (eds.): The e-Skills Manifesto. European SchoolNet, Brussels (2012)
5. Joyce, A., Dzoga, M. (eds.): Science, Technology, Engineering and Mathematics: Overcoming Challenges in Europe. European SchoolNet, Brussels (2011)
6. Marginson, S., Tytler, R., Freeman, B., Roberts, K. (eds.): International Comparisons of Science, Technology, Engineering and Mathematics. Australia Council of Learned Academies, Victoria (2013)
7. European Internet Foundation: The Digital World in 2030. European Internet Foundation, Brussels (2014)
8. Cohen, C., Paterson, D.: Teaching Strategies That Promote Science Career Awareness. Northwest Association for Biomedical Research, Seattle (2012)
9. Darling-Hammond, L.: The Flat World and Education: How America's Commitment to Equity will Determine Our Future. Teachers College Press, New York (2010)
10. Flores, A.: Examining disparities in mathematics education: achievement gap or opportunity gap? High Sch. J. **91**(1), 29–42 (2007)
11. Margolis, J., Estrella, R., Goode, J., Holme, J.J., Nao, K.: Stuck in the Shallow End: Education, Race and Computing. The MIT Press, Cambridge (2008)
12. Blikstein, P.: Digital fabrication and 'making' in education: the democratization of invention. In: Walter-Herrmann, J., Bűching, C. (eds.) FabLabs: of Machines, Makers and Inventors, pp. 203–222. Verlag Publishers, Bielefeld (2013)
13. Baek, J.S., Lee, K.P.: A participatory design approach to information architecture design for children. CoDesign Int. J. CoCreation Des. Arts **4**(3), 173–191 (2008)
14. Bowen, S.: Critical theory and participatory design. In: CHI 2010. ACM (2010)
15. Kanstrup, A.M.: A small matter of design: an analysis of end users as designers. In: 12th Participatory Design Conference: Research Papers, New York, vol. 1, pp. 109–118 (2013)
16. Spinuzzi, C.: The methodology of participatory design. Tech. Commun. **52**(2), 163–174 (2005)
17. Crabtree, A.: Ethnography in participatory design. In: Proceedings of 1998 Participatory Design Conference, pp. 93–105. Computer Professionals for Social Responsibility, Seattle (1998)
18. Dalsgaard, P., Eriksson, E.: Large-scale participation: a case study of a participatory approach to developing a new public library. In: Proceedings of CHI 2013: SIGCHI Conference on Human Factors in Computing Systems, pp. 399–408. ACM Press, New York (2013)
19. Kristensen, M., Kyng, M., Palen, L.: Participatory design in emergency medical service: designing for future practice. In: Proceedings of CHI 2006: SIGCHI Conference on Human Factors in Computing Systems, pp. 161–170. ACM Press, New York (2006)
20. Sarkkinen, J.: Examining planning discourse: how a manager represents issues within a planning frame and how the others could do the same. In: 8th Conference on Participatory Design: Artful Integration: Interweaving Media, Materials and Practices, pp. 74–82. ACM Press, New York (2004)
21. Clark, H.: Building Education: The Role of the Physical Environment in Enhancing Teaching and Research. Institute of Education, London (2002)
22. Kőnings, K.D., van Zundert, M.J., Brand-Gruwel, S., van Merriënboer, J.J.G.: Participatory design in secondary education: its desirability and feasibility according to teachers and students. Educ. Stud. **33**, 445–465 (2007)

23. Woolner, P.: Building Schools for the Future Through a Participatory Design Process: Exploring the Issues and Investigation Ways Forward. British Educational Research Association, Manchester (2009). http://www.ncl.ac.uk/cflat/news/documents/WoolnerBSFberapaper.pdf
24. Mumford, M.D., Simonton, D.K.: Creativity in the workplace: people, problems, and structures. J. Creative Behav. **31**, 1–6 (1997)
25. Partnership for 21st Century Skills: Framework for 21st Century Learning (2007)
26. Inc, Apple: Apple Classrooms of Tomorrow – Today: Learning in the 21st Century. Apple, Cupertino (2008)
27. Wilson, S.M.: Effective STEM teacher preparation, induction, and professional development. Workshop on Successful STEM Education (2011). http://www7.nationalacademies.org/bose/ISTEM_Schools_Wilson_Paper_May2011.pdf
28. Patton, M.Q.: Qualitative Evaluation and Research Methods, 2nd edn. SAGE, Thousand Oaks (1990)
29. Stake, R.: Case studies. In: Denzin, N.K., Lincoln, Y.S. (eds.) Strategies of Qualitative Inquiry, pp. 86–109. Sage, Thousand Oaks (1998)
30. Yin, R.K.: Case Study Research: Design and Methods, 4th edn. Sage, Thousand Oaks (2009)
31. George, A.A., Hall, G.E., Stiegelbauer, S.M.: Measuring Implementation in Schools: The Stages of Concern Questionnaire. SEDL, Austin (2006)
32. Bingimlas, K.A.: Barriers to the successful integration of ICT in teaching and learning environments: a review of the literature. Eurasia J. Math. Sci. Technol. Educ. **5**(3), 235–245 (2009)
33. Buabeng-Andoh, C.: Factors influencing teachers' adoption and integration of information and communication technology into teaching: a review of the literature. Int. J. Educ. Dev. Inf. Commun. Technol. **8**(1), 136–155 (2012)
34. Gaffney, M.: Enhancing Teachers' Take-up of Digital Content: Factors and Design principles in Technology Adoption. Educational Services Australia, Ltd (2011)
35. Mumtaz, S.: Factors affecting teachers' use of information and communications technology: a review of the literature. J. Inf. Technol. Teach. Educ. **9**(3), 319–342 (2000)
36. Garet, M.S., porter, A.C., Desimone, L., Birmin, B.F., Yoon, K.S.: What makes professional development effective? Results from a national sample of teachers. Am. Educ. Res. J. **38**(4), 915–945 (2001)
37. Gulamhussein, A.: Teaching the Teachers: Effective Professional Development in an Era of High Stakes Accountability. Center for Public Education, Alexandria (2013)
38. Rogers, E.: Diffusions of Innovations. Free Press, New York (1962)
39. Albronda, B., De Langen, F., Huizing, B.: The influence of communication on the process of innovation adoption. Innov. Manage. J. **4**(1), 20–29 (2011)
40. Zhao, Y., Frank, K.A.: Factors affecting technology uses in schools: an ecological perspective. Am. Educ. Res. J. **40**(4), 807–840 (2003)
41. Coalition for Psychology in Schools and Education: Report on the Teacher Needs Survey. American Psychological Association, Washington, D.C. (2006)
42. Hall, G.E.: Technology's achilles heel: achieving high-quality implementation. J. Res. Technol. Educ. **42**(3), 231–253 (2010)
43. Byrom, E., Bingham, M. (eds.): Factors Influencing the Effective Use of Technology for Teaching and Learning: Lessons Learned from the SEIR_TEC Intensive Site Schools, 2nd edn. SouthEast Initiatives Regional Technology in Education Consortium, Greensboro (2001)

Domain Applications and Case Studies

Fostering Information Literacy in German Psychology Students: Objective and Subjective Evaluation of a Blended Learning Course

Nikolas Leichner(✉), Johannes Peter, Anne-Kathrin Mayer, and Günter Krampen

Leibniz Institute for Psychology Information, Universitätsring 15, 54296 Trier, Germany
{leichner,peter,mayer,krampen}@zpid.de

Abstract. This paper reports about the objective and subjective evaluation of a blended learning course to foster information literacy skills of psychology students. The course consists of three modules delivered online and two face-to-face seminars. The evaluation is conducted using a multi-method approach with objective as well as subjective measures: Participants completed an information literacy knowledge test and standardized information search tasks before and after taking the course as well as a feedback questionnaire. A sample of N = 67 undergraduate psychology students (n = 37 experimental group, n = 30 waiting control group) participated in the course. As it was expected, students' knowledge test scores as well as performance in the search tasks improved markedly during the course. Furthermore, students were satisfied with the course, whereas online learning found better acceptance than face-to-face learning. Results are discussed with regard to the soundness of the evaluation criteria used and to further development of the course.

Keywords: Information literacy · Blended learning · Distance education · Psychology · College students

1 Introduction

The term Information literacy is used to describe the ability to realize when there is a need for information, and the ability to identify, locate, and evaluate information which is required to meet this need [1, 2]. Against the background that advances in information technology lead to a growing number of information resources, information literacy can be considered a "basic skills set" [3].

As information literacy is of importance in nearly all circumstances [3], a clear definition of information literacy has to be provided first of all. Hence, we limit our research to information literacy in higher education, especially in psychology. Our definition of information literacy is based on the ACRL Psychology information literacy standards [4], because this framework includes detailed performance indicators. This definition includes four standards of information literacy:

The research was funded by the German Joint Initiative for Research and Innovation with a grant acquired in the Leibniz Competition 2012: grant number: SAW-2012-ZPID-6 114.

S. Zvacek et al. (Eds.): CSEDU 2014, CCIS 510, pp. 359–371, 2015.
DOI: 10.1007/978-3-319-25768-6_23

1. Determining the nature and amount of information needed: exemplary performance indicator: "understands basic research methods and scholarly communication patterns in psychology necessary to select relevant resources";
2. Assessing information effectively and efficiently: exemplary performance indicator: "selects the most appropriate sources for accessing the needed information";
3. Evaluating information and incorporating information into one's knowledge system: exemplary performance indicator: "compares new information with prior knowledge to determine its value, contradictions, or other unique characteristics";
4. Using the information effectively to accomplish a specific purpose; exemplary performance indicator: "applies new and prior information to the planning and creation of a particular project, paper, or presentation".

We decided to focus on standards one to three, as our course was devoted primarily to the improvement of information seeking skills. Skills related to standard four are part of the curriculum of academic writing courses at German universities; consequently, they should not be part of our course. With regard to our curriculum, we expected the participants inter alia to be (better) able to understand scholarly communication patterns, distinguish between several research methods (e.g. meta-analysis and empirical study), to select the most appropriate resource for their information need, and to evaluate the literature found.

There is indication that incoming students are not sufficiently information literate [5] and that students do not become information literate during the course of their studies [6]. To address this need, almost every university library in Germany provides information literacy courses that complement the academic writing courses offered by university departments. However, most of these courses are two-hour events covering only a facet of academic information literacy (e.g. the use of bibliographic databases). Due to limited time, these courses offer few possibilities to practice information seeking, or to ask questions and discuss matters. As there is no standardized test to assess information literacy for German speaking populations, in most cases, evaluation efforts are based exclusively on feedback provided by participants. Finally, most courses are not tailored to specific disciplines, or fields (e.g. economics, social sciences). This is problematic, as scholarly communication patterns and information resources differ between disciplines. Course content should therefore be adapted to the needs of psychology students [7].

The aim of this study is to create a blended learning approach to teach information literacy to undergraduate students in psychology and to carry out an evaluation study based on both objective performance indicators using a control group as well as feedback by the participants.

The main reason for choosing a blended learning approach was to give participants the chance to work on the online materials adapted to their individual schedule. This is particularly important as students are often pressed for time. However, there should also be traditional face-to-face teaching as online learning alone seems to be fraught with higher dropout rates [8]. There is research indicating that blended learning can reduce dropout rates [9] and is more effective than traditional face-to-face teaching or online learning [10]. Furthermore, face-to-face teaching facilitates the organization of discussions, which are important for a deeper understanding of learning material [11]. At the start, the course will exist alongside the courses offered by university libraries. However, we hope that our materials will later on be used by university libraries or faculty to offer courses tailored to psychology students.

2 Outline of the Course

2.1 Content

The content of the course was determined based on the psychology specific information literacy standards provided by the ACRL [4] and based on our own considerations. The target group were undergraduate students, so the content was mainly basic information about

- scholarly communication patterns in psychology and common publication types (e.g. empirical article, review article, edited books);
- different information resources (inter alia bibliographic databases, internet resources) and their advantages and disadvantages;
- appropriate use of these resources (e.g. understanding of the thesaurus and of Boolean Operators);
- inclusion of resources provided by related disciplines (e.g. PubMed, ERIC) in case the topic is of interdisciplinary nature;
- options for the acquisition of literature (e.g. use of electronic journal subscriptions, the local library catalogue or interlibrary loan);
- criteria for the selecting publications beyond their content, e.g. Journal Impact Factor.

2.2 Structure

As mentioned before, the course combined online and traditional face-to-face teaching. In total, there were three modules to be completed online and two face-to-face seminars. We expected that completing the online materials would take up to four hours; both face-to-face seminars were designed to take 90 min each. The course was scheduled to be completed within two weeks, what seems a reasonable workload for college students.

The concept of the course envisaged that most of the knowledge should be imparted by the online materials, while the main purpose of the face-to-face seminars was to provide an opportunity to solve information problems under the guidance of the instructor, to ask questions, as well as to discuss the advantages and disadvantages of different search strategies and search tools. For this reason, participants had to complete certain online materials before attending the related face-to-face seminar.

Online modules 1 and 2 were related to the first face-to-face seminar. These modules dealt mainly with scholarly communication patterns, information sources (and their functions), as well as the acquisition of literature. A central element of the related first seminar was the task to find scientific literature on the question how distractions impact car driving performance. At the beginning of the seminar, the task was presented to the participants. Then, the task was split into steps (determining the information need, finding search terms, conducting the search, selecting literature) and participants worked on the steps either individually, or in small groups. The instructor was available in case questions arose. After completing each step, one of the participants (one group, respectively) had to present his/her outcome to the other participants and the outcome was discussed. Online module 3 and the related second face-to-face seminar dealt with the evaluation of publications. The online module included criteria for the selecting publications beyond their content. During the second face-to-face seminar, the students were presented several publications about a topic and were asked to apply the criteria for evaluating and selecting publications from the online module.

All online modules were provided via the e-learning platform “Moodle”. Most of the content was presented using short passages of text which were enriched by illustrations or screenshots of the relevant computer programs. This content was provided using lessons or pages inside of Moodle. The materials also included several videos. At the end of every section of the course, short quizzes were provided, so that the participants could apply their knowledge right after learning.

3 Empirical Study

3.1 Instruments

In most cases, information literacy is assessed using knowledge tests consisting of multiple choice items; at least two such tests are available commercially [12, 13]. These tests have been shown to provide a reliable, valid and economic way of measuring information literacy. However, as information literacy is a complex ability, it can be doubted whether a knowledge test can assess information literacy comprehensively. For instance, appropriate information seeking behavior is an elementary part of being information literate [14] and the assessment of information seeking behavior requires observation [15], or self-reports [14].

Besides, several authors argue that competencies should be assessed using real-life tasks instead of knowledge tests [16, 17].

For these reasons, we decided to use a multi-method approach consisting of two standardized tests which were applied in a laboratory setting: a knowledge test and information search tasks.

The knowledge test consisted of 35 multiple-choice items and had previously been developed by our research group. When developing the items, we relied on Standards 1 to 3 of the aforementioned information literacy definition [4]. A sample item is:

Which differences exist between Internet search engines (e.g. Google Scholar) and bibliographic databases?

(a) *bibliographic databases usually have a thesaurus search*
(b) *Boolean Operators can only be used with bibliographic databases*
(c) *the order of items on the results page is not affected by the number of clicks on each item*

The test had been used in a previous study with a sample of $N = 184$ participants who had completed the test online. In this study, an acceptable internal consistency of the test of Cronbach's Alpha $\alpha = 0.49$ was found. Furthermore, it was found that Master level-students scored significantly higher than undergraduate students in their first and second year. These results can be considered an indication of the validity of the test.

The information search tasks are based on a taxonomy of tasks from which instances of tasks can be derived [18]. When reviewing the literature on information search tasks, we found that the existing taxonomies are of a descriptive nature and do not provide indications for the difficulty of a certain task type, for an example, see [19]. Another problem with these taxonomies was that they had been developed to classify non-scholarly search tasks in electronic resources. There are several differences between academic and non-scholarly searches; the most important one might be the use of bibliographic databases (e.g. PsycINFO) instead of internet search engines (e.g. Google, Yahoo!).

For these reasons, we decided to develop a task taxonomy specifically for academic information search tasks in psychology. The taxonomy provides three types of information search task differing in their difficulty. To be more precise, the tasks differ in the abilities and competencies required to solve the task. The taxonomy is designed in a way that abilities required to solve tasks of the first type are also required to solve tasks of type 2. However, solving tasks of type 2 requires additional competencies, as do tasks of type 3. The taxonomy can be used to develop several tasks of the same structure and difficulty which can be used for assessing information literacy. For illustration purposes, a type 2 task (medium difficulty) is provided:

Are there meta-analyses published after 2005 investigating "risk factors" for the development of a "Posttraumatic stress disorder"? If possible, indicate two publications.

To solve this task, the participant has to understand the keyword search function in a bibliographic database, and needs an understanding of Boolean operators and complex filter functions in bibliographic databases to find publications using a certain methodology (e.g. meta-analysis). Type 1 tasks are easier as they do not require an understanding of Boolean operators and complex filter functions. Type 3 tasks are more difficult, as they additionally require the participant to identify appropriate search terms before conducting the search. To score the tasks, rubrics for scoring the search task outcome (which publications were found) and the procedure applied by the students when completing the tasks were created. In line with the rubric for scoring the outcome, scores were awarded depending on how close the publications found come to the requirements mentioned in the task description (e.g. thematic focus of the publication, publication date). As stated in the rubric for scoring the procedure, scores were awarded for working on the tasks in an efficient and information literate way as defined by the information literacy standards [4]. For example, for a type 2 task, the maximum number of procedure scores was rewarded if the participant solved the task using bibliographic databases, used Boolean operators to combine two search terms and limited the results using the corresponding functions of the database.

As the knowledge test and the information search tasks primarily assess the overall increase in skills, we additionally employed the "Inventory for the Evaluation of Blended Learning" (IEBL) [20]. This questionnaire can be used to evaluate blended learning courses based on subjective feedback by participants. It includes three scales referring to general aspects of the training:

- "Overall benefit" (usefulness of training contents, e.g., for studying, 7 items),
- "Didactic quality" (comprehensibility and clarity of the transmission of contents, e.g. using practical examples, 6 items), and
- "Appropriateness" (adequacy of course contents, e.g., difficulty, with regard to individual preconditions, 5 items).

Furthermore, it includes five scales referring to specific aspects of blended learning:

- "Acceptance of online learning" (appropriateness of online learning for the conveyed contents, 5 items),
- "Lack of social exchange in online learning" (subjective lack of social exchanges while learning online, 3 items),
- "Usability" (clarity of arrangement and ease of handling of the online materials, 7 items),
- "Acceptance of face-to-face learning" (appropriateness of face-to-face learning for the conveyed contents, 5 items), and
- "Lecturer" (quality of teaching, e.g., speaking clearly, 8 items).

In sum, the inventory consists of 46 statements which have to be rated on 7-point Likert scales (1 = "I do not agree"; 7 = "I agree"). A sample item which refers to the scale "Acceptance of online learning" is *"Training content is conveyed comprehensible in the online modules of this training"*.

For the scale "Appropriateness", which is used to evaluate the coverage of certain materials, a different labeling of the Likert scale (1 = "far too easy"; 4 = "appropriate"; 7 = "far too hard") is used. Internal consistencies (Cronbach's α) of the scales range from $\alpha = 0.69$ to $\alpha = 0.89$ [20].

3.2 Method

Participants. The sample consisted of $N = 67$ undergraduate psychology students who took the course. Out of these students, 34 were first year students, while 33 were second year students. The average age was 21.67 ($SD = 2.38$). Participants had agreed to additionally participate in three data collection sessions for which they were compensated. Participants were randomly assigned to one of two groups; group 1 (experimental group) consisted of $n = 37$ participants, group 2 (waiting control group) of $n = 30$.

Procedure. The duration of the evaluation study was four weeks, while the actual course took only two weeks. Data collection 1 took place right at the start of the evaluation study. Subsequently, group 1 participated in the course, while group 2 served as a waiting control group. Two weeks later, when the course was completed for group 1, data collection 2 took place. After that, group 2 participated in the course. The final data collection 3 took place after all participants had completed the course.
The data collections were scheduled in the computer lab of Trier University. Students were tested in groups of 15 to 22 participants under the supervision of two experimenters. They first completed three information search tasks (one task of each type), followed by two questionnaires concerning epistemological beliefs, and the information literacy knowledge test.

To complete the information search tasks, the participants could use all resources available from these computers (access to the internet, to bibliographic databases, and to the online library catalogue). The information search tasks were presented ordered by difficulty. Participants were required to record the publications found by using input boxes that were provided by the software used. After the completion of every task, the participants had to answer several questions concerning the procedure of their search. These data were the basis for scoring the procedure. As it would be beyond the scope of this paper, the results concerning the epistemological beliefs questionnaires are not reported.

The IEBL was employed after course participation. As the two groups participated at different points in time, participants from group 1 completed the IEBL during data collection 2, while participants from group 2 completed the questionnaire during data collection 3.

Hypotheses and Research Questions. With regard to the search tasks, we expected that those tasks requiring more abilities should be more difficult; in this case, we expected type 3 tasks to be the most difficult followed by type 2 tasks, which, in turn, should be more difficult than type 1 tasks (Hypothesis 1).

As explained above, there were three variables designed to assess information literacy: outcome and procedure of the search tasks, and the knowledge test. We expected to find significant correlations among these instruments. As the knowledge test had already been tried and tested in a different study, finding correlations between the test and the search tasks would corroborate the status of the search tasks as indicator of information literacy (Hypothesis 2).

Furthermore, we expected that participants would score higher on all instruments after participating in the course. Specifically, group 1 should outperform group 2 at data collection 2. At the final data collection, there should not be any difference between the groups (Hypothesis 3).

Additionally, we expected that the training should be evaluated positively by the participants, as they should benefit from the domain-specific conceptualization of the course and the time flexibility of the blended learning approach [21]. Therefore, mean scores of all scales of the IEBL were expected to be above the theoretical mean of 4, except for the scale "Appropriateness", whose mean was expected to be close to 4, corresponding to a judgment of training difficulty etc. as "appropriate" (Hypothesis 4).

For exploratory reasons, we examined additionally whether the mean scores of the IEBL scales referring to specific aspects of blended learning differed from each other, as the results can be used to derive detailed implications for the further development of the training.

3.3 Results

Before the course could be evaluated, the information search tasks had to be scored independently by two raters. The inter-rater-reliability (correlation between the scores awarded by the two raters) was in the range from $r = 0.62$ to $r = 0.92$; most correlations were above $r = 0.70$. In those cases where the scores differed, the raters agreed on one solution which was used for the analyses.

The first hypothesis to be examined was whether the expected order of task difficulties could be verified empirically. Data from data collection 1 is presented in Table 1. As can be seen, tasks of type 3 were more difficult than tasks of type 2, which, in turn, were more difficult than type 1 tasks. The table shows the percentage of the maximum score for the different tasks types.

Table 1. Percentage of maximum score for search task outcome and procedure at data collection 1.

Task type	Outcome	Procedure
1	77 %	55 %
2	50 %	46 %
3	32 %	36 %

For the following analyses, the outcome and procedure scores of each data collection were summed up separately, so that 2 scores for each data collection resulted. These scores were scaled, in order to restrict their range from 0 to 1 and are presented in Table 2. Before using these scores for evaluating the course, we determined whether there were differences between the two groups of participants before the course started. Our analysis revealed that there were no differences between the groups, neither on the outcome scores ($t[65] = 1.34$, *ns*), nor on the procedure scores ($t[65] = 1.23$, *ns*). Furthermore, the two groups did not differ in their performance on the knowledge test ($t[65] = 0.78$, *ns*).

Table 2. Mean scores (and standard deviations) for the outcome and procedure scores.

	Data collection 1	Data collection 2	Data collection 3
Outcome			
group 1 ($n = 37$)	0.45 (0.19)	0.63 (0.19)	0.78 (0.17)
group 2 ($n = 30$)	0.51 (0.16)	0.49 (0.13)	0.76 (0.18)
Procedure			
group 1 ($n = 37$)	0.43 (0.13)	0.81 (0.10)	0.78 (0.08)
group 2 ($n = 30$)	0.47 (0.13)	0.54 (0.12)	0.70 (0.11)

Scores on the information literacy knowledge test were also scaled to restrict their range from 0 to 1, and can be found in Table 3.

Table 3. Mean scores (and standard deviations) for the information literacy knowledge test.

Group	Data collection 1	Data collection 2	Data collection 3
group 1	0.59 (0.06)	0.76 (0.05)	0.75 (0.05)
group 2	0.61 (0.06)	0.62 (0.05)	0.75 (0.05)

To examine the second hypothesis, correlations between the scores on the knowledge test and the two search task variables were computed using data from data collection 1. It was decided to analyze data from data collection 1 only, as the performance at the following data collections reflects to a great extent how much the participants have benefited from the course, so the results might be distorted.

The outcome and procedure scores of the search tasks correlated significantly ($r = 0.22, p < 0.05$), even though the correlation was weak. Both scores also correlated significantly with the performance on the knowledge test (for the outcome scores $r = 0.29, p < 0.01$, and the procedure scores $r = 0.48, p < 0.01$, both one-tailed).

To evaluate the course (Hypothesis 3), the three information literacy performance indicators were analyzed separately. For each variable, a repeated measures analysis of variance (ANOVA) was computed. The time of data collection was a within-subjects factor, while group membership was a between-subjects factor. The respective information literacy performance indicator was used as dependent variable.

The performance on the knowledge test was analyzed first. The analysis revealed a significant main effect of the within-subjects factor ($F[2.130] = 216.53, p < 0.01$) and a significant interaction of the two factors ($F[2.130] = 73.13, p < 0.01$), what is depicted in Fig. 1. To analyze group differences, a t-test was computed for every data collection. At data collection 1, there was no difference between the groups ($t[65] = 0.78$, *ns*). At data collection 2, a significant difference could be found ($t[65] = 10.47, p < 0.01$), indicating that group 1 outperformed the other group. There was no significant difference at data collection 3 ($t[65] = 0.37$, *ns*).

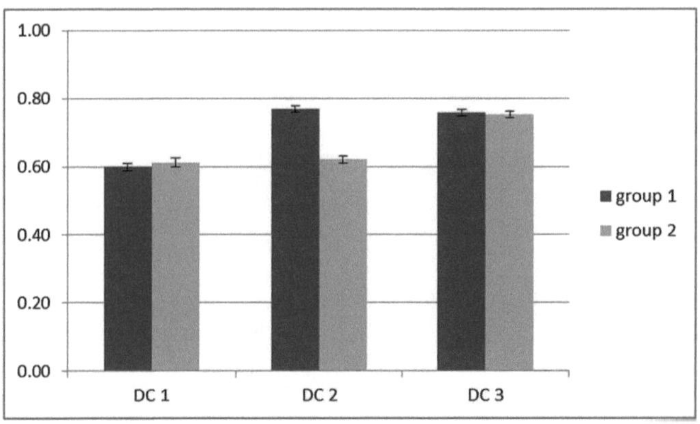

Fig. 1. Mean scores (and standard errors) on the information literacy test. DC = data collection.

Next, the outcome scores of the search tasks were analyzed. The ANOVA revealed a significant main effect of the within-subjects factor ($F[2.130] = 45.77, p < 0.01$) and a significant interaction of the two factors ($F[2.130] = 5.45, p < 0.01$). To investigate the pattern in more detail, t-tests were calculated to compare the two groups at each data collection. There were no significant differences at data collections 1 and 3 ($t[65] = 1.33$ and $t[65] = 0.32$, respectively). However, the two groups differed at data collection 2 ($t[65] = 3.32, p < 0.01$). Once again, group 1 outperformed group 2, as can be seen in Fig. 2.

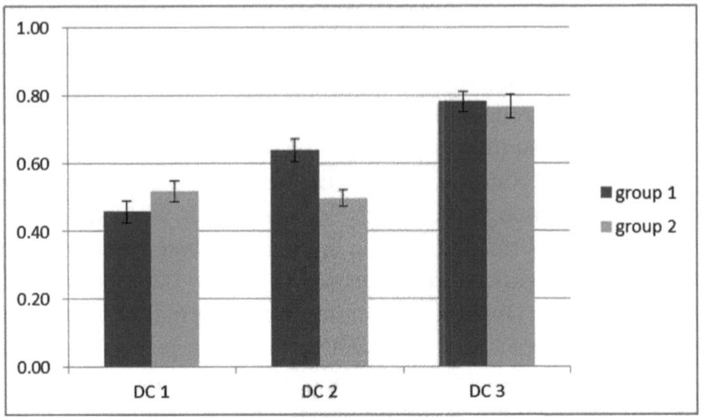

Fig. 2. Outcome scores (and standard errors) of the information search tasks.

Furthermore, the procedure scores of the search task were analyzed. The ANOVA revealed a significant main effect of the within-subjects factor ($F[2.130] = 148.46$, $p < 0.01$) and a significant interaction of the two factors ($F[2.130] = 37.38$, $p < 0.01$). Once again, *t*-tests were applied to analyze group differences. There was no significant difference at data collection 1 ($t[65] = 1.23$, *ns*), but significant differences at data collections 2 ($t[65] = 9.21$, $p < 0.01$) and 3 ($t[65] = 3.21$, $p < 0.01$) in such a way that group 1 scored higher than group 2, as is displayed in Fig. 3.

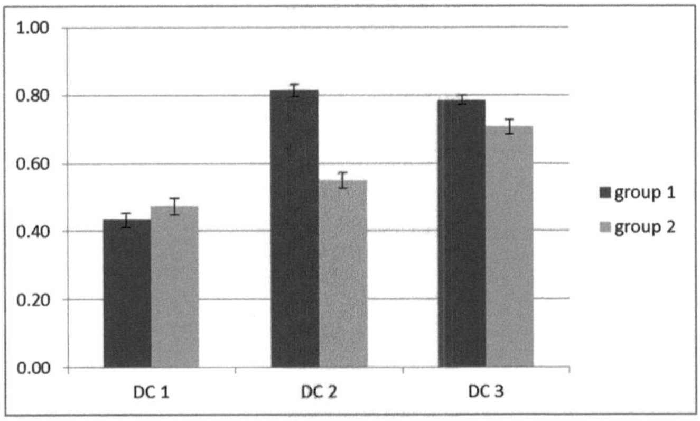

Fig. 3. Procedure scores (and standards errors) of the information search tasks.

For the analysis of the IEBL questionnaire, data from both data collections was merged; the mean scores of the scales are displayed in Fig. 4. One-sample *t*-tests revealed that the mean scores of all scales were significantly above the theoretical mean of 4 ($p < 0.01$ for all scales; alpha error level was adjusted using Bonferroni correction), except for the scale "Appropriateness", which did not differ significantly from its theoretical mean.

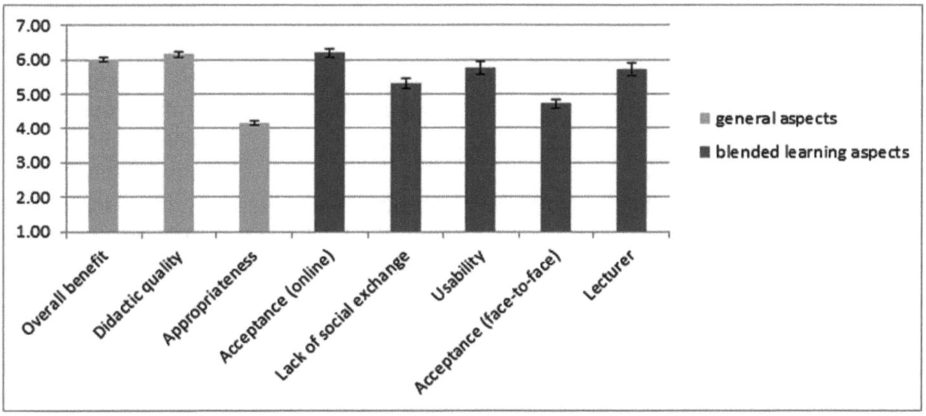

Fig. 4. Mean scores (and standard errors) of the IEBL scales.

To examine whether the mean values of the five scales referring to blended learning differed from each other, an overall mean was computed ($M = 5.54$; $SD = 0.56$), and it was examined whether each scale differed from this overall mean by one-sample t-tests (alpha error level was adjusted again). It was revealed that the mean of the scale "Acceptance of online learning" was significantly above ($t[66] = 5.91$, $p < 0.01$) the overall mean, whereas the mean of the scale "Acceptance of face-to-face learning" was significantly below the overall mean ($t[66] = -4.77$, $p < 0.01$). The mean scores of the other three scales did not differ significantly from the overall mean.

3.4 Discussion

All hypotheses were confirmed by the results. The first two hypotheses relate to the soundness of the evaluation instruments. First, the analysis of the search task difficulties indicated that the expected order of task difficulties could be verified empirically. This shows that those tasks requiring more competencies are also harder to solve for the participants, what can be seen as an indication of validity for the search tasks and the underlying task taxonomy. The second hypothesis, postulating that there would be significant correlations among all three information literacy performance indicators, could also be upheld. The fact that the correlations are far from perfect lead us to the conclusion, that all three instruments capture different facets of the concept information literacy. It is of significance that search task outcome and procedure scores both correlated significantly with the knowledge test, as this is a signal that the search tasks are valid, because the test had already been tested in a different study.

The third hypothesis was that participation in the course improves information literacy. As can be seen in Figs. 1, 2, 3, participation in the course improved information literacy on all three performance indicators. To be exact, the hypothesis was that group 1 would outperform group 2 at data collection 2. This was hypothesized because at that time, group 1 had already taken the course, while group 2 had not. At data collection 3, there should not be any group differences left. This pattern could be observed when analyzing the scores on the knowledge test and the outcome scores of the search tasks. Analysis of the procedure scores displayed the same pattern at data collections 1 and 2. At data collection 3, however, group 1 still performed better, even though at this time both groups had taken the course. A more detailed analysis revealed that both groups improved; however, group 1 performance was enhanced stronger. No substantial explanation for this result can be found except that this might be random variations due to relatively small sample size. As mentioned above, group sizes were $n = 30$ and $n = 37$, respectively. Notwithstanding that participants had been assigned to one of the groups in a randomized way, it cannot be ruled out that some group 1 participants learned more due to individual differences. As this difference can only be observed on one of the three performance indicators, it can be ascribed to random variations. The hypothesis can still be confirmed as both groups had improved by taking the course. It should also be mentioned that there were significant differences between the groups at data collection 2. At this time a treatment group was compared to a waiting control group. The group differences show that participants did not become more information literate without training, corroborating the attribution of information literacy improvements to the participation in the course.

Analyses of the IEBL scales show that the course was perceived as positive by the participants. Thus, the fourth hypothesis could also be confirmed. The participants rated the training as beneficial for their studies and appreciated its didactic quality. They felt neither overwhelmed nor insufficiently challenged.

Finally, explorative analyses revealed a comparatively high acceptance of the online learning, whereas the acceptance of the face-to-face learning was comparatively low. Although the face-to-face learning was considered to foster a deeper understanding of the learning material, e.g. through discussions, some students might have experienced it as redundant. It seems also plausible that students partly disliked the face-to-face seminars, as they were required to participate at a certain time, and there was no time flexibility as with the online materials.

To sum up, the results show that the information literacy course is effective and perceived positively. So, this research adds to the field a blended learning course that is tailored to psychology students and has been rigorously evaluated. In the future, it might be developed further by adding elements tailored to Master levels students. As this course was tailored to Bachelor students, the participants were mainly taught the essentials of seeking academic information. Furthermore, the comparatively low acceptance of the face-to-face learning should be considered when developing similar courses. One possibility is to leave out the face-to-face seminars. A further evaluation study might show whether this is equally effective. Another possibility is to enhance the personal involvement of the participants during the face-to-face seminars. For instance, in addition to discussions, the participants could be instructed to conduct literature searches for personally relevant topics, e.g. the topic of their thesis.

References

1. National Forum on Information Literacy: What is information literacy? (n.d.). http://infolit.org/?page_id=3172
2. American Library Association: Presidential Committee on information literacy. Final report (1989). http://www.ala.org/acrl/publications/whitepapers/presidential

3. Eisenberg, M.B.: Information literacy: essential skills for the information age. DESIDOC J. Libr. Inf. Technol. **28**(2), 39–47 (2008)
4. Association of College and Research Libraries: Psychology information literacy standards (2010). http://www.ala.org/acrl/standards/psych_info_lit
5. Smith, J.K., Given, L.M., Julien, H., Ouellette, D., DeLong, K.: Information literacy proficiency: assessing the gap in high school students' readiness for undergraduate academic work. Libr. Inf. Sci. Res. **35**(2), 88–96 (2013). doi:10.1016/j.lisr.2012.12.001
6. Warwick, C., Rimmer, J., Blandford, A., Gow, J., Buchanan, G.: Cognitive economy and satisfying in information seeking: a longitudinal study of undergraduate information behavior. J. Am. Soc. Inf. Sci. **60**(12), 2402–2415 (2009)
7. Thaxton, L., Faccioli, M.B., Mosby, A.P.: Leveraging collaboration for information literacy in psychology. RSR **32**(2), 185–189 (2004). doi:10.1108/00907320410537702
8. Carr, S.: As distance education comes of age, the challenge is keeping the students. Chronicle High. Educ. **46**(23), A39–A41 (2000)
9. López-Pérez, M., Pérez-López, M., Rodríguez-Ariza, L.: Blended learning in higher education: students' perceptions and their relation to outcomes. Comput. Educ. **56**(3), 818–826 (2011). doi:10.1016/j.compedu.2010.10.023
10. Clardy, A.: Distant, on-line education: effects, principles and practices (2009). http://files.eric.ed.gov/fulltext/ED506182.pdf
11. Arnold, P., Kilian, L., Thillosen, A., Zimmer, G.: E-Learning Handbuch für Hochschulen und Bildungszentren: Didaktik, Organisation, Qualität, 1st edn. BW Bildung und Wiss, Nürnberg (2004)
12. Project SAILS: Project SAILS Information Literacy Assessment (2013). https://www.projectsails.org/
13. Center for Assessment and Research Studies: Information Literacy Test (ILT) (2013). http://www.madisonassessment.com/uploads/Manual-ILT-2013.pdf
14. Timmers, C.F., Glas, C.A.W.: Developing scales for information-seeking behaviour. J. Documentation **66**(1), 46–69 (2010)
15. Julien, H., Barker, S.: How high-school students find and evaluate scientific information: a basis for information literacy skills development. Libr. Inf. Sci. Res. **31**(1), 12–17 (2009). doi:10.1016/j.lisr.2008.10.008
16. Shavelson, R.J.: On the measurement of competency. Empirical Res. Vocat. Educ. Training **2**(1), 41–63 (2010)
17. McClelland, D.C.: Testing for competence rather than for "intelligence". Am. Psychol. **28**(1), 1–14 (1973)
18. Leichner, N., Peter, J., Mayer, A.-K., Krampen, G.: Assessing information literacy using information search tasks. J. Inf. Literacy **8**(1), 3–20 (2014). doi:10.11645/8.1.1870
19. Kim, J.: Describing and predicting information-seeking behavior on the web. J. Am. Soc. Inf. Sci. **60**(4), 679–693 (2009). doi:10.1002/asi.21035
20. Peter, J., Leichner, N., Mayer, A.-K., Krampen, G.: Das Inventar zur Evaluation von Blended Learning (IEBL): Konstruktion und Erprobung in einem Training professioneller Informationskompetenz. Paper presented at 10. Fachtagung Psychologiedidaktik und Evaluation, Witten, Germany (May 2014)
21. Garrison, D.R., Kanuka, H.: Blended learning: uncovering its transformative potential in higher education. Internet High. Educ. **7**(2), 95–105 (2004). doi:10.1016/j.iheduc.2004.02.001

Ubiquitous Learning

Recommendations for Mobile Virtual Campus Design Based on Student Feedback

Pablo Rebaque-Rivas(✉) and Eva P. Gil-Rodríguez

Community Initiatives (Office of Learning Technologies), Universitat Oberta de Catalunya, Barcelona, Spain
{prebaque, egilrod}@uoc.edu

Abstract. In this paper we present a series of recommendations designed to guide universities in the development of mobile learning environments, based on a case study of the *Universitat Oberta de Catalunya* (Open University of Catalonia, UOC), an online university. A focus group was organized to gather students' views on the three mobile developments for the UOC's Virtual Campus: a hybrid app, an adapted version for mobile browsers, and an e-mail client app. The results obtained from the focus group reveal that students already use the UOC's mobile developments in their day-to-day activities and expect this use to increase in the future. The principal recommendations address the need to develop a mobile learning environment with the scalability to accommodate new functionalities and services and the multi-device capability to meet the students' choice of device, and the importance of a user-centered design (UCD) approach to meet student requirements.

Keywords: Mobile learning environment · Mobile learning · User-Centered design · Mobile strategy

1 Introduction

Smartphones and tablets are increasingly used by the general population and Spain, in particular, is among the European Union countries with the highest levels of smartphone penetration [1], with smartphones accounting for 80 % of all mobile phones sold [2]. The expansion of the apps market appears unstoppable [3], and uses are being found for mobile devices and apps in an increasing number of areas, including leisure, city management, public administration, education, etc.

The spread of mobile devices and apps has given rise to various debates, which centre around the technology itself, how this technology should be used [4–6], how to guarantee a satisfactory user experience [7, 8], and the relative merits of native, web and hybrid apps [9, 10].

In education – particularly the higher education sector – debate over mobile apps must also incorporate consideration of the use of mobile devices and apps for teaching and learning, or m-learning, (see, for example [11]).

As such, if a university wants to adapt its virtual learning environment for mobile devices it will need to take decisions regarding educational content, technological structures, and the desired form of human-computer interaction (HCI).

S. Zvacek et al. (Eds.): CSEDU 2014, CCIS 510, pp. 375–388, 2015.
DOI: 10.1007/978-3-319-25768-6_24

While there is already a body of literature on m-learning [11, 12], the relationship between m-learning and UX [13], and the types of technology and platforms that can be used to in adapting a virtual learning environment for mobile devices [14] there is an obvious lack of studies addressing the views of students, not with regard to the learning process itself but in respect of their capacity as users of both mobile devices and mobile learning environments. In other words, the literature contains little consideration of the extent to which virtual campuses are adapted to the real needs of their users (examples can be found in [15, 16]).

Questions that must be asked include the following: If a university offers a wide range of services, which are the most relevant to students when they connect from a mobile device? Would students prefer to use a virtual campus specifically adapted for mobile browsers, a native/hybrid app, or the choice of both? If the university intends to develop an app, would students prefer a single app that combines only the most relevant services or individual apps for each of the services offered?

In this paper we aim to shed light on the options open to a university when developing a mobile learning environment, based on the perspective of the student-user. Specifically, we present a series of recommendations based on a case study [17] of the Universitat Oberta de Catalunya (Open University of Catalonia, UOC), an online university. A focus group was held with UOC students to gather their views on the mobile developments currently offered at the UOC and the direction work on these developments should take in the future.

The mobile developments discussed in the focus group were: an adaptation of the UOC Virtual Campus for mobile browsers; a hybrid app of the Virtual Campus; and a native e-mail client app.

In the following sections we describe the three mobile developments and explain the objectives and composition of the focus group and the results obtained from the discussion. Finally, we present a series of conclusions and the recommendations for other universities.

2 Mobile Developments at the UOC

As stated above, the focus group was used to discuss the adapted version of the Virtual Campus for mobile browsers, the Virtual Campus hybrid app, and the e-mail client app.

The UOC Virtual Campus was developed used a proprietary UOC learning management system. The Campus works as a portal where students have access to all the different services necessary to carry out their studies, such as e-mail, the agenda, classrooms, news, library, secretariat, and so on. In addition to these basic tools and areas, which support the students' day-to-day activities, the exclusively online learning system at the UOC has required the gradual incorporation of new tools designed to improve the flow of communication between students and foster a greater sense of community. They include a geolocation tool, an instant messaging feature, and a question and answer area.

Optimized access to this learning environment from mobile devices was both a necessary step and an inevitable development. The growing use of smartphones across society as a whole, and the general profile of UOC students, who want to make the most of any chance to carry out activities related to their studies, have made it increasingly important to provide an effective means of connecting to the Virtual Campus from mobile devices [18].

Following a user-centered design methodology [19], in an initial phase a series of focus groups [20], context studies [18] and usability tests (internal document) were organized with UOC students to find out about their requirements and to assess the different design proposals deriving from their comments. The results were used to define the functions and services that students consider essential in a mobile learning environment.

Having completed the initial research in 2011 the UOC launched the adapted version of its Virtual Campus for mobile browsers [21]. The new version has three main tabs: My UOC, which gives students access to the principal range of academic services (e-mail, virtual classrooms, calendar, etc.), adapted for mobile devices; Menu, which lists the other services available in the standard Virtual Campus, which are not adapted for mobile devices but are considered useful enough for links to be provided; and Alerts, which provides direct access to the main information and notification spaces of the Campus (e-mail, virtual classrooms, work groups, teacher board, etc.). The simultaneous availability of conventional and mobile services was one of the main points considered during the focus groups.

Also in 2011, in a joint initiative between the UOC and Orange Spain, a native Virtual Campus app was developed exclusively for iPads [22]. The app was enhanced and adapted to create a hybrid Virtual Campus application for mobile devices, which was launched in 2012 and made available via Google Play and the Apple Store.

A hybrid app was preferred to the native version as it provides greater scope for development and is more suitable for the end users (students), who access the Campus from devices with various operating systems, each of which would require its own native app. A hybrid app also enables developers to make use of existing web developments and to add new functionalities as different needs emerge.

Unlike the adapted Virtual Campus for mobile browsers, the hybrid app only contains those services that students identified as essential: e-mail, virtual classrooms, alerts, news, agenda, and learning resources.

Finally, the e-mail client, launched for Android at the beginning of 2012, was the first UOC native app to be released. It is essentially a "light" version of the standard web client, providing a smaller number of key functions (inbox, folders, and compose messages).

3 Focus Group

In this section, we describe the objectives, methodology and composition of the focus group and the principal results obtained.

3.1 Objectives, Methodology and Composition

The Virtual Campus hybrid app was launched in September 2012, alongside the mobile browser version and the native e-mail client. The simultaneous availability of multiple mobile developments was considered to be a potential source of confusion among students, who would have to consider the relative usefulness of three different tools, the type of use they would be likely to make of each one, and their preference for a hybrid app or an adapted learning environment for mobile browsers.

A focus group was organized with UOC students to find out the extent to which they are aware of the mobile tools developed by the UOC, the use they make of each one, and their satisfaction with the functions provided. The students were also asked to give their opinion of the combination of sections adapted to mobile browsers and sections for traditional browsers within the mobile version of the Virtual Campus.

Specifically, we hoped to obtain information on students' patterns of use and connection habits beyond strictly quantitative data (4 % of total connections to the UOC's Virtual Campus are made from smartphones, of which 50 % are iOS handsets, 38 % are Android, 8 % are BlackBerry and 4 % are other platforms (internal document). This data differs from the Spanish market shares of the major smartphone operating systems: Android, 87 %; iOS, 6.2 %; Windows 8, 5.4 %; Symbian 0,9 %; BlackBerry 0.3 % [23]. We also aimed to determine the degree to which students are aware of the different mobile developments offered by the UOC, the use they make of each one, and their views on the simultaneous availability of different tools, as the basis for consideration of possible improvements and potential developments in the future.

For the focus groups, smartphones and tablets were used to access the different mobile developments, with demonstrations projected in real-time to facilitate in-depth discussion and evaluation of the students' views. Students were also given the chance to access and browse the tools themselves (although they used their owned devices for these tasks).

The sample taking part in the focus groups contained representative proportions of male and female students, 50 % of whom had been UOC students for more than one year and 50 % less than one year. The students were aged between 25 and 45 and were enrolled in different degree courses (Business Administration and Management, Communication, Public Relations, Systems Engineering, and Criminology). Students were selected on the basis of being regular users of a smartphone and tablet (some had actually bought their smartphone or tablet with their UOC studies in mind, together with other factors). In addition, almost all of the students divided their time between study and work.

3.2 Principal Results

In this section, we present the principal results for the main aspects discussed in the focus groups: (1) patterns of use, connection habits and choice of devices for connecting to the Virtual Campus; (2) evaluation of the adaptation of the Virtual Campus for mobile browsers; (3) evaluation of the Virtual Campus native app; (4) evaluation of the e-mail client app; and (5) future of the developments.

Virtual Campus: Patterns of Use, Connection Habits and Choice of Devices. For most UOC students, one of the main factors in choosing to study at an online university is the need to combine their studies with other activities, in particularly their jobs.

As such, the patterns of use identified in the focus groups were not completely uniform, varying according to the students' non-academic commitments. Nevertheless, a few general observations were made:

- Students connect almost every day to check for messages and notices, including updates to forums, email or messages from lecturers, work groups, debates, etc.
- Students generally browse the Virtual Campus or connect to study at night or after lunch time.
- The students' view on the importance of the flexibility that the UOC provides depends to an extent on the number of subjects in which they are enrolled (which, in turn, depends on the time available for study and each student's budget).
- The periods during which students connect are determined in part by the academic calendar, with more frequent connections registered when assessment tests are due for submission or when marks are posted.

Two distinct uses of the Virtual Campus were detected: (1) to obtain information, for example by checking for alerts and notices, viewing documents, obtaining marks and consulting documentation on continuous assessment tests; and (2) to work, for example by downloading, completing and submitting continuous assessment tests, and sharing information with other students, lecturers or tutors.

With regard to the choice of devices for connecting to the Virtual Campus, the primary options are laptops or desktop computers, complemented by less frequent use of smartphones and/or tablets.

Laptops and desktop computers are used for both of the principal activities referred to above (obtaining information and working) as the students find them easier to work with. This is due in part to the screen size, but also reflects the availability of material and the ease of carrying out continuous assessment tests on the larger devices. Students also suggested that they feel more secure about carrying out their work on laptops and desktops.

In the case of smartphones, during the initial research we found that most students were not aware of the developments we aimed to test in the focus groups and that comments on connection habits actually related to an unofficial mobile version of the Virtual Campus developed by a UOC student as a final degree project, or to the standard Virtual Campus accessed from a mobile browser. As such, the data on connection habits via mobile devices could not be considered conclusive.

Students use smartphones devices mainly to check for daily updates and notices in the communication areas of the Virtual Campus. One student explained: "Whenever I have a break from work I check my mobile to see if anything new has come up". The students value the mobility and immediacy of a smartphone for obtaining information, although they acknowledge that it is not very practical for consulting documentation; indeed, a common complaint was the incompatibility of smartphones with Office tools.

Finally, the students use tablets primarily for viewing documents. They define tablets as comfortable and practical devices that enable them to read in situations where it is easier and more user-friendly to use a handheld device than a computer. As one student described: "While you're away, at the weekend, on the train, on the sofa …".

Virtual Campus for Mobile Browsers. Following a demonstration of the mobile version of the Virtual Campus and having been given to chance to access the adapted version from their own devices, students were asked to give their opinions of the development (see Fig. 1).

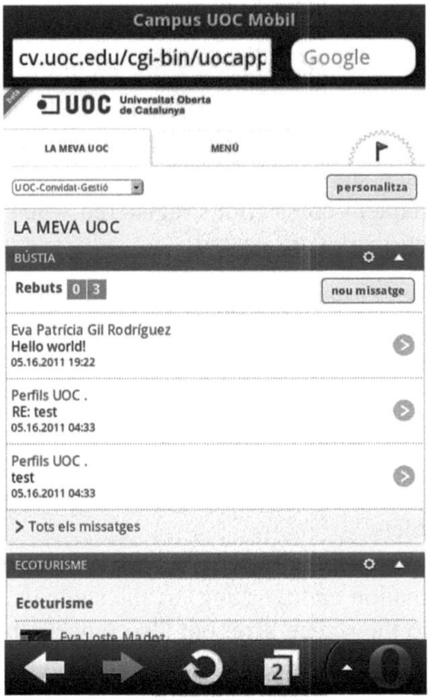

Fig. 1. Virtual campus adapted for mobile browsers.

We found that there was generally little awareness of the mobile version of the Virtual Campus. Most students were more accustomed to checking the standard Virtual Campus from their smartphone or tablet, either because the standard version opened automatically or because they had not found the link to the mobile version.

Having watched the demonstration and used some of the functions of the mobile version from their own devices, students commented that they particularly valued the practicality of the adapted Virtual Campus, in the sense that it contains all of the most relevant information for connections from a mobile device.

The most negative comments reflected the students' dissatisfaction with the fact that some sections, such as Secretary's Office and Tutor, had still not been adapted for mobile browsers, while there were links to other sections that students were unlike to use from a mobile device, including Library and News.

Students were not critical of the combination of sections adapted for mobile browsers with other sections designed for traditional browsers, as they understood that the mobile version was still in the development stage. However, students did stress that it would only be necessary to adapt those sections they were most likely to connect to from a mobile device, such as the academic record, alerts and notifications, the teacher board, forums, subject work areas and agenda.

Virtual Campus Hybrid App. Students were shown an on-screen presentation of the hybrid app and were given the chance to use it on their own devices (see Fig. 2).

We again found that only a small number of students were familiar with the app. In fact, the students who had used it were generally those who had enrolled at the UOC most recently. In some cases, as observed above, students confused the hybrid app with the unofficial tool that is also available.

The most positive comments reflected the students' satisfaction with the fact that the app meets their preferences and corrects the problems encountered with the mobile version of the Virtual Campus; in other words, it only contains the information students consider relevant for connections from a mobile device. As one student remarked: "It's like a pared-down version of the mobile version, it has everything you need". They also remarked that the app is modern, innovative and functional, which transmits a good image of the University as a whole.

The most negative comments received from students – in line with their appraisal of the adapted version of the Virtual Campus for mobile browsers – referred to the absence of the Tutor and Secretary's Office sections (particularly as this prevents them from consulting their academic records – they are less concerned about being able to manage tasks) and the lack of a general option to personalize the app.

Students also suggested that the sub-folder structure should be improved for communication in forums, virtual classrooms and via UOC e-mail, as the current structure

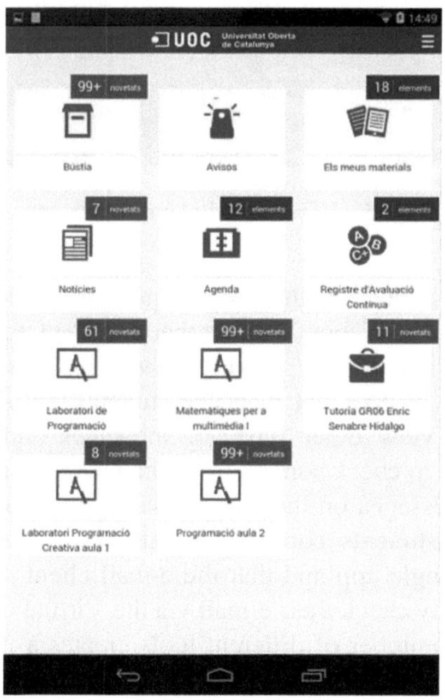

Fig. 2. Virtual campus hybrid app.

creates a feeling of uncertainty and generates concern that if students are unable to connect to the full Virtual Campus they may be missing out on information. It should be noted, however, that at the time the focus group was arranged, the hybrid app was affected by a technical issue and could only display the principal folders in the forums, classrooms and e-mail.

e-Mail Client App. Finally, the e-mail client app was presented, following the method adopted for the previous two developments (see Fig. 3).

Fig. 3. UOC e-mail client native app.

Students most highly valued that the app is a quick solution for accessing their UOC e-mail. They were less positive about the fact that the client app is basically a substitute for the hybrid Virtual Campus app, making it both too specific and not sufficiently comprehensive. As such, it does not meet the students' information requirements, as they will also need to view other types of messages and alerts. As one student explained: "When I want to check something at the UOC it's not just my in-box, it's to see whether there are messages on the notice board, the forum…".

In other words, the students considered that all of this information should be gathered together in a single app and that the e-mail client serves no useful purpose, given that they can already check their e-mail via the Virtual Campus hybrid app. They explained that having a number of different tools creates a degree of uncertainty. As one student pointed out: "If you have to check various apps, you get the feeling that you might be missing out on information".

Future of the Developments. Once the three developments had been presented, students were asked to give their views on how they should be developed in the future and what use they are likely to make of each one.

The students indicated that they would connect most frequently to the hybrid app, as they see it as the most direct form of accessing the Virtual Campus and consider that it includes enough of the necessary services (lacking only the Secretary's Office and Tutor sections, as they mentioned), unlike the adapted version for mobile browsers.

The students also suggested functions that they would like to see integrated into the hybrid app. These include a file storage and sharing system, such as an internal server or a tool along the same lines as Dropbox [24] compatible with all mobile ecosystems, in order to access their records (documents, continuous assessment tests, messages), and an instant messaging tool similar to WhatsApp [25], to facilitate interaction in specific tasks such as group projects.

With regard to the potential use of different types of hardware (conventional computers and mobile devices), the students consider that they will continue to use a combination of the two, and that mobile devices are unlikely to replace computers altogether.

As tablets becomes more widely adopted, and once assessment tasks can be carried out from these devices, students believe that use will probably increase, and that tablets could even become the principal tool for certain tasks. The consensus is that tablets could become an active part of their studies and could even be the main device for connecting to the Virtual Campus, as it was also pointed out in the NMC Horizon Report 2013 [26] in which tablets were identified as one of the key trends in education and are regarded as having immense impact on learning and teaching in the next up to five years.

With regard to smartphones, students indicate that they will continue to be an important means of connecting to the Virtual Campus, as a complement to computers and tablets.

As such, students believe that the ideal solution in the future will be an offer of services that are fully functional via mobile devices, although they acknowledge that total adoption would be difficult to achieve. Indeed, as one student commented: "It's a physical thing – It seems strange to think that I could actually write or work on a tablet, let alone a smartphone".

Finally, in relation to the availability of the three developments and the general lack of awareness among students, and taking into account the unofficial app that many students were aware of, it can be concluded that students would like improvements to be made in the way launches of new developments and tools are communicated. As one student pointed out for the specific case of the mobile app: "We could have been sent an e-mail: 'Download the app'."

4 Conclusions

The focus group with students yielded a series of conclusions from which recommendations can be drawn to guide other universities in planning the adaptation of a virtual learning environment for mobile devices. In this section we describe in detail the conclusions of the focus group. The resulting recommendations are presented in the following section.

As a general conclusion, the students were satisfied with the mobile browser adaptation and the hybrid app and considered that they provide a comprehensive answer to their current connection needs, as well as portraying the UOC as a modern, innovative university. However, students also suggested that they would only use the hybrid app, as it integrates and links to the most relevant services, and ruled out using an e-mail client app or the mobile version of the Virtual Campus. In fact, the e-mail client app is no longer maintained, and its functions have been integrated into the hybrid Virtual Campus.

For the hybrid app to be fully satisfactory, three principal improvements must be made: (1) direct access from the app to a full range of services demanded by students, who indicated that they would like to see a section for consulting marks and a link to the Tutor section; (2) an integrated instant messaging system to allow fluid and fast communication with fellow students; (3) a system for storing, sending and sharing files.

These three improvements, developed in response to student suggestions, have various implications. Interestingly, during initial surveys conducted in 2011, students did not express an interest in viewing their marks, managing documents and files, or communicating with classmates via instant messaging through a mobile Virtual Campus. The new requirements in fact emerged once the basic functionalities had been provided (e.g., access to virtual classrooms, agenda, etc.), as there was a general view among students that these features could be accessed via a mobile device, and smartphone use had become a generalized phenomenon among the UOC community.

It was discovered, for example, that students considered it unreasonable to have to wait until they reached home to check their marks on a computer, when the same task could be performed immediately from a smartphone. In the case of instant messaging, the widespread use of messaging apps such as WhatsApp or Telegram [27] and the availability of social communication tools in the standard Virtual Campus led to demand among students for a similar feature to be integrated into the mobile Virtual Campus, to make it easier to communicate with their classmates.

These new requirements clearly underline the importance of a flexible Virtual Campus, capable of incorporating new functionalities and services with minimal disruption. A hybrid application is more effective than a native app for this purpose, as it allows existing services available in the standard Virtual Campus to be integrated into the mobile version.

On the other hand, the students' regular use of smartphones and tablets to connect to the UOC Virtual Campus, their opinion about considering tablets as the potential main device for these connections in the near future, and as well as their positive appraisal of the hybrid app underline the fact that the mobile learning environment is already an integral part of students' day-to-day activities. It is therefore necessary to provide them with an optimized means of accessing the Virtual Campus from smartphones. The rise in sales of smartphones, the importance of anywhere connectivity, the general adoption of mobile apps, and the opportunities brought by mobile devices in educational settings [26], references [28, 29] underline the delay with which universities have moved to adapt their virtual learning environments for mobile devices.

Finally, it should be noted that most students were either unaware of the mobile developments described in this paper, even though they have been available for some time, or were familiar with unofficial apps before they learned about the official versions. It is clear, then, that efforts to communicate the availability of these developments failed, hence greater efforts should be made to provide students with more direct information about new tools and enhancements, rather than expecting students to "discover" them unaided.

5 Recommendations

In the following table (see Table 1) we present a series of recommendations drawn from the UOC case study which may be of assistance to other universities interested in developing mobile learning technologies.

Table 1. Recommendations to guide universities in the development of mobile learning environments.

A single app or application launcher	Developments should be unified in a single app that brings together the most relevant services for students. This is preferable to offering multiple apps, each dedicated to a different service, which may be perceived as overly specific or lacking functions, or an adapted version for mobile browsers, which would provide access to a series of services that students are unlikely to use from mobile devices. However, the gradual addition of functions and services to meet new user requirements could increase the size of a single app excessively, complicating the download process. One potential solution would be to develop multiple apps, each of which would provide a different service (for example, an agenda app, a mail app, a classroom app, and so on), and an accompanying app launcher, which would also provide shortcuts to and information on specific services within each app, such as alerts for new posts in subject forums, e-mail alerts, etc. Students would therefore download a series of different applications but the various services and functions could be viewed and used from a single app launcher. In this type of approach, it is crucial to know: (1) what information students would like to see in the app launcher; and (2) which apps students would like to see made available as downloads, i.e. which of the Virtual Campus functions and services they think should be converted into apps. It is also important to provide students with clear and easily accessible information about the degree of integration between apps and with the app launcher

(*Continued*)

Table 1. (*Continued*)

Hybrid app preferable to a native app	A standard virtual campus can house various services and functions that are, in theory, not needed in a mobile version. However, new requirements stemming from the students' interest in accessing certain services from mobile devices or from the influence of other mobile apps demand a more flexible Virtual Campus, capable of incorporating new services quickly and seamlessly. A hybrid app is therefore preferable to a native app, as it provides greater scope for recycling the existing codebase
What the student-user requests	Students periodically use a smartphone or tablet as an alternative to a computer. But the services they are expecting to find and use in the mobile learning environment may be different from the services found in the computer learning environment. Therefore it is crucial to know what these students' requirements are in order to design and develop a mobile learning environment according to their needs, and as a consequence to assure a satisfactory user experience. As referred to in the previous recommendation, offering other services that cannot easily be used via a mobile device could distract and hinder the students' goals when using the mobile learning environment and, as well as generating unnecessary development costs. Employing a user-centered design perspective is an optimal way to achieve these objectives
Devices and contexts and responsive design	Regular use of smartphones and tablets by students makes it necessary to design and develop mobile learning environments taking into account both devices and their respective contexts of use. Responsive design allows a development approach that caters for a range of possible user devices. The key is therefore to determine what devices are useful for the students' academic activities and to establish the contexts in which these devices will be used. Mobile devices are beginning to prove useful for certain tasks, but students may well go on to use other technologies in the future, such as interactive television, Google Glass, smartwatches, etc.
Document management function	Although it is difficult to create or edit documents from a smartphone, an option within the mobile learning environment to save, manage and share documents gives students greater in situ control over their work and records, without having to wait until they can use a computer
Social tools, such as instant messaging	The emergence and mass adoption of instant messaging apps typified by WhatsApp have created a need among students for rapid and efficient communication within the mobile learning environment, particularly for group work

(*Continued*)

Table 1. (*Continued*)

A good impression	The availability of a Virtual Campus app gives a good impression and portrays the university as a modern, innovative institution
Effective communication of new developments	New developments, tools and enhancements must be communicated effectively. Options include providing information on how to access a new development, for example in the form of an e-mail with a link to the tool, or clearly marking links to the enhanced version of an existing tool from the previous version. The strategy should focus especially on students who have been enrolled at the university for some time, who are more likely to have developed a routine and may be less receptive to new tools or less active in the search for new options

Acknowledgements. This paper has been done within the framework of the MAVSEL project: Mining, data Analysis and Visualization based on Social models in E-Learning, TIN2010-21715-C02-02.

References

1. El Periódico: ¿En qué países hay más 'smartphones'? (2014). http://www.elperiodico.com/es/noticias/tecnologia/mapa-penetracion-disponibilidad-smartphone-2013-3137938. Accessed 10 July 2014
2. El Mundo: En España existen 26 millones de móviles con Internet (2014). http://www.elmundo.es/tecnologia/2014/01/15/52d6a9dd22601dc2798b4570.html. Accessed 10 July 2014
3. Ticbeat: El número de aplicaciones descargadas en el mundo se duplicará en 2017 (2013). http://devs.ticbeat.com/numero-aplicaciones-descargadas-mundo-duplicar-2017/. Accessed 19 September 2013
4. Maceiras, R., Cancela, A., Sánchez, A., Casar, A., Urrejola, S.: Adaptation of a virtual campus for mobile learning devices. In: Global Engineering Education Conference (EDUCON), pp. 165–167. IEEE (2011)
5. Piguillem, J., Alier, M., Casany, M.J., Mayol, E., Galanis, N., García-Peñalvo, F.J., Conde, M.Á.: Moodbile: a Moodle web services extension for mobile applications. In: Retalis, S., Dougiamas, M. (eds.) Proceedings of the 1st Moodle Research Conference, Heraklion, Crete, Greece, pp. 148–156, 14–15 September 2012
6. Rathi, K.V., Kosale, S.S., Kumar, M., Thote, S.R.: Implementation of a mobile campus using open source software. World Res. J. Hum. Comput. Interact. **1**(1), 09–12 (2012). ISSN 2278-8476 & E-ISSN 2278-8484
7. Ballard, B.: Designing the Mobile User Experience. Wiley, New York (2007)
8. Nakhimovsky, Y., Eckles, D. Riegelsberger, J.: Mobile user experience research: challenges, methods and tools. In: Proceedings of the 27th International Conference Extended Abstracts on Human Factors in Computing Systems, Boston, MA, USA, 04–09 April 2009

9. Budiu, R.: Mobile: native apps, web apps, and hybrid apps. In: Nielsen Norman Group (2013). http://www.nngroup.com/articles/mobile-native-apps/#. Accessed 16 September 2013
10. Charland, A., Leroux, B.: Mobile application development: web vs. native. Commun. ACM **54**(5), 49–53 (2011)
11. Barnes, J., Herring, D.: Using mobile devices in higher education. In: McBride, R., Searson, M. (eds.) Proceedings of Society for Information Technology and Teacher Education International Conference, Chesapeake, VA, pp. 206–211. AACE (2013)
12. Gikas, J., Grant, M.: Mobile computing devices in higher education: student perspectives on learning with cellphones, smartphones and social media. Internet High. Educ. **19**, 18–26 (2013)
13. Dirin, A., Nieminen, M.: State-of-the-art of m-learning usability and user experience. In: The Fourth International Conference on e-Learning (ICEL2013), Czech Republic, pp. 130–139 (2013)
14. Xhafa, F., Caballé, S., Rustarazo, I., Barolli, L.: Implementing a mobile campus using MLE Moodle. In: IEEE Proceedings of International Conference on P2P, Parallel, Grid, Cloud and Internet Computing, Fukuoka, Japan, pp. 207–214 (2010)
15. Garaj, V.: M-learning in the education of multimedia technologists and designers at the university level: a user requirements study. IEEE Trans. Learn. Technol. **3**(1), 24–32 (2010)
16. Harpur, P.A.: Evaluation of Usability and User Experience of an M-learning Environment: Custom-designed for a Tertiary Educational Context. University of South Africa, Pretoria (2013)
17. Eisenhardt, K.M.: Building theories from case study research. Acad. Manage. Rev. **14**(4), 532–550 (1989)
18. Gil-Rodríguez, E.P., Rebaque-Rivas, P.: Mobile learning and commuting: contextual interview and design of mobile scenarios. In: Leitner, G., Hitz, M., Holzinger, A. (eds.) USAB 2010. LNCS, vol. 6389, pp. 266–277. Springer, Heidelberg (2010)
19. ISO: ISO 9241-210:2010 - Ergonomics of human-system interaction – part 210: human-centred design for interactive systems (2010). http://www.iso.org/iso/catalogue_detail.htm?csnumber=52075http://url/
20. Rebaque-Rivas, P., Gil-Rodríguez, E.P., Manresa-Mallol, I.: Mobile learning scenarios from a UCD perspective. In: MobileHCI 2010 Proceedings of the 12th International Conference on Human Computer Interaction with Mobile Devices and Services, pp. 389–390 ACM, New York, NY, USA (2010)
21. Office of Learning Technologies - Open University of Catalonia: Campus móvil: el campus de la UOC en tu móvil (2011). http://www.slideshare.net/olt/presentacion-campus-mvil-uoc
22. Gil-Rodríguez, E.P., Aracil, X., Manresa, I., Loste, E.: iUOC: enhanced mobile learning at UOC. In: Proceedings of EUNIS International Congress, Dublin, 15–17 June 2011
23. Kantarworldpanel: Smartphone OS market share (2014). http://www.kantarworldpanel.com/smartphone-os-market-share/. Accessed 10 July 2014
24. https://www.dropbox.com/
25. http://www.whatsapp.com/?l=en
26. Johnson, L., Adams, S., Cummins, M., Estrada, V., Freeman, A., Ludgate, H.: The NMC Horizon Report: 2013. Higher Education Edition (2013). http://www.editlib.org/p/46484. Accessed 27 September 2013
27. https://telegram.org/
28. UNESCO: UNESCO leads discussion on mobile learning at WSIS Forum (2012). http://www.unesco.org/new/en/education/resources/online-. Accessed 19 September 2013
29. Johnson, L., Adams, S., Cummins, M.: The NMC Horizon Report: 2012 Higher Education Edition (2012). http://www.editlib.org/p/48964. Accessed 27 September 2013

Author Index

MIX
Papier aus verantwortungsvollen Quellen
Paper from responsible sources
FSC® C105338

If you have any concerns about our products,
you can contact us on
ProductSafety@springernature.com

In case Publisher is established outside the EU,
the EU authorized representative is:
Springer Nature Customer Service Center GmbH
Europaplatz 3, 69115 Heidelberg, Germany

Printed by Libri Plureos GmbH
in Hamburg, Germany